Contents

W9-BBN-433

Practical information

Background information

The Guide

Maps and plans

Ground plans

Introduction

Shortly before publication of this Guide your author went hiking for a week in Abruzzo, with friends who came from as far away as Singapore for the event. The group followed a *tratturo*, one of the routes taken for centuries by the migrant shepherds of Abruzzo's western highlands who drove their flocks some 300km to Apulia in autumn, and back again in spring. Year after year, from antiquity to the dawn of the modern age (when changing socio-economic conditions made transhumance, as the migration was called, unprofitable), these robust highlanders and their flocks mowed swathes more than 100m wide through the countryside—in a sense, the region's first superhighways. These immense greenways were protected by law in their time: to obstruct them with new buildings or cultivated fields was punishable by death. Although little remains to be seen, today, of the *tratturi*, the innumerable fortresses, churches, and villages that grew up by the wayside, to offer security, spiritual solace and essential services to these extraordinary travellers, are still there. They give Abruzzo its remarkably timeless flavour, and they afford an ideal 'human' complement to the region's lofty mountains, ancient forests, emerald meadows and sparkling, clear lakes and streams.

To move slowly through this magnificent landscape, be it on foot or bycicle, snowshoes or back-couuntry skis, is, of course, the best way to see it. For Abruzzo is a land of hidden wonders, where there is little reward without effort.

Although it is a place to explore and savour slowly, and with an eye to its very special history, it is by no means an elitist place. Rock climbers have long come here to test their strength on the peaks of the Gran Sasso; naturalists to observe the fauna of the Abruzzo National Park; art lovers to admire the austere beauty of Rocca Calascio, Bominaco or San Clemente in Casauria. Lately, the extension of Abruzzo's nature reserves, the increasing attention of the travel press, the growth in popularity of 'soft' sports such as walking, and last but not least, the unquestionable authority of word-of-mouth recommendations from recent visitors, have brought thousands to Abruzzo from all over Italy and Europe. And spurred the *abbruzzesi* to rediscover their own land. Although the Adriatic beaches and Apennine ski runs are the region's main draws for mass tourism, discriminating visitors to Abruzzo have discovered the finer things, too. Many of the medieval villages, archaeological sites, museums and monuments have begun to attract the same quality of attention as their counterparts in Tuscany or Umbria—though not yet in the same quantities. As a corrolary, food and accommodation are improving to meet the new demand.

So if there is a place particularly recommendable in this edition of Blue Guide Southern Italy, it is Abruzzo. But it is certainly not the only place of interest. The guide offers a detailed description of the most fascinating cities, towns, and natural areas throughout southern Italy, from Rome to Reggio Calabria. Places have been arranged in geographic 'bundles', leaving you, the visitor, the freedom to choose the route best suited to your personal tastes. Each bundle forms a chapter, at the beginning of which you'll find suggestions on how to get there and back, what to do and when, where to stay and where to eat.

You might find yourself leafing through the guide rather more than you expect: for although its general organisation is loose and open, the specific places are dealt with in considerable depth. Wherever possible, walks have been designed to take you round the major sights, or through the finest countryside, one step at a time. But as you explore, remember: Italy possesses roughly two-thirds of the world's artistic heritage, and it's an old heritage, in constant need of conservation and restoration. If during your visit some of the works of art and architecture described in the guide are covered (in the case of buildings or public sculpture) or away for cleaning (paintings), don't let it spoil your day: just move on. The more memorable moments of a foreign journey often come unexpectedly—and southern Italy is indeed a land of the unexpected.

Acknowledgements

The author is indebted to all those people who contributed in various ways to the making of the book—especially to Judy Tither and the editorial staff of A&C Black, who have been most helpful in producing the guide. Special thanks are owed to the many friends and readers who assisted in the gathering of information, particularly to Alexandra Massini, who travelled extensively through southern Italy; Paolo Barattelli and Domenico Boccio, who revealed the hidden treasures of Abruzzo; hiking companions Bill and Juliana Cellini and friends; and Heather Killingbeck, who organised our trek. Thanks also to Alta Macadam, whose friendship and advice have been invaluable; and to Isabella Toraldo di Francia, who provided encouragement and support throughout the preparation of the guide. As with other volumes in the Blue Guide series, suggestions for the correction or improvement of the guide are gratefully welcomed.

PRACTICAL INFORMATION

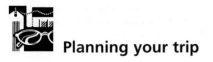

Planning your trip

When to go

Southern Italy enjoys a typically Mediterranean climate: two rainy seasons (spring and autumn); hot, dry summers and mild winters, with average temperatures almost always above 0°C (32°F) at the lower altitudes. The weather in the south—determined by the interaction of cool air masses from Central Europe and Turkey, humid air from the Atlantic and warm air from the Sahara and Central Asia—is usually warmer and sunnier than in the north, though from November to March it can be unexpectedly cool and wet, and inland in the mountains there is a risk of snow and ice. In general, however, the climate is agreeable for much of the year, and a succession of more than two or three bad days is unusual.

The heat in July and August is unpleasant in the towns and may be excessive on coasts sheltered from cooling breezes. Also, the region is subject to winds and to abrupt changes of temperature. The *maestrale* (literally, masterful), a cold, dry, northerly wind often blows in winter; and the hot, dry North African *scirocco* is not uncommon in summer. The best time to visit the region is late spring (May–June) or early autumn (particularly September), when the temperature and rainfall are moderate and the droves of summer sun-seekers (Italian and foreign) that invade the coasts, especially between 15 July and 15 August, are at home.

What to bring

Due to the difference in temperature between morning/evening and mid-day, and to the overall unpredictability of weather in the Meditereranean, you will be most comfortable if you dress in layers that can be donned or removed as the need arises. Evening dress is generally casual, except for special events such as theatre and opera, at which a jacket and tie or an evening dress are suggested. Light tennis shoes or water-resistant walking shoes are best for exploring cities; on country and mountain trails, the nature of the terrain almost always requires that you wear lightweight hiking boots with ankle support. Wherever you are, a backpack or shoulder bag will come in handy to carry snacks, water, camera, sun screen, etc., and effective rain gear (a lightweight parka or Gore-Tex jacket) will keep you dry when the odd storm breaks.

Try to travel lightly—especially if you are using public transport. Most Italian train stations require that you drag your bags up and down stairs to reach the platforms. For this important reason, and because baggage capacity of buses and trains is limited, you would do well to restrict luggage to two small bags per person. If you are starting and ending your trip in the same city, additional luggage may be left at the first hotel and picked up at trip's end.

Planning an itinerary

When planning your trip don't overfill your days: leave a bit of free time between events and at the end of the day, to wind down before dinner. This is especially true if you are driving. Remember that unforeseen circumstances (a queue at a museum, or roadwork on the highway) require that you leave a margin of error in planning your schedule. Remember also that meals in Italy take longer to prepare and consume than in Britain or North America: everything, not just the coffee, is prepared *espresso* when ordered. Most Italians have two-hour lunch hours, and with good reason.

Passports and formalities

Passports or ID cards are necessary for EU travellers entering Italy; North American travellers must carry passports. No visa is required for EU, US or Canadian citizens holding a valid passport for visits of up to 90 days. Citizens of other countries should check current visa requirements with the nearest Italian consulate before departure.

Italian law requires travellers to carry some form of identification at all times. A stolen or lost passport can be replaced with little trouble by the relevant embassy in Rome. All foreign visitors to Italy must register with the police within three days of arrival. If you are staying at a hotel, this formality is attended to by the management. If staying with friends or in a private home, you must register in person at the nearest police station (*questura*).

National tourist boards

Tourist information may be obtained from the following Italian Tourist Board offices:

UK	*Italian State Tourist Board*, 1 Princess Street, London W1R 7RA, ☎ 020 7408 1254, 🖷 020 7493 6695, 🖾 www.enit.it, italy@italiantouristboard.co.uk)
USA	*Italian Government Tourist Board*, 630 Fifth Avenue, Suite 1565, New York, NY 10111, ☎ 212 245 4822, 🖷 212 586 9249, 🖾 www.italiantourism.com, enitny@italiantourism.com
	Italian Government Tourist Board, 500 North Michigan Avenue, Suite 2240, Chicago 1, IL 60611, ☎ 312 644 0996, 🖷 312 644 3019, 🖾 www.italiantourism.com, enitch@italiantourism.com
	Italian Government Tourist Board, 12400 Wilshire Blvd, Suite 550, Los Angeles, CA 90025, ☎ 310 820 1898, 🖷 310 820 6357, 🖾 www.italiantourism.com, enitla@italiantourism.com
Canada	*Italian Government Tourist Board*, 175 Bloor Street E., Suite 907–South Tower, M4W3R8 Toronto (Ontario), ☎ 416 925 4882, 🖷 416 925 4799, 🖾 www.italiantourism.com, enit.canada@on.aibn.com
Netherlands	*National Italiaans Verkeersbureau*, Stadhoudeskade 2, 1054 ES Amsterdam, ☎ +31 20 616 8244; 🖷 +31 20 618 8515, 🖾 einitams@wirehub.nl

The London office issues free an invaluable *Traveller's Handbook* (in North America, *General Information for Travellers to Italy*, usually revised every year).

General information on travel in Italy on the web

Italian National Tourist Board ✉ www.enit.it
Italytour.com ✉ www.italytour.com
In Italy Online ✉ www.initaly.com
ITWG Travel ✉ www.itwg.com
Windows on Italy ✉ www.mi.cnr.it/WOI/woiindex.html

Tour operators

Tour operators in the **UK** who sell tickets and book accommodation, and also organise inclusive tours to some parts of southern Italy, include:

Abercrombie and Kent, Sloane Square House, Holbein Place, London SW1W 8NS, tel. 0845 070 0610, ▤ 0845 070 0608, ✉ www.abercrombiekent.co.uk, info@abercrombiekent.co.uk. Known for its absolute commitment to the highest levels of personal service.

Ace Study Tours, Babraham, Cambridge CB2 4AP, ☎ 01223 835 055; ▤ 01223 837 394, ✉ www.study-tours.org, ace@study-tours.org. Runs study tours and courses in art, archaeology, history, music, drama, literature, geology, ecology and wildlife.

Alternative Travel Group, 69-71 Banbury Road, Oxford OX2 6PJ, ☎ 01865 315679; ▤ 01865 315697, ✉ www.atg-oxford.co.uk, info@atg-oxford.co.uk. Specialises in walking tours, also courses in Italian language, cookery and wine, painting and music.

Andante Travels, The Old Barn, Old Road, Alderbury, Salisbury SP4 6EH, ☎ 01722 713800; ▤ 01722 711966, ✉ www.andantetravels.co.uk, tours@andantetravels.co.uk. Focusing on art and archaeology.

British Museum Traveller, 46 Bloomsbury Street, London WC1B 3QQ, ☎ 020 7436 7575; ▤ 020 7580 8677, ✉ www.britishmuseumtraveller.co.uk, traveller@bmcompany.co.uk. History, art and archaeology tours.

Citalia, Marco Polo House, 3–5 Lansdowne Road, Croydon CR9 1LL, ☎ 020 8686 0677, ▤ 020 8681 0712, ✉ www.citalia.co.uk, Italy@citalia.co.uk. The UK's most venerable Italian specialist, offering travel, hotels, self-catering, cruises, etc.

Headwater Holidays, The Old School House, Chester Road, Northwich, Cheshire CW9 5HH, ☎ 01606 813333; ▤ 01606 813334; ✉ www.headwater-holidays.co.uk/newlook/index.htm, info@headwater.com. Walking, cycling, canoeing, discovery and cookery.

Ilios Travel Ltd, 18 Market Square, Horsham, West Sussex RH12 1EU, tel. 01403 259788, ▤ 0143 211699, ✉ www.iliostravel.com, andrea@ilios.clara.co.uk; a small specialist company providing holidays for the discerning traveller.

Italian Escapades, 227 Shepherds Bush Road, London W6 7AS, ☎ 020 8748 2661, ▤ 020 8748 6381. A small company focusing on Italy.

Italiatour Ltd, 9 Whyteleafe Business Village, Whiteleafe Hill, Whiteleafe, Surry CR3 0AT, ☎ 01883 621900, ▤ 01883 625222, ✉ www.italiatour.co.uk, italyforlovers@italiatour.co.uk. An Alitalia affiliate offering air and accommodation packages.

Magic of Italy, King's House, 12–42 Wood Street, Kingston-upon-Thames, Surrey KT1 1JF, ☎ 0870 888 022, ✉ www.magictravelgroup. co.uk. Award-winning Italy specialist offering holidays in countryside and coastal locations as well as cultural tours.

Martin Randall Travel Ltd, Voysey House, Barley Mow Passage, Chiswick, London W4 4GF, tel. 020 8742 3355, ⎙ 020 8742 7766, ☒ www.martinran-dall.com, info@martinrandall.com. High-quality cultural tours.

Naturetrek, Cheriton Mill, Cheriton, Alresford, Hants SO24 0NG, ☎ 01962 733051; ⎙ 01962 736426; ☒ www.naturetrek.co.uk; info@naturetrek.co.uk. Birdwathing, botanical and natural history holidays.

Page and Moy Ltd, 136–140 London Road, Leicester LE2 1EN, tel. 08700 106212, ⎙ 08700 106211, ☒ www.page-moy.com, holiday @page-moy.com. History, art and architecture.

The many **North American** agents offering individual and group tours to Italy include:

Abercrombie & Kent, Inc, 1520 Kensington Road, Suite 212, Oak Brook, Illinois, USA 60523-2141, ☎ 800 323 7308, ⎙ 630 954 3324, ☒ www.aber-crombieandkent.com. Known for its absolute commitment to the highest levels of personal service.

Backroads, 801 Cedar Street, Berkeley, CA 94710-1800, ☎ 800 462 2848, ⎙ 510 527 1444, ☒ www.backroads.com. Biking, walking, and multi-sport vacations.

Butterfield & Robinson, 70 Bond Street, Toronto, Canada M5B 1X3, ☎ 800 678 1147, ⎙ 416 864 1354, ☒ www.butterfield.com, info@ www.butterfield.com. Biking, multi-active and walking trips.

Classic Journeys, 5580 La Jolla Blvd. #104, La Jolla, CA 92037, ☎ 800 200 3887, ⎙ 858 454 5770, ☒ www.classicjourneys.com, moreinfo@classicjour-neys.com. Small-group cultural walking tours and vacations.

Donna Franca Tours, 470 Commonwealth Avenue, Boston, MA 02215, ☎ 800 225 6290, ☒ www.donnafranca.com. Focusing on Italian culture.

Far and Wide, 80 S:W: 8th Street, Suite 2601, Miami, FL 33130-3047, ☎ 305 908 7555, ⎙ 305 908 7535, ☒ www.farandwide.com. Family of companies offering customised and independent foreign travel, as well as escorted, cultural, educational, adventure, ski and fitness vacations.

Grand Expeditions, Inc, 4800 North Federal Highway, Suite 307D, Boca Raton, FL 33431, ☎ 561 347 7654, ☒ www.grandex.com, info@grandex.com. Family of companies offering walking adventures, wildlife and natural history tours, photography expeditions, private yacht vacations and more.

Italiatour, USA, ☎ 800 845 3365, Canada ☎ 1-888-515-5245, ⎙ US & Canada 800 848 6286, ☒ www.italiatourusa.com. An Alitalia affiliate offering air and accommodation packages.

Disabled travellers

All new public buildings are now obliged by law to provide easy access and specially designed facilities for the disabled. Unfortunately the conversion of historical buildings, including many museums and monuments, is made problematic by structural impediments such as narrow pavements. Barriers therefore continue to exist in many cases. Hotels that are equipped to accommodate the disabled are indicated in the annual list of hotels published by the local tourist boards. Airports and railway stations provide assistance and certain trains are equipped to transport wheelchairs. Cars with disabled drivers or passengers are allowed access to the centre of towns (normally closed to traffic), where special parking places are reserved for them. For further information, contact the tourist board in the relevant city.

Maps

The **Touring Club Italiano** (**TCI**) publishes several sets of excellent maps, including *Carta Stradale d'Europa: Italia* on a scale of 1:1,000,000; the *Atlante Stradale Touring* (1:800,000); and the *Carta Stradale d'Italia* (1:200,000). The latter is divided into 15 sheets covering the regions of Italy. These are also published as an atlas (with a comprehensive index) called the *Atlante Stradale d'Italia*, in three volumes. The ones entitled *Centro* and *Sud* cover the southern mainland. These maps are available from *TCI* offices and at many booksellers. In London they can be purchased at Stanfords, 12–14 Long Acre, London WC2 9LP, ☎ 020 7836 1321, ⬛ www.stanfords.co.uk, with branches in Bristol and Manchester.

The **Istituto Geografico Militare**, Via Cesare Battisti 10, Florence, publishes a map of Italy on a scale of 1:100,000 in 277 sheets and a field survey, partly 1:50,000, partly 1:25,000, which are invaluable for the detailed exploration of the country, especially its more mountainous regions; the coverage is, however, still far from complete at the larger scales and some of the maps are out of date.

For the computer literate, *Route 66 Geographic Information Systems BV* of Veenendaal, The Netherlands, distributes software that calculates and displays routes from any origin to any destination in Italy. Road maps, city maps and custom itineraries (in English) may be found on the Web at *Mappy*, ⬛ www. mappy.fr.

Health and insurance

British citizens, as members of the EU, can claim for health treatment in Italy if they have the E111 form (issued by the DSS). There are also a number of private holiday health insurance policies. Italy has no medical programme covering US or Canadian citizens, who are advised to take out an insurance policy before travelling. First aid services (*pronto soccorso*) are available at all hospitals, railway stations, and airports. For emergencies ☎ **118** (rescue or ambulance) **113** (state police) or **112** (*Carabinieri*).

Currency

In Italy, the monetary unit is the euro (€). There are bank notes of 5, 10, 20, 50, 100 and 200 Euro and coins of 1, 2, 5, 10 and 50 Euro cents as well as 1 and 2 Euro. Travellers' cheques are the safest way of carrying money while travelling and most credit cards are now generally accepted in hotels, shops, and restaurants (and increasingly at petrol stations).

 **Getting there**

By air

Direct flights operate throughout the year between London and Naples and from several British and North American cities to Milan and Rome, where there are internal flights to Bari, Brindisi, Lamezia, Pescara and Reggio Calabria.

From the UK

Alitalia	☎ 0870 544 8259,	✉ www.alitalia.co.uk
British Airways	☎ 0845 77 333 77,	✉ www.ba.com
British Midland	☎ 0870 6070555,	✉ www.flybmi.com
easyJet	☎ 0845 605 4321,	✉ www.easyjet.com
Meridiana	☎ 0207 839 2222,	✉ www.meridiana.it
Ryanair	☎ 0905 586 0000,	✉ www.ryanair.com

Air France (☎ 0845 0845 111, ✉ www.airfrance.com), *Brussels Airlines* (☎ 0870 735 2345, ✉ www.brusselsairlines.com) and *Lufthansa* (☎ 0345 737747, ✉ www.lufthansa.com) offer connecting flights via Paris, Brussels and Frankfurt, respectively. These may cost less than the direct flights.

From the USA and Canada

AeroMexico, ☎ 800 237 6639, ✉ www.aeromexico.com, from Atlanta, Miami, New York to Milan; from Atlanta and New York to Rome.

Air Canada, ☎ 1 888 247 2262, from the USA 800 268 0024, ✉ www.aircanada.ca, from Toronto to Milan and Rome; from New York to Venice.

Alitalia, ☎ 800 223 5730, ✉ www.alitaliausa.com, from Atlanta, Boston, Chicago, Miami, Toronto to Milan; from New York, Toronto to Rome.

Continental, ☎ 800 525 0280, ✉ www.continental.com, from Atlanta, New York to Milan.

Delta, ☎ 800 221 1212, from Atlanta, Boston, Chicago, Miami, New York, to Milan; from Atlanta and New York to Rome; from New York to Venice.

United, ☎ 800 864 8331, ✉ www.ual.com, from Washington to Milan.

USAir, ☎ 800 245 4882, from Philadelphia to Rome.

Air France (☎ 800 237 2747, ✉ www.airfrance.com); *British Airways* (☎ 800 AIRWAYS), ✉ www.britishairways.com); *Brussels Airlines* (☎ 0870 735 2345, www.brusselsairlines.com), *KLM* (☎ 800 347 7747), *Lufthansa* (☎ 800 645 3880, ✉ www.lufthansa.com) and *Swiss Airlines* (☎ 1 877 359 7947, ✉ www.swiss.com) offer connecting flights via Paris, London, Brussels, Amsterdam, Frankfurt or Munich and Zurich. Again these are often more economical than the direct flights.

Web fares

The many agencies offering travel on the Internet include:

Expedia	✉ www.expedia.co.uk, www.expedia.com
Travelocity	✉ www.travelocity.com

Discounts on airfare, cars, hotels, etc., can be found at:

AAA Airline Tickets	✉ www.travel.aaa.com
AllCheapFares.com	✉ www.allcheapfares.com
Bargain Travel	✉ www.bargaintravel.com
BizRate.com	✉ www.bizrate.com
Biz Travel Brokers	✉ www.biztravelbrokers.com
Cheap Tickets	✉ www.cheaptickets.com
Discount Fares	✉ www.discountfares.com
Expedia.com	✉ www.expedia.com
Hotwire	✉ www.hotwire.com

Independent Traveler	✉ www.independenttraveler.com
Orbitz	✉ www.orbitz.com
Priceline.com	✉ www.priceline.com
SkyAuction.com	✉ www.skyauction.com
Traveller's Advantage/	
Sears Discount Travel	✉ www.travellersadvantage.com
TravelNet2000	✉ www.airtravel.net
Travelzoo	✉ www.travelzoo.com
Yahoo! Travel	✉ travel.yahoo.com

By rail

From the UK

To travel from London to Naples by train is certainly an adventure; it takes nearly two full days and is not significantly cheaper than flying. It makes sense only if you're thinking of stopping at other destinations along the way.

In the UK, information and tickets on the Italian Railways (*Trenitalia*) can be obtained from European Rail Travel Ltd, ☎ 020 7387 0444, 📠 020 7387 0888, ✉ www.raileurope.co.uk. Information and tickets with station pick-up in Italy, ✉ www.trenitalia.it. Trenitalia Help Desk, ☎ +39-06-88339537, 📠 +39-06-88339613, ✉ helpdesk@sipax.com.

From the USA and Canada

In North America, information and tickets on the Italian Railways (*Trenitalia*) can be obtained from European Rail Travel, 1 877 257 2887 in the US, 800 361 RAIL in Canada, or www.raileurope.com. Information and tickets with station pick-up in Italy, ✉ www.trenitalia.it. Trenitalia Help Desk, ☎ +39-06-88339537, 📠: +39-06-88339613, ✉ helpdesk@sipax.com.

By coach

From the UK

A coach service, which takes two days, runs between London (Victoria Coach Station) and Rome (Piazza della Repubblica) via Dover, Paris, Mont Blanc, Aosta, Turin, Genoa, Milan, Bologna and Florence, daily from June to September, and once or twice a week for the rest of the year. Reductions are available for students. Information from the *National Express* office at Victoria Coach Station in London (☎ 0990 808080), National Express Contact Centre (08705 808080), National Express Website ✉ www.gobycoach.com, or from *SITA* in Italy, ✉ www.sita-on-line.it, sitadirezione@sita-on-line.it

By car

The easiest approaches to Italy by road are the motorways through the San Bernard, Frejus or Mont Cenis tunnels, or over the Brenner Pass. The Mont Blanc tunnel is closed and will probably remain so for several years. British motorists taking their own cars via any of the routes across France, Belgium, Luxembourg, Switzerland, Germany and Austria need the vehicle registration book, a valid European Community pink version of the UK driving licence, an international insurance certificate and a nationality plate (fixed to the rear of the vehicle so as to be illuminated by the rear lights). A Swiss Motorway Pass is needed for

Switzerland, and can be obtained from the *Royal Automobile Club* (☎ 0906 470 1740, ✉ www.rac.co.uk), the *Automobile Association* (☎ 0870 600 0371, ✉ www.theaa.com), or at the Swiss border. Motorists who are not owners of the vehicle must be fully insured for its use abroad. Foreign drivers hiring a car in Italy only need a valid national driver's licence. Additional route information is available from ✉ www.autostop.it.

By sea

Adriatic Italy is connected by car-ferry and hydrofoil to Greece (Patras, Igoumenitsa, Corfu) and Croatia (Dubrovnik, Korcula, Split, Zadar). For information and reservations:

Greece From the UK: *Greek National Tourism Organisation*, 4 Conduit Street, London W1S 2DJ, ☎ 020 7495 9300, ▤ 020 7287 1369, ✉ www.gnto.gr, info@gnto.co.uk

From the US and Canada: *Greek National Tourist Organization*, Olympic Tower, 645 Fifth Avenue, 9th Floor, New York, NY 10022, ☎ 212 421 5777, ▤ 212 826 6940, ✉ www.greektourism.com, info@Greektourism.com

Croatia From the UK: *Croatian National Tourist Office*, 2 Lancasters, 162–164 Fulham Palace Road, London W6 9ER, ☎ 0208 563 7979, ▤ 0208, 563 2616, ✉ info@cnto.freeserve.co.uk; or from *Split & Dalmatia County Tourist Office*, ✉ www.dalmacija.net, tzzup-st-dalm@st.tel.hr

From the USA and Canada: *Croatian National Tourist Office*, 350 Fifth Avenue, Suite 4003, New York, NY 10118, ☎ 800 829 4416, ▤ 212 279 8683, ✉ cntonv@earthlink.net, or *from Split & Dalmatia County Tourist Office*, ✉ www.dalmacija.net, tzzup-st-dalm@st.tel.hr

 # Where to stay

Hotels

In this guide a selection of hotels has been given at the beginning of each chapter. They have been classified in a very relative manner, as expensive (€€€), moderate (€€) or inexpensive (€). Generally speaking, you should expect a double room at an expensive hotel to cost €200 or more; at a moderate hotel, €100–200, and at an inexpensive hotel, under €100. The hotels listed, regardless of their cost, have been chosen on the basis of their character or location. All have something special about them: beautiful surroundings, a distinctive atmosphere, and even the humblest are adequately comfortable. The local tourist offices will help you find accommodation on the spot; nevertheless you should try to book well in advance, especially if you're planning to travel between May and October; if you cancel the booking at least 72 hours in advance you can claim back part or all of your deposit. Hotels equipped to offer hospitality to the disabled are indicated in the tourist boards' hotel lists.

In all hotels the service charges are included in the rates. The total charge is exhibited on the back of the hotel room door. Breakfast is by law an optional extra charge, although a lot of hotels try to include it in the price of the room. When booking a room, always specify if you want breakfast or not. If you are staying in a hotel in a town, it is usually well worthwhile going round the corner to the nearest café for breakfast. Hotels are now obliged by law (for tax purposes) to issue an official receipt to customers: you should not leave the premises without this document. The hotels listed in the guide are open all year unless otherwise stated.

Bed and breakfast

B&B accommodation is now offered in most areas covered by this Guide. Rooms are usually in private homes, villas, etc, and may be booked through a central agency. Contact **Caffelletto**, Via di Marciola 23, 50020 San Vincenzo a Torri (Firenze) Italy, ☎ 055 7309145, ▤ 055 768121, ▨ www.caffelletto.it; **BedandBreakfast.com**, 1855 Blake Street, Suite 201, Denver, CO 80202 USA, ☎ 800 462 2632 (from outside the USA, 303 274 2800), ▤ 303 274 2900, ▨ www.bedandbreakfast.com, support@bedandbreakfast.com; or **Bed & Breakfast in Europe**, ▨ www.bedandbreakfastineurope.com/italia/en.htm.

Residences

A new type of hotel, called a *residenza*, has been introduced into Italy. Residences are normally in a building, or a group of houses of historic interest, often a castle or a monastery. They may have only a few rooms, and sometimes offer self-catering accommodation. They are listed separately in the *APT* hotel lists, with their prices.

Farm stays (Agriturismo)

Recently developed throughout Italy, the short-term rental of space in villas and farmhouses (*agriturismo*) provides an interesting alternative form of accommodation in the countryside. Terms vary greatly from bed-and-breakfast to self-contained flats. These are highly recommended for travellers with their own transport, and for families, as an excellent (and usually cheap) way of visiting the Italian countryside. Some farms require a stay of a minimum number of days. Cultural or recreational activities, such as horse-riding, are sometimes also provided. Information about such holidays is supplied by the local *APT* offices. The main organisations in Italy concerned with agriturismo are:

Agriturist, Corso Vittorio Emanuele 101, 00186 Roma, ☎ 06 685 2342, ▤ 39 06 685 2424, ▨ www.agriturist.it, agriturconfagricoltura.it
Terranostra, Via Nazionale 89/A, 00184 Roma, ☎ 06 482 8862, ▨ www.terranostra.it, terranostra@coldiretti.it. Terranostra publish an annual list of agriturismo accommodation under the title *Vacanze Natura*
Turismo Verde, Via Caio Mario 27, 00192 Roma, ☎ 39 06 3268 7430, ▤ 06 3600 0294, ▨ www.turismoverde.it, turismoverde@cia.it

Camping

Camping is well organised throughout Italy. Campsites are listed in the local information offices' publications. Full details of the sites in Italy are published annually by the **Touring Club Italiano**, Corso Italia 10, 20122 Milano (☎ 02 8901 1383, ▨ www.touringclub.it) in *Campeggi e Villaggi Turistici in Italia*. The national headquarters of the **Federazione Italiana Campeggiatori**, at Via Vittorio Emanuele 11, 50041 Calenzano (Firenze), ☎ 055 882 391, ▤ 055 882 5918, ▨ www.federcampeggio.it) also publishes an annual guide (*Guida Camping d'Italia*) and maintains an information office and booking service.

Hostels

The *Associazione Italiana Alberghi per la Gioventù* (*Italian Youth Hostels Association*), Via Cavour 44, 00184 Rome, ☎ 06 487 1152, ▤ 06 488 0492, ✉ www.ostellionline.org, runs many hostels, which are listed in its free annual guide. A membership card of the *AIG* or the *International Youth Hostel Federation* is required for access to Italian youth hostels. Details from the *Youth Hostels Association*, Trevelyan House, Dimple Road, Matlock, Derbyshire, DE4 3YH, ☎ 0870 770 8868, ✉ www.yha.org.uk, and from the *National Offices of American Youth Hostels, Inc*, at Hostelling International-USA, 8401 Colesville Road, Suite 600, Silver Spring, MD 20910, ☎ 301 495 1240, ▤ 301 495 6697, ✉ www.hiayh.org.

Religious institutions

Religious institutions sometimes offer simple but comfortable accommodation at very reasonable prices. For listings of convents, monasteries and other religious institutions offering accommodation, contact the Arcivescovado of the city of your choice (for Milan, for instance, the address is: *Archivescovado di Milano, Milano, Italia*), or the local tourist information office.

Food and drink

Restaurants

Italian food is usually good and inexpensive. Generally speaking, the least pretentious *ristorante* (restaurant), *trattoria* (small restaurant) or *osteria* (inn or tavern) provides the best value. A selection of restaurants has been given at the beginning of each chapter. The restaurants listed have been chosen for the quality and distinction of their cuisine and the extent of their wine lists; even the simplest are quite good. Like hotels, they have been graduated by price (expensive, moderate, inexpensive). Consider an expensive meal, one costing €80 (£50) or more; a moderate meal, €30–80 (£20–50), an inexpensive meal, under €30 (£20). As a rule, the more exclusive eating places are considerably cheaper at midday. You should telephone for details and make a reservation, as all the establishments listed provide good value for money and are likely to be very popular. Where no restaurants have been indicated in certain areas, I have felt that none merit special mention; although many establishments in the area will provide a satisfactory meal.

Restaurants are now obliged by law (for tax purposes) to issue a receipt to customers: you can be fined if you leave the premises without this document. Prices on the menu do not include a cover charge (shown separately, usually at the bottom of the page), which is added to the bill. The service charge (*servizio*) is now almost always automatically added at the end of the bill; tipping is therefore not strictly necessary, but a few euro are appreciated. Many simpler establishments do not offer a written menu, and here, although the choice is limited, the standard of cuisine is usually quite acceptable.

Bars and cafés

Bars and cafés are open from early morning to late at night and serve numerous varieties of excellent refreshments that are usually taken standing up. As a rule, you must pay the cashier first, then present your receipt to the barman in order to get served. Throughout southern Italy it has become customary to leave a small tip for the barman. If you sit at a table the charge is usually higher, and you will be given waiter service (so, you should not pay first). However, some simple bars have a few tables that can be used with no extra charge, and it is always best to ask, before ordering, whether there is waiter service or not.

Coffee

Naples is considered to have the best coffee in Italy. *Caffè* or *espresso* (black coffee) can be ordered *alto* or *lungo* (diluted), *corretto* (with a liquor), or *macchiato* (with a dash of hot milk). A *cappuccino* is an espresso with more hot milk than a *caffè macchiato* and is generally considered a breakfast drink. A glass of hot milk with a dash of coffee in it, called *latte macchiato* is another early-morning favourite. In summer, many drink *caffè freddo* (iced coffee).

Snacks

Gelato (ice cream) is always best from a *gelateria* where it is made on the spot. *Panini* (sandwiches) are made with a variety of cold meats, fish, cheeses, or vegetables, particularly *melanzane* (aubergines) or *zucchine* (courgettes) fried in vegetable oil; vegetarians may also ask for a simple sandwich of *insalata e pomodoro* (lettuce and tomato). *Pizze* (a popular and cheap food throughout Italy), *arancini* (rice croquettes with cheese or meat inside), and other snacks are served in a *pizzeria*, *rosticceria* and *tavola calda*. A *vinaio* often sells wine by the glass and simple food for very reasonable prices. Sandwiches are made up on request at *pizzicherie* and *alimentari* (grocery shops), and *fornai* (bakeries) often sell delicious individual *pizze*, *focaccie* or *schiacciate* (bread with oil and salt), cakes and so on.

Pasta

Pasta is an essential part of most meals throughout southern Italy. Today, pasta is classified according to its composition and shape. The forms that pasta may assume are countless. An ordinary Italian supermarket usually stocks about 50 different varieties, but some experts estimate that there are more than 600 shapes in all. *Pasta corta* (short pasta, i.e. *rigatoni*) is much more varied than *pasta lunga* (long pasta, i.e. spaghetti). The latter may be tubular (like *ziti* or *macaroni*), or threadlike (*spaghetti, vermicelli, capellini*); smooth (*fettucce, tagliatelle, linguine*), ruffled (*lasagne ricce*), or twisted (*fusilli*). Pasta corta comes in a limitless variety of shapes-shells (*conchiglie*), stars (*stelle*), butterflies (*farfalle*) and so on-and may be smooth (*penne*) or fluted (*rigatoni*).

The differences of shape translate into differences of flavour, even when the pasta is made from the same dough, or by the same manufacturer. The reason for this is that the relation between the surface area and the weight of the pasta varies from one shape to another, causing the sauce to adhere in different ways and to different degrees. Even without a sauce, experts claim to perceive considerable differences in flavour, because the different shapes cook in different ways.

Naples is the classic home of *pastasciutta*, which is quite different from the *pasta fresca* preferred in northern Italy (this is usually home-made, from a dough composed of flour, eggs, and just a little water). *Pastasciutta* is generally factory-made, from a simple flour and water paste rolled into sheets, cut and moulded into the desired shape and then air dried. It is hard and brittle when bought, and when correctly cooked it remains *al dente* (chewy; never soggy), additional moisture being provided by the sauce.

A short history of pasta

Whereas the invention of egg pasta is generally credited to the Chinese, the origin of pastasciutta may well be Italian. The Etruscan Tomb of the Reliefs at Cerveteri, near Rome, has stucco decorations representing pasta-making tools: a board and a rolling-pin for rolling out the dough, knives and even a toothed cutting-wheel for making decorative borders. References to lasagne may be found in Cicero and other Roman writers; the name itself is probably derived from the Latin *lagana* or *lasana*, a cooking pot.

By the end of the Middle Ages pasta was known throughout Italy. The 14C *Codice del l'Anonimo Toscano*, preserved in the library of Bologna University, contains several serving suggestions; and the poet Boccaccio, in his masterpiece, the *Decameron*, describes an imaginary land of grated parmesan cheese inhabited by people whose only pastime is the making of *'maccheroni e raviuoli'*. Of course, tomato sauce was unheard of until the discovery of America: Boccaccio's contemporaries cooked their macaroni and ravioli in chicken broth and dressed them with fresh butter. An early American appreciator of *pastasciutta* was Thomas Jefferson, who in 1787 brought a spaghetti-making machine from Italy to the United States.

Regional dishes

Southern Italian cuisine can be very different from that of the north. The number and variety of regional dishes is so great that to describe them all in detail would require several hundred pages. What follows is therefore a brief summary.

Antipasti ~ hors d'oeuvre

Crostini alla napoletana are among the simplest and tastiest of all crostini. Small, thin slices of bread are covered with mozzarella, chopped anchovies and tomatoes; seasoned with salt and oregano; then lightly toasted in the oven.

Gatto The gatto is fairly common in Neapolitan cooking, although the ingredients often change. It has little to do with the gâteaux of French haute cuisine, notwithstanding its Angevin origins. It is a humble dish, a sort of dumpling made of mashed potatoes, eggs, prosciutto, mozzarella and whatever else happens to be on hand. It is usually served piping hot.

Impepata di cozze is a simple Neapolitan dish of fresh mussels, poached and dressed with lemon juice, chopped parsley, and olive oil.

Mozzarella in carrozza (literally 'mozzarella in a carriage') consists of a slice of mozzarella fried between two slices of bread that are dipped in an egg batter, like French toast.

Pagnottine Santa Chiara, as the name suggests, were invented by the nuns of Santa Chiara. They are savoury cakes made with anchovies, tomatoes, parsley and oregano.

Panzanella alla napoletana is a favourite salad dish made of crumbled bread, onions, tomatoes, anchovies, basil and garlic (sometimes peppers and green olives are added) all dressed with olive oil.

Peperoni farciti, stuffed baked peppers, is a peasant dish existing throughout the south in a variety of versions. Three common fillings are: olives, capers, parsley, and anchovies; aubergine and tomatoes; macaroni in a savoury sauce.

Taralli col pepe are rings of crisp bread flavoured with pepper and almonds. Another version uses fennel seeds.

Zucchine a scapece may be either an antipasto or a *contorno* (see below). Courgettes are sliced and fried in olive oil, seasoned with vinegar and fresh mint leaves and served cold.

Primi piatti ~ first courses
Soups
Minestra maritata, a very old, very typical Neapolitan speciality, is also known as *pignato grasso*. It is a classic winter soup consisting chiefly of beet greens or cabbage boiled with a ham bone and sausages, served hot.

Minestrone napoletano is similar to all other Italian minestroni, with a predominance of yellow courgettes over all the other ingredients. Usually served with macaroni.

Zuppa di cardoni, a rich, tasty dish from the Campanian hinterland, is made of cardoons (an edible thistle) cooked in chicken broth with meat balls, mozzarella, chicken and sausages.

Zuppa alla marinara is made throughout the south with as many varieties of fish as possible, which are stewed together with clams and mussels in lots of tomato sauce, olive oil, garlic and hot peppers.

Pasta and rice
Maccheroni cacio e uova is simply macaroni in a cheese and egg sauce, sprinkled with chopped parsley before serving.

Frittata di pasta, or *pasta fritta*, originally a way of getting good mileage out of leftovers, is now a classic first course in its own right. Vermicelli or macaroni are seasoned with a rich sauce made with meat balls, chopped prosciutto and cheese. The whole concoction, bound together by a few well-beaten eggs, becomes a fragrant and savoury omelette, often considered a complete meal.

Fusilli alla napoletana are served in a rich sauce made with meat dripping, tomatoes, onions, celery, carrots, ricotta, salami, bacon, garlic and seasoned pecorino cheese. Sometimes spaghetti or macaroni are used instead of fusilli.

Lasagne di Carnevale is an especially rich dish, popular in Naples at carnival time. Square lasagne are baked in a sauce containing sausages and meat balls, mozzarella, ricotta, and other cheeses and hard-boiled eggs.

Pasta e fagioli all'ischitana, a speciality of the island of Ischia, is made with several pasta shapes: spaghetti, tripolini, bucatini and linguine, or whatever leftovers happen to be to hand. The sauce is made with lots of fresh beans, and is seasoned with hot red peppers. *Pasta alla sorrentina* adds diced scamorza cheese to the tomato sauce, to make it thick and stringy. The pasta thus seasoned is served with lots of grated caciocavallo or parmesan cheese.

Ragù alla napoletana, also known as *rrau*, is a delicious sauce for special occasions that is traditionally placed on the stove at dawn and left to simmer slowly all day. It is prepared by melting lard and ham fat in a pan, then adding slices of veal rolled around a filling of grated cheese, garlic, parsley, raisins and pine-nuts. As the sauce cooks, red wine and tomatoes are added. At the end the sauce is used to dress the pasta, while the meat rolls are served as an entrée.

Sartù is the richest of all Neapolitan dishes. Today only a few Neapolitan restaurants make it regularly, and to taste it at its best you should order it ahead of time.

It is a rice pie stuffed with meat balls, sausage, chicken livers, mozzarella, mushrooms, peas, etc. Baked in a mould, it is not only tasty, but also very theatrical.

Timballo di maccheroni, like *sartù* is a classic dish favoured by the Neapolitan aristocracy. It gradually spread throughout the Kingdom of the Two Sicilies to become one of the more characteristic dishes of southern Italy. It is made with macaroni baked in a pie with a sauce of chicken livers, mushrooms and black truffles.

Spaghetti aglio e olio is served with a sauce of olive oil, garlic, parsley, and sometimes peperoncini, or hot red peppers. Best enjoyed after midnight.

Spaghetti alle vongole is spaghetti in a clam sauce flavoured with onions, tomatoes, cheese and aromatic herbs. Sometimes rice is used instead of spaghetti—*Risotto alle vongole*.

Vermicelli alla carrettiera (literally 'cart drivers' vermicelli') belongs to a category of pasta (like *spaghetti alla bucaniera* (pirates' spaghetti), and *Maccheroni alla zappatora* (ditch-diggers' macaroni) whose names suggest that their seasoning is so strong that only he-men can be expected to cope with them. In *vermicelli alla carrettiera* a distinctive element is provided by the breadcrumbs that are sprinkled over the pasta instead of parmesan cheese.

Zite ripiene, a speciality of Caserta, takes the pasta known as *zite* as a basic ingredient, although *conchiglie* or *lumache* (both called 'shells' in English) can also be used. The pasta is filled with diced pork, onions, salami or sausage, cheese, spices and eggs, then covered with more cheese and baked. In a Lenten version the filling is made of ricotta, fresh basil and other herbs.

Panzerotti, a kind of Apulian ravioli, are usually filled with anchovies, capers and strong ricotta cheese (made from ewe's milk).

Spaghetti alla carbonara (spaghetti with bacon, black pepper, eggs and pecorino), and *supplì* (rice croquettes stuffed with mozzarella cheese and minced meat) are among the specialities of Lazio; and Abruzzo is famous for *Maccheroni alla chitarra* (home-made pasta with pecorino cheese and tomatoes).

Pizza

Suffice it to recall here that there is an infinite variety of pizza recipes, all based on bread dough. The secret of a successful pizza is a blazing hot oven. Only violent heat, in fact, is capable of cooking the pizza in such a way that it is soft, yet crunchy at the same time; if the oven is not hot enough, the dough becomes tough as shoe leather. A wood-fired oven is best, although it is possible to produce an acceptable pizza in an electric or gas oven.

Secondi piatti ~ main courses

Anguilla in umido (eel) is a common dish in the Agro Pontino and the Caserta area, where it is still fairly easy to find eels in the irrigation canals. They are cooked in tomato sauce and served on toast.

Anguilla alla griglia is grilled and basted with a sauce of olive oil, garlic, vinegar and fresh mint leaves.

Baccalà alla napoletana is a traditional dish of salted cod fillets first floured and fried, then stewed with tomatoes, capers, black olives, raisins, pine-nuts, and, of course, garlic.

Agnello pasquale is roast lamb seasoned with rosemary, bay leaf and sage and accompanied by tender new onions and potatoes. Considered a traditional dish at Easter, it also appears year round on the menus of many restaurants.

Braciola alla napoletana is a rich dish usually reserved for special occasions. An immense slice of beef or pork is covered with chopped provolone, prosciutto, raisins, and eggs; then tightly rolled, tied with string and cooked in tomato sauce.

Cecenielli literally means little chick-peas, but if you order *cecenielli* in a Neapolitan trattoria what you get is quite different: spicy little fish cooked in a flour and water paste, or served on a pizza.

Cervella alla napoletana is veal or lamb's brain baked with capers, black olives, pepper and breadcrumbs.

Coniglio all'ischitana In this dish the delicate meat of the rabbit is cut into pieces, browned in olive oil and cooked in white wine, tomato sauce and rosemary.

Costata alla pizzaiola is a T-bone steak served in a tomato sauce flavoured with garlic and oregano.

Genovese is the term used by Neapolitans to indicate a particular kind of beef stew—cooked slowly with much onion, olive oil, lard and tomato sauce—that crept into the local culinary tradition through the colony of Genoese merchants who lived in Naples.

Polpo alla luciana It seems that this manner of stewing octopus—with tomatoes, olive oil, garlic, and hot peppers—was developed by the wives of the fishermen of Santa Lucia. When small octopuses are used, the dish is called *purpetielle affocate*.

Ostriche (oysters) and *cozze* nere (black mussels) are specialities of Apulian cookery, as are *tordi al solso*, thrushes cooked with fennel and bay leaves and conserved in white wine.

In the mountains of Basilicata and Calabria, game dishes are plentiful, whereas lamb dishes prevail in the mountainous regions of Abruzzo and Molise although *pollo all'abruzzese* (chicken with sweet peppers), and *trota alla brace* (grilled trout) are both typical here.

Contorni ~ vegetables

Carciofi ripieni alla napoletana is baked artichokes with a delicious filling of meat, mushrooms, onions and tomatoes.

Cianfotta is a sort of vegetable stew made with potatoes, yellow peppers, onions, tomatoes, aubergines, courgettes and celery.

Insalata di rinforzo, a traditional Christmas dish, is a hodgepodge of cauliflower, olives, various pickled vegetables, anchovies and capers, mixed together and dressed with olive oil and vinegar. The name comes from the fact that the dish is eaten in more than one day and is continually 'reinforced' with other ingredients, which take the place of the ones eaten the day before.

Melanzane alla partenopea is an aubergine casserole, like *melanzane alla parmigiana* (which, despite its name, is a Campanian invention). Ingredients are aubergines, caciocavallo and parmesan cheese, tomato sauce, spices.

Peperoni in teglia alla napoletana are yellow peppers fried in olive oil with capers and anchovies. In Basilicata and Calabria, aubergines are cooked in several different ways: *in agrodolce* (sour wine with chocolate, cinnamon, walnuts and raisins); *al funghetto* (baked with garlic, pepper and oregano); or as *melanzane ripiene* (stuffed and baked).

No trip to Lazio would be complete without *Carciofi alla giudia* (tender artichokes fried crisp and sprinkled with lemon juice); and in Apulia grilled vegetables of all kinds, dressed in abundant olive oil (which has a more aggressive flavour than the Ligurian or Tuscan oils) are often served as a main course.

Desserts

Coviglie (*al caffè or al cioccolato*) is a traditional Neapolitan dessert much like a mousse. *Pastiera* is a classic that can be found in Campanian *pasticcerie* from November to March. It is a pie filled with fresh ricotta, grains of wheat, rice, or barley boiled in milk, candied fruit, eggs, sugar, spices and other ingredients. Some famous Neapolitan bakers make pastiera to order, packing it in such a way that it can stand up to long journeys.

Sfogliatelle are perhaps the most famous of Neapolitan breakfast pastries. There are two types, one made with a thin ribbon of crisp dough wound in tight spiral layers (sfogliatelle ricce) and the other a simple envelope of soft dough. Both types are filled with fresh ricotta, chopped candied fruit, cinnamon, vanilla, and other ingredients.

Sproccolati, sun-dried figs filled with fennel seeds and preserved on wooden sticks, are a speciality of Ravello and the Amalfi coast.

Struffoli, a traditional Christmas dessert, has all the characteristics typical of ancient Greek sweets: it calls for very little sugar, relying for its sweetness on honey, and, to a lesser extent, on candied fruit. It comes in two shapes: the traditional cone and the more modern ring.

Susamelli, a fusion of the Italian words for sesame and honey, sesame and miele, are S-shaped biscuits made with flour, sesame seeds (often substituted with ground almonds), sugar, honey, and candied orange and lemon peel.

Southern Italian wines

Some southern Italian wines are universally known; others, highly popular at home, are seldom exported and may even be difficult to obtain outside their own province. As elsewhere in Italy, fine wines must meet high standards of quality to earn the seals, DOC (*di origine controllata*, 'monitored appellation') or DOCG (*di origine controllata e garantita*, 'monitored and guaranteed'). The following list includes some of the better southern Italian wines.

Southern Lazio

The vine has been an important part of agricultural life in Lazio since the time of the Roman Empire, and even today much of the region is given over to vineyards. The volcanic hills around Rome produce the best wines—for instance, the famous *Colli Albani*, a dry or mellow white served with antipasti, poultry and fish (the *superiore* is stronger, the *spumante* sparkling); *Frascati*, a dry white served with antipasti, poultry, fish, desserts (the *superiore* is stronger, the *spumante* is sparkling, and the *novello* is fruity); *Montecompatri Colonna*, a mellow white good with antipasti and poultry (the *superiore* is stronger); and *Zagarolo*, a mellow white served with cold meats and poultry (the *superiore* is stronger); the lesser-known *Genazzano Bianco*, a mellow white served with minestre, poultry and fish; *Genazzano Rosso*, a mellow red served with meats, cheeses and desserts; *Velletri Bianco*, a dry or mellow white served with antipasti, soups and fish; and *Velletri Rosso*, a dry red served with roast meat and poultry and mature cheeses, also come from the hills just south of Rome.

Southern Lazio produces fewer good wines, but the reputation of this area is improving over time. *Colli Lanuvini*, a dry or mellow white served with antipasti, fish or dessert, is made in the hills between Lake Nemi and the Aprilia district, around Latina. The latter district yields the delicious *Merlot di Aprilia*, a dry red served with roast meat and poultry; *Sangiovese di Aprilia*, a dry rosé served with pastasciutta, poultry and mushrooms; and *Trebbiano di Aprilia*, a dry white served with fish, minestre, vegetables and cheeses. The wines of Cori—*Cori Bianco*, a dry, mellow, or sweet white served with antipasti, poultry and desserts; and *Cori Rosso*, a dry red served with poultry, pork, wildfowl—established a certain standing some time ago and are perhaps the most complex wines of the region.

Campania

The quality of Campanian wines is widely appreciated, even though a relatively small proportion of the region is planted with vineyards.

Possibly the best Campanian wine, *Taurasi*, a dry red (the *riserva* is aged four years), served with fine roasts, is not well known. Nevertheless, it is generally considered one of the premier wines of southern Italy. It is produced around Taurasi, in Avellino province. Made from the Aglanico grape, with the possible addition of other non-aromatic red grapes (max 15%), it has an intensely ruby red colour, tending to garnet, with orange reflections when aged; a distinctive, intense bouquet; and dry, full, harmonious flavour with a persistent aftertaste.

The same grape is used to make the tasty *Aglianico del Cilento*, a dry red served with roasted and grilled meats; the dry red *Aglianico di Guardia Sanframondi* (or *Guardiolo*; the *riserva*, aged two years, has a lighter bouquet and smoother flavour), served with roasted and grilled meat; and *Aglianico di Sant'Agata dei Goti*, a robust red rich in tannins, aged at least two years (the *riserva* is aged three years), served with roasts and stews.

If you like things with a history, try *Aversa Asprinio*, a dry, fruity white served with fish or vegetables, or *Aversa Asprinio Spumante*, a dry, sparkling white served as an aperitif or with pastry. These wines, from the provinces of Naples and Caserta, are grown with the vines trained to trees—as were the first vines planted in the Mediterranean. The special training system, called *alberata aversana*, is considered an environmental and cultural asset of the growning region. Wines from vineyards trained in this fashion bear the terms *alberata* or *vigneti ad alberata* on their labels. The dry white is made from Asprinio and other non-aromatic white grapes (>15%), the *spumante* from Asprinio only.

Several fine wines come from the volcanic soils of the Plegraean Fields and Procida. These include *Campi Flegrei Bianco*, a fresh, dry white served with fish; *Campi Flegrei Rosso* and *Piedirosso* or *Pér 'e Palummo*, dry, harmonious reds made from the Piedirosso grape and served with meats (there are also a *rosso novello* and a *Piedirosso riserva*, aged two years); *Piedirosso* or *Pér 'e Palummo Passito*, a dry-to-sweet soft, harmonious dessert wine made from grapes dried on the vine or after the harvest; *Falanghina*, a soft, dry white; and the somewhat frutier *Falanghina spumante*, served respectively with fish and desserts.

Vineyards terraced onto the steep slopes of Capri produce *Capri Bianco*, a dry white served with antipasti, risotti, soups and fried fish and *Capri Rosso*, a dry red served with meat or poultry, pastasciutta and timballi.

Castel San Lorenzo, in Salerno province, gives its name to four good wines: *Barbera di Castel San Lorenzo*, a dry red served with meats and aged cheeses; *Castel San Lorenzo Bianco*, a dry white served with fish or fresh cheeses; *Castel San Lorenzo Rosato*, a delicate, dry rosé served with antipasti di pesce, antipasti di prosciutto, or poultry; and *Castel San Lorenzo Rosso*, a dry, fruity red served with meats and roast poultry. There are also a *Moscato di Castel San Lorenzo*, a sweet, mellow white (the *lambiccato* is stronger) served with pastry or ice cream, and a *Moscato Spumante di Castel San Lorenzo*, a sweet, sparkling white served with cake or ice cream.

The hilly terrain of the Cilento Peninsula, just south of Salerno, is home to *Cilento Aglianico*, a dry, full-bodied red served with roasted meats; *Cilento Bianco*, a delicate white served with minestre, poultry, or fish; *Cilento Rosato*, a intense rosé served with minestre and roast or grilled fish; and *Cilento Rosso*, a dry red served with fried meat and stews.

The sun-baked Amalfi Coast has its own appellation, which embraces *Costa d'Amalfi Bianco*, a dry, delicate white served with fish; *Costa d'Amalfi Rosato*, a dry, fresh rosé; and *Costa d'Amalfi Rosso*, a medium-bodied red served with all meals. The red and rosé both use Piedirosso (known locally as *Pér 'e Palummo*) and Sciascinoso variety (locally, Olivella) grapes; the white is a blend of Falanghina (locally, Bianca Zita) and Biancolella (Bianca Tenera). These wines are sometimes labelled with the name of one of three sub-areas, *Furore, Ravello* or *Tramonti*.

The hills above Caserta produce several wines based on Falanghina white, and Aglanico, Piedirosso and Barbera red grapes. These include *Falerno del Massico Bianco*, a dry white served as an aperitif or with minestre and poultry; *Falerno del Massico Primitivo*, a dry red served with roasts and stews; *Falerno del Massico Riserva* (both *Rosso* and *Primitivo* aged two years); and *Falerno del Massico Rosso*, a dry red served with meats, wild game and mature cheeses.

In the province of Avellino the Fiano variety (sometimes mixed with Greco, Coda di Volpe Bianca or Trebbiano Toscano grapes) is used to make *Fiano d'Avellino*, a dry white served with antipasti, fish, and poultry; whereas the Greco and Coda di Volpe Bianca varieties go into the delicious *Greco di Tufo*, a dry, delicate white (sometimes *spumante*) served with antipasti and fish.

The beautiful, rolling countryside of Guardia Sanframondi, in Benevento province, produces the excellent *Falanghina di Guardia Sanframondi* (or *Guardiolo*, a dry, delicate white served with fish; *Guardia Sanframondi* (or *Guardiolo*) *Bianco*, a delicate, dry white served with vegetables or poultry; *Guardia Sanframondi* (or Guardiolo) *Rosato*, a dry rosé served with shellfish and rich fish dishes; *Guardia Sanframondi* (or *Guardiolo*) *Rosso*, a dry red served with roast meat (the *novello* is lighter and served at a lower temperature, the *riserva* is aged two years); and *Guardia Sanframondi* (or *Guardiolo*) *Spumante*, a delicate sparkling white served as an aperitif, with shellfish or with cake.

The wines of Ischia have been highly regarded since the 16C, when the Greco made there was thought to have therapeutic properties. You can't get Ischia Greco these days, but there are some pretty good substitutes: *Ischia Bianco*, a dry white made from Forastera Bianco, Biancolella and other white grapes (the *superiore* is stronger); *Ischia Biancolella* and *Ischia Forastera*, dry, balanced single-varietal whites served with fish and shellfish; *Ischia Rosso*, a dry red; and *Piedirosso* or *Pér e' Palummo*, a dry, medium-bodied, single-varietal red served with pastasciutta and poultry. There is also a *Piedirosso* or *Pér e' Palummo Passito* dessert wine.

The best wines from the Sorrento Peninsula are *Penisola Sorrentina Bianco*, a dry, harmonious, full-bodied white, drunk locally as an aperitif; *Penisola Sorrentina Rosso*, a medium-bodied red made from Piedirosso, Sciascinoso, and/or Aglianico grapes and served with all meals; and *Penisola Sorrentina Rosso Frizzante Naturale*, a dry-to-sweet sparkling red served throughout meals if dry, at the end if sweet.

The ancient region of Samnium gives its name to the *Sannio* appellation, which applies to wines made in Benevento province: *Sannio Bianco*, a vivacious dry white served as an aperitif or with fish (sweet and sparkling varieties are served as dessert wines); *Sannio Rosso*, a soft, tannic red (also available as a *novello* and a sweeter *frizzante*) served with meals and desserts; *Sannio Rosato*, *a* fragrant, dry, fresh rosé served throughout meals; *Sannio Spumante Metodo Classico*, a dry, fresh, harmonious white or pink bubbly involving traditional refermentation in the bottle, an excellent before-dinner drink; *and Aglianico, Barbera, Piedirosso, Sciascinoso, Coda di Volpe, Falanghina, Fiano* and *Greco* single-varietal wines. *Sannio Moscato*, *a* soft, sweet, white made from grapes dried on the vine or after the harvest, is a delicious, strong (14.5%) dessert wine.

The verdant hills around Sant'Agata de' Goti, in Benevento province, produce the excellent *Greco di Sant'Agata dei Goti*, a fresh, fruity white served with poultry; *Piedirosso di Sant'Agata dei Goti*, a robust red, rich in tannins, served with meats; *Sant'Agata dei Goti Rosato*, a delicate rosé served with poultry; and *Sant'Agata dei Goti Rosso*, a dry red served with all meats. The Solpaca district, in the same province, yields the pleasant *Solopaca Bianco*, a dry white served with pastasciutta, risotti, poultry and bolliti, and *Solopaca Rosso*, a dry, intense red served with meats, especially lamb.

The bay-side slopes of Vesuvius produce the very fine *Vesuvio Bianco*, a dry white served with antipasti di mare, zuppe, risotti, fish; *Vesuvio Rosato*, a dry rosé served with antipasti, timballi, fresh cheeses; and *Vesuvio Rosso*, a dry red served with roasts and stews. When these wines have a minimum alcohol content of 12% they are called *Lacryma Christi*. The dry white *Lacryma Christi del Vesuvio Bianco* is served with fish; *Lacryma Christi del Vesuvio Liquoroso*, a sweet amber wine, with desserts; *Lacryma Christi del Vesuvio Rosato*, a dry rosé with antipasti and poultry; and *Lacryma Christi del Vesuvio Rosso*, a dry red, with meat and poultry.

Basilicata and Calabria

The wines from the dry hills and plains of Basilicata and Calabria are excellent and have considerable alcohol levels. They also reflect a very old enological tradition, dating from before the Greek colonisation.

Basilicata is known for its exquisite *Aglianico del Vulture*, a magnificent red wine that has been cultivated on the volcanic slopes of Monte Vulture since ancient times. One of the few southern Italian wines suited to extended aging, it has an intense ruby-red to garnet colour; a delicate, vinous bouqet that improves with age, and a dry, fresh, balanced, and tannic flavour that becomes velvety over time. Excellent with roasts (it enlivened the table of Emperor Frederick II), all *Aglianico del Vulture* is aged at least one year; after three years it can be called *vecchio*; the *riserva* is aged five (!) years.

The Ionian coast of Calabria produces several appellations. From the area around Bivongi come *Bivongi Bianco*, a dry, fruity white served as an aperitif or with fish; *Bivongi Rosé*, a dry, agreeable rosé served throughout meals; and *Bivongi Rosso*, a dry, fruity, harmonious red, also available in *novello* and *riserva* versions and likewise served throughout meals.

Calabria's most famous wine is certainly Cirò, made in the province of Catanzaro, around Cirò, Cirò Marina, Melissa and Crucoli. The white *Cirò Bianco* is made from Greco Bianco grapes, with up to 10% Trebbiano Toscano; it is straw-yellow in colour, with an enticing vinous bouquet and a dry, lively, but balanced flavour. The fabulous red, *Cirò Rosso*, is made from Galioppo grapes, with the possible addition of Trebbiano Toscano and Greco Bianco, (max 5%); it is ruby-red in colour, and warm, balanced, and velvety to the taste when aged. The *classico* is grown in a special area in the townships of Cirò and Cirò Marina; the *superiore* is stronger (13.5%, rather than 12.5%) and two years of age qualifies the wine as a *riserva*. There is also a rosé, *Cirò Rosato*, made from the same grapes as the red. It has an intense rosé colour; a delicate vinous bouquet; and a fresh, dry, inviting flavour that makes it good to drink throughout a meal.

Cosenza province is known for its Donnici appelatiion. *Donnici Bianco*, a fresh, dry and, occasionally, fruity white, is good with fish; *Donnici Rosato*, a fresh, delicate, fragrant rosé, and *Donnici Rosso*, a full, dry, harmonious red), with all meals.

Greco di Bianco is produced in a tiny area in the townships of Bianco and Casignana (Reggio Calabria). It is a soft, warm, balanced white dessert wine, aged at least one year. It is best enjoyed with cake, fruit salad and ice cream.

Lamezia Terme gives its name to two whites—the full, dry, velvety *Lamezia Bianco*, and the dry, harmonious *Lamezia Greco*, made principally from Greco grapes—both served with fish. There are also a dry, fragrant rosè, *Lamezia Rosato*, and a dry, full-bodied and usually fruity red, *Lamezia Rosso*, served with all meals. Near the Lamezia growing area is that of the Savuto Valley, which yields *Savuto Rosato*, a dry rosé served with meats, poultry and fresh cheeses; and *Savuto Rosso*, a dry red served with meats, game and mature cheeses.

The township of Melissa is famous for its excellent Cirò-like wines, *Melissa Bianco*, a dry white served with antipasti, fish; and *Melissa Rosso*, a full, dry red blending Gaglioppo, Greco Nero, Greco Bianco, Trebbiano Toscano and/or Malvasia Bianca grapes (the *superiore* is aged at least two years) and served with stewed meats.

The Gaglioppo variety is also the basis of *Pollino*, a dry red grown in northern Cosenza province and served with roast meats and poultry (the *superiore* is aged two years); as well as of two wines from Crotone province, *Sant'Anna di Isola Capo Rizzuto Rosato*, a dry rosé good with 'important' meats, especially lamb; and *Sant'Anna di Isola Capo Rizzuto Rosso*, a dry red served with lighter meats or roast poultry.

Abruzzo and Molise

Italy's mountainous heart, dominated by the tall peaks of the Gran Sasso and the Majella, has rich rocky soil well suited to the production of fine grapes. Skilled craftsmanship turns the main varieties grown here, Montepulciano, Trebbiano and Sangiovese, into excellent wines.

Controguerra and neighbouring townships in Teramo province produce the delicious *Controguerra Rosso*, a dry, ruby-red, lightly tannic blend of 60% Montepulciano grapes with Merlot and/or Cabernet, with the possible addition of other local red grapes. Served with all meals, it is available also as a *novello* and can be labeled as a *riserva* afrter twelve months' aging in the cask and six months' fining in the bottle. The Controguerra appellation also includes *Controguerra Bianco*, a dry, somewhat fruity white taken by the *Abruzzesi* as an aperitif or with fish (the *frizzante* is lightly sparkling); *Controguerra Spumante*, an elegant sparkling wine with fine perlage, a persistent bouquet and fresh, full, prolonged flavor; *Controguerra Passerina*, a golden white with delicate aroma and fresh flavour good with seafood; *Controguerra Malvasia*, a straw-yellow, dry white also served with fish; *Controguerra Moscato Amabile*, a dark yellow dessert wine with a sweet, balanced flavour; *Controguerra Passito Bianco* and *Rosso*, dessert wines made from grapes crushed as late as six months after harvest (the very special *arnoso* has been aged in special casks called *caratelli* for 30 months); as well as the less distinctive *Controguerra Merlot*, *Pinot Nero*, *Chardonnay*, *Malvasia* and *Riesling*.

The Montepulciano grape, brought to Abruzzo in the early nineteenth century, is now grown throughout the region. It goes into the dry red *Montepulciano d'Abruzzo*, served with meat and poultry (the *vecchio* is aged two years); *Cerasuolo d'Abruzzo*, a dry, soft, balanced, dark cherry-red wine served with roast or grilled meats; and *Colline Teramane*, a full, robust but velvety dry purplish-red wine blending 90% Montepulciano grapes with other Sangiovese grapes. *Trebbiano d'Abruzzo*, a dry white served with fish and cheese, is made from Trebbiano d'Abruzzo and/or Trebbiano Toscano grapes.

Although agriculture is still a primary economic activity in Molise, the thrust is on cereals, forage crops, legumes, garden vegetables and forestry. Nevertheless, grape-growing is gaining momentum in the region and there are now has two registered appellations, Biferno and Pentro di Isernia. *Biferno Bianco* is a dry white blend of Terebbiano and Malvasia Bianca grapes, served with poultry and vegetables. *Biferno Rosso* is a delicious blend of Montepulciano, Trebbiano Toscano and Aglianico red grapes, with the possible addition of non-aromatic local red or white varieties, made around Campobasso; it is served with red meat and is also available as a *riserva*. *Biferno Rosato* is a dry rosé variant of the *Rosso* served with poultry, rabbit and cheeses. *Biferno Tintilia* is an interesting dry, soft red served with most foods; the *riserva* is aged two years. There are also a *Biferno Chardonnay, Falanghina, Greco Bianco, Moscato, Moscato Passito, Moscato Spumante, Pinot Bianco, Sauvignon, Trebbiano, Aglianico, Cabernet Sauvignon, Montepulciano,* and *Sangiovese.*

The province of Isernia produces *Pentro di Isernia Bianco*, a dry white served with vegetables, poultry, or cold meats; *Pentro di Isernia Rosato*, a dry rosé served with poultry, rabbit and game; and *Pentro di Isernia Rosso*, a dry red served with roast meat and poultry.

Apulia

Apulia is the only region of southern Italy that is not mountainous—which is good news for grapes. Grape-growing and winemaking understandably constitute one of the pillars of the region's economy, and Apulia is distinguished for both quantity and the quality of its wines. Also, the tradition has deep roots: the Phoenicians, who practiced viticulture as long ago as 2000 BC, introduced new varieties of grapes as well as new techniques of cultivation to the region. The science was so advanced when the Greeks arrived that they called Apulia *Enotria* (Wineland).

Aleatico di Puglia is probably the oldest of the Apulian wines. Today it is made from Aleatico grapes, with the addition of small quantities of Negroamaro, Malvasia Nera and Primitivo. It is intense garnet red in colour with purple reflections that turn to orange-red with aging. The bouquet is delicate and distinctive, the flavour moderately sweet and velvety. It is a strong wine (at least 15% alchohol; the *liquoroso*, made from lightly dried grapes, reaches 18.5%). Aged from five months to three years (*riserva*), it has a full, warm, sweet, balanced flavour best enjoyed with desserts, especially cake and ice cream.

Alezio wines, from the province of Lecce, is made from Negroamaro grapes with the possible addition of Malvasia Nera di Lecce, Sangiovese and Montepulciano. *Alezio Rosso*, a dry, warm red with a slightly bitter aftertaste, is served with meats and poultry (the *riserva* is aged two years); *Alezio Rosato*, a rosé, is coral-red, dry and velvety; it is served with minestre, fried and baked dishes, and cheeses.

The territory between Brindisi and Mesagne produces *Brindisi Rosato*, a dry rosé served with pastasciutta, vegetables and cheeses; and *Brindisi Rosso*, a dry, velvety red served with meats (the *riserva* is aged two years).

A complex blend of Montepulciano, Uva di Troia, Sangiovese, Malvasia Nera di Brindisi, Trebbiano Toscano, Bombino Bianco and Malvasia del Chienti varieties is used to make *Cacc'e Mitte di Lucera*, a full, harmonious dry red from Northern Apulia served with meat, eggs and cheeses.

Castel del Monte, one of Apulia's more famous monuments, gives its name to several wines produced in the province of Bari. These include the dry white blend of Pampanuto, Chardonnay or Bombino Bianco grapes with non-aromatic local varieties, *Castel del Monte Bianco*, served with fish and shellfish; the dry rosé *Castel del Monte Rosato*, served as an aperitif or with antipasti; and *Castel del Monte Rosso*, a dry, tannic red combining Uva di Troia, Aglianico or Multipulciano grapes with non-aromatic local varieties, served with roasts (available comes as a *novello* and as a three-year-old *riserva*). The appellation also covers single-varietal wines such as *Bombino Bianco, Chardonnay, Pinot Bianco, Sauvignon, Aglanico, Aglianico Rosato, Bombino Nero, Cabernet Franc and/or Sauvignon, Pinot Nero* and *Uva di Troia*.

From the Salentine Peninsula, south of Lecce, come *Copertino Rosato*, a dry rosé served with pastasciutta and vegetables; *Copertino Rosso*, a dry red served with roasts (the *riserva* is aged two years); and the many fine wines of *Galatina*: the delicate, fruity white, *Galatina Bianco*, served as an aperitif or with fish (also *frizzante*); *Galatina Rosato*, a cherry-red dry rosé, served with all food (also *frzzante*); the warm, hearty ruby-red *Galatina Rosso*, served with meats; and the single-varietal *Chardonnay, Negroamaro* and *Negroamaro Riserva*.

Various types of wine are produced under the appellative, *Gioia del Colle. Gioia del Colle Bianco* is a delicate dry white served with fish and poultry; *Gioia del Colle Rosato*, a dry rosé; served as an aperitif or with poultry; *Gioia del Collo Rosso*, a dry red, served with meat and poultry. *Gioia del Colle Primitivo* is made exclusively from grapes of the Primitivo variety; full, harmonious and slightly sweet, this strong (13%) dark red wine is best at the end of meals (the *riserva* is aged two years). Another good end-of-meal wine, *Gioia del Colle Aleatico Dolce* is a full, moderately sweet, velvety red. The *riserva* is aged two years; the *liquoroso* decidedly sweet, and much stronger (18.5%).

Gravina, made in a district ranging from Gravina di Puglia to Altamura, is a dry or mellow white served with poultry, fish and desserts; it also comes with bubbles (*spumante*).

Leverano, near Lecce, produces *Leverano Bianco*, a dry white served with roast or fried fish and shellfish; *Leverano Rosato*, a dry rosé served with soups, fried fish and cheeses; and *Leverano Rosso*, a dry red served with meats (the *riserva* is aged two years).

Lizzano, in Taranto province, gives its name to a variety of wines: *Lizzano Bianco*, a dry white served with antipasti or fish; *Lizzano Rosato*, a dry rosé served with fish or shellfish; *Lizzano Rosso;* a dry red served with meats, cold meats and mature cheeses. The white and rosé come in sparkling (*frizzante*) versions, and there are also single-varietal a *Negroamaro Rosato, Negroamaro Rosso and Malvasia Nera*. The fragrant rosé is served with antipasti and minestre; the red, with hot and cold meats. The *Malvasia* is a sweet, slightly aromatic dessert wine; the *superiore*, aged at least one year, is stronger.

Apulia's most famous white wines are *Locorotondo* and *Martina Franca*. The first is produced in the fairy-tale valleys between Locorotondo, Cisternino and Fasano. Made from Verdeca and Bianco d'Alessano grapes with the possible addition of Fianom Bombino, and Malvasia Toscana, it is straw-yellow in colour and dry and delicate in flavour. Ideal with fish, it also comes sparkling (*spumante*). The same grapes make up *Martina Franca* (or *Martina*). Produced nearby, around Martina Franca, Alberobello, Ceglie, Cisternino and Ostuni, this delicious dry white has enjoyed wide favour since ancient times (also available as a *spumante*).

A similar appellation, *Matino*, is applied to two wines made in the hills of the Salentine peninsula, mainly from Negroamaro grapes. These are the dry rosé *Matino Rosato*, served with pastasciutta, vegetables, and poultry; and the dry red *Matino Rosso*, served with lamb, roast pork and mature cheeses.

Moscato di Trani, best with cake and ice cream, is an exquisite, naturally sweet amber-coloured dessert wine made from the grapes known locally as Moscato di Trani or Moscato Reale. Famous since ancient times, it has a velvety flavour owed partially to five months' fining; the *liquoroso* type is aged one year and has a minimum alcohol content of 18%.

Also from the Salentine come *Nardò Rosato* a dry rosé served with soups and roast fish; and *Nardò Rosso*, a dry red served with lamb or mature cheeses. Both are made from Negroamaro grapes and have a slightly bitter aftertaste.

Orta Nova Rosato, a dry rosé served with pastasciutta and cheeses; and *Orta Nova Rosso*, a dry red served with meat and poultry and mature cheeses, are two Sangiovase-based wines from the province of Foggia, in northern Apulia.

The beautiful town of Ostuni, on the coast in Brindisi province, produces the delicious *Ostuni Bianco*, a dry white served with antipasti, pastasciutta, fish, eggs and vegetables; and *Ottavianello*, a delicate dry red made from the local grape of the same name, served with stewed and grilled meats.

Primitivo di Manduria, a soft, dry, harmonious red served with roast meats, is aged to make the sweeter dessert wines, *Dolce Naturale*, *Liquoroso Dolce Naturale* and *Liquoroso Secco*.

West of Barletta are three districts producing excellent dry, full-bodied reds: *Rosso Barletta*, served with meat and game (the *vecchio* is aged two years); *Rosso Canosa* (or *Canusium*) served with meats, especially lamb (the *riserva* is aged two years); and *Rosso di Cerignola* served with grilled meats (also available as a two-year-old *riserva*).

The appellative *Salice Salentino* covers a variety of wines grown between Lecce and Brindisi. *Salice Salentino Bianco* is 70% Chardonnay, the other 30% being made up of local grape varieties. Pleasant and dry, it is served with antipasti, shellfish and fish. Similar is the destiny of *Salice Salentino Pinot Bianco*, which contains up to 15% Chardonnay and/or Sauvignon. *Salice Salentino Rosato*, a dry rosé, goes well with soups, fried foods and cheeses. *Salice Salentino Rosso* is a dry red in which Negroamaro grapes are blended with Malvasia Nera di Lecce and/or Malvasia Lecce di Brindisi; it is served with meats, especially lamb (the *riserva* is aged two years).

San Severo Bianco, a dry white served with light antipasti, shellfish and fish, *San Severo Rosato*, a dry rosé served with antipasti, soups and poultry; and *San Severo Rosso*, a dry red served with pork, lamb or wildfowl, are made on the plain between Foggia and the Gargano Peninsula.

Last but not least, *Squinzano Rosato*, a dry, delicately scented rosé served with antipasti, minestre and poultry; and *Squinzano Rosso,* a full, dry, robust red served with meats (the *riserva* is aged two years) are two more of the many Salentine wines based on Negroamaro grapes, this time blended with Malvasia Nera di Brindisi, Malvasia Nera di Lecce and Sangiovese.

Getting around

By car

Regardless of whether you are driving your own car or a hired vehicle in Italy you must, by law, carry a valid driving licence when travelling. You must also keep a red triangle in the car in case of accident or breakdown. This serves as a warning to other traffic when placed on the road at a distance of 50m from the stationary car. It can be hired from *ACI* for a minimal charge and returned at the border.

It is now compulsory to wear seat-belts in cars in Italy, and crash helmets are compulsory when riding a motorcycle. Traffic is generally faster (and often more aggressive) than in Britain, the US or Canada. As 80 per cent of goods transported travel by road, lorries pose a constant hazard, and the degree of congestion in even the smallest towns defies the imagination. Road signs are now more or less standardised to the international codes, and state-of-the-art technology is used to enforce speed limits: 130km/h (80mph) on most motorways, 90km/h (56mph) on major roads, 50km/h (31mph in urban areas).

Certain customs differ radically from those in UK, the US or Canada. Unless otherwise indicated, cars entering a road or roundabout from the right are given right of way. Trains (including trollies) always have right of way from either left or right. If an oncoming driver flashes his headlights, it means he is proceeding and not giving way. In towns, Italian drivers frequently change lanes without warning. They also tend to ignore pedestrian crossings (although pedestrians have the right of way). In the south, they view red lights with a certain contempt. Motorbikes, mopeds and Vespas weave in and out of traffic, disregarding the right of way. The concept of the safe braking distance is unknown in Italy and if you leave a gap between your car and the vehicle in front of you, it will be filled immediately.

Roads in Italy

Italy probably has the finest motorways (*autostrade;* for information, ✉ www. autostrade.it) in Europe. They are indicated by green signs. Tolls are charged according to the rating of the vehicle and the distance covered, except on the A3 south of Salerno, which is toll free. All autostrade have service areas open 24 hours a day, and most have SOS points every 2km. At the entrance to motorways, the two directions are indicated by the name of the most important town (and not by the nearest town), which can be momentarily confusing. Similar to autostrade, but not provided with service stations, SOS points, or emergency lanes, are the dual-carriageway fast roads called superstrade (also indicated by green signs).

Southern Italy has an excellent network of secondary roads (*strade statali, regionali* or *provinciali,* indicated by blue signs marked, respectively, SS, SR or SP), usually good roads which provide fine views of the countryside. Local traffic can be extremely heavy in densely populated areas, such as the gulf coast between

Naples and Castellammare di Stabia, and on main arteries, such as the road (SS 16) between Bari and Brindisi.

Throughout Italy, buildings of historic interest are often indicated by yellow or brown signs; towns (*comuni*) and their component villages (*frazioni*), by white signs. The territory of a comune is often much larger than the town of the same name that is its administrative centre-another source of confusion.

Petrol stations

Twenty-four-hour self-service stations can also be found in or near the larger towns. Pumps are operated by €10, €20 and €50 banknotes, or by credit cards. All varieties of petrol (including diesel and unleaded) are now readily available in Italy, although they cost more than in Britain, and considerably more than in North America. Most stations offer basic maintenance service (motor oil, brake fluid and so on) but mechanical assistance must be sought from a *meccanico* (mechanic), *elettrauto* (auto electrician), *gommaio* (tyre shop), *carrozziere* (body shop) and so on. Temporary membership of the **Automobile Club d'Italia** (**ACI**) can be taken out on the border or in Italy (the headquarters of **ACI** are at 8 Via Marsala, Rome, with branch offices in all the main towns). They provide a breakdown service (*Soccorso ACI*, ☎ 116) and other advantages.

Parking

Many cities in southern Italy have taken the wise step of closing their historic centres to traffic (except for residents), which makes them much more pleasant to visit on foot. Access is allowed to hotels and for the disabled. It is always advisable to leave your car in a supervised car park, though with a bit of effort it is almost always possible to find a place to park free of charge, away from the town centre. However, to do so overnight, or even for brief periods in or around Naples and Bari, is not advisable. Always lock your car when parked, and never leave anything of value inside it.

Car hire

Car hire is available in most Italian cities. Arrangements can be made before departure through the airlines (at specially advantageous rates in conjunction with their flights) or in Italy through any of the principal car-hire firms (the best known include *Maggiore, Avis* and *Hertz*), which offer daily, 5-day, weekly and weekend rates. Special leasing rates are available for periods of 30 days and over. Trenitalia also offers special rail-car combinations (see below).

Car and driver service is a convenient, though somewhat expensive way to visit southern Italy, especially metropolitan areas such as Naples and its environs, where traffic is harrowing and a knowledge of alternative routes saves time and effort. Details from the local tourist boards, or from your hotel.

By rail

The Italian Railways (**Trenitalia**) now run eight categories of trains. The service in all categories is improving rapidly as the railways pursue their ambitious modernisation programme.

- *ES* (*Eurostar*), high-speed trains running between major Italian cities.
- *EC* (*Eurocity*), international express trains running between the main Italian and European cities.
- *EN* (*Euronotte*), overnight international express trains with sleeping car or

couchette service.
- *IC* (*Intercity*), express trains running between major Italian cities.
- *E* (*Espressi*), long-distance trains, not as fast as the Intercity trains.
- *IR* (*Interregionali*), intermediate-distance trains making more stops than the Espressi.
- *R* (*Regionali*), local trains stopping at all stations.
- *M* (*Metropolitani*), surface or underground commuter trains.

Booking seats

Seats can be booked in advance, as early as two months ahead and as late as three hours before departure, from the main cities at the station booking office (usually open daily 07.00–22.00), or at travel agencies representing ***Trenitalia***. Seats on a Eurostar can be reserved up to 30 minutes before departure at the Eurostar booking counter in the station, or directly from the conductor on the station platform. The timetable of the train services changes in late September and late May every year. Excellent timetables are published twice a year by ***Trenitalia*** (*In Treno*; one volume covers the whole of Italy; trains with facilities for the disabled are marked). These can be purchased at news-stands and railway stations.

Tickets

Tickets must be bought at the station, from travel agents representing ***Trenitalia***, or on the Internet (✉ www.trenitalia.it) before starting a journey, otherwise a fairly large supplement has to be paid to the ticket-collector on the train. Most tickets are valid for 60 days after the date of issue. Some trains charge a special supplement; and on others seats must be booked in advance. It is therefore always necessary to specify which train you are intending to take as well as the destination when buying tickets. And don't forget: you must stamp the date of your journey on the ticket in the meters located on or near the station platforms before you get on the train. If you buy a return ticket, you must stamp your ticket before beginning the outward bound and return journey. In the main stations major credit cards are now generally accepted (although a special ticket window must sometimes be used when paying with one). There are limitations on travelling short distances on some trains.

Fares and reductions

Fares in Italy are still much lower than in the UK or the USA. Children under four travel free and between four and twelve pay half price. There are also reductions for families and for groups of as few as two persons, and a frequent-travellers' points programme called *Intercity Card*. ***Trenitalia*** info phone (from Italy only) ☎ 892021.
- The *Europe Select Pass* offers up to fifteen days of free travel over a two-month period, in first or second class, in France, Germany, Italy, Spain and Switzerland; there is also an under-26 version, for travel in second class only.
- The *Inter-Rail Card* (valid one month), which can be purchased in Britain or North America by people up to the age of 26, and the Inter-rail 26+ card for those over 26 years of age, are valid in Italy.
- The *Carta Amico Treno*, valid one year, offers reductions of 10–50% on rail fares (*except* on Eurostar trains), and discounts at selected hotels, car rentals, etc.
- The *Carta Club Eurostar*, valid one year, offers a 15% reduction on first-class tickens on all trains, special VIP louunges in major stations, and discounts on hotels, car rentals, etc.

- The *Carta d'Argento* (for those over 60) and the *Carta Verde* (for those between the ages of 12 and 26), both valid one year, allow a 15% reduction on first- and second-class rail fares.
- The *Euro Domino* and *Euro Domino Junior* cards, available to those resident outside Italy, gives unlimited travel on the Italian railways for three, five, or eight day in a month. These cards can be purchased in Britain or at main stations in Italy.
- The *Carta Blu* is available for the disabled.

Other forms of discount travel include *Rail Inclusive Tours,* which offer transport, accommodation, excursions, etc, in a single package: available from travel agents only.

Websites Remember, you can view schedules, build an itinerary and purchase tickets at the ***Trenitalia*** website, ✉ www.trenitalia.it.

Restaurant cars

Restaurant cars are attached to most international and internal long-distance trains. Some trains also have self-service restaurants. Snacks, hot coffee and drinks can often be purchased from a trolley wheeled down the train during the journey. At every large station snacks are on sale from trolleys on the platform and you can buy them from the train window. These include carrier-bags with sandwiches, drink and fruit (*cestini da viaggio*) or individual sandwiches (*panini*).

Additional services

Additional services available at main stations include assistance for the disabled; special car-hire offers; automatic ticketing; porterage; and left luggage offices (open 24 hours at the main stations; often closed at night at smaller stations). Porters are entitled to a fixed amount, shown on noticeboards at all stations, for each piece of baggage.

By bus

Local and long-distance buses between the main towns in southern Italy are not as frequent as they are in the north, and as increasing numbers of residents become independently mobile, the service is diminishing. Except in areas of par- ticular interest to non-residents (such as Sorrento and the Amalfi coast), most buses now carry school children from the villages to the towns in the early morn- ing, and from the towns to the villages in the afternoon. Buses still serve most towns not reached by rail at least once a day, leaving major cities from a depot usually at or near the railway station. Excellent timetables are published twice a year by ***Trenitalia***. Accurate timetables for other areas can be obtained from the local tourist boards.

City buses are an excellent means of getting about in most towns, with the notable exception of Naples, where traffic is often paralysed; in this case, the underground railway (*Metropolitana*) is the swiftest and easiest means of moving across town. Almost everywhere, tickets must be purchased before boarding (at tobacconists, bars, news-stands, information offices and so on) and stamped in a machine on board.

By air

Frequent internal flights are operated between most main towns. Reductions are available for weekend travel and for early booking.

Cycling and walking

Biking and walking have become more popular in Italy in recent years and more information is now available locally. The local offices of the ***Club Alpino Italiano*** (***CAI***) and the ***Worldwide Fund for Nature*** (***WWF***) provide all the information necessary. Maps are published by the ***Istituto Geografico Militare*** (see Maps above), by ***Tabacco*** and by ***Kompas*** at scales of 1:50,000 and 1:25,000.

Taxis

These are hired from ranks or by telephone; there are no cruising cabs. Before taking a taxi it is advisable to make sure it has a meter in working order. Fares vary from city to city but are generally cheaper than in London, though considerably more expensive than in New York. Taxis are owner-operated, and no tip is expected. Supplements are charged for late night journeys and for luggage. There is a heavy surcharge when the destination is outside the town limits (ask roughly how much the fare is likely to be).

 # Language

Even a few words of Italian are a great advantage in the south of Italy, where English is not so widely spoken as in the north. Local dialects vary greatly and are usually unintelligible to the foreigner, but even where dialect is universally used, nearly everybody can speak and understand Italian. A simple series of instructions for pronouncing Italian words follows.

Words should be pronounced well forward in the mouth, and no nasal intonation exists in Italian. Double consonants call for special care as each must be sounded. Consonants are pronounced roughly as in English with the following exceptions:

c and *cc*	before e and i have the sound of *ch* in chess.
sc	before e and i is pronounced like *sh* in ship
ch	before e and i has the sound of *k*
g and *gg*	before e and i are always soft, like *j* in jelly.
gh	is always hard, like *g* in get
gl	is nearly always like *lli* in million (there are a few exceptions, for example, *neligere*, where it is pronounced as in English)
gn	is like *ny* in lanyard.
u and *qu*	are always like *gw* and *kw*
s	is voiceless like *s* in six except when it occurs between two vowels, when it is voiced, like the English *z* or the *s* in rose
ss	is always hard
Z and *zz*	are usually pronounced like *ts*, but occasionally have the sound of *dz* before a long vowel

Vowels are pronounced much more openly than in southern English and are given their full value (more like the pronunciation in the north of England). Every vowel should be articulated separately in Italian. The stress normally falls on the penultimate syllable; in modern practice an accent sign is usually only written when the stress is on the last syllable, for example, *città*, or to differentiate between two words similarly spelt but with a different meaning: for example, *e* (and) and *è* (is).

Customs and etiquette

Attention should be paid to the more formal manners of the Italians. It is customary to open conversation in shops and such places with the courtesy of *buon giorno* (good day) or *buona sera* (good evening). The deprecatory expression *prego* (don't mention it) is the obligatory and automatic response to *grazie* (thank you) throughout the country. The phrases *per piacere* or *per favore* (please), *permesso* (excuse me), used when pushing past someone (essential on public transport), *scusi* (sorry; also, I beg your pardon, when something is not heard), should not be forgotten. A visitor will be wished *buon appetito!* before beginning a meal, to which he should reply *grazie, altrettanto*. This pleasant custom may be extended to fellow passengers eating a picnic on a train. Shaking hands is an essential part of greeting and leave-taking. In shops and offices a certain amount of self-assertion is taken for granted, as queues are not the general rule.

Begging and unwanted offers of guidance should be met with firmness but without harshness or rudeness. You should bear in mind the fact that in the south of Italy begging is regarded as a necessary stimulus to the virtue of charity; even the poor will give something, if only a few Euro, to a beggar. In Naples the persistent attention of small boys should be firmly but kindly discouraged; further south, however, the local school children are frequently knowledgeable and genuinely anxious to show the beauties of their home town. Where this is done in the name of hospitality, no reward will be accepted.

Galleries, museums and churches

The opening times of museums, sites and monuments have been given in the text, but they often change without warning. The provincial tourist authority in major cities keeps updated timetables of most museums. National museums and monuments are usually open daily 09.00–19.00, plus evening hours in summer. Archaeological sites generally open at 09.00 and close at dusk. Naturally, as opening times are constantly being altered, care should be taken to allow enough time for variations in the hours shown in the text when planning a visit to a museum or monument.

Some museums are closed on the main public holidays: 1 January, Easter, 1 May, 15 August and 25 December. Several smaller museums have suspended regular hours altogether and are now open by appointment only. Their telephone numbers have been included in the text, and visits may be booked by calling in advance.

Entrance fees to Italian museums vary (some are free, others up to €8.00) according to your age and nationality; British citizens under 18 and over 60 are entitled to free admission to national museums and monuments because of reciprocal arrangements in Britain. During the *Settimana per i Beni Culturali e*

Ambientali (Cultural and Environmental Heritage Week), usually held early in December, entrance to national museums is free for all.

Churches in southern Italy open quite early in the morning (often for 06.00 Mass), but are normally closed for a considerable period during the middle of the day (12.00 or 12.30 to 15.00, 16.00, or 17.00). Cathedrals and some of the large churches may be open without a break during daylight hours but smaller churches and oratories are often open only in the early morning (the key can usually be found by enquiring locally). The sacristan will also show closed chapels and crypts and a small tip should be given. Some churches now ask that sightseers do not enter during a service, but normally visitors may do so, provided they are silent and do not approach the altar in use. At all times they are expected to cover their legs and arms, and generally dress with decorum. An entrance fee is becoming customary for admission to treasuries, bell-towers, and so on. Lights (operated by coins) have been installed in many churches to illuminate frescoes and altarpieces. In Holy Week most of the pictures are covered and are on no account shown.

Entertainment

Annual **music**, **drama** and **film festivals** take place in many towns, famous ones including the classical drama festival in the Roman theatre at Pompeii (July and August), and the International Film Festival in Sorrento. The **opera** season in Italy usually begins in December and continues until June: the principal opera house in southern Italy is the San Carlo in Naples.

Traditional festivals are celebrated in most towns and villages in commemoration of a local historical or religious event and are often very spectacular. The major festivals have been indicated in the text.

At present there are no agencies in the UK, the US or Canada authorised to sell opera and concert tickets. You may write directly to the theatre or ask your travel agent if he/she can obtain tickets through his/her representatives in Italy. The desk staff at hotels will also assist guests in obtaining tickets for performances.

Sport and leisure

Cycling This is Italy's leading participant sport. Every man, woman and child, from eight to eighty, has or knows someone who has a racing bicycle, and many can be seen out riding the back roads on weekends. Amateur bicycle races are numerous and fun to watch or even participate in.

Diving and fishing The clear Mediterranean waters of Italy's rocky coasts are suitable for marvellous **diving** and **spear fishing**. No license is required for spear fishing, which is allowed everywhere except in harbours. However, regulations forbid the use of oxygen tanks and nets for underwater fishing. Not more than 5kg of fish, crustacea and shellfish can be caught daily.

Italy's many lakes, rivers, mountain streams and miles of coastline offer abundant fishing. Mountain waters are rich in trout, grayling, char, etc., and other waters contain bleak, chub, carp, tench, pike, perch, etc. Sea fishing is free, but for inland waters a special license is required. The license is quite cheap and valid for one year. In addition, membership of the *Federazione Italiana della Pesca Sportiva* must be taken out, which administers 90 per cent of Italian waters. Membership can be obtained at all provincial offices of the federation or at the central headquarters in Rome, Viale Tiziano 70, ☎ 06 3685 8290, 📠 06 3685 8630, 🖂 www.fipsas.it.

Golf There are only two 18-hole golf courses in southern Italy: in Campania (Naples Afsouth Golf, Via Campiglione 11, 80072 Arco Felice, ☎ 081 867 4296), and in Apulia (Riva dei Tessali, 74011 Castellaneta (Taranto), ☎ 099 843 9334).

Horse-riding Arrangements for horseback riding can be made through most hotels. For more information, contact the *Federazione Italiana Sport Equestri*, Viale della Casina di Raffaello, 00197 Roma, ☎ 800 220077, 🖂 www.fise.it.

Hunting Restrictions are strictly enforced on the importation and use of firearms. Information from the *Federazione Italiana della Caccia*, Via Troilo Il Grande 11, 00131 Roma, ☎ 06 4140 4947, 🖂 www.fidc.it.

Skiing Downhill skiing is extremely popular in southern Italy, and there are many miles of excellent slopes. Exact locations are given in the text. Cross-country, back-country and alpine skiing, as well as snow-shoeing, are acquiring a growing public in the larger parks and nature preserves. Many trails are now marked with phosphorescent flashes.

Spectator sports Soccer is by far the most popular spectator sport in Italy. Every Sunday, from September to June, enthusiastic fans pack into Italian soccer stadiums. The most important teams in the south are *Bari* and *Lecce*. **Basketball**, **cycling** and **volleyball** are other major spectator sports. Life grinds to a halt for the *Giro d'Italia* bicycle race (June) and the World Cup soccer championships.

Swimming and water sports The clear Mediterranean waters of Italy's coasts make for marvellous swimming, water-skiing, kajaking, diving, etc. Motor boats (including jet-skis) must stay at least 300m from public beaches. Many hotels have pools, and most towns have at least one Olymic-size public pool. Details from your hotel staff.

Tennis There are numerous tennis courts in all larger cities, and most holiday centres and many hotels have at least one or two courts.

Walking, hiking and climbing These are probably the fastest growing sports in Italy. Trails and back-country lodges, from the Alps to the Aspromonte, are maintained by individuals, towns, provinces and regions, and by the *CAI* (*Club Alpino Italiano*, Via Petrella Errico 19, 20124 Milano, ☎ 02 205 7231, 🖂 www.cai.it , with local chapters in major cities and resorts.

Yachting The Italian coastline has numerous natural harbours, which make it ideal for sailing. Permission to anchor must be obtained from the *Capitaneria di Porto* (harbour master) in each harbour. Information from the *Federazione Italiana Vela* (Piazza Borgo Pila 40, 16129 Genova, 🖂 www.federvela.it) or *Federazione Italiana Motonautica* (Via Piranesi 44/b, 20137 Milan, ☎ 02 701631, 🖂 www.fimconi.it). The latter also supply lists of yacht-chartering companies.

Additional information

Banking services

Money can be changed at banks, post offices, travel agencies and some hotels, restaurants and shops, though the rate of exchange can vary considerably from place to place. The best way to obtain euros while in Italy is to use your cashpoint card or credit card: in most cities ATMs (automatic teller machines) are open 24 hours a day, require no waiting and offer the best exchange rates.

Banks are open Monday–Friday 08.30–13.30, 14.30–16.00 and are closed on Saturday, Sunday and public holidays. The afternoon one-hour opening may vary from bank to bank, and many banks close early (about 11.00) on days preceding national holidays.

Exchange offices are usually open seven days a week at airports and most main railway stations. A limited amount of euros can be obtained from conductors on international trains and at certain stations. For small amounts of money, the difference between hotel and bank rates may be negligible, as banks tend to take a fixed commission on transactions.

Crime and personal security

Pickpocketing is a widespread problem in towns all over Italy: it is always inadvisable to carry valuables in handbags, and be particularly careful on public transport. Never wear conspicuous jewellery, including necklaces and expensive watches; women, when walking, should keep their bags on the side of their bodies away from the road. Crime should be reported at once to the police, or the local *Carabinieri* office (found in every town and small village). A detailed statement has to be given in order to get an official document confirming loss or damage (essential for insurance claims). Interpreters are provided.

For emergencies ☎ **113** (*Polizia di Stato*) or **112** (*Carabinieri*).

Electric current

The electrical current in Italy is AC, 220 volts/50 cycles. If you are carrying electrical appliances having a different current (for instance, 110 volts/60 cycles), you should buy a lightweight transformer either before leaving home or at an electrical appliance shop in Italy. Check the voltage with your hotel before using electrical appliances. Plugs have prongs that are round, not flat, therefore an adaptor plug is needed for appliances manufactured in the UK, the US or Canada. Many electrical appliances, such as travel irons, hairdryers, cell phones and laptop computers are available in the UK, the US or Canada for use abroad without the need of separate transformers or adaptors.

Embassies and consulates

Help and advice is available to British, US and Canadian travellers who are in difficulty, from the British, US, and Canadian Consulates in Italy, and by the British, US and Canadian Embassies in Rome. They will help if your passport has been lost or stolen.

British Consulate in Naples Via dei Mille 40, ☎ 081 401367.

US Consulate in Naples Piazza della Repubblica 2, ☎ 081 661150.
Canadian Embassy in Rome: Via Giosuè Carducci 29, ☎ 081 401338.

Emergency numbers

For emergencies ☎ **113** (*Polizia di Stato*) or **112** (*Carabinieri*)
Medical assistance ☎ **118**

Newspapers

The most widely read newspapers are the *Corriere della Sera* (Milan), *La Stampa* (Turin), and *La Repubblica* and *Messaggero* (Rome). Among the principal papers in the south are the *Mattino* produced in Naples and the *Giornale di Sicilia* in Palermo. Foreign newspapers are sold at central street kiosks and railway stations.

Opening hours

Government offices usually work Mon–Sat 08.00/09.00–13.00/14.00; businesses Mon–Fri, 08.30/09.00–12.30/13.00 and 14.30/15.00–18.00. Shops generally open Mon–Sat 08.30/09.00–13.00 and 15.30/16.00–19.30/20.00. Shops selling clothes and other goods are usually closed on Monday morning, food shops on Wednesday afternoon, except from mid-June to mid-September, when all shops are closed instead on Saturday afternoon. In resorts, during July and August, many shops remain open from early morning until late at night.

Pharmacies

Pharmacies (*farmacie*) are usually open Mon–Fri 09.00–13.00, 16.00–19.30 or 20.00. A few are also open on Saturdays, Sundays, and public holidays (listed on the door of every chemist). In all towns there is also at least one chemist shop open at night (also displayed on the door of every chemist).

Photography

There are few restrictions on photography in Italy, but permission is necessary to photograph the interiors of churches and museums and this may sometimes be withheld. Care should also be taken before photographing individuals, notably members of the armed forces and the police. Photography is forbidden on railway stations, military installations and civil airfields, as well as in border areas and near military installations.

Public holidays

The Italian national holidays when offices, shops and schools are closed are as follows:

1 January	25 April (Liberation Day)
Easter Sunday and Easter Monday	1 May (Labour Day)
15 August (Assumption)	1 November (All Saints' Day)
8 December (Immaculate Conception)	Christmas Day (25 December)
26 December (St Stephen)	

Each town keeps its patron saint's day as a holiday.

Public toilets

There are few public toilets in Italy. All bars (cafés) should have toilets available to the public (generally speaking, the larger the bar, the better the facilities); it is customary to make a small purchase if using the toilet. Of course, all museums, theatres, and other public institutions have toilets.

Sales tax rebates

If you're a non-EU resident, you can claim sales tax rebates on purchases made in Italy provided the total expenditure is more than €150.00. Ask the vendor for a receipt describing the goods acquired and send it back to him when you get home (but no later than 90 days after the date of the receipt). The receipt must be checked and stamped by Italian customs on leaving Italy. On receipt of the bill, the vendor will forward the sales tax rebate (the present tax rate is 20 per cent on most goods) to your home address.

Telephone and postal services

Stamps are sold at tobacconists (*tabacchi*) and post offices. There are numerous public telephones all over Italy, and card-operated phones are becoming increasingly common in major cities and resort areas. Phone calls cost 10c per billing unit. Cards offering €2.50 or €5.00 in prepaid calls (particularly convenient for phoning abroad) are available at post offices, tobacconists and some newsstands. For all calls in Italy, local and long-distance, dial the city code (for instance, 080 for Bari), then the telephone number. For international and intercontinental calls, dial 00 plus the country code, then the city code (for numbers in Britain, drop the initial zero), and the telephone number (for instance, the central London number 020 7855 2000 would be ☎ 0044 20 7855 2000). You can reach an AT&T operator at ☎ 172 1011, MCI at ☎ 172 1022, or Sprint at ☎ 172 1877.

For **directory assistance** ☎ 12 (for numbers in Italy) or ☎ 176 (for international numbers). You can receive a wake-up call on your phone by dialling ☎ 114 and following the prompts (in Italian).

Time

Italy is one hour ahead of Greenwich Mean Time and six hours ahead of Eastern Standard Time in the US. Daylight savings time in Italy usually runs from April to October inclusive.

Tipping

A service charge of 15 to 18 per cent is added to **hotel** bills. The service charge is already included when all-inclusive prices are quoted, but it is customary to leave an additional tip in any case. As a guideline and depending on the category of your hotel, a tip of €1–2 is suggested for hotel staff except the concierge who may expect a little more (€2–3).

Restaurants add a service charge of approximately 15% to all bills. It is customary, however, to leave a small tip (5–10%) for good service. In cafés and bars, leave 15% if you were served at a table (if the bill does not already include service) and 10–20 cents if standing at a counter or bar to drink.

At the theatre, opera and concerts, tip ushers 50 cents or more, depending on the price of your seat.

Tourist information

The *Italian State Tourist Board* (or *ENIT, Ente Nazionale Italiano per il Turismo*) has information offices at the border crossings with Austria (*Valico autostradale Lupo di Brennero*) and France (*Casello Roverino di Ventimiglia*) as well as at Milan Linate, Rome Leonardo da Vinci and Naples Capodichino airports. Within Italy, each 'region' has information services organised at regional, provincial, and local levels; where possible, these have been indicated in the text. A general reorganisation of the Italian tourist authorities will, when completed, lead to the concentration of resources traditionally divided between the **Enti Provinciali del Turismo** (**EPT**) and the **Aziende Autonome di Cura, Soggiorno e Turismo** (**AA**) under a single authority, the **Aziende di Promozione Turistica** (**APT**). In some areas this transition has already taken place.

Weights and measures

Italians use the metric system of weights and measures. The *metro* is the unit of length, the *grammo* of weight, the *ara* of land-measurement, the *litro* of capacity. Greek-derived prefixes (*deca-, etto-, chilo-*) are used with those names to express multiples; Latin prefixes (*deci-, centi-, milli*) to express fractions (*chilometro* = 1000 *metri*, *millimetro* = 1000th part of a *metro*). For approximate calculations the *metro* (or metre) may be taken as 39 inches and the *chilometro* (kilometre) as 0.6 miles, the *litro* (litre) as 1.75 pints, an *etto* as 3.5 oz, and the *chilo* (kilogram) as 2.2 lb.

BACKGROUND INFORMATION

Historical introduction

by Alexandra Douglas

Italy is the geographical centre of the Mediterranean Sea, or *Mare nostrum* (our sea), as the Romans called it. This natural vicinity to neighbouring lands has exposed the country to foreign exploration, emigration and invasion. Time and time again her soil has been ravaged by hostile armies seeking to claim her boundaries, trade routes and resources.

Yet the inhabitants of the land today called Italy have shown an extraordinary ability to defend their shores and to extend their influence abroad. In antiquity, Rome systematically subjugated surrounding lands, proving herself to be the most indomitable of Mediterranean empires. In the late Middle Ages and Renaissance, the great power of the Italian city-states was exercised. Through the ages, Italians have varyingly reigned supreme militarily, economically, politically and culturally over much of the Mediterranean. Throughout Italy's turbulent history, her power has waxed and waned, but she has sustained the ability to emerge from adversity and destruction with remarkable resilience and strength.

Prehistory

Man first appeared in Italy about 200,000 years ago. Stone Age tools, particularly flint axes, have been found throughout the country. Neanderthal skulls of the Middle Palaeolithic (c 50,000 BC) have been discovered just outside Rome and Cro-Magnon skulls of the Upper Palaeolithic (c 10,000 BC) have also been excavated. Nevertheless, evidence of prehistoric man is sparse until the **Neolithic period** (c 5000 BC), when farmers emigrating from eastern lands gradually replaced the nomadic hunters and gatherers of earlier periods, bringing seeds for planting, domesticated animals and hut-building skills to the region.

Worked metals began to appear in the Late Neolithic period (c 3500 BC), though metallurgy seems to have developed more strongly in the northern and central regions of Italy. During the **Bronze Age** (after 1700 BC) Mycenaeans, originating from the Greek mainland, and Minoans, originating from the island of Crete, are known to have landed in southern Italy: Mycenaean influences have been found at Tarentum and there is evidence that the Mycenaeans traded throughout the heel of the peninsula, perhaps as far north as Etruria. Exploration by these Aegean cultures was a direct precursor to the Greek colonisation of Italy.

During the **Iron Age** (after 800 BC) a civilisation of Danubian origin, called Villanovans, named after a large cemetery discovered at Villanova, near Bologna, came to the area. The Villanovans cremated their dead, unlike the native Italic peoples, who had long practised the rite of inhumation (burying the dead). Towards the end of the Iron Age the Villanovan culture was absorbed by indigenous cultures and their language subsumed into the Italic languages.

Greeks and Romans

The first **Greek colonies** in Italy were established as a result of the arrival of hostile, non-Greek peoples in the Aegean (and the consequent westward migration of indigenous Greeks) and of overpopulation and economic crises within the Greek world. The Greek name for colony, *apoikia*, loosely translates as 'a home away from home'. The Greek colonists were well received by some indigenous tribes, but others met their arrival with distrust and resistance. Around 750 BC the Greeks first colonised *Cumae*, near Naples, and c 760 BC the nearby island of Ischia, naming that colony *Pithecusae*. *Parthenope* (Naples) and *Poseidonia* (Paestum) were founded soon after. Further south, the cities of *Locri Epizephyrii*, *Metapontum*, *Sybaris*, *Croton*, *Taras* (Taranto), *Hydruntum* (Otranto) and *Rhegion* (Reggio Calabria) were established. Although Greek colonisation of the Mediterranean eventually extended as far afield as France and Spain, these colonies, together with Messina and Siracusa in Sicily, customarily marked the outer edge of the region known in antiquity as *Magna Graecia* or Greater Greece.

This string of Hellenic settlements led an active trading life, carrying bronzeware and various types of Attic (from *Attica*, the area of eastern Greece surrounding the city of Athens) vases and pottery. The Italic peoples of central and northern Italy soon developed a strong taste for Greek trade goods. The **Etruscans**, a powerful group of tribes in the northern and central regions of the peninsula, were particularly fond of Greek pottery, establishing workshops to copy vase styles and filling their large, painted tombs with vases to be used in the funeral banquets of the dead in the afterlife. The colonists also introduced the cultivation of the olive, a plant that had previously existed only in the wild in Italy. The Greek alphabet, which had been adapted from the Phoenician alphabet, also infiltrated the peninsula, facilitating the development of characters for a written script.

The Greeks traded with the less civilised Italic tribes, who prospered from their close contact with the colonists. The Italic peoples were excellent apprentices to their Greek masters in the study of architecture and sculpture, as well as the rudiments of warcraft. The Greeks, however, never possessed the organisational ability that the Romans would perfect and were therefore unable to transplant their superb civilisation in its entirety. Around 400 BC, a hinterland people known as the **Sabellians** (the term embraces the Sabines and the Samnites, as well as lesser tribes) began to migrate south, bringing with them a strong opposition to Greek rule. Later, the Etruscans would also prevent the Greeks from establishing new centres north of Cumae.

When Rome finally revolted against Etruria in 509 BC, ousting the last Etruscan king, Tarquinis, the Romans allied with the Greeks against the Sabellians, Etruscans, Phoenicians, and all other hostile forces that threatened the peace of the colonists. The Romans gradually expanded their empire to encompass all of Italy, including the Greek colonies, and then Greece itself. Their long-standing admiration for Greek culture, which eventually led to the trend towards Hellenisation in Republican Rome, probably dates from this time.

The **Romans** soon learned to set up complicated individual alliances with surrounding states, in such a way that Rome should become the diplomatic centre. Allies were untaxed, protected, able to visit Rome when they wished and allowed to retain their local government; in return they were expected to provide troops for the Roman armies and to take an oath to preserve the majesty of the republic.

By proffering protection while encouraging home rule, Rome was able to instil a strong sense of duty and loyalty in her allies. She organised the state around war: militarism was her constitution, and fighting someone, somewhere, every year, was part of the Roman mentality. In 390 BC the capital was sacked by Gallic tribes from the north, inculcating a deep and abiding fear of the 'enemy' and teaching the Romans to react with a ferocity unrivalled in the ancient Mediterranean. There were no conditions of surrender: a hostile city was destroyed as an object lesson, after first being ravaged for its booty. Pacifism was unknown in the ancient world, where survival of the fittest was the rule.

In this scenario the Etruscans were the first to lose: they were unable to remain united under strong pressure from Roman armies, and as the Roman threat mounted, their large underprivileged class revolted against the aristocracy, further weakening the infrastructure of their society. Interestingly, the fall of the Roman Empire would follow a similar, though more complex pattern.

When Rome finally turned her sword on the Hellenic domain of Magna Graecia, the Greeks summoned Pyrrhus, King of Epirus, to their aid. Pyrrhus twice defeated the Romans (but at a terrible human cost: even today, the term 'pyrrhic victory' denotes a victory in which no one can experience true glory), only to be defeated at Beneventum in 275 BC. By 264 the Roman dominion stretched to Rhegion (Reggio Calabria).

Rome defeats Carthage

Once the powers of southern Italy had been subdued, Rome was in a position to challenge her Phoenician enemy across the sea, Carthage. The Romans latinised the Greek name Phoenician (derived from a word meaning purple; this Eastern Mediterranean people made a purple dye from shellfish) to Punic; and the Latin phrase *punica fides*, which translates as 'gross dishonesty', expresses the rancour the Romans felt for their formidable enemy.

The **Carthaginians** were a powerful mercantile nation which had long sought to control Sicily—an ambition that was thwarted after their defeat by the Romans in the **First Punic War**, 300–251 BC. The **Second Punic War**, also called the Hannabolic War (218–201 BC), was a relentless conflict of attrition that Rome nearly lost. After Hannibal's great victory at Cannae, the Roman allies of Capua and Taras deserted, bringing a terrible retribution upon themselves (the citizens of Capua were butchered and those of Taras sold into slavery) when the Romans finally claimed victory. Hannibal at last saw the destiny of Carthage when his brother Hasdrubal's head was delivered to him at his camp in Apulia by his enemy and he wearily sailed home, to be defeated later at Zama, in present-day Tunisia, by the great Roman general, Scipio (who consequently received the cognomen *Africanus*).

The **Third** (and final) **Punic War** ended with the destruction of Carthage and the surrender of its citizens in 149 BC. In an act of extreme savagery, even by Roman standards, the city was burned, levelled, and the ground ploughed and salted to prevent any future habitation.

The fate of southern Italy had been in the hands of the Romans since the expulsion of the Etruscans and the subjugation of the Greeks. During the Roman

Republic, unrest grew in the south, beginning with the **Social War** in Samnite territory (today western Campania, Abruzzo and Molise). It is important to remember that this war was fought by peoples seeking Roman citizenship, not independence; the central and southern portions of the peninsula strengthened their ties with the capital as a consequence and Roman Italy became more a nation than a loose federation of conquered states.

Summer villas and retreats for the Romans

In the 1C BC, southern Italy became the playground of the Roman élite, the south-west coast of the peninsula boasting the largest number of summer villas and retreats in the republic. Well-to-do Romans seeking to escape the stifling heat of the city fled to the country for solace; the island of Capri, and the coastal towns of Surrentum, Baiae, Puteoli and Neapolis were particular favourites. The ill-fated Pompeii and Herculaneum were also popular destinations. This region was appropriately called *Campania felix* ('fruitful' or 'fortunate country') for its beauty, fertility and wealth; and the export of luxury goods, such as wine and oil, to surrounding provinces served as a substantial source of income for the region.

Paestum produced roses whose luxurious oils were as desirable as they were expensive. The hills—and volcano—near Naples provided rich soil for the cultivation of fine wines, the forests abounded with game and the sea yielded a wide variety of fish and seaweeds to satisfy the most demanding tastes. Roman delicacies consisted of tree fungi in fish-fat sauce, jellyfish and eggs, boiled ostrich and dormouse with pine kernels—which were so popular that Cicero felt obliged to admonish his fellow Romans to 'eat to live, not live to eat'.

The eruption of Mount Vesuvius

Then as now, the Gulf of Naples was overshadowed by Mount Vesuvius, at once marvellous and ominous. Rivalled only by Mount Etna in Sicily as the most active volcano in Europe, it first awoke with a shudder in AD 63, during the reign of the Roman emperor Nero, causing an earthquake that nearly destroyed the Campanian towns of Herculaneum and Pompeii. In the 16 years that preceded the major eruption of AD 79, shocks and tremors provided frequent and telling warnings of what was to come. Titus was emperor when Vesuvius reaped its terrible vengeance on the Neapolitan countryside, burying the towns of Pompeii and Herculaneum (which, according to Cicero, had been founded when Hercules drove the Bulls of Geryon along their shores).

Pliny the Younger, nephew of Pliny the Elder, who was killed during the eruption, gives us our only eyewitness account of the circumstances of the eruption (see p 213). His account of that fearsome event in August of AD 79 is important, because he does not mention any flow of lava. It is now believed that the crater threw up ashes and rocks along with a dense, noxious vapour, which is probably what killed most of the hapless inhabitants of the surrounding areas. Herculaneum was covered with heavy mud, which slid down in torrents from the belching mountain, whereas Pompeii was bombarded by small pumice stones and ashes. Though the eruption preserved these ancient towns for the pleasure and instruction of visitors centuries later, one cannot escape the sense of tragedy that pervades their narrow, ghostly streets.

The relative instability of the area, however, did nothing to deter prominent Romans from retiring there. They simply built their villas further south, closer to Surrentum and Capri. The mountain remained still until AD 472, but several other eruptions were recorded shortly after that date. The dreadful eruption of December 1631 was as calamitous as the eruption of AD 79. Streams of lava, clouds of ash and a tidal wave resulting from the accompanying quakes were responsible for the deaths of over 18,000 people. Many other eruptions have followed and the last recorded disturbance occurred in 1944.

A place of erudition

Throughout antiquity Neapolis was considered a city of learning, a tradition it preserved well into the Middle Ages. As elsewhere in the Roman Republic, **boys** of the privileged classes were taught the rudiments of Latin grammar, pronunciation and enunciation as young as seven; between the ages of eight and eleven, they spent time with their fathers and tutors mastering Greek and Latin literature. Competence was measured by culture. Something as trivial as the unorthodox pronunciation of a word had the power to label a man uneducated and therefore unacceptable. Adolescent boys were required to attend the law courts to become familiar with public speaking; and history, philosophy and poetry were studied to provide a wide range of quotations to be used in future debates. Rhetoric was the focus of every young aristocrat's education, for his career would most certainly be public. The primacy of Naples as a study centre was due to its strong ties to Greek culture.

With very few exceptions, Roman **women** received little education and were excluded from public life; most were relegated to the roles of wife or prostitute. Indeed, women played so small a role in Roman society that they were virtually anonymous. Whereas men often bore cognomens that made reference to their personal achievements (such as Scipio's *Africanus*), or at least to highly individual characteristics (Cicero translates as chick-pea and supposedly refers to an acute case of acne that afflicted the famous rhetorician), Roman men, sadly, had little imagination when it came to naming their daughters. If a father was Claudius, his first daughter was named Claudia Prima, his second Claudia Seconda, and so forth.

Caesar, Cicero and the flight to Formiae

One of the leading intellectuals of the Roman Republic, but also the first man to declare himself dictator and consul, was **Julius Caesar**. His name would become a title (from which the modern words 'kaiser' and 'czar' derived), and his personage would become a symbol. He was a brilliant negotiator and a consummate opportunist. In 44 BC he arranged to be named 'dictator for life', rendering his opponents powerless and inspiring the enmity of all those in less prominent positions. The senate, whose cumulative power had been virtually absolute up to that point, loathed him.

Caesar lost respect for his rivals—a fatal error—and flagrantly abused his position. He arrogantly insisted upon being called *Parens patriae* (Father of the Country), named a month of the year after himself (July), dressed in triumphal robes every day and even refused to stand when another Roman patrician entered the room. His assassination, on 15 March 44 BC, was plotted and carried through by members of the senate and the scale and success of the plot (Suetonius recorded that 'he was stabbed with three and twenty wounds') indicate the zeal with which the Roman ruling class desired to rid itself of him. Cicero, who, after the murder, placed himself at the head of the republican party and assailed Mark Antony in his Philippic orations, upon the formation of the triumvirate by

Octavian, Antony and Lepidus (27 November 43) was condemned to death and his property forfeited to the state. The orator fled to his villa at Formiae, but was overtaken by Antony's soldiers and put to death on 7 December. A semblance of republican government was restored, though chaos ruled the land. Approximately 15 years later, with the establishment of the Roman Empire by Octavian Caesar (Augustus), lessons learned from Julius Caesar's mistakes would be applied with consummate skill—the most important being to lavish honour and prestige on the senate while surreptitiously sapping its power.

The Roman Empire and its decline

The elaborate system of political checks and balances perfected during the republic was lost under the empire. Elections thinly disguised an autocracy in which the role of the senate was minimal. The imperial prerogative became an instrument of personal power in the hands of one ambitious leader after another. Augustus ruled with discretion and intelligence, but his visions were distorted by later emperors, such as Tiberius, Caligula and Nero. Among the more judicious Roman emperors were Trajan and Hadrian, whose extensive military and building campaigns stretched as far as Asia Minor, and North Africa, encompassing Macedonia and Northern Europe (then Gallia, Hispania, and Britannia). Some of the better-preserved and more beautiful examples of Imperial Roman architecture can still be found there; in southern Italy the accomplishments of Trajan and Hadrian are celebrated on reliefs of the triumphal arch at Benevento. Even Nero, though more often remembered for burning the city of Rome in AD 64, was responsible for some spectacular building projects.

Roman law and custom endured throughout this vast region until increasing pressures from northern 'barbarian' tribes combined with civil wars to break down the fabric of all that the empire had been at its zenith. Military crises, the rise of Christianity, diminishing faith in Imperial leadership and increased poverty and strife eroded the foundations of Rome's strength. The last emperor of the West (Romulus Augustulus, who died in exile in Naples) was forced to abdicate in AD 476 and the seat of the Roman Empire was moved to Byzantium (Constantinople), destroying political unity in Italy.

The Middle Ages

Though Rome vanished as a political entity in the 5C of the common era, much of its personality was retained throughout the Middle Ages in various institutions, traditions and thought processes. Byzantium, where the Roman imperial tradition was kept alive until the Muslim conquest of the 9C, remained a centre for the study of Greek literature and ancient art. Though Italy's stronghold on European culture weakened, Greek continued to be spoken and studied in southern Italy, where the Hellenic tradition had been firmly rooted. Latin was retained as the language of the clergy and the learned, and Latin literature remained a subject of intense study, particularly in monastic communities. Modern scholars of the classics owe a considerable debt to the Church for salvaging many aspects of Roman culture.

In southern Italy, as everywhere in Europe, the fall of the Roman Empire brought a prolonged succession of social, political and cultural crises. After AD 476 the barbarian chieftain Odoacer, ostensibly acting in the name of the Eastern emperor, assumed power in Italy. He was subsequently overthrown by the Ostrogoth, Theodoric of Byzantium, who established a capital at Ravenna and ruled from AD 493 until AD 526. At the same time, Sicily was taken by the Byzantine general, Belisarius, in the name of the emperor Justinian, and though the invasion met with resistance when it extended to the southern mainland, Naples, Rome and Ravenna eventually capitulated.

Justinian's rule and Lombard invaders

Justinian's rule brought a first, brief respite to the area. The emperor left an indelible mark on the pages of art history by welding the Byzantine influence to the Classical tradition in Italian art; he restored the divine sanctions of legitimate government to Italy (the Justinian code of law is still one of the more prominent forms of Roman law studied and taught in universities and even Dante gave the emperor a place in Paradise for purging the law of the verbose and irrelevant) and he moved the seat of government from Ravenna to Rome. Nevertheless, Gothic power was not brought to an end in Italy until AD 552. In this unstable political climate, the power of the papacy grew steadily, preparing the future political destiny of Italy and Europe.

In 568 the Italian peninsula was invaded by 'barbarians' from the north: this time the Lombards (whose English name derives from the Italian *Longobardo*; perhaps inspired by the long barbs that distinguished their spears). The Byzantines' defensive strategies proved inadequate. Gregory the Great, a Roman scholar and politician deeply respected within the Church, won his title by dissuading the Lombard invaders from sacking Rome. Thanks to his skill as a negotiator, a semblance of peace was restored to the peninsula, though Lombard duchies were established throughout the land—in southern Italy at Benevento, Capua, Naples and Salerno.

The Holy Roman Empire

In AD 754 the Franks invaded, led by Charlemagne's father, Peptone. Their struggle for control over Italy, though eventually successful, met with stern opposition on the southern mainland and in Sicily. Nevertheless, on Christmas Day 800 the Frankish invaders, in alliance with the pope, established the **Holy Roman Empire**, and the title of emperor was given to Charlemagne. Power in Europe would thereafter be shared by the emperor and the pope, who became the spiritual custodian of the imperial mandate and the temporal sovereign of Rome.

This awkward division of power offered yet another group of foreigners fertile ground for invasion. In AD 827, the armies of a nomadic people from the deserts between Syria and Arabia, the **Saracens**, landed in Sicily, at Mazara. These Muslim invaders conquered Palermo and rapidly moved inland, establishing an enlightened government that restored Sicily to the grandeur of previous centuries, when the Greeks had colonised there.

Though the Sicilians took kindly to Saracen rule, the majority of their neighbours did not. Naples, Amalfi, Sorrento and Gaeta allied to defend the south-eastern mainland against the Muslims and were victorious at Ostia (the victory is celebrated by Raphael in the Vatican Stanze) in 846. Naples, however, eventually allied with the Saracens—an act that led to its excommunication by Pope John VIII. Over the subsequent decades alliances shifted constantly in Italy. Germanic invaders edged into the north, while the Lombards and the Saracens, the Byzantines and the pope, haggled over the south.

The Normans

The return of political unity to southern Italy was aided by the **Norman conquests** of 1030–1130. As early as 1015, Norman adventurers had come to the south to seek their fortunes. The volatile atmosphere of the region provided opportunities for them to sell their services to whoever was prepared to pay them in gold, horses or land. By intervening in local conflicts, a handful of Norman knights acquired a foothold in the southern hinterland, establishing their capital at Melfi.

The rapid expansion of Norman influence alarmed the papacy, which eventually took up arms against the newcomers. But Pope Leo IX was defeated and captured by the formidable Robert Guiscard at Civita, in 1053, and released only after bestowing his blessing on the conquerors. Leo's successor, Nicholas II, subsequently made an alliance with the Normans, naming Guiscard the Duke of Calabria and Apulia and future Duke of Sicily—an astute diplomatic move that legitimised Norman rule and gave the papacy a strong claim over southern Italy and Sicily.

The Normans were excellent and benevolent administrators of their territories, over which they won papal recognition as kings in 1139. By wise tolerance of the region's Arabic, Jewish, Greek and Roman traditions, they established an authoritarian government, half Oriental, half Western, unequalled in Europe. Nevertheless, when Norman rule ended in 1189 (following the death of William II, who left no legitimate heir), southern Italy again fell into chaos.

By coincidence, the power vacuum that developed in the south coincided with a more general conflict for the succession to the imperial throne—a conflict rendered all the more bitter by the ambitious new pope, Innocent III, who by supporting first one, then another of the rival claimants weakened imperial power while increasing that of the papacy. The evident incompatibility between papal and imperial interests crystallised in the political and civic conflicts between Guelphs and Ghibellines which swept the peninsula. The Guelphs opposed intervention by the Holy Roman Emperor and were pro-papal, whereas Ghibellines (whose ranks were largely made up of noble feudatories of the emperor) opposed the intervention of the Church in state affairs.

Frederick II of Hohenstaufen

Ascending the throne of Sicily in 1208, the young German Prince Frederick of Hohenstaufen (one of the more judicious and beneficent sovereigns of medieval Europe, as well as a brilliant poet and architect) restored order to the island, dislodged a northern Italian colony at Siracusa and suppressed a Saracen revolt, afterwards removing the Muslim population to Lucera on the mainland. Later, he gained the imperial crown while ostensibly acting for the papacy, then outwitted Innocent by promising to give the Sicilian throne to his young son and to lead a crusade.

As long as Honorius III was pope (1216–27) he did neither. Instead, he consolidated his position first in northern Europe, then in the south. His diplomatic conduct of the crusade of 1228, by which he obtained a ten-year truce for pilgrims, his open criticisms of the Church, and his bestowal of the title of King of Sardinia on his natural son, Enzo, widened the breach with Pope Gregory IX (1227–41), who had excommunicated him before his departure and negotiated with his enemies in his absence. This was hardly surprising, for Frederick's vision of empire was incompatible with a papacy wielding temporal power. His interest in rational science and love of Classical sculpture foreshadow the Renaissance and his summoning of the Third Estate to council anticipated Simon de Montfort's similar action in England by 25 years. Dante called him the father of Italian poetry.

After Frederick's death in 1250 imperial powers in Italy began to decline. His son, Conrad, arrived in Apulia in 1252 to claim the throne, but was opposed by Innocent IV. Conrad's sudden death during the campaign of 1254 put the papacy in the ascendant; but **Manfred**, Conrad's illegitimate brother, successfully roused Apulia against the pope. Having gained full control of southern Italy, Manfred was crowned King of Sicily in 1258. He extended his domain to include most of the peninsula, gaining victories as far north as Montaperti, where he defeated the Florentines. He was even made senator of Rome for supporting republicanism over papal autocracy.

Anjou and Aragon

Urban IV, elected to the papacy in 1261, at once searched for a worthy candidate to champion the papal cause and expel Manfred. He chose **Charles of Anjou**, the ambitious and ruthless younger brother of St Louis of France, who defeated Manfred at Benevento in 1266 and the young Conradin (son of Conrad) at Tagliacozzo two years later. The vanquished Conradin was unceremoniously beheaded in Naples, and Charles was made King of Sicily, restoring strength to the Guelph faction.

Fortunately for Charles, Rudolph of Habsburg, the new Holy Roman Emperor, focused his efforts on northern Europe and pursued a policy of non-intervention in Italy. Unlike his predecessors, he did not go to Italy to be crowned, nor did he care to dabble in its politics. Consequently Charles had the full support of the Guelph party and the tacit approval of the Ghibellines from the start. But instead of consolidating his position in Italy, he embarked on a costly policy of empire building, underestimating both the resentment of his subjects and the combined strength of his enemies.

Revolt broke out spontaneously at Palermo in a masssacre known as the **Sicilian Vespers**, and within a month the French had been cleared from the island, mainly by massacre (see *Blue Guide Sicily*). The nobles allied themselves with Peter of Aragon, Manfred's son-in-law, turning the former kingdom into a battlefield for the French and Spanish and also for rival factions of the Angevin family. Many years passed before Peter's descendant, Alfonso of Aragon, obtained complete control of the region (1435), establishing Spanish control south of Rome.

The Renaissance

Commerce in the Mediterranean found its crossroads in Italy, leading to the speedy development of an urban society of merchants and bankers. **City-states** blossomed as the demand for trade goods from the East increased in western Europe. The northern ports of Genoa, Pisa and Venice dominated trade routes, but cities throughout central and southern Italy grew as well. Despite this burgeoning of wealth (or perhaps because of it) the mercantile city-states developed an acute sense of patriotism that perpetuated the separatism of Italy's medieval consciousness. Neighbouring cities were rarely on civil terms, unless they were under a specific alliance to protect themselves against a greater offensive power.

The growth of these communal states nevertheless provided the right climate for the intellectual movement of the Renaissance, as an educated and ambitious middle class emerged from the economic and social ferment. The reconciliation between the active and contemplative life took on a new meaning as Renaissance poets and philosophers participated in the redevelopment of government.

Southern Italy was and still is very different from northern Italy. During the Renaissance, when northern cities such as Milan, Florence and Venice were enjoying various levels of republicanism and independence, the south was crushed by an oppressive baronage and torn by wars of succession. While Renaissance Humanism (the philosophical movement that stressed the dignity of man—hence the importance of an individualistic and critical spirit—over the primacy of orthodox political and religious belief) established a firm foothold elsewhere in Italy, the socio-political patterns of the Middle Ages remained substantially unchanged in the south. Today scholars attribute the huge difference in the efficiency of democratic institutions in northern and southern Italy to this historical divergence, which, they argue, led to the development of a strong social consciousness in the north, and a perpetuation of primitive (and in some cases immoral) practices, either in self-defence or to protect one's family, in the south.

In the 16C and 17C Naples and the southern mainland were separated from the Spanish kingdom of Sicily and governed by separate viceroys, of whom Don Pedro de Toledo (1532–53) was perhaps the most constructive. At the end of the War of the Spanish Succession, the Treaty of Utrecht (1713) awarded southern Italy and Sardinia to Austria; but the defeat of the Austrians at Bitonto in 1734, and the conquest of Naples by **Charles of Bourbon** in the same year, once again gave the south a dynasty of its own.

The Bourbons

The byword for misrule that the Bourbon name later became has obscured the dynasty's earlier virtues. Charles of Bourbon (1734–59) was a skilful diplomat as well as a judicious sovereign. He abolished many privileges of the nobility and clergy, built the San Carlo theatre and Capodimonte palace, initiated excavations at Pompeii and Herculaneum and began the palace at Caserta. When he went on to become King of Spain, his successor, **Ferdinand IV** (1759–99 and 1799–1806), continued his efforts to curb ecclesiastical power in the south. During the French Revolution Ferdinand was forced to abandon the throne temporarily; but with the restoration of Bourbon rule he re-entered Naples as Ferdinand I of the Two Sicilies and immediately set about establishing a severe, absolute government.

Repression worsened under his successors, Francis I and Ferdinand II, who simply imprisoned liberal sympathisers. The kingdom, reduced by indolence to squalor and by corruption, persecution and fear to moral decay, provoked Gladstone's famous denunciation of it as 'the negation of God erected into a system of government'. It is therefore no wonder that the conquest of the south in 1860–61 by **Victor Emmanuel II**, King of Piedmont and Sardinia (and first ruler of a united Italy 1861–78), met with little resistance.

The achievement of unity

The movement for political unity in Italy, the **Risorgimento**, had begun in the north as early as the mid-18C. Unification began with a group of conspirators called the Carbonari (or Charcoal Burners, because they gathered at night, in secret), who worked towards encouraging a nationalistic state of mind. They were supported by **Giuseppe Mazzini** (1850–72), a radical republican who worked to inspire nationalistic feelings in the masses, to fight the Austrian hold over northern Italy.

Count Camillo Cavour, Prime Minister (1852–61) under Victor Emmanuel II, strove to retain the state under the House of Savoy. For a while, Cavour's arguments represented a foil against the locomotive force of **Giuseppe Garibaldi** (1807–82), the flamboyant general whose volunteer army, the Thousand Red Shirts, brought Sicily under the Savoy banner in 1860, preparing the way for Italian unification. When Garibaldi effected his surprise landing on the southern mainland, Reggio Calabria fell almost immediately and Villa San Giovanni soon after. Resistance dissolved as the march became a race for Naples, which the general entered with a small staff 48 hours ahead of the vanguard of his troops, in August 1860. Francis II, the last of the Bourbon kings, fled to Gaeta with his still loyal army; but two months later a successful campaign on the Volturno led to Garibaldi's meeting with Victor Emmanuel, which sealed the unity of Italy.

Italy was created by joining Piedmont/Sardinia, Lombardy/Venetia, the Duchy of Modena, the Duchy of Parma, the Grand Duchy of Tuscany, the Papal States and the Kingdom of the Two Sicilies. Each of these seven states differed greatly from the others in its traditions, customs, government, economic life and even in its language, as much of the population was able to express itself only in local dialect. The social panorama was distressing, to say the least: terrible hygienic and nutritional conditions resulted in repeated cholera and typhoid epidemics and an extraordinarily high infant mortality rate, and illiteracy was rampant.

But the problem that most afflicted the new nation was the 'Southern Question'—the political and economic backwardness that distinguished the southern mainland, Sicily and Sardinia from central and northern Italy. Industry in these areas was absent and commerce reduced; what few roads existed were in poor condition; and the large estates were crowded with peasants who lived in conditions of extreme poverty, subject to the systematic exploitation of a corrupt aristocracy.

Problems of unification
Many of the destitute had fought bravely for Garibaldi's cause in the hope that unification would improve their condition. But they were bitterly disappointed when Garibaldi retracted his promise to redistribute land and brutally repressed peasant uprisings in Sicily. The disillusionment continued under the governments of united Italy, which promised much but delivered little.

The first reaction to the attitude of the nation's new rulers was a violent outbreak of brigandage, which ravaged the south in the 1860s. Poverty, burdensome taxation and obligatory conscription (which took strong young men off the land) motivated discontented peasants (including large numbers of women), former Bourbon soldiers, young draft dodgers, and even criminals to join the movement. Initially, the outlaws were financed by Francis II, who nurtured hopes of regaining his throne, and tolerated by the pope, whose territory was often used as a base for their operations. But the brigands also found complicity in the population's *omertà* (conspiracy of silence), perceiving them as avengers of the injustices suffered.

The solution proposed by the Piedmontese was to meet violence with violence: a full-scale military campaign conducted between 1861 and 1863 left more than 20 officers and 300 men dead in the field. Thousands of brigands were killed and thousands more imprisoned. A study of 1863 states: 'Brigandage is the savage and brutal protest of poverty against century-old injustice joined to other ills left over from the inauspicious reign of the Bourbons [namely] ignorance, superstition, and the absolute lack of faith in law and justice ... To destroy brigandage we have spilled rivers of blood but have thought little of deeper remedies. We have been good surgeons and terrible doctors.'

From unification to Fascism

Political development after unification was flawed by the imbalance that continued to exist between the 'real nation', made up largely of masses of illiterate peasants devoid of the right to vote, and the 'legal nation', whose social basis was constituted by the landed aristocracy and the wealthy middle class. Not surprisingly, half a century after the Risorgimento the 'Southern Question' was still on the agenda. Parliament had produced several studies of the problem, but little in the way of concrete results. Protests voiced by eminent intellectuals had likewise gone unanswered. The few reforms that had been passed had failed to change the prevailing system of agrarian organisation (large estates with primitive agricultural methods and an exploited labour force), and while agricultural methods gradually improved elsewhere in Europe, the impoverishment of the countryside in Italy forced hundreds of thousands of peasants to emigrate. Underdevelopment, poverty and ignorance reinforced the power of the Sicilian *mafia* and its mainland counterpart, the Neapolitan *camorra* for those who remained behind.

At the close of the First World War the young Italian nation found itself on the verge of a severe social and economic crisis. The reconversion of an industry 'swollen' by the war effort and post-war inflation sharpened the country's endemic conflicts. Faith in the established order was shaken by the socialist movement and by the widespread discontent of the middle classes, whose real income was rapidly diminishing. The frustration of the Italian claims at the Versailles peace conference introduced a further destabilising element, the myth of the 'mutilated victory', which was used to advantage by the growing nationalist movement, whose numbers included several intellectuals (such as the poet **Gabriele d'Annunzio**), veterans unable to find a place in post-war society, and members of the privileged classes frightened by the prospect of a proletarian revolt. The elections of 1919 marked the collapse of the traditional political parties and the advance of the socialists and the Catholic-inspired populists, who became essential for the creation of coalition governments in the following years.

In November 1921 the *Fasci Italiani di Combattimento*, right-wing political activist groups that advocated an expansionistic foreign policy and a socialising domestic policy (universal suffrage, employee participation in industrial management, progressive taxation of capital, confiscation of war profits, etc.) were reorganised to form the *Partito Nazionale Fascista*. In August 1922 the leftist labour unions called a general strike to protest against the violent methods of the Fascist *squadristi* (hit-squads made up of former soldiers, the unemployed, hooligans, and youths disoriented by the war). Party chief **Benito Mussolini** responded by launching an ultimatum: if the government did not take immediate action, the Fascists would themselves restore order, using every means at their disposal. On 24 October 1922, at the Fascist convention in Naples, Mussolini announced the **March on Rome**, which took place on 27 October. As the Black Shirts descended on the capital, Prime Minister Luigi Facta prepared a decree ordering a state of siege, but Victor Emmanuel III, in response to the pressures of the military and the nationalists (who viewed the Fascists favourably), refused to sign. Facta resigned and, the following day, 28 October 1922, the king called on Mussolini to form a new cabinet.

The Fascist social order

The Fascist movement, which arose as a result of resentments and as a tool of often contrasting interests, did not initially have a real ideology. 'My doctrine', Mussolini wrote in 1932, 'had been the doctrine of action. Fascism was born of a need for action and was itself action'. Only after the consolidation of the regime did Fascism seek to give itself a doctrine. The most coherent attempt was that of philosopher **Giovanni Gentile**, who contrasted liberal, democratic individualism (responsible for the disintegration of the social fabric) with the need for a collective solidarity in which the rights and aspirations of the individual were subordinated to the values and interests of the nation as a whole and for whom the State was the sole trustee and guarantor. This principle of 'class solidarity' (as opposed to the Marxist concept of class struggle) was expressed in the theorisation of the corporative state, in which employers and employees, united in organisations that were made part of the structure of government, were expected to work together in the greater interest of the nation.

After the passage of special legislation, too complicated to discuss here, which allowed what amounted to the transition from representative democracy to totalitarian dictatorship, many anti-Fascists fled to France; others were imprisoned or sent in 'forced residence' to remote parts of the country. All organised opposition to the regime was suppressed, and of the pre-Fascist political parties only the communists maintained a clandestine organisational structure.

The Italian economy went through a positive phase until 1929, supported by the government's deflationary policy and American loans. After the 1929 crisis the Fascists adopted a policy of government participation in industry which made it possible for industrial development to continue, thanks to an increase in capital, the compression of salaries, and the preservation of economic self-sufficiency. The regime had little effect on agriculture, to which it devoted, above all, propaganda.

The late twentieth century

Until the mid-1930s Fascist foreign policy followed a moderate course, favouring relations with France in order to offset the growing importance of Germany. Isolated diplomatically after the conquest of Ethiopia, however, Italy fell into line with its reactionary neighbour and, after observing the German military successes in Northern Europe, entered the Second World War with the intention of conducting a 'parallel campaign' for the conquest of the Mediterranean and the Balkans. But a series of Italian defeats forced the Germans to intervene in both regions and undermined faith in Mussolini and his regime. In the summer of 1943 a 'court conspiracy' toppled the Fascists, and the new government headed by **Marshal Pietro Badoglio** obtained an armistice from the Allies, who had already landed on the peninsula (at Taranto and Salerno). Northern Italy was occupied by the Germans (Mussolini founded the Italian Social Republic, a German puppet state with its capital at Salò), but the advance of the Allies and the bloody campaign of resistance launched by the Partisans made it clear that the end was near. On 25 April 1945 the Germans and the Fascists abandoned

Milan. Mussolini, captured while attempting to escape, was executed together with other Fascist notables. On 29 April 1945 the German forces in Italy surrendered to the Allies at Caserta, and a Special Assembly elected on 2 June 1946 drafted a new Constitution that came into effect on 1 January 1948, marking the end of the monarchy and the rebirth of Italy as a parliamentary republic.

Contemporary Italy

Between May 1946 and September 1947 the cost of living in Italy rose over 50 times with respect to pre-war levels, while the average income remained at unacceptable levels, especially in the south, where agrarian reform remained a chimera. In Lazio, Apulia and Calabria, clashes between police and an impoverished peasantry led to numerous deaths. In this difficult economic situation the nation returned to democracy in a state of 'limited sovereignty' conditioned by the authority of the United States. The affirmation of the Christian Democrats (DC) in the elections for the Constitutional Assembly marked the beginning of the prevalence of that party in Italian political life. Not long afterwards, the radicalisation of the contrasts between the US and the Soviet Union brought the exclusion of the left from government and the beginning of the 'centrist' policy of Prime Minister **Alcide De Gasperi**.

During the first years of republican legislation there was considerable social tension. De Gasperi's government—a coalition between the Christian Democrats and the lesser centrist parties—responded by repressing protest and reinforcing the police. A limited agrarian reform failed to satisfy the 'hunger for land' of the peasantry in the south, leading instead to the formation of the first system of political patronage (the *Cassa del Mezzogiorno*, or Fund for the South), with which the DC reinforced its electoral power.

In the 1950s, industry surpassed agriculture as the principal means of employment for the first time in the country's history, and production, investment and expenditure for consumer goods increased rapidly. But in 1963 the system's weaknesses became clear. Vast areas, especially in the south, had remained outside the 'boom' area. An excessive expansion of credit led to inflation, the stock market reacted with a strong downturn, and many firms that had grown too fast and had not acquired the solidity necessary to weather a period of relative stagnation, failed. Only in 1965, thanks largely to a favourable balance of payments, did the situation begin to improve.

Insecurity returned in the 1970s, caused by the global economic crisis and by the failure of the centrist majority to deal with the demands of a changing society. This led to a series of bloody episodes contrived by terrorist organisations (known as the 'strategy of tension') who wanted to destabilise the country's democratic order. The deterioration of the political atmosphere provided the ground for acts of violence by radical groups at both ends of the political spectrum (in southern Italy right-wing thugs in Reggio Calabria turned a protest over an insignificant administrative matter into a lethal street brawl in 1970, and the Neapolitan cell of the communist-inspired Red Brigade kidnapped an eminent Christian Democrat politician in 1981). In the 1980s the ineffectiveness of the State in checking the spread of organised crime and the interference of the parties in administrative and economic matters led to a general disillusionment with party politics and a widespread distrust of institutions. Intensive efforts in the 1990s to bring numerous 'untouchable' citizens (including two former prime ministers) to justice, on charges ranging from corruption, to mafia association, to murder, is slowly restoring people's faith in government.

Today, Italians again find themselves at a crossroads. The political parties that emerged at the end of the Second World War have been swept away either by scandal (as in the case of the Christian Democrats and Socialists), or by the changing tides of international events (Communists), and there is much talk of a Second Republic. But perhaps more importantly, the 'economic miracle' of north-eastern Italy, the country's fastest growing industrial region, is once again widening the gap between north and south. Unless precise steps are taken—in the private as well as the public sphere—to prevent the migration of human and financial resources to northern Italy and beyond, the savings and skills of southern Italians will never be invested in their native land. In this sense, the complete integration of the south into a united Italy has yet to be achieved.

Southern Italian art and architecture

by Alexandra Massini

Art and myth ~ the Classical past

Since ancient times, southern Italy, at the centre of the Mediterranean, has served as a catalyst for the cultural exchange between the Middle East and West, and northern and southern Europe. The many peoples that have passed through it have left an imprint on the area, contributing to its multilayered and complex character. The true value of the south is its history, and yet the peculiarity of this history is inextricable from the nature of the land and the image that was traditionally attached to it. The myth of Classical Antiquity, even though changed and transformed, was never forgotten. On the contrary, it was assimilated by the various cultures that took turns in ruling the south: from the Byzantines to the Normans, and later, from the French Angevins to the Spanish Aragonese and Bourbons.

Travelling to the south of Italy has always been regarded by those interested in art and architecture as an attempt to rediscover the Classical past. In the 18C–19C, when the 'Grand Tour' was fashionable, such a journey was even identified with a return to a fabled Golden Age.

Greek and Roman art

The long-standing fascination exerted by this region dates back to the Graeco-Roman world and the tales of Homer and Virgil who recounted the adventurous journeys undertaken by Ulysses and Aeneas to reach the coasts of Italy. Even the origins of the Greek colonies of Magna Graecia, and, later, of the Roman cities, were imbued with an aura of myth: each city was founded by a descendant of the epic heroes and protected by a god.

The Greeks settled mainly in Sicily and the areas of Campania, Lucania (modern Basilicata) and Calabria. Except for the ports of Otranto and Taranto, they could not expand into Apulia which was inhabited by Iapigian settlements. Significant traces of a Greek presence on the southern mainland are evident in the ruins of Metapontum, Eraclea, Sybaris, Crotone and Locri (all along the Ionian coast of Lucania and Calabria). Particularly impressive is the temple complex of **Paestum** in Campania, as well as the collections of the **National Museum** in Taranto and the **Museum of Magna Graecia** in Reggio Calabria.

Once the Romans took over, they rapidly assimilated Greek culture and art, and adopted the type of architecture they encountered in Greek foundations. Temples, theatres and houses became a model for Roman equivalents, although modified to fit new requirements.

More than the Greeks, the Romans were outstanding engineers: they built roads, such as the **Via Appia** down to Brindisi, the Via Latina, and the Via Traiana from Benevento; they also started to use concrete (2C BC), and perfected the use of the arch. It was the flexibility of concrete, and the technical ability in erecting arches and consequently vaults, that enabled the Romans to build acqueducts, bridges, baths with huge vaulted spaces, and amphitheatres. An admirable example can be found at **Santa Maria Capua Vetere** which was conceived as a freestanding structure, unlike Greek precedents that were always built into hillsides.

The Romans' admiration for Greek art is most evident in sculpture. If one excludes portraiture, much of Roman sculpture displays a strong Greek influence both in form and content. The Romans were in fact the first 'collectors of history', taking home the art of the cities they conquered and encouraging their artists to imitate new styles. Much of our knowledge of Greek art is due to the marble copies made in the 2C AD after bronze originals that were melted down. Some fine examples, of both copies and originals, are in the **Archaeological Museum** in Naples.

Greek influence is also felt in other arts. Although most Greek painting has been lost, hindering direct comparison to Roman painting, the frescoes from **Pompeii** and **Herculaneum** seem to imitate Greek precedents, as testified by literary descriptions, thematic recurrences and copies that have come down to us. They may even have been executed by Greek artists who complied with the demands of their Roman patrons and the change in taste reflected in the four Pompeian styles. At any rate, these two towns represent not only the best impression of a provincial, yet fashionable centre inhabited by a rich bourgeoisie, but also a unique example of Roman wall-painting, taste and culture between the last years of the Roman Republic and the beginning of the Empire.

Cultural synchretism and the adaptation of the Greek world to Roman needs also infiltrated politics and religion, and consequently visual propaganda. Once the Roman Empire took shape, much of the ideological impact of the Roman emperors relied precisely on the use of mythology and the legends inherited from the Greeks. One such case was the combination of the legend of Troy with the story of Romulus. According to Virgil, Romulus was the son of Mars and Rhea Silvia, who in turn belonged to the Trojan family of Aeneas. Virgil finished his *Aeneid* just before Augustus, the first Roman emperor, seized absolute power under the claim of divine descendancy (from Aeneas, via Romulus and the deified Julius Caesar).

From Augustus onwards, each emperor used mythology to justify his position. Art naturally played an important role in this context: images of gods and heroes were used as a powerful vehicle for imperial ideology. This is even more evident when looking at portraits or statues of emperors in the guise of gods, and the many celebratory reliefs decorating temples, altars, sarcophagi and triumphal arches. The triumphal **arch of Trajan** at Benevento aptly illustrates this point: apart from the scenes glorifying Trajan's government it also bears an image of Jupiter giving his thunderbolt to the emperor. There could not be a stronger statement: the most important of gods is investing a mortal with divine authority.

Early Christian art

The advent of Christianity introduced a different kind of art. In its early stages, when followers of the new religion were persecuted, Christian artists avoided explicit references to their faith; abstract decorations, foliage with animals and other images indirectly symbolising Christ and the afterlife (fish, birds, grapes etc.) were more common.

With the Edict of Constantine allowing freedom of worship (AD 313) mythology was no longer needed to prove the divinity of emperors, nor to transmit imperial propaganda. The new religion had other themes and meanings to get across, moreover it feared pagan myths and was well aware of the danger of idolatry. For this reason pagan representations were transformed in a spiritual sense and gradually gave way to a fully developed religious iconography. Christian art was concerned with spirituality, and served mainly didactic purposes, indeed, using the words of Gregory the Great (6C), it was meant 'to teach the Bible to the illiterate'.

Examples of this turning point can be found in the **Baptistery** at Naples (San Giovanni al Fonte), and in the **catacombs of San Gennaro** in Naples. The mosaics on the dome of the Baptistery date back to the early 5C and represent scenes from the Gospels, standing saints, and the symbols of the evangelists amid garlands of flowers, fruit and birds. A little later in date are the mosaics in the catacombs of San Gennaro, the finest being those in the crypt of the bishops, showing half-length portraits of the bishops buried there. In the same catacombs are also a number of frescoes with biblical stories, dating from the 2C to the 10C.

In Campania, near Santa Maria Capua Vetere, the chapel of Santa Matrona at **San Prisco** is decorated with mosaics of the 6C. The best preserved are two lunettes showing the Blessing Christ and an empty throne flanked by the symbols of the Evangelists Luke (the bull) and John (the eagle). The style of the mosaics in the dome, decorated with foliage and doves on a blue background, recall the naturalism of Classical art.

Moving further south, to Apulia, are the beautiful 6C mosaics of Santa Maria della Croce at **Casaranello** (Casarano). The dome is decorated with a Cross set in a starry sky, and the presbytery with geometrical patterns and lively representations of animals.

Many early Christian churches have been remodelled at a later date, and little remains of the architecture of the period. However, some interesting examples are the round church of Santa Maria Maggiore at **Nocera Superiore**, originally a baptistery of the 6C, and the martyrium precinct at **Cimitile** (also in Campania), housing the remains of four basilican structures of the late 4C and frescoes of the 10C (in the Santi Martiri).

In Apulia, near Canosa, are the remains of the once impressive 6C church of **San Leucio**. This was a centrally planned building with four exedrae, covered with imposing domes. It was destroyed in AD 1000, yet the finely carved capitals and mosaic floor are a remarkable testimony of the earliest influences of Byzantine art.

Byzantine and early medieval art

After the end of the Roman Empire and the barbaric invasions, around AD 700 half of southern Italy belonged to the Lombard duchy of Benevento, the other (south Apulia, Calabria and Sicily) was under Byzantine control. A brief and precarious unity was reached in Italy under Charlemagne and the institution of the Holy Roman Empire (crowned 25 December 800), yet the south had to face the constant threat of the Saracens who in the 9C invaded Sicily, besieged Rome and raided the coasts of the southern mainland on several occasions. By the late 9C, however, the regions of Calabria, Basilicata and Apulia had been restored to the Empire of Byzantium and would remain under eastern control for nearly two centuries.

Although patronage was limited during this troublesome period and much of the artistic output was lost through subsequent re-adaptations, what is left reflects the complex history of the south and the various cultures that left their mark on the area.

Byzantine influence started appearing in Italy once the political centre had shifted from Rome to Constantinople during the late Roman Empire. This pervaded not only art and culture, but also the liturgy and rites, court ceremonials, fashions, and even gestures and attitudes which were strictly regulated by standard formulae and are reflected in the iconography of the period. So the hieratic style developed between the 6C–11C, may well have been a deliberate choice rather than an expression of 'a decline in the arts' (as E. Gibbon dismissed it in *The Decline and Fall of the Roman Empire* [1776–88]).

An early example from the Eastern Empire is the colossal bronze statue of a Byzantine emperor at **Barletta**. The statue has been identified as Marcian, who ruled between 450–457. It was made in Constantinople and washed up in Barletta harbour in 1309, probably from an Adriatic shipwreck. The earliest evidence of Byzantine painting in southern Italy comes from the Cathedral of **Rossano** in Calabria, where a 6C illuminated copy of the Gospels has been found (we do not know when or how it got there). It is known as the *codex purpureus* (from the purple colour of the vellum leaves) and is the oldest copy of the Gospels in existence. It is written in Greek and has 16 miniatures executed by artists linked to the Byzantine court. A book of such refined quality would not have been widely circulated and, as was often the case with manuscripts, it remained an isolated work bearing little influence on the art of the region.

The church of **Santa Sofia** at **Benevento**, in Lombard territory, once attached to a prestigious monastery founded in 762 by Duke Arechi II is another example of Byzantine influence. It was restored in the 1950s to its original plan (a hexagon articulated by columns and arches, and covered by a dome) whose style imitates the centrally planned churches of the east. Remains of an important fresco cycle of the early 9C, depicting scenes from the Old and New Testaments can be seen in two apses.

Of a similar style, yet later in date (824–842), are the frescoes in the crypt of St Lawrence, attached to the Benedictine Abbey of **San Vincenzo al Volturno** (Castel San Vincenzo, in the region of Molise). The paintings represent scenes of the *Infancy of Christ*, the *Virgin Enthroned*, the *Martyrdom of Saints Stephen and Lawrence*, and the *Crucifixion* with the kneeling Abbot Epiphanius. The latter is identified by an inscription and a square nimbus indicating that he was alive at the time of painting, also providing us with a precise date. Though Byzantine in taste, both these cycles show a strong stylistic affinity with the new Carolingian art of northern Italy (e.g. Müstair), whose influence spread south along the routes of the old Lombard duchies, and was well received in the Benedictine foundations of San Vincenzo and Monte Cassino.

Strong Byzantine influences can be detected in the 10C paintings of the Grotta dei Santi at **Calvi** (Campania). Although fairly damaged, these frescoes are a particular expression of Benedictine monasticism. This type of stone sanctuary (*grotta*) is fairly common in southern Italy, particularly at **Matera**, where dwellings and entire districts (the so-called **Sassi**) were excavated from the *tufa* (a rather soft stone), creating spectacular formations over the centuries. Other interesting examples of stone villages and churches, often decorated with paintings, can be found nearby, in Apulia, around the centres of Mottola, Massafra, Laterza and Gravina. Many of these settlements were founded by Greek monks seeking refuge from the Arab invasion from the Byzantine east and from the Iconoclasm of the 8C–9C which explains the Byzantine character of the churches and paintings. Moreover, stone villages of this kind have some notable parallels in areas of Greek influence such as Cappadocia. In southern Italy the whole phenomenon should also be linked with the retreat of rural communities to inaccessible places in an attempt to escape barbaric invasions from the north and Saracen raids from the sea.

Clear evidence of Greek settlers can be found in the crypt of Sante Marina and Cristina at **Carpignano** (near Otranto), where two painted niches representing *Christ Enthroned* are signed by Greek names and dated 959 and 1020. The two painters, Theophylactos and Eusthatios, were probably Basilian monks. More important, although much later in date, are the frescoes in the crypt of **San Biagio** at San Vito dei Normanni (13C–14C).The frescoes of **San Pietro** at Otranto (10C–11C), executed by Greek monks, as the inscriptions tell us, are also Byzantine in style. The centrally planned church is believed to be the original cathedral of Otranto.

Byzantine architecture in southern Italy is most conspicuous in Calabria with churches such as the 10C **Cattolica** at Stilo, built of brick and remarkably well preserved, and the 11C **San Marco** at Rossano. Both these churches reproduce an Eastern style frequently found in the Peloponnese, Armenia, Georgia and Anatolia, with a square plan, three apses and five little domes.

At **San Demetrio Corone** (Cosenza), is a Basilian church founded in 905 and rebuilt, after a Saracen attack, in the Norman Romanesque style. Although later in date (12C), the frescoes that decorate the interior still follow the Byzantine tradition. Like San Demetrio, the so-called **Roccelletta**, near Squillace, is an example of the fusion between eastern and western elements. The church (now half ruined) was founded by Basilian monks in the 11C, and built upon a western ground plan (a single naved Latin cross) inspired by French Romanesque prototypes that were introduced by the Normans. However, the architectural details are Byzantine in character.

Besides bringing the art of Byzantium to southern Italy, these churches are also a vivid expression of the coexistence of two types of monasticism: the Greek, as introduced by eastern monks and hermits in the territories controlled by the Byzantine Empire, and the Latin as embodied by the great Benedictine abbey of

Monte Cassino and its branches. Cross influences between the two can be detected not only in art and architecture, but also in the liturgy, even though the Greek followed the orthodox rite.

The abbey of **Monte Cassino**, founded by St Benedict, played a crucial role for the development of art in southern Italy, particularly under Abbot Desiderius, the future Pope Victor III, who entirely rebuilt it from 1066 to 1071. With the intention of reviving the arts of antiquity, Desiderius designed the abbey to reflect the Early Christian basilicas of Rome, but invited the best mosaicists, sculptors, enamel and glass workers, as well as bronze- and silversmiths, from Constantinople. Unfortunately, next to nothing is left of the past glory of the abbey which suffered an earthquake, was rebuilt in the 16C–18C and eventually bombed in 1944.

Abbot Desiderius also founded the basilica of **Sant'Angelo in Formis** (Capua). It is entirely covered in frescoes which testify to the outstanding quality of craftsmanship reached by the artists in the abbot's milieu. Along the nave walls are scenes from the Old and New Testaments; on the west wall is the *Last Judgement* and in the apse is a giant figure of Christ, flanked by the symbols of the Evangelists and sitting above Desiderius (holding a model of the church), St Benedict and three Archangels. The style and iconography of the paintings are Byzantine, as exemplified by the standard formula of *Christ Enthroned*, with the Greek gesture of benediction (Christ Pantocrator).

Derivations from the style introduced at Monte Cassino and continued at Sant'Angelo in Formis can be found in the surrounding areas of Benedictine influence. The architecture of **Salerno** cathedral, built by the Norman, Robert the Guiscard and Archbishop Alfanus in 1080, closely followed the model of the abbey, while the 12C frescoes at **Ventaroli**, including a *Madonna Enthroned*, dressed like a Byzantine empress, are reminiscent of Sant'Angelo in Formis. Further examples can be found in Abruzzo with the imposing church of **San Liberatore a Maiella** (c 1080) and the 13C fresco cycles of **Fossa** (Santa Maria ad Cryptas) and Bominaco. In southern Lazio there are important paintings at **Subiaco** (Sacro Speco) and in the cathedral crypt at **Anagni** (13C).

While sculpture always remained indebted to antiquity, as exemplified by the marble sarcophagi produced at Capua and Calvi from the 11C, some highly influential artefacts were directly imported from Byzantium, such as the bronze cathedral doors at Amalfi, Atrani, Salerno and Monte Cassino, which inspired bronze workers throughout southern Italy. However, the finest doors are at **Monte Sant'Angelo**, in Apulia. Cast in Byzantium around 1076, they consist of 24 panels depicting the deeds of the Archangel Michael, to whom the sanctuary was dedicated.

Later in date are the bronze doors of the **Mausoleum of Bohemond** at Canosa (1111) showing, like the building itself, a mixture of Byzantine and Oriental influences. Closer to Byzantine prototypes are the two sets of doors on the façade and south portal of **Troia** cathedral, executed in 1119 and 1127 by Oderisius of Benevento. Another named sculptor, Barisanus of Trani, designed the doors at **Trani** (about 1175), Ravello (1179), and Monreale in Sicily (1186).

The Byzantine revival promoted by Desiderius also invested other art forms such as mosaic floors. While the work of the mosaicists called to Monte Cassino has largely been lost, the fragments of the mosaic floor in the cathedral at **Salerno** can give us an idea of the high standards reached by the artists trained at the abbey. Further away from Monte Cassino, the mosaic pavements of Apulia (at Taranto, Otranto, Trani, Brindisi) draw their inspiration from the Classical style. The impressive floor of the cathedral at **Otranto** (completed between 1163 and 1166) has a variety of scenes ranging from the Bible and episodes of court literature, to fantastic animals and signs of the Zodiac. A similar floor decorates the 12C church of **Santa Maria del Patire** in Calabria. The roundels with animals can be compared with those at Otranto but also show the influence of Arab decorative patterns, which were known through the circulation of Sicilian fabrics produced at Palermo, in the Arab style.

Trade with Sicily also brought new influences to the coasts of Campania, where mosaic floors acquired an Islamic flavour (at **Casertavecchia** and **Sessa Aurunca**). Altar fronts and church fittings were decorated with an inlay of coloured glass quite different from anything produced at or derived from Monte Cassino. Even architectural structures such as façades (at **Amalfi**), bell-towers (at Amalfi and **Gaeta**) and domes (at Casertavecchia) were enriched in the 13C with blind pointed arches and majolica decorations, whose direct precedents are at Palermo and Monreale.

The Norman conquest and Romanesque art

The artistic and cultural revival accomplished by the great Benedictine foundations needs to be placed against the background of the Norman unification of southern Italy. By 1056 Robert Guiscard had conquered Calabria and Apulia while his brother Ruggero annexed Sicily (under Arab dominion), thus preparing the ground for the Kingdom of the Two Sicilies (instituted in 1130), which, under different rulers, would remain the only monarchy on Italian soil until the Risorgimento in the 19C.

The Norman presence in the south favoured a programmatic 'latinisation', pursued by the Church of Rome in territories that were heavily imbued with Greek culture. The Normans were indeed responsible for the diffusion of Benedictine monasticism on the one hand, and the reconstruction of several town cathedrals on the other. The art of this period is defined as Romanesque and is characterised by a deliberate rediscovery of Classical forms. Yet it remained a unique kind of Romanesque, particularly in Apulia, with strong overtones derived from French art and architecture.

Among the earliest examples of Romanesque style were the newly founded cathedrals at **Taranto** (1070) and **Otranto** (1080), which adopted the Latin basilican plan for ideological reasons and are often linked to the Campanian cathedrals of Salerno and Monte Cassino. The most important event in the art of the period was the construction of the church dedicated to **San Nicola di Bari**, caused by the arrival of the saint's relics from Turkey in 1087. The sanctuary soon became an important site for pilgrims and crusaders leaving the port of Bari for the Holy Land. At the same time it was also a palatial church of the Norman princes, reflecting northern European building types, particularly in the façade. The new principles introduced at San Nicola served as model for a whole series of churches such as the cathedrals of **Trani**, Bari and Barletta, and, at the very end of the 12C, **Ruvo** and **Bitonto**. On the other hand, the influence of Byzantium was never forgotten as is shown in the cathedrals of Canosa, Siponto, **Troia** (which also follows Pisan models) and, somewhat later, **Molfetta**.

While painting remained attached to Byzantine prototypes, Romanesque art was best illustrated in sculpture. Most of the sculptural output was linked to the architectural fabric of the great cathedrals (in the form of portals, capitals and cornices) or applied to church fittings such as episcopal thrones, pulpits, altar screens and paschal candelabra. The marble throne in the cathedral of **Canosa** is of interest, being supported by two elephants, inspired by Islamic bronzes (possibly from Iran). As the inscription tells us, the throne was carved by the sculptor Romualdo for Archbishop Urso between 1079 and 1089. Of a different character and outstanding quality is the throne in **San Nicola di Bari**, commemorative of Bishop Elia (founder of the church): the three caryatid figures holding the throne at the front, the two lions at the back and the overall decoration are reminiscent of Classical sculpture and represent the most mature expression of Romanesque art in the south.

The pulpits of Campania, such as those in the cathedral of **Salerno** (1173–81) or the later one at Sessa Aurunca (13C) are also distinctive. These are decorated with geometrical compositions of inlaid glass influenced by Arab Sicily and delicate capitals in line with the Classical tradition. Standing next to these pulpits, and following the same style, are highly refined paschal candelabra. Strikingly Classical is the candelabrum of the cathedral at **Gaeta** whose superimposed registers with narrative panels recall the historiated columns of Rome. More provincial in style, yet equally inspired by Classical sculpture, are the cyboria and pulpits in Abruzzo, such as those at **Moscufo** (1159) and Cùgnoli (1166), both executed by the sculptor Nicodemo. Also in Abruzzo are the beautifully decorated apses in the 12C cathedral of **Valva** (Corfinio) and the portal of **San Clemente a Casauria** (1176–82).

The best examples of Romanesque portals can be seen in the Apulian cathedrals, such as **Troia**, where the combination of reliefs, bronze doors by Oderisius of Benevento, and the splendid rose window, contribute to the impressive beauty of the façade. Other noteworthy sculpted portals can be seen at **San Leonardo a Siponto**, Ruvo, Bitonto and **Trani** cathedral (of particular importance here are the bronze doors, now kept inside the church, executed by Barisanus of Trani in 1180).

Frederick II and the revival of Antiquity

In 1208, after a period of political unrest following the death of the last Norman king, power was assumed by Frederick II Hohenstaufen, son of the Norman heiress Constance d'Hauteville and Henry VI. The first concern of the new king was the administrative reorganisation of southern Italy, which was in a state of chaos due to the absence of a central authority. A series of castles and fortifications was erected along the territorial borders, the coast and the main routes of communication, while urban strongholds guaranteed stability against local landlords. Some of these, such as **Castel del Monte** (built from 1240), are spectacular examples of military architecture. The octagonal plan may be derived from the Syrian castles built in the 8C by the Omayyad dynasty; Frederick invited various Arab scientists to his court and had travelled to the Near East during the Sixth Crusade (1228–29).

As Holy Roman Emperor, Frederick II strived to emulate the great emperors of Rome, as Charlemagne had done before him. The coins minted at Brindisi and Messina copied those of the late Roman Empire and depicted Frederick in the guise of a Roman Caesar, crowned with a laurel wreath. He promoted a revival of Classical culture that infiltrated art and politics alike. His concept of 'Empire' was derived from Roman law and to educate his collaborators in the subject he founded a new university at Naples (1224).

As an eager collector of Classical art, Frederick instructed artists and architects to restore the myth of antiquity, as can be seen in the many examples that have come down to us.

The entrance gate of Castel del Monte combines a tympanum with a Classical cornice and pilasters, while the famous **Porta Romana** at Capua, destroyed in 1557, was modelled on Roman triumphal arches, its decoration designed to have great ideological impact. The overall theme was the legitimacy of the emperor's position: it included two busts of judges and a big female head personifying Justice (often wrongly called *Capua fidelis*). On top of these was a group of statues at the centre of which was the enthroned emperor. The sculptures and other fragments from the gateway are now in the Museo Campano at Capua.

Numerous busts imitating the antique have been found throughout southern Italy and convincingly identified as portraits of Frederick II. One such case is the bust in the Museo Civico at Barletta which, although mutilated, is characterised by such naturalism and intense individuality to find its only precedents in Roman portraits.

It is in this context that artists such as **Nicola Pisano** (1220–c 1284) were formed before moving to Tuscany. Although no work in southern Italy can be ascribed with certainty to his hand, we know from documents that he was born and trained in Apulia. Classicist works such as the pulpit at Pisa (1260) have their premise in the art of the Swabian court and contributed enormously to the development of sculpture through the art of his son, Giovanni Pisano and apprentice, Arnolfo di Cambio.

The Angevins and Gothic art

When the Angevins took over in 1266 (they were to rule until 1442 when the throne passed to the Aragonese), the capital of the kingdom moved from Palermo to Naples which also became the artistic centre of the south. A new type of court art flourished, reflecting its French origins, and foreign masters brought along the latest developments in architecture.

Elements of Gothic architecture, including the pointed arch and the cross vault, had already been introduced to the south as demonstrated by the great Cistercian abbeys of **Fossanova** (1187–1208) and **Casamari** (1203–17). The Cistercians derived from the Benedictine order but followed the stricter dictates of Bernard of Clairvaux (1109–53) who preached a more austere and rigorous observance of the rule of St Benedict while condemning the excessive wealth of the Church. Cistercian abbeys were consequently built with great simplicity of style, with little decoration. Like Fossanova, they generally follow a set type with three naves covered by cross vaults, a transept and a square choir instead of an apse. Outside Latium, other examples of this kind are Santa Maria Arabona in Abruzzo, Ripalta in Apulia, Sambucina and Santa Maria di Matina in Calabria.

Gothic elements and great simplicity were also adopted by the new mendicant orders, the Franciscans and Dominicans, although their churches were allowed fresco decoration and were often single naved. A beautiful, if somewhat atypical example, is the church of **Santa Maria del Casale** at Brindisi, founded by Philippe of Anjou at the end of the 13C and distinctive for the geometric design of the façade composed by stones of two different colours. Other examples of

Gothic architecture in Apulia are the cathedral of **Lucera**, founded by Charles II in 1302, and the church of **Santa Caterina** at Galatina which was built as late as 1391 but is still indebted to Romanesque precedents, especially in the façade. The interior of the church is more modern in character, displaying five naves, pointed arches and some remarkable frescoes that follow the style of Giotto and the Neapolitan school.

The interplay of white and pink stone also decorates the façade of a totally different church in the Abruzzo region. The beautiful **Santa Maria di Collemaggio** in L'Aquila was built in the late 13C and testifies to the persistence of Romanesque traits. By contrast, the early 14C church of San Domenico, also in L'Aquila, was built by French masters under Charles II of Anjou and is entirely Gothic. Influences of the new style further inspired the design of 14C cathedrals at **Atri**, Larino, and (to a lesser degree) Teramo. In particular, the cathedral of **Larino** (Molise) has a beautiful rose window reminiscent of Apulian precedents.

The Angevin religious foundations at Naples, such as Sant'Eligio, **San Lorenzo**, and **San Domenico Maggiore**, are also Gothic in style. Somewhat later in date (14C) and built by local architects trained in contemporary French building methods are the churches of San Pietro a Maiella, **Santa Chiara** and **Santa Maria Donnaregina**.

Besides foreign architects, the Neapolitan court attracted some of the best Italian painters, sculptors, and literary figures of the day, including Pietro Cavallini, Giotto, Simone Martini, Tino di Camaino, Petrarch and Boccaccio. **Pietro Cavallini** (active 1273–1308) decorated the Cappella Brancaccio at San Domenico Maggiore (1308–09), while his workshop completed the most extensive fresco cycle of the period at Santa Maria Donnaregina (1319–32). **Simone Martini** (c 1284–1344) executed the famous altarpiece of St Louis crowning his brother Robert of Anjou (1317), now kept at Capodimonte but originally intended for the church of San Lorenzo. Finally, in 1330 Giotto and his assistants painted the frescoes of the Palatine Chapel at Castel Nuovo (the impressive fortress built by Charles I of Anjou, and reconstructed by the Aragonese). Unfortunately all but a few fragments have been lost.

The greatest name in 14C Neapolitan sculpture was **Tino di Camaino** (c 1285–1337), a Sienese artist who was trained by Giovanni Pisano (son of the great Nicola 'de Apulia'), and established himself at Naples working as court sculptor and architect. The Classicism introduced by Nicola and continued by Giovanni also inspired Tino's art as can be seen in the seven tomb monuments that he carved for the Angevins for the major Gothic churches. Three of these are at Santa Chiara: Mary of Anjou (1329), Charles of Calabria (1333) and the beautiful tomb of Mary of Valois.

The tradition of Classicism and the Renaissance

The Middle Ages is often seen as a period of darkness during which—if one excludes the brief 'revivals' under the Carolingian and Ottonian dynasties—all contact with the Classical past was lost. As is testified by the many examples cited above, this interpretation is highly misleading and fails to take into account the continuity and transformation of antiquity sustained by close contact with Rome and the Graeco-Byzantine Empire.

Byzantine art and culture were, in fact, always considered as a continuation of the Roman Hellenistic world and Byzantine *paideia* (education) was based on the knowledge of Classical literature and the use of a highly sophisticated and archaistic language. While manuscripts of Virgil and Ovid were copied and preciously illustrated in the monastic *scriptoria* of Campania and Apulia, the study of Roman law flourished in the first Italian universities such as Naples.

In the 11C, Gregory VII was actively involved in restoring Rome to its Classical grandeur whereas Desiderius's abbey at Monte Cassino was explicitly inspired by Early Christian basilicas and decorated by Byzantine artists, reinforcing the link with the Classical east. The pulpits of the cathedrals at Salerno and Ravello drew heavily on the Classical repertoire; various paschal candelabra imitated Roman historiated columns, while sarcophagi with Classical reliefs were produced at Capua and Calvi. Further south, the sculptures decorating the great cathedrals and castles of Apulia were deliberately modelled in Classical style. Frederick II instructed his artists to imitate precise models. Such was the case in the Porta Romana at Capua, commissioned with the clear intention of presenting Frederick as the new Roman emperor.

Even the Gothic period never lost sight of Classical principles: the façade of Fossanova has a portal with a tympanum that reminds one of the gateway at Castel del Monte, while the sculptures by Nicola Pisano and Tino di Camaino would have been inconceivable without a close study of antique precedents. Such examples show that the 'recovery' of antiquity and the imitation of Classical art promoted during the Renaissance fit into a long tradition that runs unbroken from the Byzantines to the Aragonese.

When Alfonso of Aragon triumphally entered Naples in 1443, he inaugurated a long period of Spanish rule. In artistic terms his name (and that of his successors) is linked to the reconstruction of **Castel Nuovo**, and the decoration of its famous gateway was an attempt to emulate Classical emperors—as Frederick II had done at Capua two centuries earlier—and return to a celebratory and propagandist art. The gateway has two superimposed triumphal arches decorated with Classical columns, a fine relief with the entry of Alfonso, and statues of the Virtues and St Michael in the upper register. Among the sculptors employed in the project were Pisanello, the Dalmatian Francesco Laurana, Domenico Gaggini and possibly, Mino da Fiesole. None of these was a Neapolitan by birth. In fact, despite the presence of excellent works, there was no local school of merit and the best sculpture of the 15C was carried out by Tuscan or artists from northern Italy.

Once the Brancaccio tomb was completed in their workshop at Pisa, **Donatello** and **Michelozzo** sent it to the church of Sant'Angelo a Nilo at Naples (1428). **Antonio Rossellino** did the same around 1475 with the altar of the Nativity created for the church of Monteoliveto in Naples. Together with **Benedetto da Maiano**, Rossellino also carved the tomb of Mary of Aragon for the Piccolomini chapel there, an exact replica of the monument to the Cardinal of Portugal in the Florentine church of San Miniato. Also at Monteoliveto is another work by Benedetto representing the *Annunciation* (1489) and the outstanding terracotta group of the *Lamentation* executed by the Modenese, **Guido Mazzoni** in 1492.

Among the best foreign artists working in Naples at this time were the Spaniards Diego de Siloe and Bartolomeo Ordoñez. Ordoñez was responsible for the beautiful monument of Andrea Bonifacio in the church of Santi Severino and Sossio (1519).

It was only in the 16C, with **Giovanni da Nola** (1488–1558) that local sculpture emerged with some originality, as can be seen in the tomb of Don Pedro da Toledo at San Giacomo degli Spagnoli (1539), or in the Sanseverino Chapel at Santi Severino and Sossio (1539–46). Another important Neapolitan sculptor was **Girolamo Santacroce** (c 1502–37) who worked alongside Giovanni da Nola at Santa Maria delle Grazie a Caponapoli and at Monteoliveto where he executed the Del Pezzo Altar (1524). His style was formed by the Spaniards Ordoñez and Siloe, who introduced him to a greater freedom of expression.

The taste of the Neapolitan court and the link with the centres of the European Renaissance is further reflected in a number of Flemish works acquired by the Aragonese. Unfortunately none of these survive, but documents report of several paintings including a *St George* by Van Eyck (known through copies) and a series of tapestries by Rogier Van der Weyden. Some of these works must have been known to **Colantonio** (1352–1442), the main painter of 15C Naples, and to his even more gifted pupil **Antonello da Messina** (1430–79). Their style is indeed marked by a naturalism and passion for detail that has no precedent in Italy at that time. The painting of the *Deposition* at San Domenico, both in form and iconographical solutions, reveals Colantonio's debt to Petrus Christus, a Flemish painter who also influenced Antonello. The refined oil technique employed by the two artists instead of the more common tempera, may also be a result of Flemish influence. Another important work by Colantonio is the polyptych of *St Vincent Ferrer* in the church of San Pietro Martire. What the master had started was perfected by the pupil. However, except for a portrait at Capodimonte, no paintings by Antonello can be seen at Naples, because he worked mainly in Venice and Messina.

Another artist of note, active in Naples in the early 16C, was the Venetian **Antonio Solario**, who painted the frescoes with the *Life of St Benedict* in the cloister of Santi Severino e Sossio. More important and productive was **Andrea da Salerno** (1480–1530) who worked extensively throughout Campania. He was trained in Rome where he met the Leonardesque Cesare da Sesto. Together they moved back to Naples and developed a style echoing both Raphael and Leonardo. Andrea's main works are the *Madonna and Saints* of 1512 at Salerno (Museo del Duomo), and the *Adoration of the Magi* in the Girolamini church at Naples. Following the Sack of Rome by imperial troops (1527), many artists left the city. Among them was **Polidoro da Caravaggio** (1500–43), a pupil of Raphael, who sought refuge in Naples, bringing along a highly emotional narrative style. He was one of the painters responsible for introducing Mannerism to the south, a trend which was favoured by two other events: the arrival of Vasari in 1544, and the marriage of Cosimo de'Medici with Eleonore of Toledo (daughter of the Spanish viceroy governing Naples). The paintings by Vasari in the old refectory of Monteoliveto had quite an impact on subsequent artists such as **Fabrizio Santafede** (c 1560–1624) and **Belisario Corenzio** (1558–1646). These prolific painters, of mediocre quality, are a typical expression of the religious and decorative urge that animated Neapolitan churches after the Council of Trent. Much of it was financed by the newly established orders of the Jesuits, Theatines and Oratorians, whose prestigious foundations included churches, hospitals, confraternities and charitable institutions.

The Baroque age

While the Renaissance in southern Italy was mainly created by foreign artists and produced little of note in terms of originality, the Baroque age was quite different. Neapolitan art came into its own with a series of painters, sculptors and architects that formed a distinctive school and changed the appearance of the city. The patrons largely responsible for this transformation were the new religious orders (Jesuits, Theatines and Oratorians) and a few of the viceroys who governed Naples and the southern mainland (by now governed separately from Sicily) in the 16C and 17C. Among these was Don Pedro de Toledo (1532–53) who devised a new urban plan to solve the dramatic problems of overpopulation.

In 1734 Naples became the capital of the Bourbon kingdom, an event which further contributed to its development with the construction of the enormous Albergo dei Poveri, the Theatre of San Carlo and the new royal palaces at Capodimonte, Caserta and Portici. While the best artists worked in the capital (Caravaggio, Jusepe de Ribera, Mattia Preti, Luca Giordano, Francesco Solimena, Francesco de Mura, among others), the rest of the kingdom, with the exception of Lecce and Apulia, followed the Neapolitan mainstream producing a derivative art of little individuality.

The 17C opened in Naples with the construction of the new viceregal palace by the architect Domenico Fontana, and the arrival of **Caravaggio** (1571–1610) in 1606. Caravaggio's turbulent success in Rome had been brought to a sudden end when he stabbed his opponent in a game of racquets and had to flee from the city. Notwithstanding his violent temper and the reputation he had made through his non-conformist art, characterised by a vivid realism and the rejection of all idealisation and iconographic rules, the painter was immediately employed in the decoration of the **Monte della Misericordia**, a charitable institution that still exists to this day. On the altar is one of Caravaggio's masterpieces: a moving and powerful picture representing the *Seven Acts of Mercy*, which also provides an incomparable image of popular life in 17C Naples. In the side chapels are works by the first Caravaggesques, the most talented being **Battistello Caracciolo** (1578–1635) who is the author of the *Deliverance of St Peter from Prison*. During his brief stay, Caravaggio executed two other paintings, now at Capodimonte: a *St John the Baptist* and the *Flagellation*, both painted for the church of San Domenico Maggiore.

The influence of Caravaggio and the art of the Spaniard **Jusepe de Ribera** (1588–1652) changed the direction of Neapolitan painting and contributed to the creation of an independent local school. Ribera's best works (a *Deposition* and a series of prophets) are at the **Certosa di San Martino**, one of the major monuments of the Neapolitan Baroque. All the main exponents of the new school are represented at the Certosa: from Battistello Caracciolo and Massimo Stanzione (the most Caravaggesque), to Andrea Vaccaro, Micco Spadaro, Francesco Fracanzano and Bernardo Cavallino, whose paintings are characterised by dark colours, dramatic compositions and an intense religious feeling, in line with the dictates of the Counter-Reformation. Strong Caravaggesque overtones and directed lighting are also the main features of **Mattia Preti**'s works (1613–99), one of the best painters in the second half of the 17C. A native of Calabria, he left a number of paintings in the churches of San Domenico and Santa Barbara at Taverna, near Catanzaro. His main works in Naples are the canvases decorating the vault of San Pietro a Maiella.

The innovative achievement of these artists was continued by the second generation of Neapolitan painters. Their works competed against the masters invited from Rome, such as Carlo Maratta, or Domenichino and Lanfranco (rivalling each other on the vault of the Cappella di San Gennaro) who brought the taste of pontifical commissions and a more Classical style to Naples, but they were soon driven out by the hostility of the locals.

Besides Mattia Preti, the major Neapolitan artists working in the late 17C were **Salvator Rosa** (1615–73), who is well known for his landscapes and battle scenes, and **Luca Giordano** (1634–1705), whose enormous output is best represented by the spectacular ceiling with the *Triumph of Judith* at the Certosa di San Martino (1703). Before leaving for other centres such as Rome, Venice and Madrid (to decorate the Escorial), Luca Giordano trained **Francesco Solimena** (1657–1747) the greatest Neapolitan painter of the 18C as well as an architect of some credit. He was in constant demand by kings and princes, acquired great wealth and set up his own academy that trained almost an entire generation of 18C painters, sculptors and architects. His masterpieces are the frescoes in the sacristy of San Paolo Maggiore (1689–90), the *Triumph of Faith* in the sacristy of San Domenico (1706), and the *Expulsion of Heliodorus* in the Gesù Nuovo (1725). Among Solimena's pupils were **Francesco de Mura** (1696–1782), responsible for the frescoes in the royal palace at Naples, and **Corrado Giaquinto** (1703–65), who became court painter in Madrid and marked the transition from the rhetorical classicism of the Baroque to the lighthearted grace of the Rococo.

Baroque sculptors working in 17C Naples were Pietro Bernini (1562–1629), father of the more fortunate and talented Gian Lorenzo, and **Cosimo Fanzago** (1591–1678) who was also an outstanding architect, perfecting the use of coloured marbles to decorate monuments and buildings, as can be seen in the lavish interior of the Certosa di San Martino (1623–31) or the altar of Santi Severino e Sossio (1635).

The monastery of San Martino also employed the major sculptors of the 18C, **Domenico Antonio Vaccaro** (1678–1745) and **Giuseppe Sanmartino** (1720–93), whose best work is the extraordinary *Shrouded Christ* in the **Cappella Sansevero** (1753). The entire chapel is among the chief monuments of the late Baroque period. Commissioned by Prince Raimondo di Sangro to house the tombs of his family, it is decorated with statues personifying Virtues (the overall iconography remains obscure and has been tentatively connected to the prince's involvement in Freemasonry). Among the best sculptures are the so-called *Deception unmasked* by the Genoese Francesco Queirolo, and the veiled figure of *Modesty* by the Venetian Antonio Corradini, who was an expert in the subject and was probably invited to provide an adequate pendant to Sanmartino's *Shrouded Christ*.

Like sculpture and painting, Baroque architecture flourished in Naples through the work of some very interesting personalities. The Classical elements of Roman Baroque introduced at the beginning of the 17C century by Domenico Fontana (1543–1607) were combined with the Spanish passion for elaborate decoration, and ultimately created a style of great individuality. Among the architects of the early and more Classical phase are Giovan Antonio Dosio (1533–1609) who rebuilt the 14C monastery of San Martino together with his pupil Giovan Giacomo Conforto. More influential are Fra Francesco Grimaldi (1543–1613), a monk from Calabria responsible for the construction of San Paolo Maggiore (1603) and the Dominican Fra Nuvolo whose elliptical ground-plan of San Carlo all'Arena (1631) seems to anticipate Bernini's solution for Sant'Andrea al Quirinale in Rome.

The greatest architect of the 17C was certainly **Cosimo Fanzago**, already mentioned as a talented sculptor and decorator. Apart from working in Naples, he was also active in Abruzzo and Calabria, bringing innovative ideas to the con-servative south. His early work, such as the cloister at the Certosa di San Martino (1623–31), is still indebted to the restrained Classicism of his predecessors. Later, as in Santa Maria Egiziaca a Pizzofalcone (from 1651), he experiments with the same octagonal plan used by Borromini in Rome (Sant'Agnese in Agone). Much more innovative are his last churches (Pietrasanta; Santa Teresa a Chiaia) where the effective use of space, with contrasting curves and volumes, ranks among the best examples of Italian Baroque.

While the return to Classicism was deliberate and direct in the Renaissance, it was utterly transformed in the Baroque reinterpretations. All rules were broken, along with pediments and entablatures, and the clusters of columns and decora-tions had little to do with structural functionalism, becoming an art of pure aes-thetic enjoyment. Architecture became increasingly more playful and elaborate and ultimately culminated in the Rococo of the 18C.

At the turn of the century there was a group of architects, formed in the acad-emy of Francesco Solimena. Among them, **Ferdinando Sanfelice** (1675–1748) and **Domenico Antonio Vaccaro** (1681–1750) were involved in updat-ing several older buildings, following a general trend that has irreversibly changed (often for the worse) the appearance of medieval churches throughout Italy. Sanfelice's best work concerned domestic buildings, such as Palazzo Cassano (1725) and Palazzo Sanfelice (1726), where he experimented with scenographic staircases and provided unexpected solutions to the cramped Neapolitan spaces. Among Vaccaro's contributions is the charming Chiostro delle Clarisse at Santa Chiara: a garden decorated with coloured majolica tiles.

The undisputed leaders of 18C architecture were **Ferdinando Fuga** (1699–1781) and **Luigi Vanvitelli** (1700–73). The first was summoned from Rome to build the Albergo dei Poveri (begun in 1752), a huge structure with a façade 1000 feet long (305m), which was intended by Charles III to house 'the poor of the entire reign'. At the same time, Vanvitelli, son of the painter Gaspar van Wittel, was entrusted with the construction of the new royal residence at **Caserta** (1751–74). The scale of the project was immense: a palace with 1200 rooms and landscaped gardens with avenues that deliberately imitated the palace at Versailles. The rationalism of the ground plan combined with the rigorous symmetry and Classicism of the elevations place Vanvitelli among the best of Neo-classical architects. However, the interplay of scenographic vistas along straight and diagonal axes is still in the tradition of the late Baroque. The same applies to the 19 fountains in the grounds, depicting mythological subjects and culminating in a multi-figured group of *Diana and Actaeon* on either side of a great cascade.

Another extensive project of the period was the Carthusian monastery of San Lorenzo at **Padula**. The complex had been founded in the 14C and was rebuilt in the 17C–18C. Like the Escorial near Madrid, it is designed in the shape of the gridiron where St Lawrence was supposed to have been martyred, while the overall appearance, especially the great cloister, have the logic and clarity of Neoclassicism.

Outside Naples and Campania, the most original expressions of Baroque flourished in Apulia, particularly at **Lecce** and the Salentine area. Palaces, churches and interiors were decorated with an unrivalled exuberance on the southern mainland—both an explosion of vitality and a display of wealth and status. Every inch on the façade of Santa Croce at Lecce is covered with statues, garlands and friezes, while the interior space is enriched by equally elaborate details. The theatrical solemnity of the Baroque culminates here in complete irrationality. Yet in all its playfulness, it never loses sight of Classicism: it may break rules, overdecorate, distort and transform, but it still uses the Classical vocabulary (columns, entablatures and capitals, etc.), which it turns into a highly complex, though somewhat redundant, language.

The age of Neo-classicism

A reaction against these exaggerated modes, and a return to Classical simplicity, characterises the Age of Enlightenment, in the second half of the 18C. 'One should never put anything on a building for which one cannot give a solid reason' was the view of Abbé Laugier, one of the precursors of Neo-classicism.

His words were echoed by theorists like Winckelmann who advocated a return to the 'noble simplicity and calm grandeur' of Classical sculpture, while a wealth of publications and a series of prints by Piranesi (*Views of Rome* and *Imaginary Prisons*—both published 1745 onwards—and *On the Magnificence and Architecture of Rome*, published in 1761) contributed to the rediscovery of antiquity and the development of a new taste.

Knowledge of the Classical past was increased by the great discoveries of **Herculaneum** (1738) **Pompeii** (1748) and **Paestum** (1750). It must be remembered that the 18C archaeological finds had been fortuitous (the Golden House of Nero in the 15C, the Torso Belvedere and Laocoön in the 16C). The Classical world as we know it today from excavations and museums, is far removed from the reality encountered by anyone travelling southwards in the 18C–19C. Many ruins still lay half-buried and were frequently misinterpreted (a typical example, although earlier and occurring in Tuscany, is the famous case of 15C Florentines mistaking the medieval Baptistry for an ancient temple of Mars, that had been readapted for Christian usage).

While Europe had hitherto only been acquainted with one class of antique building, i.e. the grand civic monument, the discovery of the Vesuvian cities in the 18C added a totally new dimension. As a result, the goût grec soon invaded all aspects of domestic life, from architecture to interior decoration and from furniture to fashion.

In 1738, when excavations started in Herculaneum and Pompeii under the patronage of the Bourbon kings, they were more inspired by a quest for Classical collectables and *mirabilia*, than by a true archaeological spirit. Indeed, the sculptures and bronzes that were unearthed became part of the Bourbon collection and often remained inaccessible even to the greatest scholars. Collections of this kind were fashionable at the time and sanctioned by names such as the Farnese (whose collection Charles of Bourbon had inherited from his mother Elisabetta

Farnese), Cardinal Albani (the employer of Winckelmann), the Medici, the Borghese, and of course the Vatican court, whose antiquities had constituted the first public museum on the Capitoline Hill.

The Bourbon passion for the Classical past is reflected in the decorative arts and especially in the beautiful porcelain services of the Real Fabbrica di Napoli (opened by Ferdinand of Bourbon in 1772), which were inspired by the newly discovered frescoes and prints on antique subjects. Notable examples are the Hercolanese service (in the museum Duca di Martina at Naples) the Etruscan Déjeuner (now at Capodimonte) or the Classical biscuit figurines by the sculptor **Filippo Tagliolini** (1781–1812).

These artefacts should be viewed within the general context of European Neo-classicism. New aesthetic ideas circulated around Europe together with sculptures, paintings, prints and the essays of scholars and collectors. Yet it was Winckelmann and Piranesi who contributed to the creation of the false myth of the Classical world more than anything or anyone. Travellers of the 'Grand Tour' wished to view antiquity in this idealised way. Many travelled to the South in search of a lost Golden Age. Many wrote in their diaries about the great remains of the past. But only a few mentioned the fact that large parts of Pompeii and Herculaneum still lay under mud and had to be visited (if at all) by candlelight (as Goethe reports). In fact many enthusiastic descriptions were more inspired by the publications funded by the Bourbon court than by actual first-hand knowledge.

The truth of the matter is that in the 18C travelling to the south was not easy: the territory beyond Naples was infested by brigands (particularly Calabria), and foreigners had to reach Sicily by sea, because travelling overland was much too dangerous. Southern Italians were considered by many a chronicler as stinking, filthy, uncultured and dishonest, while the inns and food were at best dismissed as revolting.

The Romantic vision of the Classical south

The myth of the Classical past that was commonly associated with southern Italy, stuck in the minds of Romantic writers, artists and archaeologists, and inspired generations of painters (known as *vedutisti*) who depicted the hills of southern Latium or the Gulf of Naples bathed in sunlight. The beauty of the landscape and natural phenomena such as Vesuvius and the Phlegraean Fields, attracted the curiosity of European travellers as much as the new excavations or the grandeur of antique ruins. Moreover, they provided an adequate interest for the cultured Englishman steeped in the new aesthetics of the picturesque and the sublime.

One such personality was Sir William Hamilton, whose famous collection of antique vases was engraved and published in four volumes under the supervision of **Johann Heinrich Wilhelm Tischbein** (1751–1829), becoming an invaluable source for European Neo-classicism. Hamilton was also interested in scientific studies, as shown in his essay entitled *The Volcanoes of the Two Sicilies* (1776) which was illustrated with engravings after the *gouaches* of the German painter **Jacob Philipp Hackert** (1737–1807).

In 1782 Hackert became official painter to Ferdinand IV and his Austrian wife Marie Caroline, who had invited several northern European artists to the Neapolitan court. Many of these, including Hackert and Tischbein, were responsible for decorating the royal palace at Caserta with landscapes and antique decorations derived from Herculaneum. Others, like **Anton Raphael Mengs** (1728–79) and **Angelica Kauffmann** (1741–1807) were employed as portrait painters. Tischbein himself turned to portraiture, while Hackert became famous for his landscapes (highly esteemed by Goethe) in which he followed the trend initiated by Gaspar Van Wittel (1653–1736) a century earlier, portraying the environs of Naples with a transparent clarity typical of the northern tradition. By transforming reality into the idealised elegance of Neo-classical style, Hackert's paintings also anticipated Romantic vision.

Many other landscape painters, foreign and local, were working at Naples chiefly to provide travellers on the 'Grand Tour' with a souvenir to take home. Among them were Giovan Paolo Pannini (1692–1768), who is more famous for his accurate views of Rome, **Antonio Joli** (1700–77), the Frenchman **Claude-Joseph Vernet** (1714–89), and **Giovanni Battista Lusieri** (1775–1821), who produced some marvellous watercolours.

Major English artists working in the area were **John Robert Cozens** (1752–97), Joseph Wright of Derby (1734–97), and **Thomas Jones** (1742–1803) whose watercolours range from detailed accounts of the city, to intimate portraits of streets and houses, and impressive views of Vesuvius. **Richard Parkes Bonington** (1802–28), **J.M.W. Turner** (1775–1851) and **Jean Baptiste Corot** (1796–1875) all arrived in Naples in the early 1820s. The freer approach to landscape painting that characterised their works, exerted a tremendous influence on local *vedutisti*, introducing expressions of European Romanticism for the first time.

The painter **Anton Sminck Pitloo** (1791–1833) became a professor at the Neapolitan Academy of Arts in 1816 and had a strong influence on the new generation. A number of artists at the Academy who shared an interest with **Giacinto Gigante** (1806–76) in the lyrical depiction of landscapes and the study of colour and light effects formed a group. The **Scuola di Posillipo**, as it was called, included Ercole Gigante (the younger brother of Giacinto), Raffaele and Consalvo Carelli, and Gabriele Smargiassi. Although reminiscent of Pitloo and Turner, their work is among the few original expressions of Neapolitan painting, at a time when landscapes had turned into prettified views showing sunsets over the sea, or country idylls dotted with sheep and ruins, with Vesuvius smouldering in the background. By the 1830s there was an active market for the 'picturesque' and such landscapes were mass-produced in Naples.

Two other painters initially connected to the *Scuola di Posillipo* were the brothers **Giuseppe** and **Filippo Palizzi** from Abruzzo. Giuseppe (1812–88) moved to Paris in 1844 to work with Corot and the *Barbizonniers*, whose aim was an exact and unprettified representation of reality, painted on the spot (thereby precursing the Impressionists). Ten years later he was back in Naples to train his brother Filippo (1818–99) in the new technique. The truth to nature that characterised their approach is matched by the work of Beniamino de Francesco (1805–46), the Apulian Saverio Altamura (1826–97), and Giuseppe Abbati (1836–68), all working in Naples in the 1840s. The former two were also connected with the Tuscan *Macchiaioli* school who constructed their paintings solely through colour contrasts, regardless of contours. In the rejection of academic rules as well as in technique, style and subject, Italian artists of the 19C drew heavily from their more fortunate French contemporaries.

More in line with academic teachings were the history paintings of Domenico

Morelli (1826–1901), who was trained at the Neapolitan Academy and later went to Rome and Florence where he executed a series of sentimental and often melodramatic compositions.

The last great period of landscape painting in the south was headed by the so-called **Scuola di Resina**, a group founded in 1864 by Federico Rossano (1835–1912), Marco de Gregorio (1829–75), Giuseppe de Nittis (1846–84) and Adriano Cecioni (1836–86). The school promoted direct study from nature, emphasising the importance of colour, and absence of contours and underdrawing. Adriano Cecioni, a theorist and critic as well as an artist, defended 'art for art's sake' arguing that beauty depended upon the artist's skill and execution, rather than the subject. His theories opened the way for a variety of domestic representations and a low-key genre best exemplified by the informal portraits of Antonio Mancini (1852–1930) and the sculptures of Vincenzo Gemito (1852–1929), whose themes ranged from young fishermen to card players.

The best artist of the *Scuola di Resina* was certainly the Apulian **Giuseppe de Nittis** (1846–84) who moved to Paris, participated in the first Impressionist exhibition (1874) and became a successful painter of townscapes and society life.

At the opposite end of the scale to the fashionable De Nittis, stood Michele Cammarano (1835–1920) whose critical realism captured the terrible social problems of the south and the destitute conditions of the lower classes. A blander realism characterised the art of Paolo Michetti (1851–1929) who often represented the folklore of his native Abruzzo (and was therefore praised by his fellow countryman Gabriele D'Annunzio, one of the most famous poets of the period).

With few exceptions, the 19C in Naples closes with a rhetorical kind of art, devoid of any originality. The long artistic tradition of Neapolitan painting was over, and the lead role passed to the north.

THE GUIDE

South of Rome

If you arrive from the north—from the green, rolling hills of Tuscany and Umbria, for instance—you will certainly notice that the landscape changes radically south of Rome. Everything is somehow more intense: the hills are higher, the contrasts between their barren summits and the green lowlands more pronounced. Even the light seems brighter. It is not a 'friendly' change, and travellers of the past often found it somewhat frightening. As Charles Dickens wrote in *Pictures from Italy* (1846), 'Of all kinds of country that could, by possibility, lie outside the gates of Rome, this is the aptest and fittest burial-ground for the Dead City. So sad, so quiet, so sullen; so secret in its covering up of great masses of ruin, and hiding them; so like the waste places into which men possessed with devils used to go and howl, and rend themselves, in the old days of Jerusalem.' The area nevertheless abounds with things to see, and even the atmosphere, which made Dickens shudder, holds a subtle appeal for the more detached (or disenchanted) modern traveller.

Geographically speaking, you are in Lazio (anciently *Latium*), a hilly region of 11,000sq km lying to the west between the Apennines and the Tyrrhenian Sea, at the centre of the Italian peninsula. The region consists of five provinces, Rome, Rieti, Viterbo, Frosinone and Latina, of which only the last two are included in this volume. The name, one of the oldest place names in Italy, originally outlined a small area between the mouth of the Tiber and the Alban Hills south-east of Rome. With the Roman conquest, it was extended south-west to the Gulf of Gaeta and east to the mountains of Abruzzo, forming the so-called *Latium novum* (or *adiectum*). In Constantine's day it was re-named *Campania romana*, which distinguished it from the *Campania felix*; the area surrounding Naples (see below). The Campania romana includes the Agro Pontino, formerly the Pontine Marshes, the region's only extensive plain.

To the south and east of this rise the Lepini, Ausoni and Aurunci mountains, separated from the main body of the Apennines by the Valle Latina. This broad valley is crossed by the Rivers Sacco and Liri.

The present region of Lazio was essentially formed in 1870, with the inclusion of the Papal States in United Italy. Its southern boundary was established in 1927 with the annexation of the area around the Gulf of Gaeta, which formerly belonged to the Province of Caserta.

THE VALLE LATINA

The atmosphere that perturbed Dickens is most tangible in the long, wide Valle Latina, which stretches from the suburbs of Rome to the Neapolitan hinterland

and, unlike the coastal plain, was long isolated from outside influences. Today this is a fascinating area, dotted with ancient remains, such as the fortifications of **Alatri**, and remarkable medieval monuments, like the churches of **Anagni** and **Casamari** and the renowned abbey of **Monte Cassino**.

Practical information

Information offices
CASSINO *Ufficio Informazioni e di Accoglienza Turistica*, Piazza De Gasperi 6, ☎ 0776 25692.
FIUGGI *Ufficio Informazioni e di Accoglienza Turistica*, Via Gorizia 4, ☎ 0775 515766; Piazza Frascara 4, ☎ 0775 515019.
FROSINONE *Ufficio Informazioni e di Accoglienza Turistica*, Via Aldo Moro 467–469, ☎ 0775 833836, ✉ www.apt.froisinone.it.
Azienda di Promozione Turistica, Via Aldo Moro 465, ☎ 0775 83381, ✉ www.apt.frosinone.it, info@apt.frosinone.it.
See also ✉ www.lazioturismo.it; www.regione.lazio.it/turismo/turismo.shtml/

Getting there and getting around
By car
The AI/E45 motorway (*Autostrada del Sole*) runs the length of the Valle Latina and is the swiftest way to reach the area by car. If you are arriving from northern Italy you can bypass Rome, diverging east before reaching the capital and joining the Rome–Naples leg some 32km south. The Via Casilina (Road 6) weaves its way alongside the *autostrada* for much of the way, though local commercial traffic can make the driving slow and frustrating. For bus routes and schedules, contact *Cotral*, freephone 800 431 784.
By train
The Rome–Bari railway line runs through the Valley Latina to Caserta (roughly 2hrs 20mins with stops; 1hr 40mins by Eurostar), where you must change trains for Naples (another hour).

Where to stay
ANAGNI €€ *Villa la Floridiana*, Via Casilina, km 64, ☎ 0775 769960, 🖷 0775 774527, ✉ www.vlf.cjb.net, floridiana@applicazioni.it. A lovely 19C villa with nine spacious rooms, frescoed ceilings, antique furniture, friendly staff, and a great restaurant, 5km from Anagni; open Sept–July.
CEPRANO €€ *Villa Ferrari Relais*, Via Casilina, km 103, ☎ 0775 912852, 🖷 0775 94319. A quiet 17C villa with good views, fine cuisine, tasteful rooms, marble bathrooms, just 1km from the autostrada; open Dec–Oct.
FIUGGI FONTE €€€ *Palazzo della Fonte*, Via dei Villini 7, ☎ 0775 5081, 🖷 0775 506752, ✉ information@palazzodellafonte.com. A large luxury hotel with park and pool; open Apr–Nov.
€€ *San Giorgio*, Via Prenestina 31, ☎ 0775 515313, 🖷 0775 515012. A quiet place with a shady garden; open May–Oct.
€€ *Silva Hotel Splendid*, Corso Nuova Italia 40, ☎ 0775 506545, 🖷 0775 506546. An elegant but unpretentious place, also with park and pool; open May–Oct.
FROSINONE €€ *Astor*, Via Casilina Nord, 220, ☎ 0775 270132, 🖷 0775 270135, ✉ astor@fr.flashnet.it. A modern establishment on the outskirts of the town.
€€ *Palombella*, Via Maria 234,

☎ 0775 872163, 🖷 0775 270402. Another modern place, with a well-known restaurant.

Eating out

ALATRI € *La Rosetta*, Via Duomo 35, ☎ 0775 434568. Restaurant with rooms offering good local cooking, near the acropolis; closed Tues and three weeks in Nov.

ANAGNI € *Lo Schiaffo*, Corso Vittorio Emanuele 270, ☎ 0775 739148. Restaurant featuring good simple fare—the name refers to the insult received by Boniface VIII at the hand of Guillaume de Nogaret (see below); closed Mon and one week in Oct.

CEPRANO € *Enoteca Federici*, Piazza Martiri di Via Fani 8, ☎ 0775 914048. Wine bar serving lunch and dinner—the family also has a pastry shop on the main square; closed Tues.

€ *Ida*, Via Caragno 27, ☎ 0775 950040. Hotel restaurant, with garden seating in summer; closed 24 Dec–1 Jan.

FIUGGI €€ *La Torre*, Piazza Trento e Trieste 18, ☎ 0775 515382. Restaurant serving creative interpretations of regional dishes; closed Tues.

FROSINONE €€ *Hosteria Tittino*, Vicolo Cipresso, 2–4, ☎ 0775 251227. Restaurant; closed Sun and last three weeks in Aug.

€ *Bar Enoteca Celani*, Via Aldo Moro 401, ☎ 0775 884005. Wine bar, open for lunch only; closed Sun and two weeks in Aug.

€ *Pane e Vino*, Via Tiburtina 11, ☎ 0775 872070. Wine bar; open for lunch and dinner Fri, dinner only Sat, closed Sun.

FUMONE €€ *Vecchia Mola*, Vicinale Piè di Monte, ☎ 0775 49771. Creative seasonal cuisine and pleasant service; closed Mon and late Aug.

€ *La Taverna del Barone*, Via del Ponte 4, ☎ 0775 49655. Trattoria; closed Mon.

€ *Panificio Moriconi*, Via Provinciale per Atri, bivio Fumone. Bakery with natural-leavened, wood-oven-baked bread.

OLEVANO ROMANO €€ *Sora Maria e Arcangelo*, Via Roma 42, ☎ 06 956 4043. Traditional osteria; closed Mon evening, Wed and July.

PALIANO €€ *Taverna Colonna*, Via Lepanto 5, ☎ 0775 571044. In Filippo Colonna's ducal palace; closed Wed and late Dec.

PONTECORVO € *Primavera*, Piazzale Porta Pia 8, ☎ 333 203 8986. Small, simple family-run trattoria, open mid-day (and Fri and Sat evenings); closed Mon and Aug.

Anagni and environs

Travelling east from Rome on the A1, the first important place you encounter is **Segni** (population 9000). Set on the slopes of a hill, this is the ancient *Signia*, founded by Tarquinius Priscus and noted in antiquity for its wine, its pears and a simple, roughly patterned pavement called *opus signinum*. Pope Alexander III canonised Thomas Becket here in 1173. The town has some medieval houses, but it is particularly notable for its **cyclopean walls**, about 1km of which, including the Porta Saracena, are in good condition. There are also remains of the Temple of Jupiter Urius, for which Signia was famous.

Anagni (population 20,000) stands on high ground just north of the Rome–Naples *autostrada*. It preserves a strong feeling of the Middle Ages, with many fine 14C mansions, arched doorways, and trefoil windows.

History of Anagni

Anagnia was the ancient capital of the Hernici, and Cicero had a fine estate here. It was also a favourite country residence of the popes and the birthplace of

Innocent III, Gregory IX, Alexander IV and Boniface VIII. The last, following a quarrel with King Philip IV of France, was insulted and imprisoned at Anagni in 1303 by Guillaume de Nogaret, chancellor of France, but he was rescued by his fellow citizens three days later. The English pope Adrian IV died here in 1159.

The 14C Casa Barnekow (left) and the Romanesque tower of Sant'Andrea (right) mark the entrance to the old town. The town hall, further on, is an attractive 13C building with a vaulted passage beneath it.

The street climbs to the **cathedral**, on the top of a hill offering beautiful views. This large basilica, dedicated to the Virgin Mary, was built in Romanesque forms in 1072–1104 under Bishop Pietro da Salerno but altered in the mid-13C by Bishop Pandolfo, who introduced the Gothic arches in the nave and transept and rebuilt the choir. The exterior has an imposing campanile and a fine triple apse; a statue of Boniface VIII stands high up on the south flank. The interior is known for its very beautiful Cosmatesque floor, of 1231, and for the Caetani Chapel, with a Cosmatesque tomb (1292), on the north side. The fine ciborium on the high altar dates from 1294. Nearby are a bishop's throne of 1263 (behind the altar) and a candelabrum with mosaic decoration, both by Vassalletto.

The **crypt** has another 13C Cosmatesque floor, untouched by restorers, as well as one of the more important fresco cycles in central Italy. This is the most complete example of the 12C–13C Roman school of painting. Its splendour has led the *New York Times* to term the crypt the Sistine chapel of the Duecento.

The paintings were executed by Benedictine monks starting in 1104, and continuing up to the 13C, under the patronage of Anagni's powerful bishops. Three different hands are detectable: the first master still follows the Byzantine tradition and is the most archaic of the three. The other two, working in the 13C, and particularly the third, are stylistically more advanced.

Starting with the work of the first master, at the far left end of the crypt, is a vault with a depiction of Plato's cosmology (taken from the *Timaeus*): Man as microcosm is shown in the centre of seven circles symbolising the Universe, in turn divided into four sections (the Four Ages of Man, the Four Seasons, etc.). The lunette on the right shows Hippocrates and Galenus, the two doctors of antiquity, and at their side is a diagram of the four elements.

The work of the first master continues on the wall opposite, with the Virgin enthroned between Sts Aurelia and Neomisia, whose relics are deposited in the crypt. Below is the story of the martyrdom of St Secondina, another local saint.

Following this bay are the frescoes of the main apse, representing, in the lower section, the martyrdom of St Magnus (Anagni's patron saint), the translation of his body (which had been bought off the Saracens) and his burial in the crypt at Anagni. The upper half of the apse and the three adjoining vaults are devoted to *Visions of the Apocalypse*.

The vault over the altar of St Magnus shows the first vision of St John, with Christ seated as judge. On the apse itself is his second vision, with the 24 elders holding up their calyxes to the lamb with seven eyes (Omniscience) and seven horns (Omnipotence) and the book with the seven seals. On the right of this are the four riders of the Apocalypse (opening of the first four seals). On the left are the naked souls of the martyrs pleading for justice (fifth seal). The lunettes of the adjoining vault, on the left, depict the opening of the sixth seal, withthe dark sun, the blood-red moon and the stars falling out of the sky. The opening of the seventh seal is heralded by an angel blowing the trumpet.

Following the depiction of the Apocalypse are *Elijah on a Chariot*, and the *Encounter between Abraham and Melchisedek*, both by the first master. Next to the latter is a 17C fresco of rather poor quality.

The central nave was painted by all three masters (their different hands are clearly recognisable in the successive bays) and recounts the *Story of the Ark of Alliance* (book of Exodus), with the Philistines stealing the Ark, being persecuted by various plagues, and finally returning the Ark to the Jews.

The second and third masters also worked on the remaining walls, opposite the Apocalypse (left of the entrance). In addition to executing all the floral and geometric decorations of the arches, the second master painted the bays next to Plato's cosmology with a *Miracle of St Magnus* (saving a boy fallen into a well), the *Martyrdom of St John the Evangelist* (in boiling oil) and *Christ Pantocrator* blessing in the Byzantine manner, with the hand in the shape of an alfa and omega, symbolising the beginning and end of the world.

The two bays closest to the entrance are by the third master, depicting more miracles of St Magnus (healing cripples, resurrecting a woman). These frescoes are by far the most advanced; by virtue of their use of perspective and greater plasticity of the body, they anticipate the work of Cimabue and Giotto by half a century.

Two more interesting frescoes adorn the wall on the right of the entrance. One, representing the sainted bishop of Anagni, Peter, seated among two female saints, has been attributed to Pietro Cavallini. The other, a lactating Madonna seated among saints, is a very unusual image. The lactating Madonna is itself very rare in Byzantine iconography; on the few occasions that the nursing Mother of Christ is shown, she is always alone, without saints. If the attribution to the second master is correct, this 13C rendition seems to anticipate later iconographies by three centuries.

Adjoining the crypt is a chapel dedicated to St Thomas Becket, formerly a Roman mythraeum. It is decorated with frescoes of the Old and New Testaments, heavily retouched and in very poor condition. For climatic reasons the chapel is normally closed, and visits to the crypt are limited to 15 minutes.

The **treasury**, on the right of the choir, contains the pontifical ornaments of Boniface VIII, chief among which is a cope embroidered in *opus anglicanum* with medallions representing the lives of Christ and the Virgin. Also noteworthy are a 13C reliquary decorated in Limoges enamel with the histories of Thomas Becket, and a 13C German reliquary with stories of Hercules.

Some portions of a Roman rampart and remains of the Palace of Boniface VIII also survive at Anagni. The latter houses a small collection of documentary material on the town and its environs (Museo dell'Istituto di Storia e di Arte del Lazio Meridionale, open summer daily 09.30–13.00, 15.30–18.30; winter 09.00–12.30, 15.00–18.00, ☎ 0775 727053), of interest chiefly to historians.

About 11km south-east of Anagni on the Via Casilina, **Ferentino**, the *Ferentinum* of the Hernici, was colonised by the Romans in the Second Punic War. It is a maze of narrow alleys within a rampart of cyclopean walls with a later Roman superstructure, still pierced by four gates. At its highest point the bishop's palace rises on the massive foundations of the antique citadel. Adjoining it is the **cathedral**, notable for a 12C mosaic pavement and for its transennae and a beautiful ciborium and candelabrum of the 13C.

Lower down is Santa Maria Maggiore, a 13C church in the Cistercian Gothic style (recognisable by the square east end and overall simplicity of design); the façade has a rose window and symbols of the four Evangelists. The Museo Civico, Piazzale del Collegio, has a modest collection of local antiquities. It is rarely open.

Fumone, perched on a hill between Ferentino and Alatri, has an ancient castle (the Rocca) dating from around 1000, in which both the anti-pope Gregory VIII and Celestine V (who died there in 1296) were kept prisoners. Inside are a small museum of antiquities (open daily 10.00–12.30, 16.00–18.30; ☎ 0775 49023) and a lovely garden.

Frosinone is a hilltop town, the capital (population 48,000) of the province of the same name and the chief place in the *Ciociaria*, a district once noted for the picturesque costumes worn by the peasantry. Now it is also one of Italy's principal industrial centres.

Of the ancient *Frusino*, a town of the Hernici, only fragmentary walls and traces of an amphitheatre remain, together with a few finds of limited interest in the Museo Archeologico (Via XX Settembre 32; open Tues, Wed, Thur 09.00–13.00; Fri, Sat and Sun 09.00–12.00, 16.00–19.00; ☎ 0775 212314). Today Frosinone is a bustling modern city, and unless you have a special interest in that peculiar trait of Mediterranean culture—urban chaos—it is perhaps best avoided.

Well worth a visit, instead, is the abbey of **Casamari**, in the hills north-east of the city. This is one of the region's finer medieval monuments. Founded by the Benedictines in the 11C, it passed to the Cistercians in 1151, to the Trappists in 1717, and in 1864 was returned to the Cistercians, who still hold it. The plan of the original abbey has been remarkably well preserved. The church, fine cloister, aisled chapter house, and guest house, all dating from the 13C, adhere to the Burgundian Gothic types imported by the Cistercians and admirably embodied also at Fossanova. The conventual buildings house a photographic exhibition on Cistercian architecture, as well as a small archaeological collection and a *Cereatum Marianum* (open by appointment; ☎ 0775 283466). Casamari was visited by Holy Roman Emperor Frederick II, when he was admitted to the brotherhood. The event may be celebrated in the capital carvings of the cloister.

A scenic route to Frosinone

An alternative route from Rome to Frosinone touches on the towns high up in the hills on the east side of the Valle Latina.

Genazzano is a picturesque little town. It was the birthplace of Martin V (Oddone Colonna; pope 1417–31). The church of the Madonna del Buon Consiglio contains a venerated Madonna, miraculously transported from Scutari (Albania) in 1467; it is the scene of colourful pilgrimages on 25 March and 8 September.

The village of **Olevano Romano** lies 6km north, on the road to Subiaco. A favourite resort of landscape painters, it preserves some cyclopean walls and remains of a medieval castle.

Paliano is a fortified town on a rocky hill 3km south. It was a stronghold of the Colonna, whose simple tombs may be seen in the church of Sant'Andrea. The

Fortezza Colonna, with late 16C frescoes celebrating the triumphal entry of Marcantonio Colonna into Rome after his victory at Lepanto in 1571 (when the Turks were defeated by the alliance of the pope, Spain and Venice), can be visited by appointment (☎ 0775 578126).

Fiuggi (population 8000), situated among the Monti Ernici, consists of two separate places: Fiuggi Fonte or Fiuggi Centro, on the road from Palestrina; and Fiuggi Città, at the top of a hill 4km north. The lower resort is very busy in season, which lasts from May to October. Because of its high altitude (621m at Fiuggi Fonte), the climate is agreeable and bracing, even in summer.

Fiuggi is known for its mineral waters, whose curative properties have been known from the 13C. Their patrons have included Pope Boniface VIII (1294–1303) and Michelangelo. The waters issue at a temperature of 11°C from two springs, with a daily yield of nearly 2000 litres. Filtered through an extensive layer of porous volcanic tufa, they are tasteless and slightly radioactive.

The **Fiuggi Fonte** spa is attractively situated on a wooded upland plain between two streams, the Fosso Pantano and the Fosso del Diluvio. Most of the hotels are to be found here, as well as numerous pleasant villas. The two springs are incorporated in separate spas, the Fonte Bonifacio VIII and the Nuova Fonte Anticolana. Both have gardens, with tennis courts, bowling greens, cafés and halls for concerts and art exhibitions. It is ideal walking country.

From Fiuggi Fonte a road winds up to Fiuggi Città (747m), a medieval town without special character, known until 1911 as Antícoli di Campagna. In the Middle Ages it was ruled by the Church, and in the 16C it passed into the hands of the Colonna.

At Vico nel Lazio Bivio a turning leads north to Guarcino, the best starting-point for the ascent of Monte Viglio (2156m, 11km further north), the highest peak of the Monti Cantari. The village of Collepardo Bivio is noted for its large stalactite grotto.

About 5km further north-east, in a scenic location 825m above sea-level, reached by a long, winding road, is the huge **Certosa di Trisulti**. The monastery rises in the midst of a dark forest overlooking a valley. Established in 1211 in the grounds of an earlier Benedictine monastery, it has been rebuilt several times, most extensively in the Baroque age. At the entrance is a marble relief of St Bartholomew, patron of the certosa, by Jacopo Lo Duca, a pupil of Michelangelo. The garden is especially beautiful, and the 18C pharmacy is adorned with frescoes in a neo-Pompeian style and caricatures of Poverty and Egoism. The single-naved church has frescoes showing the *Glory of Paradise*, and other paintings, in a provincial Baroque style.

Alatri (502m), the *Aletrium* of the Hernici, is a picturesque town (population 25,000) on a hill, with narrow winding streets and some interesting medieval remains. It possesses the most perfect example of the Pelasgian (pre-Hellenic Greek) system of fortification in Italy. The great wall of cyclopean masonry that surrounded the town may still be traced, in some places with medieval or later additions. The crest of the hill is occupied by the **citadel**, c 180m round, built of immense polygonal blocks without mortar and still in perfect condition. Two gateways with monolithic architraves lead to the citadel, within which stand the cathedral and the bishop's palace. The church of Santa Maria Maggiore, in the main square, has a singular rose window (and enjoys a fine view). The **Museo Civico**, Corso Vittorio Emanuele 1, houses local antiquities and mosaics (open summer daily 09.00–12.00, 16.00–20.00; winter 09.00–13.00, 15.00–19.00; ☎ 0775 459009).

Veroli, the ancient *Verulae*, also boasts remains of polygonal walls. The church of Sant'Erasmo has a rich treasury of objects brought from the Cistercian abbey of Casamari, 9km south-east (see p 84). The curious little **Museo delle Erbe** (open daily 09.00–12.00, 16.00–19.00, Sun 09.00–12.00, closed Thur; ☎ 0755 237081) displays nearly 1000 medicinal herbs that grow in the hills here.

At **Ceprano**, Pope Gregory IX lifted the ban of excommunication from Emperor Frederick II on his successful return from Jerusalem (28 August 1230). The modern village, occupying the site of the Volscian *Fregellae*, guards the crossing of the copious River Liri (the ancient *Liris*), which becomes the Garigliano further downstream. These rivers formed the ancient boundary between the Kingdom of Sicily and the Patrimony of St Peter. Dating from Norman times, this remained the oldest surviving frontier in Europe until the 1860s. Its strategic importance is underscored by the many battles that have been fought here: failure to destroy the bridge at Ceprano before the advancing army of Charles d'Anjou was the first error of Manfred's last disastrous campaign (Jan–Feb 1266); and, more recently, the Liri valley was the scene of intensive operations in Jan–May 1944, linked with the assault of Monte Cassino.

The fortified medieval village of **Rocca d'Arce** stands on the site of the citadel of *Fregellae*, just outside Arce. The latter grew up as the castle's marketplace, gradually surpassing its parent settlement in size and importance. Roccasecca, to the south-east, is the birthplace of St Thomas Aquinas (1226?–74), son of Count Landolfo d'Aquino.

Aquino is the insignificant successor of the famous Roman colony of *Aquinum*, the birthplace of the satiric poet Juvenal (c AD 55). The ruins of the ancient town extend into the vineyards and gardens far beyond the modern village. The church of Santa Maria della Libera (1125), which lost most of its roof in the Second World War, has a 12C mosaic; it stands on the foundations of a Temple of Hercules, and beside it is a charming little Corinthian arch. Beyond the Roman Porta San Lorenzo are the ruins of a basilica, an amphitheatre, and two churches, Santa Maria Maddalena and San Pietro, incorporating the remains of temples of Diana and Ceres. Pontecorvo, 6km south, was named after a crooked bridge (Latin *pons curvus*) over the Liri. North-east of Aquino rises the bare, stony Monte Cairo (1669m), the north bastion of two formidable defensive lines built by the Germans in 1943, the Gustav Line and the Hitler Line.

The abbey of Monte Cassino

The abbey of Monte Cassino, perhaps the most famous monastery in the world, stands on a hill some 400m above the town of Cassino. It can be reached by car (the way is well marked), by bus, or on foot (a steep climb of about 1hr 30mins). The ascent commands an uninterrupted series of magnificent views.

Opening hours

Monte Cassino is open daily in summer 09.00–12.30, 15.30–18.30; winter 09.00–12.30, 15.30–17.00; ☎ 0776 311529, ✉ www.officine.it/montecassino. Women must cover their shoulders and arms and men should wear long trousers. Shawls and other concealing garments may be hired for a modest fee, at the entrance.

History of the abbey of Monte Cassino

The abbey was founded by St Benedict of Norcia in 529, after he had left Subiaco guided by three tame ravens. Reorganised several times since then, it was a beacon of civilisation throughout the Middle Ages. Here in 790 Paulus Diaconus wrote his history of the Lombards and here the tradition of learning was kept burning by the devoted labours of the Benedictines.

The tragedy of 15 February 1944, when Monte Cassino was bombed by the Allies, was the fifth in the abbey's history. The complex had previously been destroyed in 589 by the Lombards, in 884 by the Saracens, in 1030 by the Normans and in 1349 by an earthquake. The appearance of the abbey today still reflects the major building campaigns undertaken in the 16C and 18C.

Access is through the ceremonial entrance in the south-west corner. A brief ascent leads to three communicating cloisters, rebuilt along the lines of those constructed in the 16C and 18C. The cloister nearest the entrance contains a bronze of the ***Death of St Benedict*** by the modern sculptor Attilio Selfa. The lines

ABBEY OF MONTE CASSINO

Noviziato

Church

Chiostro del Priore

Chiostro dei Benefattori

0   50 yards
0   50 metres

Small Cloister   Entrance

of the destroyed church of San Martino, where the saint is reputed to have died, are marked in the pavement. In the central cloister is a well head of good design and, at the foot of the staircase, a statue of St Benedict (1736), which survived the bombardments unharmed. The staircase, of monumental proportions, leads to an elegant atrium and, beyond, to the **Chiostro dei Benefattori**, fronting the basilica, with statues of saints, popes and sovereigns, built to a design by Antonio da Sangallo the Younger.

The rebuilt **church** has entrance doors with bronze reliefs illustrating the first four times the abbey was destroyed. Its predecessor was itself a rebuilding in 1649–1717 from designs by Cosimo Fanzago. As richly Baroque as it was before, the interior is faced with marble intarsia that faithfully repeats the earlier design. Among the several paintings are works by Cavaliere d'Arpino, Francesco de Mura and Francesco Solimena. The remains of St Benedict and of his twin sister St Scholastica lie beneath the high altar, in a silver and bronze casket. In the choir of the old church were the tombs of Pietro de'Medici (d. 1503) by Antonio and Francesco da Sangallo and of Guido Fieramosca by Giovanni da Nola (1535–48). The **crypt**, only the central vault of which was seriously damaged, is built in brightly coloured granite. It bears traces of old frescoes and decorations, executed with great severity of style, by the monks of Beuron in Germany (c 1898).

The contents of the **library and archives**—over 80,000 volumes, including 500 incunabula—were deposited in the Vatican in 1943. Among the precious documents are the Paulus Diaconus collection (8C), the 11C *Biblia Hebraica* of St Gregory the Great, and the *Liber Moralium* with notes in the handwriting of St Thomas Aquinas. Also preserved is the old main **door** of the church, a wonderful piece of bronze work cast at Constantinople in 1066 and found damaged in the debris. A panorama, famous throughout Italy, can be enjoyed from the Loggia del Paradiso, above the portico.

Apart from the monastery, there is little to see in or around Cassino. The **Museo Archeologico Nazionale di Monte Cassino** (open daily 09.00–20.00; ☎ 07776 301168), at the bottom of the hill, houses Roman antiquities from local excavations.

The town of **Cassino** is one of wide streets and severe white buildings. It takes its name from the Volscian *Casinum*, which was located somewhat to the south of the modern town. The site, known in the Middle Ages as Castel San Pietro or San Pietro al Monastero, was deserted in 866 by its inhabitants in favour of the newly founded settlement of *Eulogomenopolis* (or Town of St Benedict), later called San Germano, and since 1871 Cassino.

Just north of the city centre, ruins have been left as a memorial to those killed in the bombings. Outside the town, to the north-west, the medieval fortress of Rocca Ianula tops a rocky peak that was a formidable obstacle in the fighting of 1944 (Castle Hill, 187m). The old Via Latina leads south to the remains of a Roman amphitheatre, above which are the ruins of the **Cappella del Crocifisso**; an antique tomb rebuilt as a church dedicated to St Nicholas of Bari around the year 1000 and reconsecrated by Pope Innocent III in the later 16C, it contains remains of Byzantine frescoes. On the other side of the valley stood the villa of Terrentius Varro, where Mark Antony led a life of dissipation.

South of the railway line, on the road to Sant'Angelo in Theodice, lies **Cassino**

British Military Cemetery, the largest British military cemetery in Italy, with 4267 graves of those who fell in operations in the vicinity. Here, too, is the memorial commemorating over 4000 officers and men of the Commonwealth who died in the Sicilian and Italian campaigns and who have no known grave. Designed by Louis de Soissons and unveiled in 1956, it consists of a formal garden with an ornamental pool in the centre. On each side rise 12 marble pillars on which the names of the dead are recorded.

THE MONTI LEPINI

This area lies between the Valle Latina and the sea. Access is provided by the principal railway line from Rome to Naples, and by the Appian Way, which today, as in antiquity, runs in a nearly straight line from Velletri, in the Colli Albani, to Terracina, on the Tyrrhenian coast. The most interesting sights north of Terracina lie in the rugged hills, and seeing them may entail a diversion by bus if you are travelling by train. **Cori**, **Sermoneta**, and **Sezze** are famous for their ancient and medieval remains; and the impressive abbey of **Fossanova** is the oldest conventual complex of the Cistercian Order in Italy. Its Burgundian Gothic forms would be imitated by southern Italian builders again and again. Last but not least, if you are fond of Rationalist architecture you will be intrigued by the town plan and public buildings of **Latina**, built from scratch in the 1930s. If you are not keen on this period in 20C architecture, Latina is best avoided.

Practical information

 Information offices
LATINA *Azienda di Promozione Turistica*, Via Duca del Mare 19, ☎ 0773 695404, ✉ www.aptlatinaturismo.it, info@aptlatinaturismo.it. Piazza del Popolo, ☎ 0773 348 0672.
The tourist office in **Terracina** also covers this area, see p 95.

Getting there and getting around
By car
The only way to tour through the Monti Lepini is by car, via Road 7 (the Via Appia), 7dir, 7qu, and local roads. Traffic can be heavy on all main arteries, especially the Via Appia between Rome and Terracina, and in the vicinity of Naples. Country buses are too infrequent to be practical (routes and schedules from **Cotral**, freephone 167 431784), and there is no direct rail access.

 Where to stay
LATINA €€ *De la Ville*, Via Canova 12, ☎ 0773 661281, 🖷 0773 661153. A modern hotel just outside central Latina, near the hospital.
€€ *Gabriele*, Foceverde lungomare 346, ☎ 0773 645800, 🖷 0773 648696. On the sea at Lido di Latina, with spacious rooms, many with terraces and sea-views.
SERMONETA € *Principe Serrone*, Via del Serrone 1, ☎ 0773 30342, 🖷 0773 30336. A pleasant place in the village centre, with good views over the valley and the Monti Lepini.

Eating out

CORI € *Trattoria da Checco*, Via della Repubblica 174, ☎ 06 967 8336. Trattoria; closed Thur and Nov.

€ *Da Zampi*, Via Leopardi 17, ☎ 06 967 9688. Traditional country restaurant that makes its own hams; closed Mon.

LATINA €€ *Casablanca*, SS 156 dei Monti Lepini km 51.9, ☎ 0773 241861. Restaurant known for its innovative cuisine; closed Sun evening and Mon.

€€ *Cavallino Bianco*, Via Capograssa 5, ☎ 0773 242121. Good regional dishes, nice ambience; closed Sun and Aug.

€€ *La Locanda del Bere*, Via Foro Appio 64, Borgo Faiti (8km from the city centre), t 0773 258620. Restaurant and wine shop; closed Sun and two weeks in Aug.

€€ *La Padovana*, Strada Sabotino 1 (10km from the city centre), ☎ 0773 646029. Trattoria with outside seating in summer; closed Wed and Sun evening.

€ *Assunta*, Via Pontina km 74 (5km from the city centre), ☎ 0773 241940. Trattoria between Latina and the sea; closed Sun and Tues evening and three weeks in Aug.

€ *Hosteria La Fenice*, Via Bellini 8, ☎ 0773 240225. Osteria with good country cooking; closed Sun evening and Wed, in summer Wed mid-day and Sun, late Dec and mid-Aug.

€ *Il Caminetto*, SS 156 dei Monti Lepini 176, ☎ 0773 610515. Restaurant; closed Wed, mid-Aug and Dec–Jan.

€ *Impero*, Piazza della Libertà 19, ☎ 0773 693 140. Trattoria with good home cooking; closed Sat and Aug.

PRIVERNO €€ *Antica Osteria Fanti*, Via Setina di Ceriara 56 (Road 156, km 28), ☎ 0773 924015. Restaurant popular with the locals; closed Thur, two weeks in Aug and 25–26 Dec.

€ *Caseificio Latin Lat*, Via Marittima (near Fossanova Abbey).Produces and sells fresh buffalo-milk mozzarella and ricotta.

€ *Il Ritrovo*, Via Schito, ☎ 0773 924410. Garden restaurant serving regional dishes; closed Tues.

SERMONETA €€ *La Taparita*, Via Romana Vecchia, ☎ 0773 318417. Restaurant; closed Mon.

SEZZE €€ *Angeluccio*, Via Ponte Ferraioli 48, ☎ 0773 899146. Good regional cuisine, with garden and pool; closed Mon and early Nov.

€ *Barbitto*, Via Colli, ☎ 0773 888523. Simple fish restaurant; closed Mon and a few days in Aug and Dec.

A land of tradition

The warm sea breeze, rich in moisture, makes this side of the hills of south-central Lazio more suitable for farming than the side facing the Valle Latina. The country here is therefore richer and more carefully tended than that on the east slopes of the hills, and the villages somehow seem more content.The area's agricultural vocation dates from well before Roman times.

Cori

Cori, a little town (population 10,000) combining two centres, Cori a Valle (220m) and Cori a Monte (398m), is famous for its ancient **walls**. Cori suffered grievously during the Second World War, but the walls and Roman remains escaped unharmed. It is one of the oldest towns in Italy, its foundation being attributed to

Dardanus of Troy or to Coras, brother of Tiburtus. The Roman colony of *Cora* suffered at the hands of Totila and Barbarossa and was rebuilt by the counts of Segni in the 13C. Its massive walls were constructed at four distinct periods and form a threefold circuit of the hill. The oldest portions date from the 11C.

At the entrance to the town is the surviving campanile of the church of Santa Maria della Trinità. From here Via Papa Giovanni XXIII, passing a section of Pelasgian wall, leads to the church of **Sant'Oliva**, which was formed by connecting two adjacent churches, built in the Middle Ages and the 15C respectively. In the beautiful cloister is a small collection of archaeological finds from local excavations. The road continues up to the so-called **Temple of Hercules**, which despite its present name was probably dedicated to the Capitoline deities Jupiter, Juno and Minerva. Behind the graceful Doric peristyle is the cella, which became the church of San Pietro, now reduced to a complete ruin. On a clear day the view spans the Monti Lepini and the Pontine Marshes to the sea. Descending to the Piazza San Salvatore, you find fragmentary ruins of a Temple of Castor and Pollux and, nearby, remains of a cistern, a piscina and Roman walls. Outside the Porta Ninfina are more cyclopean walls and the Ponte della Catena, a boldly constructed Roman bridge attributed to Sulla.

Just a few kilometres south of Cori are the ruins of **Ninfa** (open for guided visits Apr–Oct first Sat and Sun of the month 09.00–12.00, 14.30–18.00; July–Aug 15.00–18.30), a medieval town abandoned in the 17C because of the malaria from the Pontine Marshes, an extensive swamp land that until recently occupied much of the coastal plain between Rome and Terracina. The remains of churches, houses and other buildings, surrounded by a ruined rectangle of walls, are all overgrown with luxuriant vegetation creating a park. A spring from the Monti Lepini has formed a little lake within the ruins.

Beyond Ninfa, a road ascends the slopes of the Monti Lepini to the little town of Norma, next to which lie the remains of the Volscian city of Norba, with massive towers and cyclopean walls. The view, over the coastal plain to the sea, is magnificent. Finds from Norba are displayed at the small Museo Archeologico (open Mon–Fri 09.00–13.00, Sat–Sun 09.00–13.00, 15.00–18.00; ☎ 0773 353806).

If you turn right instead of left, at the junction for Norma, you soon come to **Sermoneta**, a charming medieval town (population 7000) dominated by the well-preserved **Castello Caetani**. This was built in the 13C, enlarged in the 14C and fortified in the early 16C, with the aid of Antonio da Sangallo the Elder. It culminates in a massive keep. The fortress was visited by Cesare and Lucrezia Borgia, Charles V and Pope Gregory XIII. The cathedral has a painting by Benozzo Gozzoli, and the church of San Giuseppe has frescoes by Girolamo Sicciolante of Sermoneta.

Just north of Sermoneta the road to Sezze (marked) passes the 13C abbey of **Valvisciolo**, with a fine Cistercian church of 1240. A little further on is Bassiano (588m), birthplace of Aldus Manutius (Teobaldo Mannucci, 1450–1516), the famous printer who set up his business in Venice.

Sezze is the Volscian *Setia*. It preserves cyclopean walls and some Roman and medieval ruins, as well as a 14C **cathedral** in the Cistercian style. The orientation of the church was reversed in the late 15C or early 16C, resulting in the unusual main façade. The Antiquarium Comunale (open Tues–Sat 09.00–

13.00, 16.00–19.00, Sun 09.00–13.00) contains archaeological material from local excavations (prehistoric finds, Roman mosaics, ceramics, architectural elements and coins) and 12C–15C manuscripts. The Museo Territoriale del Giocattolo dei Monti Lepini (open by appointment, ☎ 0773 88179) has an interesting collection of locally crafted toys. The town is famous for its yearly Passion play, enacted in the huge outdoor theatre.

Crafts of southern Lazio

Toys are not the only things that are hand-made locally. A number of the towns in southern Lazio, in fact, are renowned for their crafts. These include Alatri, for umbrellas and saddlery; Anagni, inlaid furniture; Cori, saddlery; Fiuggi, jewellery and terracotta nativity figures; Formia, wooden boats; Frosinone, jewellery, wicker, wood and leather goods; Latina, wood, straw, leather, iron and copper; and Pontecorvo for pottery.

The abbey of Fossanova

Priverno (population 14,000) has a beautiful cathedral dating from 1283 and a Gothic town hall. Known also as Piperno, it preserves the name of the Volscian *Privernum*, whose ruins lie 2km north-east. The Museo Archeologico e Area Archeologica, in Largo Ludovico Tacconi (open Mon–Sat 07.00–12.00, 15.00–16.00) has a small educational collection from this and other local sites.

To the south is the lovely Amaseno valley, where the splendid Cistercian abbey of **Fossanova** (open Mon–Sat 07.00–12.00, 15.00–16.00) is situated. St Thomas Aquinas died here while on his way from Naples to Lyons in 1274. The monastery is mentioned for the first time under the name of Santo Stefano in documents dating from the 11C. By order of Innocent II it passed in 1134–35 to the Cistercians, who built the present complex along the lines of Cistercian convents in France, in the last quarter of the 12C. It grew in wealth, becoming a leading intellectual centre and maintaining its position until the 15C, when it fell into decadence. The abbey at one time housed an important archive and library, but its documents and codices have since been dispersed.

The **church**, consecrated in 1208, has a plain façade that was meant to be preceded by a three-bayed portico (never built). It is dominated by a rose window and a Gothic door adorned with roll and fillet moulding and staggered shafts with beautifully carved capitals. The lintel bears a delicate interlace relief that is echoed in the tracery of the tympanum. The interior consists of a nave and aisles separated by compound piers, shallow transepts and a rectangular presbytery flanked by four chapels, two on each side. The ceiling is cross-vaulted, with pronounced transverse arches. In accordance with the early Burgundian style introduced to Italy by the Cistercians, the shafts attached to the piers are continued to the springing of the arches and the crossing is surmounted by an octagonal

The cloisters at the Cistercian abbey of Fossanova

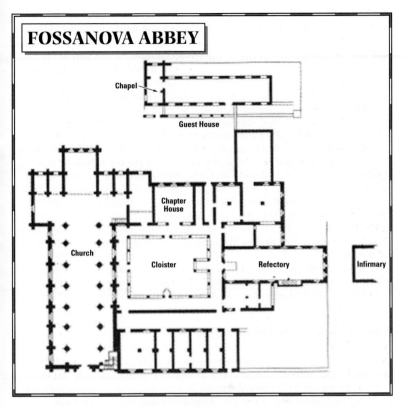

FOSSANOVA ABBEY

Chapel

Guest House

Chapter House

Church

Cloister

Refectory

Infirmary

tower with mullioned windows, terminating in a lantern, also with windows.

Adjoining the church on the right is the **cloister**, striking in its harmony of proportion and detail. The older, Romanesque sections are distinguished by sequences of five arches carried by coupled columns. The side opposite the church, rebuilt in 1280–1300 in the Burgundian Gothic style, is articulated into groups of four arches, with a small aedicule projecting into the garden midway along. The sacristy, chapter-house, refectory and kitchen occupy the ground floor; the monks' cells, the floor above. Detached from the cloister are the Casa dei Conversi (servants' quarters), the *foresteria* (guesthouse), and the infirmary. The room where St Thomas died, later made into a chapel, has an 18C relief of the saint's death.

Just beyond the abbey, a road leads left for Sonnino, whose castle preserves a drum-tower and some 13C portions of the church of San Michele. On the plain, at the foot of the Monte Lepini, Cisterna di Latina lies near the site of Tres Tabernae, where St Paul stopped on his journey to Rome (Acts xxviii, 15). The town is named after a reservoir, built by Nero to supply *Antrium* (Anzio) with water. In the Middle Ages it was a fief of the Caetani, dukes of Sermoneta. After the Allied landing at Anzio and Nettuno in January 1944 it was the scene of intense fighting and has been almost completely rebuilt since the Second World War.

Latina

Latina (population 104,000), founded in 1932 and originally called *Littoria*, is the first and largest of the new towns of the Agro Pontino, the former Pontine Marshes. Situated in the centre of the reclaimed wetland, it is perhaps the best surviving example of Rationalist town planning. Its orderly buildings, conspicuous lack of decorative detail, systematic street plan and large public spaces were intended to embody political principles dear to the Fascist regime, such as strength, authority and regimentation. Its overall design is the creation of the otherwise obscure architect, Oriolo Frezzotti.

The Corso della Repubblica crosses the town from north to south, opening out into three squares—Piazza Roma, the spacious Piazza del Popolo (the town centre) and Piazza San Marco. In Piazza del Popolo are the **town hall**, with a high tower, the chamber of commerce and other public buildings. Various important streets radiate from this square. On the west side of Piazza San Marco is the severe church of **San Marco**, which has a lofty campanile. On the east side of the Piazza del Popolo, Via Diaz and Piazza della Libertà, with the prefecture, lead to the Parco Comunale. Further north, Viale Mazzini leads east to Piazza Bruno Buozzi, with the imposing **courthouse**. A series of avenues encircle the centre of the town.

Near Latina, on the Appian Way, was the *Appii Forum*, where the brethren from Rome met St Paul (Acts xxviii, 15). In antiquity, travellers from Rome who wished to continue their journey to Anxur (Terracina) by canal set off here.

THE TYRRHENIAN COAST

Although popular among Italians, the seashore south of Rome is little known to foreigners. The main attraction in this area is the **Parco Nazionale del Circeo**, a beautiful national park well worth a visit even if you are not an ornithologist (it is one of Mediterranean Europe's largest bird sanctuaries). There are several attractive seaside resorts in this region—**Terracina**, with its imposing Temple of Jupiter Anxurus; **Sperlonga**, popular with wealthy Romans; and Gaeta, a charming medieval town with a fine beach—not to mention some of the more breathtaking landscape on the Tyrrhenian coast. From **Minturno**, where there are some interesting Roman remains, a diversion can be made inland to **Sessa Aurunca**, with its attractive 12C cathedral. The main road continues south-east after Minturno, bearing across the Phlegraean Fields to Naples. Those who are driving will enjoy magnificent views after Terracina heading down the coast, where the road runs high above the sea.

A word of warning: in summer this route is swamped with Romans (and Neapolitans) on their way to and from the seaside resorts. Traffic is congested and trains may be packed.

Practical information

Information offices

FORMIA *Ufficio Informazioni e di Accoglienza Turistica*, Via Unità d'Italia

30/34, ☎ 0771 771490.
GAETA *Ufficio Informazioni e di Accoglienza Turistica*, Piazza Traniello 4,

☎ 0771 462767; Corso Cavour 16
(open June–Sept), ☎ 0771 461165.
SCAURI *Ufficio Informazioni e di
Accoglienza Turistica*, Via Marconi 23,
☎ 0771 683788; Via Lungomare 32,
☎ 0771 168 3788.
TERRACINA *Ufficio Informazioni e
di Accoglienza Turistica*, Via Leopardi,
☎ 0773 727759.
The tourist ofice at **Latina** also covers
this area, see p 89.

Getting there and getting around

By car

From Rome, any number of routes may
be taken to Anzio, from where the main
Road (Road 601) hugs the coast to
Terracina. Road 213 continues along
the shore from Terracina to Formia.

From Naples, take Road 7a north,
along the coast, or Autostrade A2 and
A1 to Capua, then Road 7 to Formia via
Sessa Aurunca. This is the quicker of
the two routes.

By bus

Express buses run from Rome to
Terracina, with frequent connections
between Terracina, Formia and Gaeta,
and between Terracina and points in the
Parco Nazionale del Circeo.

By train

The main railway line from Rome
(Termini, Tiburtina or Ostiense) to
Naples (Centrale) follows the coast,
covering the 220km in c 2hrs. Eurostars
from Rome (Termini) to Naples
(Mergellina) take 1hr 50mins. Most
trains stop at Latina, Formia and
Aversa, in Campania. Railway passengers could travel to Naples, breaking
their journey for two or three hours in
Formia and Gaeta, in a long half-day.

By boat

Ferries travel daily between the island of
Ponza and Terracina (2hrs) and Formia
(2hrs 30mins). There is also a daily
hydrofoil service between Ponza and

Formia (1hr 20mins). For details contact, in Terracina, *Anxur Tours*, Viale
della Vittoria 40, ☎ 0773 723978; and
in Formia, *Caremar*, *Agenzia
Jannaccone*, Banchina Azzurra,
☎ 0771 22710, or (for hydrofoils only)
Agenzia Helios, Banchina Azzurra,
☎ 0771 700710.

Where to stay

FONDI €€ *Villa dei Principi*, Via
Flacca km 1, ☎ 0771 57399, ▯ 0771
57624. Especially known for its
restaurant—creative cuisine, wonderful
presentation.
GAETA €€ *Le Rocce*, 7km west of
the city centre on Road 213, ☎ 0771
740985, ▯ 0771 741633. A very
comfortable place offering garden terraces and good views of the sea and
coast; open May–Sept.
€€ *Serapo*, Spiaggia di Serapo, Via
Firenze 11, ☎ 0771 450037, ▯ 0771
311003, freephone 800 015772,
▧ www.hotelserapo.it, hotelserapo@
uni.net. On the beach, with covered
pool, tennis courts, gym.
€€ *Villa Irlanda*, Via Lungomare
Caboto 6, ☎ 0771 712581, ▯ 0771
712172, ▧ www.villairlanda.com,
villairlanda@villairlanda.com. In a
magnificent position with fine views,
occupies four buildings (a Neo-classical
villa, a convent, a nuns' home and a 1C
Roman villa) in a shady garden.
SABAUDIA €€€ *Le Dune*, Via
Lungomare 16, ☎ 0773 51291,
▯ 0773 5129251, freephone 800
638034, ▧ www.ledune.com. A
Mediterranean-style building on the sea,
with pool, tennis and bocce, sauna, private beach and seafront terraces in most
rooms; open Apr–Oct.
SAN FELICE CIRCEO €€€ *Punta
Rossa*, Via delle Batterie 37, ☎ 0773
548085, ▯ 0773 548075. Overlooking
the sea in a secluded position 5km from
the village centre, with luxuriant
gardens, cliff-top pool, private beach,

sauna and sea views from all rooms.
SPERLONGA €€ *La Sirenella*, Via
Cristoforo Colombo 25, ☎ 0771
549186, 📠 0771 549189, ✉ lasirenella.
com, albergo@lasirenella.com. A
family-run establishment on the sea,
with private beach.
€ *Parkhotel Fiorelle*, ☎ 0771 54092,
📠 0771 54092. In a shady garden 1km
west of the town centre; open
Easter–Sept.
Youth hostel

Marina degli Ulisi, Contrada Fiorelle,
☎ 0771 557031, 📠 0771 557036.

Eating out

FONDI €€ *Il Selciato*, Via
Amante 15, ☎ 0771
500556. Restaurant known for its fish
and wines; closed Wed, Nov and late Dec.
€€ *Vicolo di Mblò*, Corso Appio
Claudio 11, ☎ 0771 502385. A vener-
able establishment known for its tradi-
tional cuisine; closed Tues and late Dec.
€ *Enoteca Izzi*, Corso Claudio 14 and
Enoteca Faiola, Corso Italia 38, both
wine bars with good wines and snacks.
Buonanno, Via Mola della Corte 7-9,
Casa Bianca, Via Arnale Rosso 30, *De
Sarra*, Via Santa Anastasia and *Palella*,
Via Trento 34, make the buffalo moz-
zarella for which Fondi is rightly famous.
FORMIA €€ *Castello Miramare*,
Via Balze di Pagnano, ☎ 0771 700138,
📠 0771 700139. An early 20C faux
castle with garden seating in summer
and 10 tastefully decorated rooms; open
every day.
€€ *Chinappi*, Via Anfiteatro 8,
☎ 0771 790002. Fresh fish at its best;
closed Thur (except in summer).
€€ *Da Veneziano*, Via A. Tosti 120,
☎ 0771 771818. Good seafood
restaurant in a historic setting; closed
Mon and Dec–Jan.
€€ *Il Gatto e la Volpe*, Via Abate Tosti
83, ☎ 0771 21354. Restaurant; closed
Wed (except in summer) and Dec–Jan.
€€ *Sirio*, Viale Unità d'Italia, ☎ 0771

790047. Restaurant with indoor and
outdoor seating; closed Mon evening
and all day Tues, and Wed lunch in
summer.
GAETA € *Enoteca di Luigi Raschi*,
Via Indipendenza Vicolo I, 15, ☎ 0771
465639. Trattoria; closed Tues, Wed
and Nov–Feb.
MADONNA DELLA CIVITA
€ *Montefusco* (11km north of Itri),
☎ 0771 727560. Trattoria with rooms;
closed Tues and Nov–Mar.
MONTE SAN BIAGIO € *Hosteria
della Piazzetta*, (on Road 7 between
Terracina and Fondi), Viale Littoria 13,
☎ 0771 566793. Trattoria; closed Tues.
PONTINIA € *Capocavallo* (30km
south of Latina on Road 7), Strada del
Confine 29, ☎ 0773 853457.
Trattoria-pizzeria; closed Wed (except in
summer) and Oct.
SABAUDIA € *La Pineta*, Corso
Vittorio Emanuele II 110, ☎ 0773
515053. Trattoria with good pasta and
fish; closed Dec–Jan.
SAN FELICE CIRCEO €€
La Veranda, Hotel Maga Circe, Via
Amm. Bergamini 1, ☎ 0773 547821.
Seafood restaurant; open all year.
€€ *Stiva di Ulisse*, Lungomare Circe
32, ☎ 0773 548814. Known for its fish
and wines, with seaside seating in summer; closed two weeks in Jan.
SPERLONGA €€ *Amyclae*, Via
Colombo 77, ☎ 0771 548545. The best
place in town to taste the day's catch;
closed Wed and Nov–Jan.
€€ *Lacoonte*, Via Cristoforo Colombo 4,
☎ 0771 548122. Simple but good
seafood restaurant; closed Mon and late
Dec.
SCAURI € *L'Anfora*, Via del Golfo
50, ☎ 0771 614291. Restaurant-
pizzeria; closed Tues except in summer.
TERRACINA €€ *Bottega Sarra
1932*, Via Villafranca 34, ☎ 0773
702045. Small trattoria with good wine
list; closed Mon (closed for lunch only in
summer).

€€ *Fiordaliso*, Strada Provinciale per San Felice Circeo, km 10, ☎ 0773 780897. Hotel restaurant with good seafood and wines; closed Tues.

€€ *Il Caminetto*, Via Cavour 19-21, ☎ 0773 702623. Simply delicious fish; closed Mon and a few weeks in Sept and Jan.

€€ *La Ciprea*, Via San Francesco Nuovo 1, ☎ 0773 703921. Restaurant offering delicious traditional dishes; closed Wed.

€ *Antico Forno Terracinese*, Via Alighieri 10. Bakery, delicious breads, pizzas and cakes.

€ *Bar Enoteca del Porto*, Via del Porto 2. Wine bar, good snacks and a wide selection of wines.

€ *Rifugio Olmata*, Via Olmata 88, ☎ 0773 700821. Small, friendly trattoria; closed Wed and late Dec–early Jan.

€ *Saint Patrick*, Corso Anita Garibaldi 56, ☎ 0773 703170. Wine bar serving light dinners; open evenings only, closed Tues and Jan.

Circe's shore

The beaches of southern Lazio are dotted with places that are historically significant as well as beautiful. At **Torre Astura**, a castle on an islet joined to the mainland by a bridge and dominating the Via Severiana, Conradin, last of the Hohenstaufen, sought refuge after the battle of Tagliacozzo in 1268, only to be handed over by Giacomo Frangipani to his opponent Charles d'Anjou, by whom he was put to death. Cicero, after his proscription, embarked at Astura on the flight that ended with his death in Formiae. The magnificent **view** from the tower embraces the coast towards Nettuno and Anzio, with the Alban Hills to the north and the Monti Lepini and Ausoni to the north-east and east. In the sea on the east side of the building, at water level, are ruins commonly called the Villa of Cicero, with a fish-pond in a good state of preservation.

Continuing along the coastline (called the Lido di Latina along this section) towards the south-east, you cross the Fosso Astura, formerly the Mussolini (now Moscarello) Canal, right flank of the Anzio beach-head in the Second World War. Soon afterwards, you enter the wild, beautiful Parco Nazionale del Circeo.

The Parco Nazionale del Circeo

The park was set up in 1934 to preserve the natural beauty of the area, with its flora and fauna, and to provide a lasting reminder of what the Pontine Marshes were like before they were drained and improved. Extended in 1975 to an area of 8300 hectares, this vast reserve now includes the towns of Sabaudia and San Felice Circeo (see below) as well as the four coastal lakes of Fogliano, Monaci, Caprolace and Sabaudia. It extends from Capo Portiere, on the north side, to Monte Circeo, on the south.

Within the park are four *riserve naturali integrali*, specially protected areas to which entrance is only granted with the prior authorisation of the *Azienda di stato per le foreste damaniali* at Sabaudia. These reserves are known above all for their oaks, ashes, hornbeams, elms, sorb-apples and black alders, for their eucalyptus groves and for the dwarf palms that grow on the steep slopes of Monte Circeo.

Concerted efforts have been made to reintroduce wildfowl that once used the Pontine Marshes either as a resting-place or as a permanent abode. The park now boasts more than 200 species, among them, quail, woodcocks, herons, seagulls, storks, woodpeckers and various birds of prey, notably ospreys.

Within the park are the ruins of a so-called Villa of Domitian (visits by special permission only), Roman harbour works and the walls and Acropolis of Circeii (see below), as well as several medieval watch-towers.

Ovid on the origin of species

The Latin poet Ovid, in his *Metamorphoses* (XIV, 320–434), establishes an unusual lineage for one of the winged inhabitants of the Circeo National Park.

Picus, he relates, the young son of Saturn and King of Latium, rejected the love of Circe and was changed by her into a woodpecker. When the sorceress approached the youth in a shady glen and revealed her desire, he proclaimed, 'Another has taken and holds my love in keeping, and I pray that she may keep it through all coming time'. To this ingenuous declaration Circe replied by chanting a charm and thrice touching the youth with her wand. 'He turned in flight', Ovid narrates, 'but was amazed to find himself running more swiftly than his wont, and saw wings spring out upon his body. Enraged at his sudden change to a strange bird in his Latin woods, he pecked at the rough oak-trees with his hard beak and wrathfully inflicted wounds on their long branches. His wings took the colour of his bright red mantle, and what had been a brooch of gold stuck through his robe was changed to feathers, and his neck was circled with a golden-yellow band; and naught of his former self remained to Picus except his name'.

The road runs through sand dunes 12–15m high, separating a lagoon, the **Lago di Fogliano**, from the sea. The village of Fogliano is on the landward side. This lagoon is 5km long, with a maximum width of 1.5km and a depth of 4–5m; it is joined to the much smaller Lago dei Monaci by a short canal called La Fossella.

Between the two lagoons is the Torre di Fogliano; here the road bends sharply inland to cross the Rio Martino. At Borgo Grappa you turn right, passing through the lowlands on the landward side of the Lago dei Monaci. Further on the road passes another lagoon, the Lago di Caprolace, 5km long, connected by the Fossa Augusta, built by Nero, with the Lago di Sabaudia, formerly Lago di Paola and in antiquity *Lacus Circeus*. This is a long, narrow lagoon extending for 8km with a maximum width of 505m, as far as the base of Monte Circeo. It is separated from the sea by dunes, through which the road runs. In places it is 15m deep. It has six branches or bays, called *bracci*, running inland. On the left are picturesque woods of the Selva del Circeo. In front are the wooded slopes of Monte Circeo and in the distance, rising from the sea, the Ponziane Islands: Ponza, Zannone, and Palmarola.

Sabaudia (population 15,000), attractively situated between two of the arms of the Lago di Sabaudia, the Braccio Annunziata and the Braccio della Crapara, was founded in 1934. Its centre is the Piazza del Comune, with the **town hall**, from the tower of which there is a fine view of the surrounding country. Largo Giulio Cesare leads to the **Annunziata**, a church with an imposing mosaic (1955) on the façade; inside is the chapel of Queen Margherita, formerly in the Palazzo Margherita in Rome.

Monte Circeo (571m), wooded and rocky, rises abruptly from the south end of the plain which runs into the sea between Anzio and Terracina. On its summit are the remains of a Temple of the Sun and a lighthouse on the seaward side. On its slopes are the cyclopean walls of the vanished town of *Circeii* and numerous caves; one of these, on the west coast, is called the Grotta della Maga Circe (**Circe's cave**). In fact, Monte Circeo was once an island identified with *Aeaea*, the home of Circe, famous for her magic arts. Ulysses, who escaped the metamorphosis of his companions after they had been cast upon the island and forced Circe to restore them to human form, stayed for a year with the enchantress, who became by him the mother of Telegonus, reputed founder of *Tusculum* and *Praeneste*, now Palestrina. Boats may be hired at Paola for a sea trip round the promontory.

Circe's feast

In Ovid's *Metamorphoses* (XIV, 250–000) Ulysses' companion, Marareus, provides a delightful account of the famous lunch with Circe, at which the hero's crewmen were changed into swine. The episode was also described by the Greek poet Homer, in his *Odyssey*. The beautiful translation is by Frank Justus Miller.

'When [Circe] saw us and when welcome had been given and received, she smiled upon us and seemed to promise the friendship we desired. At once she bade her maidens spread a feast of parched barley-bread, of honey, strong wine, and curdled milk; and in this sweet drink, where they might lie unnoticed, she slyly squeezed some of her baleful juices. We took the cup which was offered by her divine hand. As soon as we had thirstily drained the cup with parched lips, the cruel goddess touched the tops of our heads with her magic wand; and then (I am ashamed to tell, yet will I tell) I began to grow rough with bristles, and I could speak no longer, but in place of words came only hoarse, grunting sounds, and I began to bend forward with face turned entirely to the earth. I felt my mouth hardening into a long snout, my neck swelling in brawny folds, and with my hands, with which but now I had lifted the goblet to my lips, I made tracks upon the ground. And then I was shut up in a pen with others who had suffered the same change (so great was the power of her magic drugs!).

'But blessed with special acumen, Ulysses avoided the ruse. He entered Circe's palace and, 'when he was invited to drink of the fatal bowl, he struck aside the wand with which she was attempting to stroke his hair, and threatened the quaking queen with his drawn sword. Then faith was pledged and right hands given and, being accepted as her husband, he demanded as a wedding gift the bodies of his friends. We were sprinkled with the more wholesome juices of some mysterious herb, our heads received the stroke of her reversed rod, and words were uttered over us which counteracted the words said before. And as she sang, more and still more raised from the ground we stood erect, our bristles fell away, our feet lost their cloven hoofs, our shoulders came back to us, and our arms resumed their former shape. Weeping, we embraced him, weeping too, and clung to our chieftain's neck; and the first words we uttered were of gratitude to him.'

The road now runs nearly due east across the base of Monte Circeo to (5km) a fork. The Via Severiana goes on from here to Terracina. You may turn right to reach (1.5km) **San Felice Circeo** (population 8000), finely situated on the eastern slopes of Monte Circeo and an excellent excursion centre. Follow the coast, passing the ends of two canals built in the 16C to drain the Pontine Marshes. On the right, modern bathing establishments stretch along the beach. Ahead, Terracina is visible below the remains of the Temple of Anxur.

Terracina

This town of 40,000 inhabitants is situated between the foothills of Monti Ausonian and the Tyrrhenian Sea. The new town lies close to the sea; the old town, on the slopes above.

History of Terracina

The Roman *Tarracina* succeeded the ancient Volscian town of *Anxur*; the names seem to have been interchangeable. Terracina was an important stage on the Appian Way from Rome to Capua and Brundisium and a favourite seaside resort of the Roman aristocracy. Ghalba, Roman Emperor AD 68–69, was born here in 3 BC. The town was noted for its Temple of Jupiter Anxurus, which crowned its fortified citadel.

In the main street of the new town, built by Pius VI, is the early 19C church of the Santissimo Salvatore. At the east end of the town is the **Pisco Montano**, a rocky promontory cut away by Trajan to a height of 36m, to make an easier path for the Appian Way, which originally climbed over the summit of the rock. The Roman poet Horace, who took the old road on his journey to Brundisium, refers to the three-mile uphill crawl in carriages to Anxur. The depth of the cutting is marked at intervals of 10 Roman feet, starting from the top; the lowest mark, near the present roadway, shows the figure CXX.

The street to the left of the Santissimo Salvatore ascends past a large (6.5m high) Roman arch (1C AD) to the **Piazza del Municipio**, a large square that occupies the site of the ancient forum. On the right rises the 14C Palazzo Venditti; on the left, the modern town hall. The Torre Frumentaria, adjacent, houses a small **Museo Archeologico** (open summer Mon–Sat 09.00–13.30, Sun 10.00–13.00, 17.00–21.00; winter Mon 09.00–13.00, Tues–Sat 08.00–13.00, 15.00–19.00, Sun 09.00–13.00, 15.00–18.00, ☎ 0773 707313), containing Greek and Roman statues and fragments from sites in and around the city.

At the far end of the square stands the **cathedral** of San Cesario, built amid the ruins of a Temple of Rome and Augustus (parts of the floor are well preserved). The church, consecrated in 1074 and rebuilt in the 17C, is approached by a portico of antique columns on medieval bases, enclosing a 12C mosaic frieze. The fine campanile dates from the 14C. In the interior is a good mosaic pavement dating from the 12C or 13C; the pulpit and candelabrum are likewise decorated with mosaics. The two ciboria and the high altar are composed of antique fragments. The carved chest in the sacristy is thought to date from the 8C or 9C.

Along the right side and at the rear of the church are vestiges of the ancient cella walls, which provided the foundation of the Christian building. The stones on the right flank bear a running acanthus-leaf pattern. Opposite, a largo contains ruins of the **Capitoline temple** dating from the 1C BC. It was revealed accidentally during the conflict in 1944. On two sides of the temple are well preserved tracts of Roman street pavement. The curved segments of Roman masonry just north of this site suggest the presence of a theatre.

The ascent to the summit (227m), to the right of the cathedral takes 30–45 minutes. Here are ruins of the walls of Anxur and of the **Temple of Jupiter**

TERRACINA

Anxurus (possibly dedicated to Venus Obsequens, the bringer of good fortune). The temple is known locally as the Palazzo di Teodorico (Palace of Theodoric). The powerful arches of its foundations (33 x 20m) dominate the surrounding landscape. Monte Circeo rises to the south-west and the view is superb.

A medieval interlude to Fondi and Itri

The inland route to Formia, followed by the Appian Way, takes you past two lovely medieval hill-towns and through superb natural scenery. Beyond the citadel of Anxur the Via Appia turns north-east with the foothills of the Monti Ausoni on the left. On the right is the outlet of the Lago di Fondi, the largest of the coastal lakes of Lazio (16km long), which you reach at Torre del Pesce. Beyond the railway you pass a turning for Monte San Biagio, a village on a hill (133m); the station is on the right.

Fondi, the *Fundi* of Horace's satires, produced the famous Caecuban wine of antiquity. The old town is built along the traditional lines of the Roman battle camp. It is rectangular in plan, each side measuring about 400m. At the ends of the *decumanus* and *cardo maximi* are four gates; the forum stood at the centre of the grid, on the site now occupied by the church of Santa Maria. Although the town was sacked and burned by the Saracens in 866 and again destroyed by fire in 1222, its street plan still follows the ancient model.

The **Palazzo del Principe** and the **castle**, once the seat of the Caetani and later of the Colonna, have been restored following war damage. The castle is noteworthy as the scene of the Conclave of 1378, when the dissident cardinals, outraged by the savage, erratic Urban VI, elected Clement VII as anti-pope, an act that marked the beginning of the Great Schism. In 1534 the corsair Barbarossa, fired by the fame of the beauty of Giulia Colonna, attempted to abduct her from the palace here; the lady, warned in time, fled inland. The baffled pirate sacked the town and massacred many of its people.

The church of **San Pietro** contains an early 14C Caetani tomb and a 13C pulpit and throne. Santa Maria Assunta and San Domenico (where St Thomas Aquinas taught) are also interesting.

The Via Appia now turns south-east, back towards the coast, and begins to climb into the Monti Aurunci. These hills were once notorious as a haunt of brigands, among whom were Marco Sciarra, the protector of Renaissance poet Torquato Tasso (16C), and Fra'Diavolo (1771–1806), a murderous partisan of the Bourbons of Naples. The road winds up to a pass between Monte Grande (776m; left) and Monte Marano (517m; right) and then descends.

Itri, an important agricultural centre, was Fra'Diavolo's birthplace. It is divided in two by the Fosso Pontone: the upper town, huddled at the foot of the ruined castle; and the lower town, which fans out on the more level land below. Beyond, the road descends, amid fabulous **views**, to Formia.

Sperlonga and environs

Today, the main route to Formia (Road 213) is the *Litoranea*, between Terracina and Gaeta. Opened in 1958, it makes a beautiful stretch of coast accessible. The road is well surfaced, has frequent lay-bys, viaducts and bridges, and is intelligently signposted. Seven years of building involved the excavation of 700,000 cubic metres of rock, the draining of 30 hectares of land and the construction of four tunnels, totalling more than a kilometre in length. Traces of the ancient Roman road, the Via Flacca, can still be seen along the rock face.

On leaving Terracina, pass the Via Appia on the left and continue to (16km) the turning for **Sperlonga**, a select resort consisting of the old quarter on the rocky headland and a new district on the landward side. Just before the first tunnel, a bit further along the road, is the charming **Grotta di Tiberio** (open daily 08.30–19.30; winter 09.00–16.00, ☎ 0771 548028), with a circular pool, where Sejanus, head of the Praetorian Guard (the household troops of the Roman emperors), took the first step towards his pre-eminence by saving the emperor Tiberius from a fall of rocks.

A little way inland, on the main road, is the **Museo Archeologico Nazionale** (open as above), which houses the sculptures, in the Hellenistic style of Pergamum and Rhodes, found during excavations in the grotto (1957–60). An inscription found in the cave, with the names of the three Rhodian sculptors (Agesander, Athenodorus and Polydorus) responsible for the *Laocoön* group in the Vatican, did not lead to the discovery of its original. Instead, a huge group, the *Struggle with Scylla*, has been reassembled, with Ulysses holding the Palladium (the archaic wooden statue of Pallas Athena that was kept in the citadel at Troy) as protection against the monster. A poem of Faustinus, a contemporary of Martial, claims the work is better than the *Laocoön*. Other notable sculptures include *Ulysses Struggling with Polyphemus*, and a bust of Aeneas as tutelary deity of the Julio-Claudian family group.

After passing through four tunnels the road becomes most attractive. On the right, cliffs drop abruptly into the sea and medieval watch-towers stand on the major promontories.

Gaeta

Gaeta is a pleasant little town (population 24,000) on a headland at the southern end of the gulf of the same name. Once an important fortress, it maintained its freedom throughout the Gothic and Saracenic invasions and became an important town under the Normans. The citadel was repeatedly attacked during the Middle Ages, but was taken only by treachery or by starving out the inhabitants. Gaeta was the last stronghold of Francis II of Naples and fell to the Italian forces in 1861. Today it is famous for its beaches; it is also a NATO naval base.

En passant

Charles Edward Stuart 'won his spurs' here, aged 13, against the Austrian garrison in 1734. During his voyage from Gaeta to Naples with Charles of Bourbon, the Young Pretender's hat blew into the sea: when it was proposed that a boat should be lowered to recover it, the young Charles told the crew not to trouble themselves, as 'he should be obliged before long to fetch himself a hat [the Crown] in England'.

Town life centres on the modern Piazza del Municipio, on the harbour front. From here the Lungomare follows the shore around the north slope of Monte Orlando to the medieval quarter, passing two sets of defensive fortifications and the scanty remains of a 2C Roman villa. The church of the **Santissima Annunziata**, midway along on the right, dates from 1302, but was rebuilt in 1621. Within are a *Nativity* and a *Crucifixion* by Luca Giordano.

Continuing to the heart of the old quarter, you soon reach the **cathedral** of Sant'Erasmo. This suffered considerable damage in the Second World War. Dating from 1106 but rebuilt in the 17C and 18C, it has a fine campanile of 1148–1279 incorporating architectural fragments from antique buildings, particularly the tomb of Sempronio Atratino (see below). In the archway beneath the tower steps lead to the interior. The passageway contains Roman sarcophagi and fragmentary reliefs from a 13C ambo. Within are the marble shaft of a candelabrum with 13C reliefs depicting the lives of Christ and St Erasmus and minor paintings by southern Italian artists. The Museo Diocesano (open Sun 10.30–12.00 and by appointment, ☎ 0771 462255), above the portico, contains a small collection of sculptural and architectural fragments, and paintings. More of these can be seen in a permanent exhibition at the library, Piazza De Vio 9 (open daily 16.30–19.30, Sun 10.00–12.30, ☎ 0771 464293).

Further west is the little 10C church of San Giovanni a Mare, commonly called San Giuseppe, surrounded by the most picturesque (or melancholy, depending on the season) of the area's narrow streets, vaulted passageways and winding steps. The **castle** stands above it, to the south. The lower part dates from c 1289, the upper from c 1435. The prominent church of San Francesco, further inland, was rebuilt in 1850.

On the summit of Monte Orlando stands the **tomb of Munatius Plancus** (died after 22 BC), founder of Lyons. The monument consists of a tower in *opus reticulatum* faced with travertine and crowned by a Doric frieze containing scenes of battle in the metopes. The hill itself is allegedly the grave of Caieta, Aeneas's nurse; the town was named after her. At the south-west point the cliff, riven by three narrow vertical chasms, is known as the Montagna Spaccata (Split Mountain). The sanctuary of the Santissima Trinità, founded in the 11C, dominates the headland; the adjacent convent, founded by the Benedictines, is now a seminary.

More ancient tombs may be seen in the environs. At the north end of the town, above the Porto Salvo area, stands the Tomba di Sempronio Atratino, a Roman patrician tomb damaged by fighting in 1815. The marble facing was removed to build the cathedral's campanile. Beyond Gaeta, between the coast road and Via Appia, stands the so-called Tomb of Cicero, which has recently been restored.

Formia

Formia (population 34,000) was praised by the Romans for its wine. The town is the ancient *Formiae*, the fabled abode of Lamus, King of the savage Laestrygones.

History of Formia

After the murder of Julius Caesar on 15 March 44 BC, Cicero placed himself at the head of the Republican Party and in his Philippic orations assailed Mark Antony with immoderate vehemence. On the formation, on 27 November 43 BC, of the triumvirate by Octavian, Antony and Lepidus, Cicero's name was put on the list of those proscribed. The orator fled to his villa at Formiae, but was caught by Antony's soldiers and killed on 7 December, aged 64. At the time, Formiae was one of the chief residential centres of Italy, second only to Baiae in terms of the number and opulence of its patrician villas. The area still contains numerous (though scanty) remains of farms and villages. Today Formia is a favourite bathing resort (as it was in antiquity) for the Romans, and the sea views are enchanting. It was virtually destroyed in the Second World War and has been rebuilt since 1945.

In Piazza della Vittoria at the centre of town, the town hall houses the small **Museo Archeologico Nazionale** (open daily 08.30/09.00–19.00/19.30, ☎ 0771 770382) containing statues and other material, dating from the 1C BC–2C AD, brought to light in local excavations. Some columns from a temple of Venus can be seen in the piazza itself, which is planted as a public garden.

Below the square and separated from it by a modern viaduct, is the Porto Nuovo, with a year-round ferry service to the islands of Ponza and Ventotene. The medieval Torre di Mola rises to the south. Along the waterfront to the north, in the grounds of the Giardini Colagrosso and the Villa Rubino, are the important remains (stuccoed vaults and fragments of wall paintings) of a Roman villa of the 1C or 2C, commonly called **Cicero's villa**, and a brief segment of defensive walls. The Porticciolo Caposele, nearby, incorporates part of the ancient harbour.

Along the Via Appia, further inland, is the **Fontana Romana di San Rimigio**, a Roman fountain behind a well-preserved tract of ancient road. The octagonal **Torre di Sant'Erasmo**, on the hillside to the south-east, marks the site of the Roman citadel. In the nearby Vico Anfiteatro is a private home built on the ancient theatre, the structure of which is still clearly visible (the amphitheatre, after which the street is wrongly named, stands in an orange grove near the station and awaits excavation). The small Roman Porticciolo di Gianola is reached by a road at the southern edge of the town.

Habitation is almost continuous between Formia and Scauri (see below). At Santa Croce, a sort of suburb of Formia, a road turns inland for **Ausonia**, a village recalling the Samnite town of *Ausona* destroyed in the Second Samnite War. On a by-road just south of it is the 15C church of **Santa Maria del Piano**, noted for its frescoes, possibly of the 12C, in its crypt. The surrounding ruins are probably those of Ausona. The road goes on to Cassino (see above).

Scauri is another sea resort, with the ruins of the villa of M. Aemilius Scaurus, consul in 107 BC. It is connected with **Minturno** (3km east), a town with a population of 18,000, where the church of San Pietro contains a Cosmatesque candelabrum and pulpit (1260–70), and the Annunziata has frescoes in the tradition of Giotto. To the south the River Garigliano, the ancient *Liris*, marks the boundary between Lazio and Campania.

Minturnae

On the west bank of the river, not far from the road, are the ruins of Minturnae (open 09.00–1hr before sunset, ☎ 0771 680093), once an important town built in the marshes formed by the flooding of the river. Here the proscribed Roman consul Marius, who had been taken prisoner in 88 BC, daunted the would-be assassin sent by Sulla.

History of Minturnae

The ancient Minturnae, the chief Tyrrhenian port of the Ausoni, became a major Roman colony in 295 BC. It is repeatedly described in the letters of Cicero, and a clue to its decline may be found in Ovid's *Metamorphoses* (XV, 716), where allusion is made to its malarial waters. The earliest settlement stood on the right bank of the *Liris* (Garigliano), roughly 3km from the river-mouth, and was enclosed within a rectangular wall in *opus polygonale*, with gates on the north and south sides and bastions at the four corners.

The Roman town was built to the west within its own wall circuit in *opus reticulatum*, with square and polygonal towers. The Appian Way, which crossed it from end to end, passed between the republican and imperial fora, forming the main street. A road flanked by *tabernae* ran along the riverbank to the harbour, beyond which stood the chief sanctuary of the town, dedicated to Marica, the Italic goddess of fertility, to whom the waters of the river and its marshes were sacred.

Excavations conducted jointly by the University of Pennsylvania and the Soprintendenza alle Antichità in Naples in 1931–33 brought to light numerous ex-voto offerings, with archaic votive statues of Italic, Etruscan, and Greek workmanship, now at the Museo Archeologico Nazionale in Naples. More sculpture, pottery and architectural fragments unearthed during the excavations are displayed in the antiquarium (Via Appia 7; opening times as the ruins, see above).

The most distinct remains are located in the area of the Roman town. Chief among these is the **theatre**, built in the 1C and later restored, of which the scena, orchestra and cavea survive. Behind the theatre lies the **republican forum**, originally surrounded by a colonnade and incorporating two fountains on the side that faced the Appian Way. To the west stood temples dedicated to the Capitoline triad (Jupiter, Juno and Minerva) and, possibly, to Roma and Augustus; to the east another large temple extended over part of the Italic town. South of the Appian Way and separated from it by another arcade stood the **imperial forum**, flanked by the basilica and public baths. Archaeologists have identified the site of an amphitheatre beyond. Along the riverbank are remains of the harbour and, 500m further on, part of a **Temple of Marica** (6C BC). Ruins of an aqueduct are also visible.

At **Minturno British Military Cemetery**, on the right bank of the river, lie the graves of 2049 men who fell in the Battle of the Garigliano, January 1944. The battle took place a few days before the landings at Anzio and Nettuno.

At an earlier battle of the Garigliano (1503), in which the Spanish general Gonsalvo de Cordova defeated the French, the Chevalier Bayard ('the knight without fear and without reproach', d. 1524) is said to have defended a bridge single-handed against 200 Spanish horsemen.

Beyond Minturnae Road 7q follows the coast south, skirting the ruins of *Liternum* (where the Roman general Scipio Africanus died in self-imposed isolation), then winds across the Phlegraean Fields to Naples.

Sessa and the road to Capua

The fastest road from Terracina to Naples (Road 7) follows a vaguely south-easterly course from Minturno through lovely countryside, joining the Via Casilina 7km north of Capua.

Along this route are several pleasant villages. **Sessa Aurunca**, a small town on the saddle between the Monti Aurunci and the spur of Monte Massico, is 2km north of the main road. This is the ancient *Suessa*, capital of the Aurunci. Remains of a Roman theatre and baths, and the fine **Ponte degli Aurunci** (now largely walled-up) may still be seen. The **cathedral**, built in the 12C using fragments from antique buildings, contains 13C Romanesque reliefs representing the lives of St Peter, Noah and Samson; a mosaic pavement and a candelabrum, ambo (with the story of Jonah) and transennae of Cosmatesque work.

The extinct volcano of Roccamonfina (1005m), c 11km north of Sessa Aurunca, has magnificent chestnut woods. **Carinola**, 6km south of Sessa Aurunca on the Piana di Carinola, has many charming 15C houses and a Romanesque cathedral. Nearby **Francolise** has a picturesque Angevin castle.

PONZA AND ITS ARCHIPELAGO

The Archipelago Ponziano comprises two groups of islands, located approximately 35km apart and 32km from the coast of Lazio at Monte Circeo. The north-west group includes **Ponza**, the largest (7sq km) island and the chief centre of the archipelago; and the islets of **Gavi**, **Zannone** and **Palmarola**. The south-east group comprises **Ventotene** and **Santo Stefano**. All are of volcanic origin; the archipelago is linked geologically to the volcanic area of the Gulf of Naples. Through the ages these lovely islands the islands of Capri, Ischia and

Procida have been the (sometimes simultaneous) home of patricians, pirates and prisoners.

A collection of brilliant white rocks and pristine beaches, the islands are among the least spoilt in the Mediterranean, although their popularity as a holiday resort is slowly eroding their primitive beauty. This development is most evident on Ponza, which nevertheless remains quiet and romantic out of season. The rocky coasts, especially around Ventotene, are a skindiver's paradise.

Practical information

 Information offices
ANZIO *Ufficio Informazioni e di Accoglienza Turistica*, Piazza Pia 19, ☎ 06 984 5147.
FORMIA *Ufficio Informazioni e di Accoglienza Turistica*, Via Unità d'Italia 30/34, ☎ 0771 771490.
LATINA *Azienda di Promozione Turistica*, Via Duca del Mare 19, ☎ 0773 695404, ✉ www. aptlatinaturismo.it, info@ aptlatinaturismo.it.
PONZA *Ufficio Informazioni*, Molo Musco, ☎ 0771 809 875, ✉ www. ponza.it
TERRACINA *Ufficio Informazioni e di Accoglienza Turistica*, Via Leopardi, ☎ 0773 727759.

 Getting there and getting around
By ferry

Daily ferry service to Ponza from Anzio (2hrs 30mins, 15 June–15 Sept), Formia (2hrs 30mins), and Terracina (2hrs). Hydrofoils run daily from Anzio (1hr 10mins) and Formia (1hr 20mins). Access for cars is severely restricted.

Boats may be hired on Ponza to visit the other islands; commercial services are available June–Sept. For details of services, contact the following offices:
FORMIA *Caremar*, ☎ 0771 22710, 0771 23800 (ferries), reservation centre ☎ 199 123199, ✉ www.caremar.it; *Vetor*, ☎ 0771 700170, 0771 700711 (hydrofoils).

TERRACINA *Mazzella*, ☎ 0773 723406; *Agenzia Anxur Tour*, ☎ 0773 723979 (ferries).
SAN FELICE CIRCEO *Pontina Navigazione*, ☎ 0773 544157, 0338 723 9299.
ANZIO *Vetor*, ☎ 06 984 5083, ▤ 06 983 40054 (hydrofoils).
PONZA *Caremar*, ☎ 0771 80565 (ferries and hydrofoils), *Mazzella*, ☎ 0771 809965 (ferries), *Vetor*, ☎ 0771 80380 (hydrofoils).

 Where to stay
PONZA €€ *Bellavista*, Via Parata 1, ☎ 0771 80036, ▤ 0771 80395, ✉ hotelballavista@ tin.it. Simple, with great views; open mid-Jan–mid-Dec.
€€ *Cernia*, Via Panoramica 7, ☎ 0771 80412, ▤ 0771 809954. Another simple place, in a shady garden with sea views and private shuttle to and from the harbour; open Apr–Oct, moderate.

 Eating out
PONZA €€ *Punta Incenso*, Via Calacapara, ☎ 0771 808517. Trattoria at Le Forna, on the north point of the island; closed Tues (except in summer).
€ *Cooperativa Unipesca*, Via Banchina, sells the day's catch.
€ *Acqua Pazza*, Piazza Pisacane, ☎ 0771 80643. Simple trattoria serving fresh fish outside; closed midday and Nov–Feb.

Ponza is famous for its scenic beauty and its tiny rocky beaches dotted with Roman remains. The coast is steep and irregular and in most areas cliffs fall 100m or more into the sea. The chief town of the island is **Ponza** (population 3000), which spreads out fan-like around its harbour. From here roads lead to (6km) Le Forna, a small village at the north end of the island and to Chiaia di Luna, a sandy beach 200m long on the west side. Paths ascend to the Punta dell'Incenso and to Monte della Guardia, respectively situated at the northern and southern tips of the island. Motor launches may be hired at the harbour for visits to the Grotte de Pilato and to the outlying islands.

Palmarola, located 5 nautical miles from the harbour, is the largest of the uninhabited islands that surround Ponza and, with its jagged coastline and rich vegetation, the one most similar to Ponza. A small harbour with a restaurant operates on the island during the summer.

Zannone, about 3.5 nautical miles from Ponza, is a resting place for migratory birds and a showcase of Mediterranean flora and fauna. Among the latter may be counted the moufflon, a wild sheep peculiar to southern Europe.

Ventotene, the larger of the two islands that make up the south-eastern part of the archipelago, differs from Ponza both in the reddish-brown tone of its rock and in the nature of its vegetation, which in contrast to the lush vegetation of Ponza, is dominated by prickly-pear and low macchia. Nero (son of Germanicus), Agrippina (sister of Caligula) and Flavia Domitilla (granddaughter of Domitian), lived in exile here. Remains of a villa of the imperial age may be seen near the Punta Eolo, at the northern end of the island. The town (population 700) spreads south-west from the Cala Rossano, where the ferry from the mainland moors. At the Punta del Pertuso, the site of the Roman harbour, natural arches have formed in the tufa. The antiquarium (Palazzo Municipale di Forte Torre; open June–Sept daily 10.00–13.00, 18.00–20.00, 21.00–24.00; other months by reservation, ☎ 0771 85345) has a small collection of local antiquities; docents lead tours of local archaeological finds.

Near Ventotene lies **Santo Stefano**, a tiny, round island, crowned by the *ergastolo* erected by Ferdinand IV in 1794–95, no longer in use. Both Ponza and Ventotene have been used as political prisons. Mussolini was interned for a short while on Ponza after his fall from power.

Naples

During the 18C the warm climate, the beauty of the setting, and the sophisticated social life of Naples drew thousands of visitors from Europe and North America—aristocrats, but also intellectuals, such as the British novelist Laurence Sterne and the American artist John Singleton Copley. Most waxed enthusiastic over the city, like the German poet, playwright and philosopher Goethe, who declared (in the *Italian Journey*, 1786–1788), 'Naples proclaims herself from the first as gay, free and alive. A numberless host is running hither and thither in all directions, the King is away hunting, the Queen is pregnant and all is right with the world.' But some viewed it with reservation. In *A Tour through Sicily and Malta* (1773), Goethe's British contemporary Patrick Brydone underscored the sometimes striking contrasts which, even today, are the city's hallmark: 'It is hard to say, whether the view is more pleasing from the singularity of many of the objects, or from the incredible variety of the whole. You see an amazing mixture of the antient and modern; some rising to fame, and some sinking to ruin. Palaces reared over the tops of other palaces, and antient magnificence trampled under foot ... Mountains and islands that were celebrated for their fertility, changed into barren wastes, and barren wastes into fertile fields and rich vineyards.'

Nevertheless the appeal of the city lasted well into the 19C. In 1817 the French novelist Stendhal wrote that it was 'the only capital of Italy,' and the British *Gentleman's Magazine* reported that 'the emigration of our countrymen to Italy is so extensive, that 400 English families now reside at Naples alone.'

By the middle of the century, however, generations of misrule and a general awakening of social conscience, on the part of its visitors, had severely tarnished the appeal of Naples. Even the least sensitive foreigner noticed the contrast between the abject misery of the *lazzaroni*, the city's disenfranchised poor, formerly seen as picturesque, and the spectacular luxury of the Neapolitan court. 'What would I give that you should see the *lazzaroni* as they really are,' wrote Charles Dickens in a letter of 1845, 'mere squalid, abject, miserable animals for vermin to batten on; slouching, slinking, ugly, shabby, scavenging scarecrows! And oh the raffish counts and more than doubtful countesses, the noodles and the blacklegs, the good society! And oh the miles of miserable streets, and wretched occupants.' By 1890 Karl Baedeker observed in his *Guide to Southern Italy*, that 'In Naples the insolence of the mercenary fraternity has attained to such an unexampled pitch that the traveller is often tempted to doubt whether such a thing as honesty is known.' This portrait of Naples, reiterated by many subsequent guides, still survives to the present day. But it is a grossly unfair image, especially in the light of developments over the past few years.

Today Naples (*Napoli*) is a fascinating place; it is one of the more populous cities in Italy (population 1,206,000), the most important port after Genoa and the intellectual and commercial centre of the south. The animated and noisy town, bright with the southern sun, enjoys one of the more wonderful situations in the world, spread out fan-wise above its beautiful gulf. Naples is a unique city for several reasons. Most importantly, it bears traces of more than twenty centuries of continuous habitation by various civilisations. Its remarkably rich past is reflected in its art and architecture, but it is also evident in the very form and structure of the city.

The city is once again flourishing. Under the guidance of mayors Antonio Bassolino and Rosa Rossi Jervolino, Naples has become a much safer city. A vast urban renovation programme has revitalised and enhanced the beauty of the city centre, buildings have been restored and repainted, and a considerable area of the waterfront, as well as several of the elegant shopping streets further inland, have become pedestrianised. In the derelict industrial district flanking the railyards, a whole new city, the *Centro direzionale*, has been built to designs by the Japanese architect, Kenzo Tange. New museums have opened in the city and its environs, volunteer organisations and private sponsors have restored and reopened major monuments, guided tours through the mysterious spaces of **underground Naples** have been organised, and the area of the abandoned steelworks at Bagnoli has been converted into a park and scientific research centre, with a hands-on museum for children.

The world-famous **Museo di Capodimonte** has been granted administrative autonomy, the galleries have been thoroughly renovated and the collections augmented. A special section devoted to contemporary art has been added on the top floor, and the Farnese Collection, which Naples inherited 'by marriage' from Parma and which contains many masterpieces by Italian and foreign artists, has been installed in specially designed quarters. The works commissioned from prominent Neapolitan painters by the wealthy Carthusian community of San Martino have returned to the monastery, where are visible together for the first time in the Museo Nazionale di San Martino; and the immense collection of figured vases (formerly in storage at the Museo Archeologico Nazionale) is once again on public display, in an arrangement reflecting state-of-the-art museological standards. With all this activity, it is no surprise that Naples has become an attractive centre for cutting-edge art as well, hosting Italy's second most intense concentration (after Milan) of world-class commercial galleries.

Exploring the city

One of the special things about Naples is that you can walk from the city centre to its garland of hills in just a couple of hours—or even less, if you hop on one of the famous *funicolari* (cable cars). On the walks that follow you can explore the heart of the city, ascend to the magnificent museums of Capodimonte and San Martino, and wander the lush paths of the Posillipo headland. And there is much more to do as well, for Naples is almost overwhelming in its wealth of art, culture and history.

Like London or New York, Naples has grown haphazardly over the centuries— which means that the modern city centre no longer corresponds to the centre of the Roman and medieval town. This makes Naples more difficult to explore than, say, Florence or Venice, where many centuries of architectural history are concentrated in a very small space. The walks are therefore designed to capitalise on the city's spread-out character, each one focusing on a significant epoch in the city's development: the ancient city; the Middle Ages and the Renaissance; the Bourbon city; and modern Naples.

Practical information

Information offices

Assessorato Regionale al Turismo, Via Santa Lucia 81, ☎ 081 7961111, ▤ 081 7962027, ✉ www.regione.campania.it.
Azienda Autonoma di Cura Soggiorno e Turismo, Palazzo Reale, ☎ 081 418744, ▤ 081 418619.
Ente Provinciale per il Turismo, Piazza dei Martiri 58, ☎ 081 405311, ▤ 081 401961, ✉ www.ept.napoli.it.
Branch offices at Capodichino airport, ☎ 081 780 5761; Piazza del Gesù Nuovo 7, ☎ 081 552 3328; Stazione Centrale, ☎ 081 268779; Stazione Mergellina, ☎ 081 761 2102.

The **Campania ArteCard** gives free or reduced admission to museums and monuments throughout the region, plus free travel; available from the information offices and most museums, in 3- or 7-day versions.

Ask your hotel receptionist for the useful monthly magazine *Qui Napoli*, in Italian and English (free).

Getting there
By air

Capodichino, 4km north of the city centre, is the airport for both international and domestic flights. Direct flights connect Naples with Amsterdam, Brussels, Cagliari, Catania, Cologne, Genoa, London (Gatwick, Stansted), Munich, Nice, Paris (Orly, Charles De Gaulle); internal flights with Bologna, Catania, Milan (Linate, Malpensa, Orio Al Serio), Palermo, Rome, Trieste, Turin, Venice, Verona. There are no direct intercontinental flights.

An airport bus runs to Piazza Municipio (Map 2; 11; ☎ 081 531164) at hourly intervals or less, 06.30–23.30. Transit time is c 30mins.

By car

Naples lies at the junction of four important motorways: Autostrade A1 and A2 from Rome and Caserta, Autostrada A3 from Salerno and Reggio Calabria, and Autostrada A16 from Bari and Taranto. East of Naples a bypass (A30) connects the A1 to the A3, diverting traffic from the *tangenziale* (ring-road), and the Naples–Salerno stretch of the A3.

By bus

Autolinee Circumvesuviana connects Naples with, Avellino, Boscoreale, Castellammare di Stabia, Pompei, Somma Vesuviana, Sorrento, Torre Annunziata and other destinations.
SITA goes to Amalfi, Bari, Battipaglia, Castellammare, Eboli, Maiori, Nocera, Nola, Pompei, Positano, Salerno, Sorrento (Cantone, Massa Lubrense, Nerano, Marciano, M. Lobra, Sant'Agata, Termini, Torca),Vietri, etc.
SEPSA will take you to the Zoo, Agnano, Bagnoli, Pozzuoli, Arco Felice and Lakes Lucrino and Fusaro.
Visit ✉ www.campaniatrasporti.it for schedules.

By train

There are four main stations for Italian Rail (*Trenitalia*) services: **Napoli Centrale** (Map 2; 4, 8); **Piazza Garibaldi** (in the same complex, but at a lower level); **Mergellina** (Piazza Mergellina); and **Campi Flegrei** (in the suburb of Fuorigrotta). There are also two minor stations for private railways that serve the Gulf of Naples: **Stazione Circumvesuviana** (Corso Garibaldi 387; Map 2; 8) for the Circumvesuviana line, which runs to Pompeii, Sarno, Sorrento, Nola, and other destinations south and east of the city; and **Stazione Montesanto** (Piazza Montesanto; Map 2; 6), for the Cumana and Circumflegrea lines, which run west to

Pozzuoli, Cuma and Torregaveta.

By boat

Naples harbour is one of the largest and busiest in the Mediterranean, with several quays (*moli*). Cruise liners moor at the **Molo Angioino** (Stazione Marittima Passaggeri; Map 2; 11); other vessels at the **Molo Pisacane** (Immacolatella Nuova; Map 2; 12) or within the inner harbour between the two. Pleasure craft may moor at **Molosiglio** (Map 2; 15), **Santa Lucia** (Map 2; 15), **Mergellina** (Map 1; 12), and **Posillipo**.

Ferries depart from **Molo Beverello** (Map 2; 11) to Capri (1hr 15mins), Ischia (1hr 15mins), Pozzuoli (30mins), Procida (1hr), and Sorrento (1hr), daily. From the **Stazione Marittima** (Map 2; 11) to Sardinia (Cagliari), Thur and Sat from mid-June–mid-Sept, Thur only from mid-Sept–mid-June; to Sicily (Palermo), daily; to the Aeolian Islands, Mon, Tues, Thur, Fri, Sat and Sun from mid-June–mid-Sept, Wed and Fri from mid-Sept–mid-June.

Hydrofoils and **catamarans** run from **Molo Beverello** (Map 2;11) and from **Mergellina** (Map 1; 12) to Capri (40–45mins), Ischia (30–45mins), and Procida (35mins), daily; to Sorrento (30mins), daily; to Palermo (4hrs 30mins) and to the Aeolian Islands (4hrs), daily June–Sept. Hydrofoils and catamaran are generally 50 per cent more expensive than ferries.

Tickets are available at the dock and from selected travel agents; schedules and other information at ✉ www. campaniatrasporti.it.

Where to stay

The best hotels in Naples are on the waterfront overlooking Castel dell'Ovo and the Santa Lucia yacht basin, or on the hill above; both positions offer marvellous views over the city and its gulf. Several of the finer establishments have roof gardens or terraces where the Neapolitan élite gather for an aperitif on warm evenings. If you are on a tight budget it is worth considering somewhere to stay in Sorrento, catching a train into Naples.

Hotels

€€€ *Excelsior*, Via Partenope 48, ☎ 081 764 0111, ▤ 081 764 9743, ✉ www.excelsior.it. A venerable establishment, famous among Neapolitans for its roof-top bar, a favourite place for cocktails.

€€€ *Miramare*, Via Nazario Sauro 24, ☎ 081 764 7589, ▤ 081 764 0775, ✉ www.hotelmiramare.com/, info@hotelmiramare.com. In a *fin-de-siècle* villa on the waterfront, with fine views, friendly staff and a sun-drenched terrace for fair-weather breakfasts.

€€€ *Santa Lucia*, Via Partenope 46, ☎ 081 764 0666, ▤ 081 764 8580, freephone 800 887014, ✉ www. santalucia.it, reservations@ santalucia.it. Overlooking the Castel dell'Ovo and Borgo Marinaro, spacious rooms, tasteful public spaces, helpful staff; open all year.

✿✿✿ *Terminus*, Piazza Garibaldi 91, ☎ 081 7793111, ▤ 081 206689, freephone 167 884066, ✉ www. starhotels.it, terminus@terminus.it. One of Naples' historic hotels, near the station but quiet and elegant.

€€€ *Vesuvio*, Via Partenope 45, ☎ 081 764 0044, ▤ 081 764 4483, ✉ www.vesuvio.it. Elegant public spaces, including a trompe-l'oeil frescoed staircase, a bounteous breakfast buffet and rooms designed with the utmost care (there are even specially furnished childrens' rooms) make this one of Italy's finest hotels.

€€ *Britannique*, Corso Vittorio Emanuele 133, ☎ 081 761 4145, ▤ 081 669760, ✉ www. hotelbritannique.it/, Reception@ hotelbritannique.it. Old-world atmosphere, a shady garden, spacious rooms with beautiful views.

€€ *Chiaia Hotel de Charme*, Via Chiaia 216, ☎ 081 415555, 📠 081 412344, 🖃 www.hotelchiaia.it, info@hotel chiaia.it. A charming place indeed, the former home of the Marchesi Lecaldano Sassola Terza, just a few steps away from Piazza del Plebiscito on Naples' fancy shopping street.

€€ *Executive*, Via del Cerriglio 10, ☎ 081 5520611, 📠 081 5520611, 🖃 www.sea-hotels.com/exec/ executive1.htm, info@seahotels.com. In a renovated convent, with nicely decorated rooms and public areas, sauna, gym and breakfast seating on a terrace in summer.

€€ *Mercure Napoli Angioino*, Via Depretis 123, ☎ 081 552 9500, 📠 081 552 9509. Centrally located, near the castle, with light-filled rooms, double glazing, courteous staff.

€€ *Paradiso*, Via Catullo 11, ☎ 081 2475111, 📠 081 7613449, 🖃 www.bestwestern.it/paradiso_na, paradiso.na@bestwestern.it. Modern comfort on Posillipo hill overlooking Mergellina harbour.

€€ *Rex*, Via Palepoli 12, ☎ 081 764 9389, 📠 081 764 9227, 🖃 www. hotel-rex.it, hotelrex@hotel-rex.it. In early 20C townhouse, with period décor and sea views from some rooms.

€€ *Splendid*, Via Alessandro Manzoni 96, ☎ 081 714 5630, 📠 081 714 6431, 🖃 www.napleshotels.na.it/ hotelsplendid, splendid@napleshotels. na.it. At Posillipo, spacious, quiet and panoramic.

Youth hostels

NAPLES *Mergellina*, Salita della Grotta a Piedigrotta 23, ☎ 081 761 2346.

POMPEI *Casa del Pellegrino*, Via Duca D'Aosta 1, ☎ 081 850 8644.

FORIO *Il Gabbiano*, Ischia, Via Provinciale Panza 162, ☎ 081 909422.

Eating out
Restaurants, osterie and trattorie

€€€ *La Cantinella*, Via Cuma 42, ☎ 081 764 8684, 📠 081 764 8769. Fancy restaurant with outstanding traditional and creative cuisine; closed Sun, late Dec–early Jan and two weeks in Aug.

€€€ *La Sacrestia*, Via Orazio 116, ☎ 081 664 186. One of the city's more distinguished restaurants, with outdoor summer seating and fine views; closed Mon, Aug and late Dec.

€€ *A'fenestella*, Via Marechiaro 23, ☎ 081 769 0020, 📠 081 575 0686. Restaurant with summer seating on a terrace overlooking the sea; closed midday July–Aug (except Sun) and two weeks in mid-Aug.

€€ *Bersagliera*, Borgo Marinari, Banchina Santa Lucia, ☎ 081 764 6016. Where you can watch the yachts come and go while enjoying the morning's catch; closed Tues and Jan.

€€ *Valdinchenia*, Via Pontano 21, ☎ 081 660265. A curious wedding of Campanian recipes and Lucanian (Basilicata) ingredients,open evenings only; closed Sun and Aug.

€ *Da Tonino*, Via Santa Teresa a Chiaia 47, ☎ 081 421533. Old-fashioned osteria, lunch only except Sat; closed Sun.

€ *Il Gobbetto*, Via Sergente Maggiore 8 (Quartieri Spagnoli), ☎ 081 411483. Trattoria much loved by musicians from the Teatro San Carlo; closed Sun and Aug.

€ *La Cantina di Masaniello*, Via Donnalbina 28, ☎ 081 552 8863. Traditional Neapolitan cuisine and great wines in a historic townhouse; closed Sun aned Aug.

€ *La Cantina di Sica*, Via Bernini 17, ☎ 081 556 7520. Traditional trattoria on the Vomero hill; closed Thur and late Aug–early Sept.

€ *La Cantina di Triunfo*, Riviera di Chiaia 34, ☎ 081 668101. Wine bar,

open evenings only; closed Sun,
holidays and Aug.

€ La Chiacchierata, Piazza Matilde
Serao 37, ☎ 081 411465. Traditional
trattoria, open for lunch only (except
Fri); closed Sun and Aug.

€ La Mattonella, Via Nicotera 13,
☎ 081 416541. A real, earthy osteria;
closed Sun evening (except in summer)
and two weeks in Aug.

€ La Stanza del Gusto, Vicoletto
Sant'Arpino 21, ☎ 081 401578. A tiny
place in a street known by another
name (Gradini di Chiaia), run by the
owner of the *Officine Gastronomiche
Partenopee* (Neapolitan Gastronomy
Workshops) and known for its *sfizi* (little
delicacies), evenings only; closed Sun.

€ Salvatore alla Riviera, Riviera di
Chiaia 91, ☎ 081 680490, 🖷 081
680494. Good traditional trattoria;
closed Tues.

Pizzerie

€ Bellini, Via Costantinopoli 79/80,
☎ 081 459774. One of the better
places in town for pizza (including take-
away), popular among the young artists
and musicians of the nearby Accademia
and Conservatorio; closed Sun evening,
all day Sun in July and Aug, and 10
days in Aug.

€ Brandi, Salita Sant'Anna di Palazzo,
1–2, ☎ 081 416928. The city's oldest
(est. 1780); closed mid-Aug.

€ Capasso, Via Porta San Gennaro 2,
☎ 081 456421; closed Tues.

€ Ciro a Mergellina, Via Mergellina
18–21, ☎ 081 681780. Great pizza
and noisy company somehow go
together; closed Mon.

€ Ciro a Santa Brigida, Via Santa
Brigida 71–74, ☎ 081 552 4072.
Where the pizza gets a special mention
from the Italian Academy of Cuisine;
closed Sun and one week in mid-Aug.

€ Di Matteo, Via Tribunali 94, ☎ 081
455262. Where the pizzas are so good
former US President Bill Clinton had
two; closed Sun and two weeks in Aug.

€ Ettore, Via Santa Lucia 56, ☎ 081
7640498. Outside seating in fair
wether; closed Sun and Aug.

€ Gorizia, Via Bernini 29–31, ☎ 081
5782248. Closed Wed and Aug.

€ Lombardi a Santa Chiara, Via
Benedetto Croce 59, ☎ 081 552 0780.
In business for over a century, in the
heart of the Spaccanapoli district;
closed Mon and three weeks in Aug.

€ Novecento, Via Scura 4-5, ☎ 081
5521634. Where the intellectuals go;
closed Wed and Aug.

€ Starita, Via Materdei 27, ☎ 081 544
1485. You'll be the only tourist here—
the others are straight out of *L'oro di
Napoli* with Sofia Loren, which was
filmed in the neighbourhood; closed
Sun and two weeks in Aug.

Cafés, pasticcerie, gelaterie and cake shops

Acquafrescaio, Via Chiaia 154. The last
of the vanishing breed known as
acquafrescaie, literally 'cold water sellers'
who now sell mineral water, fresh fruit
juice and other exquisite drinkables.

Bar Ascensione, Piazzetta Ascensione 2.
Ice creams, tiramisù, *semifreddi* and
other cold specialities, made with natural ingredients.

Bar Bellavia, Via Luca Giordano 158.
Sweet and savoury pastries from Naples
and Sicily.

Caffè Gambrinus, Via Chiaia (near the
Palazzo Reale). An historic, popular
café, with excellent coffee and pastries.

Dolce Idea, Via Solitaria 28.
Confectioner with outstanding home-
made chocolates.

Officine Gastronomiche Partenopee,
Via Rampe Brancaccio 32. Home-made
liqueurs and jams.

Panna, Zucchero & Cannella, Via Croce
50. Confectioner offering assorted
chocolates, sweets and liqueurs.

Pasticceria Girasole, Via Posillipo 362.
Outstanding *cannoli* and *sfogliatelle*.

Scaturchio, Piazza San Domenico
Maggiore 19. One of the city's older and

finer *pasticceria-gelaterie*, making pastries, cakes, ice cream, cassate and a delicious *ministeriale*, or liqueur-filled chocolate medallion.

Other specialist food shops

Cremeria D'Angelo, Via Galiani 4. Fine cheeses and dairy products.
Friggitoria Vomero, Via Cimarosa 44. Excellent *arancini*, potato croquettes, pizzas and pastries.
Guida, Via dei Mille 46. Delicious sandwiches, cheeses, cold meats, roasts, ice-cream, etc.

Getting around

There is no easy way to get around Naples—except, of course, to walk. Traffic is so heavy that it is practically at a standstill all day. **Bus** maps and schedules are available from the information office; routes and schedules at ⊠ www.campania trasporti.it.

Travellers who arrive by **car** should park in a safe place (a private or supervised car park) and use public transport while in the city.

Metropolitana

There are two Metropolitana underground lines. **Line 2**, offers a frequent service along a single east–west axis, running from Piazza Garibaldi to Pozzuoli Solfatara in c 30mins, with intermediate stops at Piazza Cavour (Map 2; 3), Montesanto (Map 2; 6), Piazza Amedeo (Map 2; 9), Mergellina (Map 1; 12), Fuorigrotta, Campi Flegrei, Bagnoli and Agnano Terme. **Line 1**, the **Metroplitana collinare** ('of the hills'), running from Piazza Municipio to the Hospital and Secondigliano, is not useful for the itineraries in this Guide. Other lines are under construction; important contemporary architects and visual artists are engaged in the design and redesign of stations; examples include Gae Aulenti (Museo e Dante) and Alessandro Mendini (Salvator Rosa and Materdei)

Funicular railways

Three services climb the Vomero Hill from 'lower' stations in the town: the **Montesanto** from Piazza Montesanto (Map 2;6), the **Chiaia** from Piazza Amedeo (Map 2; 9) and the **Centrale** from Via Toledo (Map 2;10), all with intermediate stops at Corso Vittorio Emanuele II. The fourth, the **Mergellina**, connects Posillipo (Via Manzoni) to the seafront at Mergellina (Map 1; 12) and Campi Flegrei station. Hours and frequency of service are as follows:

Chiaia, Piazza Amedeo—Corso Vittorio Emanuele II—Via Palizzi—Via Cimarosa; Mon–Thur 07.00–21.00, Fri–Sun 07.00–01.00; weekdays every 10mins (every 15mins after 21.00), Sun and holidays every 15mins.
Montesanto, Piazza Montesanto—Corso Vittorio Emanuele II—Via Morghen; daily 07.00–22.00; weekdays every 10mins (every 15mins after 21.00); Sun and holidays every 15mins.
Centrale, Via Toledo—Corso Vittorio Emanuele II—Petraio—Piazza Fuga; daily 06.00–01.00; weekdays every 10mins (every 15mins after 21.00); Sun and holidays every 15mins; non-stop every 30mins 08.00–22.00.
Mergellina, Mergellina—Via Orazio—Via Manzoni; daily 07.00—22.00; every 15mins.

Gira Napoli tickets Valid for travel on buses, trams, funiculars and the Metropolitana, Gira Napoli tickets are available at news-stands and tobacconists. There are two types, one lasting 90mins and the other all day.

Taxis

Taxis tend to get stuck in traffic, as do buses. Cabs, with ranks in all the main squares, are equipped with metres, which should be carefully watched by passengers. There are fixed supplements for holiday or night (23.00–06.00) service, for luggage, and for radio calls

(☎ 081 570 7070, 081 556 4444 and 081 556 0202). A return fee must be paid for taxis sent beyond the city limits, and the fare from Capodichino airport is double the amount indicated on the metre.

Horsedrawn carriages

In Naples, as elsewhere in Italy, the horsedrawn *carrozza* is by no means extinct, but fares are rather high, and when hiring a vehicle it is advisable to make an exact agreement with the driver before setting off.

Festivals

Though in recent years the importance of the Neapolitan festivals has diminished, they still offer an interesting insight into the life of the people. Here are a few of the main events:

Festa di Sant'Antonio Abate (17 January), horses and other animals are blessed at Sant'Antonio.

Liquefazione del Sangue di San Gennaro (when the saint's dried blood turns to liquid) on 19 September and 16 December in the cathedral and on the first Saturday in May at Santa Chiara, the phials are borne in colourful procession (late afternoon).

Ritorno dei Pellegrini da Montevergine (pilgrims' return from Montevergine; Whit Monday). You can see interesting costumes and beribboned harnesses in the streets near the harbour. People carry staves decorated with fruit and flowers as in the ancient Bacchanalia.

Struscio so-called because of the rustling of the silk dresses worn on the occasion, brings a great crowd into Via Roma on the Thursday and Friday before Easter to view the season's novelties in the shops.

Festa della Madonna del Carmine (16 July), features a mock burning of Fra'Nuvolo's campanile.

Festa di Piedigrotta New songs, specially prepared for the occasion, are sung at the Festa di Piedigrotta (September, at Piedigrotta, in commemoration of the Battle of Velletri, 1744).

Rioni Festivals In summer (Saturday night to Sunday night) the Rioni Festivals (neighbourhood celebrations) follow one another at frequent intervals, with processions, fireworks, sporting events and performances by local music clubs.

Entertainment

The major venues for concerts, drama and concerts are:

Teatro San Carlo, Via San Carlo 98 (Map 2;11), for opera and ballet.

Auditorium della Radiotelevisione Italiana, Via E. Marconi for concerts.

Conservatorio di Musica San Pietro a Maiella, Via San Pietro a Maiella (Map 2; 7), for concerts.

Teatro Politeama, Via Monte di Dio 80, for opera and drama.

Traditional theatre with plays by Italian and foreign authors at:

Cilea, Via San Domenico 11.

Sannazaro, Via Chiaia 157 (with dialect plays).

Bracco, Via Tarsia 38.

San Carluccio, Via San Pasquale 49.

Villa Patrizi, Corso Vittorio Emanuele; the exquisitely restored private theatre of an 18C patrician villa merits a visit in itself.

An **international film festival** (Incontri Internazionali del Cinema) takes place at Sorrento in October.

An annual music festival, the **Luglio Musicale**, takes place at Capodimonte in July.

Cultural associations

Fondazione Napoli 99, Riviera di Chiaia 202, ☎ 081 667599, *Napoli Sotterranea* (☎ 081 296944) and *LAES*, Via Santa Teresella degli Spagnoli 24 (☎ 081 400256), are actively involved in preserving the city's cultural-historical heritage and making it avail-

able to visitors. *Fondazione Napoli 99* is rehabilitating and opening monuments and is also engaged in a wide range of educational activities. *Napoli Sotterranea* and *LAES* offer guided tours of underground Naples (sites are described in the text).
The *Associazione Italo-Americana* (American Studies Centre), Via A. d'Isernia 36; *British Council*, Via dei Mille 48; *Goethe Institut*, Riviera di Chiaia 202; *Istituto Francese di Grenoble*, Via Crispi 86; *Istituto Español de Santiago*, Via San Giacomo 40, organise long-term cultural exchanges (largely at university level) and offer a number of foreign language study programmes.

Consulates

CANADA Via Carducci 29, ☎ 081 401338.
UK Via Crispi 122 (Map 2, 9, 13),

☎ 081 663511.
USA Piazza della Repubblica (Map 1; 8), ☎ 081 583 8111.

Sport and leisure

Events include **football** at the San Paolo stadium in Fuorigrotta; **horse-racing** at the Ippodromo di Agnano (*Gran Premio* in April and **harness-racing** in the summer); **motor-racing** (*Rally della Campania*) in April–May; **cycling** (*Giro della Campania*), also in April–May; **international regatta** (*One Ton Cup*) in June; and a **horse show** at Monte Faito, above Castellammare di Stabia, in July. **Tennis** facilities include the *Tennis Club Napoli*, Villa Comunale; *Tennis Club Petrarca*, Via Petrarca 93; *Tennis San Domenico*, Via San Domenico 62; *Tennis Vomero*, Via Rossini. There is a **swimming pool**, *Piscina Scandone*, at Fuorigrotta.

THE ANCIENT CITY

To tell the story of Naples is to tell the story of Europe, for ever since the first inhabitants of the Old Continent came to its shores nearly six millennia ago, Naples and its gulf have played a role of primary importance in European history. All the great powers—from the Greeks and Romans to the British, French and Austrians—have aspired to control it; several of the continent's more powerful rulers made it their capital. Today, Naples is the most vibrant and exciting city in Italy. But an understanding of contemporary Naples would be incomplete without some knowledge of its complex history.

History of Naples

It is now known for certain that the area around Naples was inhabited as early as the Stone Age (before 3500 BC). Human remains and stone tools have been found on the island of Capri (the first of these were discovered in the time of the Roman emperor Augustus), as well as along the coast and in the hills and valleys of the Neapolitan hinterland. Artefacts dating from the Bronze Age (after 3500 BC) and the Iron Age (after 1100 BC) are also common. Many of these early inhabitants came to Italy by sea from the Eastern Mediterranean: traces of the Bronze Age cultures of Crete and Mycenae, for instance, are visible in burial artefacts from around 15C BC onwards.

In the period around 1000 BC, when archaeological deduction gives way to recorded history, references to the Naples area may be glimpsed in the myths and legends of ancient Greece. On the northern shore of the crescent-shaped gulf stands Cumae, home of that ancient prophetess, the Sibyl; Olympian gods defeated the Giants and buried them beneath the Phlegraean Fields (Campi Flegrei), which tremble in the earthquakes characteristic of the region, whenever the imprisoned monsters try to break free. To the south lie the Isole Sirenuse, the rocks into which the Sirens were metamorphosed after they had enticed Ulysses to land.

A Greek colony

The earliest Greek colonies in the Naples area were Cumae and Pithecusae (Ischia), thought to have been founded by settlers from Chalcis in the 11C BC. These were soon followed by the neighbouring centres of *Dikaearchia* (Pozzuoli), *Parthenope* (Naples), and a little farther to the south, *Poseidonia* (Paestum).

The Gulf of Naples marked, for all practical purposes, the outer edge of what came to be called *Magna Graecia*. Sybaris, Croton, Taranto and Naples on the mainland, and Messina and Siracusa, on the island of Sicily, became the chief centres of a flourishing Hellenic civilisation that attracted distinguished visitors from the homeland and gave rise to a splendid local culture.

Etruscans and Samnites

Campania may have continued to flourish under Greek domination had it not been for the powerful **Etruscans**, who lived primarily in the area now known as Tuscany and Umbria. Attracted by the mild climate and lucrative trade, they established their first colonies in south-central Italy in the 9C. Later, as their northern homeland was invaded by the Celts, they migrated to the region en masse. The Etruscans, like the Greeks, had reached a high degree of political, social and artistic development, though they were more warlike than the Greeks and perhaps more actively colonialist. As the years passed, they gradually consolidated their foothold in the south, conquering one Greek city after another. At one point their influence was so strong that new houses in Campanian towns were built almost exclusively in the Etruscan manner.

The tide finally turned against the Etruscans, however, as a consequence of two Greek victories at Cumae, in 525 and 474 BC. The resulting decline in their power was so rapid that between these dates the Etruscan kings were also chased out of Rome. Eventually, the expanding Roman republic interposed itself between the Etruscan homeland to the north and its extension in Campania; deprived of a land connection, the southern settlements dwindled.

The expulsion of the Etruscans and the involvement of the Greek colonies in the fratricidal Peloponnesian Wars created a power vacuum in Campania (which at that time included western Campania, Abruzzo and Molise). This was filled when the indigenous **Samnites** (a simple people who lived in the hills north and east of Naples) rose up and conquered the region, with relative ease, c 420 BC. The Samnites were so keenly aware of the inferiority of their own civilisation with respect to those they had conquered, that instead of governing the occupied territory according to Samnite law and custom they created a federation of city-states, each governed by its own magistrate and faithful to its own traditions. In this way, they managed to maintain their hold over the area although they were themselves gradually being conquered by the Romans in a series of conflicts generally referred to as the Samnite Wars (343–290 BC).

Campania felix

Campania prospered once again under the Romans, who occupied the area after the Social War in 88 BC (see p 49). It became known as the Campania felix on account of its beauty and fertility (see p 49). The alluvial plains and fertile hills produced the finest grains, vegetables, olives and wines. The slopes of Mount Vesuvius produced highly prized wines, as well as the more common *vinum vesuvium*. The forests yielded wood in abundance, the mountains provided numerous varieties of building stone, and the sea supplied fish from which the ancient peoples made the sauces garum, liquamen and muria, which Pliny says were a special treat.

In the 1C AD the area developed its character as a rich man's playground. It became a place where Romans went to escape the tensions of the capital—to retire, or simply for a holiday. The coast along the Gulf of Naples was adorned with towns, residences and plantations, which spread out in unbroken succession, presenting the appearance of a single city, as it does today.

Parthenope and Neapolis

Naples proper is the modern successor of two ancient towns that had merged to form a single metropolis even before Roman times. The colony of **Parthenope**, the more ancient of the two, was founded by Rhodian navigators in the 9C BC. It stood on Mount Echia, the volcanic hill now occupied by the Pizzofalcone quarter. This site was chosen because it was easy to defend—it was surrounded by the sea on three sides, with steep cliffs, and was separated from the hinterland by a deep valley, today Via Chiaia.

After the Greek victory over the Etruscans the population of Parthenope grew rapidly, and it soon became clear that the city would have to be enlarged. This posed some serious problems: the lie of the land, which made Parthenope impregnable, also made urban development virtually impossible. So a decision was made to build a new town, **Neapolis** (from which *Napoli* is derived), on a hillside on the other side of the harbour, with its highest point, the acropolis, in the area that would later become Caponapoli. Neapolis soon surpassed the older city in importance, its population swelled by the arrival c 450 BC of Greek colonists from Chalcis, Pithecusa and Athens. Both towns were conquered, first by the Samnites in c 400 BC and then by the Romans in 326 BC.

The population of Neapolis expanded under the Romans but the town held on more tenaciously than any other city in Magna Graecia to its Greek customs, culture and institutions. Greek games, in which musical competitions alternated with gymnastic events, were held by the Neapolitans every five years, and Greek was preserved as the official language. The emperor Nero was particularly fond of Naples' Hellenic culture, and he sang there several times before going to Greece.

The city of learning

Because of its Hellenic character, Naples was regarded as the city of learning. Roman youth flocked here to cultivate the arts of rhetoric, poetry, and music. Although the city lacked an amphitheatre, it did have a famous covered theatre, and the Neapolitan actors were renowned throughout the Roman world. Plutarch, the Greek biographer and moralist, recounts that Brutus came personally to Naples to beg one of these actors, Canuzio, to come and recite in Rome. The theatres of Naples offered plays in Latin and in Greek;

among the latter, that written by Claudius to honour his brother, Germanicus. The great masters included the orator Polemone, one of whose pupils was the Roman emperor and Stoic philosopher, Marcus Aurelius.

Virgil, not yet famous, came to Naples in search of the atmosphere that his spirit demanded and that the hustle and bustle of the capital precluded. Here he wrote his exquisite Georgics, and when he died at an early age in Brindisi, his wish to be buried in Naples was fulfilled on Augustus's orders. According to Dante, his tomb is on the hill of Posillipo.

For the Romans, Naples and its splendid surroundings—the slopes of Vesuvius, the Capodimonte hill, the Phlegraean Fields, the harbours of Pozzuoli, Baia, Pompeii, Stabia and Herculaneum—afforded an extraordinary oasis of peace. Horace, the famous poet and satirist, wrote of 'restful Naples', and another poet, Ovid, claimed that 'Parthenope was born in idleness.'

1 • Some ancient architecture

Unfortunately, there are few ancient ruins in Naples to speak of—nothing, at least, as extensive as the Imperial Fora in Rome or as impressive as the Colosseum: most of Naples' ancient treasures lie buried beneath the modern city. The few remains that can be seen have been camouflaged by time: incorporated into later structures, they crop up in unexpected places.

Our first historic city walk follows the line of the *decumanus major*, the main street of Graeco-Roman Naples, now the Via dei Tribunali (Map 2; 7, 3, 4). Several buildings in this area—mainly churches, but residential buildings, too— incorporate vestiges of the very distant past. A visit to the Greek and Roman remains beneath San Lorenzo Maggiore is followed by a tour of Naples' fabulous **underground aqueduct**. The total length of the walk, aqueduct excluded, is less than 3km; it can be covered in just over an hour.

Begin at the Franciscan church of **San Lorenzo Maggiore** (Map 2; 7), one of Naples' more important medieval churches (described in full detail on p 147). Here it is not so much the details of the church, as the overall form of the building, that is interesting. San Lorenzo is built over the ancient Roman basilica. In Neapolis, as throughout the Roman world, the basilica was an oblong building ending in a semicircular apse, used as a court of justice and place of public assembly. During the first centuries of the Christian age, the Roman basilican form was used by Church architects as a prototype for their meeting places, and the term 'basilica' is now used to refer to any Christian church consisting of nave and aisles and a large, high transept from which an apse projects. San Lorenzo Maggiore is therefore a Christian basilica; its form corresponds almost perfectly to that of the Roman basilica of Neapolis. Its builders used the massive walls of the existing edifice as the foundation for their own building (a common practice in the Middle Ages). Evidence of this may be seen in the **cloisters**, where **archaeological excavations** (open Mon–Sat 09.00–17.00, Sun and holidays 09.00–13.00; ☎ 081 211 0860) have unearthed the antique walls of the treasury, in the basement of the basilica, the remains of a Roman street flanked by shops, traces of Greek buildings made of large square blocks of tufa and the ruins, on a higher level, of a medieval public building.

More Graeco-Roman remains, including fragments of a mosaic pavement, have been brought to light beneath the **cathedral** nearby (the excavations, in the basement, are open 09.00–12.00, 16.30–19.00, Sun and holidays 09.00– 12.00).

Across the street from San Lorenzo Maggiore, and running along the right flank of San Paolo Maggiore, the narrow Vico Cinquesanti leads to the Via dell'Anticaglia, the *decumanus superior* of Roman Neapolis. The street is crossed by two massive brick arches—the only existing remains of the walls that joined the baths, which were located on the far side of the street, with the ancient theatre, which stood in the area between Vico Giganti, Via dell'Anticaglia, Via San Paolo and the former Convento dei Teatrini. The theatre was built to accommodate 11,000 spectators. It was here that Claudius had the play he had written in honour of his brother Germanicus performed, and here that Nero sang to an enthusiastic audience.

LAES offers visits to the ancient **aqueduct** that runs beneath the city. Begun by the Greeks and extended by virtually all those who came afterwards, the aqueduct was Naples' main source of water until the latter half of the 19C. It was used as a clandestine quarry during the period of the Spanish viceroys, when laws intended to curb new building inside the city walls prohibited the importation of building stone. The tour covers roughly 30,000sq m at 20–40m below ground.

2 • The catacombs

Some very old legends say that St Peter visited Naples on his way to Rome, interrupting his journey to establish a diocese in the city and to name St Asprenus as its first bishop; numerous chronicles describe the martyrdom, near Pozzuoli, of Bishop Januarius (San Gennaro); and unsubstantiated legends attribute the foundation of the city's first Christian churches to the time of Constantine (AD 306–377). But recent studies show that St Peter did not visit Naples, the birth date of the Neapolitan episcopate is still uncertain, and although there is evidence that followers of the new religion existed in the city shortly after the time of Christ, it is now known that Naples' first Christian churches were erected only at the end of the 4C.

The second walk includes the **catacombs** of St Januarius (San Gennaro), excavated in two storeys in the tufa beneath the church of San Gennaro extra Moenia. A second early-Christian burial ground, dedicated to St Gaudiosus, lies beneath the church of Santa Maria della Sanità. These catacombs are among the oldest Christian monuments in Naples. The **Museo e Gallerie Nazionali di Capodimonte** may be seen at the same time as the catacombs. It is located across the street from San Gennaro's catacomb in a lovely park.

The **Catacomba di San Gennaro**, located beneath the church of San Gennaro extra Moenia (Map above 2; 2; entrance in Via Capodimonte; open daily for guided tours, 09.30, 10.15, 11.00, 11.45) dates from the 2C AD and seems to have developed around the family tomb of an early member of the Christian community. It probably became the official cemetery of Christian Naples after the burial here, in the 3C of the Bishop-Saint Agrippinus, over whose tomb a basilica was built. Later, when San Gennaro, the 5C martyr and patron saint of the city, was entombed here, the catacomb became a place of pilgrimage. The first dukes of Naples, notably Stephen I (d. AD 800) and Stephen III (d. 832), are also buried here. In 831 Sicone, prince of Benevento, carried the relics of San

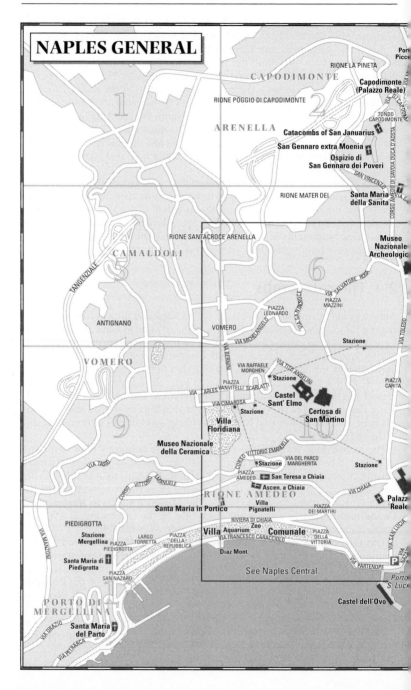

NAPLES GENERAL

Por
Picc

RIONE LA PINETA

CAPODIMONTE

Capodimonte
(Palazzo Reale)

RIONE POGGIO DI CAPODIMONTE

TONDO
CAPODIMONTE

ARENELLA

Catacombs of San Januarius

San Gennaro extra Moenia

Ospizio di
San Gennaro dei Poveri

SAN VINCENZO

RIONE MATER DEI

Santa Maria
della Sanita

RIONE SANTACROCE ARENELLA

Museo
Nazionale
Archeologic

CAMALDOLI

VIA SALVATORE ROSA

TANGENZIALE

PIAZZA
LEONARDO

PIAZZA
MAZZINI

VIA SANTACROCE

ANTIGNANO

VOMERO

VIA MICHELANGELO

Stazione

VIA TOLEDO

VOMERO

VIA BERNINI

VIA RAFFAELE
MORGHEN

VIA TITO ANGELINI

Stazione

PIAZZA
VANVITELLI SCARLATTI

PIAZZA
CARITA

VIA ARLES

Castel
Sant' Elmo

VIA CIMAROSA

Stazione

Certosa di
San Martino

Villa
Floridiana

Museo Nazionale
della Ceramica

CORSO VITTORIO EMANUELE

VIA DEL PARCO
MARGHERITA

Stazione

VIA TASSO

Stazione

PIAZZA
AMEDEO

San Teresa a Chiaia

CORSO VITTORIO EMANUELE

Ascen. a Chiaia

RIONE AMEDEO

VIA CHIAIA

Villa
Pignatelli

PIAZZA
DEI MARTIRI

Palazz
Reale

Santa Maria in Portico

PIEDIGROTTA

RIVIERA DI CHIAIA

Villa Aquarium Zoo

Comunale

Stazione
Mergellina

VIA MANZONI

LARGO
TORRETTA

PIAZZA
PIEDIGROTTA

PIAZZA
DELLA
REPUBBLICA

VIA FRANCESCO CARACCIOLO

PIAZZA
DELLA
VITTORIA

VIA SAN LUCIA

Santa Maria di
Piedigrotta

PIAZZA
SAN NAZARO

Diaz Mont.

VIA PARTENOPE

Porto
S. Luc

PORTO DI
MERGELLINA

See Naples Central

VIA ORAZIO

Santa Maria
del Parto

Castel dell'Ovo

VIA PETRARCA

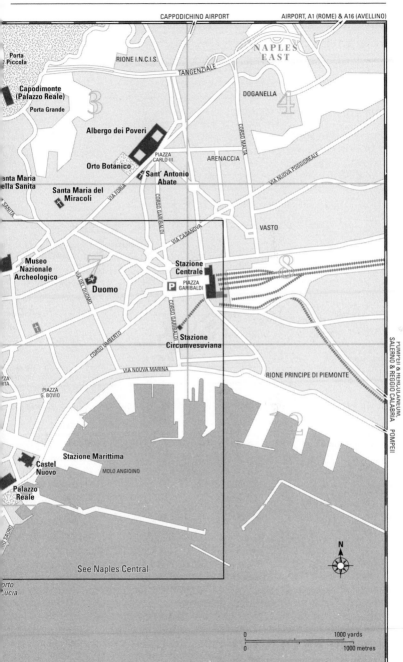

CAPPODICHINO AIRPORT

AIRPORT, A1 (ROME) & A16 (AVELLINO)

NAPLES EAST

Porta e Piccola

RIONE I.N.C.I.S.

TANGENZIALE

DOGANELLA

Capodimonte (Palazzo Reale)

Porta Grande

3

4

Albergo dei Poveri

PIAZZA CARLO III

ARENACCIA

CORSO MALTA

VIA NUOVA POGGIOREALE

Orto Botanico

Sant' Antonio Abate

anta Maria ella Sanità

VIA FORIA

Santa Maria del Miracoli

SANITÀ

VIA CASANOVA

VASTO

CORSO GARIBALDI

Museo Nazionale Archeologico

VIA DEL DUOMO

Duomo

Stazione Centrale

P PIAZZA GARIBALDI

CORSO GARIBALDI

Stazione Circumvesuviana

CORSO UMBERTO

VIA NOUVA MARINA

PIAZZA G. BOVIO

RIONE PRINCIPE DI PIEMONTE

ZA TA

Stazione Marittima

MOLO ANGIOINO

Castel Nuovo

Palazzo Reale

DSADIO

See Naples Central

orto ucia

PUMPEII & HERCULANEUM, SALERNO & REGGIO CALABRIA POMPEII

N

0   1000 yards

0   1000 metres

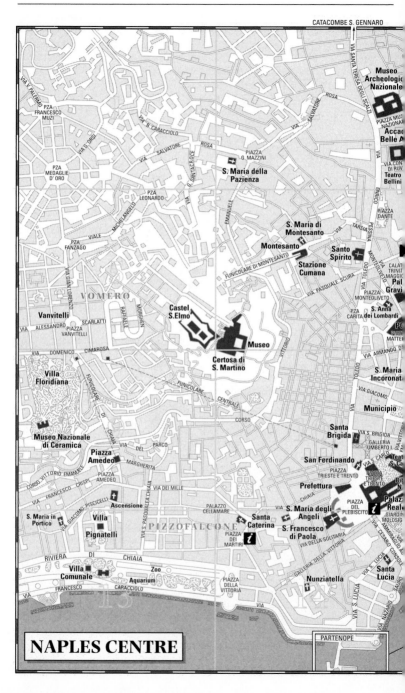

NAPLES CENTRE

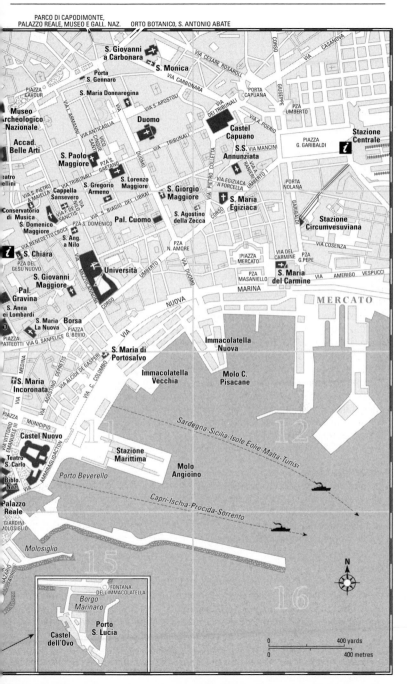

PARCO DI CAPODIMONTE,
PALAZZO REALE, MUSEO E GALL. NAZ.   ORTO BOTANICO, S. ANTONIO ABATE

S. Giovanni
a Carbonara
S. Monica
Porta
S. Gennaro
VIA CESARE ROSAROLL
CORSO
VIA CASANOVA

PIAZZA
CAVOUR
S. Maria Donnaregina
VIA CARBONARA
PORTA
CAPUANA
GIUSEPPE
PZA
UMBERTO

Museo
Archeologico
Nazionale
Duomo
VIA S. APOSTOLI
VIA
DEI TRIBUNALI
Castel
Capuano
VIA A. POERIO
Stazione
Centrale

Accad.
Belle Arti
VIA TRIBUNALI
S.S.
Annunziata
VIA MANCINI
PIAZZA
G. GARIBALDI
i

S. Paolo
Maggiore
PZA S.
GAETANO
VIA EGIZIACA
A FORCELLA
PORTA
NOLANA

Teatro
Bellini
S. Gregorio
Armeno
S. Lorenzo
Maggiore
S. Giorgio
Maggiore
S. Maria
Egiziaca
Stazione
Circumvesuviana

Cappella
Sansevero
VIA S. BIAGIO DEI LIBRAI
S. Agostino
della Zecca
VIA COSENZA

Conservatorio
di Musica
S. Domenico
Maggiore
Pal. Cuomo
PZA S. DOMENICO
CORSO
PZA
N. AMORE

i S. Chiara
S. Ang.
a Nilo
PIAZZA
MERCATO
PIAZZA
CARMINE
PZA
G. PEPE

PZA DEL
GESU NUOVO
Università
S. Maria
del Carmine
VIA   AMERIGO   VESPUCCI

S. Giovanni
Maggiore
UMBERTO I
PZA
MASANIELLO

Pal.
Gravina
MARINA
MERCATO

S. Anna
ei Lombardi
Borsa
NUOVA

S. Maria
La Nuova
PIAZZA
G. BOVIO
Immacolatella
Nuova

PIAZZA
MATTEOTTI
S. Maria di
Portosalvo

MEDINA
Immacolatella
Vecchia
Molo C.
Pisacane

S. Maria
Incoronata

PIAZZA
MUNICIPIO

Castel Nuovo
11
Stazione
Marittima
12

Teatro
S. Carlo
Sardegna-Sicilia-Isole Eolie-Malta-Tunisi

Biblio.
Naz.
Porto Beverello
Molo
Angioino

Palazzo
Reale
Capri-Ischia-Procida-Sorrento

GIARDINI
MOLOSIGLIO

Molosiglio
15

N

FONTANA
DELL'IMMACOLATELLA
Borgo
Marinaro
16

Castel
dell'Ovo
Porto
S. Lucia

0   400 yards
0   400 metres

Gennaro off to his city; and around the mid-9C the bishop-saint John IV trans-ferred the remains of his illustrious predecessors to the cathedral. But he, like his successor St Athanasius (d. 877), was buried here, and the catacomb remained in use throughout the 10C and probably the 11C. The catacomb contains burial cells and fragmentary frescoes and mosaics, but is interesting above all for its extent and overall ambience.

The **Catacomba di San Gaudioso** (Map 2; 3; guided tours Sun, 09.45 and 11.45), which lies beneath Santa Maria della Sanità, was named after the African Bishop-Saint, Gaudiosus. According to a very old legend, San Gaudioso was deposed by the Vandal king, Genseric, and set adrift in a small boat, along with Quodvuldeus and several followers. After many vicissitudes, the ecclesias-tics landed at Naples, where they founded a monastery. San Gaudioso died in 451 or 452 and was venerated as a saint. An extensive cemetery grew up around his tomb, of which only a small part remains today.

3 • The National Archaeological Museum

By far the most extensive collection of ancient art in Naples is to be found in the **Museo Archeologico Nazionale** in Piazza Museo 18 (Map 2;3). This is one of the larger and more interesting museums of antiquities in the world. Universally famous for its magnificent series of exhibits of every kind from Pompeii and Herculaneum, it is also of prime importance for the study of Greek sculpture. The building that houses it was designed as a barracks in 1586 but occupied by the university after 1599. In 1790 it was remodelled to receive the antiquities from Pompeii and Herculaneum, the Farnese Collections (inherited by King Charles of Bourbon from his mother, Elisabeth Farnese of Parma) and the picture gallery. Alexandre Dumas, père, held the office of Keeper in 1860–64.

The museum's vast stock of antique painting, sculpture, ceramics and jew-ellery has survived amazingly well. The building suffered only superficial damage during the Second World War. Many of the treasures had been removed for safety; of those sent to Monte Cassino a few were lost, but most were carefully preserved. The picture gallery was moved to Capodimonte in 1957.

Opening times

The museum is open daily except Tues 09.00–19.00; ☎ 081 292823. Ideally it should be seen after visiting Pompeii and Herculaneum, which provide a context for much of the work displayed.

The museum operates on a rotating gallery basis, so not everything men-tioned in the following description can be seen in a single visit.

Ground floor

The ground floor is devoted mainly to sculpture from the Farnese Collection, the Borgia Collection from Velletri and the cities of Campania. The main entrance opens into the **Grande Atrio dei Magistrati**, containing statues and tombs of the Imperial Age of Rome, notably a marble sarcophagus from Pozzuoli, with Prometheus moulding man out of clay in the presence of the gods (4C AD).

Room 1. The **Galleria dei Tirannicidi** (right), contains archaic sculptures, including severe style torsos, and the *Aphrodite Sosandra* from Baiae, the best surviving imitation of the celebrated work by Kalamis. The room takes its name from the sculpture of **Harmodius and Aristogeiton**, slayers of the tyrant Hipparchus, from Tivoli; this is a 2C AD copy of the bronze group made by Kritius and Nesiotes in 477 BC for the Agora in Athens. The present arrangement of the figures is of doubtful authenticity; various alternatives have been suggested, of which the most probable are Aristogeiton set on the left of Harmodius, or the two statues on separate bases, at a distance from each other. The rooms to the right contain sculpture from the golden age of Greek art (5C BC).

The *Athena* in **room 2** is a copy, of imperial date (1C–3C AD), of a bronze statue of the school of Phidias; here, too, are a low relief of **Orpheus, Eurydice and Hermes**, the best of the three known copies of a work by Phidias; *Aphrodite Genetrix*, from Herculaneum; a Hellenic votive relief from Herculaneum; a head of Artemis (the so-called *Farnese Artemis*), a 2C AD copy of a Greek original from the 5C BC; a herm of Athena with a mild, youthful cast of features, probably from a Greek original of c 450–425, from Herculaneum; and a statue of *Apollo*, from the House of the Cithara Player at Pompeii.

Room 3 is dominated by the *Doryphorus* (from Pompeii), the most complete copy of the famous spear-bearer of Polyclitus (c 440 BC), which was considered the 'canon' or perfect model of manly proportions. In **room 5** is a statue of *Diomedes*, from Cumae, from an Attic original (450–430 BC) attributed to Kresilas; and in **room 6**, *Nereids*, possibly Greek originals of the 5C or 4C, from a Roman villa at Formia, and a statue of *Hera*.

Returning to the Galleria dei Tirannicidi, pass through **room 7**, which includes, among several marble works, Roman imitations of archaic Greek heads and herms; a statue of a boxer, from Sorrento; and a two-figure group representing *Eros and Psyche*, according to one version, or *Orestes and Electra*, according to another.

Rooms 8–16. The next few rooms contain sculpture from the Baths of Caracalla, formerly in the Farnese Collection, together with other works. **Room 8**, a long hall, is divided into two sections. Highlights in the first room are *Dionysus and Eros*, a 2C Roman copy of a 4C BC Greek original; two crouching figures of *Venus* (both AD 2C copies of a 3C BC Greek original attributed to Doidalsas); and an alabaster statue of *Artemis of Ephesus* with bronze face, hands and feet (the many breasts symbolise fertility). Between the two sections stands the *Venus Callypige* from Nero's Domus Aurea, in Rome. The second half of the gallery is a re-creation of the sculptural arrangement of the **Galleria dei Carracci**, in the Palazzo Farnese in Rome—the gallery painted in 1597 by the Carracci for Odoardo Farnese. The statues include *Antinous* (Hadrian's favourite), a *Dionysus* after a Praxitelean model; a *Satyr with Infant Dionysus*; and *Ganymede* with the eagle and a lifelike dog.

Stairs descend to the basement level, where the Egyptian and Epigraphical collections (see below) are displayed.

Adjoining room 8 is the **Galleria del Toro Farnese**, a long hall of six bays (rooms 11–16). At the far end (right), beyond a vestibule, are two small rooms (**rooms 9, 10**) displaying the Farnese gems, including the famous **Tazza Farnese**, a cup made from veined sardonyx, one of the largest known examples of the cameo-maker's art, of the finest Alexandrian workmanship of the Ptolemaic age.

Returning through **room 11**, the *Farnese Heracles*, another work from the Baths of Caracalla, is a copy by Glycon of a work by Lysippus. **Room 13** is dominated by the *Flora Farnese*, a huge statue; also here a Claudian-age well-head with a relief showing various male gods. **Room 16** hosts the work that gives its name to this section, the *Farnese Bull*. This is the largest known work of antique sculpture, representing the vengeance of Zethus and Amphion on Dirce, Queen of Thebes. It also comes from the Baths of Caracalla.

In the long gallery (**29**) to the left is a collection of busts of Roman emperors, none particularly noteworthy. The five rooms (**rooms 24–28**) leading from this gallery are occupied by a collection of decorative sculpture and reliefs with interesting details of hunting and other scenes. The rooms are closed at present and their contents will probably be relocated elsewhere.

Basement ~ the Egyptian Collection

The stairs at the end of the Galleria di Flora lead down to the Egyptian collection where hieroglyphics, mummies, sculptures of sacred animals and funerary statuettes (Uschebtia) are displayed. Particularly noteworthy is a mummy case of the 22nd Dynasty, dating from the 9C BC. Also on this level is the Epigraphical Section, beyond which another staircase ascends to the museum entrance.

Entresol ~ mosaics from Pompeii

The main staircase ascends from the Grande Atrio to the mezzanine floor. The east wing houses the **coin collection**, with some 200,000 ancient and medieval coins. The west wing of the entresol is occupied by **Pompeian mosaics**. Among them are some of the finer known examples of the art; all three types, tessellated, vermiculated and *opus sectile* are represented. Notice especially, in **room 59**, the *Comic Actors* (sometimes described as begging musicians), a very fine mosaic from Cicero's villa, representing two women, a man and a dwarf, all masked and playing musical instruments; *Consulting the Sorceress*, a scene from a comedy, both of these mosaics signed by Dioscorides of Samos; the *Academy at Athens*, seven figures (Plato in the centre) with the Acropolis in the background; a pattern of fish, crustacea and marine creatures, featuring over 20 species, including an octopus, which is zoologically correct (another may be seen in room 60); also, panels showing Nile scenes, with crocodiles, hippopotami, ibis and other creatures, originally the frame of the *Battle of Issus*. **Room 60** also contains the *Winged Boy riding a Tiger*.

Room 61 hosts **mosaics from the House of the Faun**, as well as the celebrated *Dancing Faun* from which the house takes its name; a decorative band with festoons and theatre masks; a still life in two registers, with a remarkably life-like cat catching a quail; and *Darius and Alexander at the Battle of Issus* (333 BC). This mosaic, finely executed in minute tesserae, may be compared in scale with the hunting scenes at Piazza Armerina, in Sicily (see *Blue Guide Sicily*). The composition is thought to follow a 4C Greek painting, probably by Philoxenos, and is one of the few ancient works that develops perpendicularly to the picture plane as well as horizontally. Beyond rooms 61–62 is the so-called **Gabinetto Segreto** with paintings, mosaics, statuettes and reliefs of erotic subjects found in the Vesuvian excavations.

First floor

At the top of the stairs, between the east and west wings, is the immense **Salone dell'Atlante**, which takes its name from a Hellenistic statue of *Atlas*. The ceiling

MUSEO ARCHEOLOGICO NAZIONALE

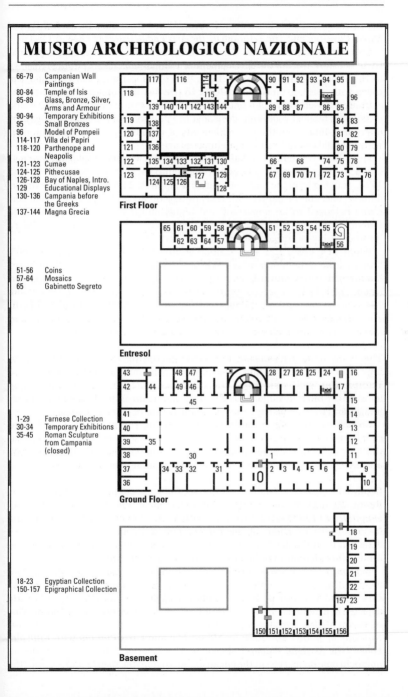

First Floor

Entresol

Ground Floor

Basement

has a fresco by Pietro Bardellino showing *Virtue Crowning Ferdinand IV and Maria Carolina* and *The Triumph of the Arts and Sciences* (1781).

Cross the Salone and enter the west wing from the recently opened **prehistoric section**, tracing the development of Campanian cultures from prehistory to the Greek colonisation. From here, the exhibit continues in chronological order, with a section on **Greek culture in the Bay of Naples**. It starts with the extraordinary discovery of a house of the 8C BC at Punta Chiarito, on the island of Ischia. The next rooms are dedicated to Pithecusae and Cumae, followed by interesting finds from the two settlements of ancient Naples. The section ends with splendid examples of Roman Imperial art.

From here you enter the **Sala della Villa dei Papiri**, displaying artefacts found in the celebrated villa at Herculaneum, excavated between 1750 and 1761. Judging from the finds (50 marble sculptures, 21 bronzes and an extraordinary collection of papyri with texts on Epicurean philosophy), the villa certainly belonged to an important and highly cultured figure—possibly Lucio Calpurnio Pisone (Julius Caesar's father-in-law) or Appio Claudio Pulcro (brother-in-law of the general and epicure Lucullus).

Room 115. Cases 1, 2, and 3: small bronzes from the atrium. Case 4: small bronzes from a room on the west side of the villa. Case 5: small portrait busts, mainly from the 3C onwards; dancing and playing satyrs. In the adjoining rooms (**rooms 110–114**) are several murals and carbonised fragments of papyri. **Room 116** is home to the so-called *Dancers* (1C BC), a sleeping satyr, a drunken *Silenus* and *Hermes* resting. In **room 117** are several fine bronzes: a portrait head (*Seneca?* 1C BC); *Heracles*, a copy after Polycletus; and a bust of an ephebe.

The rooms in the east wing are numbered from the front to the rear of the building. Their contents fall into three groups: the south rooms are devoted to **Campanian wall paintings**; the north rooms, to bronze objects; and in between are other miscellaneous objects including furniture, household utensils, images and so on, which give a very complete idea of ancient domestic life.

Cross the Grande Salone and turn into **room 66**. This and the long hall, adjacent (**room 68**) contain a wealth of paintings which show the difference between the 'four styles' of Pompeian painting—a conventional definition, used to classify and date the various frescoes found at Pompeii and similar Roman frescoes.

Room 69 contains a famous cycle of second-style paintings from Boscoreale. **Room 70** displays more mural paintings, including a fine *Hercules and Omphale*; a *Childhood of Dionysus*, with a boy of charming vivacity; and the famous fresco of *Dido Abandoned by Æneas*. **Room 71** has four frescoes detached from the 'basilica' of Herculaneum, including a very beautiful representation of *Hercules Finding his Son Telephus in Arcadia*.

In **room 72** is a fresco of *Perseus and Andromeda*, considered the most faithful copy of the original painted by Nikias; *Achilles Discovered at Skyros*, by the Greek painter Theon of Samos; *Nuptials of Jupiter*; *Sacrifice of Iphigenia* depicted in a manner similar to that of traditional representations of the sacrifice of Isaac; *Medea*, perhaps copied from a celebrated painting by Timomachus; *Nuptials of Jupiter and Hera on Mount Ida*; and *Girls Playing with Knucklebones* (*The Astragal Players*), signed by Alexander of Athens and executed in monochrome on marble, in the encaustic technique (the scene may represent the

Four styles of fresco

The **first style** was common throughout the Mediterranean world during the 2C BC and was hardly a matter of painting at all. It consisted simply in covering the wall with plaster, painted and shaped to look like coloured stone, especially marble. It is a plain type of decoration, imitating the exteriors of Doric pfiublic buildings. The best examples are the **House of Sallust** and the **House of the Faun** at Pompeii, or the **Samnite House** at Herculaneum.

The **second style** was an original Roman creation, fashionable from about 80 BC to the end of the 1C BC. It consisted in painting the walls with illusionistic perspectives, creating a trompe l'œil effect. The preferred themes of the figured paintings seem to be mythological or religious narratives: a magnificent example is the **Villa dei Misteri** in Pompeii.

The **third style** returns to a flat decorative idiom with no attempt at illusionism. It developed from about 20 BC to AD 45 and makes use of a unified background decorated with a calligraphic ornamentation of various motifs, small-scale architectural features, and light-hearted figurines. This style was heavily criticised for its daintiness and frivolity by Vitruvius, who considered it illogical and immoral. You can see it in the House of Marcus Lucretius Fronto.

The **fourth style** developed after AD 62, when Pompeii was shaken by an earthquake and many houses needed redecorating. It lasted until AD 79, when another eruption in Pompeii buried the city, and survived longer in other centres. It is an eclectic synthesis of the illusionism of the second style and the flat elegance of the third style, often combined with narratives, best exemplified in the **House of the Vetii** in Pompeii.

vengeance of Leto, as narrated by Ovid in Metamorphoses VI). In **room 73** are two outstanding images, of *Meleager and Atalanta*, and of *Iphigenia in Tauris*.

The paintings continue in **room 74**, with cupids at work and play, and four small paintings of women—*Medea, Leda and the Swan, Diana*, and a girl gathering flowers (so-called *Spring*), with delicate colouring, from Stabiae.

Room 77 contains images of everyday life: *Paquius Proculus and his Wife*, portraits of convincing realism; a baker selling (or by another interpretation, a public official distributing) bread; *Bacchus and Mount Vesuvius*, generally considered an allegory of Pompeii; a *Brawl in the Amphitheatre at Pompeii* between Pompeians and Nucerians (59 BC); and a *View of the Port of Puteoli*, strangely reminiscent of the style of Canaletto. The display continues in rooms 78 and 79.

Rooms 80–84 contain the entire pictorial decoration from the Temple of Isis at Pompeii.

Rooms 85 and **86** are devoted to glassware. Among the more notable pieces are a 1C **blue glass vase** of fine workmanship, beautifully ornamented with Dionysiac scenes in cameo technique (**room 85**) and the glass of Sepinus, from the early 4C, with a bacchic procession of Dionysus, satyrs and mæneads, showing a strikingly modern design emblematic of the return to stylisation in the art of the late Roman Empire.

Room 87. Arms and armour, including gladiators' helmets with delicate reliefs. **Room 88**. Terracotta collection, with figurines, cups and other vessels, plus a case containing ivory objects and figurines.

Room 89 displays silverware of various provenance, including tableware from the House of the Menander; the service was found untouched in a deposit underneath the house in Pompeii. It contains cups and other vessels of silver (118 pieces in all), some produced by a late Hellenistic workshop, others by Roman workshops of the Augustan age.

Rooms 90–94 are used for temporary exhibitions. **Room 95** contains **small bronzes** from Pompeii and Herculaneum. Here are various household implements, finials and appliqués, as well as little animals (used as amulets) and figurines, most of which have a votive purpose. Examples include the Lares, the protectors of the house, which personified ancestors' souls and were kept in a niche in the atrium.

The exhibits end in **room 96**, with a huge scale-model of Pompeii—a delight for children and people of all ages.

THE MEDIEVAL AND RENAISSANCE CITY

History of medieval and Renaissance Naples

The decline of the Roman Empire is too complicated to go into in detail here. Suffice it to say that the Romans were simply unprepared—economically, politically and psychologically—for the enormous military effort that three centuries of barbarian invasions required of them. The eastern provinces, with their capital at Constantinople (or Byzantium as it was then called), managed to defend their borders and preserve Imperial institutions of law and government.

But the weaker provinces of the west were overrun one by one by the Germanic peoples who, driven from their homelands by other invaders, sought a safe refuge on Roman soil. These historical events found concrete expression in the art and architecture of our area. The early Christian churches and catacombs that appeared in Naples and its environs in the late Roman period reflect both Classical and medieval values, setting the spiritual tone for much of the art produced in later centuries. The finest of these works—the 5C mosaics in Naples (in the Baptistery of San Giovanni in Fonte and in the Catacomb of San Gennaro) and at San Prisco, near Santa Maria Capua Vetere (in the chapel of Santa Matrona, attached to the parish church)—are distinguished by an explicit naturalism that is rarely seen outside Rome.

During the 5C Campania fell prey to the **Goths**, and for the next five centuries the region lacked both the financial resources and the political stability necessary for major artistic undertakings. In 535 the area was conquered by the **Byzantine** general, Belisarius, but Totilla, another Gothic leader, drove the Byzantines from the region in 547; ten years later, it reverted to Byzantine rule. Towards the end of the 6C, the already weak hold of the eastern emperors relaxed still further under pressure from the **Lombards**, who gained control of the important provinces of Capua, Benevento, Nola, Acerra and Nocera, reaching the sea at Salerno in 646.

While the Lombards ruled over the interior of Campania, the part of the province remaining under the Byzantine Empire gave its allegiance to the

Duke of Naples, who was originally a Greek envoy, but in 661 became a Neapolitan. In 763 Duke Stephen II, while ostensibly maintaining his loyalty to Byzantium, secured the privilege of hereditary power for his family and gradually detached Naples from the direct domination of the empire. His allies in Sorrento, Amalfi and Gaeta soon followed suit. Their dukes, likewise separated by distance and political interest from their nominal allegiance to Byzantium, disengaged themselves from the Eastern Empire in 768, 786 and 899, respectively. During the age of the **Independent Duchy** (763–1139), Latin replaced Greek as the official language in Naples, and the Roman image of St Januarius (San Gennaro) replaced the Greek effigy of the emperor on municipal seals and coins.

Naples developed one of the strongest fleets in Europe, and in the 9C it joined forces with other Campanian cities: Gaeta, Sorrento and Amalfi, to rid the Tyrrhenian Sea of the marauding Saracens, who terrorised the coasts and interfered with vital maritime trade. In so doing they avenged the Saracen sack of Rome (846), and with a famous victory over the Saracens three years later at Ostia, celebrated by Raphael in the Vatican Stanze, they saved the Eternal City from a new catastophe.

The Normans

The Norman conquest (1030–1130) restored political unity to southern Italy. The Norman adventurers who first came to the area in 1016 to seek their fortunes in Apulia and Calabria seem to have had no political ambitions. Lacking organisation and experienced leadership, they were prepared to live as mercenaries in the service of the Byzantines or the Lombards.

It was not until 1030 that Sergius of Naples, by awarding the Norman leader Rainulf the county of Aversa in payment for services rendered, gave them the opportunity to begin an organised conquest of the land. In the years that followed, Norman knights, led by the sons of Tancred de Hauteville, intervened in local conflicts and by so doing gradually gained control of Capua (1062), Salerno (1076) and Amalfi (1137). Naples was the last to fall: it maintained its independence until 1139, its citizens resisting even after the submission of its duke.

By the middle of the 12C, Campania had been overpowered by the conquerors, whose dominion extended over all southern Italy and Sicily. This vast territory became the Norman **Kingdom of Sicily**, with its capital at Palermo. It was administered efficiently and with great tolerance of the region's Arab, Jewish, Greek and Roman traditions. It is a pity that in this scheme of things Naples was reduced to the status of a provincial town.

Norman art around Naples

The Norman influence is most clearly seen in the maritime cities, which prospered through trade with Sicily and the Orient and were the chief channels through which the Norman court of Palermo administered its holdings on the mainland. Siculo-Norman artists, or local artists trained in the Norman schools of Sicily, were active at Salerno, Ravello, Sessa Aurunca, Gaeta and elsewhere in this area throughout the 11C and 12C. They left an extraordinary series of sculptures—mainly decorated episcopal thrones, pulpits, paschal candelabra and altar screens, incorporating coloured glass inlay and marble tarsia work inspired by Saracenic art. The Normans were also responsible for introducing French architectural forms and styles, which are most harmoniously expressed in the abbey of Fossanova (see p 92), consecrated in 1208.

The rebuilding of the Benedictine abbey of Monte Cassino (see p 86), which also took place in the 11C, under the enlightened direction of the abbot Desiderius, stimulated artistic activity in the area. From Monte Cassino, Desiderius masterminded a real revolution of the arts. He brought in architects from Lombardy and artists from Constantinople and trained his monks in their methods, giving rise to a new artistic sensibility that combined the splendour of Oriental mosaic and allied crafts with revived early Christian narrative methods. Although Monte Cassino has lost most of its medieval grandeur, a reflection of this 11C blend of styles may be seen in the marvellous series of contemporary frescoes in the basilica at Sant'Angelo in Formis, near Capua.

Further contacts between eastern and western artistic cultures are evident in the bronze doors that appeared on Campanian cathedrals in the 11C and 12C. The first of these were installed at Amalfi in 1065. They had been commissioned in Constantinople by the wealthy Amalfitan merchant, Pantaleon, who had business interests in the Byzantine capital and must have seen bronze doors on churches there. Desiderius of Monte Cassino was so impressed by these doors when he visited Amalfi that he ordered a pair for the abbey. The fashion spread from there to Salerno, Atrani, Ravello, Benevento and other southern Italian cities.

Frederick II

In 1194 the crown of Holy Roman Emperor was claimed by Henry IV of Hohenstaufen in the name of his wife, Constance (daughter of the Norman king, Roger II). He was succeeded as emperor and as King of Sicily by his son Frederick II (1197–1250), whose splendid court at Palermo drew on Islamic and Jewish, as well as Christian cultures. Frederick's belief in the principles of just government is reflected in the famous code of laws known as the *Constitutiones augustales.* His interest in rational science and love of Classical sculpture foreshadow the Renaissance.

Naples initially challenged Frederick's sovereignty and suffered a humiliating defeat at the hands of an imperial army. In a gesture of calculated magnanimity, Frederick regained the favour of the Neapolitans by making their city, and not Palermo, the intellectual capital of his kingdom: in 1224 he founded the university, where many famous men of letters—including Pier delle Vigne, Andrea d'Isernia, Bartolomo Prignano, and Cino da Pistoia—were teachers.

Frederick's son, Conrad, died before he could inherit the kingdom, and Pope Urban IV at once set about finding a rival candidate for the Sicilian throne. He chose **Charles of Anjou**, the younger brother of St Louis of France. In two fortunate battles, at Benevento (1266) and Tagliacozzo (1268), Charles defeated the last of the Hohenstaufen, establishing himself as the first French king of Naples and Sicily. To mark the sharp contrast between his monarchy and that of his predecessors, he transferred his capital from Palermo to Naples, which naturally grew in importance.

The Angevin court

The Angevin court of Naples was as sophisticated and cosmopolitan as any contemporary court in Provence. As allies of the pope the French kings employed Florentine bankers and patronised Florentine intellectuals, many of whom, like the poet Giovanni Boccaccio, became quite fond of their adopted home.

The gaiety of the Angevin court unfortunately did not extend to the rest of the kingdom. Indeed, the political life of these years was as turbulent as the social life was exuberant. Charles initially enjoyed the favour of his subjects, but his political ambitions, which necessitated oppressive taxation, led to resentment. Revolt broke out in Palermo on Easter Tuesday, 1282, in the uprising known as the **Sicilian Vespers**. Within a month the French garrisons on the island had been either expelled or massacred, and the Sicilian nobles had summoned the Catalonian, Peter of Aragon, to be their king.

Charles died in 1286, and his heir, Charles II, was not crowned until 1288. He was succeeded in 1309 by his second son, **Robert** (the Wise), who proved a capable ruler and patron of the arts (it was he who financed Boccaccio's literary endeavours), but whose authority was limited by a turbulent and rebellious baronage. His death was followed by a whirlwind of coups and counter-coups. He was succeeded (1343) by his granddaughter Joan I, whose husband and crown prince, Andrew of Hungary, was assassinated in 1345, probably with the queen's complicity. Joan nominated Louis of Anjou her heir, and he was recognised by the anti-pope Clement VII. Pope Urban VI, however, named Charles of Durazzo, great-grandson of Charles II, king of Naples. Charles conquered the kingdom, took Joan prisoner in 1381 and had her murdered the following year. Louis died in exile three years later. The anarchic reigns of Charles III and his son Ladislas were followed (1414) by the dissolute rule of Joan II, which was torn by the rival claims of Louis III of Anjou and of **Alfonso of Aragon** to be her heir. Alfonso seized Naples at Joan's death in 1335, and in 1443 assumed the title, King of the Two Sicilies (i.e. of Sicily and Naples).

Art under the Angevins

During the 13C and early 14C the artistic impetus in Naples, which came through the Angevin dynasty, was understandably foreign. The Angevins generally imported their architects from France, but they chose their artists from among the representative masters of the major Italian schools: Pietro Cavallini from Rome, Giotto from Florence, Simone Martini and Tino di Camaino from Siena. By so doing they established a pattern of patronage (favouring foreign artists or artists from further north over local masters) that would continue, with rare exceptions, until the 17C.

Fifteenth-century Naples

During the brief reign of Alfonso of Aragon, called the Magnanimous, Naples was again united with Sicily. The kingdom enjoyed a period of renewed splendour, for Alfonso was at once a brilliant ruler, a scholar and a patron of the arts. When he died (1458) his brother John II succeeded to the throne of Sicily, while Naples adopted his illegitimate son Ferdinand I (Ferrante) as king. Like his father, Ferrante surrounded himself with artists and humanists and was in this respect a typical Renaissance prince, though often perverse and cruel (it was his policy to imprison his enemies in the Castel Nuovo until they died; they would then be mummified and exhibited to his guests, dressed in the clothes they had worn when living).

Ferrante was succeeded by Alfonso II, who in September 1491 surrendered the kingdom to Charles VII of France. Many months later Alfonso's son Ferdinand II (Ferrandino), with the help of Spain, returned to his capital, where he died in 1496. During the reign of his successor, Frederick, the country was torn by civil war and brigandage as both the French and the Spanish continued to press their claims. A series of victories by Spanish forces under **Gonzalo de Cordoba** secured the kingdom for Spain in 1503. Naples was not united with Sicily, but governed by a separate viceroy, Gonzalo being the first.

Renaissance art in Naples

While Renaissance painters in Florence, Rome, and Venice produced works of art that are known the world over, very little of note was done in 15C Naples. Like the Angevins, the Aragonese entrusted their most important commissions to the famous names of the north (notably the Florentines Donatello, Michelozzo, Antonio Rossellino and Benedetto da Maiano). This was only to be expected, as they could afford the best works and considered themselves to be on a level with the great families of northern cities.

The major Neapolitan painter of the 15C is Colantonio, whose style shows a debt to Flemish painting. Andrea da Salerno, too, has left many fine works throughout Campania. Despite the fine sculptured works by northern Italian artists in the major churches of Naples, there was no local school of any merit. The most successful architects were Tommaso and Giovanni Tommaso Malvito and Giovanni Francesco Mormanno, whose creations we shall encounter shortly.

4 • From the castle to the cathedral

This walk begins in the heart of the city, at the great Castel Nuovo on the waterfront. From here you cross the Piazza del Municipio and follow the broad, modern Via Medina and Via Monteoliveto, busy with traffic, to the former convent of Monteoliveto. The Calata Trinità Maggiore then curves up to the old city centre, which is entered from Piazza del Gesù. From here you proceed along the street popularly known as the Spaccanapoli (the *decumanus inferior* of Neapolis), which changes its modern name several times during its length, but never its straight and narrow course, emerging in Via del Duomo (another modern thoroughfare) just south of the cathedral. This dark, crowded quarter gives you a feeling for medieval Naples. And here, in fact, are the major monuments of the Middle Ages: the great conventual complexes of **Santa Chiara**, **San Domenico** and **San Gregorio Armeno**, on the west side of the city centre; and the **cathedral**, the churches of **Santa Maria Donnaregina** and **San Giovanni a Carbonara**, and the **Porta Capuana**, on the east side.

The walk is roughly 3km long (the first kilometre of which, from the Castel Nuovo to Santa Chiara, is uphill) and requires about 2 hours. It may be combined with the walk that follows the Via del Tribunali, two blocks north.

The Castel Nuovo

Above Naples harbour rises the royal residence of the Angevin kings, the Castel Nuovo (Map 2, 11), commonly, but less correctly, called the Maschio Angioino. Built for Charles I by Pierre de Chaulnes (1279–82), it was largely reconstructed under Alfonso of Aragon and rearranged by Ferdinand IV for use as the royal

Boccaccio in Naples

The Florentine writer Giovanni Boccaccio (1313–75) is best known as the author of the *Decameron*, a collection of tales recounting medieval life, brilliantly adapted to the screen by Italy's most controversial filmmaker, Pier Paolo Pasolini.

Boccaccio came to Naples as a young man, around 1327, to gain practice as a merchant and banker. He served a long (but fruitless) apprenticeship at the Bardi bank in the lively Portanova neighbourhood, an experience that brought him into daily contact with clients from all areas of the Mediterranean. Boccaccio's life could not have been that of an ordinary apprentice-clerk, for he was the son of a partner of the Bardi who in 1328 became a 'counsellor and chamberlain' of King Robert. The refined, gay life of the Neapolitan upper classes, divided between the aristocratic opulence of the city and the carefree, voluptuous idleness of the gulf-shore resorts (particularly Baia), is delightfully portrayed in his early works. In his *Rhymes*, for instance, he voices a curious lament.

> If I fear the sky and sea of Baia,
> the ground and waves and lakes and fountains,
> the wild and the domestic places,
> no one should be surprised.
> Here one spends all one's time celebrating
> with music and song, and with vain words
> seducing wandering minds
> or telling of love's victories.

Against this background he chose to set his great romantic novel, *Elegia a Madonna Fiammetta*.

and viceregal residence. Now beautifully restored, it houses the offices and library of the Società Napoletana di Storia Patria, the Biblioteca Comunale Cuomo, and the meeting rooms of the city Council of Naples and the Regional Council of Campania, as well as a fine museum (see 138).

Among the events that have taken place here are the abdication of Pope Celestin V and the mock marriage of Ferdinand I's granddaughter to a son of Count Sarno, at which the king arrested Sarno and other barons who were conspiring against him. The emperor Charles V stayed at the castle on his return from Tunis, and the revolt of Masaniello (described on p 152) was formally ended here in the pacts signed by the viceroy and the Prince of Massa.

Fronting the square across the dry moat is the long north wall between two massive 15C towers, the Torre del Beverello at the seaward end and the Torre di San Giorgio. Beyond this is the impressive main façade, which you enter between two further towers, under the famous **triumphal arch**, erected between 1454 and 1467 to commemorate the entry of Alfonso I into Naples (1443). This masterpiece of the Italian Renaissance was probably inspired by the celebrated Capua Gate of Frederick II. However, it differs in that it is not free-standing, but adapted to serve as the entrance to the castle. In this sense it is unique among the architectural inventions of its day, having no parallel in Tuscany or Lombardy. Many prominent sculptors, including Domenico Gagini, Isaia da Pisa, and Francesco

Laurana, were brought to Naples to assist in its decoration. The large bas-relief shows the *Triumph of Alfonso*. Above the second arch stand the four *Cardinal Virtues*, followed by two large river gods and, topping the whole, *St Michael*.

The castle is best seen in the morning. Pass through the arch into a vestibule, then enter the polygonal courtyard. The **Museo Civico di Castel Nuovo** (open Mon–Sat 09.00–19.00; ☎ 081 420 1241) includes the **Cappella Palatina** or church of Santa Barbara. It has a delicate Renaissance door surmounted by a *Madonna* by Francesco Laurana and contains 14C and 15C sculptures and frescoes. There is also an extensive, if undistinguished, collection of 15C–19C painting, and silver and bronze objects in the south wing. The chapel is lit by a large rose window of Catalan design and by tall Gothic windows, the splays of which contain frescoes attributed to Maso di Banco. The adjacent **sala dei baroni**, a large (26m x 28m) hall damaged by fire in 1919, is now the meeting place of the city council. The door next to the entrance leads to the **viceregal apartments**, which occupy the north side of the castle; on the wall opposite there is a monumental fireplace and choir lofts of Catalan workmanship.

The seaward side of the castle affords an impressive view of the huge bastions, with the Torre del Beverello on the right and the Torre dell'Oro set back to the left; between them rises the restored east end of the chapel, flanked by two polygonal turrets.

Piazza del Municipio

The long Piazza del Municipio (Map 2; 11), with a central monument commemorating Victor Emmanuel II, overlooks the harbour. On the west side stands the **town hall** (Palazzo di San Giacomo; 1819–25), the Palace of the Ministers under the Bourbons, which incorporates the church of **San Giacomo degli Spagnoli**. The latter, founded by Don Pedro de Toledo in 1514 and rebuilt in 1741, follows a Latin cross plan. The first chapel in the south aisle contains a *Madonna and Child* by Marco Pino. Above the altar in the south transept is a *Martyrdom of St James* by Domenico Antonio Vaccaro, who also painted the *Dead Christ* in the frontal above the main altar. In the apse the **tomb** of the founder can be seen, executed in his lifetime by Giovanni da Nola.

Two churches dedicated to the Virgin Mary

From the Piazza del Municipio take Via Medina. You soon reach (left) the Gothic doorway of **Santa Maria Incoronata** (Map 2; 11), a church built and named by Joan I (1352) to commemorate her coronation of 1351 and embodying the chapel of the old Vicaria, where she had married Louis of Taranto, her second husband, in 1345. The interior has kept its original form. In the vault are remarkable frescoes of the seven sacraments and the *Triumph of the Church* by Roberto Oderisi (c 1370); the Cappella del Crocifisso contains other frescoes of similar date.

The street rises gently between huge new buildings of varying merit to an important crossroads: Via Sanfelice leads right to Piazza Bovio; Via Diaz, realigned since 1945, leads left, opening almost at once into Piazza Matteotti (Map 2, 10), the focal point of Naples' business district. Its north side is dominated by the **post office**, a vast edifice in marble and glass (1936). Leaving this to your left you enter Via Santa Maria la Nova.

The church of **Santa Maria la Nova** (Map 2; 11), built by Charles I for Franciscans expelled from the site of Castel Nuovo (1279), was redesigned by

Agnolo Franco in the 16C. The façade is a fine Renaissance work. The aisleless nave has a richly painted ceiling incorporating works by Fabrizio Santafede, Francesco Curia and others. The first chapel on the south side contains a *St Michael* by Marco Pino. The angels on the dome are by Battistello Caracciolo. The second chapel on the north side (San Giacomo della Marca), built by Gonzalo de Cordoba (1504), contains the tomb of Marshal Lautrec (who died in 1528 of the plague while besieging Naples), by Annibale Caccavello, and statues by Domenico d'Auria. In the transept is a wooden *Crucifixion* by Giovanni da Nola. The high altar, which combines complex and unusual architectural members with fine floral inlay, is one of the more important works of the Baroque master Cosimo Fanzago. The two cloisters contain 15C tombs and later frescoes.

Monteoliveto and Santa Chiara

Now retrace your steps and turn right in Via Monteoliveto. Behind the post office is the cloister of Monteoliveto (the church is described below). The double order of arcades, built to compensate for the sloping land (monks entering the cloister from the church emerged on the upper level), open directly onto the street, a reminder that the convent was once surrounded by gardens. The poet Torquato Tasso took refuge from the persecution of Alfonso d'Este, in 1588, in the former Olivetan monastery here. On the opposite side of the street, a bit further on, is **Palazzo Gravina**, a beautiful Renaissance building in the purest Tuscan style, by Gabriele d'Agnolo and Giovanni Francesco Mormanno (1513–49), spoilt by the addition of a storey in 1839. It now houses the university's Faculty of Architecture.

The church of **Monteoliveto** (Map 2; 6), or Sant'Anna dei Lombardi, stands in the piazza of the same name, fronted by a Baroque fountain. Begun in 1411, the church contains a wealth of Renaissance sculpture, mostly undamaged in spite of a direct bomb hit in March 1944. The façade, shorn of its 18C additions, has been reconstructed in its original style. The vestibule contains the tomb (1627) of Domenico Fontana, architect to Pope Sixtus V. Inside, on either side of the entrance, are marble altars, by Giovanni da Nola (right) and Girolamo da Santacroce. On the south side, the first chapel (Cappella Mastrogiudice) contains an *Annunciation* and other sculptures by Benedetto da Maiano (1489) and the tomb of Marino Curiale (1490), in a similar style. The third chapel has an altar attributed to Giovanni da Nola. Beyond the fifth chapel a passage leads to the Chapel of the Holy Sepulchre, with a terracotta *Pietà* by Guido Mazzoni (1492); the eight life-size figures are said to be portraits of the artist's contemporaries. A corridor on the right leads to the Old Sacristy, which is frescoed by Vasari and contains fine intarsia stalls by Giovanni da Verona (1510).

The apse contains 16C stalls and the tombs of Alfonso II (d. 1495), by Giovanni da Nola, and Guerello Origlia, founder of the church. The sixth chapel on the north side was designed by Giuliano da Maiano; it also contains some repainted 16C frescoes. In the fifth chapel are a *St John the Baptist* by Giovanni da Nola and a *Pietà* by Santacroce. The third chapel has a *Flagellation* (1576) in marble relief and the first chapel, an *Ascension* (on wood) by Riccardo Quartararo (c 1492). From here entrance is gained to the Piccolomini Chapel, with a charming *Nativity* by Antonio Rossellino (c 1475). The beautiful tomb of Mary of Aragon (d. 1470), daughter of Ferdinand I, was begun by Rossellino and finished by Benedetto da Maiano.

Calata Trinita Maggiore climbs to the right, past the Baroque church and square of the del Gesù Nuovo. In the centre of the square stands the **Guglia dell'Immacolata**, a fanciful Baroque column (1747–50) typical of Neapolitan taste. Its ornate marble is emphasised by the severe west front of the church of the **Gesù Nuovo** (also called Trinità Maggiore), built between 1584 and 1601 for Isabella della Rovere. The embossed stone façade, once a wall of the palazzo of Roberto Sanseverino (by Novello da San Lucano, 1470), is pierced by three sculptured doorways. Those on the sides date from the 16C, the central doorway from 1685.

The rich interior (1601–31), ornate with coloured marbles, has frescoes by the Baroque painters Corenzio, Stanzione and Ribera. That of *Heliodorus Driven from the Temple*, above the entrance, is by Francesco Solimena (1725). The original design, by Giuseppe Valeriano, one of the more distinguished architects working in Naples at the end of the 16C, was much more severe, featuring white plaster walls and a discreet use of coloured marble and black piperno. A highly original design, it differs considerably from the Gesù in Rome, which served as the model for many Jesuit churches of the day. Its centralised plan and the flat, continuous wall surface which defines the space with maximum clarity, are still visible beneath the beautiful decoration of inlaid coloured marbles, the inventors of which, working under the direction of Cosimo Fanzago, seem to have gone to great lengths to respect the intrinsic qualities of the spatial design. The original dome was damaged by an earthquake in 1688 and replaced by the present structure in 1744.

At the far end of Piazza Gesù Nuovo is the great church and Franciscan convent of **Santa Chiara** (Map 2; 7), built in 1310–28 for queen Sancia, wife of Robert the Wise, who died here a nun. The church was completely burnt out by incendiary bombs on 4 August 1943, when the magnificent Baroque interior of 1742–57 was destroyed and most of the large monuments wrecked. The reconstruction has preserved the original Provençal-Gothic austerity, a quality so foreign to Naples as to be all the more striking. The Gothic west porch was undamaged.

The aisleless **interior**, the largest in Naples, has a new open roof 45m high and tasteful modern glass in the lancet windows. Of the glorious series of Angevin royal monuments, the principal survivals are the lower portions of the tombs of Robert the Wise (d. 1343), the work of the Florentine brothers Giovanni and Pacio Bertini (behind the high altar) and of Charles, Duke of Calabria, by Tino di Camaino and his followers (to the right). Also undamaged is the beautiful monument (1399) to their daughter, Mary of Durazzo (to the left). Every chapel has some tomb or Gothic sculpture that merits inspection.

The conventual buildings on the ground floor are open daily (09.30–12.30, 14.30–17.00/18.30). The entrance is reached by passing between the north side of the church and the detached campanile (not finished until 1647), passing through the first court and turning right. The parts seen include a particularly fine 18C Nativity crib and the huge 14C **cloister**, transformed in 1742 by Domenico Antonio Vaccaro, into a rustic garden adorned with majolica tiles and terracottas. The friars' austere refectory, with a charming fountain in the centre, lies off the east side. The Museo dell'Opera di Santa Chiara (open daily 09.30–13.00, 14.30–17.30, holidays 09.30–13.00; ☎ 081 552 6280) traces the history of the complex.

The Spaccanapoli

Via Benedetto Croce marks the beginning of the Spaccanapoli, whose decayed medieval and Renaissance palaces make it the most characteristic of old Neapolitan streets. Beyond the house (see plaque) where the eminent philosopher Benedetto Croce spent his last years, is Piazza San Domenico, with the Baroque Guglia di San Domenico (1737), enclosed by 16C mansions.

On the left rises **San Domenico Maggiore** (Map 2; 7), a noble Gothic church built in 1289–1324, rebuilt after earthquake and fire damage (1465 and 1506) and much altered since. The church of the Aragonese nobility, its chief interest lies in its Renaissance sculpture and monuments, which include some of the finest expressions of the Tuscan manner in Naples.

The **interior**, with aisles and transepts, is 76m long. In the south aisle, on the right of the entrance, is the Cappella Saluzzo, with decorated Renaissance arches (1512–16) and the monument to Galeotto Carafa (1507–15), all the work of Romolo di Antonio da Settignano. The tomb of Archbishop Brancaccio (d. 1341) in the second chapel is by a Tuscan follower of Tino di Camaino. The seventh chapel leads to the **Cappellone del Crocifisso**. Here is the little painting of the *Crucifixion* that spoke to St Thomas Aquinas when he was living in the adjacent monastery. To the left stands the fine tomb of Francesco Carafa (d. 1470), by Tommaso Malvito, and behind is a side-chapel (1511) with other family tombs and frescoes by Bramantino. From the eighth chapel you enter the **sacristy**, the ceiling of which hosts a brilliant fresco by Solimena. Above the presses are the coffins of ten princes of Aragon and 35 other illustrious people, including the Marquis of Pescara (d. 1525), leader of the forces of Holy Roman Emperor Charles V against the French king Francis I at the battle of Pavia. The sacristan can be persuaded to show these.

The south transept contains the tomb of Galeazzo Pandone (1514), a fine work probably by a Tuscan artist; above, the tomb slab of John of Durazzo (d. 1335), by Tino di Camaino. Perhaps the best of the tombs in the **chiesa antica** (Sant'Angelo a Morfisa) is that of Tommaso Brancaccio by Jacopo della Pila (1492); note also that of Porzia, wife of Bernardino Rota, by Annibale Caccavello and Giovanni Domenico d'Auria (1559), in the vestibule. The beautiful altar and recessed seats at either side of the choir are adorned with inlaid marbles by Fanzago (1646); the paschal candlestick (1585) is supported by nine sculptured figures from a tomb by Tino di Camaino.

In the north transept, the first chapel contains a contemporary copy, by Andrea Vaccaro, of the *Flagellation* by Caravaggio (1607); the original, formerly on the opposite wall, is now at Capodimonte. The second chapel houses the Spinelli monument (1546) by Bernardino del Moro. The north aisle chapels have many good 15C–17C tombs, including that of the poet, G.B. Marino (d. 1625) in the eighth, where there is a lovely group by Giovanni da Nola. In the fourth chapel, there is a *St John the Baptist* by the same artist and two paintings by Mattia Preti above. In the end chapel is a *Crowning of St Joseph* by Luca Giordano.

Beyond San Domenico Maggiore the Spaccanapoli changes its name to Via San Biagio ai Librai. The little church of **Sant'Angelo a Nilo** (Map 2; 7), on the south-east corner of the street, has a fine Renaissance doorway. It contains the **tomb of Cardinal Rinaldo Brancaccio**, the first Renaissance sculpture to be brought to Naples (in 1428). The tomb was executed in Pisa and sent by ship. The architectural framework, the Classical detail of which represents a clean break with Angevin Gothic style, is designed by Michelozzo; the relief of the *Assumption* is by Donatello.

Keeping straight on, you pass (left) an antique statue of the Nile. Also in this street are the former Palazzo Carafa, birthplace of Pope Paul IV, and (right; no. 121) the Palazzo Santangelo (1466), an elegant townhouse in the Tuscan style.

San Gregorio Armeno

A little to the north lies San Gregorio Armeno (Map 2; 7), a convent of Benedictine nuns, whose charming **cloister**, an oasis of tranquillity in contrast with the noise of the streets outside, is overlooked by the 17C campanile and a tiled cupola. At the centre of the garden is a Baroque glorification of the *Well of Samaria*, with figures of Jesus and the Samaritan woman, carved by Matteo Bottiglieri in 1730, which from a distance appear to be walking among the orange trees.

The **church** has a fine gilded ceiling of 1582, a gilded bronze *comunichino* (1610), and frescoes by Luca Giordano of the life of St Gregory. The nuns here were traditionally the daughters of noble families, accustomed to a life of luxury that they could hardly be expected to renounce. An 18C English traveller provides an account of a royal visit to the convent, and of the somewhat unusual conventual cuisine:

> The company was surprised, on being led into a large parlour, to find a table covered, and every appearance of a most plentiful cold repast, consisting of several joints of meat, hams, fowl, fish and various other dishes. It seemed rather ill-judged to have prepared a feast of such a solid nature immediately after dinner; for those royal visits were made in the afternoon. The Lady Abbess, however, earnestly pressed their Majesties to sit down; with which they complied...The nuns stood behind, to serve their royal guests. The Queen chose a slice of cold turkey, which, on being cut up, turned out [to be] a large piece of lemon ice, of the shape and appearance of a roasted turkey. All the other dishes were ices of various kinds, disguised under the forms of joints of meat, fish, and fowl, as above mentioned. The gaiety and good humour of the King, the affable and engaging behaviour of the royal sisters (Queen Maria Carolina and the Princess of Saxe-Teschen), and the satisfaction which beamed from the plump countenance of the Lady Abbess, threw an air of cheerfulness on this scene; which was interrupted, however, by gleams of melancholy reflection, which failed not to dart to mind, at sight of so many victims to the pride of family, to avarice and superstition. Many of those victims were in the full bloom of health and youth, and some of them were remarkably handsome.

Via San Gregorio is famous for its craftsmen, called *pastorari*, who make the figures for Neapolitan Nativity scenes (*presepi*).

From San Gregorio Armeno it is a short walk along Via San Biagio ai Librai to **San Giorgio Maggiore**, founded by St Severus in the late 4C, destroyed by fire in 1640 and rebuilt by the Baroque architect Cosimo Fanzago, who reversed its orientation. Just inside the entrance are the extensive remains of the apse of the early Christian basilica. These include a half-dome resting on three arches that spring from two columns. The Corinthian capitals were taken from ancient Roman buildings. The walls are made of alternating courses of brick and tufa, in the Roman manner.

A shepherd for your Christmas crib

There are at least three schools of thought regarding the making of the small clay 'shepherds' and other folk figures that appear in Neapolitan Nativity scenes. For many connoisseurs of local folklore, the only authentic kind are crude, roughly modelled figures; some are more concerned with detail (in this case much of the figures' authenticity is created by the colouring); others favour a combination of the two: plebeian power combined with a refinement worthy of a sculptor. Via San Gregorio also has many workshops where *pastori* (shepherds) in clay and wax, and wooden statues (usually of religious subjects) are restored. Several shops specialise in making elaborate bouquets of silk flowers, a tradition that dates back to the 18C.

The cathedral

The cathedral (San Gennaro; Map 2; 3), two streets north by the Via del Duomo, was founded in the 4C on the site of a Greek sanctuary dedicated to Apollo. The present building was begun in the French Gothic style by Charles I in 1294 and finished by Robert the Wise in 1323. The façade, shattered by an earthquake, was rebuilt by Antonio Baboccio in 1407; only his portal remains, however, the rest being mainly from a Gothic Revival design by Enrico Alvino (1877–1905). The remainder of the church was rebuilt after the earthquake of 1456.

The nave has an elaborate painted ceiling by Fabrizio Santafede (1621), supported on 16 piers incorporating over 100 antique columns of Oriental and African granite. On the walls above the arches are 46 saints, painted by Luca Giordano and his pupils. Over the central doorway are (left to right) the tombs of Charles I of Anjou (d. 1285), Clementina of Habsburg and her husband Charles Martel (King of Hungary and son of Charles II; d. 1296), all moved from the choir in 1599, when the monuments were executed by Domenico Fontana.

In the south aisle the **Capella di San Gennaro** or treasury, was built by Francesco Grimaldi in 1608–37 in fulfilment of a vow made by the citizens during the plague of 1526–29. It is closed by an immense grille of gilded bronze, based on a design by Cosimo Fanzago (1668). The luminous interior, faced with marble, has seven ornate altars, four of which have paintings by Domenichino (Domenico Zampieri), who began the frescoes; these were completed by Lanfranco after Domenichino had been hounded from the city. Above the altar on the right side is a large oil painting by Giuseppe Ribera. The balustrade of the main altar is by Cosimo Fanzago, with small doors by Onofrio d'Alessio. The sumptuous silver altar-front is by Francesco Solimena. In a tabernacle behind the altar are preserved the head of St Januarius (martyred at Pozzuoli), in a silver-gilt bust (1305), and two phials of his congealed blood, which, according to tradition, first liquefied in the hands of the sainted Bishop Severus, when the saint's body was translated to Naples from Pozzuoli. The miracle has been documented since 1389 and is reported to occur three times a year: on the first Saturday in May at Santa Chiara, and in the cathedral on 19 September and 16 December. The prosperity of the city is believed to depend on the speed of the liquefaction. The ceremony attracts an enormous crowd, and if you wish to be present you should secure a place near the altar in advance by applying to the sacristan. The fifth chapel on this side of the church contains the tomb of Cardinal Carbone (d. 1504) under a Gothic canopy.

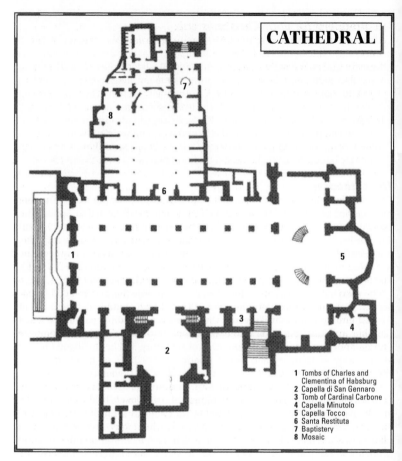

CATHEDRAL

1 Tombs of Charles and
  Clementina of Habsburg
2 Capella di San Gennaro
3 Tomb of Cardinal Carbone
4 Capella Minutolo
5 Capella Tocco
6 Santa Restituta
7 Baptistery
8 Mosaic

The outer chapel on the right of the **choir** (Cappella Minutolo), paved with majolica, contains the tomb of Cardinal Arrigo Minutolo, crafted by Roman marble-workers who came to Naples with Baboccio (1402–05), other tombs by a follower of Arnolfo di Cambio, and repainted 14C frescoes. The polyptych on the side altar is by Paolo di Giovanni Fei. The adjacent Cappella Tocco, also Gothic, has frescoes (1312; restored). Below the high altar is the **crypt of St Januarius** or Cappella Carafa (apply to the sacristan if closed), by Tommaso Malvito (1497–1506), perhaps the masterpiece of Renaissance art in Naples. Entrance is gained through two fine bronze doors. Within, note the delicate ornamental carving; likewise the statue of the founder, Cardinal Oliviero Carafa, near the altar which covers the remains of the patron saint. In the north transept (right to left) are: the tomb of Innocent IV (d. 1254), the opponent of Frederick II (*stravit inimicum Christi, colubrum Federicum*), a Cosmatesque work of 1315 partially reconstructed in the 16C; the tomb of Andrew of Hungary, murdered in 1345; and the cenotaph of Innocent XII (1703; buried in St Peter's, Rome).

Half-way along the north aisle is the entrance to the basilica of **Santa Restituta**, founded in the 4C on the site of a temple of Apollo, rebuilt in the 14C and again after an earthquake in 1688. This is the city's oldest surviving church. Recent restorations have revealed the bases of various columns and fragments of the early Christian mosaic floor. The 27 columns may be relics of the old temple. The ceiling painting, showing the *Arrival of Santa Restituta at Ischia*, is by Luca Giordano. Beneath the chapel is an archaeological area with Graeco-Roman remains, including fragments of a mosaic pavement (open 09.00–12.00, 16.30–19.00, Sun and holidays 09.00–12.00).

At the end of the right aisle is the **baptistery**, or chapel of San Giovanni in Fonte. It is square in plan, with a small dome, and is believed to be the earliest (5C) example of this form of building in Italy. It preserves fragmentary 5C mosaics. In the centre of the dome is a gold Cross on a blue background with white and gold stars, flanked by the Greek letters Alpha and Omega (signifying that Christ represents both the beginning and the end) and surmounted by the hand of God holding a gold crown (a sort of warning that those who aspire to the crown must first bear the cross). Around this runs a band of flowers, fruit, and birds, including a phoenix with a halo, symbol of the Resurrection. Eight radial bands containing flowers, fruit, festoons, and birds divide the cupola into eight wedges, four of which are well preserved. The mosaics depict a turquoise drapery with gilded detail, a vase with two birds, the *Women at the Sepulchre* (largely ruined), *Christ Saving Peter from the Waters*, the *Miracle of the Fish*, the *Tradito Legis* (haloed Christ giving the book of laws to St Peter), and *St Paul* (ruined).

The fifth and seventh chapels on the left contain beautiful 13C bas-reliefs in marble; in the sixth is a fine mosaic (1322) of the *Virgin Enthroned*, by Lello da Roma, showing Byzantine influence.

North of the cathedral

North of the cathedral, the Archbishop's Palace extends towards the church and convent of **Santa Maria Donnaregina** (Map 2; 3), often closed. Dating originally from the 8C, the church was reconstructed by Mary of Hungary, Charles II of Anjou's queen, following an earthquake of 1293. A second church, in the Baroque style, was added when the nuns were incorporated in the Theatine Order. The 14C church is reached from the Vico Donnaregina. The presbytery, stripped in 1928–36 of later additions, ends in a plain polygonal apse. To the right is the Cappella Loffredo, to the left the tomb of Queen Mary by Tino di Camaino and Gagliardo Primario (1326). In the nuns' choir, a rectangular gallery built over the west end of the church, are the celebrated **frescoes** by Pietro Cavallini and his pupils (begun 1308) representing the *Passion*, the *Legends of Saints Elizabeth of Hungary, Catherine and Agnes*, and the *Last Judgement*. Another Cavallini fresco may be seen above the choir roof. The 17C church, elaborate but in good taste, has coloured marbles, majolica pavements and paintings by Luca Giordano.

Further north, in Via San Giovanni a Carbonara is the little chapel of **Santa Monica**, with a Gothic doorway and a fine tomb by Andrea da Firenze (1432), and, adjoining it, **San Giovanni a Carbonara** (Map 2; 3), built in 1343 and enlarged by King Ladislas at the beginning of the 15C. Within, facing the entrance, is the Cappella Maroballo, a richly decorated Renaissance monument with 15C statues. Behind the high altar towers the tomb of Ladislas (d. 1414), a masterpiece by Marco and Andrea da Firenze; a three-storeyed composition of trefoil arches, statues and pinnacles. Beneath this, entrance is gained to the Cappella Caracciolo del Sole (1427), with Andrea da Firenze's unfinished tomb of Sergianni Caracciolo, steward of Joan II, stabbed at the Castel Capuano in 1432. On the walls are 15C frescoes by Leonardo da Besozzo and Perrinetto da Benevento. The tiled floor dates from 1440. To the north of the sanctuary is the marble-lined Cappella Caracciolo di Vico (1517), attributed to Tommaso Malvita; one of the more remarkable early 16C designs in Naples, this contains tombs and statues by Giovanni da Nola. In the sacristy is the tomb of Scipione Somma (d. 1553).

East of the cathedral, Via dei Tribunali ends at the **Castel Capuano** (Map 2; 4), also called *La Vicaria*. Begun by William I and finished by Frederick II, this was the residence of the Hohenstaufen and of some of the Angevin kings. It was here that Sergianni Caracciolo, lover of Joan II, was murdered in 1432. Much altered, the castle has been used as the Court of Justice since 1540.

Across the square to the north-east, near the little Renaissance church of Santa Caterina a Formiello, rises the beautiful **Porta Capuana**, between two mighty Aragonese towers. The extant exterior decoration of this former city gate was begun by Giuliano da Maiano and completed, after his death in 1490, by Luca Fancelli. Smaller and more delicate than Alfonso of Aragon's triumphal arch at the Castel Nuovo, it is a rare and particularly fine application of late 15C Florentine sculptural style to a town gate. The only other project of this kind undertaken during the Renaissance was Agostino di Duccio's gate at Perugia, dating from around 1475. The open space in front of the gate is used as a market-place and is always animated and colourful.

5 • From the cathedral to the castle

This walk loops back through Naples' historic centre and takes about 2 hours. In addition to visiting the area's major religious monuments—the **Girolamini**, **San Lorenzo Maggiore**, **San Paolo Maggiore**, the Capella di Santa Maria della Pietà dei Sangro (**Cappella Sansevero**) and **San Pietro a Maiella**—look into doorways along the way to discover the magnificent interior courtyards and open staircases of Neopolitan patrician homes. Keep an eye open as well for the details of religious architecture: in Piazza del Gesù Nuovo and Piazza San Domenico Maggiore, for instance, stand two *guglie*—respectively the **Guglia dell'Immacolata** and the **Guglia di San Domenico**—fanciful Baroque spires typical of Neopolitan taste, erected as neighbourhood ex-votos for deliverance from the plague of 1656.

South and west of the cathedral

Just south of the cathedral, in Via del Duomo, is the **Monte della Misericordia**, a charitable institution founded in 1601. In its octagonal church (1658–78; entrance in Via dei Tribunali) is a huge painting by Caravaggio of the *Seven Acts of Mercy* (1607). The pinacoteca has paintings by Fabrizio Santafede, Francesco de Mura, Luca Giordano and others (church and pinacoteca open by appointment; ☎ 081 446994).

Turn west (right) into the narrow Via dei Tribunali (Map 2; 7, 3, 4). The street broadens before the **Girolamini** church (or San Filippo Neri), built in 1592–1619 by Giovanni Antonio Dosio and Dionisio di Bartolomeo, with a façade by Fuga (c 1780), now blocked up. You enter from the side facing the cathedral.

The **interior** is richly decorated and has 12 monolithic granite columns; the fine wooden ceiling was damaged in 1943. Over the principal entrance is a fresco by Luca Giordano of *Christ Driving the Moneylenders from the Temple*. Near the last column on the left is the tomb of Giovanni Battista Vico (1668–1744), pioneer of the philosophy of history. The apse contains paintings by Corenzio; and the chapel of St Philip Neri (left) is decorated with frescoes by Solimena. In the convent, a small **pinacoteca** (open Mon–Sat 09.30–13.00; ☎ 081 449 139) has paintings by Andrea da Salerno, Guido Reni, Massimo Stanzione, and others. The entrance is opposite the cathedral at Via Duomo 142. Also interesting is the Girolamini's **library**, which occupies a fine room by Marcello Guglielmelli (1727–36).

San Lorenzo Maggiore

West of the Girolamini, in Via dei Tribunali, stands the Franciscan church of San Lorenzo Maggiore (Map 2; 7), one of Naples' more important religious buildings. This great medieval church was begun by Charles I to commemorate the victory at Benevento and completed by his son, Charles II. There is a fine doorway of 1325 in the 18C façade. It was here, on Easter Eve, 1334, that Boccaccio first saw Maria, natural daughter of Robert of Anjou, whom he immortalised as Fiammetta in his *Elegia a Madonna Fiammetta.*

Inside, the nave has been patiently restored to that Gothic simplicity retained unaltered by the transepts and the apse, which are by an unknown French architect of the late 13C. The **apse** has nine radiating chapels; the high altar is by Giovanni da Nola. There are two chapels of inlaid coloured marbles by Cosimo Fanzago—the third chapel on the right, the Cappella Cacace, 1643–55, and the magnificent, bold **Cappellone di Sant'Antonio**, c 1638, in the left transept—and a number of good medieval tombs, notably that of Catherine of Austria (d. 1323), first wife of Charles the Illustrious, possibly by Tino di Camaino. In the chapels are two large canvases by Mattia Preti: a *Crucifixion with St Francis and Franciscan Saints*, and a *Madonna and Child with St Clare and Franciscan Saints*. The cloister, where Petrarch experienced a storm of 1345, is entered through a 15C doorway to the left of the campanile (1507). The chapter house is supported on Roman columns. Beneath the cloisters archaeological excavations (open Mon–Sat 10.00–17.00, Sun and holidays 10.00–13.30) have unearthed traces of Greek, Roman and early medieval buildings (see p 120).

The 16C church of **San Paolo Maggiore** (Map 2; 7) stands on the site of a Roman temple dedicated to the Dioscuri—Zeus's twin sons Castor and Pollux, who were reunited after Castor's death by Zeus's decree that they live in the upper and lower worlds on alternate days. The front of the temple originally included six fluted Corinthian columns. It was used as the façade of the church until 1688, when it was destroyed in an earthquake. Today all that remains of the ancient edifice are two tall columns with their architrave and the bases of two more columns in front of the church, another column along the right side, and, beneath the statues of St Peter and St Paul, some weathered sculptures of the Dioscuri. The **Chiostro di San Paolo** incorporates 22 ancient granite columns. These did not apparently belong to the Temple of the Dioscuri.

In 1603 the church was rebuilt by Francesco Grimaldi. The spacious **interior** has alternating large and small bays in the nave arcade that create an unprecedented sense of movement. The transept and apse are less ingenious. The church is decorated with frescoes by Stanzione (1644), and (in the sacristy) by Solimena. There are also two interesting Baroque chapels: the first chapel left of the high altar, the Cappella Firrao (1641) by Dionisio Lazzari, decorated with inlaid coloured marbles and mother of pearl; and the fourth south chapel, the Cappella della Purità (1681) by Giovanni Domenico Vinaccia, again with inlaid coloured marbles and paintings by Massimo Stanzione.

The Sangro palaces and the Conservatorio

Continue along Via dei Tribunali. Reached by the Via Nilo (left) and Via De Sanctis is the **Cappella di Santa Maria della Pietà dei Sangro** (Cappella Sansevero, 1590; Map 2; 7), the tomb-chapel of the princes of Sangro di San Severo (open as a museum, daily except Tues, 10.00–17.00/19.00, Sun and holidays 10.00–13.30, ☎ 081 561 8470). It is remarkable for its 18C interior decoration, a profusion of frescoes, marbles and statuary. Most notable among the allegorical figures are those of *Modesty* (completely veiled), by Antonio Corradini, and *Disillusion* (a man struggling in the net of Vice), by Francesco Queirolo, a marvel of technical ability. The *Dead Christ*, a veiled statue in alabaster, by Giuseppe Sammartino (1753), is a work of astounding realism.

The neighbourhood is dominated by the **Sangro family palaces**. In Piazza San Domenico Maggiore, at no. 3, is the Palazzo del Balzo, built in the early 15C and renovated after the earthquake of 1688; the marble doorway and the court-yard, with its low arches and elegant first-floor portico, elements typical of the Catalan architectural style brought to Naples by the Aragonese, belong to the original building.

To the right, at no. 17, is an 18C palace of the Sangro family designed by Mario Gioffredo and remodelled by Luigi Vanvitelli. The impressive portico is carried by Greek columns unearthed during the construction of the building.

Across the square, at no. 12, is the palace of Giovanni di Sangro, with a fine 18C doorway. No. 9 is the Neapolitan residence of the main line of the family, Dukes of Torremaggiore and Princes of Sansevero. It was built in the early 16C and later enlarged. The magnificent portal was made by Vitale Finelli, on a design by Bartolomeo Picchiatti (1621). The stucco bas-reliefs of the foyer were exe-cuted by Giuseppe Sammartino, when the palace belonged to Raimondo di Sangro (1711–71), well known for his mechanical inventions.

Return to Via dei Tribunali and turn left, past the Policlinico, with its 17C chapel, and the ruined church of Santa Maria Maggiore, in front of which is the graceful chapel, in the Tuscan Renaissance style (1498), of the poet and human-ist Giovanni Pontano (1426–1503). Just beyond it is a decayed tower of Roman material and early construction, called the Campanile della Pietrasanta.

The church of **San Pietro a Maiella** was built in 1313–16. It contains a mag-nificent series of paintings by Mattia Preti (1656–61) depicting the life of Celestin V and the legend of St Catherine of Alexandria. Adjoining the church, in the former convent of San Pietro, is the **Conservatorio di Musica San Pietro a Maiella**. The oldest music school in existence, it was founded in 1537 and moved here in 1826. The conservatorio evolved from the gradual merger of four institutions—Santa Maria di Loreto, the Pietà dei Turchini, Sant'Onofrio a Capuana, and the Poveri di Gesù Cristo—established in the 16C and 17C as homes for foundlings. Catechism and singing were taught in these institutions.

Later on, when the private donations that were their only source of income dwindled or ceased altogether, the young musicians began to offer their services in churches, theatres, and private palazzi. In time, the conservatorio produced singers, instrumentalists, virtuosi, and composers, the demand for which was insatiable. Domenico Cimarosa, Nicola Antonio Porpora, Giovanni Paisello, Domenico and Alessandro Scarlatti, and Giovan Battista Pergolesi all graduated from the Conservatorio di Musica San Pietro a Maiella and its illustrious predecessors. The library has an extraordinary collection of autograph manuscripts and the museum has portraits of eminent musicians and memorabilia such as Martucci's piano and Rossini's desk. Both are opened on request.

From Via San Pietro a Maiella pass under Port'Alba to Piazza Dante (Map 2; 7). The difference in atmosphere is remarkable as you leave the narrow, dark lanes of the medieval city centre and enter the wide, luminous avenues of the Bourbon city. Piazza Dante and its environs are the subject of walk 7. You turn southwards (left) in Via Roma and left again in Via Santa Brigida to return to the Castel Nuovo, described in walk four.

THE VICEREGAL AND BOURBON CITY

History of viceregal and Bourbon Naples

The Spanish viceroys

During the period of the Spanish viceroys, and during that of the Austrian viceroys who followed them after 1707, Naples was oppressed by excessive taxation and delegated rule. Brigands terrorised the countryside, and pirates roamed the seas, discouraging trade and endangering travellers. The scarce attention that the Spanish governors dedicated to the provinces brought increasing numbers of immigrants to the capital, causing severe overcrowding—at the end of the century, Naples had 240,000 inhabitants; 300,000 counting the suburbs. Several viceroys, especially Don Pedro de Toledo (1532–53), tried to alleviate the problem by constructing new roads and buildings, but they were outpaced until the terrible plague of 1656 killed or dispersed half the population.

In the provinces, as in the capital, life was dominated by the burden of high taxes. Despite reduced profits, country dwellers devoted themselves as always to the cultivation of fields and orchards, and the sale of agricultural products remained their principal source of income. In the cities an educated and ambitious middle class climbed steadily to wealth and political power, the successful buying titles and estates (it is estimated that 17C Naples had at least 119 princes, 156 dukes, 173 marquesses and several hundred counts). In contrast to these, and to the virtual army of clergy (which came to represent one-fortieth of the population), stood the hoards of ragged beggars known as *lazzeroni*. On one hand, they were considered as thieving, treacherous, seditious, lazy, and corrupt ('There is not such another race of rogues as the common people of Naples', Henry Swinburne commented); but on the other their 'way of being satisfied with so little, of living on the air of time', was idealised, especially by northern Europeans, like Goethe, who attributed to them a peculiarly Mediterranean sense of freedom.

The French never fully accepted the idea that they had lost the Kingdom of Naples to the Spanish (a French army under Lautrex de Foix, Viscount of Lautrec, laid siege to the capital in 1528), and the Neapolitans themselves considered the foreigners tyrants whose unjust rule was to be cast off at the earliest possible opportunity. When Viceroy Pedro de Toledo levied a new round of taxes in 1535, the people appealed in vain to Spanish emperor Charles V, who passed through Naples on his way back from his Tunisian campaign. The city rose up with more success in 1547, when Don Pedro, as he was known, tried to revive an old project to introduce the Inquisition, in full swing at that time in Spain.

Naples is nevertheless deeply indebted to this energetic viceroy, for he undertook the most ambitious (and successful) urban development programme in the city's history. He curbed ecclesiastical building (a sticky political problem throughout the viceregal period) by acquiring property in the city centre so that tenement houses would not be torn down and convents built in their place. He alleviated day-to-day 'commuter' traffic by moving administrative offices out of the downtown area (it was by his order that the law courts were moved to their present seat at the Castel Capuano). Most importantly, he doubled the area available for building within the city walls by constructing a new set of fortifications that ran from the Castel Capuano, on the east side of town, to the Castel Sant'Elmo (rebuilt in the form of a six-pointed star) on the Vomero hill, and from the latter to the Castel dell'Ovo, on the sea to the west. In place of the now obsolete Aragonese walls, he built the great thoroughfare known as Via Toledo (now also Via Roma), in his honour.

To the west of this road he constructed a whole new quarter to house the Spanish garrison at Naples (the labyrinthine lanes and steep staircases that characterise this area have changed little since then and repay a visit). Via Toledo became the fashionable residential street of the aristocracy. At the southern end of the street, Don Pedro erected a new viceregal palace. It became known as the Palazzo Vecchio at the beginning of the following century when Viceroy Ferrante di Castro commissioned Domenico Fontana to build the magnificent Palazzo Reale, in anticipation of a visit by King Philip III that never took place.

Art and architecture in 16C–18C Naples

By the end of the 16C, Naples bristled with churches and convents—at least 400 of the former, not counting private chapels, and about 200 of the latter. At the beginning of the 18C, a petition was sent to the viceroy, urging him to prevent the clergy from acquiring more property, which suggests that Don Pedro de Toledo's nightmare remained a major political concern of his successors.

Yet the construction of churches and convents led to the great artistic flowering of the 17C and 18C, characterised by the presence of architects, sculptors, and painters who were famous throughout Europe—Cosimo Fanzago, Caravaggio, Giuseppe Ribera, Domenichino, Giovanni Lanfranco, Giovan Battista Caracciolo, Massimo Stanzione, Bernardo Cavallino, Salvator Rosa, Mattia Preti, Luca Giordano and others. In the words of a contemporary observer, 'That which seemed to us most extraordinary at Naples was the number and magnificence of the churches. It may be justly said, that in this respect it surpasses imagination ... If you would look upon rare pictures, sculptures, and the rarity of vessels of gold and silver, you need but go to the churches: the roofs, the wainscots, the walls are all covered with pieces of precious marble, most artificially laid together, or with compartments of basso relievo, or of joiner's work gilded, and enriched with the works of the most famous painters. There is nothing to be seen but jasper, porphyry, mosaic of all fashions, all masterpieces of art.'

Another connoisseur of the **Neapolitan Baroque**, the eminent British art historian Anthony Blunt, warned that 'the architecture of Naples is like its inhabitants: lively, colourful, and with a tendency not to keep the rules,' adding that 'if you go to Naples expecting its architecture to behave like that of Rome, you will be as surprised as if you expected its traffic to behave like Roman traffic, though you will be in less physical danger.' Many of the architects who worked in Naples at this time were not natives of the city—**Cosimo Fanzago**, the most imaginative architect and sculptor of the period, came from Bergamo—yet they all seem to have become acclimatised. They either ignored or, in some cases, anticipated the accomplishments of their contemporaries in Rome and elsewhere in Europe to a remarkable degree.

In ecclesiastical architecture, the most characteristic examples of the Neapolitan Baroque style are those that combine simple ground plans with rich, varied decoration; for Neapolitan architects were accomplished at carrying out elaborate decorative schemes without bringing confusion to the overall form of their buildings. Consequently, the great churches of 16C and 17C Naples show a lack of interest in new spatial forms that distinguishes them from the ecclesiastical architecture in Rome during the same period. It was not until the 18C and the Rococo creations of Domenico Antonio Vaccaro and Ferdinando Sanfelice that Neapolitan church architects displayed inventiveness in planning.

In domestic architecture, the pressure of overcrowding caused Neapolitans to build higher than their counterparts in other Italian cities. This permitted them to move the *piano nobile*, the most sumptuous level of lordly palaces, from the first to the second floor and to introduce the vast, monumental doorways or *portes cochères* which, together with the magnificent external staircases, are the most striking and individual features of Neapolitan palaces.

In painting, the 17C was dominated by the dark, dramatic styles of the Spaniard **Ribera** and of **Caravaggio** (the latter, exiled from Rome where he had killed a man in a moment of rage, and from Malta, where he had insulted the Grand Master of the Order of St John, took refuge in Naples until his involvement in a brawl in a waterfront tavern got him expelled from this city, too). Ribera and another foreigner, the Greek Corenzio, joined forces with the native Caracciolo in the 'Cabal of Naples' to prevent competition from northern Italy. Using methods of intimidation characteristic of the south—sabotage and the hired assassin—they hounded Annibale Carracci, the Cavaliere d'Arpino and Guido Reni from Naples, and Domenichino to his death (1641). After Caracciolo's death in the same year, and Ribera's in 1652, the soul of Naples found its most perfect expression in the exuberant compositions of **Luca Giordano**, who also frescoed the rooms of the Medici-Riccardi palace in Florence.

The first school of sculpture in Naples was founded in the 16C with

Girolamo da Santacroce and Giovanni da Nola and their pupils, alongside whom worked the Florentines Michelangelo Naccherino and Pietro Bernini (the father of Gian Lorenzo Bernini, of Vatican fame). In the 17C the fanciful **Fanzago** was prominent, followed in the 18C by the disciples of Gian Lorenzo Bernini and the technicians of the Cappella Sansevero.

The Bourbons

The last years of Spanish rule were undistinguished. The usual burdensome taxation roused the Neapolitans to insurrection (1647) under **Masaniello**, an Amalfi fisherman who was used as a figurehead by liberal reformers seeking to undermine the power of the nobility. The ensuing Parthenopean Republic lasted only a few months. In 1707, after the War of the Spanish Succession, Naples passed to the Archduke Charles of Austria (Charles VI), but the succession of viceroys was continued. In 1734, however, the Infante **Charles of Bourbon** (Charles VII, known as Charles III) seized Sicily and subsequently Naples and in 1744 defeated the Austrians at Velletri, near Rome, thus founding the Neapolitan Bourbon dynasty.

Charles (1734–59) was the first of the Bourbon kings who ruled Naples until the Unification of Italy in the 19C. Although not without his faults, he was certainly the most generous and enlightened member of this controversial dynasty. He restored order to public finance, curtailed ecclesiastical jurisdiction and immunities and taxed ecclesiastical property, then about one-third of the whole kingdom. He modernised the university and gave it a new home in the Palazzo degli Studi (now the National Museum). He also began the excavations at Pompeii and Herculaneum and published the finds in nine splendidly illustrated volumes. Sir James Gray, resident English minister at Naples, described Charles III as follows:

'The King of Naples is of a very reserved temper, a great master of dissimulation, and has an habitual smile on his face, contracted by a constant attention to conceal his thoughts; has a good understanding and a surprising memory, as his father had, is unread and unlearned, but retains an exact knowledge of all that has passed within his own observation, and is capable of entering into the most minute detail. He is in many things his own Minister, passing several hours every day alone in his cabinet.' (This and other contemporary accounts quoted in Sir Harold Acton's *The Bourbons of Naples*.)

Charles was an absolute ruler. 'He has too good an opinion of his own judgement, and is so positive and obstinate, that he is seldom induced to alter his resolutions,' says Gray. 'He has very high notions of his prerogative and his independency, and thinks himself the most absolute monarch in Europe.' Yet the king chose his servants wisely, in spite of his autocratic character. Beginning with Bernardo Tanucci, the Tuscan law professor whom he made his prime minister, and the architect Vanvitelli, who designed the magnificent palace and gardens of Caserta, he appointed to high office men of competence and unquestioned personal integrity.

Charles was uncommonly generous as a patron of the arts. His ambition to make Naples the most brilliant centre of musical culture in Italy (a position it would maintain throughout the 18C) culminated in the construction of the famous San Carlo Theatre, so named because it was inaugurated on his saint's day, November 4, 1738. These and many other improvements made in public and private life bear witness to this sovereign's acute mental vision, especially if one considers the brevity of his reign (25 years, compared to Frederick the Great's 46 and Louis XV's 59) and the sound political and economic position in which he left the kingdom at the end of it.

Charles's son and heir Ferdinand IV (1759–1825), or **Ferdinand I** as he called himself after the Congress of Vienna, unfortunately possessed few of his father's virtues. He reigned with the enthusiastic approval of the Neapolitan mob, which fondly called him 'Nasone' on account of his bulbous nose. To his peers he was known as the Lazzarone King, 'beloved by the vulgar Neapolitans ... from his having been born amongst them,' and inclined 'rather to seek the company of menial servants and people of the very lowest class than those of a better education.' Ferdinand was famous for his indolent bonhomie, his love of hunting, his inclination for crude practical jokes and his indifference to anything not directly related to his physical well-being. Sir William Hamilton, who succeeded Gray as resident English minister in 1764, called him insensitive, choleric, and obstinate, commenting that at the end of his regency 'the young King ... seems to have been more desirous of becoming his own master to follow his caprices, than to govern his kingdoms.' When Ferdinand married Maria Carolina of Austria (daughter of Maria Theresa and sister of Marie Antoinette), Sir William described the young husband as follows:

'On the morning after his nuptials, which took place in the beginning of May 1768, when the weather was very warm, he rose at an early hour and went out as usual to the chase, leaving his young wife in bed. Those courtiers who accompanied him, having inquired of his majesty and how he liked her: "*Dorme come un'ammazzata,*" replied he, "*e suda come un porco*" [she sleeps as if she had been killed, and sweats like a pig]. Such an answer would be esteemed, anywhere except at Naples, most indecorous; but here we are familiarized to far greater violations of propriety and decency... When the king has made a hearty meal and feels an inclination to retire, he commonly communicates that intention to the noblemen around him in waiting, to the favoured individuals, whom, as a mark of predilection, he chooses shall attend him. "*Sono ben pranzato,*" says he, laying his hand on his belly, "*adesso bisogna una buona panciata*" [I've eaten well, now I need to move my bowels]. The persons thus preferred then accompany his majesty, stand respectfully round him, and amuse him by their conversation during the performance.'

The Bourbons and the arts

The numerous building projects undertaken during the reigns of Charles III and his successors changed the face of Naples. The architects who were most involved in these initiatives (which to a large extent gave the city the appearance that it has today) were **Ferdinando Sanfelice**, **Domenico Antonio Vaccaro**, **Ferdinando Fuga** and **Luigi Vanvitelli**.

Other art forms also played a major role in making Naples a truly European capital. **Francesco Solimena** was the last and perhaps the greatest of the Neapolitan Baroque painters, Giuseppe Sammartino made hundreds of statuettes for the presepi that filled the churches and palaces of the city, and the Capodimonte Porcelain Works produced some of the finest porcelain in Europe.

War with France

At the outbreak of the French Revolution (1789) Ferdinand was not at first hostile to the new movement; but in the months that followed he was compelled to take action against republicanism at home and abroad. Every tremor that emanated from Paris was registered with particular anxiety in Naples, where the opposing forces had polarised more sharply than elsewhere in Italy. Rightly or wrongly, the Neapolitan liberals believed that they had suffered more under the Bourbons than the inhabitants of other regions of Italy had under their sovereigns; and they saw in the cause of revolutionary France the glimmer of hope for a free and united Italy.

The royalists, on the other hand, rallied in defence not only of their beloved Nasone, but also of their queen, the sister of the martyred Marie Antoinette. Sir John Acton, the French-born English baronet who became Ferdinand's prime minister, counselled prudence; but Maria Carolina, who exercised considerable influence over the king, maintained that the best defence was a strong offence. In 1793 Naples joined the first coalition against republican France, severely persecuting all those who were even remotely suspected of French sympathies. The eruption of Vesuvius in May 1794, widely regarded as an expression of divine wrath over the execution of Louis XVI and Marie Antoinette, won popular approval for the initiative.

In 1798, during Napoleon's absence in Egypt and after British admiral Horatio **Nelson**'s destruction of the French fleet at the Nile, Maria Carolina persuaded Ferdinand to go to war with France. The king promptly sent an army against French-held Rome, which fell without resistance. For a few ecstatic days that December, the Neapolitans occupied the Eternal City; but the French under Championnet quickly counter-attacked, recaptured Rome and entered Naples so swiftly that the royal family had to be evacuated by Nelson himself, with the aid of Emma Hamilton, the lovely young bride of Sir William, who had her servants carry the crown jewels of Naples aboard the British flagship before it set sail for Sicily.

On 23 January 1799 the second **Parthenopean Republic** was proclaimed, but like its predecessor (instituted during the revolt of 1647), it was short-lived. Governed by local liberals and precariously supported by the French army, it claimed dominion over the peninsular portion of the former kingdom while Ferdinand and Maria Carolina ruled Sicily from Palermo, protected by the British navy patrolling the Strait of Messina.

Although the republicans had noble aims, they were doctrinaire and unpractical, and they knew very little about the ordinary people in their own country. A violent anti-French feeling in southern Italy coincided with French defeats by Austro-Russian forces in the north. The following year the king and queen, with the aid of Nelson and Cardinal Ruffo, who swept up from Calabria with a band of peasants, brigands, convicts and a few soldiers, managed to reconquer the mainland provinces of the kingdom. The French and their republican allies found themselves confined to Naples proper, and before long surrendered on the promise of an amnesty. The foreigners were allowed to leave with the implicit blessing of St Januarius, whose liquefied blood was supposedly helped along in that year by the President of the Parthenopean Republic (who held the archbishop at gunpoint during the ceremony). Had the miracle not taken place, the French might well have been seized and lynched by the angry mob, whose sympathies were, as always, with their king.

A period of severe repression followed. Nelson, prompted by Emma Hamilton (now his mistress) and Maria Carolina, set out to eradicate all traces of the Parthenopean Republic, while the two husbands gave him carte blanche. Sir William was too busy lamenting the loss of much of his precious collection of antiquities, which had gone down with the ship that was transporting them to England, and Ferdinand had grown so fond of his Sicilian hunting grounds that he could barely be persuaded to return to the throne in Naples.

While the *lazzeroni* plundered the republicans' property to cries of *Chi tien pan' e vino ha da esser giaccobino* (He who has bread and wine is surely a Jacobin), Nelson unabashedly violated the terms of surrender, summarily executing the liberal leaders—among them Admiral Francesco Caracciolo, the philosopher Mario Pagano, the scientist Domenico Cirillo, and other prominent Neapolitan intellectuals.

Bonaparte and Murat

After Napoleon's successful second Italian campaign, Ferdinand was forced to grant another amnesty to the surviving republicans, to close all the ports of his kingdom to the British fleet and to allow a French garrison to be stationed deep within his territory, at Taranto. Even so, the Neapolitans could consider themselves lucky, for Napoleon had treated them more leniently than his other, more powerful enemies. Only when he found out that they had been negotiating with Austria with a view to joining the third coalition, did his patience give out: after the Austerlitz campaign (1805), he issued the famous proclamation, 'the Bourbon dynasty has ceased to reign,' and sent his brother Joseph to dethrone Ferdinand, who again fled to Sicily under the protection of a British fleet.

Joseph Bonaparte, though certainly no genius, was a cultivated and well-meaning man. He abolished the privileges of the nobility and the clergy and introduced several important reforms. But his taxes and forced contributions were resented, and royalist risings undermined his authority in much of the kingdom. In 1808 Napoleon gave Joseph the crown of Spain and appointed his colourful and flamboyant brother-in-law, **Joachim Murat**, king of Naples. Murat continued Joseph's reforms, quashed the Bourbon guerilla bands in the provinces and instituted a programme of public works that included new roads to Posillipo and Capodimonte.

Meanwhile, in Sicily, where King Ferdinand's extravagance and methods of police espionage rendered the royal presence a burden instead of a blessing, a bitter conflict broke out between the court and parliament. In 1812 Sir William Bentinck, the British minister, obliged Ferdinand to grant a liberal constitution. But the wind changed as a result of Napoleon's defeat at Waterloo, and the king dissolved parliament in May 1815, having concluded a treaty with Austria for the recovery of his mainland dominions.

A month later Ferdinand re-entered Naples, amid some discontent, while Murat fled to Corsica. At first the king abstained from persecution and received many of the usurper's officers into his own army. Murat, believing he still had a strong following in the kingdom, landed with a few companions at Pizzo in Calabria, but was immediately captured, court-martialled and shot.

The struggle for a constitution

Ferdinand proclaimed himself King of the Two Sicilies at the Congress of Vienna, incorporating Naples and Sicily into one state and abolishing the Sicilian constitution of 1812. In 1818 he signed a Concordat with the Church, reinstating ecclesiastical jurisdiction over education and censorship. But ideas of national unity and personal gain continued to make progress throughout the country. In 1820 a spontaneous insurrection, which began in the army at Nola, quickly took fire under the leadership of General Guglielmo Pepe, the mutineers demanding a new constitution while assuring the king of their continued loyalty. Ferdinand, feeling himself helpless to resist, agreed to their demands. These events seriously alarmed the powers responsible for the preservation of the peace in Europe, who at the Congress of Troppau (October 1820) issued the famous protocol affirming the right of collective 'Europe' to interfere to crush dangerous internal revolutions.

The following year Ferdinand abandoned his agreement with the rebels, and the powers authorised Austria to march an army into Naples and restore the autocracy of the monarchy. General Pepe was sent to the frontier at the head of 8000 men, but was defeated by the Austrians at Rieti on 7 March 1821. A period of severe repression ensued, the inevitable State trials resulting in the usual harvest of executions and imprisonments.

The conditions of the country continued to worsen under Ferdinand's successors, **Francis I** (1825–30) and **Ferdinand II** (1830–59). Francis I refused several opportunities to strike an alliance with Victor Emmanuel, King of Piedmont and Sardinia, for the division of Italy. But the desire for a constitution became ever more fervent. Revolution broke out in Sicily on 12 January 1848, under the leadership of Ruggero Settimo, while demonstrations also shook Naples. On 28 January 1848, King Ferdinand II granted the constitution; but the following spring he refused to open parliament and sent an army under Carlo Filangieri against the revolutionary government of Palermo, which fell on 14 April 1848. Open despotism followed, during which liberal sympathisers were condemned to prison or the galleys for life. Thousands of respectable citizens were thrown into prison, including Luigi Settembrini, Carlo Poerio and Silvio Spavento.

Garibaldi's victory over the Bourbon rule

On 5 May 1860 the Piedmontese general **Giuseppe Garibaldi** embarked at Quarto, near Genoa, with 1000 hand-picked followers on board two steamers, and sailed for Sicily. On 11 May the expedition reached Marsala and landed without opposition. Garibaldi was somewhat coldly received by the astonished population, but he set forth at once for Salemi, where he issued a proclamation assuming the dictatorship of Sicily in the name of Victor Emmanuel, with Francesco Crispi as Secretary of State. On 15 May he attacked and defeated 3000 Bourbon loyalists under General Landi, at Calatafimi. The news of this brilliant victory revived revolutionary agitation throughout the island. By a clever ruse, Garibaldi avoided General Colonna's forces, who were expecting him on the Monreale road, and entered Palermo from Misilmeri, receiving an enthusiastic welcome.

After three days' street fighting the Bourbonist commander, General Lanza, not knowing that the Garibaldians had scarcely a cartridge left, asked for and obtained a 24-hour armistice (3 June). Garibaldi went on board the British flagship to confer with the Neapolitan generals Letizia and Chrétien; then he informed the citizens by means of a proclamation of what he had done, and declared that he would renew hostilities on the expiration of the armistice. Lanza became so alarmed that he asked for an unconditional extension of the armistice, which Garibaldi granted, and 15,000 Bourbon troops embarked for Naples on 7 June, leaving the revolutionaries masters of the situation.

The news of Garibaldi's astonishing successes entirely changed the situation in the capital, and on 25 June 1860 the king again granted a constitution. He appealed to Great Britain and France to prevent Garibaldi crossing the Straits of Messina and only just failed. On 19 August Garibaldi crossed with 4500 men and took Reggio by storm. He was soon joined by the rest of his troops—15,000 in all—the Neapolitan army collapsed before Garibaldi's advance, and the people rose up in support almost everywhere. As the Piedmontese entered Naples Francis II retired to Gaeta, where he capitulated in October 1860 after a last, desperate stand on the Volturno.

6 • Pizzofalcone and environs

This walk leads through the historic area south and west of the Castel Nuovo (Map 2; 11). The first part takes in some of the city's more notable public buildings, which grew up as the Spanish viceroys and their Austrian successors, anxious to mark the distinction between their rule and that of the Aragonese, moved the civic centre of Naples from the Castel Nuovo to the area immediately to the south-west. Highlights in this area include the **Palazzo Reale**, the centre of viceregal government, and the monumental church of **San Francesco di Paola** with its square, today called Piazza del Plebiscito. The latter is now closed to traffic, allowing you to imagine the extraordinary visual and symbolic impact that such an immense open space had, when first built, on the inhabitants of the crowded city.

The second part of the itinerary explores the city's finest old residential quarter, **Pizzofalcone**, which stands on a hill (the site of the ancient Parthenope) between the gulf shore and Via Chiaia, Naples' elegant shopping street. Here some truly spectacular examples of Neapolitan palace architecture (as well as one or two small churches supported by aristocratic families) can be seen. Finally, the walk ends on the busy Via Partenope, a scenic boulevard carved out of the slums when the old fishing port of Santa Lucia was 'improved' in the late 19C and now home to many of the city's luxury hotels.

The total length of the route is about 3km; it may be walked comfortably in just over two hours. Care should be taken when crossing the street at all major intersections, as Neapolitan drivers rarely stop at crossings.

From the **Castel Nuovo**, follow Via Vittorio Emanuele II south-west to Via San Carlo, which branches right. On the left, at the entrance to the Giardino Reale and the Biblioteca Nazionale (see below), are groups of *Horse Trainers*, by Baron Clodt, presented by Czar Nicholas I. Further along on the left lies the Teatro San Carlo (Map 2; 11).

The Teatro San Carlo

This is the largest opera house in Italy (open to visitors by appointment except on performance days, ☎ 081 797 2331). It was built for Charles of Bourbon by the contactor and impresario Angelo Carasale on a plan by court architect Giovanni Antonio Medrano. Begun in March 1737, it was finished in the following October and opened to the public on 4 November, the king's saint's day in the Roman Catholic calendar. In the decades that followed it was remodelled a number of times, notably in 1762 by Giovanni Maria Bibiena, in 1768 by Ferdinando Fuga, in 1797 by Domenico Chelli and in 1812 by Antonio Niccolini (who added the courtyard and loggia). Destroyed by a fire on the night of 12 February 1816, the old theatre was rebuilt in its present form by Niccolini (who, it is said, inserted hundreds of clay pitchers in the walls in order to improve the acoustics). The foyer on the garden side was added in 1938.

The **concert hall**, seating 3000, is famous for its perfect acoustics. The 185 boxes are arranged in six tiers; above the centrally located Royal Box, the fifth and sixth tiers open up in the manner of an amphitheatre. Throughout the theatre red upholstery and gold trim combine to create an opulent, festive atmosphere. The ceiling is adorned with a painting of *Apollo Introducing the Greek, Latin, and Italian Poets to Minerva*, by Giuseppe Cammarino, and the curtain bears a representation of *Homer and the Muses with Poets and Musicians*, the work of Giuseppe Mancinelli. The premières of Rossini's *Lady of the Lake* and *Moses*, Bellini's *Sonnambula* and Donizetti's *Lucia di Lammermoor* were all performed on this stage.

Opposite the Teatro San Carlo is the main entrance to the arcades of the cross-shaped **Galleria Umberto I** (1887–90, rebuilt since 1945), less lively than in former days. The dome is 56m high and is one of the first major iron-and-glass constructions in Italy. The street ends in the busy Piazza Trieste e Trento (Map 2;11), still generally known as Piazza San Ferdinando, with a modern fountain in the centre. The square lies at the junction of several important streets: to the north runs Via Toledo; to the west, Via Chiaia (described below). Turning south you come immediately to Piazza del Plebiscito (Map 2; 10, 14), a wide hemicycle with a Doric colonnade and frigid equestrian statues of Charles III of Bourbon and Ferdinand IV, by Antonio Canova and Antonio Calì. Here rises the church of **San Francesco di Paola**, founded by Ferdinand IV to celebrate the restoration of the Bourbon dynasty after the Napoleonic interlude and designed by Pietro Bianchi (1817–32) in obvious imitation of the Roman Pantheon. The north and south ends of the piazza are occupied respectively by the Prefecture and the Palazzo Salerno, residence of the military commandant.

The Palazzo Reale

On the east side of the square is the majestic façade (167m wide) of the Palazzo Reale (Map 2; 14), built by Domenico Fontana in 1600–02, in anticipation of a visit by Philip II of Spain. Occupied only by viceroys, it was restored in 1838–42 after a fire, and again after damage in the Second World War. The statues in the ground-floor niches represent the eight dynasties of Naples: Roger the Norman, Frederick II the Swabian, Charles I of Anjou, Alfonso of Aragon, Charles V of Austria, Charles III of Bourbon, Joachim Murat, and Victor Emmanuel II of Savoy.

King Charles and music in Naples

The Teatro San Carlo was built at a time when Italy was the centre of European musical culture and Naples was the centre of music in Italy, thanks to Charles III's generous patronage of composers and performers. Rousseau, in his famous essay on genius, advised aspiring musicians to go to Naples to study; his eminent contemporary Lalande declared that music could be discerned in the gestures, the inflection of the voice and even the cadence of everyday conversation in Naples. 'Music is the triumph of the Neapolitans,' he wrote. 'Everything there expresses and exhales music.'

In the light of these considerations it is hardly surprising that Charles should have desired to provide his capital with a large, splendid opera house, even though he had no personal passion for this particular art form. Indeed, as one observer noted, the king often talked during one half of the performances and slept during the other—a habit that scandalised his foreign guests. The 18C English traveller Samuel Sharp has left a description of the original appearance of the theatre (which today is lost), as well as an amusing account of the Neapolitan manner of enjoying a performance.

'The King's Theatre, upon the first view, is, perhaps, almost as remarkable an object as any man sees in his travels. The amazing extent of the stage, with the prodigious circumference of the boxes and the height of the ceiling, produce a marvellous effect on the mind ... Notwithstanding the amazing noisiness of the audience during the whole performance of the opera, the moment the dances begin there is a universal dead silence, which continues so long as the dances continue. Witty people, therefore, never fail to tell me, the Neapolitans go to see not to hear an opera ... It must be confessed that their scenery is extremely fine; their dresses are new and rich; and the music is well adapted, but, above all, the stage is so large and noble, as to set off the performance to an inexpressible advantage ... It is customary for gentlemen to run about from box to box between the acts, and even in the midst of the performance; but the ladies, after they are seated, never quit their box the whole evening. It is the fashion to make appointments for such and such nights. A lady receives visitors in her box one night, and they remain with her the whole opera; another night she returns the visit in the same manner. In the intervals between the acts, principally between the first and second, the proprietor of the box regales her company with iced fruits and sweetmeats.' (Acton, cit.)

The palace interior is now the **Museo dell'Appartamento Storico del Palazzo Reale** (Royal Apartments), open daily except Wednesday 09.00–20.00; ☎ 081 794 4021.

The **Cappella Palatina**, attributed to Cosimo Fanzago (1668), stands at the foot of the grand staircase (1651, restored 1837), which ascends to various fine halls with period furniture, tapestries, paintings, and porcelain, preceded by the small Teatro di Corte, built by Ferdinando Fuga in 1768 for Maria Carolina of Habsburg's wedding to Ferdinand IV and restored after war damage in 1950. Here also are the original bronze doors of the Castel Nuovo, by Guillaume le Moine and Pietro di Martino (1462–68), on which six reliefs depict Ferdinand of Aragon's struggle with the barons. The cannon-ball lodged in the lower relief on the left door is a relic from the naval battle between the French and the Genoese; the doors and other booty en route to France from Naples were recovered and returned to the city.

Part of the great building houses the **Biblioteca Nazionale Vittorio Emanuele III**, or National Library, open weekdays 09.00–18.30, Sat 09.00–13.30; entrance in Via Vittorio Emanuele III. The library was founded in 1734 and is the most important in southern Italy. It holds over 1,500,000 volumes and 17,000 incunabula and manuscripts. Annexed are the Lucchesi-Palli Library of Music and Dramatic Literature, and the J.F. Kennedy Library of American Studies.

Pizzofalcone

From the north-west corner of Piazza del Plebiscito the steep quarter of Pizzofalcone (Map 2; 13) is reached by Piazza Carolina and Via Serra, which lead to the piazza and church of **Santa Maria degli Angeli**, by the cleric, Francesco Grimaldi. The church, begun in 1600, is built to one of the more daring designs of its day. The architect's clear, decisive treatment of solids and voids and his handling of architectural ornament are well ahead of contemporary developments in Naples or even in Rome. The third south chapel contains a *Holy Family* by Luca Giordano; the second on the north an *Immacolata* by Massimo Stanzione.

From the piazza, turn left and ascend Via Monte di Dio. In the Middle Ages this street was lined with convents, but in the 18C it became the centre of a fashionable residential area. Today it is known for its aristocratic palaces, the most noteworthy of which is **Palazzo Serra a Cassano** (nos 14–15), built in the early 18C to plans by Ferdinando Sanfelice and recently restored. With two courtyards and a scenographic double staircase, it is perhaps the most impressive of all Neapolitan palaces. Also interesting are **Palazzo Sanfelice** (nos 4–5), **Palazzo Caprocotta** (no. 74), and **Palazzo Carafa di Nola**, the courtyard of which gives on to a lovely garden.

Via Parisi leads west to the former convent of the Nunziatella, now a military college, with an 18C church begun by Ferdinando Sanfelice at the request of the Jesuits.

Returning by Via Parisi, and continuing along the north side of Palazzo Serra a Cassano, turn left into Via Egiziaca a Pizzofalcone. The Baroque church of **Santa Maria Egiziaca a Pizzofalcone**, attributed to Cosimo Fanzago, is sumptuously adorned with marble (over the high altar is a painting of the saint by Andrea Vaccaro). Just beyond it Via della Solitaria descends to the Istituto d'Arte, with a small museum of applied arts (open by appointment; ☎ 081 764 7471). From here, steps go back down to Piazza del Plebescito.

Via Chiaia and the Borgo Marinaro

Walk through to Piazza Trieste e Trento turning west towards Via Chiaia (Map 2; 14). You pass under a bridge linking Pizzofalcone with Via Nicotera; nearby a lift ascends to Santa Maria degli Angeli and Pizzofalcone (see above). Further down the street, **Palazzo Cellamare**, begun in the 16C and restored in the early 18C, stands on a bend, beyond which (right) is the church of **Santa Caterina** (c 1600), with the simple tomb of Cleotilde of France (1755–1802). From here Via Santa Caterina opens immediately into Piazza del Martiri, with a column by E. Alvino (1868) commemorating the martyrs of four revolutions (1799, 1820,

1848, and 1860). To the left, Via Morelli leads to the west end of the Galleria della Vittoria (see below). Here, turn south to the waterside and follow the shore eastward along Via Partenope (Map 2; 14), a broad promenade enjoying a magnificent view across the gulf.

On the right is the **Borgo Marinaro**, the ancient island of *Megaris*, once the site of a villa belonging to the Roman patrician Lucullus. It was later joined by a pier to the shore to form the little Porto di Santa Lucia. Restaurants line the quay. On the island is the **Castel dell'Ovo** (Map 2; 11), a fortress dating from 1154. The odd name (literally *ovo* is egg) is a corruption of *lowe* (German for lion); the lion was the emblem of Frederick II, whose troops were garrisoned here. After Frederick's death in 1250, the castle became the prison of the luckless Conradin and of Beatrice, daughter of Manfred, the last of the Swabians. Restored in 1975, it is now used for meetings, lectures, and exhibitions. The Museo di Etnopreistoria, operated by the Club Alpino Italiano, is open by appointment (☎ 081 764 5343).

At the end of Via Partenope stands the huge Baroque **Fontana dell' Immacolatella** (1601), with statues by Pietro Bernini and caryatids by Naccherino. Turn left into Via Nazario Sauro, which affords a further splendid **view** right across to Vesuvius with a wide terrace overlooking the sea halfway along.

The **Santa Lucia** quarter is reached by any of the streets leading inland. Once highly characteristic, with fishermen's houses and the old shellfish market, it is now quite ordinary. It is crossed by the broad Via Santa Lucia, which takes its name from the church of Santa Lucia, rebuilt after 1945.

At the end of Via Nazario Sauro, from which Via Cesario Console ascends back to Piazza del Plebiscito, go along Via Ammiraglio Acton for the Molosiglio, the embarkation point for pleasure boats. Up to the left, at the bottom of the hill, is the mouth of the Galleria della Vittoria, a tunnel 623m long, opened in 1929, beneath the hill of Pizzofalcone. Via Acton bears right here, skirting the south side of the Palazzo Reale, to the Molo Beverello, where you can catch ferries for Ischia, Procida, Capri, and Sorrento. With the Castel Nuovo high above the harbour, you reach the wide quayside where the largest passenger liners dock; the **Stazione Marittima Passeggeri** (Map 2; 11) was built on the Molo Angioino, designed by C. Bazzani in 1936 and rebuilt after 1945.

7 • The road to Capodimonte

This walk explores the neighbourhoods of central Naples that were transformed, during the 17C and 18C, to accommodate the numerous new inhabitants—soldiers, aristocrats, and clergy—who thronged the city. It follows the long, almost straight thoroughfare that connected the Palazzo Reale down by the sea, with the huge Bourbon hunting lodge on the hill at Capodimonte, now home to the **Museo e Gallerie Nazionali di Capodimonte**, one of the larger and more opulent museums in Europe. The 4km uphill trek from one palace to the other takes roughly 2hrs, including stops. Traffic permitting, bus no. 24 makes the run in about half an hour. If you wish, you can make a small detour (described below) to visit Naples' luxuriant **botanical gardens**.

Via Toledo

Via Toledo, so called after the Spanish viceroy who had it built, Don Pedro de Toledo, begins on the north side of Piazza Trieste e Trento (Map 2;11). This is Naples' high street. Although closed to traffic, it is filled by a noisy and lively throng all day, especially in the late afternoon. Numerous streets and alleys diverge from it: those on the right are broad and modern up to the south side of Piazza della Carità, descending through the business district of Carità towards the harbour, while those on the left are narrow and often squalid, ascending steeply, sometimes in steps, towards Corso Vittorio Emanuele. There are plans to build a parallel road to the west, which may eventually cut through the chess-board of populous streets with their lofty tenements.

On the corner facing Piazza Trieste e Trento is San Ferdinando, a Jesuit church. Begun by Giovanni Giacomo Conforto and altered by Cosimo Fanzago, it was again modified and renamed, after expulsion of the order in 1767, in honour of Ferdinand I, whose morganatic wife, Lucia Migliaccio (d. 1826) is buried within. Beyond the Galleria Umberto I, on the right, is the church of **Santa Brigida** (Map 2; 11), built in 1612 in honour of St Brigid of Sweden. Here Luca Giordano is buried; his

A fish stall in the Quartieri Spagnoli, off Via Toledo

ingenious perspective paintings add apparent height to the dome. Luca was known to his contemporaries as 'Fast Hand Luke' (*Luca Fa Presto*) because of his ability to turn out works like these with amazing speed. The painting of *St Francis Receiving the Stigmata*, in the transept, is by Massimo Stanzione.

The Banco di Napoli, further on, has been in business since the 16C. Behind its modern building lies the new but architecturally uninteresting business quarter centred on Piazza Matteotti (Map 2; 7, 11) but taking its name from Piazza della Carità. The church of Santa Maria della Carità, at the north-west corner of the piazza, contains paintings by various 18C artists.

Via Roma and Via Pessina

North of Piazza della Carità Via Toledo changes its name to Via Roma. At the intersection with Via Benedetto Croce stands the Baroque Palazzo Maddaloni (right), an ancient building redesigned by Cosimo Fanzago. A bit further up, on the opposite side of the street, is the church of **Santo Spirito**. Altered between 1757 and 1774 by Mario Gioffredo, it rivals Vanvitelli's Annunziata as the most masterful expression of the new Classical taste that grew up in Naples under Charles III. Within, Gioffredo's main order of powerful columns almost swamps the earlier interior. But the architect remains faithful to the Neapolitan tradition in such devices as the choir gallery above the main altar, the design of the altar itself and the overall proportions of the building. At the sides of the entrance are the tombs of Ambrogio Salvio and Paolo Spinelli, by Michelangelo Naccherino. In the south transept, a *Madonna and Saints* by Fedele Fischetti. In the apse, *Pentecost*, by Francesco de Mura. The first north chapel has a *Purification*,

Conversion of St Paul, and *Fall of Simon Magus*, by Fischetti; the fourth chapel, a *Madonna del Soccorso* by Fabrizio Santafede. The tomb on the left is also by Naccherino. In the fifth chapel is a *Baptism of Christ*, by Santafede. The façade, which is much less advanced than the interior, adheres to the contemporary Roman type.

Opposite Santo Spirito is the Palazzo d'Angri, by Luigi and Carlo Vanvitelli (1755), where Garibaldi stayed in 1860. Continuing up Via Roma you pass (left) Via Tarsia, which leads to Montesanto Station and the Montesanto Funicular. Alessandro Scarlatti is buried in the church of Santa Maria di Montesanto, opposite. Via Roma ends in Piazza Dante (Map 2; 7), enclosed on the east side by Luigi Vanvitelli's hemicycle and the 17C Port'Alba; the monument to **Dante Alighieri** (1265–1321), medieval Italy's most famous poet, prose writer, literary theorist, moral philosopher and political thinker, dates from 1872.

Beyond Piazza Dante Via Roma becomes Via Pessina. Three blocks on, Via Conte di Ruvo (Map 2; 7) leads right to Via Bellini and the **Accademia di Belle Arti** (with a small gallery, open daily 09.00–14.00). Across the street is the little church of **San Giovanni Battista**, with paintings by prominent 18C artists. These include *St Mary Magdalene*, by Mattia Preti, above the entrance; *Annunciation*, by Andrea Vaccaro and *Immacolata*, by Bernardo Cavallino, in the first south chapel; *Crowning of the Virgin* by Massimo Stanzione, in the south transept; *St John the Baptist*, by Luca Giordano, above the high altar; and *St Luke Painting the Virgin*, by Andrea Vaccaro, in the first north chapel. In Via Santa Maria di Costantinopoli, the church of the same name has a noteworthy ceiling by Belisario Corenzio.

Via Pessina continues northwards to the Museo Archeologico Nazionale, Naples' immense museum of antiquities, described on p 126. Beyond the Museo Archeologico Nazionale, Via Santa Teresa degli Scalzi and Corso Amedeo di Savoia wind their way up the hill of Capodimonte. At Via Santa Teresa 94, the writer Giacomo Leopardi died in 1837.

A detour to the botanic gardens

About 1km north-east of the museum, along Via Foria are the **botanic gardens** (Map above 2; 4). The gardens were founded by Joseph Bonaparte in 1807. They cover about 12 hectares (open Mon–Fri 09.00–14.00; ☎ 081 449759) and contain an early 19C Neo-classical greenhouse in addition to numerous varieties of **exotic plants**. Sant'Antonio Abate, the church of a 14C hospital for lepers opposite the north end of the gardens, retains 14C and 15C frescoes. Just beyond is the Albergo dei Poveri, a workhouse built by Ferdinando Fuga for Charles III in 1751. The immense façade, 345m long, occupies the north side of Piazza Carlo III. From the other side of the piazza the busy Corso Garibaldi descends to Piazza Garibaldi (1km), the Stazione Centrale and the docks.

8 • The palace and park at Capodimonte

The Palazzo Reale di Capodimonte (Map above 2; 3), begun in 1738 and completed in 1838, is magnificently situated in a fine park, enjoying a wide view of Naples and Campania. In May 1957 the palace was opened as the new seat of the **Museo e Gallerie Nazionali di Capodimonte**, comprising the National

Gallery of Naples (formerly in the Museo Nazionale) and important exhibitions of tapestries, furniture, armour, porcelain, and ivories from the royal collections. A large section on the arts in Naples from the 13C to the 18C and an exhibit of drawings has recently opened on the second floor. The store-rooms and restoration laboratories on the third floor have been turned into galleries housing a good collection of 19C Italian paintings, formerly in the Accademia di Belle Arti, and a selection of photographs and contemporary art.

Getting there

The palace is situated at the north end of Via Toledo and its extensions, 4km from Piazza del Municipio and 3.5km from Piazza Garibaldi (Stazione Centrale). Regular bus services run from the city centre to the museum. Nos 137 and 160 from Piazza Dante to the Porta Piccola entrance; no. 24 from Piazza Vittoria via Piazza Dante, stops at the Porta Grande, the more usual entrance to the magnificent **park** (open 09.00–dusk; free). Kilns from the famous porcelain works founded by Charles of Bourbon in 1739, which were working until 1805, may be seen within. The entrance to the palace is through the most northerly of the building's three courtyards. The **museum** is open Tues–Sun 08.30–19.30; ☎ 081 749 9111. The Gabinetto Stampe e Disegni (print and drawing room) on the mezzanine floor is opened by appointment. It has 2500 drawings and 22,000 prints. Refreshments are available in the museum café.

Intended by Charles III of Bourbon to be the most important summer hunting-lodge in Europe, the **Palazzo Reale di Capodimonte** was begun in 1738 by Giovanni Antonio Medrano, and the park was designed by Ferdinando Sanfelice. The construction by Joachim Murat of the Sanità bridge and of a new approach road stimulated further enlargements, which were completed by Antonio Niccolini for Ferdinando II in 1838. After the decline of the Bourbons the palace became a favourite haunt of Victor Emmanuel II, and in 1906–47 of the Dukes of Aosta.

First floor ~ the Farnese collections

The fabulous **Farnese collections**, which constitute the core of the museum's holdings, have been brought together in the monumental rooms on the main floor. The arrangement highlights the museum's oldest and most important collection of master paintings and drawings, inherited by Charles of Bourbon from his mother, Elisabetta Farnese. The rooms are reached by the grand staircase designed by Tommaso Giordano. At the bottom, introducing the richness of the collection, is the impressive *Jupiter Shooting Arrows at the Titans*, a group in biscuit porcelain by Filippo Tagliolini.

    Room 1. Vestibule.

    Room 2. Works celebrating the Farnese family and its most important member, Pope Paul III. Here are some famous portraits by **Titian** including *Paul III* (1543), *Paul III with his Nephews Alessandro and Ottavio Farine* (1545–46), a painting of great psychological insight in which the young men are shown as continuing the family's ecclesiastical and secular traditions; *Cardinal Alessandro Farnese* (1545–46), famous for the detail of his gloves, which suggests that Alessandro (cardinal at the age of fourteen) was something of a dandy; *Charles V*; *Philip II*. Also in this room is a portrait of *Cardinal Alessandro Farnese*, future Pope Paul III (1509–11), attributed to **Raphael** and painted on the occasion of Alessandro's election as Bishop of Parma, the first step in his climb to power; accompanied by **Giorgio Vasari's**, *Allegory of Justice, Truth and Vice*; a fine Medici tapestry showing the *Sacrifice of Alexander*, after a cartoon by Francesco Salviati (post 1542); and **Andrea del Sarto's** *Leo X with Two Cardinals* (1525) showing the pope with his cardinal-nephews Giulio de'Medici (the future Pope Clement VII) and Luigi de'Rossi. This is a copy of the famous work by Raphael, secretly commissioned by Ottaviano de'Medici and sent in guile to Federico Gonzaga instead of the original, which Federico had demanded as a gift from Clement VII. The composition is meant to express approval of the transfer of ecclesiastical power along blood lines. Two marble portraits of *Paul III* and five bronzes after the antique (busts of *Caracalla, Lucius Verus, Elius Verus, Antinous and Hercules Strangling Snakes*), all by **Guglielmo della Porta**, form a complement to the paintings.

Room 3. Masaccio, *Crucifixion* from a polyptych painted in 1426 for the private chapel of Giuliano da San Giusto, a wealthy notary, in the Carmine in Pisa. The polyptych is now dismembered, its parts on display in London (main panel: the *Enthroned Madonna Holding the Christ Child*, eating grapes as a prefiguration of the Passion), the Getty Museum in Malibu (*St Andrew*); Pisa (*St Paul*) and Berlin (the three predella panels and four side panels with saints).

Room 4. Famous cartoons from the private collection of Fulvio Orsini, librarian and artistic adviser to Ranuccio and Alessandro Farnese. **Michelangelo**, group of *Soldiers* (c 1546), a cartoon for the fresco of the *Crucifixion of St Peter* in the Vatican; copies after Michelangelo attributed to **Pontormo** and Hendrik van der Broeck; Giovanni Francesco Penni, *Madonna del Divino Amore*; **Raphael**, *Moses Before the Burning Bush* (c 1514), a cartoon for another Vatican fresco, in which the scale and sculptural quality of the figure recall Michelangelo's ceiling in the Sistine Chapel (unveiled in 1512).

Room 5. Masolino, *Assumption of the Virgin* and *Foundation of the basilica of Santa Maria Maggiore* (c 1428), two panels of a triptych commissioned by Pope Martin V from Masolino and Masaccio (the latter died before they were completed for that church).

Room 6. The paintings exhibited here illustrate the development of the Early Renaissance in Tuscany and Umbria. **Sandro Botticelli**, *Madonna and Child with Two Angels* (1468–69); **Perugino** (or after), *Madonna and Child* (1496–98); and a tondo by Sebastiano Mainardi depicting the *Madonna and Child with Angels*, belong to the Farnese Collection. **Luca Signorelli**, *Adoration of the Child* (1493–98); **Filippino Lippi**, *Annunciation with St John the Baptist and St Andrew* (1483); Lorenzo di Credi, *Adoration of the Child* (1523); and fragments of an early altarpiece by Raphael painted with an assistant for the church of Sant'Agostino at Città di Castello (1501) are of Bourbon provenance. The small *Christ Carrying the Cross* by the Emilian painter Francesco Zaganelli, showing the influence of Dürer, is also interesting.

Room 7. *Objets d'art* and paintings from the eclectic collection of Cardinal Stefano Borgia (1731–1804) including Bernardo Daddi, *Madonna and Child*; a beautiful triptych by **Taddeo Gaddi**; **Andrea Mantegna**, *St Eufemia* (1454); Bartolomeo Caporali, *Madonna and Child*; and panels by Bartolo di Fredi.

Room 8. 15C and 16C Venetian art. **Giovanni Bellini**, *Transfiguration* (1478–79), perhaps the artist's masterpiece, showing perfect command of light and atmosphere and an extraordinary humanisation of Christ; **Lorenzo Lotto**,

Madonna and Child with St Peter Martyr (1503), the artist's earliest known work, commissioned by Bishop Bernardo de'Rossi as a votive offering for having escaped a murder plot; *Bernardo de'Rossi, Bishop of Treviso* (1505), a work of unmitigated realism; **Andrea Mantegna**, *Francesco Gonzaga* (1406–62), cardinal at seventeen, later portrayed by the artist in the *Camera picta* in Mantua; Bartolomeo Vivarini, *Enthroned Madonna with Saints*; Alvise Vivarini, *Madonna and Child with Saints Francis and Bernardino da Siena*; portrait of the mathematician *Luca Pacioli* attributed to Jacopo de'Barbari (1495).

Room 9. Painting in Rome in the first half of the 16C. **Giulio Romano**, *Madonna della Gatta* (c 1523), clearly indebted to Raphael in its compositional scheme; school of Raphael (Giovanni Francesco Penni), *Madonna del Divino Amore*; school of Raphael, *Holy Family* (Madonna of the Veil); **Sebastiano del Piombo**, two wonderful portraits of *Clement VII* (one showing the pope seated, his red robe against a green background; the other, a small-scale profile of the head only, painted in very dark colours, interesting for that age) and the *Madonna of the Veil* (1533–35), drawing on the styles of Raphael and Michelangelo; Marcello Venusti, copy after Michelangelo, *Last Judgement* (the copy was executed before Daniele da Volterra overpainted the fresco to cover the nakedness of the figures).

Room 10. Painting in Florence in the first quarter of the 16C. Franciabigio, *St Bartholomew*; *St Bruno*; **Iacopo Pontormo**, *Scene of Sacrifice* (c 1540), a mysterious exercise in anticlassicism executed in grisaille; Fra Bartolomeo, *Assumption of the Virgin with Saints John the Baptist and Catherine* (1516); Brescianino, *Madonna and Child with the Infant St John*; Domenico Puligo, *Madonna and Child with the Young St John*; Francesco Salviati, *Gentleman* (c 1545), a work of singular psychological intensity, possibly the artist's self-portrait; **Rosso Fiorentino**, *Young Man* (c 1527), thought to represent Parmigianino; Agnolo Bronzino (attributed), *Lady*; copy after Bronzino, *Madonna and Child with St Anne and the Infant St John*.

Room 11. 16C Venetian painting. **El Greco**, *Giulio Clovio* (1571–72), the famous Croatian illuminator, holding his *Golden Book* (now in the Pierpont Morgan Library in New York); the freedom of the brushwork suggests the influence of Titian, under whom El Greco worked on his arrival in Venice in 1567; *Young Man Lighting a Candle with a Coal* (*El soplón*, c 1575), in which the artist brings Venetian colourism to bear on a subject celebrated by Pliny in the *Naturalis Historia*; **Titian**, *Danäe* (1544–46), painted for the private rooms of Cardinal Alessandro Farnese and representing the story, from Ovid's *Metamorphoses*, of a young princess seduced by Zeus in the form of a shower of gold; the provocative sensuality of the figure contributes to the ambiguity of the scene, which some scholars believe depicts Alessandro's mistress; *Young Lady* (1545–46), thought by some to represent the artist's daughter, Lavinia Vecellio, and by others, Alessandro's young lover, subject of the Danäe; *Mary Magdalen*; Palma Vecchio, *Sacra Conversazione with Two Donors*; Schiavone, *Christ and Herod*.

Room 12. 16C Emilian (Parma, Ferrara) painting. **Correggio** (Antonio Allegri called Correggio), *St Anthony Abbot*; *St Joseph and a Devotee*; *Madonna and Child* (La Zingarella); *Mystic Marriage of St Catherine*; Michelangelo Anselmi, *Madonna and Child with Mary Magdalen and St Apollonia*; *Nativity*; *Adoration of the Shepherds*. Anonymous (Michelangelo Anselmi?), *Gentleman* (Giovan Battista Castaldi); Girolamo Mazzola Bedoli, *Holy Family with St John the*

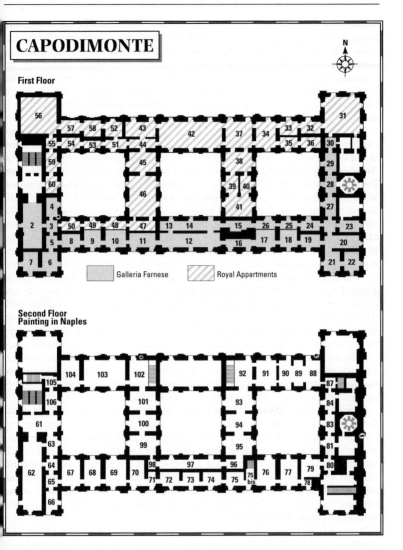

CAPODIMONTE

N

First Floor

Galleria Farnese   Royal Appartments

Second Floor
Painting in Naples

Baptist and Angels; *St Claire*; *Portrait of a Tailor*; *Annunciation*;
Parmigianino, *Galeazzo Sanvitale* (1524), showing the spatial ambiguity and
disquieting effects of light and shadow on which the artist built his reputation;
Holy Family; *Young Woman* (1530–35) identified with the courtesan Antea,
possibly the artist's mistress during his years in Rome; *Lucretia*; Nicolò
dell'Abate, *Young Man with a Book*; Girolamo da Carpi, *Gentleman in Black*
(Girolamo de Vincenti?); **Sofonisba Anguissola**, *Self-portrait at the Spinet*;
Lelio Orsi, *St George and the Dragon*; *Sacrifice of Abraham*; Bastianino,
Madonna and Child; Scarsellino, two landscapes with mythological scenes;

Dosso Dossi, *Holy Family*; *Sacra Conversazione*; *Madonna and Child with the Infant St John*; *Madonna and Child with a Bishop Saint*; Garofalo, *St Sebastian*; *Madonna and Child with the Saints Jerome and Sebastian*; Giovanni Battista Benvenuti (l'Ortolano), *Deposed Christ*.

Rooms 13–14. These make up a sort of *Wunderkammer*, or room of marvels, displaying a wealth of precious and rare objects. On the entrance walls between rooms 12 and 13 are a portrait miniature of *Settimia Iacobacci* by Giulio Clovio and an amber plaquette of the *Holy Family with the Infant St John*. The paintings in room 13 belong to the artistic climate of the Farnese court at Parma: Girolamo Mirola, *Intervention of the Sabine Women in the Battle Between the Romans and Sabines*; Jacopo Zanguidi (Bertoja), *Madonna and Child*; Jan Sons, *Tabula Cebetis Thebani*; *Baptism of Christ*; *St Cecily* and the *Vision of St John*, *Loves of the Gods* (ceiling). Renaissance bronze statuettes are displayed here and in the adjoining room 14: **Giambologna**, *Rape of the Sabines* (1578), a small bronze prototype of the marble group in Florence, commissioned by Duke Ottavio for his study; *Mercury*; Giacomo della Porta, *Cupid*; **Francesco di Giorgio Martini**, *David* (1475–85), combining iconographic traditions of the Middle Ages (David as elderly prophet) and the Renaissance (as young hero); L'Antico (Pier Jacopo Alari Bonacolsi), *Venus*; Baccio Bandinelli, *Cleopatra*; Niccolò Roccatagliata, *Minerva*; bronzes by Riccio (Andrea Briosco); and a female figure by Alessandro Vittoria. Also in room 14 are the **Farnese casket** (1548–61), a box in gilt silver, lapis lazuli, enamel and carved crystal made for Cardinal Alessandro Farnese by Manno di Bastiano Sbarri and Giovanni Bernardi da Castelbolognese; as well as the crystal Farnese bread-tray incised with a drunken Silenus from a design by Annibale Carracci. The display cases contain Renaissance medals (Pisanello, Matteo de'Pasti among others), plaquettes, incised crystals, ambers, ivories, goldsmiths' work (centrepiece of *Diana the Huntress* (1610), by Iacob Miller the Elder, and the majolica Farnese dining service made for Cardinal Alessandro in the Castelli manufactory.

Room 15. Paintings of the *Seven Deadly Sins* by the Flemish artist Jacques de Backe.

Room 16. 15C and 16C Lombard painting. Boccaccio Boccaccino, *Adoration of the Shepherds*; **Bernardino Luini**, *Madonna and Child*, showing a strong Leonardesque influence; Cesare da Sesto, *Christ of Sorrow with Cardinal Oliviero Carafa in Prayer*; Giampietrino, *Madonna and Child, St John the Baptist* and *St Jerome*; Alessandro Bonvicino (Moretto da Brescia), *Christ at the Column*; Camillo Procaccini, *Jesus at Gethsemane*; Giulio Cesare Procaccini, *Madonna and Child with Angel*.

Room 17. Flemish and German painting: **Peter Bruegel the Elder**, *The Misanthrope* (1568); the Flemish proverb at the bottom reads, 'As the world is so untrustworthy, I am in mourning'; *The Blind Leading the Blind* (1568), illustrating the well-known New Testament parable ('when one blind man leads another, both will fall into the ditch'); Herri met de Bles (Civetta), two landscapes with the Good Samaritan; *Coastal Landscape*; *Landscape with Temptation of Christ*; *Landscape with Storm at Sea*; *Moses Before the Burning Bush*; anonymous Italianising Flemish artist, *Deposition*; anonymous Franco-Flemish artist, *Young Prince*; Bernard van Orley, *Charles V as a Young Man*; Marinus van Reymerswaele, *The Avaricious*; workshop of Konard Witz, *Sacra Conversazione*.

Room 18. Joachim Beuckelaer, *Street Market*; *Country Market*; *Vendor of*

Exotic Animals; *Game Vendor*; *Butcher's Shop*; *Fish Market*; Marten de Vos, *Jesus Among the Youths*.

Room 19. This room is almost entirely dedicated to the art of the Bolognese brothers Annibale and Agostino Carracci and their cousin Ludovico. Founders at Bologna of the Accademia degli Incamminati, they called for a return to the classical and balanced art of Raphael, avoiding the contrived and intellectual style of late Mannerism. In 1595 Annnibale was called to Rome by Cardinal Odoardo Farnese to decorate the gallery in the family's palace with the *Loves of the Gods*. His art proved to be extremely influential on the first generation of Baroque painters working in Rome in the early 17C, many of whom followed their master from Bologna. Particularly noteworthy are: **Agostino Carracci**, *Lute Player* (Orazio Bassani?); *Arrigo Peloso, Pietro Matto and Amon Nano* (c 1598), representing three characters from the Roman court of Cardinal Odoardo Farnese, Pietro the buffoon, Rodomonte the dwarf, and Arrigo Gonzalez, the 'wild man of the Canary Islands'; **Annibale Carracci**, *Marriage of St Catherine* (c 1585), a masterpiece of Classicism commissioned by Ranuccio Farnese as a gift to his brother, Cardinal Odoardo; *Musician* (Claudio Merulo); workshop of Annibale Carracci, *Annunciation* (recto); *Madonna and Child with St Francis* (verso); **Ludovico Carracci**, *Rinaldo e Armida* (1593), an entertaining literary subject drawn from Tasso's *Gerusalemme Liberata*.

Room 20. The paintings exhibited here show the influence of Bolognese art in Rome in the late 16C and early 17C. Sisto Badalocchio, *Deposition*; Agostino Carracci, *St Jerome*; *Holy Family with St Margaret*; Annibale Carracci, *Satyr* (perhaps directed against Caravaggio; the smiling head in the corner is a portrait of the artist); *Bacchus*; *River Allegory*; *Hercules at the Crossroads* (1596), executed for Cardinal Odoardo Farnese and showing the choice between the 'easy way' of earthly pleasure, indicated by *Voluptuousness*, and the rocky path to glory, pointed out by *Virtue*; *Pietà* (1599–1600), a painterly homage to Michelangelo's sculpture in St Peter's; *Rinaldo e Armida*; *St Jerome*, unfinished; Giovanni Lanfranco, *Jesus Served by the Angels*; *Assumption of Mary Magdalene*; *Noli Me Tangere*.

Room 21. This room is dedicated to the art of the Emilian painter **Bartolomeo Schedoni**, (1578–1615) who worked almost exclusively for the Farnese court at Parma. Noteworthy are the *Announcement of the Massacre of the Innocents*; *Cupid*; *Charity*; *St Sebastian Healed by the Pious Women*; portrait of *Vincenzo Grassi* (shoemaker of Ranuccio I Farnese).

Room 22. 17C Emilian painting, with highlights on **Guido Reni** and **Lanfranco** as key examples of two opposite trends: a return to Classicism on the one hand and early Baroque solutions on the other. Guido Reni, *Atalanta and Ippomene*: the painting is based on Ovid's *Metamorphoses* and shows the moment in which the nymph Atalanta, who challenged her suitor Ippomene to a race, stops to pick the golden apples that he had intentionally thrown to the ground in order to win the competition; the *Four Seasons*. Giovanni Lanfranco, *Madonna and Child with Saints Charles Borromeo and Bartholomew*; *Madonna and Child with Saints Mary of Egypt and Margaret*; Michele Desubleo, *Ulysses and Nausicaa*.

Room 23. Bedroom of Francesco I and Maria Isabella decorated *alla Pompeiana* by Antonio Niccolini (1830).

Rooms 24–26. Flemish and Netherlandish paintings of the 17C including **Antonie van Dyck**, *Crucifix*; *Portrait of an Old Man*; Pieter Paul Rubens, *St*

George and the Dragon (post 1603). Landscapes by Sebastiaen Vrancx, Pieter Brueghel the Younger, and others. Still lives of game and hunting scenes by David de Koninck.

Room 27. More 17C Emilian painting. Domenico Zampieri (**Domenichino**) *Guardian Angel*; Francesco Albani, *St Elisabeth in Glory*; Lodovico Carracci, *Fall of Simon Magus*; Alessandro Tiarini, *Madonna and Child with Angels*; Carlo Maratta, *St Peter*.

Room 28. Late 17C Tuscan painting. Luca Cambiaso, *Venus and Adonis*; *Death of Adonis*; Ludovico Cardi (Cigoli), *Pietà*; Domenico Cresti (Passignano), *Deposition*.

Room 29. Carlo Saraceni, six landscapes with scenes from Ovid's *Metamorphoses*; Claude Lorrain (Claude Gellée), *Landscape with the Nymph Egeria*; Giovanni Battista Gaulli (Baciccia), *Cardinal Louis of Vendôme*; Bernardo Strozzi, male portrait; Orazio de'Ferrari, *St Peter's Denial*; Pietro Testa (Lucchesino), *Emperor Titus Consulting the Hebrew Prophets*.

Room 30. Sebastiano Ricci, *Christ and the Centurion*; *Christ and the Adulteress*; *Assumption of Mary Magdalen*; *Virgin Interceding for the Souls in Purgatory*; Giuseppe Maria Crespi, *Holy Family with Saints*.

The Royal Apartments

From room 30 you pass directly to the Royal Apartments, a rich showcase of European decorative arts from the 18C and the first half of the 19C.

Room 31, the **Sala della Culla** (cradle room), has an elliptical floor from Tiberius' villa at Capri (extensively restored); two 19C history paintings by Vincenzo Camuccini, two landscapes by Alexandre Hyacinthe Dunoy and Jean Joseph Xavier Bidauld; Neapolitan clocks and furniture, a model of the Temple of Isis at Pompeii.

The next two rooms are decorated with paintings and furniture from the time of Charles of Bourbon.

Room 32. Giovanni Paolo Panini, *Charles of Bourbon Visiting Pope Benedict XIV in the Coffee House of the Quirinal Palace*; *Charles of Bourbon Visiting St Peter's in Rome* (both 1745); Antonio Sebastiani, *Charles of Bourbon in Hunting Costume*; English black lacquer furniture (first quarter of the 18C) with chinoiseries; an English clock by Joseph Martineau (second half of the 18C).

Room 33. Wonderful landscapes by Antonio Joli, *Departure of Charles III Viewed from the Sea*; *Departure of Charles III Viewed from the Dock* both painted in 1759 when Charles, upon the death of Ferdinand VI, became King of Spain and left Naples; *Ferdinand IV with his Court on Horseback*; Claude-Joseph Vernet, *Charles of Bourbon Hunting Ducks at Lake Licona*; Anton Raffael Mengs, *Ferdinand IV* as a child painted in 1759 when he became king of Naples at the age of eight, following the abdication of his father, Charles of Bourbon. English red lacquer furniture (first half of the 18C) with chinoiseries; two Neapolitan sedan chairs (second half of the 18C).

Room 34 has an important portrait collection of royal couples, including Francesco Liani, equestrian portraits of Charles of Bourbon and Maria Amalia of Saxony; Ferdinand IV and Maria Carolina of Austria; Francisco Goya, *King Charles IV of Spain and Queen Maria Luisa of Spain*; Neapolitan furniture of the first quarter of the 19C.

Rooms 35–36 display an outstanding collection of porcelain, including the fabulous **Servizio dell'Oca** from Capodimonte (1739–95). The service takes its name from the putto strangling a goose (after a Roman figure group in the Capitoline museums), which decorates the lids. It should actually be called the Neapolitan View service, as it is decorated with a series of views, probably inspired by prints or paintings by Antonio Joli and Philip Hackert. The miniatures on the pieces were executed by various artists, first amongst them Giacomo Milani. The set, comprising some 300 pieces, was commissioned by Ferdinand IV from the royal manufactory at Capodimonte in 1793–95. Notable among the other pieces are a series of biscuit figurines of various subjects executed by Filippo Tagliolini; an altar set comprising a porcelain Crucifix and six candelabra by Giuseppe Gricci; a déjeuner set from the *Real fabbrica* (royal manufactory) of Naples, decorated with Etruscan subjects taken from a series of prints by Tischbein and d'Hancarville; a déjeuner set from Vienna sent by Queen Maria Carolina to her husband Ferdinand IV, while she was in Vienna between 1800-1801 (remarkable quality); and 4 Meissen white figure groups.

Room 37 is the **Sala da Pranzo** (dining room). At the two ends of the room are two large scale family portraits: Angelika Kauffmann, *Family of Ferdinand IV* and Giuseppe Cammarano, *Family of Francis I* (son of Ferdinand IV).

Room 38–41, housing the Raccolta De Ciccio, a collection of 1300 *objets d'art*, were closed at the time of writing.

Adjoining the Sala da Pranzo is **room 42**, the **Salone delle Feste**. This is the ballroom, adorned in pale blue, pastels and gold by Salvatore Giusti (1835–38); the wall paintings, curtains and furnishings have been restored to their original splendour. The room also has three large crystal chandeliers and a collection of musical instruments.

The adjoining rooms contain an elaborate *Aurora* in Capodimonte biscuit, by Filippo Tagliolini (c 1807), paintings of Vesuvius by Pierre Jacques Volaire, landscapes by Jacob Philipp Hackert (1737–1807) and a beautiful, anonymous *presepio* (crib). **Room 45** has tapestries depicting stories about Henry IV and a display of precious objects in cases. From here you enter the famous **armoury** of the Farnese family (rooms 46–51), notable for its fine examples of 15C–17C ceremonial armour.

Room 52 is the **Salottino di Porcellana**, a little room covered with Chinoiseries entirely executed in Capodimonte porcelain in 1757–59. It was originally intended for the Palace of Portici and was moved here in 1866. **Room 53** has portraits of infant royals by Elisabeth Vigée-Lebrun; and a *View of the Gulf of Naples* by Antonio Joli. Portraits of Napoleon and Murat hang in **room 54**; the following room contains a plaster replica of Canova's Letitia Bonaparte, c 1808 (the original in marble is at Chatsworth, Derbyshire). **Room 56** has five paintings by Vincenzo Camuccini and Neo-classical sculptures including a relief with the personification of *Night* by Bertel Thorvaldsen. In the centre is a round Neo-classical table designed by Antonio Niccolini and inlaid with a late antique mosaic. **Room 57** has landscapes of Neo-classical and Romantic taste as well as some remarkable examples of Empire furniture. **Room 58**. Paintings and Neapolitan furniture of the early 19C (noteworthy is the Mechanical table 'in the Herculaneum style' and the *Jardinnière* table with miniatures depicting views of Naples and market scenes). **Room 59**. Church furnishings in coloured marble executed by Matteo Bottiglieri (17C) for the church of the Trinità delle Monache. **Room 60**. Cyborium in coloured marbles and precious stones by Cosimo Fanzago. This fine example of miniature architecture was completed in 1624 and cost the enormous sum of 5000 ducats.

Second floor ~ painting in Naples from 1200 to 1700

This vast section (44 rooms) illustrates the development of painting in Naples, at the hands of local artists and of foreigners working in the city. The core of the collection was formed during the 19C when many paintings entered the Royal Museum following Napoleon's suppression of monasteries. Many others were donated, acquired, or relocated, for reasons of conservation, from Neapolitan churches.

Room 61 has a wonderful alabaster polyptych with the *Passion of Christ*, produced in Nottingham in the first half of the15C; and a tapestry with the *Deposition*, from the workshop of Pieter van Aelst (1531–33).

Room 62 houses the splendid **Arazzi d'Avalos**, a set of seven tapestries illustrating the famous battle of Pavia (1525) fought between Charles V and François I for supremacy on Italian soil and ending with the imprisonment of the French king. The tapestries were executed in Brussels, in the workshop of Bernaert van Orley, and were donated by the city's administration to Charles V. In 1571 they passed into the hands of Francesco Ferdinando d'Avalos, the commander who had orchestrated the emperor's victory, and in 1862 were donated by his descendants to the Italian State.

Room 63. Works of the 13C including Giovanni da Taranto, *St Dominic*; and a panel with a *Madonna* (c 1290) by an unknown Campanian painter working in a Byzantine style.

In the next three rooms are works produced under the Angevin kings. They reflect the refined taste of the French court that brought to Naples figures such as Giotto and Simone Martini, as well as other Tuscan artists. **Room 64**. Lippo Vanni, *Christ the Redeemer*; Andrea Vanni, *St Jacob*; two works by the Neapolitan Roberto di Oderisio, *Crucifixion* and *Madonna of Humility*, from the church of S. Domenico Maggiore. **Room 65**. Master of the Franciscan temperas, *Madonna of Humility*; Niccolò di Tommaso, *St. Anthony Abbot and other Saints* (signed and dated 1371). **Room 66** has the stunning *St Louis of Toulouse Crowning Robert of Anjou*, by **Simone Martini** (signed and dated 1317) painted for the church of S. Lorenzo Maggiore.

In the next three rooms are paintings executed under the Aragonese. **Room 67**. Important works by **Colantonio** including *St Jerome in his Study* (from S. Lorenzo Maggiore); *Polyptych of St. Vincent Ferrer* (from the church of St. Peter Martyr) and *Deposition* (1455–60) from S. Domenico Maggiore. The latter shows a strong influence of Rogier van der Weyden, whose work was known to Colantonio through a set of Flemish tapestries acquired in 1455 by Alfonso of Aragon. Also in this room are the *Polyptych of St Severinus*, by the master of the same name; and a *St Anthony Abbott*, by the Master of San Giovanni da Capestrano. **Room 68** has works by Spanish and northern Italian artists working at the court of Naples, as well as the beautiful *Polyptych of Archangel Michael* by the Neapolitan Francesco Pagano. **Room 69**. Central Italian and Tuscan artists working at Naples including **Pinturicchio**, *Assumption of the Virgin* (from the church of Monteoliveto); Matteo di Giovanni, *Massacre of the Innocents* (1468); Guido Mazzoni, a bronze portrait of *Alfonso of Aragon* (or *Ferrante II*).

Room 70. Andrea da Salerno, *Deposition*; *St. Benedict and Doctors of the Church*; Cesare da Sesto, *Adoration of the Magi*; Giovan Filippo Criscuolo, *Polyptych with the Adoration of the Child*. **Room 71**. 16C sculpture.

Room 72. Works by Polidoro da Caravaggio, *Deposition*; *Road to Calvary*; etc.
Room 73. Mannerist works inspired by Polidoro da Caravaggio; Pedro Machuca, *Death and Assumption of the Virgin*.

Room 74. Tuscan mannerism, including Giorgio Vasari, *Presentation at the Temple*; Sodoma (Giovanni Antonio Bazzi), *Resurrection*; Marco Pino, *Adoration of the Magi*.

Room 75. Titian, *Annunciation* (1557). **Room 75 bis.** Giovanni Bernardo Lama, *Road to Calvary*; Silvestro Buono, *Pietà with Saints*.

Room 76. Flemish Mannerists and their Neapolitan followers. **Room 77.** Late 16C artists of Tuscan inspiration: Scipione Pulzone, *Annunciation*; Ippolito Borghese, *Deposition*; Fabrizio Santafede, *Adoration of the Shepherds*.

Room 78 has the fabulous *Flagellation* by **Caravaggio** (1607). **Room 79.** Caravaggeschi (Battistello Caracciolo, among others). **Room 80** gives access to the collection of Contemporary art (see below), while **room 81, 83, 84** have an exhibition of prints and drawings from the 16C to the 18C.

Room 87 opens the extensive section on 17C painting (the golden age of Neapolitan art), with the famous *Judith and Holophernes* by **Artemisia Gentileschi** (1612–13). A second version of this painting hangs in the Pitti, in Florence. **Room 88–90.** More paintings by Artemisia Gentileschi; Battistello Caracciolo; Massimo Stanzione; as well as Simon Vouet's *Circumcision*; and a number of works by **Giuseppe Ribera**, in particular *St Jerome and the Angel of Judgement*. **Room 91.** Pietro Novelli's version of *Judith and Holophernes*; Giuseppe Ribera, *Drunken Silenus*. **Room 92.** Works by Matthias Stomer heavily influenced by Caravaggio. **Room 93.** Works by the second generation of 17C Neapolitan painters. Caravaggio's inspiration is still recognisable, but it is mediated by the Classical achievements of the Bolognese school and French masters such as Poussin and Vouet. Noteworthy in this sense are Andrea Vaccaro, *Triumph of David*; *Adoration of the Golden Calf*; **Francesco de Rosa**, *Susanna and the Elders*; Francesco Guarino, *St Agatha*; *St Cecily*.

Room 94. Works by the Neapolitan Bernardo Cavallino (1616–56), in particular *Female Singer*; *St Cecily in Ecstasy* (the only signed work of the artist, dated 1645). **Room 95.** Genre paintings including battle scenes by Micco Spadaro and Aniello Falcone.

Room 96. Still lives by the Tuscan Bartolomeo Bimbi; the Genoese Grechetto (Giovan Benedetto Castiglione); and the German Christian Berentz (in collaboration with Carlo Maratta author of the figures). **Room 97** has an important collection of **still lives** by Neapolitan artists such as Luca Forte; Giovanni Battista Recco; Paolo Porpora and Giovanni Battista Ruoppolo.

In **rooms 98–101** is the **Collezione d'Avalos**, constituted in the 17C by Prince Andrea d'Avalos and given to the Italian State in 1862. It includes still lives by Luca Forte, Giuseppe Recco and Giovanni Battista Ruoppolo; and paintings by Giuseppe Ribera (*Apollo and Marsyas*); Francesco de Rosa (*Bath of Diana*); Luca Giordano and Andrea Vaccaro (*Rinaldo and Armida*).

Room 102. Paintings by **Mattia Preti**, active in Naples from 1653.

Room 103. Paintings by **Luca Giordano**: perhaps the most important and certainly the most prolific Neapolitan artist of the second half of the 17C.

Room 104 introduces 18C painting with **Francesco Solimena**, whose painting of *Aeneas and Dido* (1739–41) takes up the teachings of Luca Giordano. To the same generation belong Paolo de Matteis and the eclectic Domenico Antonio

Vaccaro (painter, sculptor and architect). Francesco de Mura, pupil of Solimena, takes to the extreme his master's work using an exuberant style that announces the Rococo. **Room 105** has a number of *bozzetti* or studies for ceiling frescoes by the aforementioned artists. **Room 106**. Rococo painting by Corrado Giaquinto and Pietro Bardellino, as well as a series of witty portraits of the aristocratic world by Gaspare Traversi.

Third floor ~ 19C art

The recently opened gallery offers a selection of 19C art ranging from the history paintings of Domenico Morelli (*The Sicilian Vespers*; *The Iconoclasts*) to the Naturalism of Filippo Palizzi. Also well represented are the Realist painters, in particular Gioacchino Toma, Francesco Paolo Michetti, and Michele Cammarano. Some rooms are dedicated to the Impressionist paintings of Giovanni Boldini, Antonio Mancini and Giuseppe de Nittis. Also exhibited are sculptures by Vincenzo Gemito, and paintings by Francesco Saverio Altamura and Giuseppe Pellizza da Volpedo. Interesting is the presence of a portrait, *The Carelli Family*, by **Giacomo Balla** painted in 1901 before the artist adhered to the Futurist movement.

Contemporary art

The works exhibited document the recent acquisition policies of the Soprintendenza and include Italian masters such as Alberto Burri, *Grande Cretto Nero* (1975); Carlo Alfano, *Room* (1987); Michelangelo Pistoletto, *Reliefs–White Year* (1989); Mario Merz, *Shock Wave* (1987); Luciano Fabro; Enzo Cucchi; Mimmo Paladino; Augusto Perez; Guido Tatafiore; as well as international artists such as Joseph Kosuth, *A Grammatical Reflection*, *Modus Operandi* (1986–96); Jannis Kounellis; Sol LeWitt; Hermann Nitsch, *Bodentusch* (1978); Sigmar Polke, *Sfumato* (1991); Andy Warhol, *Vesuvius* (1985). An interesting exhibition of photographs concludes the contemporary section.

The **Osservatorio Astronomico di Capodimonte** has a small museum (Salita Moiariello 16; open by appointment, ☎ 081 293266) featuring astronomical instruments in use from the establishment of the observatory by Ferdinand IV in 1819, until the early 20C. The collection is displayed, in part, on the original premises.

9 • Castel Sant'Elmo, San Martino & Villa Floridiana

This itinerary takes in three of Naples' finer museums—**Castel Sant'Elmo**, a former fortress now used for temporary exhibitions; the **Certosa di San Martino**, with displays representing the history of the Carthusian Order and of Naples; and **Villa Floridiana**, a beautiful mansion housing a museum of ceramics. All are set in splendid surroundings on the slopes of the Vomero hill.

Castel Sant'Elmo

The Castel Sant'Elmo, built in 1329–43 and altered to its present star-shaped form in the 16C by Pier Luigi Scrivà of Valencia, was originally intended to discourage popular insurrection. Long used for political prisoners, it has been restored and reopened to the public as an exhibition space. It hosts many of the city's larger temporary exhibitions and commands an extensive, magnificent view of Naples and its bay. The castle is open Tues–Sun 08.30–19.30.

Getting there

The best way to follow this route is to take a funicular to the top of the hill (bus connections are too complicated), then walk down. To see the museums and return to the centre of Naples requires about 2hrs.

Take the **Montesanto** funicular from Piazza Montesanto (Map 2; 6) to Via Alessandro Scarlatti (Map 2; 9, 5), just behind the museums of Castel Sant'Elmo and San Martino. Alternatively, take the **Centrale** from

Via Toledo (Map 2; 10) or the **Chiaia** from Via Parco Margherita (Map 2; 9) to Via Cimarosa (Map 2; 9) 5mins away from Via Scarlatti by Via Raffaele Morghen. From the upper station of the Montesanto funicular in Via Scarlatti, follow Via Morghen right to Via D'Auria, Via D'Auria right to Via Angelini, and Via Angelini right to Castel Sant'Elmo and the Certosa di San Martino.

Monastery of San Martino

Adjoining Castel Sant'Elmo is the Carthusian monastery of San Martino (Map 2; 10, 6), founded in the 14C but transformed in the late 16C and early 17C by Giovanni Antonio Dosio (active at San Martino 1589–1609) and **Cosimo Fanzago** (director of works 1623–56). Architecturally beautiful in themselves, the conventual buildings now also provide an admirable setting for the treasures of the **Museo Nazionale di San Martino**. The extensive museum illustrates the history, life, and art of Naples. It is open Tues–Sun 08.30–19.30; ☎ 081 558 5942.

The church

From the outer gate you enter the Cortile Monumentale and the church, one of the few instances in which Baroque decoration has been satisfactorily applied to a Gothic building (the original ribs of the 14C vault are still visible) and certainly the most cogent expression of the Baroque aesthetic in Naples. The church originally had three aisles, which were unified into a single space with side chapels.

The first plans to change the medieval structure were produced by Giovanni Antonio Dosio (1580), although the interior decoration, with its extraordinary wealth of inlaid marble, was executed much later under Cosimo Fanzago. The marble floor is the work of Fra'Bonaventura Presti (1664–67). At the sides of the entrance are Fanzago's statues of *St John the Baptist* and *St Jerome* (finished by Alessandro Rondone), and two paintings of *Moses* and *Elias* by **Giuseppe Ribera** (1638); two frescoes, of the same subject, by **Cavalier d'Arpino**, have been discovered beneath. Over the door is the *Deposition*, **Massimo Stanzione**'s masterpiece of 1638. In the spandrels above the chapels more *Prophets* by Giuseppe Ribera complete the series (1638–46). The remarkable ceiling fresco, by **Giovanni Lanfranco**, represents the *Ascension of Christ* (1637–40).

The **side chapels** contain many notable works of art. The first chapel on the right (not visible from the nave and entered from the second chapel) is decorated with fine stucco work, paintings and a marble floor by the versatile **Domenico Antonio Vaccaro**, who, together with his father Lorenzo, was responsible for the greater part of the sculptural work in the first three chapels on either side of the nave (c 1700). The fourth chapel on the right and its pendant on the left were furnished in the mid-18C by Nicola Tagliacozzi Canale and Giuseppe Sammartino, who made the fine statues of *Fortitude* and *Charity*. The fourth chapel on the left also contains three canvasses by **Francesco de Mura** (*Assumption of the Virgin*, *Annunciation*, *Visitation*), and magnificent frescoes with stories of Mary by **Battistello Caracciolo** (1623–26). More frescoes by the same artist are in the second chapel on the left. The two central chapels, with frescoes by Massimo Stanzione, were begun by Fanzago in 1656 and completed in the 18C.

The **presbytery** is divided from the rest of the church by a balustrade of coloured marbles designed by Nicola Tagliacozzi Canale. Beyond is the **high altar**, actually a gilded wooden model by **Francesco Solimena** for a final design that was to have been executed in pietre dure. The **monks' choir** was commissioned to Orazio de Orio in 1629. The ceiling above is decorated with scenes from the Old and New Testaments by **Cavalier d'Arpino**. At the back are statues of the *Contemplative Life* by G.B. Caccini (on the left) and the *Active Life* by Pietro Bernini (on the right). On the back wall is a *Nativity* by **Guido Reni** (1642) and, in the lunette above, a *Crucifixion* by Lanfranco (1638). On the wall to the left *Institution of the Eucharist* by Ribera and *Washing of the Disciples' Feet* by Caracciolo; on the wall to the right, *Last Supper* by Stanzione and *Institution of the Eucharist* by a son and pupils of Paolo Veronese.

Leading off the choir is the **sacristy**, with ceiling frescoes by Cavalier d'Arpino (1596–97) and walnut wardrobes decorated with late 16C intarsia of biblical stories. Over the entrance is a canvas of the *Crucifix* by Cavalier d'Arpino (1589–91) flanked by perspectives by Viviano Codazzi. By the same artist is the double staircase painted in the lunette over the exit, whereas the figurative composition showing an *Ecce Homo* is by Massimo Stanzione. From the sacristy, passing through an antechamber with ceiling frescoes by Stanzione (1644) and two paintings by **Luca Giordano** (*Calling of the Apostles*), one enters the **treasury**. Here, above the altar, is Ribera's masterpiece, the *Deposition*. The fresco on the vault showing the *Triumph of Judith* is Luca Giordano's last work (1704).

Returning to the presbytery, by a door on the right, you enter the **coro dei conversi** with frescoes by Domenico Gargiulo (called Micco Spadaro) executed around 1640, and beautiful intarsia stalls (1510–20), depicting saints, and views, including two representations of the Gothic monastery. From here a passageway leads to the **Cappella della Maddalena** with early-18C frescoes by Giovan Battista Natali and an altarpiece by Andrea Vaccaro (1636). Returning to the monks' choir, a door on the right leads to the **chapter house**, richly decorated with wooden stalls, 17C frescoes (the vault is by Belisario Corenzio) and a number of paintings, including Simon Vouet's *St Bruno Receiving the Rule of the Order*. The adjoining parlour gives access to the Great Cloister.

Returning to the Cortile Monumentale, proceed to the **Chiostrino dei Procuratori**, built by Giovanni Antonio Dosio in the late 16C, and cross the courtyard to the **Salone Carrozze e Stemmi** (carriages and coats of arms; **room 1**). From here you may enter the **pharmacy** with frescoes by Paolo de Matteis (1699), and the beautiful convent **gardens**, arranged on three levels, with extraordinary views over the city and the bay. The topmost level was once the herbarium of the pharmacy. The prior's vegetable garden, with an 18C pergola, was on the intermediate level. Below were the monks' vineyards: visitors can still take part in the grape harvest, at the end of September. The other rooms

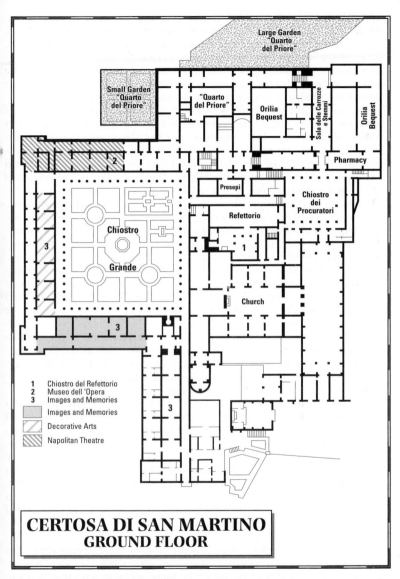

Large Garden "Quarto del Priore"

Small Garden "Quarto del Priore"

"Quarto del Priore"

Orilia Bequest

Sala delle Carozze e Stemmi

Orilia Bequest

Pharmacy

2

Presepi

Chiostro dei Procuratori

Refettorio

1

Chiostro Grande

3

3

Church

3

1 Chiostro del Refettorio
2 Museo dell 'Opera
3 Images and Memories

Images and Memories

Decorative Arts

Napolitan Theatre

CERTOSA DI SAN MARTINO
GROUND FLOOR

in this part house the **Maria Teresa Orilia bequest** of porcelain, Castelli majolica, furniture, fans, walking sticks and other *objets d'art*; as well as 15C and 16C polychrome wood sculpture from Neapolitan churches.

The prior's apartment

From the Salone Carozze e Stemmi you can also descend to the Quarto del Priore (the former prior's apartment), with ceiling frescoes by Micco Spadaro. Here an outstanding series of artworks, representing four centuries of Carthusian patronage in Naples, is displayed. The works range from an important triptych by Jean Bourdichon (*Virgin and Child*, 1494) to the art of the major figures of the 17C and 18C (Pietro Bernini, Santacroce, Caracciolo, Corenzio, Guarino, de Rosa, Vaccaro and others). Pietro Bernini's statue of the *Virgin and Child*, in **room 8**, shows both the influence of Michelangelo and the development of Mannerism. Spadaro's frescoes in **rooms 14** and **15**, begun in 1642, represent landscapes with hermit saints. They show the influence of northern European landscape painters such as Herman Swanevelt and Gaspard Dughet, active in Rome at about the same time. Although retouched, the central landscape decorating the ceiling of **room 15** is particularly interesting. It shows a view of Naples and the still-bare hill of San Martino, on which the Certosa would later be erected. A model of the monastery is held by Charles of Anjou (son of Robert of Anjou), who ordered its construction in 1325.

Adjoining the Quarto del Priore, in **rooms 32** and **33**, is the **biblioteca** (library), decorated in 1741 with frescoes by Crescenzo La Gamba, depicting the *Triumph of Faith*, *St Martin in Glory* and *St Bruno Receiving the Rule of the Order*, bordered with the Rococo chinoiseries typical of the age. The lower frescoes in **room 32** show the monogram CAR SM (standing for the Carthusian Order of St Martin). The floor of **room 33** is decorated with astrological symbols and a meridian (by Leonardo Chiaiese, 1771). The decorative scheme of the two rooms is linked by a common iconographical programme, which is both a summary and a celebration of the bases of the Carthusian order.

Close by is the **sezione presepiale**, with a renowned collection of **presepi** (or representations of the Nativity, elaborate compositions with hundreds of statuettes), some by prominent Neapolitan sculptors. One, the *Presepe Cuciniello*, includes 180 shepherds, 10 horses, 8 dogs and 309 objects.

In front of the *sezione presepiale*, across a corridor, is the **refectory**, built in the 18C by Nicola Tagliacozzi Canale and adorned with a big painting of the *Wedding at Cana* by Nicola Malinconico (1724). Adjoining the refectory is a pretty inner courtyard called the Chiostrino Fanzago although it was rebuilt by NicolaTagliacozzi Canale in the 18C.

The corridor also leads to the **Chiostro Grande** (Great Cloister) which, with its white and grey marble ornamentation and beautifully kept gardens, is undoubtedly one of the more striking achievements of Italian Baroque architecture. The original plan of the cloister is by Giovanni Antonio Dosio (16C), but its present character results largely from the sculptural and architectural programme developed by Cosimo Fanzago in the 17C. His design, conceived in 1623, is strongly conditioned by the style of the Florentine Bernardo Buontalenti (note especially the curved and twisted framework of the niches above the doors), introduced to Naples in the first quarter of the century by Michelangelo Naccherino and other Florentine artists. Five of the seven busts (*St Martin of Tours*, *Bishop Nicola Albergati*, *St Bruno*, *St Hugh*, and *St Dionysius*) are by Fanzago's hand, whereas the last two (*St Januarius* and *St Martin*) are an early work of Domenico Antonio Vaccaro. Fanzago is also either partly or wholly responsible for the eight statues at the corners and centre of the arcade (that of the *Resurrected Christ* was begun by Naccherino).

In the south wing of the cloister is the **Museo dell'Opera** displaying works that reconstruct the history of the complex. It includes portraits of the various *priori* and images of the founder saints; plans, views and a model of the Certosa; decorative marbles and architectural elements by Cosimo Fanzago as well as a *Self-portrait*; paintings by Giacinto Gigante, Frans Vervloet, Gabriele Carelli and others; temperas by Edoardo Dalbono with the *Eruptions of Vesuvius*; views from S. Martino by Antonio Senape. The balcony commands a wonderful view over the city and the bay of Naples.

In the east and north wings of the Chiostro Grande is a section dedicated to **images and memories of the city**, with a rich collection illustrating the history of Naples. Among the exhibits is the famous *Tavola Strozzi*, showing the return of the Aragonese fleet, and, in the background a view of Naples in the 15C. The painting is attributed to Francesco Rosselli di Lorenzo. The exhibition continues with 16C maps of the city; portraits of Charles V; 17C maps and views, including the interesting *Bird's-eye View of Naples* by Didier Barra (1647). Next are ebony and ivory cabinets and numerous views of Neapolitan squares. The next rooms are dedicated to the Revolt of Masaniello, with portraits of its protagonists and paintings illustrating some episodes (note Micco Spadaro's *The Revolt of 1647*); and the plague of 1656 (more paintings by Micco Spadaro and others). Continuing through the rooms you pass two views by Gaspard van Wittel; 18C maps; portraits of Bourbon royals; genre paintings and a map of Naples by the Duke of Noja. More 18C maps are displayed on the upper floor, along with paintings of the city and life in the early 19C. A room is dedicated to the events of 1799; another to the ten years of French rule. The last rooms are dedicated to the return of the Bourbons.

The rooms beyond house important collections of **decorative arts**. Among these is the Bonghi collection of 18C mirrors, Murano glass, majolica from the Castelli manufacture and Sicily, terracotta and biscuit pieces. The Canessa collection concentrates on 19C porcelain; the Savarese collection comprises various types of arms; the Ricciardi has medals, coins etc. There are also sections devoted to furniture, costumes, jewellery, corals, ivories and precious stones (including a large topaz that was to decorate the Palatine Chapel of the Palazzo Reale). Also on the first floor, in the south wing of the cloister, is a section on the history of **Neapolitan theatre** from the refined San Carlo and San Carlino opera houses, to the more popular expression of the *opera dei pupi* puppet theatre.

Left of the main entrance, stairs lead up to a series of rooms with 19C Neapolitan art. Here are a model for Gianbattista Amendola's statue of *Murat* at the Palazzo Reale; a statue of *Salvator Rosa* by Achille d'Orsi; portraits by Domenico Morelli; sculptures by Vincenzo Gemito; views by Frans Vervloet; paintings by the artists of the Posillipo School: Gabriele Smargiassi, Gaetano Gigante, Consalvo Carelli, Anton Sminck Pitloo, Giacinto Gigante and Ercole Gigante; paintings by Domenico Morelli (including *The Kiss*) and his followers; genre paintings by Vincenzo Migliaro showing Neapolitan places that have long disappeared; paintings by Antonio Mancini (the famous Prevetariello); the naturalistic paintings of Filippo and Giuseppe Palizzi and their followers; small paintings by Francesco Paolo Michetti.

Villa Floridiana: the Museo Nazionale della Ceramica

Return to the Montesanto funicular station (see above) then continue along Via Raffaele Morghen. The second street to the left leads into Via Cimarosa. This runs parallel to Via Scarlatti, passing the upper station of the Chiaia funicular, to the shaded park of the Villa Floridiana (Map 2; 9). The **gardens** (open 09.00–1hr before sunset), beautifully sited on a spur overlooking the sea, are famous for their camellias; the view from the terrace is particularly fine.

The mansion houses the **Museo Nazionale della Ceramica Duca di Martina** (open Tues–Sun 08.30–14.00; ☎ 081 578 8418), based on the original porcelain collection of Placido de Sangro, Duke of Martina, augmented by his nephew, Count De Marzi and presented to the city by the widow of the latter, Maria Spinelli. The museum now contains over 6000 pieces of European and Asiatic porcelain and pottery, as well as goldsmiths' work, ivories, and 17C, 18C and 19C paintings.

In the ground-floor foyer are portraits of Ferdinand I of Bourbon and his morganatic wife Lucia Migliaccio, Duchess of Floridia (to whom Ferdinand gave the villa and for whom he had it renovated in the Neo-classical style); the duchess's portrait is attributed to Vincenzo Camuccini.

From the foyer, a stair ascends to the precious and beautifully arranged main collections.

First floor

Rooms 2–4 contain porcelain from Meissen, the first place in Europe to use *pâte dure*, among the best pieces are the **Augustus Rex vases**, with chinoiseries on a pink background (rooms 2 and 3), and the figure groups (*Lovers with a Puppy Dog*; *Couple of Lovers with a Bird Cage*, by J.J. Kaendler) in room 4.

Room 5, the former ballroom, is dedicated to Bourbon porcelain. The collection of **Capodimonte porcelain** is particularly impressive; notice, among other fine pieces, the *Pietà* by Giuseppe Gricci. Other highlights include pieces from the Buen Retiro manufactory (1765–70); plates from the *Servizio Ercolanese* (which was given by Ferdinand of Bourbon to his father, then King Charles of Spain) and from the set of the *Vestiture del Regno*, both produced by the *Real fabbrica* (royal manufactory) of Naples (1771–1806). Also displayed here are works by Filippo Tagliolini and pieces from the Doccia manufactory (1735–1838). **Rooms 6–7.** More Meissen ware. **Room 8.** Vienna and Meissen ware. **Room 9.** Pieces from the Ginori works at Doccia and other Italian manufactories (Venice). **Room 10.** French porcelain of various manufacture (Rouen, Saint-Cloud, Sèvres, Paris). **Room 11.** German porcelain from manufactories other than Meissen and English porcelain (Bow, Derby, Wedgwood, Chelsea). **Room 12.** A collection of some 755 tortoise-shell artefacts brought together at the turn of the century, ranging from jewellery (necklaces, rings, brooches) to toiletries (brushes, combs, hairclips, shoecombs) as well as candlesticks, snuff-boxes, cigarette-holders, etc. In the same room are also a number of precious miniatures and other *objets d'art*. **Room 13.** Asian (Chinese Ming and Japanese Arita) porcelain. **Room 14. Donazione Riccardo Di Sangro**, a rich, varied collection of Chinese, Neapolitan and Delft ware (plus a Meissen chocolate service of 1735–40), given to the museum in 1978. The small room adjacent contains two cases of Meissen services and another case of Meissen figurines and animals.

Ground floor

The galleries on this floor begin with an extensive collection of 16C Italian majolica from Faenza, Deruta, Gubbio, Pesaro, Urbino and Venice; Hispano-Moresque majolica, notably Manises lustreware; Iznik ware from Turkey and Persian ceramics; 18C ware from Castelli d'Abruzzo, Naples, Palermo and Venice; 18C ceramics from Delft and Rouen. **Rooms19–20** contain Murano glass and 'façon de Venise', as well as Bohemian crystal. **Rooms 21–22**. Medieval and Renaissance *objets d'art*: Limoges enamels, ivories, corals, metalwork.

Basement

The **Oriental Art** section has been re-opened in the basement. The collection, comprising over a thousand pieces of Chinese and Japanese manufacture—mostly ceramics and porcelain but also items in bronze, jade, lacquer and enamel—is one of the more important in Italy. There is an impressive display of 18C Chinese porcelain classified according to its dominant colour as blue and white, *blanc de Chine*, *famille verte*, *rose*, and *noire*. There are also several pieces of Japanese porcelain from the Edo period in the Kakiemon and Imari styles.

Via Cimarosa continues, eventually joining the winding Via Falcone, which can be reached on foot much further down the hill by taking the Via Luca Giordano (left). Continue the descent, turning left into Via Tasso, passing the Ospedale Internazionale, where you emerge into Corso Vittorio Emanuele. To the left, the Corso returns back up to Piazza Mazzini, from which Via Salvator Rosa descends to the Museo Archeologico Nazionale. To the right, skirting the Rione Amedeo, it leads to Piazza Piedigrotta and the Stazione Mergellina. At no. 292 is the **Raccolta d'Arte della Fondazione Pagliara**, part of the University Institute of Suor Orsola Benincasa, with paintings by Neapolitan masters, mainly of the 18C and 19C (open by appointment, ☎ 081 252 2225).

MODERN NAPLES
• • • • • • • • • • • • • • • • • •

History of modern Naples

In 1884 a terrible cholera epidemic swept Naples, taking many lives, particularly in the crowded alleys and tall tenements of the medieval city centre. As a result special laws were passed to hasten urban renewal. Wide thoroughfares were driven through the slums, the waters of the Serino River were brought into the city, and complete new quarters were built. Naples lost much of its picturesqueness without gaining in improved health, as the population evicted from the condemned buildings was housed in neighbouring blocks, increasing density even further.

The greatest achievement of the *Risanamento*, as the urban renewal programme was called, was the construction of the Corso Umberto I (popularly the Rettifilo) from Piazza Garibaldi and the railway station to the Piazza del Municipio, the centre of local government. Other 'improvements' included the rebuilding of the quarter of Santa Lucia, the founding of a new residential district on the Vomero hill and the establishment of the first industries in the Vasto Arenaccia area, the most easterly link in the chain of industrial suburbs that encircles Naples today, presenting a serious obstacle to the successful expansion of the city.

Quite independently of the Risanamento, wealthier Neapolitans began to build their luxurious villas in the area around the Riviera di Chiaia around the turn of the 20C (Piazza Amedeo, Parco Margherita). Many of these elegant dwellings, which continued to be built up until the eve of the First World War, are in a curious local variant of the Art Nouveau style.

The period between the wars witnessed a revival of building without any precise guidelines. During the Fascist period both urban expansion and rebuilding activity in the city centre were important. The suburban quarters grew rapidly, particularly at Fuorigrotta, where development was stimulated by the construction of the Mostra d'Oltremare fairground and of the tunnel under Posillipo Hill.

In central Naples the most striking changes took place in the Carità quarter, between Via Toledo, Via Monteoliveto, and Via Medina. Here the central post office, the provincial office building and the police headquarters were erected, concentrating administrative services even more in an already overburdened area. Finally, in 1939 the need for an organic design stimulated the drafting of a general town plan, which was not, however, applied until many years after the war.

The events of the Second World War nullified many earlier improvements. Naples was heavily bombed on 4 August 1943 by the advancing Allies, then attacked and captured by the Germans after the armistice of 8 September. A Neapolitan uprising (Le Quattro Giornate, 28 September–1 October) drove out the Germans, who before retreating destroyed the port, utilities and public archives. A typhus epidemic followed by a bad winter added to the distress and aggravated the age-old problem of the *scugnizzi*, deprived children who managed to survive only by resorting to crime.

The contemporary city

Commercial and industrial development has radically changed the city's appearance in the post-war years. The coastline from Pozzuoli to Castellammare di Stabia and the inland suburbs now host an array of industrial plants (including ironworks, food processing plants, an oil refinery, cement works, aircraft and automobile assembly plants), and residential building has expanded over the surrounding hills and to the eastern plains. This apparent burgeoning of wealth and activity is illusory, however, and does not reflect the true economic condition of the city which, notwithstanding costly and elaborate plans for development, remains substantially poorer than its northern counterparts.

Naples has the highest population density of any European city and is severely lacking in social services. Despite the efforts of the local authorities to provide adequate housing, many Neapolitans still live in *bassi*—street-level, single-roomed dwellings in which light and air are admitted by a double door alone. At the same time, illegal building activity has altered the appearance of the town beyond recognition. A special investigatory committee of the Ministry of Public Works revealed in 1971 that almost everything built in Naples since 1945 was in violation of the law. Judiciary action in 1975 resulted in the incrimination of a former mayor, the demolition of 22 buildings erected on lands destined for parks, schools, and other public facilities and the arrest of several contractors. In spite of intimidatory actions brought by the profiteers and their sympathisers, the effort to restore Naples to her former elegance continues.

The task is not an easy one, for even the force of nature must be taken into account. The violent earthquake that rocked Campania and the neighbouring region of Basilicata on 22 November 1980 claimed over 3000 victims and caused incalculable damage. In Naples, the largest city affected by the earthquake, 200,000 people were left homeless. An effort is now being made to make all new buildings part of an overall design for urban renewal. Countless monuments have been cleaned, renovated, or restored; attempts have been made to extend restricted traffic zones and major renovation programmes have been launched in the area behind the Stazione Centrale (the **Centro Direzionale** or Management Centre, designed by the internationally acclaimed architect, Kenzo Tange) and at the former steel works at Bacoli, now home to the fascinating science museum, **Città della Scienza**.

10 · Parks and promenades

In the early and mid-19C, the Romantic fashion for broad, open spaces and breathtaking views led to the construction of parks and panoramic carriage roads in and around major Italian cities, such as the Pincio in Rome and the Viale dei Colli in Florence. In Naples the old mule tracks to **Posillipo** (Map 1; 11, 13 and beyond) were improved to make a parkway, and the waterfront at **Mergellina**, west of Pizzofalcone (Map 1; 12), was developed as a wooded quayside promenade, for the benefit of the chic new residential quarter on the hillside to the north. Both areas correspond extremely well to the Romantic ideal. A stroll through the park at Posillipo, in particular, is rewarding.

The itinerary described here is 5–6km long, so good walking shoes (and a free morning or afternoon) are musts. If using public transport, take bus 140 from Piazza della Vittoria to its terminus at Capo Posillipo (Rotonda) and make the tour of the park on foot (this way you may walk as much or as little as you like). Bus 152 crosses the city from Corso Garibaldi to the modern precinct of Mostra d'Oltremare (an area devoted to leisure activities in the Quartiere Flegreo), continuing to Pozzuoli.

The Riviera di Chiaia

From Piazza dei Martiri, Via Calabritto leads south to the fine Piazza della Vittoria (Map 2; 14). On the seaward side of the piazza a column of ancient marble commemorates Neapolitans who lost their lives in the various revolts against the Bourbons. From the landward side the Riviera di Chiaia, a broad, busy street, extends westward for c 1.5km. Along the left side of the street is the **Villa Comunale**, a popular public garden beautifully shaded by sub-tropical trees. In the centre is the Zoological Station (Map 2; 13, 14), founded in 1872 for research into the habits of marine flora and fauna. Its chief attraction is the famous **Aquarium** (open summer Tues–Sat 09.00–18.00; Sun and holidays 10.00–18.00, winter Tues–Sat 09.00–17.00; Sun and holidays 09.00–14.00), remarkable for its structure, which enables sea water to enter the tanks directly from the sea, preserving the most delicate marine organisms. The collection includes more than 200 species that inhabit the Gulf of Naples.

In front of the Villa Comunale a wide seaside promenade, Via Caracciolo, extends all the way to Mergellina, with an uninterrupted view all round the bay. Halfway along it is the Armando Diaz Monument (1936).

Across the Riviera di Chiaia, set in a walled garden, is the Neo-classical **Villa Pignatelli** (Map 2; 13). Built in 1826 for the Acton family by Pietro Valente, this once handsome mansion was acquired in 1841 by the Rothschilds, who refurbished much of the interior in the Second Empire style. It was sold in 1867 to the Pignatelli di Monteleone and bequeathed by Princess Rosina Pignatelli to the Italian State in 1952.

The villa now houses the **Museo Principe Diego Aragona Pignatelli Cortes**. The collection (open Tues–Sun 08.00–14.00; ☎ 081 761 2356) includes Italian and European porcelain (from Capodimonte, Venice, Doccia, Vienna, Berlin, Meissen, Thuringen, Bow, Chelsea and Zurich); biscuits from Naples, Vienna and Sèvres; Chinese vases; period furniture, and some paintings and sculptures, including family portraits. Highlights include the four Chinese Edo vases in the circular vestibule; a beautiful Meissen coffee set with marine landscapes; a Doccia coffee set with pastoral landscapes, of Ginori manufacture; and a service from the *Real fabbrica di Napoli* with landscape and genre scenes by Raffaele Giovine. Also noteworthy are a late 18C French *sécretaire* imitating Martin Carlin furniture and decorated with marquetry and Sèvres plaquettes of flowers. The **biblioteca** has restored leather wall hangings, from the turn of the 19C, exemplifying a fine technique of imprint decoration successively gilded *a pastiglio*, and two Neapolitan tortoise-shell cabinets; and the **sala da pranzo** has a table laid with a fine Limoges service expressly made for Princess Rosina Pignatelli.

The rooms on the first floor have been recently opened to house the **Banco di Napoli collection**, comprising Neapolitan art from the 16C to the 20C.

The villa also hosts temporary exhibitions of contemporary art. In the garden is the **Museo delle Carrozze Mario d'Alessandro Marchese di Civitanova**, with English, French and Italian carriages of the 19C and early 20C.

The area to the right of the Riviera di Chiaia is the **Rione Amedeo**, a modern, fashionable quarter worth a short detour. Either walk up northwards from Villa Pignatelli or ascend Via Santa Maria in Portico, passing the church of Santa Maria in Portico (begun 1632, with a façade of 1862) on the left. A little further on is the church of the Ascensione a Chiaia, begun in the 14C but rebuilt by Cosimo Fanzago in 1645. The interior contains canvases by Luca Giordano. Further on, another church, designed by Cosimo Fanzago but ruined by later restorations, Santa Teresa a Chiaia (1650–62), also contains paintings by Giordano. To the west lies Piazza Amedeo, the centre of the district. From here the Parco Margherita winds up to join Corso Vittorio Emanuele.

Piedigrotta

The Riviera di Chiaia passes the north side of Piazza della Repubblica, with the *Monumento allo Scugnizzo* by Mazzacurati (1969), commemorating the Quattro Giornate di Napoli. Shortly afterwards, it ends at Largo Torretta (Map 1; 8), an open space named after a former tower erected as a defence against pirates. Here the road divides. Via Giordano Bruno (left) leads to Piazza Sannazzaro and the harbour at Mergellina, described below. Via Piedigrotta (right) leads to Piazza Piedigrotta and Mergellina station.

On the left of the piazza is **Santa Maria di Piedigrotta** (Map 1; 7, 8), a 14C church remodelled in 1822 and restored at the beginning of the 20C. The façade is by Enrico Alvino with a campanile rebuilt in 1926. Within are a 15C Neapolitan painting of the *Descent from the Cross* on wood, and, in the large chapel near the choir, tombs of the Filangieri family. On the high altar stands a wooden figure of the *Madonna*, after the manner of Tino di Camaino, much restored and much venerated. On the night of 7–8 September this forms the focal point of a lively **festival** celebrating the Battle of the Velletri.

Some local curiosities

In Piazza Piedigrotta, beneath the railway viaduct and to the left of the entrance to the Galleria Quattro Giornate (a tunnel leading to Fuorigrotta), steps lead to the **Parco Virgiliano**. A pillar here marks the remains of the writer, Giacomo Leopardi, moved to the park from a demolished church. Nearby is the Roman columbarium in *opus reticulatum*, restored in 1927 and known (although there is no concrete evidence to support the claim) as Virgil's tomb. Immediately below the columbarium is the mouth of the Grotta Vecchia or Crypta Neapolitana (710m long; closed), a remarkable feat of Roman engineering, planned by Cocceius for Agrippa and Octavian to provide a direct road from Neapolis to Puteoli (Pozzuoli).

Today much the same route is followed by the Galleria della Laziale (or di Posillipo), a straight, modern tunnel 900m long (no pedestrians), entered from Piazza Sannazzaro (see below).

At the far end of the tunnel, Via Fuorigrotta leads directly into the **Quartiere Flegreo** (Map 1; 9, 10), a new district developed from the little village of Fuorigrotta after 1938. The broad principal thoroughfare, Viale Augusto, and the parallel Via Giulio Cesare both terminate at the vast Piazza Vincenzo Tecchio, in the north-west corner of which is the entrance to the **Mostra d'Oltremare**. This is a modern development, set in gardens below the north slope of the Phlegraean hills, comprising a number of pavilions designed to house exhibitions, fairs, congresses and all sorts of entertainment. Among the more important constructions are the Arena Flegrea (10,000 seats), the Teatro Mediterraneo, a large swimming pool, and the Palazzo dei Congressi; there are also ice- and roller-skating rinks, a dance hall and restaurants.

To the south, Viale Kennedy leads (1km more) to the **zoo** (open daily summer 09.00–19.00, winter 09.00–17.00; refreshments, no restaurant), opened in 1950. The zoo is located in a beautiful park with tropical trees and has a fine collection of well-housed animals. Viale Kennedy continues across the Phlegraean Fields to Pozzuoli.

Mergellina

From Largo Torretta Via Mergellina leads south to Piazza Sannazzaro. To the right is the entrance to the Galleria della Laziale. From Piazza Sannazzaro (Map 1; 12), take Via Sannazzaro to reach the shore again at the little bay of **Mergellina**, affording a good view back to Santa Lucia. Here is the lower station of the Mergellina funicular, which runs from the seafront to Via Manzoni.

Above the south end of the bay rises the church of **Santa Maria del Parto**, or del Sannazzaro, founded in the 16C by the Neapolitan poet, Jacopo Sannazzaro. It contains the well-known painting nicknamed the 'Diavolo di Mergellina' (*St Michael overthrowing Satan*), by Leonardo da Pistoia (1542). At the back of the apse, which is decorated with paintings and stucco, is the tomb of Jacopo Sannazzaro, by Fra Giovanni da Montorsoli (1537).

Posillipo

From Santa Maria del Parto, Via Posillipo (Map 1; 11, 15) hugs the shore for some way and then climbs away up the slopes of the hilly promontory known as Posillipo, a name said to be derived from *Pausilypon* (the carefree), a villa belonging to the Roman patrician Vedius Pollio and afterwards to Augustus. This picturesque road, begun in 1808 under Murat, passes many handsome villas amid rich vegetation and commands lovely views, especially fine at sunset. In 1839, the two-year-old W.S. Gilbert was kidnapped here by brigands and held to ransom; the incident is alluded to in *The Gondoliers*.

On the left side of the road is the **Palazzo di Donn'Anna** (Map 1; 15), built in 1642–44 by Fanzago for Anna Carafa, wife of the Duke of Medina, Viceroy of Naples. Perhaps the most ingeniously planned and dramatically situated of all Neapolitan palaces, its construction was interrupted by the death of the patron in 1642. Further on is the Ospizio Marino, a home for retired sailors and fishermen, with a monument to Ludovico da Casoria, its founder. The view becomes increasingly fine as the road climbs to Piazza San Luigi (c 85m; restaurants), on the far side of the **Parco della Rimembranza**, which contains an Egyptian-style mausoleum; a memorial to victims of the First World War. The exceptional view is reflected in the name of the church, Santa Maria di Bellavista. Close to the church Via Ferdinando Russo winds down in 10 minutes to **Capo di Posillipo** (view), near which is the sumptuous **Villa Rosebery**, the Neapolitan residence of the President of the Republic.

Via Posillipo continues its winding course, reaching a major intersection known as the Quadrivio del Capo. To the south Via Marechiaro, a road through villas and vineyards, leads down to (1km) **Marechiaro**, an unspoilt fishing hamlet with stone houses rising in steps from the sea. A plaque marks the window celebrated by Salvatore di Giacomo in a well-known Neapolitan song set to music by Tosti. From here you can take boat trips to the **Grotta dei Tuoni** (where the waves produce thunderous echoes) and **La Gaiola**, a rocky island near which the remains of Pollio's Villa (see above) may be seen.

Return to the Quadrivio del Capo and take Via Boccaccio (right), climbing up to Via Manzoni. About 150m beyond the Quadrivio del Capo, Viale Tito Lucrezio Caro, to the left, winds up to the top of Monte Coroglio and the entrance to the **Parco di Posillipo** (153m). A road encircles the park; at the point nearest the sea a **belvedere** offers a splendid view of Capri, Vesuvius, Ischia and Capo Miseno. The island of Nisida lies immediately below.

From the park entrance, you can either go directly to Posillipo Alto along the Viale Virgilio and on to Mergellina (see above) or return along Via Caro for Pollio's Villa. Turn left, passing under the Montagna Spaccata viaduct to reach the **Rotonda di Posillipo**, another famous viewpoint overlooking the Campi Flegrei, the Gulf of Pozzuoli and Procida (though the view is somewhat marred by the railway sidings and chemical works in the foreground). The road turns towards the sea and descends, passing the entrance to the Grotto of Sejanus, a tunnel c 950m long leading to Pollio's Villa and (in spite of its name) believed to have been cut in AD 37.

At the foot of the hill a byroad crosses the modern causeway to the island of **Nisida**, an extinct volcano known to the ancients as *Nesis*. This little isle once belonged to Lucullus and later became the retreat of Marcus Brutus, who was visited here by Cicero. The conspiracy against Caesar was planned at Nesis by Brutus and Cassius, and Brutus bade farewell to his wife Portia here. The castle (now a school) was used as a prison for the Italian patriot Carlo Poerio, whose plight horrified the visiting Gladstone.

From the park Viale Virgilio crosses a viaduct to join Via Boccaccio above the Quadrivio del Capo. From here you ascend Via Manzoni (left; view towards Agnano) or Via del Casale (right) to arrive at the Torre Ranieri crossroads. From here Via Petrarca drops gradually to Mergellina, offering unimpeded seaward views; Via Manzoni (left) runs along the whole length of the Posillipo hills through magnificent countryside, dotted with modern villas, passing the upper station of the funicular from Mergellina (see above).

Via Stazio descends from the Quadrivio di Posillipo Alto (160m) in steep bends to Mergellina. Via Manzoni continues, still affording pleasant views, to the Villa Patrizi, where a road diverges (left) for Agnano, and Largo Europa. From here another road to the left, Via Tasso, drops (with a great part of the city spread out below) to join Corso Vittorio Emanuelle, and Via Falcone ascends to the Vomero.

11 • The Rettifilo, the market and the harbour

Corso Umberto I, popularly called the **Rettifilo** (Map 2; 7, 8) was laid out in 1888–94 to connect the city's civic and financial centre to the main railway station. This long, straight thoroughfare is a typical example of late 19C town planning in Italy, which, as a rule, had little regard for local needs or traditions. It dominates the area between the medieval Castel Nuovo and the Stazione Centrale cutting through Naples' eastern districts in a merciless way, destroying the area's medieval flavour and introducing an academic, pretentious architectural style vaguely related to the Neo-classicism of the Bourbon era. A few impressive monuments of the city's past do survive, however, and amply repay a visit. Two hours are more than enough for the 4km-long visit to this living example of how-not-to-treat-a-city.

The Rettifilo and its environs

From the Piazza del Municipio the wide Via Agostino Depretis leads straight to Piazza Giovanni Bovio (formerly Piazza della Borsa; Map 2; 11). In the centre of the piazza is the graceful **Fontana del Nettuno**, designed in 1601, probably by Domenico Fontana. The sea-monsters are by Pietro Bernini, and the figure of Neptune by Michelangelo Naccherino. To the left stands the **Palazzo della Borsa** (1895), engulfing the 8C chapel of **Sant'Aspreno al Porto**, which was transformed in the 17C and incorporates columns from San Pietro ad Aram.

Corso Umberto I, or the *Rettifilo*, starts from the north-east side of the piazza. After a few metres, Via Mezzocannone leads left to **San Giovanni Maggiore**.

The church, built in the 6C on the ruins of a pagan temple, but remodelled in 1685 and again in 1870, retains its basilican plan. A chapel on the south side contains an 18C terracotta *presepio*; the third chapel on the north side a *Baptism of Christ*, attributed to Giovanni da Nola; the fifth chapel, a late 16C bas-relief of the beheading of John the Baptist. The magnificent **high altar** (1732–43) is the work of Domenico Antonio Vaccaro.

The church of **San Pietro Martire**, built in 1294–1347, stands in a small square to the right along the Corso. Much damaged during the Second World War, it contains a number of 14C–16C works of art, including (in the third north chapel) a naïvely realistic 15C Catalan painting on wood of *St Vincent Ferrer*, as well as paintings by Solimena and Stanzione.

Immediately opposite the church is the imposing façade of the **University of Naples** (Map 2; 7) by Pier Paolo Quaglia and Guglielmo Melisborgo (1897–1908), with a pediment sculptured by Francesco Ierace. The university was founded in 1224 by Frederick II. In 1777 it was moved to the 16C rooms of the former Jesuit convent behind the present building. The Musei di Antropologia, Mineralogia, Zoologia e Paleontologia are located here, in Via Mezzocannone 8 and Largo San Marcellino 10 (open Mon–Fri 09.00–13.30, Sat and Sun 10.00–13.00). They contain the study collections of the Faculty of Science.

Three blocks further along the Corso, on the left, a crooked alley and a flight of steps lead up to the church of **Santi Severino e Sossio**, built over an earlier structure in 1494–1561 and decorated in the 17C. The façade was restored after earthquake damage in 1731. The interior has ceiling paintings by Corenzio, who fell to his death while retouching them and is buried near the entrance to the sacristy. In the fourth chapel on the south side is a 16C polyptych. On the same side is the sacristy vestibule, in which are two Cicaro tombs of the 16C, both with inscriptions by Sannazzaro. The **Cappella Sanseverino** (right of the choir) contains the tombs, by Giovanni da Nola, of three Sanseverino brothers, all of whom were poisoned on the same day (1516) by their uncle. The choir stalls (1560–75) are by Bartolomeo Chiarini and Benvenuto Tortelli.

The **Benedictine convent**, with four cloisters, was the repository of the State Archives. They were removed for safety during the war, but wantonly destroyed in reprisals by the retreating German forces. The **Chiostro del platano**, named after a plane tree said to have been planted by St Benedict, is accessible by a door to the left of the vestibule. It is frescoed by Andrea Solario.

With the church behind you, turn immediately left to the Via del Duomo. One block up, on the right, is **San Giorgio Maggiore** (see p 142), founded by St Severus in the late 4C.

Museo Civico

Across the street from San Giorgio is the **Palazzo Cuomo** (Map 2; 7), a severely elegant 15C Florentine building (1464–90) that now houses the attractive **Museo Civico Gaetano Filangieri** (open Tues–Sat 09.30–14.00, 15.30–19.00; Sun and holidays 09.30–13.30; closed for renovation at the time of writing; ☎ 081 203175), established in 1881. The original collections of Prince Gaetano Filangieri (1824–92) were burnt by the Germans in 1943, but a new collection has since been formed.

On the ground floor are objects from various excavations and Oriental arms;

above, sculpture (notably a boy's head by the Della Robbia) and paintings by Ribera, Mattia Preti, Luca Giordano and others. Note particularly Ribera's gruesomely realistic head of *St John the Baptist*; Mattia Preti, *Meeting of Peter and Paul at the Gates of Rome*; Bernardino Lanino, *Madonna and Child*; Battistello Caracciolo, *Ecce Homo*. The gallery has a good collection of porcelain, and the library has a number of manuscripts and documents dating from the 13C–19C.

Return to the Corso via **Sant'Agostino alla Zecca** (Map 2; 8), a 14C church transformed in the mid-17C by Bartolomeo Picchiatt and Giuseppe Astarita with the tomb of Francesco Coppola, Count Sarno. The fine 14C **chapterhouse**, opening off the Baroque cloister, is reached by a door beneath the 17C campanile.

Back on the Corso, and further on to the left, is the little church of **Santa Maria Egiziaca** (Map 2; 8), originally of the 14C, but in its present form designed by D. Lazzari (1684), with paintings by Andrea Vaccaro, Luca Giordano and Francesco Solimena. The oval plan is rare in Naples.

Santissima Annunziata

By taking Via Egiziaca to the left and then turning right in Via dell'Annunziata you reach the Santissima Annunziata (Map 2; 8); rebuilt by Luigi Vanvitelli and his son Carlo in 1761–82 after a fire, important as one of the first examples of the new Classical taste in ecclesiastical architecture that was championed by Vanvitelli and Fuga as official architects of Charles III.

The **interior** is a Latin cross with barrel-vaulted nave and choir and short transepts. The nave arcade is replaced by a colonnade bearing a flat entablature. The crossing, the choir, and the semicircular apse, as well as the gallery at the west end of the nave, provide interesting variants in the use of columns. The white and grey stucco underscores the severity of the design. The slender cupola, badly damaged in 1943, has been well restored. The **treasury**, containing frescoes (in a bad state) by Corenzio, and the **sacristy**, on the south side (likewise decorated by Corenzio and containing sculptured 16C presses), are relics of the former church of 1318, in which Joan II was buried (plain tomb before the high altar). The altars of the unusual, circular crypt are adorned with 17C terracotta statues.

To return to Corso Umberto I turn right and take Via Antonio Ranieri. The church of **San Pietro ad Aram** flanks the left side of the Corso. The 17C façade faced Via Santa Candida, but the usual entrance is by the south door from the Corso. The church stands on the site where St Peter is said to have baptised St Candida and St Asprenus (who later became the first bishop of Naples). A fresco in the porch depicts St Peter celebrating Mass with them. The church has a finely stuccoed interior. The high altar is decorated with mosaics, and the presbytery is adorned with early works of Luca Giordano. Restoration work in the crypt in 1930 uncovered remains of an aisled church dating from the early Christian era.

Towards the market

Corso Umberto I ends in the vast Piazza Garibaldi (monument by Cesare Zocchi, 1904) in front of the **Stazione Centrale** (Map 2; 4). From here Corso Garibaldi leads shortly into Piazza Nolana, where the massive **Porta Nolana**, part of the ancient enceinte, has a 15C relief of Ferdinand I. From the piazza, Corso Garibaldi continues southwards, passing the Stazione Circumvesuviana, to Piazza Guglielmo Pepe. Here Via del Carmine, to the right, leads to the church of

Santa Maria del Carmine (Map 2; 8), rebuilt at the end of the 13C. The campanile was begun in the 15C, but not completed until 1631, when Fra Nuvolo added the spire; the façade, by Giovanni del Gaizo, dates from 1766. The interior of the church is decorated with polychrome marble; the modern roof replaces a 17C coffered ceiling destroyed in 1943. On the north side is the monument, designed by the Danish sculptor Thorvaldsen, to Conradin of Swabia (p 97), who is buried behind the altar. Under the transept arch stands a 13C wooden crucifix and above it a painting, *God the Father*, by Luca Giordano. The frescoes in the north transept and in the sixth chapel on the north side are by Solimena; in the south transept is an *Assumption*, also by Solimena. Behind the high altar a much-venerated 14C painting, the *Madonna della Bruna*, occupies a 16C marble shrine. In the north transept is a 15C crucifix.

West of Santa Maria del Carmine is the Piazza del Mercato, centre of trade in medieval Naples and still the site of the city's lively general market. Here you can buy virtually anything; the fruit and vegetable stands are particularly colourful. In 1269, Conradin and his kinsman, Frederick of Baden, were beheaded here by Charles I of Anjou. Here also Masaniello's rebellion against Spanish rule broke out in July 1647. Plague victims were buried on this site in the 17C, and the leaders of the 1799 revolution were also executed here. In the church of Santa Croce al Mercato a porphyry column, from a chapel erected on the site of Conradin's scaffold, is preserved. On the west side of the piazza stands Sant'Eligio, restored after war damage, with a good Gothic doorway showing French influence. On the south side lie the remains of the Castello del Carmine.

The harbour

The Porta del Carmine, with its massive pillars, leads to the Via Nuova della Marina, along which you turn right. This busy street skirts the extensive installations of the harbour. Already famous in Greek and Roman times, this was developed greatly under Charles II of Anjou and went on expanding as the volume of shipping increased. The enormous damage sustained during the Second World War reduced it to a third of its pre-war efficiency, the passenger terminal being all but destroyed. Reconstruction began in 1946 and the city rapidly regained its former status as a major Mediterranean port, only to lose it again by not converting promptly to container shipping. Among the more notable modern works is the 330m-long **dry dock** (1955), by the Molo Cesario Console at the east end of the harbour. Further along and facing the south end of Via del Duomo is the Immacolatella Nuova quay.

Continuing west, Via De Gasperi branches right, leading to Via Depretis and the starting point of this walk. Emerging from the tenements, beneath which it has long been buried, is the church of Santa Maria di Portosalvo, erected in 1544. To the left, Via Cristoforo Colombo passes another pier, the Immacolatella Vecchia (seat of the Capitaneria di Porto) and leads towards the seaward end of Piazza Municipio and Castel Nuovo.

Campania

Campania, the region of which Naples is capital, is not for everyone. 'Here the beautie of all the World is gathered as it were into a bundle,' remarked the British traveller Fynes Moryson in 1617. But by 1973 another writer, Peter Nichols, could call Campania an 'Eden which produces poverty.' Indeed, although the region is strikingly beautiful, centuries of misrule have left a deep mark here, which time is only very slowly erasing. The Neapolitan hinterland is one of the more impoverished areas of Italy, with unemployment rates in certain towns and age groups reaching peaks above 80 per cent. And facilities to provide the education and training that are the keys to qualified employment are sadly lacking or, at best, dysfunctional.

Outside the more desperate areas, which lie between Naples and Caserta to the north, and along the gulf shore at the foot of Vesuvius, to the south, there is a certain, carefully cultivated order to the neglect in Campania. As Leslie Stephen pointed out over a century ago, 'the squalor of [a Campanian] town surrounds monuments of incomparable beauty, and somehow does not seem altogether out of harmony with them.' As cynical as this comment may seem, it does contain an element of truth that British or North American visitors may find shocking: the people who live on the shores of the Mediterranean have a very different relationship with what we consider 'decency'. Perhaps they lack our Puritan sense of decorum; or perhaps they just have less to hide.

Campania occupies the Tyrrhenian coast and the western slopes of the Apennines, between Lazio and Molise on the north, Apulia on the east and Basilicata on the south. It is a fertile region, with an astonishing variety of coast, plain, and mountain. Administratively it is divided into five provinces with capitals at Avellino, Benevento, Caserta, Salerno, and Naples. Anciently known as *Ausonia* or *Opicia* (after the Italic tribes who first lived here), it received its civilisation from the Greeks and the Etruscans. Its present name, originally used to designate the fertile plain of Capua (the *Ager campanus*), dates from the Samnite conquest (5C BC). Under the Romans, who occupied it after the Social War (88 BC), it rose to great prosperity and soon won the appellative *Campania felix* on account of its beauty and fertility.

With the fall of the Roman Empire the region passed to the Goths, to the Byzantines, and finally to the Lombards, who partitioned it into the duchies of Benevento, Capua, Naples and, later, Salerno. In its subsequent history the region followed the fortunes of Naples, its chief city.

Many of the more interesting places in Campania are conveniently visited from Naples.

THE PHLEGRAEAN FIELDS

The **Phlegraean Fields** or *Campi Flegrei* (burning fields), is the name given to the volcanic region to the west of Naples, as far as Cumae. Eruptions have apparently ceased, but have left their trace in 13 low craters, some filled with water, which give the countryside its distinctive appearance. It still abounds in hot springs and *fumarole*, or steam jets, notably the **Solfatara** at **Pozzuoli**. Both Greek colonists and the Romans were quick to appreciate the glorious climate and delightful surroundings close to the sea. Innumerable villas sprang up at Baiae and Puteoli, places renowned for their unbridled luxury under the empire, in keeping with the excesses of the imperial court. Of all this nothing remains except for a few ruined buildings and the names that evoke the memory of past glories.

Practical information

A tour of the principal sights may comfortably be made by car in half a day (actual driving time is just over 1hr); but if you can, spend a day or two on foot exploring this delightful region. The most important sites are the Roman **baths at Baia**, the Greek and Roman **ruins at Cumae** and the Roman **amphitheatre at Pozzuoli**.

 ### Information offices

POZZUOLI *Azienda Autonoma di Cura Soggiorno e Turismo*, Via Sacra 1, ☎ 081 850 7255, ▣ 081 863 2401.
See also **Naples** tourist information offices, p 111.

 ### Getting there and getting around
By road

The swiftest way to reach the Phlegraean Fields from Naples is to take the ringroad (*tangenziale*) to Pozzuoli, then proceed along local roads; the towns and sights are marked. If you are arriving from the coast of Lazio follow Road 7q south to Cuma. From Rome, take Autostrade A1 and A2 to Napoli Nord, then follow the *tangenziale* west to Pozzuoli.

By rail

Frequent trains are operated by the *Cumana* railway from Naples Montesanto station (Piazza Montesanto; Map 2, 5); trains run every 20mins to Pozzuoli (27mins), Baia (40mins) and Torregaveta (50mins). The *Circum Flegrea* railway, also departing from Montesanto station, goes to Torregaveta via Cuma and Lago Fusaro. The *Metropolitana* (*FS*) also runs from Naples Piazza Garibaldi, every 30mins, as far as Pozzuoli Solfatara (c 30mins). Further information from ▣ www.campaniatrasporti.it.

By sea

There are ferries to Pozzuoli from Procida (30mins) and Ischia (1hr), and hydrofoils to Pozzuoli from Procida (15mins). Details at ▣ www.campania-trasporti.it.

By bus

SEPSA bus departs Piazza Garibaldi, calling at Solfatara, Pozzuoli and Baia. From Baia, connections to Cumae, Bacoli and Cape Misenum.). Details from ▣ www.campaniatrasporti.it

 ### Where to stay

BACOLI €€ *Cala Moresca*, at Capo Miseno, Via Faro 44, ☎ 081 5235595, ▣ 081 5235557, ▣ www.calamoresca.it. Nicely located at Capo Miseno, with sea views from most rooms.

 ### Eating out

BACOLI €€ *Garibaldi*, Via Spiaggia 36, ☎ 081 523 4368. Traditional fish restaurant by the sea; closed Mon and Aug.
POZZUOLI € *La Cucina Flegrea*, at Monterusciello, Via Monterusciello 20, ☎ 081 5247481. Restaurant-pizzeria; closed Mon and briefly in Aug.

Of mud and mussels

The first signs of volcanic activity in this rather eerie region appear as soon as you leave Naples. **Agnano Terme** is a spa with hot springs on the south side of the crater of Agnano. The crater, 6.5km in circumference, became flooded with water in the Middle Ages and was drained in 1866, the waters flowing out through a tunnel beneath Monte Spina, the south-west eminence. Its marshy surface abounds with mineral springs.

The **spa** (open throughout the year, ☎ 081 618 9111) and the principal springs (mostly in the south-east part of the crater) are Agnano's chief claims to fame. On the right of the central hall are the Stufe di San Germano, a series of rooms with gradually increasing temperature; to the left is a cave like the famous nearby **Grotta del Cane** or Dog Grotto, in which carbon dioxide covers the floor to the height of half a metre, instantly extinguishing lights held in it and stupefying and killing animals: a phenomenon once demonstrated to visitors at the expense of stray dogs. The most important sources are a hot spring near the spa (72.5°C), regulated in 1921, the intermittent Sprudel (70°C), further north, and the abundant Ponticello (87°C). Further on is the Fanghiera, or mud reservoir, kept moist by springs, of which the most important is the Salvatore Tommasi (70°C). About 1km north near a hot chalybeate spring (39°C) is **Agnano racecourse**, extending to the foot of the Astroni hills.

Adjacent to the spa are the ruins of the Roman **Thermae Anianae**, a six-storeyed building with passages leading to the *sudatoria*, or vapour-chambers, hollowed out of the hillside. Excavations have revealed some interesting mosaics and pipes for water and steam. A road skirting the east side of the Agnano crater leads to the **Parco degli Astroni**, another extinct volcano.

The road to Pozzuoli climbs above Bagnoli under hills anciently called *Colles Leucogaei* on account of their white soil, which was used for bleaching barley. From the base of one of them issue the **Pisciarelli**, hot aluminous springs. Out to sea appears the island of Nisida with Capri behind it, and ahead is Capo Miseno backed by Monte Epomeo on Ischia.

The road turns away from the coast and passes the convent of **San Gennaro**, built in the 16C on the supposed site of the beheading of St Januarius. A stone stained with the martyr's blood is preserved in the church, which turns bright red on the occasion of the liquefaction of his blood in Naples. There is a fine view from the convent across the gulf.

The Solfatara di Pozzuoli

About 500m further on is the entrance to the **Solfatara di Pozzuoli** (open 08.30–1hr before sunset), a half-extinct volcano known to the Romans as *Forum Vulcani*. The huge elliptical crater, 752m across at its widest point, has changed little in appearance since Roman times. The path along the bottom passes (left) a well of hot water 9m deep and soon reaches the *fumarole*, a number of violent jets of steam emerging from the ground at a high temperature (c 143°C) and charged with sulphurous vapour. The nature of the gas varies considerably. The ground is hot and makes a hollow sound when stamped on. About 100m south-east, behind a small pavilion, is the largest fumarola, or **Bocca Grande**, from which steam issues at a very high temperature (162°C) with a whistling noise. The barren north-west part of the crater is at the lowest level and was probably covered with hot muddy water until the 18C. At various dates since, funnel-shaped cavities containing hot mud have formed here. About 240m north of the Bocca Grande are the **Stufe**, more fumaroles in an artificial excavation.

Pozzuoli

Beyond the Solfatara the road curves back towards the sea and, passing beneath the railway and just to the left of the entrance to the amphitheatre (see below), descends to (6km) Pozzuoli, a curious town (28m, population 77,000) that stands partly on an isolated promontory of yellow tufa and partly on the landward slopes, with its main street passing between. In 1970 part of the town was damaged by bradyseism, a 'slow earthquake' that raised the ground more than 75cm in six months. Further movement was registered in 1983.

History of Pozzuoli

The Greek colonists from Samos called Pozzuoli *Dikaearchia*. It became a commercial post subject to Cumae and was later conquered by the Samnites. The Romans established a colony here in 194 BC and the Romanised town, renamed *Puteoli*, soon became the principal Italian port for trading with the East. It was adorned with buildings appropriate to its wealth, so that Cicero was able to describe it as *pusilla Roma* ('little Rome'). Puteoli was the end of St Paul's perilous voyage from Caesarea in AD 62. The fall of Rome, the barbarian invasions, the eruption of Monte Nuovo, and the increase of malaria reduced the once prosperous port to a fishing village and today only its ruins testify to its former glory.

At the east end of the town, just beyond the sea-girt **Capuchin convent** where the composer G.B. Pergolesi (1710–36) died, is Piazza Matteotti (Porta di Città), where the buses from Naples terminate. Here, Via del Duomo ascends to the **cathedral** (San Procolo), which incorporates a temple erected in honour of Augustus by the architect Cocceius. The church was completely rebuilt in 1643 by Bishop Martino de Leon y Cardenas, but a fire in May 1964 destroyed the Baroque structure, revealing the Roman building, in marble, as well as remains of a Samnite temple, in tufa, dating from 3C to 2C BC. Pergolesi's tomb was undamaged by the fire.

From the Porta di Città Corso Vittorio Emanuele leads north and Corso Garibaldi leads west to the theatre and **public gardens**. Here are busts of Pergolesi and of the native composer Antonio Sacchini (1734–86). The harbour extends to the left and incorporates the surviving remains of the **Roman port**. The *Moles Puteolana* or *Opus Pilarum* consisted of a breakwater of 25 piers connected by arches, cleverly arranged to prevent the silting up of the harbour. At the end was a triumphal arch to Antoninus Pius, who restored the harbour in AD 120 after a violent storm. In calm weather, the foundations of a double line of piers and a number of columns can be discerned below the surface. The mooring rings by which ships were attached are now covered by more than a fathom of water, owing to the subsidence of the land. Offshore, on the south side of the town, are the remains of three submerged docks.

The Serapeum

The so-called Serapeum (open daily 09.00–1hr before sunset) is set in a park along the waterfront. This was not a temple dedicated to Serapis, as the name

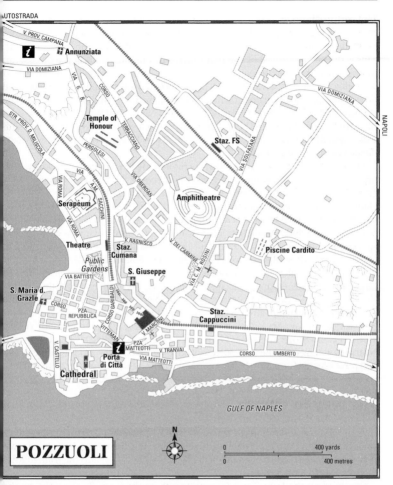

POZZUOLI

implies, but a *macellum* or rectangular market-hall (75 x 58m). It dates from the 1C AD. Opposite the entrance on the seaward side was an apse, preceded by four Corinthian columns, three of which are still standing. These have been eroded, from 3.5m to 5.5m above ground, by a species of shellfish, *Lithodomus lithophagus*, that still abounds in the Tyrrhenian Sea. This suggests that the columns were at some time buried for 3.5m and submerged for another 2m. Perhaps during the eruption of 1538, they were again raised above sea level; they became dry at the beginning of the 20C. Today water again covers the floor, although the 'slow quake' of 1970 raised the ground level by nearly 90cm.

Within the building is a courtyard, 32m square, surrounded by a gallery of 48 cipollino and granite columns beneath which were 35 booths and two marble-lined public latrines. A second storey probably existed on the same plan. The central *tholos*, or domed circular building, was supported by 16 columns of *giallo antico* which are now at Caserta, only their bases remaining in situ.

The amphitheatre

Now cross the railway and walk up the steps (5mins) to join Corso Terraciano near the entrance to the amphitheatre (open daily 09.00–1hr before sunset). This is the best preserved of the monuments of Puteoli, rivalling the Colosseum in Rome and the amphitheatres of Capua and Verona in size. The building you see today measures 149 x 166m. It was finished under Vespasian and replaced an older amphitheatre whose ruins (discovered during construction work on the Direttissima railway line connecting Rome and Naples in 1926–27) may be seen near the railway bridge to the north-east. It is built on three rows of arches and was originally surrounded by a brick arcade. The cavea had three ranges of seats divided by stairs into cunei.

The arena (72 x 42m) has an open corridor along its greater axis, below which are substructures (dens for wild beasts and rooms for stage machinery) in a remarkably good state of preservation. These were added under Trajan or Hadrian. Sixty openings connecting the substructures with the arena served for letting loose the wild beasts, for ventilation and for erecting the *pegma*, a wooden scaffold on which the gladiators fought and which could be run up very quickly. In Vespasian's time, reservoirs around the amphitheatre (the largest of which, the Piscina Cardito, still exists on the right of the Solfatara road) supplied water for flooding the arena on the occasion of a *naumachia* (mock sea battle). St Januarius and his companions were imprisoned here under Diocletian before their executions near the Solfatara. Here too Nero amazed the Armenian king Tiridates by his exploits among the beasts in the arena.

To the north-west are remains of what was probably a Roman villa, the ruined **Tempio dell'Onore** and some fragments of thermae, known as the **Tempio di Nettuno**, dating from the time of Nero. The so-called underground city may be visited June–Nov, Sat and Sun, by appointment, ☎ 848 800288 or 06 3996 7500).

The way to Cumae

As long as you don't do it in the torrid midsummer heat, the 16km (4hours) walk from Pozzuoli to Cumae is well worth your while (for the return by public transport see p 190). Of course, no one will object if you drive it; and the train follows more or less the same route.

Continue north along Corso Terracciano above the town. To the right, by the church of the Annunziata, Via Provinciale Campana diverges inland, lined on either side with sepulchral monuments, more of which were discovered when the Direttissima railway was constructed parallel to the road. About 2km beyond Pozzuoli leave the new road (which continues towards Cumae, see below) and descend to the left, joining the old road; this, with the Cumana railway, follows the lovely coastline of the Gulf of Naples.

To the right is **Monte Nuovo** (140m), a volcanic cone of rough scoriae and tufa, entered (tip required) from about half way between Arco Felice and Lago Lucrino stations. It takes c 20 minutes to reach the summit, and 10 minutes more to descend into the crater (15m above the sea). This crater was thrown up during the earthquake of 29 September 1538, when the Lucrine Lake was half filled and Pozzuoli deluged with mud and lapilli.

Lago Lucrino (Lake Lucrine) is separated from the sea (fine beach) by a narrow strip of land, the Via Herculea (whereby Hercules drove the bulls of Geryon across the swamp). The lake is much shrunken since the time (c 100 BC) when Sergius Orata began the cultivation of oysters here. Cicero's villa, which he called *Academia*, stood on the shore nearby.

A road running straight inland leads to **Lago d'Averno** (Lake Avernus), a crater 8km around and 34m deep, entirely surrounded by hills except for a narrow opening on the south side. It has been encirled by a stone edging to prevent the formation of malarial swamps; its waters are only 40cm above sea level.

Surrounded, in the heroic age, by dense forest, which gave it a dark and gloomy atmosphere, Avernus was said to be the home of the Cimmerians (Homer, *Odyssey* XI), who lived in eternal darkness, and the entrance to Hades. The Greek name *Aornos* (held to mean without birds) gave rise to the legend that birds flying over the lake fell into it, suffocated by poisonous fumes.

Hannibal, as an apparent mark of respect for local superstition, but what was in fact a pretext for a reconnaissance of Puteoli, visited Lake Avernus and offered a sacrifice; the custom of making a propitiatory sacrifice to the infernal deities of Avernus lasted beyond the days of Constantine.

Agrippa completely altered the appearance of the countryside surrounding the lake. To counter the threat of Sextus Pompeius' fleet (37 BC) he cut down the forest and connected Lake Avernus with the sea by a canal, via Lake Lucrine, and to Cumae by a tunnel (see below), thereby constructing a military harbour of perfect security, the Portus Julius. This was later abandoned, and finally wrecked by the eruption of 1538. Despite Agrippa's improvements, the association between Avernus and Hades, sung by Virgil and regenerated by Pliny and Silius Italicus, survived even among 6C Byzantine writers.

On the east shore of the lake are ruins of **thermae**. The most remarkable remains, arbitrarily known as the Tempio d'Apollo, are of an octagonal building with a round interior broken by niches, the dome of which (now fallen) once spanned a space of over 36m. The overgrown ruins on the west side probably represent a shipbuilding and repair yard.

Agrippa's tunnel to Cumae, a passage more than 1km long executed by Cocceius, leads away from the north-west shore. It is known as the **Grotta della Pace**, after Pietro della Pace, who explored it in 1507. Straight and wide enough for chariots to pass, it is the most ambitious underground work attempted by the Romans and, being lighted at intervals by vertical openings, it could be travelled through with ease, even without a light, until it was damaged by fighting in 1943.

A path along the south side of the lake, rising above it to the left, leads in c 3 minutes to a long gallery cut into the rock, off which opens a chamber blackened with torch smoke. Once a rival claimant to be the Sibyl's cave, this is now thought to have been part of Agrippa's defensive works.

Road and railway now follow the Via Herculea. The railway then tunnels through the Punta dell'Epitaffio, whereas the road follows the coast. Here is the site of *Bauli*, where Agrippina, having escaped the previous day from a planned accident at sea, was murdered, in the bedroom of her villa, on her son Nero's orders. On the right of the road are some ruins of **thermae**, called the Stufe di Nerone or di Tritoli, including a remarkable **sudatorium** (vapour chamber) hewn out of the tufa.

Baia

Baia, the ancient *Baiae*, extolled by the Latin writers Horace and Martial, is a large village standing on the bay that bears its name. It enjoys a splendid view across the Gulf of Pozzuoli.

History of Baia

In the early days of the Roman Empire, *Baiae*, which, according to legend, owed its name to Baios, Odysseus' navigator, was the fashionable bathing resort of Roman society. Successive emperors rivalled each other in the construction of magnificent seaside palaces, and Caligula built his famous bridge of boats here. However, the reputation of the town was tarnished by Nero's murder of his mother, Agrippina, and his sanguinary suppression of the conspiracy of Piso. Hadrian died here on 17 July 138. *Baiae* was plundered by the Saracens in the 8C and gradually deserted as malaria spread. The palace ruins now extend some distance beneath the sea, owing to ground subsidence. Finds made in the harbour in 1923–28 included statues and important architectural fragments. The best of these, the *Aphrodite Sossandra*, is displayed in the Museo Archeologico Nazionale in Naples. Others can be seen in the Museo Archeologico dei Campi Flegrei, described below.

A palatial summer house

Behind the station is the so-called **Temple of Diana**; one of several buildings once thought to be temples but now known to be baths. Octagonal without and circular within, it preserves four niches and part of its domed roof. From the piazza, steps ascend to the **Scavi di Baia** (open Tues–Sun 09.00–1hr before sunset). Systematic excavations began in 1941 and were completed ten years later. A group of buildings, some of which were already known in the Middle Ages, were identified, comprising an **imperial palatium** built between the 1C and 4C AD. From the entrance, a long avenue leads to a portico where architectural fragments are displayed. Here, steps lead to the upper terrace, one of several such areas set into the hillside at various levels. A row of rooms with shallow exedrae extends along the right. In the first of these the statue of Sossandra, a marble copy of a 5C Greek original, was found. The second contains a statue of *Mercury*, beheaded by thieves (who in antiquity enjoyed the god's protection!) in 1978.

A staircase descends to the central terrace, along one side of which a series of rooms forming a semicircle suggests the previous existence of a theatre-nymphaeum. From here, more steps descend to the lower terrace, occupied by a large (35 x 29m) rectangular bathing pool, surrounded by a graceful portico. To the east lies the complex of buildings traditionally called the **Temple of Venus**, which includes a large vaulted hall surrounded by apsidal openings, also believed to be a nymphaeum, and numerous smaller rooms.

Across the street, outside the archaeological park, is a hall of circular plan, 26m in diameter. Although the vault has collapsed, the rest of the structure is intact. From the north side of the pool a corridor partially covered by arches leads to the **Temple of Mercury**. These buildings appear to have made up another **thermal complex**; principal among them is a great circular hall nearly 22m in diameter, similar in structure to the Pantheon in Rome. Like the smaller halls to the rear, it is now filled with water to the base of the dome, creating the unusual acoustic effects from which it derives its nickname, Tempio dell'Eco.

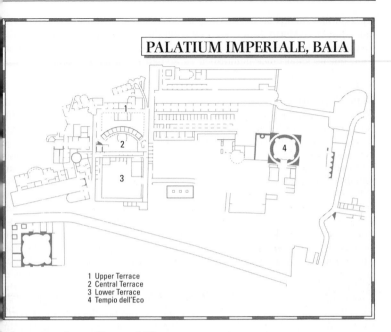

PALATIUM IMPERIALE, BAIA

1 Upper Terrace
2 Central Terrace
3 Lower Terrace
4 Tempio dell'Eco

The road to Capo Miseno

Beyond Baia, the road to Capo Miseno ascends a gentle slope along the shore, passing several columbaria (fine view). O n the left is the 16C **Castello di Baia**, built by order of Don Pedro de Toledo. The castle houses the **Museo Archeologico dei Campi Flegrei** (open Tues–Sat 09.00–14.00/19.00, Sun 09.00–19.00; ☎ 081 523 3797), with material from excavations at Baia and other sites in the area. At the bottom of a hill is the village of **Bacoli** (population 27,000). The Via della Marina, to the left, at the entrance to the village, descends to the so-called **tomb of Agrippina**, really the ruins of a small theatre. From the main road Via Ercole and Via Sant'Anna ascend to the church of Sant'Anna. Walking round this, you may go on to (15 minutes) the **Cento Camerelle**, a two-storeyed ruin of which the upper part was a reservoir; the function of the lower storey is not known. At Via Creco 10 you may obtain the key for the **Piscina mirabile**, 10 minutes south of the village (open 09.00–1 hour before sunset; tip required). This is the largest and best-preserved reservoir in the district (70 x 25m). Its form recalls that of a basilica, with five pillared aisles of equal height. It once lay at the extremity of an aqueduct and was used for supplying the Roman fleet stationed at Misenum.

At the southern end of the town is the **Lago di Miseno** or **Mare Morto**—the 'dead' (landlocked) sea. Leave the main road (see below) heading south, following the causeway that separates the lagoon from the picturesque harbour of **Misenum**. The harbour was built by Agrippa in 41 BC as a temporary refuge for the Tyrrhenian fleet during the construction of the Portus Julius (see above); it was while stationed here with the fleet that Pliny the Younger witnessed the fatal eruption of Vesuvius in AD 79. The port consisted of two basins, of which the inner, the Mare Morto, is now shut off from the Porto di Miseno proper by the road causeway. The colony of Misenum was founded at the same time as the harbour, but its importance diminished as Roman naval power declined. It was destroyed by the Saracens in the 9C.

Capo Miseno

The byroad continues to the village of Miseno. Cars are not allowed beyond this point. A path turns to the right near the church, to the right again just before a farmhouse, and then to the left, passing various ruins (see below). The ascent (1 hour there and back) leads to Capo Miseno (155m), a promontory commanding a wonderful view over the Gulfs of Pozzuoli, Naples, and Gaeta, and the surrounding lakes and islands.

The headland is a segment of an ancient crater, the rest of which has sunk below the sea. The remaining portion so resembles an artificial tumulus that it has given rise to the legend that it was the burial-place of Misenus, Aeneas's trumpeter. The headland was already covered with villas when the colony was founded, and among its distinguished residents was the general Caius Marius, whose country house passed into the possession of his eminent colleague Lucullus and later to the emperors. Tiberius died there in AD 37. The ruins of Marius's villa are on the south side of the harbour; near the church are the remains of the circular baths; and to the north-west stands a theatre commanding a fine view of Ischia. On the west side of the headland is the **Grotta Dragonara**, an excavation supported by 12 pillars, probably a storehouse for the fleet. A lighthouse marks the furthest point on the cape. Walkers may follow the **Spiaggia di Miliscola** (the name comes from the Latin *militis schola*, roughly, navy training ground), a narrow sandbar 2km long between the Mare Morto and the sea, and rejoin the main road c 1km before Cappella (see below).

Back on the main road, bear left along the north side of the Mare Morto, turning sharply right for Cappella, a village between Monte Grillo or Monte di Procida (144m) on the south, and Monte dei Salvatichi (123m). About 1km beyond Cappella, a road on the left leads to (1km) **Torregaveta** (the terminus of the Cumana and Circumflegrei railways). From here another road running south ascends to the village of **Monte di Procida** (3km; bus from Torregaveta), on a tufa hill covered with ruined villas among vineyards (which produce an excellent wine). **Acquamorta**, on the end of the promontory beyond, commands a fine view of Procida and Ischia.

Leaving the Torregaveta road on the left you reach the semicircular **Lago di Fusaro**, the ancient Acherusian Swamp, separated from the sea by a sandbar pierced by two canals, one Roman and one modern (1858). On the slopes of the hill north of Torregaveta is the ruined villa of Servilius Vatia. Since 1784 the lake has been a centre for oyster culture and fish breeding. On the lake is a casino, built for Ferdinand IV by Vanvitelli (1782), now a marine biological station (admission to both establishments on application).

Cumae

The road crosses the railway near Cuma Fusaro station. Leaving a road to Baia on the right, follow the lake shore and then pass through vineyards to reach (15mins from the station) Cumae, perhaps the oldest Greek colony in Italy, now a mass of scattered ruins in a romantic situation where excavation fights a losing battle with nature.

History of Cumae

By tradition, the foundation of Cumae dates from c 1050 BC, the first settlers being the Chalcidians and the Aeolians of Kyme. In fact, though it was one of the earliest colonies, there is no proof that it antedates Syracuse. Its prosperity and population increased rapidly, and colonies were dispatched to *Dikaearchia* (Pozzuoli) and, after the conquest of Parthenope, to found the settlement of Neapolis. Cumae was a centre of Hellenic culture, and from its alphabet all other Italian alphabets were derived. Tarquinius Superbus (who later died in exile at Cumae) here purchased the Sibyline Books from the Cumaean Sibyl, according to Pliny, and regretted his attempt to bargain with her.

In 474 BC the Cumaeans, in alliance with Hieron of Syracuse defeated an Etruscan fleet, a victory immortalised by Pindar in the first Pythian Ode. In 421 BC Cumae was conquered by the Samnites, passing later, with the rest of their possessions, to Rome. In the reign of Nero it was the scene of the voluntary death of Petronius Arbiter. No longer of importance, Cumae fell easy prey to the Sacracens in the 9C and was utterly destroyed by Naples and Aversa in 1207.

The ruins of the ancient city lie mainly beneath farmland; a visit requires at least two hours. A short distance before a fork, where the main road bears inland to the right, are the ruins of an amphitheatre, easily traced through the vineyards and olive groves that cover it. Taking the little road to the left at the fork you pass (right; on cultivated land) the **Temple of the Giants** and, further away, the **Temple of the Forum**. Along the ascent towards Monte di Cuma (78m), the city's acropolis, traces of many other buildings can be seen over a wide area.

Sibyl's cave

Beyond the entrance to the excavations (open daily 09.00–1hr before sunset; refreshments), notice the massive **walls** of cyclopean stone, Greek in the lower courses, Roman above.

Go through a tunnel hewn out of the rock. Beyond, to the left, is the entrance to the **Cave of the Cumaean Sibyl**, one of the more famous of ancient sanctuaries, brought to light in 1932. Aeneas came to consult the Sibyl here; on either side of the entrance marble plaques now recall Virgil's account of the visit (*Aeneid* VI 42–51). The cave consists of a dromos, or corridor, c 44m long, nearly 2.5m wide and c 5m high, ending in a rectangular chamber, all hewn out of the rock. The dromos, of trapezoidal cross-section, markedly Minoan in style, runs due north–south in the shoreward side of the hill, and is lit by six galleries opening to the west (so it is best visited in the afternoon). From the other side open three lower chambers, apparently designed for lustral (purificatory) waters and later used for Christian burials. The *oikos*, or secret chamber, at the end, probably redesigned in the 4C or 3C BC, has three large niches.

At a lower level (reached by a path to the left) a huge **Roman crypt** c 180m long, tunnels through the hill; this lies on the same axis as the 1km long tunnel —the Grotta della Pace (see p 197) and is probably a continuation of it. Many dark passages leading from it show traces of Christian occupation.

A paved Via Sacra climbs to the first terrace where (right) some remains of the

Temple of Apollo, a Greek structure altered in Augustan times and transformed into a Christian church in the 6C or 7C, survive. On the summit is the so-called **Temple of Jupiter**, a larger construction, also of Greek origin and also transformed (5C–6C) into a Christian basilica of five aisles. Behind the presbytery are remains of a large circular pool for baptism by immersion. Here the beauty of the view and the stillness, broken only by the rustle of lizards and the murmur of the sea, make an indelible impression.

The chief **necropolis**, which has provided many interesting additions to the archaeological museum in Naples, lies between the acropolis and, to the north, Licola, a modern village on the site of a drained lake. From the ruins a path (which you cannot enter from the other end) leads down to the deserted shore. Towards the sea the outer wall of the town is still traceable. An extension of the railway is planned from Torregaveta, which may be reached by a pleasant walk (of 4km) along the beach or by a well-preserved stretch of the Roman road that linked Cumae with Misenum. This was a branch of the Via Domitiana, engineered in AD 95 to link Rome directly with Puteoli (Pozzuoli). Along its course to the north lie the **Lago di Patria**—once the harbour for the Roman colony of *Liternum* (scanty ruins)—where Scipio Africanus died in 184 BC; and *Sinuessa* (near the modern Mondragone), where it joined the Via Appia.

Returning to Naples

To return to (20km) Naples, take the road running north-east (right) from Cumae; in 5 minutes a path (right) leads to the mouth of the Grotta della Pace (closed). The road then passes beneath (c 2km from Cumae) the **Arco Felice**, a massive brick archway, 20m high and 6m wide, in a deep cutting made in Monte Grillo by Domitian to secure direct communication between Cumae and Puteoli. To the west is a good stretch of Roman paving. Pass the north side of Lake Avernus and the Monte Nuovo, diverge right to reach Arco Felice station (4km away), then follow the shore road to (6km) Pozzuoli. Continue by the sea past thermal spas (hotels) and pozzolana quarries to Bagnoli.

Bagnoli is a bathing resort and spa much frequented by the Neapolitans. Here is the fabulous new **Città della Scienza**, a multimedia hands-on science museum and planetarium occupying the 19C factory buildings of the former Italsider Iron and Steel Works. Directly overlooking the Bay of Pozzuoli, the 12,000 square-metre facility offers an instructive and entertaining journey through the worlds of science and technology. Although there is a special childrens' section (*Officina dei Piccoli*), the museum is a must for everyone. Located at Via Coroglio 104, it is open Tues–Sat 09.00–17.00, Sun 10.00–19.00; ☎ 081 735 2260; bus and metro connections at ✉ www.cittàdellascienza.it.

Continuing along Via Coroglio you come shortly to the entrance to a fascinating new archaeological site, the **Grotta di Seiano and Area di Pausilypon** Here are the remains of *Pausilypon* (the carefree), the villa belonging to the Roman patrician Vedius Pollio and afterwards to Augustus. The villa proper comprises living areas, an odeon and a large and small theatre; it is connected by the 800m Grotta di Seiano to Marechiaro on the other side of the Posillipo promentory. At the time of writing the site can be entered from the Bagnoli side only; it is open Mon–Sat 09.00–13.00, with escorted tours leaving at 09.30, 10.30 and

11.30. On Monday, Wednesday and Friday visits are restricted to the Grotto only.

From Bagnoli the old road runs straight to Naples. Leisurely travellers may choose to follow the coast past the huge chemical works of Coroglio, then climb up to the **Rotonda** (with a view of Nisida), re-entering Naples along the Posillipo peninsula.

THE CAPUAN PLAIN

The extinct volcano of Monte Roccamonfina, today little more than a wild, wooded hill, marks the northern limit of the Capuan plain. This is the most intensively cultivated area of Campania, and although modern mechanised farming has taken away much of its original charm, it still appears as a huge, well-tended garden.

As might be expected of a place where people have lived and worked for thousands of years, sites of historic and artistic interest abound here. Suffice it to mention **Capua**, where the museum contains a unique collection of Italic *Deae Matres* (earth goddesses); **Santa Maria Capua Vetere**, known for its great ancient amphitheatre; and **Caserta**, nicknamed the Versailles of Naples after the royal palace, built here by Charles III of Bourbon. Around these major monuments are a constellation of minor sights—some, like the little church of Sant'Angelo in Formis, are equally impressive. All are easy to visit regardless of whether you arrive from Naples, or from Rome and points north.

Practical information

 Information offices
CASERTA *Ente Provinciale per il Turismo*, Palazzo Reale, ☎ 0823 322233, ▯ 0823 326300.
See also **Naples** tourist offices, p 111.

 Getting there and getting around
By road

The main cities in this area can be reached by car via Autostrada A1/E45 (from Rome) and A2/E45 (from Naples). Heavy traffic makes travel to and from the area on the smaller roads problematic.

By rail

A choice of two routes (either the old main line to Rome via Cassino, or the line to Benevento and Foggia) provides a frequent service from Naples (Centrale)

to Caserta in 30–45 mins. To reach Santa Maria Capua Vetere and Capua, on the Naples–Rome line, takes an extra 10–15mins. Intercity trains from Rome to Naples stop at Caserta only (2hrs 10mins).

Where to stay
See Naples (p 112) or the Valle Latina (p 80).

 Eating out
The best restaurants in this thriving agricultural district are in the countryside.
CAPUA €€ *Osteria a San Giovanni dei Nobiluomini*, Piazza De Renzis 6, ☎ 0823 620062. Creative cuisine and good wines, in the historic city centre; closed Mon and two weeks in Aug.
CASAGIOVE (3km north of Caserta at Caserta Nord interchange) €€ *Le*

Quattro Fontane, Via Quartiere Vecchio 60, ☎ 0823 468970. Traditional trattoria; closed Sun, Aug and late Dec.
€ *La Botte*, SS Appia 168, ☎ 0823 468130. Wine shop and delicatessen with fine wines and liqueurs, extra virgin oil, fresh cheeses and pastries.
CASERTA **€€** *Le Colonne*, Via Nazionale Appia 7–13, ☎ 0823 467494. Quiet, comfortable restaurant, dinner by reservation only; closed Tues and two weeks in Aug.
€€ *Massa*, Via Mazzini 55, ☎ 0823 456527. In a historic palace with garden seating in fair weather; closed Mon and two weeks in Aug.
PIANA DI MONTE VERNA (15km from Caserta), **€€** *Carpe Diem*, Masserie Corte 101, ☎ 0823 861371. Traditional food and wines; closed Sun evening, Mon and two weeks in Aug.
PIETRAVAIRANO (8km east of

Autostrada A2, Caianello exit) **€€** *La Caveja*, Via Roma 1, ☎ 0823 984824. Restaurant; closed Sun evening and Mon and one week in late Dec.
SAN GREGORIO MATESE (55km north of Caserta; take Road 87 from Caserta, then Road 158dir)
€ *San Donato*, Road 158, ☎ 0823 919161. Restaurant in a former hunting lodge splendidly located in the cool Monti del Matese; closed Tues and Nov.
SAN POTITO SANNITICO (44km north of Caserta on Road 265) **€€** *Quercete*, Strada Provinciale per Gioia 2, ☎ 0823 911520. Restaurant on a farm specialising in lamb dishes; closed Mon and Tues.
SANTA MARIA CAPUA VETERE **€** *Ninfeo*, Via Cappabianca, ☎ 0823 846700. Restaurant; closed Mon, two weeks in Aug and one week in Dec.

Capua

Capua (population 20,000) is situated within a narrow bend of the River Volturno, 5km west of Monte Tifata (604m). It bears the name of the ancient *Capua*, an Italic city that stood on the site today occupied by Santa Maria Capua Vetere.

History of Capua

The town was founded in 856 by refugees from ancient Capua (see below). They built a new town on the ruins of *Casilinum*, noted for its heroic defence against Hannibal in 216 BC and deserted in 2C AD. The new Capua became the medieval centre of the agricultural *Terra di Lavoro* (which occupied most of the Capuan plain and the surrounding hills) and an important frontier town of the Norman realm of Sicily. Its famous gate, designed by Frederick II in 1247, was destroyed in 1557.

The town fell, after a bloody siege, to the French under d'Aubigny and their ally Cesare Borgia, in 1501. Pope Honorius I (625–638) and Ettore Fieramosca (hero of Barletta, d. 1515) were both natives. The first Battle of the Volturno (1 October 1860), when Garibaldi defeated the Bourbons of Naples, took place on the plain and hills to the east of Capua. Afterwards he occupied the town.

The atmosphere of Capua combines the grace of a noble past with the hustle and bustle of a busy marketplace. The Via del Duomo crosses the town from Piazza dei Giudici, on the south, where the façade of the **town hall** (1561) displays seven marble busts from the amphitheatre at Santa Maria Capua Vetere (see below), to Via Roma and the Museo Campano, on the north. The **cathedral** founded in 835 and almost completely rebuilt, was destroyed in 1942 except for part of the apse, right outer wall, and side chapels. Of the 24 columns in the atrium (slightly damaged), 16 are original; the beautiful campanile dates from 861. The **crypt**, with 14 antique columns, contains mosaics.

The **Museo Provinciale Campano** occupies Palazzo Antignano, the former palace of the Dukes of San Cipriano, at Via Roma 68; the portal is in a late Catalan Gothic style. The collections (open Tues–Sat 09.00–13.30, Sun 09.00–13.00, closed holidays; for reservations, ☎ 0823 961402) focus on sculptures from ancient Capua, notably the extraordinary series of *Deae matres*, or earth goddesses, from the Temple of Mater Matuta. These small, stone women hold or suckle stone babies, children of the Earth, who depend on her fertility and generosity for survival. In early agrarian societies such statues would have been set in a place sacred to the earth-goddess in the hope of ensuring a fruitful harvest (and providing a secure future). Uncovered in 1845 near Santa Maria Capua Vetere, the statues displayed here date from the 6C to the 1C BC.

The museum also contains inscriptions from the amphitheatre (see below), a fine series of Campanian terracottas (mostly salvaged), a colossal head of *Capua Imperiale* and medieval sculptures. A small picture gallery is devoted to southern Italian art from the 15C to 18C. In the centre of the town is the Gothic palazzo of Ettore Fieramosca, one of the champions of the *Disfida di Barletta*, the famous contest between French and Italian knights (see p 438).

To the north-east of Capua the Cappella dei Morti commemorates the 5000 victims of the French siege of 1501. Beyond the chapel, at the foot of Monte Tifata, is the 11C basilica of **Sant'Angelo in Formis** (open by appointment; ☎ 0823 960492), reconstructed in 1073 and adorned with 12 columns and 11C frescoes of scenes from the Old and New Testament, featuring prophets, kings, and saints. These are by artists of the Monte Cassino school and show a strong Byzantine influence.

Teano and Calvi Risorta

On the eastern flank of Roccamonfina lies the town of **Teano**. Here, in 1860, Victor Emmanuel II on his march southward met Garibaldi returning from the Expedition of the Thousand and the overthrow of the Bourbon dynasty of Naples. The town occupies the site of the ancient *Teanum*, capital of a pre-Roman Italic people, the Sidicini. Its main monuments are a Roman theatre and amphitheatre (near the road to the station), the Romanesque church of San Paride (just beyond), and a medieval cathedral (restored). The **Museo Archeologico di Teanum** (open Tues–Sun 09.00–19.00; ☎ 0823 657302), in the Gothic Loggione e Cavallerizza, originally part of the Marzano castle beautifully situated at the top of the old town, displays finds from the ancient *Teanum Sidicium* and its territory. Highlights include votive offerings from the sanctuaries at Loreta and Fondo Ruozzo, grave finds from thhe 5C BC to the Roman Imperial age, and material unearthed during the recent excavation of the theatre.

At nearby **Calvi Risorta**, the ancient *Cales* (famous for its wine), the little Romanesque cathedral, with a Cosmatesque pulpit and bishop's throne, is intact; so are the small 10C castle and the Grotta dei Santi (30 minute walk up the Rio de Lanzi), with its remarkable collection of 10C mural paintings of saints.

Santa Maria Capua Vetere

Santa Maria Capua Vetere (population 33,000) occupies the site of the ancient Capua.

History of Santa Maria Capua Vetere

An Oscan settlement here was transformed by the Etruscans into a city called *Capua*. It soon became the most important place in Campania and the richest city in southern Italy. Constantly assailed and sometimes defeated by the war-like Samnites, it placed itself under the protection of Rome in 343 BC.

It was always a hotbed of unrest, however, and it opened its gates to Hannibal in 216 BC; explorations in 1976 revealed a military camp of the 2C BC, believed to be that of the Carthaginian forces, in the vicinity of the amphitheatre. According to the legend, the Carthaginians were so softened by the *luxuria* (idle self-indulgence) they learned from the Capuans that they never achieved another success. (Or as Fynes Moryson wrote in 1617, 'the delicacies of Capua were such that the Army of Hanibal grew effeminate thereby.') The city was retaken by the Romans in 211 and severely punished.

In 73 BC the revolt of the gladiators headed by Spartacus broke out here in the amphitheatre. Under the empire Capua was one of the wealthier towns in southern Italy, but it was razed by the Saracens, and its inhabitants fled in 856 to found the modern Capua. The present town on this site grew from a small settlement that clustered round the church of Santa Maria, which survived the Saracen raid.

The Roman amphitheatre

Just outside the town, as you arrive from Capua, are two interesting and well preserved Roman tombs, the second of which is the largest in Campania. The imposing amphitheatre (open daily 09.00–dusk) was built in the 1C AD under Augustus and restored by Hadrian and Antoninus Pius. Although it has been exploited for building stone over the centuries, it escaped damage in the Second World War. It measures 170 x 140m, and is second in size only to the Colosseum in Rome. It had four storeys and was surrounded by 80 arches; only two survive. Under the arena are three covered galleries, with a fourth around the circumference, and six vaulted passages lit by square apertures. Fragments of the building's sculptural decoration and other antiquities (notably a 2C mosaic pavement showing Nereids and Tritons) are set in the park at the south side of the monument. Several statues (including those of *Eros*, *Venus* and *Psyche*) have been removed to the Museo Archeologico Nazionale in Naples, and seven of the busts of deities that adorned the keystones of the arches have been incorporated into the façade of the town hall at Capua. The new **antiquarium** houses an archaeological collection focusing on gladiatorial activity at Capua and elsewhere in Roman times.

In 1923 an interesting subterranean **Mithraeum**, with well-preserved frescoes, was discovered nearby; visitors are conducted (10 minute walk) by the custodian. Further on, in Corso Umberto I, is a ruined arch erected in honour of Hadrian. The **cathedral of Santa Maria** contains 51 antique columns from Capuan temples.

In the environs

At **San Prisco**, 2km north-east, the church contains 5C and 6C mosaics in the tomb-chapel of St Matrona, Princess of Lusitania. **Aversa**, 13km south-west, has several interesting monuments. Andrew of Hungary, Joan I's husband, was murdered in the Norman **castle** in 1345. Three years later, Charles of Durazzo, who had instigated the murder, was killed by Louis of Hungary, Andrew's brother. The **cathedral** preserves some original Norman work. The church of **San Lorenzo** has a Lombard façade and a beautiful cloister, and **San Francesco** houses a small collection of religious art brought here, for reasons of security, from country churches.

Aversa's white wine, called *Asprinio*, is locally esteemed. Domenico Cimarosa (1749–1801), the composer, was born here. The Roman town of *Atella*, which stood nearby, was the home of the *Fabulae Atellanae*, satirical farce in the Oscan language that became a tradition in the Roman theatre. A collection of antiquities from Atella may be seen at the lovely **Museo Archeologico dell'Agro Atellano** at Succivo (Via Roma 7; open Tues–Sun 09.00–19.00; ☎ 081 501 2701).

The royal palace and gardens at Caserta

Though some 69,000 people live in Caserta, the only building anyone ever visits is uninhabited. This is the famous **Reggia**, the most sumptuous royal palace in Italy and one of the more impressive buildings in Europe. The vast palace, originally a summer home, was begun by King Charles III of Naples in 1752 and completed by Ferdinand I in 1774 from the plans of **Luigi Vanvitelli**. The first stone was laid by the king on his 36th birthday, 20 January 1752; for the occasion the perimeter of the future palace was marked by regiments of infantry and squadrons of cavalry, and two cannons with artillerymen were placed at each corner. The army of work-men engaged on the building was swelled by convicts and galley-slaves.

Construction proceeded briskly until 1759, the year in which Charles left Naples to take the throne of Spain. Work then slowed, coming to a complete halt in 1764 when, in the midst of a severe plague and famine, the half-finished building was occupied by the poor and homeless. After the death of Vanvitelli in 1773 his son, Carlo, continued the construction, but he ran into difficulties of various kinds and was unable to complete the building according to his father's plan. Eliminated from the design were four corner towers and a central dome—which undoubtedly would have relieved the gravity of the building's present configuration—and the guards' quarters, which were to enclose the vast forecourt on all sides.

During the long reign of Ferdinand IV the palace was enlivened by balls, recep-tions, hunting parties and theatrical performances. It was the favourite residence of Ferdinand II and, after the Unification of Italy, it was visited by the Savoyard kings. It was presented by Victor Emmanuel III to the State in 1921. On 29 April 1945, it was the scene of the unconditional surrender of the German forces in Italy to Supreme Allied Commander in the Mediterranean, Field Marshal Harold Alexander.

The two principal façades, 247m long and 36m high, are pierced by 243 win-dows and several monumental entrances. The palace consists of five storeys—a ground floor, mezzanine, first floor, second floor, and attic—containing 1200 rooms served by 43 staircases, all arranged around four monumental court-yards, whose decoration was never finished.

Swinburne at Caserta

The design of the building was controversial even in its own day. Although many contemporaries regarded it as one of the nobler edifices of its kind in Europe, some considered it a megalomaniac construction. The English poet Henry Swinburne visited it in the 1770s and left this account:

'The vast dimensions of its apartments, the bold span of their ceilings, the excellence and beauty of the materials employed in building and decorating it, and the strength of the masonry, claim the admiration of all beholders, who must confess it is a dwelling spacious and grand enough to have lodged the ancient masters of the Roman world. It is a pity that its enormous bulk drowns the minuter members of its architecture, and gives too much the idea of a regular monastery, where the wealthy chief of some religious order presides over long dormitories of segregated monks; by the gigantic range, and the number of windows, too great a sameness is produced, the few breaks in the front become imperceptible, and the lines too long and uniform, consequently fatiguing to the eye; the colonnades sink into the walls, and variety is in vain sought for in the prodigious expanse; bolder and greater projections, massive towers, arcades or porticoes, would have shown the parts of this great building to more advantage, and formed those happy contrasts that are so necessary in works of so very large a dimension. Upon a nearer approach, the parts and proportions are better distinguished, and the objection ceases.'

The **interior** (open daily 08.30–19.30; ☎ 0823 277 4111) is fascinating. The main portico is divided into three vestibules by 64 columns. The **state staircase** ascends to the first-floor vestibule, an octagon surrounded by 24 pillars of yellow marble. Opposite the head of the stairs is the **palatine chapel**, usually closed. Modelled on the chapel of the Palace of Versailles, it contains the finest marble ornaments and several noteworthy paintings, including an *Immaculate Conception* by Giuseppe Bonito, a *Presentation in the Temple* by Antonio Raffaele Mengs and five works by Sebastiano Conca.

A door on the left leads to the **royal apartments**, beautifully decorated with tapestries, paintings, frescoes, and period furniture. The **room of the Halabardiers**, the first to be entered, has a Bourbon coat of arms borne by Virtues in the ceiling. The **guard room**, following, is decorated with the *Apotheosis of the Farnese family* (of which Charles's mother was an eminent member) and the *Twelve provinces of the kingdom*, in the ceiling. Scenes from ancient history are depicted in the bas-reliefs around the walls. On the right is a marble statuary group of *Alexander Farnese crowned by Victory*, carved, according to tradition, out of a column from the Temple of Peace in Rome.

The adjacent **room of Alexander**, which corresponds to the centre of the main façade, enjoys a good view of what was once the tree-lined high road to Naples. The ceiling fresco and the stucco reliefs show scenes from the life of Alexander Farnese; the other paintings celebrate deeds of Charles of Bourbon. The porphyry portrait medallion over the fireplace is of Alexander the Great. The room is furnished in the Empire style; particulary noteworthy is the large clock on the right wall, made in Naples in 1828.

The **new apartment**, so-called because it was the last to be completed (1845), is reached by a door on the right. It consists of three rooms, also furnished in the Empire style and decorated with paintings and reliefs of mythological subjects. Notice, in the centre of the first room, an Oriental alabaster cup presented by Pope Pius IX to Ferdinand II.

The **throne room**, the largest room of the palace, is adorned with a frieze containing medallions of the kings of Naples from Roger the Norman to Ferdinand II (Joseph Bonaparte and Joachim Murat have been tactfully omitted). The ceiling painting shows Charles III laying the first stone of the palace. The living quarters of the king are beyond the throne room. The **council room** contains a fine table given by the city of Naples to Francis I as a wedding present. An antechamber, where majolicas are displayed, gives access to **Francis II's bedroom**, containing a magnificent mahogany bed and the first known example of a roll-top desk. The ceiling painting of *Theseus killing the Minotaur* is by Giuseppe Cammarano. Adjoining the bedroom are the king's **bathroom** and **study**. Beyond two handsome **drawing rooms** decorated with mythological subjects lies the **bedroom of Joachim Murat**, containing perhaps the finest Empire-style furniture in the palace; on the far side of the room are an antechamber and a small chapel.

Returning to the central room of Alexander, enter the east wing of the palace, inhabited by Ferdinand I from 1780 until his expulsion in 1806, and from 1815 until his death in 1825. The **reception room**, **drawing room**, **dining room**, and **fumoir** are decorated with allegories of the *Four Seasons*, by Antonio de Dominici and Fedele Fischetti. Here Maria Carolina held her famous receptions, one of which is recorded in a particularly delightful manner by an English guest, Lady Anne Miller:

After mounting a staircase, you enter several large rooms, hung and adorned in the Italian taste with crimson damask, velvet, etc., and amply illuminated. The chairs are placed all round against the walls, and each sits down where they choose. These rooms were so full, that there was a double row of chairs placed back to back down the middle. Accident placed me exactly opposite the Queen, who took the first chair she found empty. There are no tables in any of the rooms; but every person being seated, the supper is served thus: The best looking soldiers, chosen from the King's guards, carry about the supper with as much order, regularity, and gravity as if they were performing a military manoeuvre. First appears a soldier bearing a large basket with napkins, followed by a page, who unfolds and spreads them on the lap of each of the company as they happen to sit; but when it comes to the Queen's turn to be served, a lord of the Court presents her majesty's napkin. The first soldier is immediately followed by a second, bearing a basket of silver plates; another carries knives and forkes; then follows a fourth, with a great pâté, composed of macaroni, cheese, and butter; he is accompanied by an ecuyer tranchant, or carver, armed with a knife a foot long, who cuts the pie, and lays a large slice on the plate (which has been placed on the lap of each of the company); then a fifth soldier, with an empty basket, to take away the dirty plates; others succeed in the same order, carrying wine, iced water, etc.; the drinkables are served between the arrival of each eatable: the rest of the supper consisted of various dishes of fish, ragouts, game, fried and baked meats, perigord-pies, boar's-heads, etc. The dessert was formed into pyramids, and carried round in the same manner; it consisted of sweetmeats, biscuits, iced chocolate, and a great variety of iced fruits, creams, etc. The Queen ate of two things only, which were prepared particularly for her by her German cooks; she did me the singular honour to send me some of each dish.

Beyond the public rooms is the **study**, with lacquered furniture from Frankfurt am Main, and a small **drawing room**. The **bedroom of Ferdinand II** follows. From here you enter the queen's apartments: first her **sewing room**, with a small **bathroom** adjacent; then a tiny **dressing room**, beyond which lie the **drawing room** and a room for the queen's ladies-in-waiting. From the last, several richly decorated rooms lead to the **library**, containing some 10,000 volumes and a huge nativity scene (*presepio*), with over 1200 pieces made by Giuseppe Sammartino and other eminent sculptors.

The next ten rooms comprise the **gallery**, where an extensive, but dull collection of still-lifes, historical scenes, and family portraits is displayed. The small Museo Vanvitelliano contains the architect's original drawings and models for the palace.

The palace is the temporary home of the **Terraemotus Collection** of international contemporary art, assembled by the Neapolitan dealer/collector Lucio Amelio following the 1980 earthquake. The collection is shown hourly, 09.00–18.00.

Return to the ground floor and cross the second courtyard to the **palatine theatre**. This charming 18C period piece hosted concerts, plays, and balls. Lady Anne Miller describes the original appearance of the theatre and the use that was made of it during a ball she attended in 1771:

> There is no precedence observed at these balls, the King and Queen go in and out promiscuously, which is the reason why the company is not so numerous as one might expect to find it. None but such as the Queen esteems proper to receive and converse with sans cérémonie are ever admitted; and there are many of the Neapolitan nobility, even to the rank of dukes, who are allowed only to see the ball from the upper boxes ... The theatre is in the palace; it is approached through spacious courts, and then through large passages lined with a double row of guards under arms. The plan is circular, the proscenium appeared to me to cut off about a third from the circle; the boxes are larger than those in any other I have yet seen, they are lined, gilt, and decorated with a profusion of ornaments ... The stage was covered with the musicians upon benches, rising pyramidically one above the other, the top of the pyramid is crowned by the kettle-drums. The musicians are all in a livery, their coats blue, richly laced, their waistcoats red, and almost covered with silver, small black hats, with long scarlet feathers stuck upright in them: large wax candles are placed between, so that they form a striking coup d'oeil upon our entering the theatre; the whole is so artfully illuminated that the effect is equal, and seems as if the light proceeded from a brilliant sun at the top ... The pit (which is more like an antique arena) is floored with a composition coloured red, very hard, and rather slippery; here it is they dance. The boxes are appropriated to the foreign ministers and great officers belonging to the Court.

Inaugurated by Ferdinand IV in 1769, the theatre has been restored to its original form, with a horseshoe-shaped auditorium and five tiers of boxes. The ceiling painting, by Crescenzo della Gamba, shows *Apollo killing the serpents*.

The gardens

From the main portico you enter the gardens (open 08.30–1hr before sunset), which extend to the north, east and west sides of the palace. Among the more enchanting achievements of Italian landscape architecture, they were laid out by Martin Biancour under the supervision of Luigi Vanvitelli. They are famous for their fountains and ornamental waterworks adorned with statuary groups. The crowning glory of the gardens is the **great cascade**, a waterfall some 75m high that can be seen clearly from the palace 3km away (shuttle bus). The central promenade leads across a broad lower garden bordered by holm oaks and camphor trees (paths diverge into the woods on the left and right) to the circular **Fontana Margherita**, which is linked by a bridge over a sunken road to the impressive **pescheria superiore**. Beyond, a long, narrow lawn ends at the semi-circular **Fontana di Aeolo**, inhabited by statues of 29 zephyrs and wind gods (54 were originally planned). This is followed by the **Fontana di Cerere**, containing seven stepped cascades and statues of Ceres, nymphs, tritons, and river gods; then more lawn and the **Fontana di Venere**, with its group of Venus and Adonis.

From here a scenographic staircase flanked by men and women in hunting garb leads up to a basin with groups of Diana surrounded by nymphs and Actaeon being turned into a stag, into which the Great Cascade plunges. The water is brought from Monte Taburno by a lofty aqueduct. The view from the top of the wooded hill is especially fine.

To the east of the cascade is another, later garden laid out in the so-called English style; visitors are accompanied by a custodian. Here are more modest fountains and romantic groves of holm oaks, artificial ruins adorned with statues from Pompeii and Herculaneum, a large fish-pond, a miniature fort for Prince Ferdinand's mock battles, a swan lake, an apple orchard, a Classical temple, a bath of Venus, covered walks and greenhouses.

Some country excursions

San Leucio, 3km north-west of Caserta, was founded as a model town and social experiment by Ferdinand IV in 1789. He built the Casino Reale di Belvedere (also called the Casino di San Leucio) here and introduced the culture of silkworms and silk manufacture. On the outskirts north-east of Caserta lies Caserta British Military Cemetery, with 769 graves. It is immediately east of the civil cemetery.

Caserta Vecchia, 10km north-east (bus) by the road passing the cemetery, was founded in the 8C and preserves the aspect of a medieval town. The **cathedral**, a fine example of southern Norman architecture, dates from 1123–53; the central cupola and campanile (the latter with a roadway through it) were added c 100 years later. The exterior is adorned with sculptures; inside are 18 antique columns, a paschal candlestick and (in the transepts) the tombs of Count Francis II (d. 1359) and Bishop Giacomo (d. 1460), as well as many mosaic details. The ruins of the 13C castle lie to the east.

MOUNT VESUVIUS

I stood within the city disinterred
And heard the autumnal leaves like light footfalls
Of spirits passing through the streets; and heard
The mountain's slumberous voice at intervals
Thrill through those roofless halls ...
Around me gleamed many a bright sepulchre
Of whose pure beauty, Time, as if his pleasure
Were to spare Death, had never made erasure.

Percy Bysshe Shelley, *Ode to Naples*, 1820

Mount Vesuvius (Monte Vesuvio), the most familar feature in the Neapolitan landscape, is one of the smallest active volcanoes in the world (1277m; 1202m before 1944), but certainly the most famous, its development having been studied since Roman times. It is the only active volcano on the continent of Europe. In fact the name Vesuvius, or *Vesbius*, means 'the unextinguished'. It consists of a truncated cone, **Monte Somma**, which rises to 1152m—known as **Punta del Nasone**—on the north side. Within is an enormous crater, broken on the west side, called the **Atrio del Cavallo** and **Valle dell'Inferno**. From the centre of this crater rises a smaller cone, variable in size and shape, which is Vesuvius proper.

The volcanic activity started about 10,000 years ago. Ever since, periods of frequent eruption have alternated with periods of absolute tranquillity, sometimes lasting more than 2000 years. Before the disastrous eruption of AD 79, the volcano had been quiet for more than 1200 years

Practical information

Information offices
Tourist information offices in **Naples** provide information for this area, see p 109.

Getting there
By road
From Naples or Salerno, take Autostrada A3 to the Ercolano exit, then follow the signs to the Osservatorio Vesuviano. There are buses to the observatory from Ercolano.
By rail
Circumvesuviana railway from Naples to Pugliano (20–35mins). The State Railway (**FS**) to Portici-Ercolano is more useful for visitors arriving from Salerno and the south.

Where to stay
See Naples listings (p 110), or Sorrento and the Amalfi Coast listings (pp 269–270).

Eating out
SANT'ANASTASIA
€ *'E Curti*, Via Padre Michele Abete 4, ☎ 081 8972821. Excellent traditional osteria; closed Sun and Aug.
SOMMA VESUVIANA € *La Fregola*, Via Santa Maria a Castello 45, ☎ 081 893 2229. Simple restaurant on the road to Santa Maria a Castello; closed Mon and two weeks in Nov.
€€ *La Lanterna*, Via Colonnello Aliperta 8, ☎ 081 8991843. Regional dishes and good pizza; closed Mon and mid-Aug.

TORRE DEL GRECO €€ *Casa Rossa*, Via Mortelle 128, ☎ 081 883   1549. Restaurant; closed Mon.

It all began 13 or 14 million years ago

Why are there active volcanoes in Italy? The theory of plate tectonics provides a convincing answer. First the collision between the African and European plates caused the Italian boot to kick back towards the Balkan Peninsula, pulling the floor of the Tyrrhenian Sea along with it. As the sea floor stretched it became thinner, like pizza dough in the hands of a skilful *pizzaiolo*. This in turn created alterations both in the earth's crust, where fissures appeared, and in the mantle, which melted, partially, due to the diminished pressure of the layers above. Through the cracks in the lithosphere the magma from below rose to the surface, spewing forth in the volcanic areas of Lazio, Campania and Sicily.

The activity of Vesuvius is characterised by what geologists call effusive eruptions, marked by the emission of basaltic lava, and by powerful explosive eruptions. Over the past 25,000 years there have been 7 eruptions like the one of AD 79. The last eruption of the 'Plinian' variety took place in 1631; the last effusive eruption, in 1944. Since then Vesuvius has been 'asleep', but it is expected to reawaken any day now, with a new Plinian-type eruption that will be the more violent the longer the wait for it. It is important to remember, in this connection, that it was not the rain of ash or the flow of mud that killed most inhabitants of Pompeii and Herculaneum (although these caused extensive physical damage and took their toll among the early survivors). The culprit was the ring of toxic gasses and incandescent dust, the 'base surge' in technical jargon, which raced away from the crater at lightning speed, reaching the ancient cities and reaping its bitter harvest in a mere moment.

History of Vesuvius

In ancient times the lower slopes of Vesuvius were planted with vineyards, above which was a thick belt of woods noted for their wild boar. Pliny the Elder wrote that no region on earth was more joyously touched by nature. Its volcanic nature was unsuspected except by men of science such as Diodorus Siculus, Vitruvius and, especially, Strabo, who inferred its igneous nature from its conical shape and the ashy nature of its barren summit.

'In early times', he wrote, 'this district was on fire and had craters of fire, and then because the fuel gave out, was quenched' (*Geography* V, 4). To this he attributed the fertility of the lands around the mountain, saying that it had already been shown at Mount Etna that volcanic ash was particularly suited for growing vines. Today the Vesuvian soil produces grapes for the excellent wine called *Lacrima Christi*.

The peak observed by Strabo was much higher than the present summit, the now broken cone of Monte Somma. Within its seemingly dead crater, Spartacus and the rebel slaves took refuge in 73 BC, escaping via an unguarded rift from the besieging force of praetor Clodius Pulcher.

In AD 63 a violent earthquake, mentioned by Seneca, caused serious damage in Pompeii, Herculaneum, Naples and Pozzuoli:

'We have heard that Pompeii, the very lively city in Campania where the shores of Surrentum and Stabiae and that of Herculaneum meet, and hem in a lovely, gently retreating inlet from the open sea, has been destroyed by an earthquake which also struck the entire vicinity. This occurred in winter, a time which our forefathers always held to be free from such perils ... The region had never before been visited by a calamity of such extent, having always escaped unharmed from such occurrences and having therefore lost all fear of them. Part of the city of Herculaneum caved in, the houses still standing are in ruinous condition ...' (Naturales Quaestiones VI, De Terrae Motu)

The eruption in AD 79

This was followed by other shocks, and in AD 79 the central cone blew out. Pompeii, Herculaneum, and Stabiae were destroyed, the first and last buried in cinders and lapilli, or small stones, while Herculaneum was drowned in a torrent of mud; the flow of lava does not seem to have extended very far. Catastrophe struck on the morning of 24 August, ironically only a day after the annual celebration of the *Volcanalia*, the festival of the god of fire and forge, Vulcan. History owes an inestimable debt to Pliny the Younger, who witnessed the event and left a description of his observations in two letters addressed to the historian Tacitus. This is altogether the oldest realistic description, in Western literature, of a major natural disaster:

'To Tacitus:
Your request that I would send you an account of my uncle's end, so that you may transmit a more exact relation of it to posterity, deserves my acknowledgments; for if his death shall be celebrated by your pen, the glory of it, I am aware, will be rendered for ever deathless ...

'He was at that time with the fleet under his command at Misenum. On the 24th of August, about one in the afternoon, my mother desired him to observe a cloud of very unusual size and appearance. He had sunned himself, then taken a cold bath, and after a leisurely luncheon was engaged in the study. He immediately called for his shoes and went up an eminence from whence he might best view this very uncommon appearance. It was not at that distance discernible from what mountain this cloud issued, but it was found afterwards to be Vesuvius. I cannot give you a more exact description of its figure, than by resembling it to that of a pine tree, for it shot up a great height in the form of a trunk, which extended itself at the top into several branches; because I imagine, a momentary gust of air blew it aloft, and then falling, forsook it; thus causing the cloud to expand laterally as it dissolved, or possibly the downward pressure of its own weight produced this effect. It was at one moment white, at another dark and spotted, as if it had carried up earth or cinders.

'My uncle, true savant that he was, deemed the phenomenon important and worth a nearer view. He ordered a light vessel to be got ready, and gave me the liberty, if I thought proper, to attend him. I replied I would rather study, and, as it happened, he had himself given me a theme for composition. As he was coming out of the house he received a note from Rectina, the wife of Basus, who was in the utmost alarm at the imminent danger (his villa stood just below us, and there was no way to escape but by sea); she earnestly entreated him to save her from such deadly peril. He changed his first design and what he began with a philosophical, he pursued with an heroical turn of mind. He ordered large galleys to be launched, and went himself on board one, with the intention of assisting not only Rectina, but many others; for the villas stand extremely thick upon that beautiful coast. Hastening to the place from whence others were flying, he steered his direct course to the point of danger, and with such freedom from fear, as to be able to make and dictate his observations upon the successive motions and figures of that terrific object.

'And now cinders, which grew thicker and hotter the nearer he approached, fell into the ships, then pumice-stones too, with stones blackened, scorched, and cracked by fire, then the sea ebbed suddenly from under them, while the shore was blocked up by landslips from the mountains. After considering a moment whether he should retreat, he said to the captain who was urging that course, 'Fortune befriends the brave; carry me to Pomponianus.' Pomponianus was then at Stabiae, distant by half the width of the bay (for, as you know, the shore, insensibly curving in its sweep, forms here a receptacle for the sea). He had already embarked his baggage; for though at Stabiae the danger was not yet near, it was full in view, and certain to be extremely near, as soon as it spread; and he resolved to fly as soon as the contrary wind should cease. It was full favourable, however, for carrying my uncle to Pomponianus. He embraces, comforts, and encourages his alarmed friend, and in order to soothe the other's fears by his own unconcern, desires to be conducted to a bathroom, and after having bathed, he sat down to supper with great cheerfulness, or at least (what is equally heroic) with all the appearance of it.

'In the meanwhile Mount Vesuvius was blazing in several places with spreading and towering flames, whose refulgent brightness the darkness of the night set in high relief. But my uncle, in order to soothe apprehensions, kept saying that some fires had been left alight by the terrified country people, and what they saw were only deserted villas on fire in the abandoned district. After this he retired to rest, and it is most certain that his rest was a most genuine slumber; for his breathing, which, as he was pretty fat, was somewhat heavy and sonorous, was heard by those who attended at his chamber-door. But the court which led to his apartment now lay so deep under a mixture of pumice-stones and ashes, that if he had continued longer in his bedroom, egress would have been impossible. On being aroused, he came out, and returned to Pomponianus and the others, who had sat up all night. They consulted together as to whether they should hold out in the house, or wander about in the open. For the house now tottered under repeated and violent concussions, and seemed to rock to and fro as if torn from its foundations. In the open air, on the other hand, they dreaded the falling pumice-stones, light and porous though they were; yet this, by comparison, seemed the lesser danger of the two; a conclusion which my uncle arrived at by balancing reasons, and the others by balancing fears. They tied pillows upon their heads with napkins, and this was their whole defence against the showers that fell round them.

'It was now day everywhere else, but there a deeper darkness prevailed than in the most obsure night; relieved, however, by many torches and diverse illuminations. They thought it proper to go down upon the shore to observe from close at hand if they could possibly put out to sea, but they found the waves still ran extremely high and contrary. There my uncle having thrown himself down upon a disused sail, repeatedly called for, and drank, a draught of cold water; soon after, flames, and a strong smell of sulphur, which was the forerunner of them, dispersed the rest of the company in flight; him they only aroused. He raised himself up with the assistance of two of his slaves, but instantly fell; some unusually gross vapour, as I conjecture, having obstructed his breathing and blocked his windpipe, which was not only naturally weak and constricted, but chronically inflamed. When day dawned again (the third from that he last beheld) his body was found entire and uninjured, and still fully clothed as in life; its posture was that of a sleeping, rather than a dead man.

'Meanwhile my mother and I were at Misenum. But this has no connection with history, and your inquiry went no further than concerning my uncle's death. I will therefore put an end to my letter. Suffer me only to add, that I have faithfully related to you what I was either an eye-witness of myself, or heard at the time, when report speaks most truly. You will select what is most suitable to your purpose; for there is a great difference between a letter and an history; between writing to a friend, and writing for the public. Farewell.'

'To Tacitus:
The letter which, in compliance with your request, I wrote to you concerning the death of my uncle, has raised, you say, your curiosity to know not only what terrors, but what calamities I endured when left behind at Misenum (for there I broke off my narrative). Though my shock'd soul recoils, my tongue shall tell.

'My uncle having set out, I gave the rest of the day to study—the object which had kept me at home. After which I bathed, dined, and retired to short and broken slumbers. There had been for several days before some shocks of earthquake, which the less alarmed us as they are frequent in Campania; but that night they became so violent that one might think that the world was not merely shaken, but turned topsy-turvy. My mother flew to my chamber; I was just rising; meaning on my part to awaken her, if she was asleep. We sat down in the forecourt of the house, which separated it by a short space from the sea. I know not whether I should call it courage or inexperience—I was not quite eighteen—but I called for a volume of Livy, and began to read, and even went on with the extracts I was making from it, as if nothing were the matter. Lo and behold, a friend of my uncle's, who was just come to him from Spain, appears on the scene; observing my mother and me seated, and that I have actually a book in my hand, he sharply censures her patience and my indifference; nevertheless I still went on intently with my author.

'It was now six o'clock in the morning, the light still ambiguous and faint. The buildings around us already tottered, and though we stood upon open ground, yet as the place was narrow and confined, there was certain and formidable danger from their collapsing. It was not till then we resolved to quit the town. The common people follow us in the utmost consternation, preferring the judgement of others to their own (wherein the extreme of fear resembles prudence), and impel us onwards by pressing in a crowd upon our rear. Being got outside the houses, we halt in the midst of a most strange and dreadful scene. The coaches which we had ordered out, though upon the most level ground, were sliding to and fro, and could not be kept steady even when stones were put against the wheels. Then we beheld the sea sucked back, and as it were repulsed by the convulsive motion of the earth; it is certain at least the shore was considerably enlarged, and now held many sea animals captive on the dry sand. On the other side, a black and dreadful cloud bursting out in gusts of igneous serpentine vapour now and again yawned open to reveal long fantastic flames, resembling flashes of lightning but much larger.

'Our Spanish friend already mentioned now spoke with more warmth and insistancy: 'If your brother—if your uncle,' said he, 'is yet alive, he wishes you both may be saved; if he has perished, it was his desire that you might survive him. Why therefore do you delay your escape?' We could never think of our own safety, we said, while we were uncertain of his. Without more ado our friend hurried off, and took himself out of danger at the top of his speed.

'Soon afterwards, the cloud I have described began to descend upon the earth, and cover the sea. It had already begirt the hidden Capreae [Capri], and blotted from sight the promontory of Misenum. My mother now began to beseech, exhort, and command me to escape as best I might; a young man could do it; she, burdened with age and corpulency, would die easy if only she had not caused my death. I replied, I would not be saved without her, and taking her by the hand, I hurried her on. She complies reluctantly and not without reproaching herself for retarding me. Ashes now fall upon us, though as yet in no greater quantity. I looked behind me; gross darkness pressed upon our rear, and came rolling over the land after us like a torrent. I proposed while we yet could see, to turn aside, lest we should be knocked down in the road by the crowd that followed us and trampled to death in the dark. We had scarce sat down, when darkness overspread us, not like that of a moonless or cloudy night, but of a room when it is shut up, and the lamp put out. You could hear the shrieks of women, the crying of children, and the shouts of men; some were seeking their children, others their parents, others their wives or husbands, and only distinguishing them by their voices; one lamenting his own fate, another that of his family; some praying to die, from the fear of dying; many lifting their hands to the gods, but the greater part imagining that there were no gods left anywhere, and that the last and eternal night was come upon the world.

'There were even some who augmented the real perils by imaginary terrors. Newcomers reported that such or such a building at Misenum had collapsed or taken fire—falsely, but they were credited. By degrees it grew lighter; which we imagined to be rather the warning of approaching fire (as in truth it was) than the return of day: however, the fire stayed at a distance from us: then again came darkness, and a heavy shower of ashes; we were obliged every now and then to rise and shake them off, otherwise we would have been buried and even crushed under their weight. I might have boasted that amidst dangers so appalling, not a sigh or expression of fear escaped from me, had not my support been founded in miserable, though strong consolation, that all mankind were involved in the same calamity, and that I was perishing with the world itself.

'At last this dreadful darkness was attenuated by degrees to a kind of cloud or smoke, and passed away; presently the real day returned, and even the sun appeared, though lurid as when an eclipse is in progress. Every object that presented itself to our yet affrighted gaze was changed, cover'd over with a drift of ashes, as with snow. We returned to Misenum, where we refreshed ourselves as well as we could, and passed an anxious night between hope and fear; though indeed with a much larger share of the latter, for the earthquake still continued, and several enthusiastic people were giving a grotesque turn to their own and their neighbours' calamities by terrible predictions. Even then, however, my mother and I, notwithstanding the danger we had passed, and that which still threatened us, had no thoughts of leaving the place, till we should receive some tidings of my uncle.

'And now, you will read this narrative, so far beneath the dignity of a history, without any view of transferring it to your own; and indeed you must impute it to your own request, if it shall appear scarce worthy of a letter. Farewell.'

(Melmoth–Hutchinson translation, quoted in Wolfgang Leppmann's *Pompeii in Fact and Fiction*, London 1968).

Later eruptions

In the centuries that followed the eruption of AD 79 only nine comparatively unimportant eruptions are recorded, and after 1500 a period of absolute quiescence set in, during which the mountain was again cultivated up to the cone and the crater, covered with trees. On 16 December 1631, however, a violent eruption destroyed nearly all the towns at the foot of the mountain; the lava reached the sea near Portici and killed over 3000 people.

During the next 300 years there were 23 eruptions at intervals of one to 30 years. Sir William Hamilton forecast that of 1767 and went up the mountain while it was in progress. The most serious were those of 1794, which destroyed Torre del Greco; of 1871–72, which damaged San Sebastiano and Massa di Somma; and of 1906, in which the towns of Ottaviano and San Giuseppe suffered severely. In August 1928 and in June 1929 the lava descended into the Valle dell'Inferno, menacing Terzigno. An eruption in March 1944 altered the shape of the crater; the little inner cone disappeared, and in the following month the main fissure closed.

Vestiges of the Roman age

At Boscoreale, overlooking Pompeii, several Roman villas were unearthed in 1887–1907; they yielded a large find of silverware (now in the Louvre) and frescoes, some of which may be seen in Naples, others in the Metropolitan Museum of New York. A modest collection of finds from these and other sites may be seen in the Antiquarium (Villa Regina, Boscoreale; open daily 08.30–18.00; ☎ 081 536 8796), where there is a display devoted to the Vesuvian environment.

With reference to the tragic end of Pompeii, Herculaneum, and the other Campanian towns destroyed in AD 79, the poet Statius asked, 'Will future centuries, when new seed will have covered the waste, believe that entire cities and their inhabitants lie under their feet, and that the fields of their ancestors were drowned in a sea of flames?' As memory of the event waned and other misfortunes befell the empire, future generations did not believe because they did not know of the catastrophe. Pompeii was discovered inadvertently in 1592 and Herculaneum in 1709, but a systematic programme of excavation was not undertaken until the middle of the 19C.

The ascent of Vesuvius

Those who wish to make the ascent of the volcano may do so easily; the area was declared a National Park (a term used loosely in Italy to indicate land protected by law) in 1991. As the expedition is most easily made by car or by public transport, via the modern town of Ercolano, it can conveniently be combined with a visit to Herculaneum.

Some historic precedents

Today the great volcano is ominously silent; but it was not always so. The eminent English philosopher George Berkeley offers this account of an early 18C expedition:

'With much difficulty I reached to the top of Mount Vesuvius, in which I saw a vast aperture full of smoak, which hindered the seeing its depth and figure. I heard within that horrid gulf certain odd sounds, which seemed to proceed from the belly of the mountain; a sort of murmuring, sighing, throbbing, churning, dashing (as it were) of waves, and between whiles, a noise, like that of thunder or cannon, which was constantly attended with a clattering, like that of tiles falling from the tops of houses on the street.'

Shelley, who climbed the mountain at about the same time, was so deeply impressed by the volcanic phenomena that he fell into a state of semi-paralysis. He relates his experience in a letter of 1818 to Thomas Love Peacock:

'Vesuvius is, after the glaciers, the most impressive exhibition of the energies of nature I ever saw. It has not the immeasurable greatness, the overpowering magnificence, nor, above all, the radiant beauty of the glaciers; but it has all their character of tremendous and irresistible strength. From Resina to the hermitage you wind up the mountain, and cross a vast stream of hardened lava, which is an actual image of the waves of the sea, changed into hard black stone by inchantment. The lines of the boiling flood seem to hang in the air, and it is difficult to believe that the billows which seem hurrying down upon you are not actually in motion. This plain was once a sea of liquid fire ... On the summit is a kind of irregular plain, the most horrible chaos that can be imagined; riven into ghastly chasms, and heaped up with tumuli of great stones and cinders, and enormous rocks blackened and calcined, which had been thrown from the volcano upon one another in terrible confusion. In the midst stands the conical hill from which volumes of smoke, and the fountains of liquid fire, are rolled forth for ever. The mountain is at present in a slight state of eruption; and a thick, heavy white smoke is perpetually rolled out, interrupted by enormous columns of an impenetrable black bituminous vapour, which is hurled up, fold after fold, into the sky, with a deep hollow sound, and fiery stones are rained down from its darkness, and a black shower of ashes fell even where we sat. The lava, like a glacier, creeps on perpetually, with a crackling sound as of suppressed fire. There are several springs of lava; and in one place it gushes precipitously over a high crag, rolling down the half-molten rocks and its own overhanging waves; a cataract of quivering fire. We approached the extremity of one of the rivers of lava; it is about twenty feet in breadth and ten in height; and as the inclined plane was not rapid, its motion was very slow. We saw the masses of its dark exterior surface detach themselves as it moved, and betray the depth of the liquid flame. In the day the fire is but slightly seen; you only observe a tremulous motion in the air, and streams and fountains of white sulphurous smoke.

'At length we saw the sun sink between Capreae and Inarime [Ischia], and, as the darkness increased, the effect of the fire became more beautiful. We were, as it were, surrounded by streams and cataracts of the red and radiant fire; and in the midst, from the column of bituminous smoke shot up into the air, fell the vast masses of rock, white with the light of their intense heat, leaving behind them through the dark vapour trains of splendour. We descended by torchlight, and I should have enjoyed the scenery on my return, but they conducted me, I know not how, to the hermitage in a state of intense bodily suffering.'

For some observers, the sight of the volcano was profoundly disquieting, as this passage from John Ruskin's *Praeteria* (1885–89) suggests:

'The first sight of the Alps had been to me as a direct revelation of the beneficent will in creation. Long since in the volcanic powers of destruction, I had been taught by Homer, and further forced by my own reason to see, if not the personality of an Evil Spirit, at all events the permitted symbol of evil, unredeemed; wholly distinct from the conditions of storm, or heat, or frost, on which the healthy courses of organic life depended. In the same literal way in which the snows and Alpine roses of Lauterbrunnen were visible Paradise, here, in the valley of ashes and throat of lava, were visible Hell. If thus in the natural, how else should it be in the spiritual world? ... The common English Traveller, if he can gather a black bunch of grapes with his own fingers, and have his bottle of Falernian brought to him by a girl with black eyes, asks no more of this world, or the next; and declares Naples a Paradise. But I knew from the first moment when my foot furrowed volcanic ashes, that no mountain form or colour could exist in perfection, when everything was made of scoria, and that blue sea was to be little boasted of, if it broke on black sand.'

The way to the top

The road to the summit of Mount Vesuvius (marked) climbs to the Eremo, site of the **Observatory** (597m) built in 1848 on a spur of the crater of Monte Somma and so far spared by lava flows. Luigi Palmieri, curator in 1872, remained at his post throughout the eruption of that year. The building houses a library, specimens of minerals thrown up by Vesuvius, relief plans and seismic apparatus and meteorological instruments.

The road continues to a car park (1017m), from which the summit is just 10 minutes away by foot. Here visitors are met by an official guide (fee) of the comune of Ercolano, who conducts parties by a path to the edge of the crater. If you like, you can continue around the crater to the end of the path (45mins there and back). The landscape is unsettling, to say the least; the views, spectacular. Some 3–5km below the crater floor is the first, superficial magma chamber, which was responsible for explosive eruptions like that of AD 79. There are also two smaller magma chambers deeper down (perhaps as far as 10km below the surface), responsible for the more recent effusive eruptions.

To visit the vast, beautiful **Foresta Demaniale**, a protected forest of oaks and maritime pines, contact the *Corpo Forestale dello Stato*, Via Tescione 125, 81100 Caserta, ✉ www.corpoforestale.it.

POMPEII

Pompeii (in Italian, *Pompei*), one of the Roman Campanian towns buried by the Vesuvian eruption of AD 79 and painstakingly brought back to light during the last two centuries, has provided fundamental knowledge of the domestic life of the ancients. 'Nothing is wanting [here] but the inhabitants,' wrote Henry Matthews in 1820. 'Still, a morning's walk through the solemn silent streets of Pompeii, will give you a livelier idea of their modes of life, than all the books in the world.' Here you see the greater part of a Roman town as it was when disaster overtook it more than 1900 years ago, in a setting sufficiently isolated from modern surroundings to preserve the illusion of antiquity. The contrasting beauty of white stone against a background of azure sky, and the ever-changing patterns made by sun and clouds on the slopes of the volcano, combine with the intrinsic interest of the ruins to make this one of the more fascinating archaeological sites in the world.

Practical information

Information offices
POMPEII *Azienda Autonoma di Cura Soggiorno e Turismo*, Via Sacra 1, ☎ 081 850 7255, 🖷 081 863 2401. See also **Naples** tourist information offices, p 111.

Getting there
By road
From Naples or Salerno, take Autostrada A3 to the exit marked Pompei, then follow the signs to the *scavi* (excavations). **Coach excursions** daily from Naples, Piazza Municipio.
By rail
The *Circumvesuviana railway* (Sorrento line) runs from Naples to Pompei Villa dei Misteri at 35–50mins intervals. The State Railway (*FS*) to Pompei station is more useful for visitors arriving from Salerno and the south.

Where to stay
See Naples, p 112 or Sorrento and the Amalfi Coast, pp 271–272.

Eating out
POMPEII €€€ *Principe*, Piazza Bartolo Longo 8, ☎ 081 850 5566. Refined restaurant offering traditional and creative cuisine; closed Sun evening and mid-day Mon. The €€ restaurant (*Posto di Ristoro*) located behind the Forum is quite acceptable; open same times as the ruins. TORRE DEL GRECO €€ *Casa Rossa 1888*, Via Mortelle 128, ☎ 081 883 1549. Restaurant; closed Mon.

Visiting the ruins
The excavations may be entered on the south by the Porta Marina, or by the Porta Anfiteatro. They are open daily Mar–Sept 08.30–19.30; Oct–Feb 08.30–17.00; ☎ 081 857 5347. Only large groups must reserve tickets. Individuals may book in advance by calling ☎ 081 857 5111 and asking for the Ufficio Prenotazione. Conservation and restoration at Pompeii are ongoing

processes, so expect many of the houses to be closed when you visit. The official custodians, stationed in different quarters of the ancient town, will open some of the closed houses and give all necessary information. They are not supposed to accept gratuities or accompany visitors.

At least half a day is necessary for an adequate visit, which should at least touch upon the buildings around the **forum**; one of the three complexes of **thermae**; the two theatres; the **Fullonica Stephani**; the houses of **Menander**, of **Loreius Tiburtinus**, of the **Faun** and of the **Tragic Poet**; the **Villa of Julia Felix** and the **Villa of the Mysteries**. To commemorate the excavations' 250th anniversary, two special itineraries have been marked out: one is an *Extra moenia* walk, running around the outside of the walls from Porta Ercolano to Porta dell'Amfiteatro and taking in the newly excavated necropolis; the other is the *Circuito borbonico*, comprising the houses that were excavated between 1748, when digging began, and the end of the Bourbon reign.

The **restaurant** at the *Posto di Ristoro* (near the forum) is a good place to stop for lunch. In hot weather the absence of shade is noticeable and some sort of hat is a must. Be sure, also, to wear comfortable shoes: the paving-stones of the street are notoriously uneven.

History of Pompeii

Although it is not known exactly when Pompeii was first established, an Oscan village probably existed on the site as early as the 8C BC (the name Pompeii is of Oscan derivation, it seems). There is no archaeological or documentary evidence to support this date, however, and the oldest building that can be identified and reconstructed from its ruins—the Doric temple in the Triangular Forum—dates from the 6C, when Pompeii was already a flourishing commercial centre and one of the chief ports on the coast of Campania. Like the Greek coastal towns of Cumae and Neapolis, Pompeii fell under the domination of the Etruscans c 530 BC. Certain aspects of the ruins, such as the layout of the oldest section and the design of the 6C city wall, as well as some family names (the Cuspii, for instance) are thought to be of Etruscan origin. The city fell to the Samnites c 425 BC and remained under their dominion for more than two centuries. In 200 BC it became a subject ally of Rome, but with the outbreak of the Social War it joined the Italic League and was besieged in 89 BC.

After the war ended Pompeii sank back into the near-anonymity of provincial life. As a token of Romanisation it was now called *Colonia Cornelia Veneria Pompeiianorum* after the clan name of its conqueror, L. Cornelius Sulla, and the Venus Pompeiiana, patron deity of the city. In AD 59, after a brawl in the amphitheatre between the Pompeians and the citizens of Nuceria, the gladiatorial spectacles were suspended for ten years. It was possibly in compensation for this that, in AD 62, it was allowed to call itself *Colonia Neroniana*.

The following year Pompeii was devastated by an earthquake, an unwelcome token of the renewed activity of Mount Vesuvius. Heedless of this warning, however, the town continued to flourish and even increased its wealth and influence. The final catastrophe took place on 24 August, AD 79, when the famous eruption of Vesuvius overwhelmed Pompeii, Herculaneum, and Stabiae. Pompeii, like Stabiae, was covered with a layer of fragments of pumice stone (*lapilli*), mostly very minute, and afterwards by a similar layer of ashes. The flow of lava stopped at the base of the mountain and did not reach the inhabited district.

All who had not left the city in the first hours died—from the base surge, the accumulation of volcanic debris, the collapse of buildings, or in many cases, the poisonous vapours. It is estimated that of an approximate population of 20,000, two thousand, who were trapped in the city or who for some reason chose to remain, perished. Among the victims of the catastrophe, the most illustrious was Pliny the Elder, a distinguished naturalist and commander of the Roman fleet at Misenum. Warned by his sister of the appearance of an ominous cloud in the east and by a letter from Popilla Rectina, wife of the magistrate Cn. Pedius Cascus, he hurried to the help of the fugitives, but could not reach Pompeii because of the huge mounds of lapilli. He therefore sailed to Stabiae, where he found his friend Pomponianus, but was here overtaken and suffocated by the stifling vapours.

Pompeii was left a sea of ashes and lapilli, from which emerged the upper parts of the buildings that had not been totally destroyed. These later served as guide-posts to the inhabitants who returned to dig among the ruins, and, still later, to the searchers for treasure and building material.

By the 3C a number of buildings had been erected at *Civita*, to the north of Pompeii. This second Pompeii was, however, abandoned in the 11C because of the frequent earthquakes, the eruptions of Vesuvius, and the incursions of the Saracens.

'It was Goethe,' observes Norman Douglas in *Old Calabria* (1915), 'who, speaking of Pompeii, said that of the many catastrophes which have afflicted mankind, few have given greater pleasure to posterity.'

Unearthing and preserving the town

Between 1594 and 1600 Domenico Fontana, the Roman architect, in constructing an aqueduct from the sources of the Sarno River to Torre Annunziata, tunnelled through the Pompeian mound and discovered some ruins and inscriptions. But it was not till 1748 that antiquarian excavations were begun. These have continued ever since, with more or less activity, revealing the larger and more important half of Pompeii. In 1860 a regular plan of excavation was organised by the Italian government; however, a chronic shortage of funds has made the task of unearthing and preserving the city a slow and arduous one. The site has now been systematically photographed, some of the gardens have been restored (there is even an attempt underway to grow grapes and make wine in the Roman manner), and the first comprehensive catalogue of its artistic assets is in preparation. Despite efforts to protect and preserve the city, however, the greatest threat to Pompeii remains that of theft and the clandestine resale of artworks and artefacts, of which the worst recent example, the removal of three marble and two bronze statues from the House of the Vetii, is only too typical.

The ancient city

The elliptical form of Pompeii was determined by the configuration of the prehistoric lava flow on which it is built, the southern fortifications following the natural bulwark made by the limit of the flow. The town was first surrounded by an *agger* (earthwork), buttressed by wooden boards and crowned by a palisade (*vallum*). About 450 BC this earthwork was replaced by a rampart of tufa and limestone, 3220m in perimeter, elaborated by the Samnites in the 4C BC and again in the 2C BC. In the late 2C or early 1C BC (just before the Social

War) this was reinforced by towers. The entire enceinte has now been located, though the south-west wall remains to be excavated; all the eight gates are visible, the oldest being the Porta Stabiana.

The streets were paved in the Roman period with large polygonal blocks of Vesuvian lava, bordered by kerbed pavements. Stepping-stones for pedestrians are set at regular intervals in nearly all the roadways. These stones did not impede the heavy vehicles that have left deep ruts in the roadway, because the draught-animals, attached to the end of a pole, enjoyed great freedom of movement. When the Pompeian ladies or gentlemen did not wish to walk, they used litters.

The present names of the streets—Via di Mercurio, Via dell'Abbondanza, Vicolo del Gallo, and so on—have been taken from the street-corner public fountains, adorned with the heads of gods and goddesses, etc. You will notice numerous inscriptions on the outside walls of the houses and shops, generally in red lettering; these include recommendations of candidates for the post of *aedile* or *duumvir*, dates, records, poetical quotations or short poems, the outpourings of lovers, jests and ribaldry. The character of Pompeii as an important maritime town is indicated by the numerous shops (sometimes attached to large private houses), taverns (*cauponae*), public bars (*thermopolia*), inns (*hospitia*, one with an elephant on its sign) and stables (*stabula*), especially near the gates. The shops rarely have trade-signs, but frequently exhibit either a phallus (carved, painted, or in mosaic), intended to ward off the evil eye, or one or two painted serpents, regarded as the *genii loci*.

The principal public buildings, grouped round the forum, lie not in the centre but in the most level part of the city, near the south-west corner. The houses built of large blocks of limestone, the Etruscan column, the Etruscan capitals, the Doric temple of the Triangular Forum and the Porta Stabiana belong to the most ancient period of the town's history. The Samnite monuments include the other gates and the walls, the Temples of Jupiter and Apollo, the Basilica, the portico of the forum, the Thermae Stabianae, the open-air theatre, the portico of the Triangular Forum and the gladiatorial barracks and palaestra. The Thermae of the Forum, the *comitium* (polling booth, used for the election of Civic magistrates), the covered theatre, the amphitheatre and the Temple of Zeus Meilichios are Augustan or earlier. The other public buildings are of later date. The Doric temple alone corresponds to the Greek model; all the others reveal an Etruscan scheme.

The site

Pompeii is divided (though not very regularly) into a chessboard of streets, the main thoroughfares being the Via Stabiana, Via di Nola and Via dell'Abbondanza. Archaeologists have devised a street plan that divides the town into nine **regions** (marked by Roman numerals), with varying numbers of **insulae**, or blocks (Arabic numerals). These generally consist of a group of dwellings, but may be wholly occupied by one building.

The entrance to the excavations for visitors arriving by road, or by railway from the Sorrento or Salerno lines, is the **Porta Marina**. In antiquity this had an archway covering two passages, each with its own gateway: a steep track for mules and an easier pathway for pedestrians. The adjoining antiquarium, which once showed the historical development of the city, is now closed to the public.

The Via Marina leads directly from the Porta Marina to the forum. To the right you can see the remains of the **Temple of Venus Pompeiana** (Map 1), guardian deity of the town. This building, having been partly destroyed by the earthquake of AD 63, was in the process of restoration and enlargement when overtaken by the final catastrophe in AD 79. Further on, on the same side, is the **basilica** (VIII, 1; Map 2), the most monumental of the city's public buildings, used as a court of law. It was built in a distinctly Hellenistic style and probably dates from the 2C BC; the interior is divided into nave and aisles by 28 Ionic columns of brick, covered with stucco. The Corinthian pilasters in tufa, now leaning against the wall, adorned the upper storey. At the end of the hall (badly damaged by the earthquake) was the raised tribunal for the judges (*duoviri jure dicundo*).

Leave the basilica by its north door and enter the **Temple of Apollo** (VII, 7; Map 3), a Samnite structure on the site of a 6C *sacellum* (sacred place). The 48 columns of the portico were originally Ionic, with a Doric entablature, but after the earthquake they were converted into Corinthian columns by means of stucco, and the entablature took the form of a large zoöphorus. The stucco has now fallen off and the original design has come to light.

The portico was formerly decorated with paintings of scenes from the *Iliad*. The large tripod, painted on the first pilaster of the east wing, is one of the attributes of Apollo. In the middle of the uncovered area stood a large altar of travertine. The Ionic column to the left of the steps bore a sundial, emblematic of Apollo Helios. The bases placed against the columns of the portico supported statues, now in the Museo Archeologico Nazionale in Naples. At the sides are copies of the *Apollo Sagittarius* and *Diana Sagittaria*.

The actual temple stands on a high podium, accessible by steps in front, leading to the Corinthian *pronaos* (a porch in front of the cella of a temple). This enclosed the cella, which contained the statue of Apollo and the conical *Omphalos*, the symbol of the god. The latter is still in situ. An Oscan inscription in the pavement of the cella records that it was laid at the instance of Oppius Campanius, the *quaestor* (magistrate). Beside the rear door is the priest's chamber.

The forum

The forum, the most perfect example known of a Roman central square, is planned so that Vesuvius dominates its major axis. When the basilica was built the opportunity was taken to furnish the square with a colonnade enclosing its two long sides and its southern extremity. Above this colonnade was a gallery, reached by small staircases (traces of which remain) designed to accommodate spectators of the fêtes and games held in the forum before the construction of the amphitheatre. The conversion of the colonnade from tufa to travertine stone, begun in the 1C AD, was interrupted by the earthquake. The area enclosed by the colonnade, 142m long and 38m wide, was adorned with statues of officials and other distinguished people. Twenty-two of the pedestals of these are extant, five with inscriptions. The larger base halfway down the west side is the orator's tribune. The passages leading to the central space were barred to vehicles. In a niche at no. 31 is a *tabula ponderaria* (table of weights and measures) made of travertine, showing the standard measures of capacity.

Adjacent to the forum is the entrance to an inner court, and at no. 29 is a portico, possibly used as a vegetable market. No. 28 was a public latrine and no. 27 the municipal treasury.

The Pompeian house

The dwellings at Pompeii are a marvellous example of the evolution of domestic architecture from the 4C–3C BC Italic model to the Imperial Roman one of the 1C AD. The main feature of the Pompeian house was the atrium or interior courtyard, surrounded by a roofed arcade. On the side opposite the entrance was the *tablinum* or chief living room, where the family dined and received their guests. To the right and left were the *alae* (wings), the *cubicula* (bedrooms) and the *cellae*, used for various purposes. In front of the tablinum stood the *cartibulum* or table for the utensils used in serving meals. Near this was the *focus* or hearth. This early Italic plan was introduced by the Etruscans. Later on, the chambers adjoining the main façade, and sometimes also those at the sides, were converted into shops (*tabernae*) opening on the street. To the primitive house was added the Hellenic *peristylium* (peristyle, or porticoed courtyard). The tablinum ceased to be the general living room and was occupied by the family archives. Its former role was taken by the *triclinium*, one of the rooms opening off the peristyle. Some of the houses, even in the imperial epoch, maintained the simple original plan of atrium and tablinum. Even in the commercial districts of the last period, where its intimacy was encroached upon by shop and factory, the house remained a separate entity in Pompeii; nowhere will you find the blocks of flats typical of Ostia.

The characteristic dwelling of the fully developed style shows the rooms grouped round two quadrilateral spaces, the atrium and the peristyle, usually with the tablinum between them. Air and light were admitted through openings in the roof. The roof of the atrium sloped inwards so as to leave a quadrilateral opening in the middle (*compluvium*). Below this was the *impluvium*, a basin that collected the rain-water from the gutters of the compluvium and passed it on to the *puteus* or cistern.

The commonest form of atrium, seen in the **House of Lucretius Fronto**, for example, is the so-called *atrium tuscanicum*. The courtyard has a roof borne by strong beams which cross from one side-wall to the other. A

At the north end of the forum stands the **Temple of Jupiter** (VII, 8; Map 4), built in the Italic manner, with a wide cella and pronaos enclosed by Corinthian columns. Later, it became the *capitolium* of the Roman town. The pronaos is reached by a flight of 15 steps, originally flanked by equestrian statues and interrupted by a platform on which an altar stood. The cella, with its Ionic columns, had a marble pavement bordered by mosaics. Apertures in the flooring of the pronaos and cella admitted light to some lower chambers (such as the *aerarium* or treasury), which was linked directly to the forum. The podium against the back wall, reached by steps, is believed to have borne statues of Jupiter, Juno, and Minerva. After the temple had been reduced to ruins by the earthquake, the cult of these deities was carried on at the small temple of Zeus Meilichios (see below).

To the right and left of the main steps were two triumphal arches. That on the right was demolished by the ancients to open up the view of the arch behind, which had an equestrian statue of Tiberius on its top and statues of Nero and Drusus in its niches.

less common style (visible in the Houses of the Labyrinth and of the Silver Wedding) is the *atrium tetrastylum*, where the roof is sustained by four columns placed at the four corners of the impluvium. Still more rare is the Corinthian form, in which there are many columns (as seen in the Houses of Castor and Pollux and of Epidius Rufus). In some houses, as in the second atrium of the House of the Centenario, there is no opening in the roof.

Nearly every house had a second floor and some had a third; these were narrower than the first floor and were used by slaves or let out as lodgings. Few windows opening onto the street have been discovered. In some cases the floor and ceiling of the upper rooms extended to form a small pillared loggia, the so-called *cenacula*. The second floor was reached by small flights of steps, either inside or outside. A small passage adjoining and parallel to the tablinum led in to the peristyle, which was in the form of a **garden** (*viridarium*) surrounded by an arcade, but not always completed on all four sides.

Opening off the peristyle were smaller rooms for domestic purposes (*cubicula, triclinia, apothecae* or storeroom for food, especially wine) or for the reception of guests (*oeci, exedrae*). The triclinia are distinguishable by their larger size, their mosaic floors and the recesses in the lower part of their walls. The *lararium* or domestic sanctuary, in the form of an *aedicula*, or small temple, was usually found in the atrium, in an adjoining room, or in the peristyle. Sometimes it was reduced to a mere painting, even placed in the kitchen. Most houses had a second entrance (*posticum*) near the peristyle.

The shops extended along the entire front of the house and were open to the street, though they could be closed by wooden shutters or sliding doors. The counting-house or cashier's office, in front of the entrance, was often lined with marble. Many of the shops had a back room for the use of clients or a bedroom for the shopkeeper on the mezzanine floor. The number of shops lent great animation to the principal streets. Lamps hung at the doors provided lighting for the town, along with others placed on municipal altars at the street-corners.

Return along the east side of the forum, which was rebuilt in the 1C AD. The **macellum** (VII, 9, 4; Map 5), or general market, was fronted by a graceful colonnade and the shops of the *argentarii* or money-changers. Bases for statues stand against the marble columns of the arcade and the pilasters between the shops. The interior courtyard was enclosed by another colonnade (destroyed by the earthquake). The walls were adorned with frescoes: those surviving include **Io guarded by Argus** and **Ulysses and Penelope**. The frieze shows fish, game, amphorae of wine and the like. On the south side are shops, with an upper storey. In the open centre of the courtyard was a dome borne by 12 columns, of which only the bases remain; it probably sheltered a tank or basin for fish. A chapel at the back contained statues of the imperial family, to the right and left of this are the shops of a fishmonger and of a butcher.

The **Sacrarium of the Lares** next door (Map 6), is fronted by a marble colonnade and was originally paved and lined with marble slabs. A podium in the apse bore several statues. There are niches for eight other statues around the walls, probably representing the *Lares Publici*, or tutelary deities of the town.

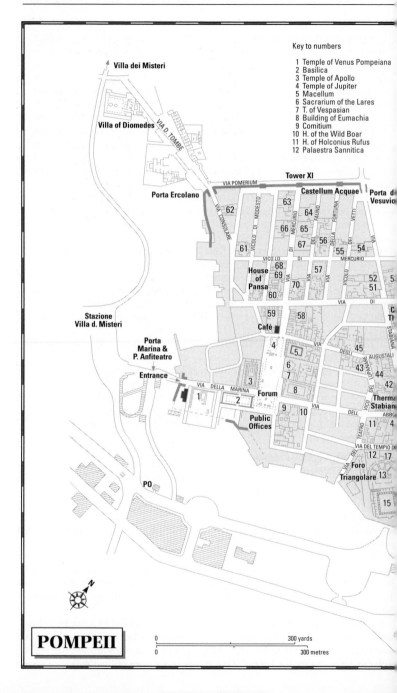

Villa dei Misteri

Villa of Diomedes

Key to numbers

1 Temple of Venus Pompeiana
2 Basilica
3 Temple of Apollo
4 Temple of Jupiter
5 Macellum
6 Sacrarium of the Lares
7 T. of Vespasian
8 Building of Eumachia
9 Comitium
10 H. of the Wild Boar
11 H. of Holconius Rufus
12 Palaestra Sannitica

VIA D. TOMBE

VIA POMERIUM

Tower XI

Porta Ercolano

Castellum Acquae

Porta di Vesuvio

VIA CONSOLARE

62

63

64

66 65

61

VICOLO DI MODESTO

VIA DI MERCURIO

VICOLO DEL FAUNO

VIA DELLA FORTUNA

VIA DEI VETTI

67 56

55 54

VICO LO DI

DI MERCURIO

House of Pansa

68
69

70

57

60

VICOLO DI

52
51

5

VIA DI

Stazione Villa d. Misteri

59

58

Café

4

5

Porta Marina & P. Anfiteatro

Entrance

VIA DELLA MARINA

1

6
7

8

2 **Forum**

3

45

VIA

DEGLI

VICO DEL LUPANARE

AUGUSTALI

43 44

42

Therma Stabian

C
Th

VIA
STABIANA

Public Offices

9 10

VIA DELL

11 4

VICO DEL TEATRO

ABBO

VIA DEL TEMPIO D

12 17

Foro Triangolare

13

15

PO

POMPEII

0   300 yards

0   300 metres

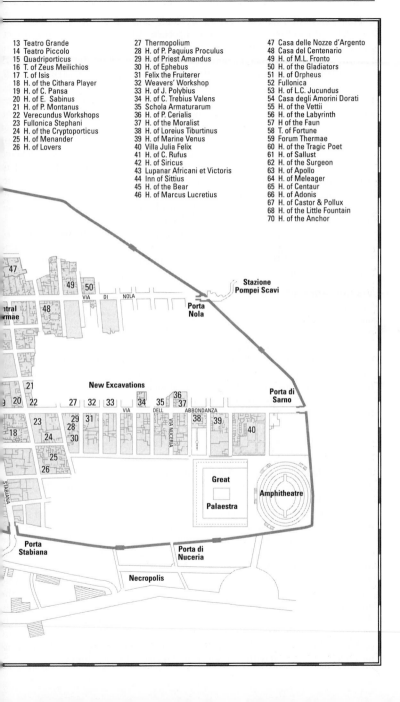

13 Teatro Grande
14 Teatro Piccolo
15 Quadriporticus
16 T. of Zeus Meilichios
17 T. of Isis
18 H. of the Cithara Player
19 H. of C. Pansa
20 H. of E. Sabinus
21 H. of P. Montanus
22 Verecundus Workshops
23 Fullonica Stephani
24 H. of the Cryptoporticus
25 H. of Menander
26 H. of Lovers

27 Thermopolium
28 H. of P. Paquius Proculus
29 H. of Priest Amandus
30 H. of Ephebus
31 Felix the Fruiterer
32 Weavers' Workshop
33 H. of J. Polybius
34 H. of C. Trebius Valens
35 Schola Armaturarum
36 H. of P. Cerialis
37 H. of the Moralist
38 H. of Loreius Tiburtinus
39 H. of Marine Venus
40 Villa Julia Felix
41 H. of C. Rufus
42 H. of Siricus
43 Lupanar Africani et Victoris
44 Inn of Sittius
45 H. of the Bear
46 H. of Marcus Lucretius

47 Casa delle Nozze d'Argento
48 Casa del Centenario
49 H. of M.L. Fronto
50 H. of the Gladiators
51 H. of Orpheus
52 Fullonica
53 H. of L.C. Jucundus
54 Casa degli Amorini Dorati
55 H. of the Vettii
56 H. of the Labyrinth
57 H of the Faun
58 T. of Fortune
59 Forum Thermae
60 H. of the Tragic Poet
61 H. of Sallust
62 H. of the Surgeon
63 H. of Apollo
64 H. of Meleager
65 H. of Centaur
66 H. of Adonis
67 H. of Castor & Pollux
68 H. of the Little Fountain
70 H. of the Anchor

Stazione
Pompei Scavi

VIA   DI   NOLA

Porta
Nola

Central
Thermae

New Excavations

Porta di
Sarno

VIA   DELL   ABBONDANZA

VIA NUCERIA

STABIANA

Great

Palaestra

Amphitheatre

Porta
Stabiana

Porta di
Nuceria

Necropolis

The **Temple of Vespasian** (VII, 9, 2; Map 7) was begun after AD 63 but neve completed. It was fronted by a columned portico. An altar, with bas-reliefs depict ing the sacrifice of a bull, the sacrificial utensils and a civic crown between two lau rels (the symbol of the imperial house), stands in the middle of the open courtyard

The **Building of Eumachia** (VII, 9, 1; Map 8), an imposing structure dedi cated to Concordia Augusta and Pietas, was erected by the priestess Eumachia acting also for her son, M. Numistrius Fronto. It was occupied by the *fullone* (fullers who shrank and thickened woollen cloth by moistening, heating an pressing). They probably used it as a saleroom. In front is a *chalcidicum* o vestibule, with a portico of two rows of columns, at the ends of which are fou niches for statues of Aeneas, Romulus, Julius Caesar and Augustus. A covere corridor (*crypta*) runs round the other three sides. A marble **portal** with splen did acanthus leaf decoration gives access to an open courtyard (*porticus*), sur rounded by a colonnade with two rows of columns on top of each other withou a second storey in between. The statue of Eumachia now in the Muse Archeologico Nazionale, in Naples, stood at the back.

On the other side of Via dell'Abbondanza stands the **comitium** (Map 9), o polling booth. At the south end of the forum are three large halls; the central on was probably used by the *ordo decurionum* (town council), the others by th *duumviri* and *aediles*.

Via dell'Abbondanza

Now descend Via dell'Abbondanza, the name of which is due to a misinterpreta tion of the bust of *Concordia Augusta*, the goddess who was the personification o concord or agreement, on a fountain at the back of the building of Eumachia.

Behind the comitium (Map 9) a steep quarter spreads down the slope of th lava flow; this neighbourhood represents one of the last expansions of th Augustan age, when the now superfluous walls on this side were demolished t make way for terraced houses of the Herculanean type (here somewhat ruined)

To the right is the **House of the wild boar** (VIII, 3, 8; Map 10), named afte the mosaic on the entrance floor. Further on, at the corner of Via dei Teatri stands the **House of Holconius Rufus** (VIII, 4, 4; Map 11), one of the mor prominent citizens of Pompeii, honoured by a statue at the neighbouring cross road. The rich decoration of his elegant dwelling is unfortunately much faded.

The Foro Triangolare and Palaestra Sannitica

From here, Via dei Teatri leads south to the **Foro Triangolare** (Triangula Forum). This is reached by a fine Ionic portico giving access to two gates openin onto the forum, which is surrounded by a Doric colonnade. Obliquely set withi it are the ruins of a Doric temple dating from the 6C BC, 30m in length and 20m in width. This is a heptastyle and pseudodipteral edifice, with 11 columns o each side. The remains include the elevated stylobate, a few capitals and frag ments of the cella walls. Apparently dedicated to Hercules, it seems to hav already been a ruin in the 2C BC and was used both as a public dumping groun and a quarry of building material. Towards the end of that century, however, th area appears to have been cleared for the erection of a sacrarium dedicated t Athena. Near the left rear of the temple was a semicircular seat, on the back c which was a sundial. Opposite the steps leading to the pronaos is an enclosure perhaps a *heroön* to Hercules. To the left are three altars and (further back) a cis tern, formerly covered with a cupola raised on eight Doric columns.

Wall paintings

Among Pompeii's most striking attractions are the wall paintings on its stucco-covered interior walls. These are arranged in three horizontal bands: dado, central zone and frieze. The colours are very vivid, predominantly red and yellow. The central field is occupied by small pictures, groups of flying figures or isolated figures. In this decoration four periods may be distinguished by their stylistic variations. In the **first** or Samnite period, the stucco ornamentation imitates the marble panelling of important Greek or Roman mansions; there are no human figures. In the **second** period (1C BC), the marble decoration is imitated in painting and figures are introduced in scenes depicting mythical, heroic, or religious subjects. In the **third** and best period (first half of the first century of the Roman Empire), the architectural framework takes on a distinctly decorative quality, and figures become more numerous. In the **fourth** period, the figures are accompanied by bizarre architectural effects, the colouring is less delicate, and the ornamental details are coarser. Many of the wall paintings from Pompeii are on view at the Museo Archeologico Nazionale in Naples, see pp 128–129.

Adjoining the Triangular Forum, near the corner of Via del Tempio d'Iside, lay the **Palaestra Sannitica** (Map 12), where young men trained for the games. To the south of this is a large reservoir for water used by the theatre.

Pompeii's theatres

Pompeii actually had two theatres, the larger one open-air, the smaller (Teatro Piccolo) with a roof. The **Teatro Grande** (Map 13), which could hold 5000 spectators, dates from the 2C BC. Built on the model of the Hellenic theatres and especially resembling that of Antioch, it was provided with large tanks or basins installed in the orchestra and connected to the reservoir mentioned above, making it both a theatre and a *nymphaeum*. The water below the stage is said to have acted as a sounding-box. The theatre was restored in the reign of Augustus.

The *cavea*, or auditorium, is divided into three tiers: the *summa cavea* placed above a corridor and accessible by several staircases, the *media cavea* with 15 rows of seats arranged in five wedges, all also reached from the corridor, and the *ima cavea*, accessible from the orchestra only. The ima cavea consisted of four broad, low tiers; the seats (*bisellia*) were reserved for the town councillors (*decuriones*). After the restoration of the theatre, seats for distinguished spectators were also placed in the orchestra. The stone rings at the top of the wall were for the poles supporting the *velarium* or awning that protected the audience from the sun. The whole of the upper part overlooking the Triangular Forum is a modern reconstruction. Above the entrances to the orchestra are two small boxes (*tribunalia*), one of which was reserved for the president of the spectacle, the other (perhaps) for the priestesses. The stage (*pulpitum*), which had a wooden flooring, was reached from the orchestra by flights of steps. Between the stage and the orchestra was a narrow slit for the curtain. The wall at the back of the stage (*scena*) represented the façade of a palace with three doors, the usual background of an ancient theatre.

The more recent **Teatro Piccolo** (Map 14), could hold an audience of 1000. The roof was probably pyramidal. It was constructed soon after 80 BC by the Duoviri C. Quintius Valgus and M. Porcius, and was used as an *odeion* for concerts. The cavea is crossed by one *praecinctio* or corridor. The lower part consists of four wide tiers, the upper of 17 tiers, arranged in five sections. The marble pavement was presented by the Duovir M. Oculatius Verus.

Behind the theatre there was a **Quadriporticus** (Map 15), a vast square piazza, surrounded by an arcade of 74 columns, that originally served as a foyer. Later, this was converted into a barracks for gladiators, with two rows of cells, the upper ones entered from a wooden gallery, part of which has been reconstructed. Here fine weapons were found (now in the Museo Archeologico Nazionale in Naples), as well as iron fetters and 63 skeletons. The palaestra of this building, the walks and colonnades of the Triangular Forum, and the Great Palaestra (described below), collectively formed the Gymnasium of the Samnite period.

You emerge from the Teatro Piccolo into the Via Stabiana, which leads (right) to the ancient Porta Stabiana. Following it in the other direction you soon reach the **Temple of Zeus Meilichios** (Jupiter the Placable; once erroneously assigned to Asclepius; Map 16) on the corner of Via del Tempio d'Iside. This is the smallest temple in Pompeii. The dedication indicates a Greek cult probably imported from Sicily. The temple had a tetrastyle vestibule. The cella had a small two-columned portico, and at the back of it were the terracotta statues of Jupiter, Juno, and Minerva (now in the Museo Archeologico Nazionale). A large altar stands in front of the steps.

The Temple of Isis

Turn left along the side street to reach the Temple of Isis (Map 17), which was almost entirely rebuilt, after the earthquake, by Numerius Popidius Celsinus. In keeping with the mysterious character of the cult of Isis, this temple is somewhat curious in form, its lateral entrance provided with a triple door. The sacred enclosure was surrounded by a colonnade, the front walk of which has a central bay formed of two pilasters with half-columns, wider than the others. Opposite was a recess, the back of which bore a painted figure of Harpocrates (now in the Museo Archeologico Nazionale). In the open courtyard is a small shrine, from which steps descend to a subterranean reservoir intended for the lustral water. Small calcined bones were found on the main altar. Seven steps ascend to the pronaos, the roof of which is borne by six Corinthian columns. To the right and left of the entrance to the cells are niches for statues, and in front, to the left, is an altar. At the back, to the left, is a small staircase by which the priests entered the cella. Underneath this temple runs Fontana's aqueduct.

Now return to Via Stabiana, in which, to the right (Map 18), is the large **House of the Cithara Player** (I, 4), or house of Popidius Secundus Augustianus, with two atria and three peristyles. The statue of Apollo Citharoedus—now in the museum of Naples—was found here. On reaching the intersection of the Via Stabiana with Via dell'Abbondanza (once adorned with a statue of M. Holconius), turn to the right. No. 20 (left; Map 19) is the **House of Cuspius Pansa** or of the Diadumeni and no. 22 (Map 20), that of **Epidius Sabinus.**

The new excavations

At this point begin the new excavations (*nuovi scavi*), first undertaken in 1911. They stretch east for some 500m, to the Porta di Sarno or Urbulana, and include some of the more striking remains in the town. The original aim of these excavations was to trace the general line of the thoroughfare and to restore to their proper places the roofs, balconies, windows, stalls, doors, and the like which ormed the street-front. On the north side little further has been done, and hough the façade is complete for much of the distance, you cannot penetrate far nto any building. On the south side, however, every insula has now been excavated back to the next parallel street.

The characteristic feature of the new excavations is that the fittings and articles of domestic use, wall paintings, mosaics, statues and stucco ornamentation have all been left, as far as possible, in their original places. Fallen walls have been re-erected and rough-cast in their original colours; the painted stucco ceilings have been restored; some of the **gardens** have been replanted in accordance with what is known of Classical horticulture, and water plays once more in the private and public fountains. Mural inscriptions, including unauthorised scrawls relating to the games or elections, are seen in full force. Here the ruins come nearest to capturing the atmosphere of everyday urban life in the Roman era.

The **House of Popidius Montanus** (no. 9; Map 21) was a great resort of chess-players (*latruncularii*), who were responsible for the notice to the left of the portal. The door, studded with large bronze nails, was wide open at the moment of the catastrophe (plaster cast). Note also the cast of the closed door of no. 10 (left). Nos 7–5, in front of which was a projecting penthouse, show the façade of the **Workshops of Verecundus** (Map 22), maker of cloth, woollen garments, and articles in felt (*coactilia*). The entrance of no. 7 is decorated by four paintings. Two of these show the patron deities of the workshops: Venus Pompeiana, in a quadriga drawn by elephants, and Mercury. The others depict the coactiliari or felt-makers at work (right) and the saleroom for the finished products (left). The plaster cast of the door shows the iron mechanism for fastening it.

At no. 2, also with a penthouse, and surmounted by a pillared loggia, are the **Workshops of the Dyers** (*infectores*). To the right of the threshold is one of the vats used in dyeing, projecting from a furnace bearing phallic emblems. No. 1, above which is a large balcony used as a drying-room, was also (as a notice tells us) occupied by felt-makers. The painted frieze shows busts of Apollo, Mercury, Jupiter, and Diana, and the processional figure of Venus Pompeiana which was carried through the town.

The greater part of insula 6, on the south side of the street, belonged to one owner who lived at no. 11 and converted the neighbouring house (nos 8–9) into domestic quarters. The legs of a marble table, bearing the inscription P. Casca Longus, probably belonged to the conspirator who dealt the first blow to Julius Caesar and may have been acquired at auction after his banishment. No. 7 is the **Fullonica Stephani** (Map 23). The double door was closed at the time of the eruption, but the small hatch in the right half had been left open, as is shown by the position in which its fastenings were discovered. Cloth and garments were handed in here to be washed (either in the impluvium or in the three tanks at the back), cleaned (in the five *saltus fullonici* adjoining the two hindmost tanks), bleached (by sulphur vapour), dried (on the wide terraces of the first floor), or pressed in the *pressorium* (by the wall to the left, on entering).

The house at no. 4 was being redecorated during the last days of Pompeii. This is suggested by the heaps of material for making stucco in the peristyle and the triclinium, the plinths still waiting for their rough-casting, the state of the rooms

adjoining the entrance and the one completed frieze, in the chamber at th
south-east corner of the atrium. The decorations of the **cabinet** (perhaps
lararium) to the right of the tablinum are unusually fine.

The small vaulted roof, reconstructed from hundreds of minute fragments, i
adorned with scenes from the last books of the *Iliad* executed in a band of whit
stucco against a blue background. At the top: Hector, driven by a Fury, resists th
appeal of his parents at the Scaean Gate of Troy; Hector's combat with Achilles
Hector's corpse dragged behind the chariot-wheels of Achilles. On the sides
Priam loading his treasures on the car and setting out, under the guidance c
Hermes, to offer them to Achilles as a ransom for the body of Hector. On th
south side are a large hall and cubiculum displaying the red colouring of the sec
ond style. The hall has a magnificent **mosaic floor** and its walls show traces c
an extensive wall painting.

No. 3 on this block is the shop of **Verus the Blacksmith**, who dealt in bronze
ware. The lamp and other objects on view here are just a few of those which wer
found. Among the technical instruments were the valuable fragments in bronz
and iron, probably for repair, which enabled a reconstruction of the *groma*, th
Roman surveyor's theodolite, to be made.

The House of Menander and its vicinity

By passing through the house at no. 2 you reach its *cryptoporticus* (Map 24), o
underground portico, with semicircular vaulting and elaborate decoration i
white stucco. Latterly, the cryptoporticus had been degraded to the status of
wine-vault (*cella vinaria*). The walls, in the second style, are divided into vertica
sections by female and phallic *hermae*. The frieze showed more than 50 picture
of episodes from the Trojan War, taken not only from the *Iliad* but also from th
Aethiopis of Arctinus and possibly other cyclic poems. Only about a score of thes
have been preserved, whole or mutilated. The existing chamber is just a fragmen
of the whole, the rest having been filled up to enlarge the garden.

Plaster casts of the impressions made by the bodies of several occupants of thi
house are shown in a glass case. During the eruption they took refuge under th
portico but, when the rain of lapilli ceased, they climbed up to the garden with th
aid of a ladder. The showers of ashes overwhelmed them here, and they all suffo
cated in one huddled group. Adjoining the east wing are some well-preserve
rooms, including a striking triclinium, the vaulting of which, with fine whit
stucco-work, rested on painted caryatids of *rosso antico*. In the frieze are remain
of paintings, in which heroic or mythical scenes alternate with banquets.

The door at the south-west corner of the cryptoporticus opens onto a littl
street containing the **House of L. Ceius Secundu**s (no. 15), notable for it
beautiful façade with white rustication, protected by the original overhangin
roof. In the vestibule are a plaster model of the door and a ceiling, reconstructe
from fragments. Beyond the tetrastyle atrium, admirably preserved and contain
ing a plaster cast of a wooden cupboard, is a pseudoperistyle. Its walls ar
adorned with hunting scenes (*venationes*) and Nile landscapes with pygmies.

Across the little street is the **House of Menander** (I, 10, 4; Map 25), a fin
dwelling belonging to a kinsman of the empress Poppaea, where silver plate–
now in the Naples museum—was found in 1930. At the time of the catastroph
this house was also being redecorated. At the onset of the eruption the family
with their slaves, took refuge in the room with the strongest roof, but they wer
trapped by the collapse of part of the peristyle and eventually killed when th

roof came down on their heads. The beautifully appointed Tuscan atrium contains a lararium in the form of a tiny temple. In an exedra to the left are three Trojan scenes. The peristyle has stuccoed columns, and in the centre of the mosaic floor a panel depicts a Nile scene. On the north side are two elegantly decorated *oeci*. A series of exedrae contain a rich selection of paintings, including the seated figure of the poet Menander, from which the house takes its name. The *calidarium* (warm room) of the private baths is well preserved.

No. 11 on the south-west corner of the insula is the **House of the Lovers** (Map 26), a charming small house with elegant decoration and a splendid inscription beneath the portico, reading, *amantes ut apes vitam mellitam exigunt* (lovers, like bees, desire a honey-sweet life).

Back on the main street

Return by the side lane between insulae 6 and 7 to the *compitum* (crossing) where, under a canopy, figures of the twelve *Dei Consentes* (Olympian gods) are painted on the wall. Continue along Via dell'Abbondanza. On the north side (IX, 10, 2; Map 27) is a *thermopolium*, or tavern, that served hot and cold drinks on the ground floor, while on the first floor the wares included the favours of such complaisant *puellae* as Asellina, Smyrna, Maria, and Aegle. The objects found, including a phallic lamp, have been placed where they once might have stood. The sign, to the right of no. 4, represents large wine jars, goblets and a wine funnel.

In contrast, the opposite side of the street (I, 7) consists of a series of respectable middle-class houses. No. 1 (Map 28) is the imposing **House of P. Paquius Proculus** with rich mosaics in its vestibule, atrium, tablinum, and a room adjoining the peristyle. The restoration of the first floor, behind the tablinum, is noteworthy. An exedra on the north side of the peristyle contains the skeletons of seven children caught together by the catastrophe. Beyond the modest but tasteful **House of Fabius Amandio** (nos 2–3) is the **House of the Priest Amandus** (no. 7; Map 29), where the triclinium is decorated in the third style; the panels show Polyphemus with the ship of Ulysses and Galatea riding a dolphin, Perseus and Andromeda, Hercules in the garden of the Hesperides and the Fall of Icarus. The charming garden was shaded by a tree, the stump of which remains.

Entered from the side lane is the **House of the Ephebos** (nos 10–12, Map 30), where the rich decoration added to an agglomeration of modest dwellings indicate the rise to wealth of its owner, the tradesman P. Cornelius Teges. The ephebos now in the Museo Archeologico Nazionale in Naples was found here. Opposite (I, 8, 19) is a **dyeworks** with four boilers, washing vats and pressing-tables.

On the corner of Via Abbondanza is the shop of **Felix the Fruiterer** (or *pomarius;* I, 8, 1, Map 31). The saleroom, in which the fruit was exhibited on wooden shelves, is adorned with Bacchic motives. Opposite, on the north side (Map 32), are *textrinoe* or **Weavers' Workshops**, with a high-columned upper storey. No. 6, the **Workshop of Crescens**, has a painted figure of Hermes-Priapus to the right of the entrance. Continue on the north side to the next insula (IX, 13). The plain façade of the **House of C. Julius Polybius** (nos 1–3, Map 33) has carved lintels over the side doors. Adjoining the entrance of no. 5 are paintings of *Aeneas, Anchises,* and *Ascanius* (right) and of *Romulus with the spoils of King Acron* (left). At the corner is an *amphora urinaria* (urinal) placed there by the fullers.

On the opposite side of the street, excavations behind the frontage were resumed in 1951, revealing (I, 9) three interesting dwellings. The **House of the**

Beautiful Impluvium (entered from no. 2) has well-preserved decoration in the atrium and tablinum. In the **House of Successus** (no. 3) the painting of the boy being chased by a duck and the statue of the boy bearing a dove probably portray a favourite child of the house. The **House of the Fruit Orchard** (no. 5) is entered through the adjacent shop, as a plaster model of the original door closes the main portal. The walls of two cubicula are finely painted in the third style, with pictures of fruit trees, including the then rare lemon. In the alley beyond is the public altar of the serpent Agathodoemon, the life-giving earth principle. Proceed past a thermopolium of the next insula, which ends with another cross road altar, then return to the north side.

The **House of C. Trebius Valens** (III, 2, 1; Map 34) has no shops on its front. On the façade were three announcements of forthcoming shows at the amphitheatre and numerous electoral 'posters', with the householder's recommendations of different candidates: all these were destroyed by bombs in 1943. Among the interesting features of this large house are the black-walled room at the south-east angle of the atrium; a cubiculum decorated in the second style, to the left of the atrium; the tablinum, with its fine frieze (north wall) and its reconstructed east wall; the calidarium behind the *praefurnium* (kitchen), to the right of the tablinum; and the reconstruction of the east door in the portico. The garden has been replanted, and the twelve jets of the fountain spout again. At the end of the garden is a summer triclinium. The skeletons of the occupants were found under the portico (reconstructed). On the same side, at no. 5 of insula 3, some carbonised fragments of mats (*tegetes*) are preserved.

The **Schola Armaturarum** at no. 6 (Map 35) was probably the headquarters of a military organisation and not of the Collegium Juventutis Pompeianae, as was formerly supposed. The decorations of this building all refer to its function. On the exterior are two trophies of arms and on the door-jambs, two palm trees, the leaves of which were the reward of victory in the gymnasium. Inside are ten female genii, each holding a buckler and some kind of weapon. A plaster model of one of the cupboards, which contained gymnastic apparatus and fencing gear, stands by the west wall. The modern fastening of this *armamentarium* was made from a cast of the ancient one.

Cross the narrow *cardo orientalis* or Via Nuceria, which enters the city by the Porta Nuceria (see below). In this street to the left is the entrance (right) to the small but charming **House of Pinarius Cerialis**, identified as a lapidary from 114 gems found here (some uncut). The fine decorations of a little room on the north side depict a theatrical representation of *Iphigeneia in Tauris*.

On the corner of Via Nuceria and Via dell'Abbondanza is the **Tavern of Zosimus**; the rest of the insula, known as the **House of the Moralist** (Map 37) consists of two inter-communicating houses belonging to the related families of T. Arrius Polites and M. Epidus Hymenaeus. In no. 2, two ceilings have been reconstructed: a coffered black ceiling in the triclinium, a yellow one in a cubiculum. The garden has been replanted. A wooden staircase (a reconstruction) ascends to the rooms on the upper floor, the details of which have been reproduced as far as possible. The remains of the ornamentation have been affixed to the walls and ceilings. A small loggia, overlooking the inside garden, is almost intact. At the south-east corner is a perfectly preserved window-ledge. From the foot of the staircase, pass (without re-entering the street) into no. 3, skirting a black-walled room with flying female figures (left) and a small courtyard garden (right). Below the loggia already noted, in immediate contact with the garden, is a summer triclinium in masonry, with the usual table in the middle. On the three black walls were painted, in white, three maxims for polite conduct at table. One of these was destroyed by bombs in 1943.

At the south corner of the crossroads is the **Hermes Caupona** (a tavern) with the customary downstairs bar and a first-floor balcony (reconstructed). To the left is a private cistern (*castellum aquae*), the only one yet discovered, which retains the leaden tank from which pipes conveyed the water to the neighbour-members of the *consortium* or user-group. On the walls of the next alley to the north are inscriptions in large white letters, almost literally fulminating against committers of nuisance, by invoking the thunderbolts of Jove against offenders.

A special house

Further along Via dell'Abbondanza, on the right (II, 2, 5; Map 38), between two taverns, is the **House of Loreius Tiburtinus**, one of those that give us a perfect idea of patrician Pompeian life. A special charm is lent by the beautiful garden, now flourishing again after a rest of nearly 2000 years. A wide portal, closed by a bronze door and flanked by benches, opens into the atrium where the water-jet of the impluvium plays once again. A cubiculum in the east wing contains a *Rape of Europa* and a charming medallion of a girl.

To the left is a room with two rows of paintings. The first, on a black ground, presents a summary of the *Iliad* in a series of twelve pictures. The other shows the *Labours of Hercules*, taken from a Hercules cycle. The peristyle is bordered on the garden-side by a series of communicating basins (*euripus*). At the east end is a cascade where the water gushes out between paintings of **Narcissus** and **Pyramus and Thisbe**. Below is a *biclinium* (or dining bed for two), the table of which seems to rise from the water. On the right couch of the biclinium you can glimpse the signature of the artist Lucius, who executed the adjoining paintings. When the north arm of the euripus was full, it overflowed through conduits, passing under the little tetrastyle temple in the middle, into another branch, crossing the garden from north to south. Beneath the temple are ornamental carvings from which issued the water for a second cascade. In the large garden numerous plaster casts have been taken of roots of ornamental plants, shrubs, and trees.

The small house at no. 4 has a painted stucco relief of the imperial emblem over its entrance—a civic crown between two laurels. The **House of the Marine Venus** (II, 3, 3; Map 39) was damaged by a bomb in 1943 and not completely excavated until 1952, when the great painting of *Venus* was brought to light. The stuccoed decoration of the portico around the garden was completed just before the eruption.

The Villa of Julia Felix

The whole of the next insula, excavated in 1755–57 and reburied, and completely disinterred in 1952–53, is occupied by the Villa of Julia Felix (II, 4; Map 40) and its magnificent garden. The villa seems to have been a luxury hotel, with three sections: the residential quarter of the proprietress; a bath for public use; and an inn, a shop, and a series of rooms, some with independent street doors. The fine private rooms have big square windows overlooking the garden. They lost their wall paintings in the 18C; that of one room (Apollo and the Muses) is now in the Louvre.

The portico has slender rectangular marble columns with delicate capitals; the tiled roof is a copy of the antique one. Below it the couches of the triclinium face the marble fish-ponds in the middle of the garden and the rustic stucco colonnade beyond. The baths are the most complete and perfect in Pompeii; their charming vestibule is linked to the adjacent inn by a hatch. The rented apartments, one still displaying its 'to let' notice, were on two floors.

The amphitheatre

Behind the villa rises the amphitheatre (I, 6), the most ancient structure of its kind known. Begun c 80 BC through the munificence of the Duoviri C. Quintius Valgus and M. Porcius, it was not completed until the time of Augustus (27 BC–AD 14). The inscriptions beneath the north entrance probably refer to restorations undertaken by C. Cuspius Pansa after the period of disuse that followed the fatal brawl of AD 59 and the earthquake. The axes of the amphitheatre measure 135 x 107m, and it held 12,000 spectators.

The cavea was divided into three tiers, containing 5, 12, and 18 rows of seats. A space on the east side, as wide as two rows, was reserved for the president of the games. In construction it differs from later amphitheatres in that the gallery from which the first and second tiers are reached is constructed in four unconnected sections, whereas the upper gallery, reserved for women and children, is entered from a corridor reached only by an external staircase. There are no subterranean chambers beneath the arena.

To the west lies the **Great Palaestra**, a space c 110m square once shaded by great plane-trees, surrounded by a portico, with a large swimming pool in the centre. When the Samnite palaestra proved inadequate, the youth of the city exercised themselves and held their gymnastic competitions here. At the southeast corner (the latrine) were found many skeletons of youths who had fled in vain to its shelter during the eruption of Vesuvius.

From the west side you may pass between insulae 8 and 9 and, by turning left, descend to the **Porta di Nuceria**. Outside the gate, modern excavations have exposed a street (Via Nuceria) running east–west and flanked by sumptuous tombs that date mainly from the second half of the 1C BC. Particularly noteworthy are (right) the painted announcements of games at neighbouring cities (Nuceria, Herculaneum, and so on), tombs with portrait statues and busts and the Sepulchre of Eumachia, the builder of the cloth market in the forum. Just outside the gate are casts of three further victims of the disaster. To the west the extramural view of the town is impressive.

Now return along the Via dell'Abbondanza to its intersection with the Via Stabiana. To the left is the House of Cornelius Rufus.

Around the thermae

To the right lie the **Thermae Stabianae** (VII, 1). These were the largest baths in Pompeii. They originally date from the Samnite era, but were enlarged soon after the establishment of the Roman colony and again under the empire. The entrance leads to the **palaestra**, enclosed by a portico; some of the beautiful stucco decorations are visible to the left. Along this stretch are the bowling alley and the swimming pool, with its appurtenances. Opposite these are another bowling alley, a latrine and some private baths.

To the right are the **men's baths**. These include the *apodyterium* (dressing-room), consisting of two chambers with marble floor, vaulted stucco and recesses for the clothes; the circular *frigidarium* or cold bath; the *tepidarium* with a plunge-bath; and (at the back) the *calidarium* or warm room, with a plunge-bath and a basin for washing. Hot air circulated below the tepidarium and the calidarium.

The **women's baths** are adjacent. From a corridor enter the dressing-room, with two entrances from the street and the usual recesses. Beyond the cold and tepid rooms is the calidarium, with hollow walls and flooring for the hot vapour to pass through. The *praefurnium*, or heating apparatus, stood between the two warm rooms (calidaria); you can still make out the furnace and the position of three cylindrical boilers.

Beyond the baths turn right into Vico del Lupanare. The **House of Siricus** (right) (VII, 1, 47; Map 42) is composed of two communicating apartments. On the threshold is the inscription *Salve lucru(m)*, a candid salute to lucre. The handsome triclinium contains paintings of **Neptune and Apollo helping to build the walls of Troy**, **Hercules and Omphale** and **Thetis with Vulcan**. Opposite the entrance is a painting of two large serpents (*agathodeomones*), with the inscription (nearly effaced) *Otiosis locus hic non est, discede morator* (loitering forbidden).

Further on, to the left, is the **Lupanar Africani et Victoris** (Map 43); the coarse paintings and inscriptions on the ground floor indicate what sort of place this was. The first floor has a balcony (carefully restored after bomb damage). Opposite is the **Inn of Sittius** (Map 44), the sign of which was an elephant.

Vico del Lupanare ends at Via degli Augustali, where, almost opposite, is the **House of the Bear** (VII, 2; Map 45), so-called from the mosaic at the entrance. To the right is a **shoemaker's shop**. Keeping to the right, regain the Via Stabiana and turn left. To the right (no. 12) is a restored **mill** (*pistrinum*). No. 5, on the same side, is the **House of Marcus Lucretius** (IX, 3; Map 46), priest of Mars and *decurion* of Pompeii. This was once one of the more luxuriantly decorated houses in the city. In the atrium, to the right, is the aedicula of the two tutelary deities of the house. Opposite is the tablinum. At the back is a pretty little garden, with a fountain and some marble figures among its flowers. The best of the well-preserved paintings, in the fourth style, are now in the Museo Archeologico in Naples.

The whole of the next insula on the right is occupied by the **Central Thermae** (IX, 4), built between the earthquake and the eruption, with the usual features on a more sumptuous scale and, in addition, a *laconicum* or *sudatorium*, a hot-air chamber of circular shape with domed vaulting. The building was unfinished at the time of its destruction.

Leave the thermae by the north side to emerge in the Via di Nola. On the right side of the lane opposite is a tavern in which three large bronze trumpets, apparently deposited here by the gladiators of the amphitheatre fleeing from the shower of lapilli, were discovered.

Further on, to the right, is the entrance to the **Casa delle Nozze d'Argento** (House of the Silver Wedding Anniversary; V, 2, Map 47), so-called because the excavations were made in the presence of King Umberto and Queen Margherita in 1893, the year of their silver wedding. This is a real Pompeiian palace, with a spacious tetrastyle atrium. The front colonnade of the well-preserved peristyle is higher than the others. The triclinium is a large, handsome apartment. The cubicula on the south side have well-preserved decorations in the third style, and their private baths have been wonderfully restored. The garden, with its stonework triclinium, is also noteworthy.

Returning to the Via di Nola and following it to the left, you soon reach (right) the large, magnificent **Casa del Centenario** (House of the Centenary), so-named because it was excavated in 1879, the 1800th anniversary of the eruption. It has two atria (that on the left handsomely decorated) and a spacious peristyle. A graceful fountain plays in a small court adorned with paintings of gardens, a fish-pond and scenes of the chase. To the west are the bathrooms and two chambers adorned with paintings. A secret chamber with erotic decoration opens from one. Of interest also are the decorations of two rooms entered from the front walk of the colonnade, one with white walls, the other with black.

Off the alley opposite stands the **House of Marcus Lucretius Fronto** (V, 4; Map 49), which dates from the early imperial period. The roof of the atrium is a modern restoration, in strict keeping with the maxims of Vitruvius. Among the notable paintings in this house are *Neoptolemus slain by Orestes* (first room on the right), *Theseus and Ariadne*, *Toilet of Venus* (second room on the right), *Wedding of Mars and Venus*, *Triumph of Bacchus*, *landscapes* (tablinum), *Narcissus at the fountain*, *Pero and her father Micon condemned to death by starvation* (room to the right of the tablinum), *Pyramus and Thisbe*, *Bacchus and Silenus* (first garden-room to the right).

Further on in the Via di Nola, to the left, is the **House of the Gladiators** (Map 50) with a four-sided porticus. The Porta Nola, at the end of the street, dates from the Samnite era. It is decorated, on the side facing the city, with the head of Minerva.

Return to Via Stabiana and turn right. At the corner on the left are a fountain, an altar to the Lares of the crossroads, and an aqueduct pillar. No. 20 (left) is the **House of M. Vesonius Primus** (VI, 14; Map 51), known as the House of Orpheus from the large painting in the peristyle. In the atrium is a portrait-herm of Vesonius. No. 22 is the **Fullonica of Vesonius**. The impluvium contains a marble table and a fountain, and there are three water tanks behind the atrium. Opposite stands the **House of L. Coecilus Jucundus** (V, 1, 26; Map 53), the banker, where the famous receipts, now in the Museo Archeologico Nazionale, were discovered. The tablinum has good decorations. The sign for the **Taberna Lusoria** (no. 28), a vase between two phalli, indicates its business, a gambling house below with rooms for hire above.

Beyond the next crossroads on the left is the **Casa degli Amorini Dorati** (House of the Gilded Cupids) (VI, 16.7; Map 54), which belonged to the Poppaei, and which demonstrates the refined tastes of the age of Nero. The porticus has been restored on its old lines. The marble sculptures in the garden remain as they were. The marble bas-reliefs in the south wing of the colonnade represent satyrs, maenads, etc. At the south-east corner of the peristyle is a shrine devoted to the cult of Egyptian deities. The lararium in the north colonnade has the conventional form of a small temple.

The mosaic on the floor of the interesting cubiculum to the right indicates the place occupied by the beds. On the walls, under antique glass, are the flying and gilded cupids that give the house its name. In the east colonnade is a large room with paintings of *Thetis and Vulcan, Jason and Pelias* and *Achilles in his tent with Patroclus and Briseis*. The stucco ceilings of two cubicula in the west colonnade are unusually fine.

The cardo ends at the **Porta Vesuvio**, adjoining which is a *castellum aquae* or conduit-head, where water entering from an aqueduct was distributed to three channels. Outside the gate, beneath cypresses, is the **Tomb of the Aedile Vestorius Priscus**, with scenes from his life painted on the inner walls.

To the right is a terminal cippus of the ancient *pomerium* (zone of defence) set up by T. Suedius Clemens, a military tribune. Further on are the ruins of the village, with factories, reoccupied in the 2C and 3C AD but later abandoned. Turning back, notice the fine stretch of **pre-Samnite wall**, which is visible to the east; to the west are three fine towers.

An extraordinary neighbourhood

Now take the Vicolo dei Vettii. The **House of the Vettii** is at no. 1 (VI, 15; Map 55). It belonged to Aulus Vettius Restitutus and Aulus Vettius Conviva, two wealthy merchants of the Roman colony. Its beautiful paintings (still in their original positions) and the skilful reconstruction of its apartments make it one of the more interesting houses to visit.

To the right of the entrance, under lock and key, is a characteristically salacious image of Priapus. The atrium has delightful paintings of amorini and putti. To the right and left are strongrooms. Also on the right is the porter's lodge. In the corresponding little room to the left are paintings of *Ariadne deserted, Hero and Leander*, and a fish pond. The larger room to the left of the entrance has pictures of *Cyparissus, Amor and Pan wrestling for the entertainment of Bacchus and Ariadne, Leda and the Swan*, and *Jupiter enthroned*. Opening off the atrium are two cubicula and the alae, in one of which (left) is a cleverly painted picture of a cock fight. To the right of the main atrium is a small rustic atrium (with a lararium), followed by the kitchen, with its fire-grate and boilers. Adjoining is a closed room with equivocal pictures and a statuette of Priapus.

The **peristyle** offers an enchanting spectacle. Against the columns surrounding it are statuettes from which jets of water spouted into marble basins. Two other jets rise in the middle of the colourful garden. In the east colonnade are two handsome rooms (oeci). In one of them are paintings of the *Infant Hercules and the serpents, Pentheus torn limb from limb by the Bacchantes, Dirce and the wild bull*; in the other, *Daedalus showing Pasiphaë the wooden cow, Ixion on the wheel, Bacchus and the sleeping Ariadne*, and beautiful arabesques.

In the north colonnade is a separate group of triclinium, cubiculum, and small garden. The triclinium is the exquisite **Sala Dipinta** probably used for banquets on special occasions. On a black band round the room are charming little *amorini* at work and play (right to left): hurling at a target, weaving and selling wreaths, distilling perfume, driving a biga (two-horsed chariot), forging metal, dying cloth, celebrating the Vestalia, harvesting grapes, worshipping Bacchus, and selling wine. On the black panels below are *Winged nymphs gathering flowers; Agamemnon forcing his way into the Temple of Artemis to slay the sacred hind; Apollo as conqueror of the Python; Orestes and Pylades with Thoas and Iphigeneia*. On the dado, *Amazons and women with sacrificial vessels* and a *Bacchante and satyr*. On the large red panels, separated by candelabra-pilasters corresponding to the small black panels, are flying groups of *Perseus and Andromeda, Dionysus and Ariadne, Apollo and Daphne*, and *Poseidon and Amymone*. On the door-jambs, *Hermaphroditus and Silenus*.

Follow Vicolo di Mercurio to the right; on the corner (left) are an aqueduct pillar and some leaden pipes. No. 10 (right) is the **House of the Labyrinth** (VII, 11; Map 56), dating from the Samnite era and taking its name from a mosaic of Theseus and the Minotaur.

Turn south by Via del Fauno to reach Via della Fortuna. Here, to the right, is the entrance to the famous **House of the Faun** (VI, 12, 2–5; Map 57). This house, belonging to the Casii, is 80m long and 35m wide, occupying a whole insula. Its popular name comes from the celebrated bronze statuette of the *Dancing Faun* found near the impluvium (now in the Museo Archeologico in Naples, and replaced here by a copy). On the pavement in front of the house is the salutation *have* (welcome). There are two atria and two peristyles. The beautiful stucco decoration successfully imitates marble. The fine flooring of the first peristyle is, unfortunately, badly damaged. The mosaic floors of the four triclinia (one for each season of the year) are now in the museum at Naples. The 28 Ionic columns of the peristyle are coated with stucco. The well-known mosaic of the *Battle of Alexander* (also at Naples) was found in the red-columned exedra. The second peristyle is in the form of a large garden, with a Doric porticus.

Continue along Via della Fortuna. To the left, at its intersection with the Strada del Foro and Via di Mercurio, stands the **Temple of Fortune** (VII, 4; Map 58), constructed in 3 BC by M. Tullius and restored after the earthquake of AD 79. The Corinthian pronaos has two columns on each side. The architrave of an aedicula in the cella bears the name of the founder. At the north (right) corner is a triumphal arch (also used as a reservoir), which bore an equestrian statue of Caligula. Refreshments are sold in the adjoining building.

Beyond the crossroad, to the left (no. 2), are the **Forum Thermae** (VII, 5; Map 59), built in the time of Sulla by the Duovir L. Cesius and the Aediles C. Occius and L. Niremius. The layout resembles that of the Thermae stabianae (p 238). The shelves in the *apodyterium* are decorated with a frieze of telamones. The large bronze brazier in the tepidarium and the benches were presented by M. Nigidius Vaccula. The marble basin in the calidarium was placed here in AD 3 or AD 4 and cost (according to the inscription) 5250 sesterces. Inside are some more plaster casts of victims of the eruption, in glass cases.

Opposite the baths, on the other side of Via di Nola, is the **House of the Tragic Poet** (VI, 8, 5; Map 60), adopted by Bulwer Lytton, in his *Last Days of Pompeii*, as the house of Glaucus. Among the valuable mosaics found here was one of a theatrical rehearsal, now in the Museo Archeologico in Naples. On the threshold is a mosaic dog, with the inscription *cave canem* (beware of the dog). Beyond the peristyle is the household sanctuary, in the form of an aedicula. In the triclinium are paintings of *a Youth and maiden looking at a nest of cupids, Marsyas teaching Olympus the flute, Theseus and Ariadne, Dido and Aeneas,* and personifications of the *Seasons*. Another important picture found here was the *Sacrifice of Iphigeneia*.

A little further on, to the right, is the large **House of Pansa** (VI, 6), or *Domus Allei Nigidi Mai*, notable for the regularity of its construction. Along the entrance wall and the wall to the left were rows of shops. The rooms on the right were to let.

Follow Vicolo di Modesto to the right, then take the first turning on the left, for the **House of Sallust** (VI, 2, 4; Map 61), more properly known as the House of

CASA DI PANSA

1 Entrance
2 Atrium
3 Alae
4 Tablinum
5 Peristylium
6 Oecus
7 Kitchen
8 Shed
9 Portico
10 Garden
11 Cubicula
12 Triclinium
13 Rented rooms
14 Tabernae
15 Impluvium
16 Rooms with first floor
17 Piscina

A. Cassius Libanus, a fine mansion of the Samnite period damaged by a bomb in September 1943, when its well-known picture of Diana and Actaeon was destroyed. A partial restoration was paid for by American funds.

Take Via Consolare, which bears left, passing a storehouse for salt (no. 13; right) and the **House of the Surgeon** (Map 62), a massive structure of Sarno stone. Several surgical instruments, now at the Museo Archeologico Nazionale in Naples, were found here.

Outside the walls

The **Porta Ercolano** (Herculaneum Gate), at the end of Via Consolare, dates from the close of the 2C BC and is the most recent and most important town gate. In antiquity it seems to have been called *Porta Salina* or *Saliniensis*. Of its three archways, that in the centre, for vehicles, was vaulted at the ends only; the lateral openings for pedestrians were vaulted throughout. Beyond the gate runs the Via delle Tombe, lined with the sepulchral monuments of prominent Pompeians. To the left is the tomb of the Augustalis (priest of Augustus) M. Cerrinius Restitutus, followed by those of the Duoviri A. Veius (in the form of a semicircular seat) and M. Porcius (altar), and the priestess Mamia (seat with an inscription). Behind the last is the family sepulchre of the Istacidii.

To the left, at the end of a lane, is a terminal cippus marking the outer limit of the Pomerium, or sacred area. The major tombs on the right side of this part of the street are those of the Aedile M. Terentius Felix Major, the Tomb of the Garlands and the Tomb of the Blue Glass Vase (no. 8). The semicircular red bench (no. 9), belongs to the House of the Mosaic Columns, which takes its name from four mosaic columns, now in Naples.

Keeping to the left, beyond the so-called Villa of Cicero, a building that was excavated in the 18C and covered up again, you pass a tomb in the form of an altar, a circular tomb with a columbarium (a niche for cinerary urns), the tomb of the Augustalis C. Calventius Quietus, the enclosure of Numerius Istacidius Elenus and his family, the tomb of Noevoleia Tyche and the sepulchral triclinium of Cn. Vibrius Saturninus. On the other (right) side of the street is the fine sepulchre of M. Alleius Luccius Libella and his son. A little further on is a tomb with a marble door. On a low hillock are the monument of L. Ceius Labeo, the tomb of M. Arrius Diomedes and other unfinished sepulchres. The suburban villas (see below) are just beyond this point.

Returning to Porta Ercolano, take the Pomerium road to the left for a glimpse of Pompeii's fortifications. The **town rampart** is c 6m thick. It consists of an outer wall (2C BC) and the pre-Samnite inner wall, with earth in the intervening space. The walls were originally of tufa or limestone, but they were repaired with blocks of lava shortly before the Social War. There were twelve towers between the Porta Ercolano and the Porta Marina, and several others on the north side, where the natural defences were weakest. It was this part of the wall that was chosen for attack by L. Sulla in 89 BC, and the damage caused by his missiles can still be seen.

Enter the city again through the **Porta Vesuvio**. Inside the wall Tower XI (which you can climb) commands an extensive panorama. Follow Via di Mercurio downhill, passing (right) the **House of Apollo** (VI, 7, 23; Map 63), with a picturesque fountain, a handsome cubiculum, a mosaic of Achilles at Scyros, and a painting of *Apollo and Marsyas*.

On the other side of the street is the **House of Meleager** (Map 64), with its tasteful fountain and Corinthian oecus. Beneath a marble table in the atrium is an apparatus for cooling wine and food in water.

The **House of the Centaur** (Map 65) is decorated in the first style. In the **House of Adonis** (Map 66) is a large painting of the *Wounded Adonis tended by Venus and cupids*. The **House of Castor and Pollux** (Map 67) has a Corinthian atrium with twelve columns and paintings of *Apollo and Daphne*, *Birth of Adonis*, *Minos and Scylla*. Like many other dwellings, it is an amalgamation of several earlier buildings.

On the east corner of the crossroads with Vicolo di Mercurio is a **caupona** or tavern (VI, 10, 1). In the back shop are scenes of tavern life. In the **House of the Little Fountain** (VI, 8, 23; Map 68), a mosaic fountain is adorned with a boy and goose in bronze (copies). The **House of the Large Fountain** (Map 69) has another mosaic fountain. Across the street is the **House of the Anchor** (VI, 10, 7; Map 70), so-called from a mosaic on the threshold. The garden, on a lower level, is surrounded by a cryptoporticus. Here you are again within a short distance of the Posto di Ristoro and the forum.

The Villa of Diomedes and Villa dei Misteri

To reach these two surburban villas, walk along Via delle Tombe, or take the road that leads north from Villa dei Misteri station on the Circumvesuviana line.

The famous **Villa of Diomedes** is so-called on the slender grounds that the burial place of M. Arrius Diomedes is on the opposite side of the road (see above). The villa had the largest garden in Pompeii, with a colonnade containing various chambers. Steps ascend to the peristyle, adjoining which are (right) a luxurious private bath with cold-water pool and (left) a large apsidal chamber, possibly a sitting room. The tablinum, opposite the entrance, opens onto a large terrace, from which steps and a ramp descend to the garden. In the middle are a *piscina* (tank) and a summer triclinium, with fountain, and an arbour borne by six columns.

In a vaulted cellar extending below three sides of the garden-colonnade were found amphorae of wine and 18 skeletons of adults and children who had vainly taken refuge in the cellar. The owner of the villa, probably a wine-merchant, was

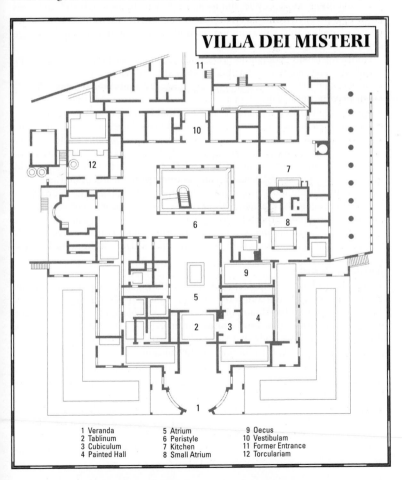

VILLA DEI MISTERI

1 Veranda	5 Atrium	9 Oecus
2 Tablinum	6 Peristyle	10 Vestibulam
3 Cubiculum	7 Kitchen	11 Former Entrance
4 Painted Hall	8 Small Atrium	12 Torculariam

found near the garden door, with the key in his hand; beside him was a slave with money and valuables. A small staircase with two columns formed the main entrance from Via delle Tombe and led directly to the peristyle.

About 200m to the west of the Villa of Diomedes stands the **Villa dei Misteri** (Villa of the Mysteries), a complex dwelling that started in the 2C BC as a town house, developed into a manor and declined into a farmhouse. It takes its name from a hall with 24 life-size **painted figures** thought to have been executed by a Campanian painter in 1C BC on a second style background. Entrance is gained from the rear of the villa, through what was once a broad gallery with a central exedra (1) and two lateral wings. Straight ahead is the tablinum (2), with black-ground paintings in a vaguely Egyptian style. Here you turn right and walk through a cubiculum (3) adorned with Dionysiac figures (such as a dancing satyr, a hallmark of the cult of the young god of excess) to reach the marble-floored **Sala del Grande Dipinto** (4).

The paintings form a cycle, the meaning of which, although still under discussion, is probably connected with the initiation rites into the Dionysiac mysteries, a practice that was common in southern Italy despite prohibitory measures adopted by the Roman Senate.

According to the leading interpretation, the scenes, starting on the wall to the left of the door, represent (a) a child reading the rite before a young bride and a seated matron; (b) a priestess and three female assistants making a sacrifice; (c) Sileni playing musical instruments in a pastoral setting; (d) the flight of the frightened initiate and a group of two satyrs and a silenus with a mask; (e) the marriage of Dionysus and Ariadne (damaged); (f) a kneeling woman unveiling (or, by a differing interpretation, protecting) the sacred phallus while a winged demon raises a *flagellum* to strike the young initiate, who seeks refuge in the lap of a companion; (g) the orgiastic dance of Dionysus; (h) the dressing of a bride for initiation and a seated woman who has undergone the initiation rite.

Returning to the tablinium, turn right through the atrium to the peristyle, then right again to the kitchen, with its two fireplaces. The adjacent small atrium gives access to a room gracefully decorated with architectural motifs. Around the peristyle are the *vestibulam*, leading to the former main entrance (opposite the atrium), and a *torcularium*, where grapes were pressed (across from the kitchen).

Modern Pompei

The modern village of Pompei (population 26,000) has sprung up round the pilgrimage shrine of Santa Maria del Rosario, built in 1876–91 and enlarged in 1938 as a shrine for the Madonna of the Rosary, an old picture, framed with gold and precious stones that now adorns the high altar. The **Museo Vesuviano** (Piazza Longo 1; open daily 09.00–13.30) has Vesuvian stones, and prints and paintings representing the eruptions of the volcano.

HERCULANEUM
. . . .

Not everyone draws aesthetic pleasure from a visit to Pompeii and Herculaneum. One 19C visitor, for instance, left this curious account, in which the sense of death and desolation overwhelms interests of a purely intellectual nature, resulting in a sour-grapes attempt to pass the whole experience off as a waste of time: 'We saw the theatre at Herculaneum, which had been buried sixteen centuries; and passed under vaults to view it by torch-light—while wandering about the galleries, I was of course obliged to express surprise and pleasure; but in truth I wished myself away, for there were neither singers nor dancers, nor pretty women there, and I never had any taste for antiques.' Too bad.

Herculaneum (Ercolano), destroyed with Pompeii in AD 79 and rediscovered in 1709, was a residential town without Pompeii's commercial importance, surrounded by villas of wealthy Romans. The excavations are on an attractive terraced site. Although they are small in extent compared with those of Pompeii and less immediately striking, the domestic buildings, especially their upper storeys and wooden parts, are better preserved. Gardens have been replanted, contributing to a feeling of life and humanity not always achieved at Pompeii. Herculaneum also has the interest of a richer artistic life and of contrasting styles of house construction.

Practical information

Information offices
Tourist information offices in **Naples** provide information for this area, see p 111.

Getting there
By road
The modern town of Ercolano can be reached by Road 18 or Autostrada A3/E45. Once in Ercolano, Road 18 passes the entrance to the excavations.
By rail
Take the *Circumvesuviana* railway (Sorrento line) from Naples or Sorrento to Pugliano station, then proceed by foot along the wide road descending seaward

from the station (10mins walk).

Where to stay
See Naples, p 112 or Sorrento and the Amalfi Coast, pp 269–270.

Eating out
ERCOLANO € *Casa Rossa 1888, al Vesuvio*, Via Vesuvio 30, ☎ 081 777 9763. Restaurant-pizzeria, the little sister of the famous Casa Rossa at Torre del Greco; closed Tues.
TORRE DEL GRECO €€ *Casa Rossa 1888*, Via Mortelle 128, ☎ 081 883 1549. Restaurant known for its delicious pasta; closed Mon.

Visiting the ruins
Visitors who have time to see only one of the two ancient cities are advised to go to Herculaneum, where the most outstanding features can be seen in about two hours. These include the House of Opus Craticium, the House of the Wooden Partition, the Thermae, the Samnite House, the House of the Deer, and the House of the Relief of Telephus. As at Pompeii, ongoing conservation work requires the

closure of certain houses from time to time. On the other hand, 'new' buildings are opened as soon as they have been made safe for visitors. Recent openings include the House of Aristides, near the House of Argus on Cardo III and, possibly, the underground theatre. The excavations are open daily, Mar–Sept 08.30–19.30, Oct–Feb 08.30–17.00, info and reservation ☎ 081 536 5154.

History of Herculaneum

The foundation of Herculaneum, called *Herakleia* by its Greek settlers, was attributed by them to its patron deity, Hercules. The town passed through periods of Oscan and Samnite domination, before falling to Titus Didius, a lieutenant of Sulla, in 89 BC, after which a colony of veterans seems to have been established here. The damage done by an earthquake in AD 63 was being repaired, under Vespasian's patronage, when the catastrophe of AD 79 overwhelmed the town. Unlike Pompeii, Herculaneum was submerged by a torrent of mud containing sand, ashes, and bits of lava, which raised the level of the soil by 12–25m and hardened into tufa, preserving many timber features and household objects that were burnt at Pompeii. Subsequent layers of volcanic matter buried the ruins to a depth of 39m and the town remained untouched for 1630 years.

The first discoveries were made in 1709 when Emmanuel de Lorraine, Prince d'Elbeuf and cavalry commander of the Kingdom of Naples, came upon the back of the theatre's stage while sinking the shaft for a well. He distributed a large group of statues and much of the scena among various museums.

Charles III continued the exploration (1738–65), without any very clear plan, but the theatre, forum, and five 'temples' were located. The Villa of the Papyri was also explored and its treasure of sculpture and library recovered and transferred to Naples. The *Accademia Reale Ercolanese*, founded in 1755 for the purpose of investigating the discoveries, published a work in eight volumes on the mural paintings and bronzes (1757–92) and a volume on the papyri (1797; by C. Rosini).

Desultory explorations were carried out in 1828–35 and in 1869–75, but systematic excavation was not begun until 1927. The excavations continue, and you will probably have the opportunity to watch a 'dig' in progress. The new excavations have disinterred three cardines (III, IV, and V), two roads (the *decumanus inferior* and part of the *decumanus maximus*) as well as the suburban area outside the walls, which descends towards the harbour. Houses are designated by insula (block) and street number only.

The ancient city

The extent of the city is still uncertain, but in both area and population it was probably only about one-third of the size of Pompeii. With *decumani* (the main street) running parallel with the coast (then much nearer the town than it is today) and *cardines* at right angles to the decumani and the shore, the town suggests a Greek rather than a Roman plan and has affinities with Neapolis (Naples). The streets are paved with local volcanic stone, but are noticeably free from both the wheel ruts and the stepping-stones so characteristic of Pompeiian streets. On the seaward side the town ended in a terraced promontory, lined with patrician villas, beneath which the cardines descended abruptly through narrow archways to the extramural quarter round the harbour.

The site

The avenue that leads from the entrance gate to the excavations commands a wonderful **view** across Herculaneum to the sea. This allows you to appreciate the natural beauty of the site, the magnitude of the disaster which transformed it, and the difficulties that face the excavators. Looking down on the city from above you can also see the variety of its dwellings and the topography of its streets.

As an alternative to the itinerary described here, the ruins may be entered via the Terme Surburbane (described at the end of this account).

Descend to Cardo III at the west corner of the site. To the left are insula II and, beyond the decumanus inferior, insula VII, both brought to light in 1828–35 when much of their interest was spoiled by inexperienced excavators. The **House of Argus** (II, 2; Map 1) must have been one of the finer mansions in the town: some idea of its grandeur may still be gained from the wall fronting the street and the noble columns of its peristyle. To the left of Cardo III is the back entrance to the house usually, but wrongly called the **hotel** (II, 1). Occupying well over half the insula, this was the largest and perhaps the richest dwelling in the south quarter of the city. When the earlier excavations exposed its west side, it was assumed because of its proportions to be a hotel; but its plan, though complex, is almost certainly that of a private villa, designed to exploit all the advantage of its site. The house had already fallen on bad times and at the date of the catastrophe was undergoing modifications: the whole south wing had been converted into a self-contained dwelling and a room on the north side into a shop. The private bath of the Augustan period had been abandoned (hypocaust exposed). The house was badly damaged in the eruption and further mutilated by Bourbon excavators, but even in decay its extent is impressive.

Herculanean houses

Unlike Pompeii, which was entirely dominated by the commercial classes, Herculaneum was a city of wealthy citizens, small artisans, and fishermen. The Herculanean house is more evolved, freer, and further advanced in the adoption of new ideas than the Pompeiian house. The Samnite type of construction described at Pompeii also exists at Herculaneum, but frequently with the atrium daringly modified for the addition of an extra floor.

In the richer type of dwelling the Hellenistic plan of building round a peristyle is frequently followed, but the peristyle itself is often modified to a closed corridor with windows overlooking the central garden. In many middle-class houses the traditional plan has been abandoned and a central courtyard, more akin to the modern 'well', has been substituted. Finally, 'apartment houses' with several floors have been discovered (though not on the scale developed in Ostia), in which the poorer artisans lived the crowded life of their modern Neapolitan counterparts.

House of the Mosaic Atrium

Emerge by the main entrance (19) into Cardo IV. Opposite is the House of the Mosaic Atrium (IV, 1–2; Map 2), another panoramic house beautifully placed for enjoying the view. From the street (no. 2), pass through the *fauces* (entrance passage) to the atrium, both of which retain their geometric mosaic floors, though the pavement was corrugated under the weight of the invading tufa. Facing the atrium are the unusual basilican tablinum, and, at right angles, a closed gallery formed by partially filling in the intercolumnar spaces of a peristyle. The door and window frames are remarkably well preserved. Off the narrow east walk are four cubicula with red walls, and a raised central exedra, adorned with mythological scenes, with a wooden table. This room enjoys a charming view of the garden with its marble fountain. The main living-rooms beyond, including a lofty triclinium paved in marble, open onto a terrace formerly shaded by a colonnaded roof, with a solarium, at either end of which is a *diaeta*, or siesta room, with low windows for maximum enjoyment of the view.

Continuing up Cardo IV, notice on the left the **House of the Bronze Herm** (III, 16; Map 3), with typical though diminutive characteristics of the Samnite house. The base of a staircase leading to an upper floor can be seen in the blind corridor leading off the atrium. On the other side of the street is the **House of the Alcove** (IV, 3; Map 4), its façade in *opus reticulatum* pierced with iron gratings and overhung by the remains of a first-floor balcony. The smaller door (no. 4) gave on to the stairs. The ground floor comprises two separate dwellings thrown into one, that to the left modest, and that to the right more distinguished with a tessellated atrium and a richly painted room with wooden couches. At the end of a long corridor is a small court with the alcoved room that gives the house its name.

The **House of Opus Craticium** presents a unique example of the wood and plaster construction, called *opus craticium*, used for plebeian dwellings, the defects and impermanence of which were noted by Vitruvius. The building, which consists of a shop with a back-parlour or workroom, and two self-contained flats, preserves its upper floor with balcony room over the pavement. The inner rooms overlook a small yard. The staircase (restored) still has several of the original steps. The houses on the other side of the street also have interesting features; two rooms at the rear of no. 6, lit by circular windows, retain their barrel-vaulting, floors, and mural decoration (of the first period; see p 231).

House of the wooden partition
Next on the left is the House of the Wooden Partition (III, 11–12; Map 6), whose façade, which rises to the second storey, offers a striking picture of the external appearance of the Roman private house. The open gallery above the cornice belonged to a second floor, added to the structure when the house declined in status; this was reached from a separate entrance in the decumanus. In the imposing atrium the double lining of the impluvium tank in *opus signinum* (mosaic or paving of small stones set in a rough or random pattern) and marble is notable; also the dogs'-head spouts (some original) of the compluviate roof. The most striking feature, giving its name to the house, is the wooden partition that closes the tablinum, reconstructed in situ with its ancient hinges and lamp brackets. Glass cases preserve remains of toilet articles, beans, etc., found in the house. The cubiculum to the right of the *fauces* has a geometrical floor design and a marble table; the further room on the left, a well-preserved frieze. Behind the house is a charming small garden. The side of the house abutting the decumanus inferior was occupied by shops which, with one exception, link directly to the house. The corner shop (no. 10) contains a unique wooden **clothes-press** in an astonishing state of preservation.

Behind is the **House of the Skeleton** (III, 3; Map 7), so-called from the

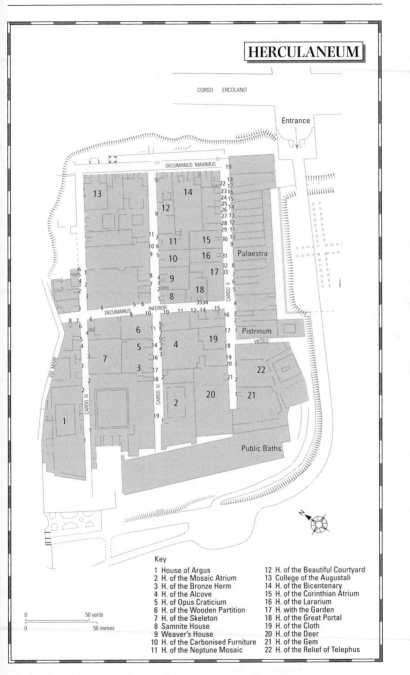

HERCULANEUM

CORSO ERCOLANO

Entrance

DECUMANUS MAXIMUS

13

12

14

11

15

10

16

9

17

8

18

Palaestra

CARDO V

DECUMANUS INFERIOR

6

5

4

19

Pistrinum

7

3

VICOLO

CARDO III

CARDO IV

2

20

22

21

Public Baths

VIA MARE

1

0   50 yards
0   50 metres

Key

1 House of Argus
2 H. of the Mosaic Atrium
3 H. of the Bronze Herm
4 H. of the Alcove
5 H. of Opus Craticium
6 H. of the Wooden Partition
7 H. of the Skeleton
8 Samnite House
9 Weaver's House
10 H. of the Carbonised Furniture
11 H. of the Neptune Mosaic

12 H. of the Beautiful Courtyard
13 College of the Augustali
14 H. of the Bicentenary
15 H. of the Corinthian Atrium
16 H. of the Lararium
17 H. with the Garden
18 H. of the Great Portal
19 H. of the Cloth
20 H. of the Deer
21 H. of the Gem
22 H. of the Relief of Telephus

remains discovered in 1831 on the upper floor. The small rooms are tastefully disposed and decorated.

The baths

Cross the decumanus inferior, passing a shop selling postcards. The greater part of insula VI (left) is occupied by the **thermae**, public baths erected early in the reign of Augustus (c 20 BC) on a plan similar to that used at Pompeii and decorated somewhat later. They survive, finely preserved and without modification, almost as they were planned. In the centre is the **palaestra**, the main entrance of which was in Cardo IV (no. 7). To the south, with separate entrances from the decumanus, was a covered hall with a penthouse roof, probably a *sphaeristerium*, where the ball game *pila* was played. A second entrance to the palaestra from Cardo III (no. 1), flanked by a porter's lodge and a latrine, led also to the **men's baths**. From the corridor you enter the apodyterium (dressing-room), with a convex floor in *opus segmentatum*, shelves for clothes, and vaulted stucco. A *cipollino* marble basin stands in an apse. A vestibule, to the left, leads down marble steps to the circular *frigidarium* or cold bath, the domed ceiling of which is painted with fish on a blue ground, pierced by a skylight. From the other side of the dressing-room, pass through the *tepidarium* to the *caldarium* or warm room, with the usual plunge-bath and a scalloped apse for a hand basin; the fallen vault has exposed the heating pipes and smoke vents.

The **women's baths**, entered from Cardo IV (no. 8), though smaller and simpler, are even better preserved. You enter a waiting-room and pass through a small linen-room to the dressing-room, whose mosaic (as in the men's tepidarium) shows a triton surrounded by dolphins and cuttle-fish. Beyond, the small tepidarium and calidarium are virtually complete. Behind (no. 10) are the service quarters, where the well can be seen, and the staircase leading up to the attendant's living quarters and down to the *praefurnium* or heating apparatus; the heavy iron door and the poker survive, though the boilers were removed by Bourbon excavators.

Further along Cardo IV (no. 11) is the **House of the Black Hall**, still largely buried, with an elegant tetrastyle portico. The paintings of the little vaulted rooms and of the black hall are particularly lively. The model temple, with wooden columns, surmounted by marble capitals, was a shrine for the Lares.

Visit next the houses on the other side of Cardo IV, starting at the crossroads. The **Samnite House**, fronted by a stretch of fine paving, has an imposing portal and an open gallery (approached by a stair from no. 2) that led to a separate apartment added at a later date. The interior decoration is beautifully executed; that of the fauces in the first style of architectural imitation. The atrium has a blind gallery of graceful proportions. Beyond a simple **Weaver's House** (V, 3–4; Map 9) and workshop is the small but dignified **House of the Carbonised Furniture** (V, 5; Map 10), in the Samnite style, with an elegantly decorated triclinium and a delightful little courtyard. The lararium is placed to be seen from the window of an inner room, the divan and table of which survive. Some furniture remains also in the upper rooms of the **House of the Neptune Mosaic** (V, 6–7, Map 11), which stand open to the street. Below is the best-preserved **shop** in the town. A fine wooden partition separates the shop from the attractive living quarters behind, where a little court is enlivened by the fresh blues and greens of the mosaic of Neptune and Amphitrite (that gives the house its name), and of the nymphaeum. The **House of the Beautiful Courtyard** (V, 8; Map 12) has an unusual plan grouped around a wide hall that precedes the court. The **College of the Augustali** (Map 13), seat of the cult of the emperor established in the Augustan age, contains some very well-preserved wall paintings. The cardo continues between high pavements (once arcaded, as may be seen from the remaining columns) to the crossing with the usual public fountain and altar. A painted inscription on a pillar records rules of the street police.

Turn into the broad decumanus maximus, reserved for pedestrians, the left side of which still lies beneath the tufa. On the right is a **shop** (V, 10) with a little room over the pavement. Built into the counter and sunk into the floor are the *dolia*, or large jars, in which foodstuffs could be preserved at an even temperature. This and the adjoining shops originally formed part of the **House of the Bicentenary** (V, 15–16; Map 14), a rich dwelling disinterred in 1938, two hundred years after Charles III began the excavations. Despite later modifications, the ground floor preserves its original plan. The fine atrium still has its lattice partition and the tablinum is decorated with mythical scenes and paved in mosaic. The outline of a cross on the wall of an upstairs room suggests that a private Christian oratory existed here, although the crucifix is not thought to have become established as a Christian symbol as early as AD 79.

Cardo V is admirably paved in limestone. To the left is a public fountain with a mask of Hercules; turn right, towards the sea. The **corner shop** (V, 21) is interesting for the wooden window-fittings remaining in the dwelling above (entered from no. 22). Beyond on the right the houses continue to be in styles already familiar; three of them, preceded by a stretch of marble pavement once shaded by a portico, have features worthy of note.

In the **House of the Corinthian Atrium** (V, 30; Map 15), small but in good taste, the compluviate roof, supported by six tufa columns faced with stucco, feeds a graceful fountain. A mosaic, in a room to the right, shows the sacred two-edged axe, or *labrys* in its pattern. A glass case contains a wooden table and a small basket. Note also the elegant decoration of the cubiculum, lit by three skylights (two restored). Next door is the **House of the Lararium** (V, 31; Map 16), an earlier and smaller dwelling showing good examples of decoration in the first and third styles. Most wonderfully preserved is a wooden *sacellum*, which consists of a cupboard surmounted by a shrine in the form of a small temple *in antis*, with Corinthian columns, where the Lares were kept. Beyond is the so-called **House with the Garden** (V, 33, Map 17), though the garden probably belonged to one of the more distinguished houses in the decumanus.

The other side of the street is quite different, foreshadowing the style developed at Ostia a hundred years later. The whole block (insula Orientalis II), c 90m long, is of uniform construction in *opus reticulatum* and was apparently planned as a unit. The street frontage consists of shops with flats above, on a plan having no resemblance to the traditional Campanian house, but such as might be seen today.

The chief interest of the plain rectangular shops is in their use and contents. No. 16 contains a marble casket and an almost perfect wooden partition door; no. 13 has a counter with remains of its vegetable wares; no. 9 preserves its stove and sink and a little painting of Hercules pouring a libation between Dionysus and Mercury. No. 8 was a bakery, where two mills for grinding flour, 25 bronze baking pans, the seal of the proprietor and an oven carved with a phallic emblem were found. The main staircase to the flats was at no. 7.

Behind this workaday façade a series of finely decorated and vaulted rooms overlook a huge open space surrounded by a portico, of which only the north and west sides have been unearthed. This area, the **palaestra**, where the public games were held, is approached by two great entrance halls (nos 19 and 4), each with a prostyle porch. No. 4, by which you enter, had a black tessellated floor and white walls and vault, a fitting entrance to the impressive colonnade within. Bourbon tunnels beneath the avenue give a vivid impression of the difficulties of excavation as well as of the size of the cruciform swimming-pool that occupied the centre of the palaestra. Its central **fountain** of bronze, cast in the form of a five-headed serpent entwined round a tree-trunk, has been re-erected.

Rejoin Cardo V by the Neptune fountain, the usual rectangular basin formed of limestone slabs joined at the corners by lead clamps. On the right side of the decumanus inferior is the imposing entrance of the **House of the Great Portal** (V, 35; Map 18), its engaged brick columns surmounted by Corinthian capitals carved with winged Victories and an architrave decorated in terracotta; within are several good paintings, and, in the floor of the *diaeta*, a picture executed in marble *opus sectile*. The other side of the street is occupied by shops; no. 14, a *caupona* (tavern) well stocked with amphorae. The largest shop, on the corner (IV, 15–16), has an impressive counter, faced with polychrome marble and containing eight *dolia* for the storing of cereals.

Continuing the descent of Cardo V, note a small **shop** (right; IV, 17) with a priapic painting next to the counter, remains of nuts, lamps and utensils, etc., and a Judas window from the adjoining house. In the lane to the left, flanking the palaestra, is another pistrinum, or bakery, where the iron door of the oven remains closed despite the collapse of the vault, and with a stable for the asses that turned the mills. The **House of the cloth** (IV, 19–20; Map 19) yielded pieces of ancient fabric in which the design is still discernible. Note the unusual arrangement of the stairs. Beyond, you again approach the terraced quarter occupied by the houses of the rich.

House of the Deer

On the right is the House of the Deer (*Casa dei Cervi*; IV, 21; Map 20), the grandest dwelling yet discovered at Herculaneum, with a frontage of 43m. The entrance leads into a covered atrium, from which opens the spacious triclinium. The latter is painted with architectural motifs on black and red panels and paved in marble intarsia. Within are the two delicately executed groups of **deer at bay**, after which the house is named. Behind, in an equally elegantly decorated oecus, stands a statuette of a satyr with a wineskin. The kitchen, latrine, and apotheca form a compact little block to the right. The garden is surrounded by an enclosed corridor, lit by windows and decorated with panels of cupids playing (most of these have been removed to the Museo Archeologico Nazionale in Naples); in this, the latest development of the peristyle, the columns have finally disappeared. In the centre is a summer triclinium flanked by two lovely smaller rooms, in one of which is a vigorously indelicate statue of the drunken Hercules. The far walk opens onto a terrace where an arbour, flanked by flower beds and siesta rooms, overlooks a sun balcony. Originally, this terrace opened directly onto the sea, commanding a view from Posillipo to Sorrento and Capri.

Cross the street to insula Orientalis I. This consists of only two houses, both planned in an individual manner dictated by their situation; some of their rooms lie at a lower level and have yet to be explored. The **House of the Gem** (no. 1), named from an engraved stone found in it, has an unusual atrium with buttress-like pilasters and a side door that opens through a *diplyon* (or double door)towards the irregular sunken garden. The latrine preserves an inscription (perhaps the work of a servant) recording a visit by a famous doctor. The floor of the triclinium is 'carpeted' in fine mosaic.

House of the Relief of Telephus

The House of the Relief of Telephus (no. 2–3), the most extensive of Herculanean mansions, is built around two sides of the House of the Gem and at two levels on the hillside. The walls were partially overthrown by the rush of mud that brought down the *Quadriga* reliefs (seen on either side of the entrance) from some higher public building. The atrium has colonnades on three sides. The original *oscilla*, circular marble panels depicting satyrs, have been rehung between the columns. On the north side, small doors lead to the servants' quarters and stables. Descend a steep passage to the peristyle, which surrounds the garden, at the centre of which is an azure basin. Off the south walk are the ruins of a once grand room (8.5 x 6m), with a polychrome marble floor; the reconstructed marble dado of one wall demonstrates the palatial standards of this rich dwelling. In an adjacent room is a relief of the myth of Telephus, a late work executed academically in the Classical manner.

Below the terrace are the public baths known as the **terme suburbane** (open 08.30–13.00), probably of late construction and surviving in a good state. Nearby is the plinth of a statue to M. Nonius Balbus, a celebrated citizen of the town. The base of another statue to his memory stands before the proscenium of the **theatre**, which lies partially buried to the west (entrance at no. 119 Corso Ercolano: apply at the office). The visit is interesting less for the theatre, the best of which was rifled by d'Elbeuf, than for the impression it gives of the daring of the 18C excavators. The great suburban **Villa of the Papyri**, from which many works of art in Naples museum came, was abandoned to the tufa in 1765.

Ercolano and its environs

Ercolano (population 63,000) was built in the Middle Ages on the lava covering the stream of mud that overwhelmed Herculaneum. Just south of the excava-tions is the Miglio d'Oro, where the road is flanked by sumptuous 18C summer homes. One of these, **Villa Campolieto**, has been restored to its original splen-dour and occasionally hosts special events. Open to visitors Tues–Sun 10.00–13.00.

Nearby **Portici** (population 72,000), smoky with factories, is the alleged birthplace of the rebel leader Masaniello (1620–47). It is noted for its **Palazzo Reale**, begun in 1739 by Canevari, which now houses the Faculty of Agriculture of Naples University; this was the birthplace of Charles IV of Spain (1748) and was occupied by Pius IX in 1849–50. Between Naples and Portici (Granatello) the first Italian train was inaugurated on 3 October 1839, by Ferdinand II. The **Museo Ferroviario Nazionale** (National Railway Museum; Corso San Giovanni a Teduccio, open Mon–Sat 09.00–14.00) occupies the restored premises of the railway works at Pietrarsa and is largely devoted to steam engines.

CAPRI

• • • • • •

Unfortunately, you are not the only one who knows that Capri is one of the more beautiful spots on our small planet. Obviously, the best time to visit the island is out of season (November–March), or mid-week, when the crowds are elsewhere. But in all fairness it must be said that the island's appeal as a resort is a boon as well as a burden to the modern traveller: it was Capri's natural beauty that led an eminent Roman, probably the emperor Tiberius, to build a luxurious beach house here (the famous Villa Jovis); and Swedish physician Axel Munthe's Villa San Michele, which stands on the site of another Roman patrician home, is hardly less impressive. Development in the late 19C and early 20C has given the towns of **Capri** and **Anacapri** an aristocratic air that other southern Italian resorts lack; and everywhere the views over sea and coast more than compensate for any inconvenience that sharing them with varying numbers of fellow travellers may cause.

Automobile traffic on the island is severely restricted, so if you are driving, leave your car on the mainland and use the bus to get around. It is possible to visit Capri from Naples in one day by taking an early morning hydrofoil, catching the bus to Anacapri at midday and returning by a hydrofoil leaving Marina Grande in the late afternoon or evening. Even better, you could combine Capri with Sorrento by spending the night on the island and leaving for Sorrento by an early-morning boat. All who can, however, should devote two or more days to Capri, to allow time for the ascent of **Monte Solaro** and a trip by boat along the east coast of the island.

Practical information

 ### Information offices

A N A C A P R I *Ufficio Informazioni e di Accoglienza Turistica*, Via G. Orlandi19/A, ☎ 081 837 1524.
C A P R I *Ufficio Informazioni e di Accoglienza Turistica*, Piazza Umberto I, ☎ 081 837 0686.
Azienda Autonoma di Cura Soggiorno e Turismo, Piazzetta I. Cerio 11, ☎ 081 837 0424, 081 837 5308, ✉ www.capritourism.com,touristoffice@capri.it.
M A R I N A G R A N D E (the harbour) *Ufficio Informazioni e di Accoglienza Turistica*, Banchina del Porto, ☎ 081 8370634.

 ### Getting there and getting around
By sea

Ferries run daily from Naples (1hr 15mins), Sorrento (45mins) and Ischia (1hr, Apr–Oct), from Amalfi and Positano. There is also a daily **hydrofoil** service from Naples (40–45mins), Sorrento (20mins–1hr) and Ischia (50mins, Apr–Oct), Positano (50mins) and Amalfi (65mins). Visit ✉ www.campaniatrasporti.it for schedules.
By land

Frequent **buses** scurry from the main square in Capri town to Marina Grande, Marina Piccola and Anacapri; and Capri is famous for its convertable-limousine **taxis**, though most of the antique models are now gone. A **funicular railway** connects the town and its harbour (services every 15mins).

Where to stay

ANACAPRI €€€ *Capri Palace*, Via Capodimonte 2, ☎ 081 9780111, 📠 0039 081 8373191, ✉ www.capri-palace.com, info@capri-palace.com. Recently renovated, transformed and promoted to a luxury hotel, with classical Mediterranean architecture, exquisite Louis XVI style furnishings, majolica and stone paving and stunning views over the open Mediterranean Sea and the Gulf of Naples.

€€ *Casa Caprile*, Via Follicara 9, ☎ 081 837 3948, 📠 0818371881, ✉ www.casacaprile.com/indexeng.htm, info@casacaprile.com. 24 rooms, all pleasantly furnished, and a garden with ficus, mangroves, palms, pines, cypress and other exotic plants.

€€ *Cesare Augustus*, Via G. Orlandi 4, ☎ 081 8373395, 📠 081 8371444, ✉ www.caesar-augustus.com. On a cliff 1000 feet above the sea, offering the most spectacular vistas and recently renovated interiors; open April–Oct.

€€ *Mulino*, Via La Fabbrica 9, ☎ 081 8382084, 📠 081 8382642, ✉ www.mulino-capri.com, mulino@capri.it. A new establishment at the verdent west end of the island; each room has a private terrace with view over the surrounding park.

€€ *San Michele*, Via G. Orlandi 113, ☎ 081 837 1427, 📠 081 837 1420, ✉ www.sanmichele-capri.com, smichele@capri.it. Pleasant atmosphere and comfortable rooms, pool and large garden; open Apr–Oct.

€ *Bouganville*, Viale Tommaso de Tommaso 6, ☎ 081 837 3641, 📠 081 838 2847, ✉ www.capri-bougainville.com, bouganville@italyhotel.com. A new establishment of just 12 rooms with enchanting view of the centre.

CAPRI €€€ *Casa Morgano*, Via Tragara 6, ☎ 081 8370158, 📠 081 8370681, ✉ www.caprionline.com/morgano, casamorgano@capri.it. A boutique luxury hotel with luxuriant gardens, pool and private panoramic terraces.

€€€ *Grand Hotel Quisisana*, Via Camerelle 2, ☎ 081 837 0788, 📠 081 837 6080, ✉ www.quisi.it, info@quisi.com. One of Italy's finer hotels, with sumptuous rooms, two restaurants, two pools, tennis courts, sauna, Turkish bath, and a famous bar with panoramic terrace; open Apr–Oct.

€€€ *La Scalinatella*, Via Tragara 8, ☎ 081 837 0633, 📠 081 837 8291, ✉ casamorgana@capri.it. Romantic and refined, spacious rooms, splendid views, attentive staff; open April–Oct.

€€ *La Certosella*, Via Tragara 13, ☎ 081 837 0713, 📠 081 837 6113. Comfortable rooms, excellent cuisine.

€€€ *Punta Tragara*, Via Tragara 57, ☎ 081 837 0844, 📠 081 837 7790, ✉ www.hoteltragara.com, h.tragara@capri.it. Designed by the French Modern architect Le Corbusier, magnificently set on a clifftop amid lush gardens, two salt-water pools (one heated, with whirlpool); open Easter–Nov.

€€ *La Minerva*, Via Occhio Marino, ☎ 081 8370374, 📠 081 8375221, ✉ www.laminervacapri.com, laminervacapri.it. Situated on the coast, in an authentic oasis of tranquillity just a few minutes walk down the shopping streets Via Camerelle and Via Vittorio Emanuele.

€€ *Luna*, Viale Matteotti 3, ☎ 081 837 0433, 📠 081 837 7459, ✉ www.caprionline.com/luna, luna@capri.it. Quiet and central, in a luxuriant garden with good views; open Easter–Nov.

€€ *Villa Brunella*, Via Tragara 24, ☎ 081 837 0122, 📠 081 837 0430, ✉ www.caprionline.com/villabrunella, villabrunella@capri.it. Cordial atmosphere in a renovated villa with stepped terraces leading down to pool and sea; open Easter–Oct.

€€ *Villa Sarah*, Via Tiberio 3a, ☎ 081 837 7817, 📠 081 837 7215,

✉ www.villasarah.it, reserve@
villasarah.it. Another family-run
establishment with rooms facing sea or
garden, home-made cakes and jams at
breakfast; open Easter–Oct.
€ *Villa Krupp*, Via Matteotti 12,
☎ 081 837 0362, ▯ 081 837 6489.
12 spacious rooms, in a renovated villa
owned and managed by a charming
family; open Mar–Oct.

Eating out

ANACAPRI €€ *Da
Gelsomina*, at *La Migliara*
(shuttle from Anacapri on request),
☎ 081 8371499. Restaurant with
rooms; closed Tues (except in summer)
and Jan-Feb.
€€ *Lido del Faro*, Punta Carena,
☎ 081 837 1798. Restaurant and lido;
closed Oct–Mar.
€ *Rondinella*, Via G. Orlandi 145,
☎ 081 837 1223. Simple but good
traditional fare, including pizza; closed
Thur (except in summer) and Feb.
CAPRI €€€ *Quisi*, Via Camerelle 2,
☎ 081 837 0788. The island's most
elegant (at the Hotel Quisisana), with
indoor and outdoor seating, wonderful
cuisine and impeccable service; closed
Nov–Mar.
€€ *Cantinella*, Viale Matteotti 8 (giardini di Augusto), ☎ 081 837 0616.

Fine cuisine and beautiful terraced
garden overlooking the Faraglioni;
closed Oct and Mar.
€€ *La Capannina*, Via delle Botteghe
14, ☎ 081 837 0732. Traditional
Neapolitan cuisine, served under a
pergola in summer; closed Wed and
Nov–Mar.
€€ *Le Grottelle*, Via Arco Naturale 13,
☎ 081 837 5719. A secluded restaurant serving excellent seafood, in a
grotto with terrace overlooking the sea;
closed Thur except July–Sept.
€€ *Pergola*, Traversa Palazzo 2, ☎ 081
837 7414. Garden restaurant with
views, a good place to go for pizza;
closed Jan–Feb.
€€ *Villa Brunella*, Via Tragara 24,
☎ 081 837 0122. Good food and
cordial atmosphere, with a youngish
clientele; closed Nov–Mar.
MARINA GRANDE €€ *La
Scogliera*, Hotel Palatium, Via Marina
Grande 225, ☎ 081 837 6144.
Restaurant, closed Jan–Feb.

Special events

CAPRI *San Costanzo*
(patron saint of the island) 14
May; *Sant'Antonio* (at Anacapri) 13
June; *Festival of the Madonna* (with a
Mass on Monte Solaro and festivities all
around the island) 7–8 September.

The island

A small island 6km long and 3km wide, Capri lies 5km from the Punta della
Campanella on the Sorrentine Peninsula, of which it forms the geological continuation. It is a mountainous island, with a precipitous and almost inaccessible coast,
abounding in caves and fantastic rocks. With its perennial sunshine, its pure air,
and its luxuriant, almost tropical vegetation, it is the pearl of the Gulf of Naples.

The appearance of the inhabitants, especially of the women (who wear a highly
picturesque costume on special occasions), is distinctly Greek. The population is c
12,000 and the chief town is also called Capri. **Anacapri**, in a somewhat less
sheltered position, is the only other centre of any size. Monte Solaro (590m) is the
highest point. The chief products of the island are fruit, oil and wine.

History of Capri

Capri was inhabited in prehistoric times; later, it became Greek and then Roman. Augustus, who visited it personally, obtained it from the Neapolitans in exchange for the larger and more fertile island of Ischia. His contributions to Capri included roads, aqueducts and villas.

The wider fame of the island began with Tiberius, who retired to Capri in AD 27. The story of the magnificence, profligacy, and horrors of his ten years' residence was unknown before the writings of Tacitus and Suetonius, but the publicity value of these undoubted exaggerations ensures their perpetuation. On the dominant points of the island Tiberius erected several villas, dedicated (probably) to the major deities of the Roman Pantheon. The most important of these structures was the Villa Jovis. In 182 the Emperor Commodus, son of Marcus Aurelius, assigned the island as a place of exile for his wife Crispina and his sister Lucilla.

During the Middle Ages Capri was occupied at length by the Saracens, whose lasting influence can be seen in local building conventions, especially the barrel-vaulted roofs of many homes and churches. In 1806 the island was taken by the British fleet under Sir Sidney Smith and strongly fortified; Sir Hudson Lowe was appointed governor. In 1808, however, it was retaken by the French, under Lamarque, and in 1813 it was restored to Ferdinand I of the Two Sicilies.

The island is much frequented by foreigners, and for more than 150 years has provided a home for expatriates, artists and eccentrics.

The town of Capri

Travellers arriving in Capri generally land on the north coast, in the bay of the **Marina Grande**. From here you get to the town of Capri by funicular railway, by road (3km), or by footpath (Strada Campo di Pisco).

Capri (142m, population 7000), a small, quaint town with vaulted houses and labyrinthine streets, lies in the saddle between Punta del Capo on the east and Monte Solaro on the west. Hard by rise the hills of San Michele and Castiglione.

The road from the Marina Grande passes the church of **San Costanzo**, built in the 10C and 11C and enlarged c 1330, with a Byzantine dome and small, characteristic campanile. Within, the crossing is marred by the loss of its ancient cipollino columns, four of which were removed in 1755 to decorate the royal chapel at Caserta (four remain); these came originally from the nearby **Palazzo a Mare** (surviving *exedra* below the cliff to the west). Further on, the road joins up with those from the Marina Piccola (south-west) and Anacapri (north-west), and after a few more paces ends on Piazza Umberto Primo. Here stands the 17C church of **Santo Stefano**, approached by a flight of steps. The interior contains, at the foot of the left (north) altar, a fragment of inlaid pavement from the Villa Jovis (see below) and the tombs of aristocrats Giacomo and Vincenzo Arcucci by Naccherino.

Across the way is the **Palazzo Cerio**, where Joan I used to stay. The mansion now houses a small private museum of natural history and antiquities (**Museo del Centro Caprese Ignazio Cerio**; open Tues, Wed, Fri, Sat 10.00–13.00; Thur 15.00–19.00; ☎ 081 837 6681) found in excavations on the island at the turn of the century by the physician and naturalist Ignazio Cerio, as well as an interesting library and archive. Close to the upper station of the cable railway from the Marina remains of a megalithic wall may be seen.

Walks around Capri

Several fine walks may be taken in the environs of Capri. To the south-west are (20 minutes) the ruins of the Castiglione (249m; closed to the public), a medieval castle constructed with ancient materials, and the **Punta Canone**, which affords a superb view of the Faraglioni rocks and the Marina Piccola. To reach the latter, you ascend the steps of the church of Santo Stefano, follow (right) Via Madre Serafina and pass the church of Santa Teresa. About 500m further on, a narrow path to the right climbs to the Castiglione. Bear left. More steps and a shaded path lead to the scenic overlook. On the north slope of the hill, in 1786 the antiquary Hadrawa, secretary to the Austrian ambassador, discovered five ancient rooms with painted and marble decoration.

To reach the **Certosa di San Giacomo** (6 minutes), leave the piazza by a vaulted passage in the south corner and follow Via Vittorio Emanuele to the Quisisana Hotel. Via Federico Serena, to the right of the hotel, descends past a large garden (bear left) to the Carthusian monastery founded in 1371 by Giacomo Arcucci, Secretary to Joan I; it was sacked by Torgud in 1553 and suppressed in 1807. The conventual buildings house the **Museo Diefenbach** (open Tues–Sun 09.00–14.00, ☎ 081 837 6218), with works by the 19C German artist. The fresco above the portal of the Gothic church, showing the Madonna and Child with the founder and his queen, might be a work of Andrea Vanni. From Via Federico Serena (see above) Via Matteotti leads to Via Augusto, a paved path built by Friedrich Krupp, the German armaments manufacturer, which descends to the Marina Piccola.

The **Punta di Tragara**, like the Punta Canone, can be reached in about 20 minutes. Via Camerelle, to the left of the Quisisana Hotel (see above), skirts a series of brick vaults known as the Camerelle, probably the arches of a roadconnecting the villas of Tragara and Castiglione. You ascend slightly to reach the Belvedere di Tragara (view of the Faraglioni and towards Marina Piccola); steps by the café and a path lead from here to the Punta di Tragara, from which the

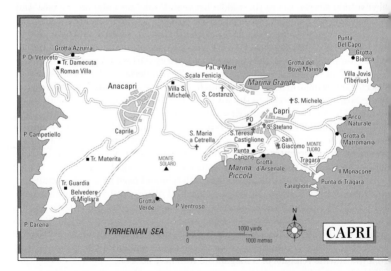

Impressions of Capri

Would you like to know what the literati thought of Capri? Here are a few quick impressions:

'I am very sick of Capri: it is a stewpot of semi-literary cats.' D.H. Lawrence, letter to Catherine Carswell, 5 February 1920.

'The place is full of fairies.' F. Scott Fitzgerald, letter to Maxwell Perkins, 31 March 1925.

'Capri is not the place for moralizing.' Norman Douglas, *Footnote on Capri*, 1952.

When Goethe visited Naples in 1787, he exclaimed: 'Naples is a paradise, in it every one lives in a sort of intoxicated self-forgetfulness. It is even so with me ... Were I not impelled by the German spirit, and desire to learn and to do rather than enjoy, I should tarry a little longer in this school of a light-hearted and happy life, and try to profit from it still more.'

In the 19C, Sorrento, Capri, Ischia and the villages of the Amalfi coast came into their own as alternative resorts for visitors to Naples and the south. Sorrento and Ravello were favourite haunts of Wagner and Nietzsche. Residents of Capri have included Emil von Behring (1854–1917), discoverer of a successful inoculation against tetanus, and Axel Munthe, the Swedish physician; Maxim Gorky (1868–1936), who lived here in 1907–13 and ran a school for revolutionaries visited by Lenin, Stalin, and Chaliapin; C.C. Coleman (1841–1928), American painter of genre scenes; and the writer Norman Douglas (1868–1952). Today these areas, which are known principally for their natural beauty, attract hundreds of thousands of visitors each year.

view includes (to the east) the flat rock, known as Il Monacone, from a species of seal once native to Capri. From the steps another path continues east to the Arco Naturale (see below).

What is perhaps Capri's most famous nature walk includes the **Arco Naturale** (20 minutes) and the **Grotta di Matromania** (10 minutes more). From the north-east corner of the piazza follow the narrow Via Botteghe, Via Fuorlovade, and Via Croce. Where the latter divides take Via Matromania (right); after 8 minutes keep to the left, and after 8 minutes more descend the steps (left) to the Arco Naturale, a fantastic archway in the rock (view). Returning to the path continue to descend to (10 minutes) the Grotta di Matromania, which opens towards the east. The cave ends in a semicircular apse, and there are various small chambers with walls in *opus reticulatum*. This is probably a **sanctuary of Cybele**, the *Mater Magna*; the erroneous belief that it was a Mithraeum was exploded when it was learned that a Mithraic relief in the Naples museum, supposedly discovered here, had in fact been found elsewhere on the island.

Villa Jovis

A lovely walk of just under an hour leads to the Villa Jovis (open daily 09.00–1hr before sunset; ☎ 081 837 0381), known to the Capriotes as the Palazzo di Tiberio. From Via Croce (see above) take the rising Via Tiberio (left; follow the central strip of paving) and pass the small church of San Michele Arcangelo. Further on bear to the right, passing near the remains of a *pharos*, or lighthouse, probably built by Augustus and overthrown by an earthquake after the death of Tiberius. Here is the **Salto di Tiberio** (296m), the almost vertical rock off which, it is fabled, Tiberiu pushed his victims. A few more paces lead to the ruined villa, a residence of pala tial proportions with several storeys. It was systematically explored for the first time in 1932–35, by which time most of its mosaic pavements and other decorative ele ments had already been carried off. The ruins cover an area of 7000 sq m, centring around a rectangular zone occupied by four large cisterns hewn out of the roc' and divided into intercommunicating cells.

From the entrance to the archaeological park a path leads left to the **vestibule** conserving the bases of four marble columns. The rooms of the guard corps, con verted during the Middle Ages into cisterns, are adjacent. Brick steps ascend from the entrance past the **thermae**, consisting of a dressing-room, a *frigidarium*, a *tep idarium*, a *calidarium* (with two semicircular apses), and rooms for the heating and distribution of the water. To the east, built in a hemicycle, are the **state rooms**.

Along the west wing of the palace, are servants' quarters, to the **imperia apartments** (remains of mosaic floor), from where a corridor and steps descend to the Loggia Imperiale or Belvedere, a long (92m) straight porch set into the north rim of the cliff, 20m below the level of the palace. Steps along the wes (inland) flank of the villa descend to vaulted store rooms and to the kitchens, se apart from the rest of the structure.

At the highest point of the promontory, on an ancient substructure, is the chapel of **Santa Maria del Soccorso**, commanding the finest **view** in Capri embracing the island itself, the sea, the Punta della Campanella, and the two gulfs. Restored in 1979, the church stands behind an enormous bronze Madonna brought to the site by a United States Navy helicopter and solemnly blessed by Pope John Paul II.

Anacapri

The trip from Capri to Anacapri is a mere 3km and may be made on foot or by bus. The windy road, hewn out of the rock in 1874 and restored in 1923 ascends, affording a series of beautiful views. On the way you pass the Torre Quattro Venti, near which is the **Palazzo Inglese**, built c 1750 by Sir Nathaniel Thorold and a key point in the French assault of 1808. Formerly, the only mean of communication between Anacapri and the rest of the island was by the **Scala Fenicia**, a flight of 800 steps attributable to the Greeks or to Augustus, descend ing to the Marina Grande. This (now, however, with fewer steps) crosses the road at the chapel of Sant'Antonio, above which are the ruins of the Castello d Barbarossa, destroyed in 1535 by the corsair of that name. Near the top of the steps is the Villa San Michele (see below).

Anacapri (284m), a village of 5000 inhabitants, recalls Sicily with its white houses and quasi-oriental roofs. From Piazza della Vittoria the main street bears right. To the north, in Piazza San Nicola, the octagonal church of **San Michele** finished in 1719, possesses a majolica pavement showing the Story of Eden, exe cuted by Leonardo Chiaiese in 1761 to a design by Solimena. The plan of the church is ascribed to Domenico Antonio Vaccaro. The four sides on the main axes are slightly longer than those on the diagonals, and the vestibule and choi are deeper than the other areas leading off the central space, imparting a longi tudinal emphasis to the plan. The architect also uses the pilasters at the point where the vestibule and choir join the central space to lead the eye from one area of the church to the next, placing them at an angle to the main axis.

Piazza Armando Diaz is at the centre of town. In the piazza is the **Chiesa Parrocchiale** (parish church, or Santa Sofia; 1510, enlarged 1870). From here, the street continues (left) to the smiling village of **Caprile** (500m). Via San Michele leads up (15 minutes) from Piazza della Vittoria to the **Villa San Michele** (open daily Jan–Feb 10.30–15.30, Mar 09.30–16.30, Apr 09.30–17.00, May–Sept 09.00–18.00, Oct 09.30–17.00, Nov–Dec 10.30–15.30; ☎ 081 837 1401), built by the Swedish doctor, Axel Munthe (1857–1949) on the site of one of Tiberius's villas and containing a small collection of antiquities. The beautifully kept garden is one of the more luxuriant in Italy; the views from its parapets are stunning.

Walks around Anacapri

The plateau of **Migliara** (304m), reached in 40 minutes, commands a striking **view** of the Faraglioni and the precipices of Monte Solaro. To reach it, take any one of the stony paths that climb southwards from Caprile, joining the former mule track that leads to the Belvedere di Migliara; or simply pick up the old mule track left of the Monte Solaro funicular station in Anacapri. Then return via the Torre della Guardia, above the Punta Carena, and the 15C Torre di Materita.

A road runs west from the Chiesa Parrocchiale to the Mulino a Vento and to the 12C Torre di Damecuta, a watch-tower against pirates. Next to the tower another **Roman villa** (open daily 09.00–1hr before sunset), smaller but similar to the Villa Jovis, has been excavated. Damaged in AD 79, it was fortified by the French and British in the 19C. From the long belvedere the **view** of the Phlegraean Fields is particularly fine at sunset. A path descends to the Blue Grotto (described below).

The ascent of **Monte Solaro** may be made in about 1hour (or by chair-lift from Piazza della Vittoria in 12 minutes). From Via Capodimonte take Via Solaro south (left if you are coming from Villa San Michele, right from Piazza Vittoria) to reach the path (signpost), along the slope, which winds south. A steep ascent passes by remains of the English fortifications of 1806–08 to the Crocella saddle (45 minutes), where a shrine of the Virgin stands. It takes c 15 minutes more to reach the summit of Monte Solaro (589m), which is crowned by a ruined castle rebuilt to form a system of panoramic terraces (refreshments). The wonderful **view** extends over the Gulfs of Naples and Salerno to the Ponziane Islands (northwest), the Apennines (east), and the mountains of Calabria (south).

A famous marine grotto

On the north coast of the island is the **Grotta Azzurra** (Blue Grotto), a visit to which is the most popular excursion on Capri. The approach is made by sea (daily 09.00–dusk, except when strong north or east winds blow, making entrance to the cave impossible), from the Marina Grande, or from the landing at the base of the footpath from Anacapri (Via Lo Pozzo). The boat from Marina Grande skirts the north side of the island, affording a view of the ruins known as the Bagni di Tiberio. The light effects are best 11.00–13.00.

A marine cavern, the Blue Grotto owes its geological formation to gradual subsidence of the coast, probably since the Roman epoch. Though known in antiquity, it seems then to have lacked the curious effects of light that are now its great charm. Its possibilities were realised in 1822 by Augusto Ferrara, a Capri fisherman, who in 1826 led Kopisch, a German poet, and some others to its 'accidental' discovery. Kopisch entered the facts in the register of Pagano's hotel, and these were published in Hans Christian Anderson's novel, *The Improvisator*.

Once a nymphaeum of Tiberius, the cavern has yielded a wealth of archaeological material, including several large statues (these objects are awaiting collocation in the planned archaeological museum). In addition, underwater explorations in 1976 revealed the existence of niches, platforms, and broad apses hewn out of the rock, in c 2m of water. The mouth of the cave is barely 1m high, so that even in calm weather, heads have to be ducked.

The **interior** is 57m long, 30m wide, and 15m high. The sun's rays, entering not directly but through the water, fill the cave with a magical blue light and objects in the water have a beautiful silvery appearance. Near the middle of the grotto is a ledge where boats can land. An adjoining cleft, once supposed to be the beginning of an underground passage to the Villa of Damecuta, has been proved to be a natural orifice. Outside the grotto is the beginning of a path ascending to Anacapri.

Boat trips for salty dogs

Those who prefer open horizons to tight spaces like caves will enjoy the **giro** or voyage around the island by boat. The non-stop trip takes 3–4 hours and begins either from the Marina Grande or the Marina Piccola. Excursions take place daily during the season, Apr–Sept; on request at other times.

Heading east from the Marina Grande, you pass, in succession, the Grotta del Bove Marino, the strangely shaped little point of Fucile (musket), and the rock named La Ricotta (cream-cheese). After doubling round Il Capo, you reach the Grotta Bianca and Grotta Meravigliosa, both with stalactites (the second accessible from the land). Further on are the Faraglione di Matromana and Il Monacone, the latter with Roman remains.

Off the Punta di Tragara are three gigantic rocks called the **Faraglioni**, one of which, La Stella (90m), is connected with the island. The outermost, Lo Scopolo (89m), resembles a sugar-loaf and is the habitat of a rare species of blue lizard.

The boat passes through a natural arch in the central rock. Next comes the Grotta dell'Arsenale, supposed to have been used for repairing ships. Beyond the Marina Piccola, at the foot of Monte Solaro, is the **Grotta Verde**, with beautiful green light effects (best 10.00–11.00; inaccessible in a strong south wind). Not far off is the Grotta Rossa. The voyage along the west side of the island up to the Blue Grotto is less interesting.

PROCIDA AND ISCHIA

'Capri or Ischia?' is a dilemma that faces every first-time visitor to the Naples area, and the answer is: 'Procida'. Perhaps because it is nearer to the mainland than the other islands in the bay, or perhaps because it is the least dramatic, Procida has suffered less from the domesticating influence of tourism. For this reason it remains the most characteristic—the noisiest and most chaotic, but also the most colourful—of the three islands. Ischia, alas, is a prime destination of package tours; fortunately these focus on the thermal resorts on the north coast—**Casamicciola Terme**, **Lacco Ameno** and **Forio**—leaving the west and outh of the island relatively untouched. You will not find Ischia as rich in history as Capri, but the geology of the island is thoroughly fascinating: its volcanic origin is responsible for the hot mineral springs that are its chief claim to fame, as well as for the rich soil that yields the excellent Ischia Bianco and Ischia Rosso wines.

Practical information

Information offices
PROCIDA *Ufficio Informazioni*, Via Roma 92, ☎ 081 896 9594.

ISCHIA *Azienda Autonoma di Cura Soggiorno e Turismo*, Corso Colonna 108, ☎ 081 507 4211, ▤ 081 507 4230.

Getting there and getting around
By sea

TO PROCIDA Ferries sail daily to Procida from Naples (1hr), Pozzuoli (30mins), and Ischia (30mins). There is also a daily **hydrofoil** service from Naples (35mins), Pozzuoli (15mins) and Ischia (15mins).

TO ISCHIA Ischia is served by daily **ferries** from Naples (1hr 15mins), Pozzuoli (1hr), Procida (30mins), and Capri (1hr, Apr–Oct); and there is a daily **hydrofoil** service from Naples (30–45mins), Procida (15mins), and Capri (50mins, Apr–Oct). Details and schedules at ▨ www.campania trasporti.com.

By bus

Frequent buses make a circuit of Ischia, starting from Ischia Porto.

Where to stay
Hotels

FORIO €€€ *Grande Albergo Mezzatorre*, Via Mezzatorre 23 (at San Montano Nord), ☎ 081 986111, ▤ 081 986015, ▨ www. mezzatorre.it, info@mezzatorre.it. Quiet luxury in a shady park; open Apr–Oct.

€€€ *Grand Hotel Punta Molino Terme*, Lungomare Cristoforo Colombo 25, ☎ 081 991544, ▤ 081 991562, ▨ reservationspointel.it. Another luxury venue, with thermal-water pool; open Apr–Oct.

€€ *La Bagattella Terme*, Via Tommaso Cigliano 8, at San Francesco, ☎ 081 986072, ▤ 081 989637, ▨ www. labagatellaflashnet.it. Garden setting and cordial atmosphere, away from the hustle and bustle; open Apr–Oct.

€€ *Paradiso Terme*, Via San Giuseppe 10, at Cuotto, ☎ 081 907014, ▤ 907913, ▨ www. hotelparadisoterme.it,info@ hotelparadisoterme.it. Quiet and pleasant, with beautiful sea views and thermal-water swimming pool; open Apr–Oct.

€€ *Punta Chiarito*, Via Sorgeto 35, at Panza, ☎ 081 908102, ▤ 081 909277, ▨ puntachiarito@pointel.it. On a headland overlooking the sea; open Mar–Nov and Dec–Jan.

ISCHIA TOWN €€€ *Grand Hotel Excelsior*, Via Emanuele Gianturco 19, ☎ 081 991522, ▤ 081 984100, ▨ excelsior@pointel.it. Elegant and luxurious, in a pine wood, with heated pool; open Apr–Oct.

€€ *La Villarosa*, Via Giacinto Gigante 5, ☎ 081 991316, ▤ 081 992425. In a shady garden, with thermal-water pool and excellent restaurant; open Apr–Oct.

€ *Il Vitigno*, Via Bocca 31, ☎ 081 998307, ▤ 081 998307. B&B with restaurant, on a farm amidst olive groves and vineyards.

LACCO AMENO €€ *San Montano*, ☎ 081 994033, 📠 081 980242, 📧 www.sanmontano.com, info@sanmontano.com. 1.5km from the village centre, in a quiet shady setting with thermal pool and outstanding restaurant; open Apr–Oct.

SANT'ANGELO €€ *San Michele*, at Serrara Fontana, ☎ 081 999276, 📠 081 999149. Garden, sea views and thermal pool; open May–Oct.

€€ *Miramare*, Via Commandante Maddalena 29, ☎ 081 999219, 📠 0811 999325, 📧 www.hotel miramare.it, hotel@hotelmiramare.it. Quiet and panoramic, with tennis courts; open Mar–Oct.

Spas

ISCHIA The most famous are *Ischia Thermal Centre*, Ischia; *Terme Belliacci* and *Terme Piro*, Casamicciola; *Regina Isabella*, Lacco Ameno. Many hotels on the island have thermal swimming pools.

Eating out

ISCHIA (CASAMICCIOLA) € *Il Focolare di Loretta e Riccardo D'Ambra*, Via Cretaio 78, Casamicciola, ☎ 081 980604. A very special family-run place in the hills above Casamicciola. Open daily except Wed; evenings only (all day Fri–Sun); closed two weeks in Nov.

ISCHIA (PORTO) €€ *Alberto*, Passeggiata Cristoforo Colombo, ☎ 081 981259. Restaurant serving traditional and creative dishes, by the sea; closed Nov–Mar.

ISCHIA (TOWN) €€ *Cocò*, Piazza Aragonese, ☎ 081 981823. Good regional dishes, by the sea; closed Jan–Feb.

FORIO €€ *Grusoni*, Strada Statale 270, ☎ 081 907272. Traditional fish restaurant with outdoor seating in fair weather; closed Nov–Feb.

€€ *Il Melograno*, Via Mazzella 110 (Cava dell'Isola), ☎ 081 998450. Garden restaurant, known for its delicious innovative cuisine; closed Nov.

€€ *La Romantica*, Via Marina 46, ☎ 081 997345. Trattoria-pizzeria with outdoor seating; closed Wed and Nov–Mar.

€ *Da Peppina*, Via Bocca 23, ☎ 081 998312. Trattoria-pizzeria, open Mar–Nov evenings only; closed Wed except in summer.

€ *Gelateria di Elio e Stani del Deo*, Via Castellaccio 35. Delicious ice cream, especially fruit flavours.

LACCO AMENO €€ *Negombo*, Spiaggia di San Montano, ☎ 081 986152. By the sea, with gardens spa-pool and good views; closed evenings and Oct–Apr.

PROCIDA € *Crescenzo*, Via Marina Chiaiolella 33, Chiaiolella, ☎ 081 8967255. Restaurant with rooms by the beach, always open.

Special events

LACCO AMENO (ISCHIA) *St Restituta* (17 May), celebrated with fireworks and bonfires on Monte Vico, etc.

PROCIDA *St Michael*, 26 September and 8 May.

Procida

The island of Procida (3.5km long, population 11,000), the ancient *Prochyta* was created from four craters of basaltic tufa and pumice stone, partly destroyed by the sea to form semicircular bays. The islet of Vivara represents a fifth crater. The main local industries are fishing and vine growing and the islanders have long been famed for their seamanship.

The town of **Procida**, with flat-roofed white houses of Eastern aspect flanked by steep cliffs, stretches along the north coast and rises in terraces on the hills beyond. The winding streets have changed little since the Middle Ages. Italian actor-director Massimo Troisi drew on their old charm in the urban scenes of his last film, *Il Postino* (The Postman).

Ferries and hydrofoils land at the marina. In Piazza dei Martiri are a tablet commemorating twelve of the inhabitants of Procida executed after the rising of 1799 (the Parthenopean Republic, see p 55), and a statue of the statesman, Antonio Scialoia, who died on the island in 1877. The **castle** (now a prison) commands a fine view over Ischia and Monte Epomeo in one direction and Cape Miseno and the Gulf of Naples in the other. In bygone days, escaped prisoners were famous for their appetites; hence the term *sprocidato*, escaped from Procida, (in popular slang, famished). Via San Michele climbs to the Terra Murata (91m), the highest point of the island, where the abbey church of San Michele features, in the ceiling, Luca Giordano's *St Michael defeating Lucifer*. At the south-west end of the island, beyond the castle of Santa Margherita, is the Bay of Chiaiolella, facing the tiny olive-clad islet of Vivara and Ischia.

Ischia

Ischia is a collection of craters and lava streams of which the highest point is the conical Monte Epomeo (788m), the north side of an extinct volcano. Adjoining its slope are other craters—Monte Rotaro and Monte Montagnone on the north-east, Monte Trippiti on the east and Monte Imperatore and the hills extending to the Punta dell'Imperatore on the west. Lava streams also formed the promontories of Monte Caruso and Punta Cornacchia on the north-west. About 34km in circumference, Ischia is the largest island in the Gulf of Naples. It has a mild climate, and its volcanic slopes are richly covered with sub-tropical vegetation.

Celebrated for its hot mineral springs (season May–Oct; some open all year) and for sea-bathing, boating and its delightful walks, the whole island is well supplied with hotels, restaurants and bathing establishments.

History of Ischia

According to the ancient poets, Ischia was the abode of the giant Typhoeus who, when struck by Jupiter's thunderbolts, expressed his vengeful fury in volcanoes and earthquakes. The Greeks who colonised it called it *Pithecusa* or *Pithecusae*, the Latins *Aenaria* or *Inarime*. In the 9C it was known as Iscla, a corruption of insula or, simply, the Island, from which its modern name is derived.

The earliest recorded volcanic eruption on the island dates from c 500 BC; the last was in 1301. Ischia was seized in 474 BC by Hieron of Syracuse, c 450 by the Neapolitans, and by the Romans in 326. Augustus exchanged it with the Neapolitans for Capri. It was later taken by the Saracens in 813 and 947, by the Pisans in 1135, by Henry VI and Frederick II. Finally it came to share the fortunes of Naples.

Ischia was the birthplace of the Marquis of Pescara (1489), and his widow Vittoria Colonna retired here in 1525. The island was sacked by the pirate Barbarossa in 1541 and captured in 1547 by the Duke of Guise; it was occupied by Nelson, and in 1815 provided a brief refuge for Murat. The self-portrait of Scottish painter Allan Ramsay in the National Portrait Gallery in London was executed on the island in 1776, and the sculptor Canova was rewarded with the title of Marquis of Ischia in 1816.

> ## *An epitome of the earth*
> Ischia's beauty, interest, and variety prompted George Berkeley to describe it, in a letter to Alexander Pope (1717):
>
> 'The island ... is an epitome of the whole earth containing within the compass of eighteen miles, a wonderful variety of hills, vales, ragged rocks, fruitful plains, and barren mountains, all thrown together in a most romantic confusion. The air is, in the hottest season, constantly refreshed by cool breezes from the sea. The vales produce excellent wheat and Indian corn, but are mostly covered with vineyards intermixed with fruit-trees. Besides the common kinds, as cherries, apricot, peaches, etc., they produce oranges, limes, almonds, pomegranates, figs, water-melons, and many other fruits unknown to our climates, which lie every where open to the passenger. The hills are the greater part covered to the top with vines, some with chestnut groves, and others with thickets of myrtle and lentiscus. The fields in the northern side are divided by hedgerows of myrtle. Several fountains and rivulets add to the beauty of this landscape, which is likewise set off by the variety of some barren spots and naked rocks. But that which crowns the scene is a large mountain rising out of the middle of the island (once a terrible volcano, by the ancients called Mons Epomeus). Its lower parts are adorned with vines and other fruits; the middle affords pasture to flocks of goats and sheep; and the top is a sandy pointed rock, from which you have the finest prospect in the world, surveying at one view, besides several pleasant islands, lying at your feet, a tract of Italy about three hundred miles in length, from the promontory of Antium to the Cape of Palinarus: the greater part of which hath been sung by Homer and Virgil, as making a considerable part of the travels and adventures of their two heroes.'

Touring the island

A tour of the island by road (30km) may be made comfortably in half a day. The comune of **Ischia** (population 18,000) consists of the picturesque **Ischia Ponte**, which stretches for c 2km along the shore, north of the castle, and the modern **Ischia Porto**, built around the harbour to the north-west. The two are separated by a fine beach backed by pine woods.

The town was built around a crater lake, the seaward side of which was pierced in 1854 to form the circular harbour, where ferries and hydrofoils dock. The **Punta San Pietro** on the east and the public park and the mole on the west side command good views. Via Roma and its continuation, Via Vittoria Colonna, lead to **Ischia Ponte**, beyond which the Ponte Aragonese (1438), a causeway 228m long, leads to the rocky islet fortress of Alfonso the Magnanimous (private).

On the island is the 14C **cathedral**, ruined when the English fleet bombarded the invading French in 1806, with a huge crypt (frescoes). The **castle**, where Vittoria Colonna stayed, rises 111m above the sea (open summer 09.00–1hr before sunset; ☎ 081 984340). It houses a small collection of arms and armour.

A road diverging to the south from the main road, about 600m west of Ischia Porto, leads to (35 minutes walk) **Fiaiano** (198m; view) and (north-west) in 10 minutes more to the top of Monte Montagnone (311m).

Casamicciola Terme, on the north slope of Monte Epomeo, is a pleasant bathing resort and spa, the first on Ischia to be frequented for its mineral waters.

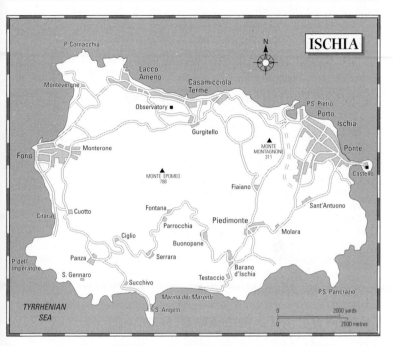

The town (population 7000) was rebuilt after the earthquake of 1883 in which 1700 people perished. The mineral waters (80°C) of the Gurgitello, prescribed for arthritis and rheumatism, are used in the establishments of Manzi and Belliazzi, and similar waters feed the Castagna Spa. At the Villa Ibsen (at the time, Villa Piseni) the Norwegian poet and novelist Henrik Ibsen started *Peer Gynt* in 1867. The **Osservatorio Geofisico** (observatory) on the Grande Sentinella commands a fine view.

Lacco Ameno (population 4000) is another thermal resort (considered the most exclusive on the island) with the most radioactive waters in Italy. At the little church of Santa Restituta, dedicated to the patron saint of the island (d. 284), traces of an early sanctuary have come to light (open Mon–Sat 09.30–12.30, 17.00–19.00, Sun 09.30–12.30; ☎ 081 980538; afternoons on request; apply to the parish priest). The 18C Villa Arbusto houses a **Museo Archeologico di Pithecusa** containing finds from the excavations of Greek colony, remains of which occupy the gardens (open Tues–Sun 09.30–13.00, 15.00/16.00–19.00/20.00; ☎ 081 900356). In addition to Greek and Italic material, the finds include Egyptian and Syrian objects that demonstrate the colony's ancient commercial ties with the eastern Mediterranean. Highlights include Pithecusan vases from the San Montano necropolis.

The road now ascends over the lava stream of 464 BC and descends to **Forio** (population 12,000), the centre of Eptomeo wine production and the focus of the foreign (particularly German) community on the island. The Santuario del Soccorso, above the village, commands an enchanting view.

The road passes above the radioactive sands of Citara, traversing Cuotto, where a path diverges to the right for the Punta dell'Imperatore (232m; lighthouse), the south-west extremity of the island. 4km Panza; view of Capri. To the south lie the rich orchards of Succhivo, and **Sant'Angelo** (2.5km), a health resort with submarine springs, from whose sandy beach, the Marina dei Maronti, issues plumes of steam.

Beyond Panza the road turns east and ascends, with many turns and magnificent views all the way, to (4km) Serrara Fontana (331m); higher up is Parrocchia, a hamlet with a colour-washed church. 2km **Fontana** (449m) has a church of 1374. This is the best starting place for the **ascent of Monte Epomeo** (788m; 1 hour on foot; mules for hire); the summit commands a **view** extending from Terracina to Capri; a small restaurant serves light lunches, May–Oct. The prominent iron crucifix commemorates 44 people killed in an air crash. The descent to Forio or Casamicciola takes 2 hours. All trails are clearly marked.

Descend through a ravine to (1.5km) Buonopane (286m), separated by another ravine from (2km) Barano d'Ischia, a small town among its vineyards. To the south is the village of Testaccio, from which you may descend on foot to the Marina dei Maronti (see above). Turn north-east and Procida, Capo Miseno and the Castello d'Ischia come into view. Beyond Molara leave Sant'Antuono on the right, and following the Lava dell'Arso lava flow, join the coast once more between Ischia Ponte and Ischia Porto at (5km) the Piazzetta di Ferrocavallo.

SORRENTO AND THE AMALFI COAST

This chapter focuses on Sorrento and Amalfi, two great maritime republics that once vied with Venice, Genoa and Pisa for control of trade routes in the Mediterranean. From Colli San Pietro, above Sorrento, to Vietri, on the outskirts of Salerno, the road follows the rugged, lofty **Costiera Amalfitana**, one of the more scenic roads in Italy. The area is widely renowned for its natural beauty and is ideally suited for walking—provided you don't mind 300m altitude gains, which are quite common along its rocky, precipitous coasts. Swimmers and sunbathers might find the lack of fine beaches disappointing.

The art and architecture of the region is predominantly medieval in flavour, the cathedrals of **Amalfi** and **Ravello** being among the most impressive in the south. The vernacular architecture also hails from the Middle Ages, whereas the distinctive majolica-tiled church domes belong to the area's colourful Baroque heritage. The many lovely **gardens** combine Renaissance formalism with the Romantic flair for shade and seclusion.

Practical information

Information offices
AMALFI *Azienda Autonoma di Cura Soggiorno e Turismo*, Corso delle Repubbliche Marinare 19, ☎ 089 871107.
CASTELLAMMARE DI STABIA

Azienda Autonoma di Cura Soggiorno e Turismo, Piazza Matteotti, 34, ☎ 081 871 1334.
MAIORI *Azienda Autonoma di Cura Soggiorno e Turismo*, Corso Regina 73, ☎ 089 877452.

POSITANO *Azienda Autonoma di Cura Soggiorno e Turismo*, Via del Saracino 4, ☎ 089 875067.

RAVELLO *Azienda Autonoma di Cura Soggiorno e Turismo*, Piazza Duomo 10, ☎ 089 857096.

SORRENTO *Azienda Autonoma di Cura Soggiorno e Turismo*, Via L. De Maio 35, ☎ 081 807 4033, ✉ www.sorrentotourism.com.

VICO EQUENSE *Azienda Autonoma di Cura Soggiorno e Turismo*, Via San Ciro 16, ☎ 081 879 8826, 🖷 081 879 9351.

See also Naples listings p 111.

Getting there and getting around
By road

Access to Sorrento and the Amalfi Coast is provided by Autostrada A3/E45, Roads 145 and 163, and local roads. Frequent buses run between Naples (Piazza Municipio), Salerno (Piazza della Concordia) and towns on the peninsula. Deluxe coaches (*SITA*) make a circular tour of the **Sorrentine Peninsula**, closely following the itinerary described here. They leave from Piazza Municipio, in Naples, in the early morning, returning in the evening. For travellers without their own transport, a tour of the Sorrentine Peninsula may conveniently be combined with Capri; the night is spent at Sorrento, with departure next day by ferry or hydrofoil to Capri, returning from there to Naples. This journey may also be made in reverse, spending the night on Capri.

By rail

The *Circumvesuviana* railway goes hourly from Naples to Sorrento in 60–80mins. Fast Intercity and Eurostar trains connect Salerno to Naples in about 40mins, and to Reggio Calabria in 3hrs 30mins–4hrs.

By sea

Hydrofoils run several times daily, in 30mins, from Naples (Mergellina) to Sorrento, from where there are daily hydrofoil and ferry connections to Capri. Visit ✉ www.campaniatrasporti.it for information and schedules. In the holiday season (June–Sept) boat trips run daily from Salerno (Molo Mattuccio Salernitano) to the Amalfi Coast.

Where to stay

AMALFI €€€ *Santa Caterina*, Strada Statale Amalfitana 9, ☎ 089 871012, 🖷 089 871351, ✉ www.hotelsantacaterina.it, info@hotelsantacaterina.it. An elegant, luxurious place with terraced gardens, spacious rooms, great food and enchanting views.

€€ *Luna Convento*, Via P. Comite 33, ☎ 089 871002, 🖷 089 871333, ✉ www.lunahotel.it, info@lunahotel.it. In a 700-year-old monastery, with sea views from most rooms and breakfast in a Byzantine cloister.

MASSA LUBRENSE €€ *Delfino*, Via Nastro d'Oro 2, ☎ 081 878 9261, 🖷 081 808 9074, ✉ www.hoteldelfino. com. Quiet and comfortable, on a lovely little bay overlooking Capri and the sea; open Apr–Dec.

POSITANO €€€ *Le Agavi*, at Belvedere Fornillo, ☎ 089 875733, 🖷 089 770186, ✉ www.leagavi.it, info@leagavi.it. Outside the town, with marvellous views and private beach; open Apr–Oct.

€€€ *Le Sirenuse*, Via Cristoforo Colombo 30, ☎ 089 875066, 🖷 081 811798, ✉ www.sirenuse.it, info@sirenuse.it. A superb place with spacious rooms, lovely terraces, magnificent sea views, stupendous pool, excellent restaurant (cooking lessons in Apr and Nov).

€€€ *Poseidon*, Via Pasitea 148, ☎ 089 811111, 🖷 089 875833, ✉ poseidon@ starnet.it. In a lush garden with magnificent views over the town and sea, restaurant seating on a vine-shaded terrace, heated pool, sauna, gym; open Apr–Oct.

€€€ *San Pietro*, Via Laurito 2, ☎ 089 875455, 📠 089 811449, 🖃 www. ilsanpietro.it, info@ilsanpietro.it. Possibly the most spectacular hotel in Italy (though not the most discreet), with glass-walled rooms descending in flowering terraces to the sea and the highest level of luxury; also an excellent restaurant; open Apr–Oct.

€€ *Casa Albertina*, Via della Tavolozza 3, ☎ 089 875143, 📠 089 811540, 🖃 www.casalbertina.it, alcaal@ starnet.it. Small but comfortable, with good rooms and pleasant atmosphere.

€€ *Villa Rosa*, Via C: Colombo 127, ☎ 089 811955, 📠 089 812112, 🖃 www.villarosapositano.it, info@ villarosapositano.it. All rooms have private terraces and breakfast in bed is free; open Mar–Nov.

R A V E L L O **€€€** *Palazzo Sasso*, Via San Giovanni del Toro 28, ☎ 089 818 181, 📠 089 858900, 🖃 www. palazzosasso.com, info@palazzosasso. com. Simply one of Europe's top hotels: quiet luxury, unforgettable views, impeccable service; open Mar–Nov.

€€€ *Palumbo*, ☎ 089 857244, 📠 089 858133, 🖃 www.hotelpalumbo.it, palumbo@hotel-palumbo.it. A small (13 rooms) but elegant establishment in a 12C building, known for the breathtaking views from its garden terrace; open Mar–Dec.

€€ *Rufolo*, Via San Francesco 1, ☎ 089 857133, 📠 089 857935, 🖃 www.hotelrufolo.it , info@ hotelrufolo.it. Near the gardens of the same name, in a lovely part of town; open Mar–Nov.

€€ *Villa Cimbrone*, Via Santa Chiara 26, ☎ 089 857459, 📠 089 857777, 🖃 www.villacimbrone.it, info@ villacimbre.it. In a medieval palace set in magnificent gardens; open Apr–Oct.

€€ *Villa Maria*, Via Santa Chiara 2, ☎ 089 857255, 📠 089 857071,

🖃 www.villamaria.it, villamaria@ villamaria.it. A renovated villa with panoramic garden and spacious rooms lovingly furnished by the owner, a collector of antiques; closed 24–25 Dec.

S O R R E N T O **€€€** *Bellevue Syrene*, Piazza della Vittoria 5, ☎ 081 878 1024, 📠 081 878 3963, 🖃 www. bellevuesyrene.it, info@bellevue.it. Quiet and comfortable, with wrought-iron beds and breathtaking views from lovely rooms facing the sea.

€€€ *Excelsior Vittoria*, Piazza Tasso 34, ☎ 081 807 1044, 📠 081 877 1206, free phone 800 890053, 🖃 www.exvitt.it, exvitt@evitt.it. A charming place with a venerable past and spacious rooms enjoying marvellous views.

V I C O E Q U E N S E **€€** *Capo la Gala*, Via L. Serio 8, ☎ 081 801 5758, 📠 081 879 8747, 🖃 www.capolagala.com, info@capolagala.com. A charming place in a panoramic position just outside the town, with thermal-water pool, private beach, majolica-tiled bathrooms; open Apr–Oct.

Youth hostel

S O R R E N T O Via Capasso 5, ☎ 081 878 1783, 📠 081 878 1783.

Eating out

A G E R O L A is famous for its cheeses, especially the exquisite *fior di latte*; best at *Caseificio Belfiore*, Via Belvedere 35; *Fior di Agerola*, Via Galli 74; *Agerolina*, Via Tutti i Santi 6.

A M A L F I **€€** *Ciccio Cielo*, Mare e Terra, Via Nazionale per Sorrento 17, at Vettica Ovest, ☎ 089 831265. Restaurant known for its fresh, simple cuisine and its marvellous views; closed Tues and Feb.

€€ *Da Gemma*, Via Fra' Gerardo Sasso 9, ☎ 089 871345. Old-fashioned trattoria overlooking the Duomo; closed Wed and mid-Jan–mid-Feb, Aug open evenings only.

€€ *Eolo*, Via P. Comite 3, ☎ 089 871241. Fish restaurant by the sea; closed Tues and Jan–Feb.

€€ *La Caravella*, Via Matteo Camera 12, ☎ 089 871029. Excellent fish restaurant; closed Tues (except July–Aug) and Nov–Dec.

Andrea Pansa, at the foot of the cathedral steps, for candied fruit and pastries (try the *delizia al limone*).

ATRANI €€ *A Paranza*, Via Dragone 1–2, ☎ 089 871840. Locally famous trattoria (and rightly so); closed Tues (except in summer) and Dec.

CETARA €€ *Acquapazza*, Corso Garibaldi 38, ☎ 089 261606. Traditional osteria in the Amalfi coast's last remaining fishing village; closed Mon (except in summer) and Jan.

€€ *San Pietro*, Piazza San Francesco 2, ☎ 089 261091. Family-run trattoria with rooms; closed Tues (except in summer) and Jan–Feb.

Cetara is famous for its canned tuna and sardines, best at **Pescheria Battista Delfino**, Via Umberto I, 78 and **Pescheria San Pietro**, Via Umberto I, 72.

FURORE €€ *Hostoria di Bacco*, at San Giacomo, Via G.B. Lima 9, ☎ 089 830360. Restaurant with rooms on a cliff overlooking the sea; closed Fri (except in summer) and Nov–Dec.

MASSA LUBRENSE € *La Primavera*, Via IV Novembre 3/g, ☎ 081 878 9125, 📠 081 808 9556. Restaurant with 10 rooms overlooking Capri and the Gulf of Naples; closed Tues and Jan.

€€ *Antico Francischiello da Riccardo*, Via Partenope 27, ☎ 081 533 9780, 📠 081 808 1813. Restaurant (with rooms) much renowned among the locals; closed Wed (except June–Sept).

NERANO €€ *Quattro Passi*, Via Marina del Cantone 13, ☎ 081 808 1271. Garden restaurant serving delicious regional food; closed Wed.

€€ *Salvatore*, Piazza Santa Croce 8, at Termini, ☎ 081 808 1107. Garden restaurant with seasonal menu; closed Wed and Dec–Feb.

€€ *Taverna del Capitano*, Piazza delle Sirene 10/11, at Marina del Cantone, ☎ 081 808 1028. Seaside restaurant with 16 sunny rooms facing the Gulf of Salerno; open Mar–Dec.

POSITANO €€ *Bucca di Baco*, Via Rampa Teglia 8, ☎ 089 875699. Traditional fish restaurant by the sea; closed Tues and Nov.

€€ *Donna Rosa*, Via Montepertuso 97–99, at Montepertuso, ☎ 089 811806. Informal, family-run restaurant; closed Tues and Jan–Mar.

€€ *Il ritrovo*, Via Montepertuso 77, at Montepertuso, ☎ 089 875453. Trattoria offering delicious home-made pasta dishes under a cool pergola in summer; closed Wed (except in summer) and Jan–Feb.

€€ *Le Tre Sorelle*, Via del Brigantono 23. Another traditional fish restaurant, on the beach; closed Nov–Dec.

PRAIANO € *La Brace*, Via Capriglione 146, ☎ 089 874 226. Restaurant known to the locals for its good, down-home cooking; closed Wed (except Apr–Sept).

SANT'AGATA SUI DUE GOLFI €€€ *Don Alfonso 1890*, Corso Sant'Agata 1, ☎ 081 878 0026, 📠 081 533 0226. Restaurant (with rooms) featuring traditional cuisine with a creative twist, a spectacular selection of wines (in a cellar possibly of Etruscan construction) and a boutique selling products from the owners' organic farm; closed Mon from June–Sept, Mon and Tues other months, closed Jan–Feb.

SORRENTO €€ *Caruso*, Via Sant'Antonio 12, ☎ 081 807 3156. Excellent food, both traditional and creative, and pleasant atmosphere; closed Wed (except in summer) and Nov–Mar.

€€ *Tasso*, Via Correale 11D, ☎ 081 878 5809. Restaurant in the pedestrian

district, with fair-weather seating outdoors.

Special events
POSITANO *Sbarco dei
Saraceni*, when a mock land-
ing from the sea is defeated amid fireworks, etc (14 Aug).

RAVELLO *Classical music festival*
June–July.
SORRENTO Annual **regatta** (15
Aug), **classical music festival** (summer), **film festival** and **jazz concert
series** (autumn), and international
tennis competitions. The Good Friday
procession is particularly colourful.

South of Naples

The Vesuvian shore, whose black sands Ruskin found so threatening, extends
south and east of Naples. The area today is a big, sprawling suburb, with really
only one place of interest. **Torre Annunziata** (population 56,000), the flourishing centre of the pasta industry, was founded in 1319 beside a chapel of the
Annunciation. A bathing and thermal resort, it is crowded with Neapolitans in
summer. Excavations here have revealed two patrician villas, probably belonging
to a residential suburb of Pompeii called *Oplontis*. The larger of the two (open
Mar–Sept 08.30–19.30, Oct–Feb 08.30–17.00; 081 8622 1775), with a vast
peristyle, baths and a monumental *piscina*, is thought to have been the summer
house of Nero's wife, Poppea.

The fertile coastal strip of black volcanic earth is thickly populated and dotted
with pines, palms, prickly pears and Oriental-looking houses. On the left, on the
summit of a small extinct volcano (184m), rises the monastery of Camaldoli della
Torre. Both the motorway and main road cross the lava flow of 1767; on the right
the coast stretches away to Sorrento, with Castellammare nestling in its bay.

Castellamare di Stabia
The Sorrentine peninsula begins at Castellammare di Stabia, a modern town
(population 68,000) with an arsenal, on the south-east shore of the Gulf of
Naples. It is visited as a climatic resort.

History of Castellamare di Stabia
The ancient city of *Stabiae*, north-east of the present town, was destroyed by
Sulla in 89 BC but was afterwards rebuilt, only to be swallowed up by the eruption of AD 79. On the beach at Stabiae, Pliny the Elder met his death. The site
was repopulated and takes its name from a 9C castle, which Charles I of
Anjou restored when he built the town walls. In 1738 some ancient villas
were brought to light by excavation, and further Roman remains are visible
on the neighbouring hill of Varano.

In the centre of the town, the shady park of the Villa Comunale gives a wide vista
over the gulf. To the left lies Piazza del Municipio with the observatory, the
duomo (1587, much altered), and the municipio, formerly Palazzo Farnese.
Further south-west are the harbour and the arsenal (1783), where some of the
more powerful Italian warships have been built, and the Terme Stabiane, a spa.
On a hill to the left is the castle, enlarged by the Swabians (1197) and again by
Charles I of Anjou (1266). A pleasant walk may be taken to (2km) the Villa

Quisisana (now a hotel), a royal residence from 1310 to 1860, where the park commands a fine panorama.

But the best thing to do is leave the hustle and bustle of Castellammare for the cool, green hills above the town, popular with Neapolitans seeking respite from the summer heat.

The ascent of **Monte Faito** (1100m) by cable railway, from the *Circumvesuviana* station, takes roughly 8 minutes, services connecting with the trains. The road (15km of switchback bends) climbs round the Villa Quisisana. The Belvedere di Monte Faito commands an extensive view; a track of 7km offers a magnificent circular walk along the ridge and round a fine wood. The ascent of **Monte Sant'Angelo** (1443m), the highest of the Monti Lattari, may be made (guide desirable) either from Monte Faito or from Pimonte (see below); it takes 4–5 hours, the descent almost as much. The **panorama** encompasses the Gulfs of Salerno and Naples, extending northwards to the Gulf of Gaeta.

If you are bound for the Amalfi coast, **Agerola** and **Amalfi** can be reached by a beautiful road across the Altopiano di Agerola. From the north end of the town you climb to Gragnano, known for its excellent macaroni and wine. The road passes Pimonte, affording good views of the Monti Lattari beneath whose crest it passes in a tunnel, c 1km long, to emerge at Agerola, a village consisting of several *frazioni* or hamlets, all frequented by summer visitors. From here the road descends the zigzag Vallone di Furore, with vistas over the Gulf of Salerno, to join the Costiera Amalfitana road near Vettica Minore, and then on to Amalfi.

A turning on the left at the beginning of the road for Gragnano (see above) leads to **San Marco**, on the Varano plain. Here are the extensive remains of two **Roman villas** (open daily 09.00–dusk; ☎ 081 871 4541), both with remnants of fresco decoration, unfortunately damaged in the 1980 earthquake. The **Antiquarium di Stabiae** (Via Marco Mario 2, open daily 09.00–18.00; closed for renovation at time of writing; ☎ 081 871 4541) contains objects from the Bronze Age to the Middle Ages, and material from the excavations in particular: frescoes, pavement fragments, Greek, Samnite, Italic and Roman vases.

The Piano di Sorrento

Beyond Castellammare the road hugs the shore, passing the pleasant beaches of Pozzano and Scraio, both with sulphur springs.

Vico Equense (population 19,000) is the ancient *Aequana*, destroyed by the Goths and restored by Charles II of Anjou. The 14C ex-cathedral church of San Salvatore contains the tomb of the jurist, Gaetano Filangieri (d. 1788). In Corso Umberto is a small Museo Comunale (open Mon–Sat 09.30–13.00) containing material from a necropolis of the 7C–5C BC, discovered beneath the present town. The Museo Mineralogico (Via S. Ciro 2, open 09.00–13.00, 16.00–19.00, closed Sun afternoon and Mon; ☎ 081 801 5668) has a small but fascinating collection of minerals and fossils from around the world. The Angevin Castello Giusso, rebuilt in 1604, is now private. Below the sheer cliff is a pleasant beach. The road rounds the head of the pretty valley behind Seiano; beyond, it turns the promontory of Punta di Scutolo, and you get a first view of the magical **Piano di Sorrento**.

This famous plain, about 80–100m above sea level, is a huge perennial spring garden, covered with orange, lemon, and olive groves, interspersed with fig trees, pomegranates and aloes. The temperature is fresh and cool even in summer. It was a favourite resort of the emperors and other wealthy Romans, and its praises have been sung by numerous poets. The villages are rather closely crowded, but an indefinable spirit of peace pervades them all.

Meta (population 8000), a pretty village, is connected by a lift with its two small harbours. The church of Santa Maria del Lauro is believed to occupy the site of a temple of Minerva. The road to Positano, Amalfi, and Salerno here branches to the south. The Sorrento road winds across the plain, crosses some deep-set torrents and touches the villages of Carotto and Pozzopiano which, together with Meta, make up the *comune* (township) of Piano di Sorrento. Sant'Agnello (3km; see below) is now almost an extension of Sorrento, which you enter via the Corso Italia; the views are restricted by garden walls and orange groves.

Sorrento

Sorrento (population 18,000), *Surriento* in Neapolitan dialect, surnamed *La Gentile* (the fair), is perched on a tufa rock rising 50m above the sea and bounded on three sides by deep ravines. Situated in an area of singular beauty, it is an enchanting place in all seasons. The district is noted for its oranges, lemons, and nuts, and the town for inlaid woodwork (*intarsia*), lace and straw-plaiting. The seat of an archbishop, Sorrento is the subject of the 19C song, *Torna a Surriento*, popularised by the tenor Luciano Pavarotti.

History of Sorrento

In antiquity *Surrentum*, of Pelasgic, Etruscan, or Greek origin, was never a town of importance, but the Romans frequented it for the sake of its scenic beauty and climate. The seat of an independent duchy in the 7C, in 892 it fought a naval battle with Amalfi in defence of its rights as an independent republic. It became part of the Norman kingdom of Sicily in 1137, but was ravaged by the Turks in the 16C. Its most illustrious native is the poet, Torquato Tasso (1544–95). In the 19C, Sorrento was a favourite winter residence of foreigners; here, in 1867, Ibsen finished *Peer Gynt*, and, some ten years later, Wagner and Nietzsche had their famous quarrel here.

The long Corso Italia leads past the railway station and Santa Maria del Carmine to Piazza Tasso, the centre of the town. Embellished with a monument to Torquato Tasso by Gennaro Cali (1870), it commands a view of the Marina Piccola, 48m below. Corso Italia continues to the west, passing the campanile, with its four columns and antique ornamentation. The vault space beneath the Arcivescovado, leading to the neglected palazzi of Via Pietà, was once the scene of council meetings. The **duomo** has a marble side-portal of 1479; the façade was rebuilt in 1913–24. Inside, the first chapel on the right has reliefs of the 14C or 15C. In the nave are the archbishop's throne with a marble canopy and a pulpit (both 1573), below which is a *Virgin with Saints John the Baptist and John the Evangelist*, a painting on panel by Silvestro Buono of Naples (1582). The stalls show typical local inlay work.

Behind the cathedral is the south wall of the town, rebuilt in 1558–61 on the line of the Greek or Roman wall, after a raid by pirates; an arch from the Roman gate survives in Via Parsano.

Via Tasso, opposite the cathedral, leads towards the sea. In Via San Nicola (left,

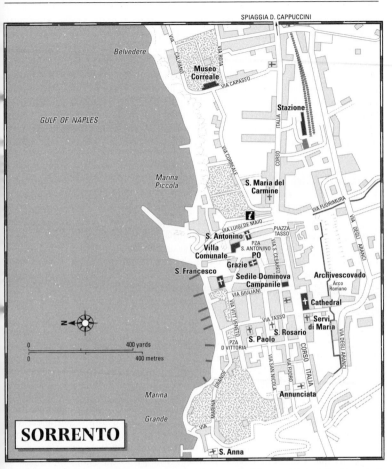

SPIAGGIA D. CAPPUCCINI

Belvedere

**Museo
Correale**

Stazione

GULF OF NAPLES

*Marina
Piccola*

**S. Maria del
Carmine**

VIA FUORIMURA

VIA LUIGI DE MAIO

PIAZZA
TASSO

S. Antonino

PZA
S. ANTONINO

**Villa
Comunale**

PO

Grazie

S. Francesco

Sedile Dominova

Campanile

Archivescovado

Arco
Romano

VIA GIULIANI

Cathedral

VIA VITT VENETO

VIA TASSO

**Servi
di Maria**

S. Rosario

N

S. Paolo

PZA
D VITTORIA

0   400 yards

0   400 metres

Marina

CORSO   ITALIA

VIA SAN NICOLA

VIA FUORO

Grande

Annunciata

SORRENTO

VIA DEGLI ARANCI

✝ **S. Anna**

no. 29) is the Casa Fasulo (formerly Sersale), marked by a tablet as the house of
Cornelia Tasso, who received her illustrious but fugitive brother here in 1577. In
Via San Cesareo (right) is the **Sedile Dominova**, a 15C loggia with capitals in an
archaic style. Beyond the Baroque church of San Paolo is Piazza della Vittoria,
which overlooks the sea. Below, on the shore, are remains of a Roman
nymphaeum. To the left a road descends, the last part in steps, through an arch
(Greek ?) to the Marina Grande. Turning right you pass the *Tramontano Hotel*,
which incorporates the remaining room of the house in which Tasso was born, and
come to the church of San Francesco d'Assisi. The annexed convent, now an
art school, preserves a 14C cloister. Just behind the church is the little **Villa
Comunale** (view). Continue to Piazza Sant'Antonino, with the church and
statue of Sant'Antonino Abate (d. 830), the patron saint of Sorrento, where he
found refuge from the Lombards. In the little streets near the church of the Grazie
are some attractive early 15C doorways. At the piazza join the winding Via Luigi
De Maio on its way from the Marina Piccola to Piazza Tasso.

From the east side of Piazza Tasso, Via Correale leads to the **Museo Correale di Terranova** (open daily, except Tues and holidays, 09.00–14.00; ☎ 081 878 1846) a charming old villa containing an important collection of Campanian decorative art from the 15C to 18C. The collection includes furniture, intarsia and intaglio work, and porcelain; archaeological finds from the Sorrentine peninsula; medieval sculpture and a small library of Tasso's works. Among the pictures is a unique collection of works by the Posillipo school, in particular by Giacinto Gigante. The belvedere commands a superb view. On the coast 1.5km further east, near the Convento dei Cappuccini, is the Villa Crawford, the residence of the novelist F. Marion Crawford, who died here in 1909. The villa stands above Sant'Agnello beach.

Coral fishing

Throughout Sorrento and the Amalfi coast towns, shops sell coral jewellery made in Torre del Greco. Though today it is little more than a sprawling suburb of Naples, this was once a proud, independent town with a time-honoured tradition of coral fishing and manufacturing. The *coralline* were boats that, from the 15C until quite recently, swept the sea floor with an intelligent tool aptly called an *ingengo*. Part of the raw coral was sold at market in Livorno, then Italy's chief centre of coral-working; but before long Torre developed its own workshops for cutting and modelling the 'red gold'. In the early 19C, thanks to a French entrepreneur named Martin, the making of coral jewellery reached a semi-industrial level, as large numbers of master coral cutters were brought in from Trapani and Rome. So a craft centre emerged, offering objects of a deliberately 'antique' nature, inspired by the ongoing finds at Pompeii and Herculaneum, to the foreign visitors who flocked to the shores of the Gulf of Naples. Examples of these may be seen, by appointment, at Torre del Greco's Museo del Corallo, Via Montedoro 61 (☎ 081 881 1225).

Today, Torre del Greco is the only centre of coral-working in Europe. Its craftsmen transform anything from 30 to 90 tonnes of raw material every year. The coral reefs of the Gulf of Naples are long gone, of course, as are most of the immense reefs discovered off the coast of Sicily in 1880. Most of the necklaces and other coral jewellery you see in the shops of Naples, Sorrento, Positano and Amalfi, are made from Pacific Ocean coral. But there is no notion of sustainable growth in the coral industry, and these resources, too, will one day come to an end ...

Walks and other excursions

The neighbourhood of Sorrento provides an opportunity for many excursions, a few of which are described below. Pleasant boat trips may also be made to the Grotte delle Sirene, the Grotta Bagno della Regina Giovanna (at the Villa Pollio Felix, see below), and other points, many showing vestiges of Classical buildings.

A walk of just over an hour takes you to the **Piccolo Sant'Angelo**, a hill commanding wide views of the Sorrento plain and the Gulfs of Naples and Salerno. The trail (marked) starts from Piazza Tasso in the city centre.

The walk (1 hour 20 minutes) to Sant'Agata sui due Golfi and the Deserto combines breathtaking panoramas with local charm. Take the narrow lane along the left flank of the little church of Santa Lucia, in Sorrento. The lane winds its way steeply uphill between high walls topped by luxuriant lemon groves. The trail (waymarked) leaves the road from time to time, affording steep short-cuts for strong walkers. At a T-intersection turn left to (15mins) **Sant'Agata sui due Golfi** (390m), a favourite summer resort and an excellent centre for excursions. The church has a Florentine altar of inlaid marble, executed in the 16C and moved here in 1845 from the Girolamini church in Naples. The road (marked) continues to the **Deserto** (10 minutes, 454m), a suppressed convent, commanding a wonderful **view** of Capri and the two bays. From Sant'Agata more waymarked trails lead to Punta Campanella (via Termini; see below), the **Baia di Jeranto** (via Nerano), and the delightful little fjord known as **Marina di Crapolla**.

Massa Lubrense is an hour's walk away by a road that runs some distance from the sea but is high up enough to afford a series of uninterrupted, delightful views. On leaving Sorrento, cross the Conca gorge. A little further on, the Strada di Capodimonte branches left. At Capo di Sorrento a track on the right descends to (7 minutes) the seaward extremity of the cape, with the ruins of the Roman Villa of Pollio Felix, worth visiting for the view alone. Next is Villazzano, at the landward end of the Punta di Massa; the view of the Capo di Sorrento with its dense groves of olives is more extensive from the Telegrafo (239m), a hill (25 minutes) to the left. On rounding the point you can see Capri and the Faraglioni.

The road turns inland and reaches the village, in an exquisite setting. **Massa Lubrense** derives its name from Baebius Massa, a freedman of Nero, and the church of Madonna della Lobra. From the Villa Rossi, Murat watched the French assault on Capri in 1808. The lovely descent to the little harbour follows Via Palma, Via Roma (right) and Via Marina, passing the church of the Madonna della Lobra (1528), near the supposed site of the legendary Temple of the Sirens. Remains of a Roman villa lie in the fishing hamlet of Marina della Lobra. Beyond Massa Lubrense the road passes below the Annunziata and the remains of a castle (1389), leaves the attractive road to Termini on the right, and ascends to Sant'Agata (see above). The byroad to Termini continues as a steep path (well-preserved sections of Roman paving) to the **Punta della Campanella** (47m; 1 hour 30 minutes from Massa Lubrense), the *Promontorium Minervae* of the Romans, which takes its modern name from the warning bell of a tower, built in 1335 by Robert of Anjou. The lighthouse commands an enchanting view of Capri.

Over the ridge to Positano

The Sorrentine peninsula's south shore is known as the **Amalfi Coast**. The quickest way to get there from Sorrento is via **Colli San Pietro** (305m; incomparable views in both directions); the road climbs abruptly from Meta, and then drops steeply to Positano. A longer but more beautiful road passes through the little village of Sant'Agata sui due Golfi, near the peninsula's south-western tip. Country buses ply both routes. On the peninsula's south side the road, here known as the **Costiera Amalfitana**, remains high above the sea, offering what may well be the most breathtaking (and heart-stopping!) drive in the Mediterranean.

Positano

Positano (population 4000) is a favourite resort, where the characteristic square, white houses and luxuriant gardens descend in steep steps to the sea. The road crosses the upper part of the town. Further on, the terrace behind the solitary little church of San Pietro offers an admirable viewpoint. Beyond Vettica Maggiore the road passes through Capo Sottile by the first of a series of short tunnels. Praiano, on the hillside above, has a charming little church.

Delightfully situated on the shore is Marina di Praia, a fishing village with a fine sandy beach. On the steep slopes above the road lie the scattered hamlets of Penna and Furore, and between two tunnels a viaduct crosses the **Vallone di Furore**, one of the more picturesque gorges in southern Italy. Narrow and fjord-like, it runs inland between imposing rocky walls that rise almost vertically below the plateau of Agerola.

The road passes close above the **Grotta di Smeraldo**. The cavern may be reached by steps or by lift; a visit takes c 1 hour (open Mar–May 09.00–17.00, June–Sept 08.30–18.00, Oct–Feb 10.00–16.00). Its name derives from the apparent colour of the interior, which glows with a remarkable green light. It was dry before the sea eroded the coast. Stalagmites may now be seen under the water, and columns have formed where stalagmites have joined to stalactites.

Paris, Milan ... and Positano

The whole world knows that Positano is a fashionable resort. Few, however, realise that the influx of money-laden travellers from Italy and abroad has transformed this once-sleepy little town into a frenetic centre of the fashion industry.

Positano began its career as a resort in 1943, when the newly arrived Allies established a rest and rehabilitation centre here. Later it was targeted by the international jet set—a development that was turned to advantage by wise public officials and private entrepreneurs. The result: for some time now, the local fashion industry has surpassed tourism as the town's prime source of income.

The leading players in this success story are the *pezze di Positano*, simple, dignified, practical garments whose bright colours and ingenious designs have a broad, popular appeal with just a touch of snobbish sophistication. Cottons, linens, and crèpes are the main materials; the designs, large, brightly-coloured flowers taken from the area's almost overwhelmingly sensual natural environment, or whites adorned with lace or embroidery borrowed from the traditional popular costume.

The main road cuts across the Capo di Conca, beyond which it offers a vista of the Amalfi coastline stretching to the Capo d'Orso. Further on you pass Tovere and Vettica Minore, two villages amid vineyards and lemon and orange groves; between them a tortuous road winds inland to Agerola.

Medieval Amalfi

Amalfi (population 6000) nestles in the ravine of the Valle dei Mulini. Its churches, towers and arcaded houses, grouped together with attractive irregularity, rise above a small harbour, and are backed by precipices of wild magnificence.

History of Amalfi

Though known as early as the 4C AD, the city did not attain any degree of prosperity until the mid-6C, in the time of the Byzantine Empire. During the early Middle Ages it developed an important Asian trade, its ships visiting the most remote seas. It has been the seat of an archbishop since 987 and its maritime republic once vied with Genoa and Pisa. Governed by its own doges, it attained great wealth and a population of 70,000, but it was subdued by King Roger of Naples in 1131 and twice captured by the Pisans soon after (1135 and 1137). Much of the ancient town was destroyed by the sea in 1343. Its maritime laws, the *Tavole Amalfitane* (now on display in the Museo Civico, see below), remained effective until 1570. Merchants from Amalfi maintained the Hospital of St John the Almoner in Jerusalem, the nucleus upon which the Crusader knights built the Order of St John after 1099. Webster's *Duchess of Malfi* is based on the life of the hapless Joanna of Aragon (c 1478–1513), consort of Alfonso Piccolomini, Duke of Amalfi.

From Piazza Flavio Gioia, on the waterfront, near which are the remains of the 13C republican arsenal (now used for temporary exhibitions), Via del Duomo leads to Piazza del Duomo, with a fountain of 1760.

The duomo

On the east side of the piazza stands the 9C duomo (Sant'Andrea), the richly coloured façade of which (1203) is approached by a flight of steps. Both façade and steps were restored to their original Lombard-Norman style by Enrico Alvano, Luigi Della Corte, and Guglielmo Raimondi in 1875–94. The mosaic at the top is by Domenico Morelli. The campanile, built in 1276 and restored in 1768, is partly Romanesque and partly Saracenic in form.

The imposing porch is divided into two by columns. The magnificent bronze **doors**, with cross and saints in inlaid silver, were commissioned by the head of the Amalfitan colony in Constantinople and made there before 1066 by Simeon of Syria. The frescoes on either side of the entrance, executed in 1929 to a design by Domenico Morelli, add little to the decorative integrity of the whole.

The **interior**, thoroughly restored in the 19C, consists of nave (fine ceiling), aisles, and chapels. From the fourth chapel on the right a flight of steps descends to the crypt, constructed in 1253 and restored in 1719 (knock on the door at the left of the gate for entrance). It contains an altar by Domenico Fontana and a statue of *St Andrew* by Michelangelo Naccherino. Below the altar rests the body of St Andrew the Apostle, brought here from Constantinople in 1208. At the entrance to the choir are two large columns from Paestum and two can-

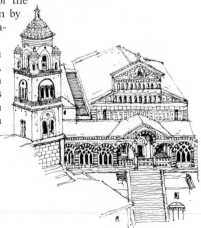

The duomo and tower at Amalfi

delabra adorned with mosaic. Ancient ambones, also with mosaics, flank the high altar.

The 13C **cloister** (*Chiostro del Paradiso*; entered from the portico, open daily 09.00–13.00, 15.00–20.00 in summer, 08.00–14.00 in winter), with inter-laced arches of marked Saracenic appearance, was once the burial-place of famous citizens. It is now a museum of architectural fragments.

Seaward of the duomo is the municipio, where the *Tavole Amalfitane* (see above) are displayed (in the Museo Civico, open Mon–Sat 08.00–14.00, 15.00–20.00; winter, Mon–Fri 09.00–13.00). From the main road west of the town (see above) you may climb the long flight of steps mounting to the former **Convento dei Cappuccini**, now a hotel. It was founded in 1212 and was originally a Cistercian house. The cloisters are picturesque, and the beautiful flower-screened verandah commands a justly famous view.

Walks in the area

A pleasant **walk** leads through the cool **Valle dei Mulini**, with its water-operated paper mills (now ruined) and tall rocky sides. On the outskirts of the old town a small **Museo della Carta** (open Tues–Sat 09.00–13.00; ☎ 089 873 6211) occu-pies a restored mill. Guided tours (in English) reveal the fascinating process of paper-making as it has been practiced for centuries in Amalfi, and you can even make a sheet or two of your own. The museum collections include engravings, manuscripts, printed books, bills and posters, as well as tools and machines for making paper; and there is an outstanding museum shop where fine hand-made paper products are sold. Beyond the Mulino Rovinato, c 1 hour from the piazza, the trail winds through the hills to (2 hours more) Scala and Ravello.

A creative interlude

No one knows for certain just when the Amalfitans started making paper, but an educated guess would be the early 12C. The earliest client for their mills seems to have been the Curia, which used paper rather than parch-ment for public documents; in later years paper was adopted at the various Neapolitan courts, as well. After the invention of moveable type, foreigners came to Naples from all parts of Europe to have their works printed on Amalfi paper, which was famous for its superior quality.

The oldest machinery at Amalfi's mill-cum-museum dates back half a millennia. It includes the water-powered beaters and mallets used to reduce cotton, linen and hemp rags to a fine pulp; the basin where the pulp was dis-solved in water, then lifted out on fine mesh screens; the felt-covered drums on which the sheets so formed were left for the first stage of drying, and the presses in which the residual moisture was squeezed out before the paper was air dried. Later equipment include a 'hollander'—a high-tech gizmo installed in 1745, which largely automated the first phases of the process.

At the paper museum you'll acquire hands-on familiarity with many of these contraptions as you make your own sheet of Amalfi paper (though you'll have to come back to get it another day, when it has dried). You'll also have an excellent opportunity to spend more than a few pennies, as you peruse the products of hands more skilled than yours, in the museum store. Don't be surprised if you succumb, as we in the book business do every day, to the subtle appeal of this most sensual material.

Another, more strenuous walk leads to Ravello by a steep, stepped mule path. From the cathedral square follow the signs for the Valle dei Mulini, but leave the main road opposite a bronze statue of the Franciscan Padre Pio. Turn right at the statue, and right again at a picture of the Madonna. Roughly 2000 steps ascend from here to Scala, from where a road continues to Ravello. The ascent takes about two and a half hours.

The Salerno road leaves Amalfi along the shore, passing between the Albergo Luna, in another convent with a good 12C cloister, and a 16C tower.

The village of **Atrani** rises in an amphitheatre shape at the end of the Dragone Valley. The road spans the gorge between the village and the sea. From the bridge you descend underneath the arches, to the little piazza, with the church of **San Salvatore de'Bireto** (940, restored in 1810). Its name refers to the capping of the doges of the Republic of Amalfi. The handsome bronze doors, executed at Constantinople in 1086, resemble those at Amalfi. The church of **La Maddalena**, beyond the bridge, has an elegant campanile and a painting of the *Incredulity of St Thomas* by Andrea da Salerno.

Ravello and its gardens

The road to **Ravello** diverges to the left beyond Atrani and winds up the hillside, affording beautiful views of the Dragone Valley. This isolated and markedly individual little town (350m, population 2000), in a charming situation, is a bishop's see and one of the more famous beauty spots in Italy. The contrast between its dramatic situation and its seductive and richly coloured setting, between the rusticity of its hilly streets and the delicate perfection of its works of art, the gaiety of its gardens and the melancholy of its Norman-Saracenic architecture, is extraordinarily impressive.

Walkers may shorten the distance a little (making the climb in just over 1 hour) by taking a mountain path from Atrani, but this is much less open than the road. Ascend the steps to the right of the church of La Maddalena, turn to the right, pass another church, follow a vaulted lane and climb a long flight of steps. Then enter the Dragone Valley and join the road, profiting by various short cuts. At a fork, turn to the right around the small church of Santa Maria a Gradillo: here you get your first view of Ravello. Passing below the ruined castle, you then reach the piazza.

History of Ravello

Built in the 9C under the rule of Amalfi, Ravello became independent in 1086 and maintained its liberty until 1813. It enjoyed great prosperity in the 13C, and its wealthy citizens, forming relations with Sicily and the East, introduced the Norman-Saracenic style of architecture to their native town. Characteristic of the doorways in Ravello are the antique colonnettes, on either side, which give them the appearance of the Graeco-Roman *prothyrum*.

The duomo

The duomo (San Pantaleone), built in 1086, was remodelled in 1786. The façade has three portals and four ancient columns. The fine bronze **doors** in the middle, by Barisano da Trani (1179), are divided into 54 panels with saints, scenes of the Passion, and inscriptions. They are protected on the inside as well as the outside by a double set of wooden doors, and are shown on request by the sacristan. In the nave (right) is a magnificent marble **ambo**, borne by six spiral columns and adorned with mosaics. It was executed in 1272 by Niccolò da Foggia at the order of Niccolò Rufolo, husband of Sigilgaita della Marra. The beautiful 13C bust of **Sighelgaita Rufolo**, which was above the door of the stairs, is now in the museum in the crypt. A smaller ambo on the left, of earlier date (c 1131), has a mosaic of *Jonah and the Whale*. In the south aisle are two sculpted sarcophagi and in the choir, the bishop's throne (decorated with mosaics) and two paschal candlesticks. The largest chapel, on the left, is dedicated to St Pantaleon, whose blood (preserved here) liquefies on 19 May and 27 August. The sacristy hosts a Byzantine *Madonna* and two pictures by Andrea da Salerno, and the crypt contains a small collection of 12C and 13C sculpture and 13C and 14C goldsmiths' work.

The gardens

Pass to the south side of the cathedral, noting its fine 13C campanile, and enter the grounds of the **Villa Rufolo** (open daily, June–Sept 09.30–13.00, 15.00–19.00; Oct–May 09.30–13.00, 15.00–17.00), begun in the 11C and occupied in turn by Pope Adrian IV (1156; Nicholas Breakspeare), Charles of Anjou and Robert the Wise. An ensemble of Norman-Saracenic buildings, partly in ruins, the palace is enhanced by tropical gardens; here Wagner found his inspiration for the magic garden of Klingsor in *Parsifal*. The arcading of the tiny cloister-like court is striking, and the little antiquarium set up in the chapel displays items found by the villa's late 19C owner, the Scot, Francis Neville Reid. The terrace (339m) commands an extensive **panorama**. The palace houses a small collection of antiquities and fragments from the cathedral.

On leaving the garden turn right and immediately left, to Via dell'Episcopio, which climbs the low hill behind the cathedral. The house at no. 4 was home to two eminent 20C writers: André Gide (who wrote *L'Immoraliste* here in 1902) and E.M. Forster (who wrote *The Story of a Picnic* in 1928). The street continues, past the old bishop's palace, to reach the Palazzo d'Afflitto with its bizarre portal (both these buildings are now hotels). Opposite is **San Giovanni del Toro**, a 12C church with a characteristic low campanile. Within, the nave is borne by ancient columns. The ambo, resembling those in the cathedral, has mosaics, Persian majolica tiles (1175) and ancient frescoes. A chapel off the south aisle contains a statue of St Catherine, in stucco.

A little further on is a small piazza with a Norman fountain, enjoying a view of Scala (see below). From here you may return by the long Strada Vescovado, which passes the 12C church of Santa Maria a Gradillo and continues south from the cathedral, passing Palazzo Rufolo. Beyond the churches of San Francesco, in the house next to which (marked) D.H. Lawrence wrote *Lady Chatterley's Lover*, and Santa Chiara, is **Palazzo Cimbrone**, with an open vaulted terrace-room (reconstructed). At the end of a straight avenue through the lush gardens (open daily 09.00–dusk) is the **Belvedere Cimbrone**, the furthest point of the ridge on which Ravello lies. The palace was frequented in the early 20C by the Bloomsbury Circle of English writers, whose rejection of the informality of Romantic gardens is said to have inspired the Renaissance-like formalism of the Cimbrone gardens. The open view of the gulf is unrivalled.

A short (1.5km) **walk** may be taken round the head of the valley to **Scala** (374m), once a populous, flourishing town, but ruined by pestilence and the rivalry of Ravello. The **cathedral** has a handsome Romanesque portal and contains a mosaic ambo, a mitre with enamels of the 13C, and a spacious crypt. The nearby villages of Santa Caterina, Campidoglio and Minuto all have interesting medieval churches, though that of Campidoglio has been extensively altered by Baroque additions. From Minuto walkers may cross Via Pontone into the Valle dei Mulini (see above) to reach Amalfi.

Towards Salerno

From Atrani the road skirts the shore to **Minori**, a delightful village at the mouth of the Reginuolo. To the left of the road lie the remains of a 1C **Roman villa** (open daily 09.00–1hr before sunset; ☎ 089 852893), excavated in 1954. The large peristyle, the nymphaeum and some vaulted rooms with frescoes are worthy of inspection. The antiquarium houses paintings found in the ruins of other Roman villas destroyed by the eruption of Vesuvius in AD 79, a *lararium* from Scafati, assorted pottery and architectural fragments.

At **Maiori**, a fortified village with a sandy beach at the mouth of the Tramonti Valley, a road leads inland across the Valico di Chiunzi (685m) to Angri. The church of Santa Maria a Mare has a majolica-tiled cupola and an English alabaster altar-frontal.

The scenery becomes wilder as the road twists away from the sea and back again round the Capo d'Orso, passing through a rocky defile. Beyond Capo Tomolo it makes a long detour round the savage Erchie Valley, affording the first glimpse of Salerno. The road crosses the wooded Vallone di San Nicola. From Cetara, a colourful fishing village, the road is so high up that it commands the whole gulf as far as Punta Licosa, with a glorious prospect of Vietri and Salerno. **Vietri sul Mare** is entered by a lofty bridge.

The **Museo Provinciale della Ceramica**, in the Villa Guariglia (open Tues–Sun 09.00–13.00, 15.00/16.00–18.00/19.00; ☎ 089 211835) contains a collection of ceramics from Vietri and the Province of Salerno, from the 17C to the present day, with a particularly rich collection of modern designs from the 1920s–40s. Beyond Vietri the road approaches Salerno through scattered suburbs.

SALERNO AND THE CILENTO

Salerno is the main place in southern Campania and one of Italy's leading university cities. Though somewhat overshadowed by Naples, it possesses a strong, individual character, which is expressed with particular flair in its handsome cathedral and two fine museums. A stone's throw from the Roman ruins of Pompeii, it is also close to the medieval centres of the Amalfi coast and the splendid Greek cities of **Paestum** and **Velia**.

Salerno is a perfect starting point for exploring the **Cilento**, one of the more beautiful and unspoilt areas of the south. Along this broad mountainous peninsula local journeys are sometimes still made by mule or by the traditional cart. A considerable part of the area was declared a National Park in 1991. The coast, known in ancient times for its unpredictable winds and currents, is particularly rich in literary allusions to Homer and Virgil.

The Cilento is also the site of two of the more important colonies of Magna Graecia, Paestum and Velia. Paestum is known primarily for its well-preserved Doric temples and its excellent museum, modern home of the remarkable set of Greek wall paintings from the so-called Tomb of the Diver; Velia, though considerably less spectacular, merits a visit because of its attractive setting and its curious layering of Greek, Roman, and medieval remains.

Practical information

Information offices
PAESTUM *Azienda Autonoma di Cura Soggiorno e Turismo*, Via Magna Grecia 151, ☎ 0828 811016.
SALERNO *Ente Provinciale per il Turismo*, Piazza Vittorio Veneto, ☎ 089 231432; Via Velia 15, ☎ 089 230411; *Azienda Autonoma di Cura Soggiorno e Turismo*, Via Roma 258, ☎ 089 224744.

Getting there and getting around
By road
To reach Salerno and the Cilento you can use any number of combinations of Autostrada A3/E45, Roads 18, 267, 447, 562 and local roads. Bear in mind that traffic can be quite slow during the summer, even on the motorway, when the beaches are crowded.

By bus
Buses connect Salerno to destinations throughout the province. The most useful services are those from Piazza della Concordia to Paestum and the Costiera Amalfitana, and from Piazza Ferrovia to Pompeii. Visit ✉ www. campaniatrasporti.it for more details.

By rail
Fast Intercity and Eurostar trains connect Salerno to Naples in about 40mins, and to Reggio Calabria in 3hrs 30mins–4hrs. Most Intercity trains stop at Battipaglia (where you can change on to a local train to Paestum), Agropoli, and Sapri; Eurostars stop at Sapri only.

By sea
Boats ply daily, May–Oct, from Salerno (Molo Mattuccio Salernitano) to the Amalfi Coast; hydrofoils (Molo Manfredi), to Capri and Ischia. Tickets at the quay; schedules at ✉ www.campaniatrasporti.it.

Where to stay
AGROPOLI € *La Colombaia*, Via Pianno delle Pere Sud, ☎ 0974 821800, ▤ 0974 823478. Country B&B with garden and pool; open Mar–Oct.
CASTELLABATE € *Giacaranda*, Conrada Cenito, ☎ 0974 966130, ▤ 0974 966800, ✉ giaca@ costacilento.it. Green and restful B&B.
CENTOLA € *Sant'Agata*, Contrada Sant'Agata, ☎ 0974 931716, contact Ms Elena De Rosa. 7 rooms on a beautiful farm (olives, vines, prickly pears) in a panoramic position in the hills above Palinuro; open Feb–Dec, restaurant evenings only.
PAESTUM € *Tenuta Seliano*, Via Seliano at Borgonuovo, ☎ 0828 723634, contact Ms Cecilia Baratta. An estate just a few kilometres from the temples, with 12 guest rooms, a lovely garden with patio and pool, and excellent cuisine featuring home-grown olives and vegetables, fresh mozzarella, etc.; closed Nov–Feb.

PALINURO €€ *King's Residence*, ☎ 0974 931324, 🖳 0974 931418. A restful place with splendid views of the sea and coast; open Easter–Oct and Dec–Jan.

SALERNO € *Plaza*, Piazza Vittorio Veneto 42, ☎ 089 224477, 🖳 089 237311, 🖳 info@plazasalrno.it. Simple and friendly, across the square from the station and on the edge of the pedestrian district.

SANTA MARIA DI CASTELLA-BATE €€€ Palazzo Belmonte, ☎ 0974 960211, 🖳 0974 961150, ✉ www. belmonte@costacilento.it. On the beach in a quaint little fishing village, spacious rooms, suites and apartments in the 17C hunting lodge of the Prince of Belmonte.

🍴 *Eating out*

CAVA DE' TIRRENI €€ *Incanto*, Via Pineta La Serra, at Annunziata di Cava dei Tirreni, ☎ 089 561820. Reserved and romantic, with views; closed Tues and Dec–Jan.

€ *L'Arcara*, Via Lambiase 7, ☎ 089 345177. Traditional restaurant-pizzeria; closed mid-day (except in summer), Mon and Nov.

€ *Le Bistrot*, Corso Umberto I, 203, ☎ 089 341617. Restaurant, closed Mon and two weeks in Aug.

€ *Taverna Scacciaventi*, Corso Umberto I 38–40, ☎ 089 443173. Osteria; closed Mon and two weeks in Jan.

CENTOLA € *Sant'Agata*, Contrada Sant'Agata, ☎ 0974 931716. Farm in the hills between Palinura and Marina di Camerota, outdoor seating with sea views, open daily, evenings only; closed Jan.

MARINA DI CAMEROTA €€ *Pepè*, Via Nazionale 41, ☎ 0974 932461. Simple but good fish restaurant; closed Tues.

€€ *Valentone*, Via Marina di Camerota, ☎ 0974 932004. Family-run trattoria known for its grilled fish; closed Sun (except in summer) and Oct–Dec.

NOCERA SUPERIORE €€ *Terrasanta*, Piazza Materdomini 46, at Materdomini, ☎ 081 933562. Friendly osteria beneath the basilica; open evenings (also mid-day on Sunday); closed Tues, Aug and Dec–Jan.

PALINURO €€ *Carmelo*, Strada Statale 562, at Isca. Traditional fish restaurant with good grill; closed Wed (except in summer) and late Jan.

PAESTUM €€ *La Pergola*, Via Nazionale 1, at Capaccio, ☎ 0828 723377. Restaurant-pizzeria with garden seating in summer; closed Mon and Sept.

€€ *Nettuno*, Zona archeologica, ☎ 0828 811028. Restaurant adjoining the excavations near the south gate, with good views over the temples; closed evenings and Mon from Sept–June.

PISCIOTTA € *Perbacco*, Contrada Marina Campagna 5, ☎ 0974 973849. Osteria and wine bar; closed Oct–May.

€ *Angiolina*, Via Passeriello 2, at Pisciotta Marina, ☎ 0974 973188. Restaurant with garden seating, crowded in summer, open evenings; closed Nov and Easter.

POLLICA € *Costantinopoli*, Contrada Costantinopoli 6, ☎ 0974 901134. Family-run restaurant in the hills between Acciaroli and Pioppi, open weekends (daily in summer); closed Oct–Mar.

SALERNO €€ *Cenacolo*, Piazza Alfano I, 4–6, ☎ 089 238818. Delicate, refined cuisine in a historic setting; closed Sun evening, Mon and Aug.

€ *Antica Pizzeria del Vicolo della Neve*, Vicolo della Neve 24, ☎ 089 225705. Oldest wood-oven pizzeria in the city; open evenings only; closed Wed, mid-Aug and late Dec.

€ *Caffè dei Mercanti*, Via dei Mercanti. Café serving excellent coffee, pastries and light lunches.

€ *Hostaria il Brigante*, Via Fratelli Linguiti 4, ☎ 089 226592. Traditional osteria by the cathedral; open evenings only (lunch by reservation); closed Mon and Aug.

€ *La Botte Piccola*, Traversa E. da Corbilia 7, ☎ 089 254101. Tiny but good, open for dinner only (lunch by reservation); closed Sun and Aug.

€ *Manzoni*, Via de Granita 11 and Corso Garibaldi 244. Bakery and wine shop.

€ *Santa Lucia*, Via Roma 182, ☎ 089 225696. Restaurant-pizzeria (with rooms) much loved by Salernitans; closed Mon and early Jan.

SAN GIOVANNI A PIRO €
U'Zifaro, Lungomare Marconi 43, at Scario, ☎ 0974 986397. Traditional fish restaurant by the sea; open weekends (daily in summer); closed Dec–Jan.

SANTA MARIA DI CASTELLABATE (near San Marco)
€ *La Taverna del Pescatore*, Via Lamia, ☎ 0974 968293. Osteria; closed Mon (except in summer), Jan and Feb.

SAPRI €€ *'A Cantina i Mustazzo*, Piazza Plebiscito 27, ☎ 0973 604010. Simple trattoria with a staff of one; closed Wed (except in summer) and late Sept.

Salerno

Salerno, a provincial capital with a population of 151,000, is beautifully situated on the gulf to which it gives its name (the Roman *Paestanus Sinus*). The old quarter, inland, has narrow streets, and the modern quarter extends along the shore behind an excellent beach.

History of Salerno

Salerno succeeds the ancient *Salernum*, which became a Roman colony in 194 BC. In the early Middle Ages it was subject to Benevento, but from the 9C–11C it was practically an independent Lombard principality until it fell to the Normans in 1076. Pope Gregory VII, rescued by Robert Guiscard from the Castel Sant'Angelo in Rome, took refuge in Salerno, where he died in 1085. The city was destroyed by Henry VI in 1198, and soon after that it became part of the Kingdom of Naples.

Salerno is considered by many to be the cradle of modern medicine. The famous medical school of this *Civitas Hippocratica* reached its zenith in the 12C, before the rise of Arabic medicine. Petrarch calls it *Fons Medicinae*, and St Thomas Aquinas mentions it as being pre-eminent in medicine as Paris was in science and Bologna in law. Salerno was the native town of John of Procida (1225–1302), a prominent figure in the Sicilian Vespers, and of Andrea Sabbatini da Salerno (1480–1545), the painter. Alfonso Gatto, the poet, was born here in 1909. During the Second World War, Salerno was the site of the Allied invasion of the southern Italian mainland. Much of the town was destroyed in the heavy fighting.

The city's misfortunes continued in the post-war period. After the bombing, Salerno suffered from an eruption of Vesuvius, two serious floods (that of 1954 caused 460 deaths and left 20,000 homeless), and an earthquake (in 1980). All these natural disasters brought a sizeable number of immigrants from the neighbouring regions of Irpinia, Sannio and Basilicata. The need for new homes was desperate, and sordid suburban quarters cropped up without building permits. *Abusivismo*, as unauthorised building is known, was a serious problem until 1990, when the city council decided to re-do the zoning

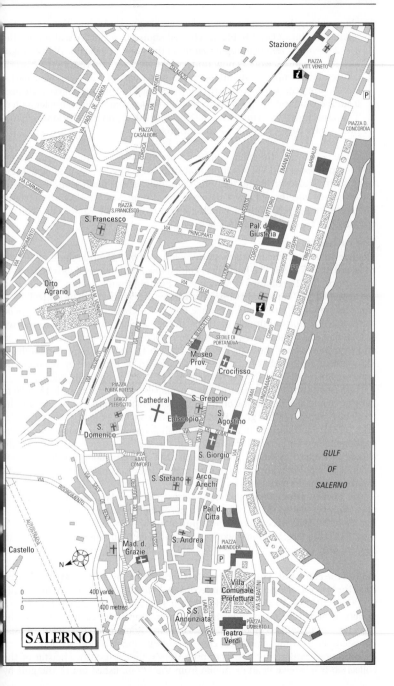

SALERNO

plan, calling in several renowned town-planners. Among them was the Spanish architect Oriol Bohigas, who redesigned Barcelona's seafront for the 1992 Olympics and was appointed to do the same in Salerno. With Bohigas as a leading force, work is now underway to recover and restore the historic centre and to improve conditions in the upper part of the town. New parks, streets and pedestrian areas are being designed in the empty areas left over from the war, and a sophisticated rapid-transit system is being implemented. The master plan was completed in December 2002 and international competitions have been called for 17 specific projects.

Near the waterfront, the main Naples access road divides into two long streets (Via Indipendenza and Via Sabatini) that run parallel to the sea, passing left and right of the Teatro Verdi and the Villa Comunale. 400m further on, the Via del Duomo leads into the old town, between the churches of Sant'Agostino (right) and San Giorgio (left) both of which contain paintings by Andrea da Salerno, crossing the Via dei Mercanti (see below).

The cathedral

Further on is the cathedral (San Matteo), founded in 845 and rebuilt by Robert Guiscard in 1076–85. The Porta dei Leoni, a fine Romanesque doorway, leads to the atrium, the 28 columns of which were brought from Paestum. To the right, the detached 12C campanile (55m) rises above the colonnade. The central doorway, decorated in 1077, has a bronze door with crosses and figures of niello work, made at Constantinople in 1099. In the nave are two splendid **ambones** (1173–81) and a paschal candlestick, resembling in their mixture of Saracen and Byzantine styles those in Palermo. The north aisle contains the tombs of Margaret of Anjou (d. 1412), wife of Charles III of Durazzo, by Baboccio da Piperno, and of Bishop Nicolò Piscicelli (d. 1471), by Jacopo della Pila.

The east end terminates in three apsidal chapels; in the one on the left is a *Pietà* by Andrea da Salerno; the one on the right contains, beneath a mosaic vault, the tomb of Gregory VII, the great Hildebrand, who died in exile in 1085 while the guest of Robert Guiscard. To the left Archbishop Carafa is buried in a pagan sarcophagus showing a relief of the rape of Proserpine. Other interesting tombs should be noticed at the end of the south aisle. The little door, beside a curious relief of a ship unloading, leads to the crypt, in which is preserved the body of St Matthew, brought here in 954.

The **Museo Diocesano** (Palazzo Arcivescovile, Via Monsignor Monterisi 2; open daily 09.00–13.00, 16.00–19.00; closed for renovation at the time of writing; ☎ 089 239126) contains a large **paliotto**, or altar-front, of 54 ivory panels (late 11C), the largest known work of its kind. The high altar is decorated with 12C mosaic.

Behind the cathedral, **Via San Benedetto** leads past the **Museo Archeologico Provinciale e Galleria Provinciale d'Arte** (Via San Benedetto 28; open daily 09.00–19.30, Sun 9.00–13.00; closed Mon, Oct–Apr; ☎ 089 225578), where a variety of finds from excavations in the surrounding province may be seen. The museum occupies two floors of the Lombard Romanesque convent of San Benedetto and contains medieval coins, paintings and a folklore section, as well as antiquities ranging in date from prehistory to late antiquity. The star of the collection is a bronze head of Apollo from the 1C AD, fished out of the gulf by

hance in 1930; also notable is a late 5C or early 4C burial treasure from
oscigno, with over 40 objects including a magnificent silver-and-gold crown.

The **Via dei Mercanti**, typical of the old quarter, leads west from the Via del
)uomo to the Arco Arechi, part of an 8C building, beneath which the road con-
inues to the Fontana dei Delfini. From here a street to the right leads to the
hurch of Sant'Andrea, with a small 12C belfry. The view from the old **Castello
legli Arechi** (273m) behind the town makes the climb well worthwhile. This
syzantine, Lombard and Norman fortress, whose recently restored interior has
een reopened to the public, now houses a small collection of ceramics (open
aily 09.00–13.00, 15.00–1hr before sunset; ☎ 089 225578).

The **Area Archeologica di Fratte**, in Via Fratte (open daily 09.00–1hr before
unset; closed Mon, Oct–Apr) has remains of a pre-Roman sanctuary (an
truscan acropolis and Samnite necropolis) dating from the 6C BC.

xcursions from Salerno

'o the east of Salerno rise the sparsely populated **Monti Picentini**, which derive
heir name from Picentine settlers who fled here (c 268 BC) before the Roman
dvance in the Marches. Their chief city, *Picentia* (see below), sided with
lannibal in the Second Punic War, and its people took refuge in the foothills on
is defeat. At **Pontecagnano**, just outside Salerno, excavations have brought to
ght 900 tombs in a large necropolis of the 9C–4C BC, now visible in the Museo
Jazionale dell'Agro Picentino (Piazza del Risorgimento 14; open daily
9.00–20.00).

Montecorvino, 10km further east, is the site of Salerno British Military
'emetery, with 1850 graves of those who fell in the landings of 1943.

To the north-west of Salerno, **Cava de'Tirreni** is a busy town (population
3,000) frequented by Neapolitans in summer. The cylindrical towers on the sur-
ounding hills were used for netting wild pigeons by a curious local method, now
arely seen. The main street, Corso Italia, is arcaded. The principal place of inter-
st is the Benedictine abbey of **La Trinita di Cava**, 4km southwest, romantically
ituated near the hamlet of Corpo di Cava beneath a crag on the Bonea torrent.
'he abbey, founded by the Cluniac St Alferius, was built in 1011–25 and conse-
rated in 1092 by Urban II in the presence of Roger of Sicily, whose second wife
ibylla is buried here. So too are the founder and the anti-pope Theodoric
d. 1102). The structure was radically altered in 1796; the campanile dates from
622. The church contains a fine Cosmatesque ambo and a candlestick from the
riginal building, as well as the 11C altar frontal. The crypt has 14C frescoes. The
hapter house has carved and inlaid stalls, perhaps designed by Andrea da
alerno. An earlier chapter house is reached from the beautiful 13C cloister. The
ibblioteca now houses a museum (open Mon–Sat 08.30–13.00; ☎ 081
63922) containing items from the archives, which, with c 15,000 Lombard
nd Norman documents, makes this one of the more important centres for the
tudy of local medieval history.

Nocera Inferiore, the *Nuceria Alfaterna* destroyed by Hannibal in 216 BC, is
low an agricultural centre of some 48,000 inhabitants. Queen Beatrice, first
vife of Charles of Anjou, died here in 1267. In captivity in the castle, Helena,
lanfred's queen, died in 1271; and Urban VI put six cardinals to the torture and

was himself kept a prisoner by Charles of Durazzo (1384). Francesco Solimena (1657–1743), the painter, was born here. The Museo Archeologico dell'Agro Nocerino Sarnese (open Mon–Sat 09.00–13.00, 16.00–20.00, Sun 09.00–13.00; ☎ 081 929880) occupies the 14C church and convent of Sant'Antonio. Opened in 1965, it houses the Pisani collection of prehistoric material from the Sarno Valley and material from recent local excavations. Highlights include a Roman marble statue of Athena.

More finds may be seen in the Museo Archeologico at **Nocera Superiore** (Palazzo del Municipio; open Mon–Fri 09.00–13.00). Just outside Nocera is the village of **Santa Maria Maggiore**, which has a round **church** of the 4C or 5C probably built as a baptistery. The double cupola, resting on 32 monolithic columns, covers a large octagonal font.

Paestum

South of Salerno extends the alluvial plain of the River Sele, one of the prime areas of Greek colonisation in antiquity. Here stands Paestum, for a thousand years a romantic ruin in the midst of a solemn wilderness. Its Doric temples, unsurpassed even by those of Athens in noble simplicity and good preservation, produce an incomparable effect of majesty and grandeur.

Opening hours

Paestum is open daily 09.00–1hr before sunset (last admission 2hrs before sunset). A complete visit requires about 3hrs; ☎ 0828 811023. Information and reservations ☎ 06 841 2312.

History of Paestum

Originally called *Poseidonia*, the city of Neptune, it was founded by Greeks from Sybaris around 600 BC together with a sanctuary (the Heraion) located further north at the mouth of the river Sele. Its strategic position next to tradeways, water courses and fertile lands rapidly turned the city into a thriving agricultural and maritime centre whose wealth lead to the construction in less than a century (530–450 BC) of its three magnificent Doric temples. In 400 BC the city was taken by the Lucanians and in 273 BC by the Romans who Latinised its name to Paestum and enriched it with a Forum, an Amphitheatre, thermae, and the so-called Temple of Peace.

Paestum was famed in antiquity for its roses, which flowered twice a year, and for its violets, from which scented oils were made. The city decayed during the Late Empire when the political centre of the Roman world shifted to Constantinople and the inhabitants of Paestum were reduced to a little Christian community concentrating in the area of the temple of Cerere (turned into a church). The majority fled to the surrounding hills founding the town of *Caput Aquis* (Capaccio) in order to escape malaria and the incursions of the Saracens who destroyed Paestum in 877 AD.

All but overgrown by tangled vegetation it was rediscovered during the building of the coach-road in the 18C and became the myth of writers, poets and artists such as Goethe, Shelley, Canova, Piranesi and the must of any traveller engaged in the fashionable Grand Tour that completed a gentleman's education.

The site

The ancient ruins comprise remains of numerous public, private and religious buildings, including four major temples, a forum and an extensive residential quarter. The town walls are constructed of square blocks of travertine and are 4750m in circumference. Their extant ruins rise to a height of 5m–15m and include four gates (of which the most important is the Porta Sirena on the east side) and several towers. The town is crossed by a *cardo* and a *decumanus*, both of which preserve paved segments. Excavations have shown that the temples belong to two groups, that to the south (dedicated to Hera) including the so-called basilica and Temple of Neptune and 11 smaller temples, that to the north (dedicated to Athena) focusing on the Temple of Ceres. Between the two ran the Via Sacra, now excavated. In the middle, immediately east of this main street, are the forum and a few public buildings; the residential area develops to the north and west. Botanists have restored some of the antique rosebeds, and in May and June the flowers' soft colours and delicate scents offer a fitting complement to its venerable old stones.

The Temple of Hera

From the Porta della Giustizia, on the south side of the excavations, the Via Sacra leads first to the Temple of Hera, the earliest temple at Paestum. It was misnamed the 'basilica' by its discoverers in the 18C who, judging by its lack of traditional temple fronts at either end, thought it was used for civic, not religious functions. Measuring 54 x 24m, it is an enneastyle peripteros with 50 fluted columns, nine at the ends and 18 along the sides. The colonnade is still standing, as are the entablature and part of the inside of the frieze. The columns are 6.5m high, with a lower diameter of 146cm and an upper diameter of 98cm. They belong to the Doric order and show distinct features of the early style: rapid tapering, a marked entasis (or swelling profile) and a bulging moulding of the capital. These and other features enable archaeologists to date the temple to c 530 BC.

Inside the colonnade stood the *cella*, or sanctuary, approached via a porch-like structure (*pronaos in antis*) formed by three columns standing between two great pilasters at the ends of the cella walls. A colonnade at the centre of the cella divided the interior into two small naves, suggesting that two deities, not one, were worshiped here. Three columns are still standing and the capital of two others are lying on the ground. There were probably seven in all, and also perhaps a half-column against the end wall, which separated the cella from the treasury.

Temple of Neptune

About 50m further north stands the Temple of Neptune. This temple, built in the 5C BC, is the largest in Paestum and ranks with the Theseion at Athens and the Temple of Concord at Agrigento as one of the three best-preserved temples in Europe. It stands on a basement (*stylobate*) of three steps and is 60m long by 24m wide. It is a hexastyle peripteros with 36 fluted columns (14 at the sides, six at the ends). These are 9m in height and taper from 270cm at the base to 146cm at the top. The cella, with a pronaos in antis, and *opisthodomos* (enclosed rear part) is divided into three aisles by two rows of two pilasters and seven columns 1m in diameter, with smaller columns above, of which three remain on the north side and five on the south. The entablature is well preserved and the pediments are almost intact. The roof, however, has gone. Shelley, the English Romantic poet, wrote that 'the effect of the jagged outline of the mountains through the groups

of enormous columns on one side, and on the other the level horizon of the sea is inexpressibly grand.' To the east are the remains of a large sacrificial altar.

The forum

Continuing to the north, the Via Sacra crosses the decumanus maximus (which joins the Porta Sirena to the Porta Marina) on the site of the forum, which replaced the earlier Greek agora. Measuring 157 x 57m, it was sur rounded on all four

Temple of Neptune

sides by a fine Doric portico, of which some fragments are still visible on the three remaining sides. The two long sides of the forum were lined with *tabernae* (shops), behind those, on the south side are the remains of Roman Imperial baths, a basilica of the late 1C AD (the so-called *curia*) with a long semicircular seat in the centre, and the *macellum* (covered market). To the south-east, unfor tunately crossed by the modern road, is the **Asklepeion**, the sanctuary of the god of health Asclepius, built around 300 BC and made into a farm in Roman times. The building included a series of rooms providing shelter for the sick and possibly functioning as school of medicine, as was customary in the great sanc tuaries of Asclepius.

On the north side of the forum is the so-called **Temple of Peace**, actually dedicated to *Mens Bona*, erected around the beginning of the 1C BC with a north south orientation and an entrance directly on the square. The temple encroached on the adjoining **Comitium** (2C BC). This was the most important public building of the Latin colony; elections and trials took place here. It consisted of a stepped circular structure (the *cavea*), flanked on the north side by the Curia. The temple of Mens Bona was later built above a section of the cavea thereby considerably reducing the number of seats.

Further to the right and partly under the modern road built by the Bourbons in 1829 is a Roman amphitheatre of the 1C AD.

Adjoining the Via Sacra just north of the forum are the ruins of the sanctuary of **Fortuna Virilis** (3C BC) consisting in a square courtyard with a central pool (*natatio*) and a platform rising on one side (of which only the foundation survives). These were used during the *Veneralia*: festivities in honour of Venus whose statue was taken in procession, immersed in the water, then placed upon the platform (thereby re-enacting the birth of the goddess). This was performed as a propitiatory rite by married and pregnant women in order to ensure happy childbirth. The pool was interred during the Imperial Age and the sanctuary transformed into a *Cesareum* (a temple for the cult of the emperors).

From here the Via Sacra leads north past an underground *sacellum*, a tomblike structure whose exact significance has long been a matter of dispute among archaelogists. It is now believed to have been a **heroön**, an empty tomb conse crated to the cult of a hero, possibly Is, the mythical founder of Sybaris, erected at

PAESTUM

Porta Aurea

Key to numbers

1 Temple of Hera I (Basilica)
2 Temple of Hera II (Temple of Neptune-Poseidon)
3 Curia
4 Macellum
5 Asklepeion
6 Temple of Peace
7 Comitium
8 Amphitheatre
9 Fortuna Virilis
10 Heroon
11 Temple of Ceres

National Museum

PORTA SIRENA

Forum

0   1000 yards
0   1000 metres

Paestum by Sybarite refugees after their city was destroyed in 509 BC. Inside th
tomb were found six *hydriai* (water jugs), two extraordinary bronze amphorae
and a black figure vase from Attica representing the apotheosis of Herakles.

Temple of Ceres

Further north along the Via Sacra stands the Temple of Ceres, more accuratel
an *Athenaion* (a temple dedicated to the goddess Athena), of a date intermediat
between the two surviving southern temples. It is the smallest of the three, a
hexastyle peripteros of 34 fluted colums (6 x 13), 6m high; it is raised on a sty
lobate of two steps and measures 33 x 14m. The cella is quite simple and th
pronaos of unusual depth. The architrave is the only remaining part of the
entablature, but much remains of the pediments.

In front of the temple are the remains of a large sacrificial altar and a votive
column, suggesting that the temple once stood at the centre of a small sanctuary
To the south east are traces of a small archaic temple, possibly the firs
Athenaion and the oldest structure of the whole town.

Excavations on the west side of the Via Sacra have brought to light an exten
sive residential quarter in which some homes appear to have been quite luxuri
ous; at least one had a private *piscina*, probably of Hellenistic workmanship.

The atmosphere of Paestum may best be appreciated by a tour of the **wall**
(c 4km). The lower and outer courses date from the 5C BC, the inner parts dat
from the Lucanian period. The Porta Sirena retains its arch and the Porta Marina
its towers and bastions. From the latter the Torre di Pesto, a medieval watch-towe
lies c 1km south-west. It commands a good view of the magnificent sandy beach
unfortunately marred by bathing establishments, extending in both directions
About 9km to the north, near the mouth of the Sele, lie the remains of anothe
Greek temple, referred to by Strabo and Pliny but undiscovered until 1934.

The Sanctuary of Hera

This extra-mural religious precinct was built during the 6C BC in honour of th
goddess Hera of Argo and as a defense against the Etruscans, who had settled on
the other side of the Sele. The sanctuary became famous throughout the Gree
world and its construction, as told by Strabo (63 BC–26 AD) and Pliny the Elde
(23 BC–79 AD) was attributed to Jason and his Argonauts. The cult of Hera out
lived the site and was transposed in the Christian cult of the Madonna de
Granato (Madonna of the Pomegranate, the latter being the traditional symbo
of Juno/Hera) that is still venerated in nearby Capaccio.

Although very little is visible today, inside the sacred precinct (*temenos*) wer
an archaic building (a treasury or temple) of the mid-6C BC, the main temple c
a later date (end of the 6C BC), two sacrificial altars and possibly a number o
minor temples, treasuries and other functional structures. The archaic buildin
was decorated with a magnificent Doric frieze of triglyphs and metopes (33 c
these survive in the museum at Paestum). The main temple was a pseud
dipteros with a pronaos and opisthodomos on the short sides of the cella. It mea
sured 38 x 18m and originally had 50 Doric columns (8 x 17) and a sandston
frieze of which 12 metopes are exhibited in the museum at Paestum
Unfortunately only the foundations survive, as the temple was damaged by
earthquakes, fires and the eruption of Vesuvius of 79 AD. During the 2C BC, as th
terrain became increasingly marshy, the sanctuary fell in to disuse and much o

he sandstone was re-employed for the production of lime. In the course of time he sanctuary was completely forgotten and searched for in vain during the 18C, only to be found in 1934 by two tenacious archaeologists, Paola Zancani Montuoro and Umberto Zanotti Bianco.

As a 'didactic integration' of the few remains of the site there is a new museum open Tues–Sat 09.00–14.30) with audio-visual material as well as a virtual reconstruction of the sanctuary and the friezes, casts of the metopes and a thematic study of the different myths that these represent.

Museo Nazionale

The Museo Nazionale, adjoining the archaeological area (open daily, Sept–June 09.00–19.00, closed first and third Mon of each month; a ticket to one gives admission to the other), was designed in 1952 to display many fine objects from the excavations, including prehistoric and protohistoric material, burial treasures, an important group of tomb paintings, architectural and sculptural fragments, and votive terracottas of Greek, Lucanian and Roman provenance. Most notable is the collection of archaic sculpture from the sanctuary of Argive Hera at the mouth of the Sele, including 33 **metopes** with Homeric and other scenes; and the truly extraordinary cycle of mural paintings from the so-called **Tomb of the Diver**, perhaps the only extant examples of Greek painting (c 480 BC). The four panels forming the coffin are decorated with a funeral banqueting scene in which singing, games, lovers, and music accompany the deceased into the other world. The fifth panel, the lid, shows the diver from whom the tomb takes its name—a naked youth who executes a perfect dive into a blue sea—in an unusual allegory of death.

About 30km north east of Paestum are the **Grotte di Castelcivita**, an impressive complex of limestone caverns situated at the foot of the Monti Alburni. They are 4.8km long, though only 1.7km are open to the public. They were inhabited in prehistoric times and present some fantastic stalactite and stalagmite formations.

Towards Sapri

The traditional route across the Cilento to **Sapri** (and Calabria) and points south bypasses Agropoli and the coastal towns to Policastro, crossing the mountainous interior of the peninsula, where some of the wilder landscape in Campania is to be found. Although the driving is slow and difficult, the scenery is magnificent.

South of Paestum the road (no. 18) climbs away from the Sele plain to Ogliastro Cilento (350m), which commands a view over the Gulf of Salerno to Amalfi and Capri. Prignano Cilento was the birthplace of Urban VI (Bartolomeo Prignano, 1378–89). The road descends the west side of the Alento Valley. At Procoio, the railway and a byroad diverge towards the coast. The main road climbs to **Vallo della Lucania** (population 8000), where the church of Santa Maria delle Grazie contains a polyptych by Andrea da Salerno. To the east rises Monte Sacro (1705m) with a sanctuary, already a place of pilgrimage before 1323. Beyond the town, the view over the hills to the sea opens up to embrace Pioppi and the Torre di Punta (see below).

The road continues through oak woods to Laurito (population 1000), perched on a spur of Monte Bulgheria. Torre Orsaia is known for its textile industry.

Beyond, the main road descends to Policastro, where it rejoins the coast road to Sapri.

Along the wine-dark sea

The more scenic route to Sapri follows the coast from Paestum, touching place of Homeric and Virgilian fame.

Across the River Solofone from Paestum lies **Agropoli**, a popular resort. The medieval town stands on a headland above a small, picturesque bay. A short distance to the west is the convent of San Francesco, situated on a cliff 60m above the sea. Beyond Agropoli the road runs inland, to the east of Monte Tresino, returning to the coast near the village of Santa Maria di Castellabate.

San Marco, a fishing village and a growing resort, has remains of ancient walls and, in the sea, of a Roman breakwater carved out of the rock. Mule track lead along the coast past (3.5km) **Punta Licosa** (the ancient *Enipeum* o *Posidium Promontorium*), which takes its name from the siren Leucosia, whe threw herself from the headland into the sea after failing to enchant Ulysses. The tracks continue to (3.5km) Ogliastro Marina, on the south side of the peninsula. Opposite the point stands the tiny isle of **Licosa**, containing remains of ancient walls and the modern navigational light, visible at a distance of 12 nautical miles. The antiquarium at Castellabate has underwater archaeological finds from wrecks in the area (open summer evenings 18.30/19.00–21.00/22.00)

Velia

From San Marco the road cuts inland once again to the tiny hamlet of Case de Conte, then returns to the coast, offering good views over the sea, punctuated by groves of maritime pine. Beyond Agnone, the main road hugs the coast to **Acciaroli**, on a lovely promontory, a favourite resort of Ernest Hemingway Leave the town to the right and wind past the houses of Pioppi, where there are fine views of Capo Palinuro. At Marina di Casal Velino, you cross the valley of the Alento (the *Hales* of the ancients). Above the river, now marked by a medieval ruin, lie the remains of the ancient **Velia**.

History of Velia

Elea, as the city was called by the Greeks, was founded in the mid-6C BC by Phocaean colonists driven from their homeland by the attacking Persians One of the last Greek colonies to be founded on the Italian peninsula, it retains the typically Phocaean system of town planning, by which residential quarters were divided into independent zones separated by walls.

The town derived its livelihood from fishing and commerce, as the rocky arid hinterland was unsuitable for agriculture. Its ties with *Massalia* (the modern Marseilles) developed to such an extent that at one time Elea was considered a sub-colony of the latter. In the 3C BC the inhabitants threw in their lot with Rome; nevertheless the city retained its Hellenic culture, language, and customs, supplying the capital with priestesses of Ceres, who tradition dictated must be Greek. Although it never attained great civic or economic importance, Elea became a leading intellectual centre, giving its name to the Eleatic school of philosophy of Xenophanes, Parmenides, and Zeno. It decline became evident in Roman times, as its harbours (there were apparently two, on the north and south sides of the headland, which once projected into the sea) filled with silt. By the 12C it had disappeared altogether, and the medieval town of Castellammare della Bruca had grown up in its place. This in turn was abandoned in the 17C.

Opening hours

The ruins were discovered in 1883. They are open 09.00–20.00 May–Oct, 09.00–1hr before sunset other months, and may be visited comfortably in about two hours; ☎ 0974 971409)

The ruins

The city was surrounded by walls (about 4.5km long) and was organized in quarters north and south of the headland, scenically exploiting the natural terracing of the hill. On the highest point, looking out over the sea, was the acropolis, today replaced by the ruins of a medieval castle. On the south side of the archaeological site, close to the entrance, are the remains of a Roman necropolis which, according to Roman burial customs, was placed outside the city walls. Here you can see a section of the seaward walls, built of sandstone blocks and later fortified when the area beyond filled with silt. Just beyond stands the Porta Marina Sud, one of the two gates (the other is at the north end of the town), which initially opened on to the harbours. Within extends the south quarter, the centre of residential and political life. Facing a large paved road with pedestrian sidewalks are the living quarters of Insula I and a large building of the Augustan age conventionally termed Insula II. It consists of a triporticus with an altar in the centre and a U-shaped cryptoporticus; notice, near the entrance to the latter, the collection of bricks, of a type peculiar to Velia, impressed with the town's mark. Numerous statues, including a portrait of Parmenides, were found here.

Further along the road, in an olive grove to the east are **Roman baths** dating from the 2C AD, of which some rooms preserve their mosaic floors. Going uphill, on the right are the remains of a monumental complex of the 3C BC that once consisted of three terraces with porticoes and fountains. Only the lowest terrace is visible today. This was probably a sanctuary dedicated to Asklepios, god of medicine, whose statue was found nearby. The cult had a particular relevance at Elea, which was famous for hydrotherapy. The main street now ascends more sharply.

Near the top of the hill stand the Porta Arcaica, built in the 6C BC, in a position of obvious defensive importance, and the **Porta Rosa**, a remarkable structure of the 4C BC brought to light in 1964. Towards the end of the same century the lofty arch was walled up and this tract of the road, threatened by landslides, was replaced by another road that runs along the viaduct above.

To reach the **acropolis** you have to double back and return to a pathway leading west off the main street. This is located opposite the ruins of Hellenistic baths. Along the pathway are the foundations of Elea's oldest settlement (6C BC) built in small polygonal blocks of sandstone. The houses were abandoned in the 5C BC when the hill was entirely devoted to religious and public functions and the residential quarters moved further south. On the terrace above lie the remains of a Greek **theatre** of the 4C BC but heavily restored in Roman times. It could hold up to 2000 spectators and remained in use until the 5C AD. Behind the *cavea*, and replaced today by a 12C chapel, was the *propylon*, the monumental entrance to the **acropolis.** Here remains of an Angevin tower overlie the foundations of an Ionic temple dating from the second half of the 5C BC and possibly dedicated to Athena. Two new museums will open shortly: one in the chapel (hitherto a lapidary museum) with exhibits pertaining to the Archaic and Classical phase of the Greek Elea. The other, with finds from the Hellenistic phase and the Roman Velia will be housed in the 18C church of Sta. Maria di Porto Salvo further below.

On the ridge to the east excavations have revealed a small Hellenistic temple and an open sanctuary dedicated to Poseidon. From here it is possible to continue the ridge walk and to follow the course of the walls. These come together at the north-east corner of the site to form the Castelluccio, a tall tower dating from the 4C BC and subsequently rebuilt. Alternatively, a path descends directly from the acropolis toward the main entrance passing the so-called House of the Frescoes of the early 2C BC.

Palinuro and points south

A series of curves leads through wild valleys and groves of giant olives, past the villages of Ascea and Pisciotta to **Palinuro**, a fishing centre and a popular resort splendidly set in a small bay. An antiquarium (closed at the time of writing) contains finds from the necropolis of Molpa. At the entrance to the harbour you can see the ruins of what popular belief holds to be the cenotaph erected to Palinurus who, overtaken by sleep, fell into the sea and drowned, appearing to the hero here, asking to be buried (*Aeneid*, V, 838–871; VI, 337–383).

A walk along the coast may be made to the ruins of **Molpa** (2km, 30mins) Originally an outpost of the Greek colony at Velia, it was later converted into a castle, where Emperor Maximian withdrew after renouncing his title. The path which runs through olive groves and along the beach, is difficult in places.

The Capo Palinuro headland contains numerous caves accessible from the sea (boats may be hired at the harbour), some of which were occupied in prehistoric times. Also of interest are the natural arches at Foce del Mingardo and Archetiello.

Marina di Camerota is a modern resort. Here, as at Palinuro, excursions may be made to numerous caves along the coast. The road leaves the coast, penetrating the rocky hinterland in a series of tortuous bends. Beyond the village of Lentiscosa the going improves somewhat, offering a view to the left of the sheer face of Monte Bulgheria (1225m). Beyond San Giovanni a Piro, the descent to the sea begins. You rejoin the main road (no. 18) on the west slope of the Valle del Bussento and cross the river to reach **Policastro** (the Greek *Pixous*), on the bay of Policastro, set against a beautiful backdrop of hills. The cathedral of **Santa Maria Assunta** dates from 1177. Follow the rocky coast east.

Sapri, a pleasant resort (population 7000) on a sheltered bay, is known for its fine beaches, its olive oil, and its wood and marble industries. It achieved a certain notoriety during the Risorgimento, giving its name to the sad expedition of Carlo Pisacane and Giovanni Nicotera, who landed on the beach to the west of the town in 1857 with a handful of patriots, freed from the political prison on the Isle of Ponza, in the hope of stirring a popular rebellion against the Bourbons. Though they planned their mission meticulously, they grossly misjudged the psychological inclination of those they were to liberate; after a brief clash with the Bourbon troops the party dispersed and was largely cut down by local peasants.

THE HILLS OF EASTERN CAMPANIA

The major artistic attractions in eastern Campania are **Benevento**, with its magnificent Roman ruins and museums, and the Baroque **Certosa di San Lorenzo**, set like a huge jewel in the countryside near Padula.

More important, however, and more satisfying, is the seemingly limitless variety of stunning views that slow travel along the area's back roads and minor rail lines affords. The train journey from Naples to Benevento is particularly beautiful. Beyond Caserta, the line passes under the **Ponti della Valle**, the colossal bridge that carries the Acquedotto Carolino across the Maddaloni Valley. The bridge was designed by Luigi Vanvitelli and has three tiers of arches (96 in all); its height is 65m. The 48km-long aqueduct carries spring waters from Monte Taburno (1394m) to feed the park of the palace at Caserta. Beyond Frasso Telesino-Dugenta the line approaches the Volturno and shortly after crosses the River Calore near its confluence with the Volturno. After that it follows the lovely Calore and Miscano valleys to Benevento.

The roads are equally beautiful, especially the one that connects Benevento with Foggia, in Apulia, winding its way amid verdant hills and touching upon little medieval towns like Buonalbergo, Lucera and Troia. In the **Vallo di Diano** Autostrada A3 and Road 19 both cross magnificent countryside, which becomes increasingly arid as you travel southwards.

Practical information

Information offices
AVELLINO *Ente Provinciale per il Turismo*, Via Due Principati 5, ☎ 0825 74695; *Ufficio Informazioni*, Piazza Libertà 50, ☎ 0825 74732.
BENEVENTO *Ufficio Informazioni e di Accoglienza Turistica*, Piazza Roma 11, ☎ 0824 319938, ✉ www. eptbenevento.it , info@eptbenevento. it; *Ente Provinciale per il Turismo*, Via N. Sala 31, ☎ 0824 319911, ✉ www.eptbenevento.it, info@eptbenevento.it.

Getting there and getting around
By road

The Benevento area can be reached via Autostrada A16 from Naples or Bari, road 7 from Caserta, road 17 from Campobasso and Isernia, and road 90/90b from Foggia. Avellino is on Autostrada A16. Access to the Vallo di Diano is given by Autostrada A3/E45 and road 19.
By rail

The only station with convenient trains is Benevento, which is located midway along the Naples–Foggia line (c 1hr 10mins from each city).

Where to stay
AVELLINO €€ *Hermitage*, 5km south-west on road 88, ☎ 0825 674788, 📠 674772. An 18C villa with garden; open Apr–Oct.

Eating out
As on the plain of Capua, the best eating places in this farming district are in the country.
ANTRIPALDA (4km east of Avellino) €€ *La Tavola del Duca*, Via Manfredi 124, ☎ 0825 610471. At the Hotel Civita—traditional regional cui-

sine, indoor and outdoor seating.

€ *Valleverde*, Via Pianodardine 112, ☎ 0825 626115. Family-run trattoria (with rooms); closed Sun and Aug.

ARIANO IRPINO €€ *Pignata*, Via Due Tigli 7, ☎ 0825 872571. Rustic charm and good wines; closed Tues and two weeks in Sept.

AVELLINO €€ *Antica Trattoria Martella*, Via Chiesa Conservatorio 10, ☎ 0825 31117. Trattoria just off the main square, known for its genuine *cucina avellinese*; closed Sun evening and Mon, Aug and late Dec.

€ *Evoè*, Via del Gaizo 12–14. Wine bar with broad selection of Italian and foreign wines and light lunches.

€€ *Malaga*, Via Francesco Tedesco 347, ☎ 0825 626045. Good fish restaurant; closed Tues.

€€ *La Maschera Locanda d'Autore*, Rampa San Modestino 1, ☎ 0825 37603. Regional cuisine served in a garden or in the cellar of an old church; closed Sun evening Mon and two weeks in Aug.

BENEVENTO € *Nunzia*, Via Annunziata 152, ☎ 0824 29431. Traditional trattoria run by a dynasty of women chefs; closed Sun and Aug.

€ *Traiano*, Via Manciotti 48, ☎ 0824 25013. Trattoria-pizzeria in the old town centre; closed Tues and mid-Aug.

MANOCALZATI (7km north of Avellino) € *Antichi Sapori*, Via Calzisi, ☎ 0825 675441. Trattoria-pizzeria; closed Mon.

MOSCHIANO (15km south-west of Avellino) € *Santa Cristina*, Via Nazionale, ☎ 081 824 0383. Restaurant known for its good country cooking; closed Mon.

OSPEDALETTO D'ALPINOLO (8km north of Avellino on Road 374d) € *Osteria del Gallo e della Volpe*, Piazza Umberto I 12, ☎ 0825 691225. Osteria in the green heart of Irpinia; closed Mon two weeks in July and Dec.

SALA CONSILINA € *La Pergola*, Trinità 239, ☎ 0975 45054. Restaurant with rooms, once a coach station on the old road to Calabria; open daily.

 Special events
BENEVENTO **Opera**, **classical** and **modern theatre** in the Roman theatre in the summer. *Città Spettacolo*, drama festival (Sept).

East of Naples

The area immediately east of Naples is rich in Roman allusions, although there is little to see in the way of hard archaeological evidence. **Acerra** (population 41,000) takes the place of the ancient *Acerrae*, destroyed by Hannibal and subjected to frequent inundations from the River Clanius (now canalised) on which it stood. Its Castello Baronale houses the small **Museo Civico Archeologico dell'Antica Acerra** (open Tues–Sun 09.00–19.00). Cancello stands near the fragmentary ruins of *Suessula*, a town founded by the Ausoni or the Aurunci and destroyed by the Saracens in 879. Near Arienzo the Via Appia crosses the ravine generally supposed to be the **Caudine Forks** (*Furculae Caudinae*), where the Romans were trapped by the Samnites in 321 BC. The memory of the disaster is preserved in the names of the hamlet of Forchia, south of the road (where the church of Santa Maria in Iugo marks the supposed site of the battle), and of the Valle Caudina.

Benevento

Benevento, roughly translated, means 'fair breeze', and on some days, when the cool north wind sweeps away the exhaust fumes that beleaguer this and other southern Italian towns, the name rings true. It is a city of ancient importance, whose 65,000 inhabitants live on a ridge between the Calore and Sabato rivers in an amphitheatre of mountains. It was badly damaged in the Second World War, the lower town and the cathedral being almost completely destroyed.

History of Benevento

This is the Oscan or Samnite city of *Malies*. Latinised as *Maleventum*, supposedly because of the bad air of the place, it changed its name to *Beneventum* on its establishment as a Roman colony in 68 BC, soon after the decisive defeat in 275 of Pyrrhus nearby at the hands of Curius Dentatus. An important place under the empire, it stood at the end of the first extension from Capua of the Via Appia, which was later continued as far as Brundisium. It rose to fame again in 571 as the first independent Lombard duchy and preserved its autonomy until 1053, when it passed to the Church. It has been the see of an archbishop since the 10C. On 26 February 1266 Manfred was defeated here by Charles of Anjou and sought a voluntary death in battle after the treacherous defection of his allies. The title of Prince de Bénévent was conferred on Talleyrand by Napoleon. As a consequence of continuous neglect in recent years, the present city is one of the least hospitable in Italy.

The principal artery of the city centre, Corso Garibaldi, crosses the town from east to west. At its east end stands the **castle** (Rocca dei Rettori), built in 1321 by John XXII; here Attendolo, first of the Sforza, was once imprisoned. The historical section of the Museo del Sannio, housed in the castle, contains material relating to the town's past. The adjoining public garden affords a good view.

In a little piazza on the right of the corso stands the church of **Santa Sofia**. Built in 760 and rebuilt in 1668, it has a dome borne by antique Corinthian columns and a 12C **cloister** with interesting columns, capitals, and carved impost blocks. The decorative scheme is the work of local masters and combines late Roman, Moorish, Byzantine and Lombard motifs in Old and New Testament, mythological, and historical scenes. Adjoining the cloister is the **Museo del Sannio** (open Tues–Sun 09.00–13.00; ☎ 0824 21818), with a collection of Samnite antiquities and sculpture from a Temple of Isis erected by Domitian in AD 88, paintings from the Middle Ages to the contemporary period (chiefly by local artists), and prints and drawings.

Via Arco Traiano leads (right) to the **Arch of Trajan**, or Porta Aurea, a single triumphal arch of Parian marble, 15m high. It was erected across the Via Appia in honour of Trajan (114–166) and is one of the finer and better preserved arches of its kind. The bas-reliefs, set between composite columns, depict scenes from the life of Trajan and mythological subjects. The side facing Beneventum and Rome bears a glorification of Trajan's home policy, including, in the attic level, Roman consuls receiving Trajan and Hadrian, and Jupiter offering the emperor his thunderbolt; in the middle level, Trajan conferring benefits on the Roman people; in the lower level, The emperor's triumphal return after the Germanic campaign. The façade facing Brundisium and the overseas provinces celebrates Trajan's provincial policy and benefits, including, in the top registers, river gods welcoming the emperor; in the middle level, Trajan recruiting troops and forming new colonies, and in the lower levels, foreign peoples swearing loyalty or bearing gifts. A continuous frieze in the form of a triumphal procession runs around all four sides of the monument. Beneath the arch are personifications of cities and scenes of Trajan inaugurating a new road and distributing funds to the poor.

Continuing along Corso Garibaldi you reach the tiny Piazza Papiniano, with an Egyptian obelisk of red granite from the Temple of Isis (see above), found nearby in 1872. Beyond this is the **duomo**, a 13C Romanesque building shattered by bombardment in the Second World War. Its richly sculptured façade, badly damaged, and its campanile of 1279, still standing, incorporate fragments of Roman and Lombard architecture. The famous bronze doors, possibly of Byzantine workmanship, were injured beyond repair, but two-thirds of their plaques were saved and placed in the seminary. The treasury is notable for a **golden rose** and a **bronze coffer** of the 11C or 12C, and the chapter library includes interesting Lombard manuscripts, illuminated choir-books, and the 13C death registry, the *Necrologio di Santo Spirito*.

To the north, Corso Vittorio Emanuele descends to the Ponte Vanvitelli, which crosses the Calore River. The bridge, built by Luigi Vanvitelli, has been restored several times; remains of a medieval bridge survive 100m upstream. Beyond the river the long Viale Principe di Napoli leads to the Stazione Centrale. Corso Garibaldi continues, changing its name to Corso Dante and then Viale San Lorenzo, towards the Madonna delle Grazie, a huge 19C church containing a 6C wooden statue; in front of the church stands a granite bull from the Temple of Isis.

Below the cathedral to the south-west are the pillaged remains of another triumphal arch and the **Roman theatre**, built in the reign of Hadrian and enlarged by Caracalla to accommodate 20,000 spectators. The first and part of the second of three tiers survive, the remainder having been destroyed to make way for the modern buildings that encroach on its perimeter. Beyond the stage ran a peristyle, possibly intended as a promenade for spectators, which was reached from the exterior by three flights of steps. A lower corridor behind the auditorium remains intact. Notice also the extant fragments of the stage buildings. Further west are the ancient Port'Arsa; the Torre della Catena, part of a Lombard fortress; and, beyond the railway, four arches of the Ponte Leproso, by which the ancient Via Appia crossed the Sabato.

Around Benevento

A pleasant drive of 84km winds through cultivated upland country to Volturara, on the Foggia–Isernia road, passing Pesco Sannita, and San Marco dei Cavoti. Oak forests cover the hills round Foiano. Beyond San Bartolomeo in Galdo, the road commands a fine view of the Abruzzo mountains.

Another pleasant road, road 90/90b, winds in a north-easterly direction towards Foggia, offering good views back over Benevento and its plain. Each of the small villages visible in the surrounding hills has a castle of some interest. The road descends to the broad Calore Valley in a region rich in the remains of Roman towns (the ancient *Irpinia*); crosses the Calore near a ruined Roman bridge of the Via Traiana; then ascends the gentle slope of Monte Sacro, through olive and oak groves. A turning on the left leads to **Paduli** (population 5000), the ancient *Batulum*, on the ridgetop between the Tammaro and Calore rivers. Once the seat of a duchy, it is now an important farming town, known for its olive oil.

Buonalbergo (population 2000), in the highlands of Monte San Silvestre, consists of two distinct towns, Terravecchia, to the south, and Terranova, to the north. The latter, with its rectilinear street plan, is thought to be the Roman *Forum Novum*. The town preserves a 7C Lombard fortress known as the Castello di Boemondo; and remains of a bridge from the Via Traiana, the Ponte delle Chianche. The little 17C church of the Madonna della Macchia, just beyond the town, contains a wooden *Madonna and Child* of the late 12C, supposedly found in the woods (*macchia*).

A road on the right (road 414) diverges south to **Ariano Irpino**, a town (population 24,000) on a ridge, with an imposing castle of Norman origin. On the way is **Montecalvo Irpino**, where the Collegiata dates from the 14C and the Cappella Carafa contains a curious baptismal font consisting of a sarcophagus borne by pillars carved by local craftsmen.

A turning on the left ascends to **Montaguto** (population 1000), in a wonderful position enjoying broad **views** over the highlands of Irpinia, the Monti del Matese and the Tavoliere di Puglia to the Adriatic Sea. You enter Apulia near Stazione Orsara where the valley widens. At the Quadrivio di Giardinetto road 90 continues across the flat Tavoliere di Puglia to Foggia. The road on the left leads to Troia and Lucera (described on pp 427–428).

Avellino

Avellino (population 56,000) lies in a wide basin surrounded by mountains, at the junction of several important roads. The town ultimately derives its name from *Abellinum*, an ancient city of the Hirpini, whose site is 4km east. Raised to the status of provincial capital in 1806, it has a spacious, modern aspect, having been devastated by earthquakes many times.

In the town are the scanty remains of the Lombard castle, where the anti-pope Anacletus II recognised Count Roger as King of Sicily in 1130, and the Palazzo della Dogana, rebuilt in 1657 and adorned with antique statues. The **duomo** has a Romanesque crypt and is adjoined by a museum (open daily 09.00–13.00) containing works of religious art from throughout the province, brought here and restored after the earthquake of 1980. The collections of the **Museo Irpino** are housed in a modern building in Corso Europa (open daily except Sat afternoon and Sun, 08.00–14.00 and 16.00–19.00; ☎ 0825 782382). These include archaeological finds from the Neolithic to the late Roman age, from Mirabella Eclano, Iriano Irpino, Cairano and other sites in the Ofanto Valley; a collection of 15C–19C paintings; ceramics of Neapolitan and foreign manufacture; a *presepio*; and a section dedicated to the Risorgimento.

The place of hazel nuts

The hazel (or filbert) tree is found throughout Europe, in Asia Minor and in North Africa. It was well known to prehistoric man, for whom its nuts were a very useful resource, given that they do not spoil in winter. But the Romans alleged that they caused headaches, stomach problems and lethargy. They called hazelnuts *abellanae* because they were a speciality of that Campanian city. When *Abella* later became Avellino, the French called large hazelnuts *avelines* (Italian *avellana*, Spanish *avellano*), a word later substituted by *noisette* (little nut), in Italian, *nocciola*. Today, country cuisine around Avellino uses hazelnuts to make everything from breads, to stuffings, to sweets.

Just below the summit of Monte Partenio, to the north-west, stands the sanctuary of **Montevergine** (1493m; reached by a tortuous road of 18km), celebrated for a greatly venerated picture of the Virgin and visited by pilgrims at Whitsuntide and on 8 September (Nativity of the Virgin). The head of the Virgin, in Byzantine style, was rescued in 1265 from Constantinople by Baldwin II and brought here by Catherine of Valois in 1310. It is reputed to have been painted by St Luke. The remainder was executed in 1310 by Montano d'Arezzo. The church in which it is honoured, built by William of Vercelli in 1119–24 on the ruins of a temple of Cybele and rebuilt in the 17C after an earthquake, contains 14C tombs.

Catherine of Valois (d. 1347) and her son, Louis of Taranto (d. 1362), second husband of Joan I, are both buried here. Below the sanctuary is the **Convento di Loreto**, the winter residence of the abbot, designed in 1735 by Domenico Antonio Vaccaro, where 16C Flemish tapestries and the important archives may be seen.

Caves and Carthusians

Beyond Salerno, Autostrada A3/E45 proceeds east-south-east, leaving the road to Potenza on the left and entering the lovely, long **Vallo di Diano**, once a lake, drained when the River Tanagro was canalised.

Near the north end of the valley **Eboli** (population 35,000) stands on a hill, to the left of the road. The Collegiata contains an *Assumption* by Andrea da Salerno, and San Pietro alli Marmi has a plain Romanesque interior (restored). Just beyond the town a road climbs over the mountains to Grottaminarda. The motorway follows the Diano Valley, crossing first the River Sele, then the Tanagro.

Signs mark the way to the **Grotta di Pertosa** (open daily, June–Sept 08.00–19.00; Oct–May 09.00–12.00, 14.00–16.00), an extensive cavern 2.5km long that may be explored by boat and on foot; the stalactites are impressive.

In the hillside village of **Teggiano** (population 8000), the **cathedral**, rebuilt after an earthquake of 1857, has a richly carved portal, ambo and paschal candlestick, all of the 13C; the 14C tomb is by followers of Tino di Camaino. Above the town stands the castle, erected by the Sanseverino in 1285 but later rebuilt.

Sala Consilina (population 13,000), dominated by its castle, is set against a backdrop of mountains rising well above 1200m. The Museo Archeologico (Via Cappuccini; open Mon–Sat 09.00–13.00; ☎ 097 522026) contains finds from local excavations dating from the 9C–6C BC.

The Certosa di San Lorenzo
On the plain just below the town of Padula is the magnificent Certosa di San Lorenzo (open daily 09.00–19.30☎ 097 577117)

History of the Certosa di San Lorenzo

San Lorenzo was founded in 1306 by Tommaso Sanseverino, who paid for and erected the Carthusian monastery on his own land. The decision to found a monastery for a French order is likely to have been made for political reasons, as Tommaso was close to the Angevin kings of Naples and the valley, situated between the capital and the remote province of Calabria, was of considerable strategic importance: through the feudal organisation of its land, the Certosa maintained a strong influence over the entire area. For similar reasons the

Angevins favoured other Carthusian foundations such as the splendid S. Martino at Naples (1325), the Certosa at Capri (1356), at Guglionesi in the region of Molise (1338), and at Chiaromonte in Basilicata (1334). San Lorenzo retained its importance until its suppression in 1810. It was used during World War II as a concentration camp and afterwards, as an orphanage.

The outer buildings

The plan of San Lorenzo follows the standard pattern of a Carthusian monastery, in keeping with the order's religious and administrative organisation. A long wall, once acting as an enceinte, encloses the complex. The arrangement of the building within is determined by the rigorous division between 'lower' and 'upper' houses—or in lay terms, between communal and secluded activity. The main gate opens onto the outer courtyard, which gave access to the pharmacy, the vegetable garden, the stables and storage rooms. In the right wing, which is decorated by an 18C fountain imitating a grotto, were the living quarters of the *conversi*, or lay brothers. These were the only ones, besides the Prior and the Procuratore (see below), who could have relations with the exterior world in order to provide for the community's practical needs and the sale of products. In the left wing were lodgings for pilgrims. The second entrance, the principal one in architectural terms, leads into the monastery itself, where visitors were only rarely admitted. One eminent visitor was Charles V, who stayed here in 1535, while on his way from Naples to Reggio Calabria. For the occasion the monks are said to have prepared the emperor and his train an omelette made with 1000 eggs.

The **main façade**, built in the second half of the 16C, has more the appearance of a secular building than of a religious one. It has a two-storeyed, rusticated front with engaged Tuscan columns. The statues in the niches represent St Bruno, founder of the Carthusian order, St Lawrence to whom Padula is dedicated, St Peter and St Paul. The busts on the second storey represent the four Evangelists, the Virgin with St Anne and the Virgin with the Child. The figurative decoration as well as the attic balustrade, the urns, the pinnacles and the elaborate crowning niche with a statue of the Virgin and Child are all 17C additions. They reflect a Neapolitan tradition of terminating a façade with a horizontal line broken in the centre by an emphatic vertical element.

The heart of the complex

Inside, a long corridor terminates in the monumental staircase (described below). To the right is the small **Chiostro della Foresteria**, or guest cloister made up of a double loggia with a fountain in the middle. On the upper floor are ten guest rooms for distinguished visitors, the only ones to be admitted inside the monastery, while pilgrims found accommodation in the outer courtyard. Besides Charles V other illustrious personalities stopped here, notably Frederick of Aragon, Alfonso duke of Calabria and Ferdinand of Bourbon.

Together with building plans and architects, Carthusian monasteries often shared the same decorative artists: not surprisingly the architecture of the chiostro recalls the work of Giovanni Antonio Dosio who had been active in the Neapolitan Certosa di S. Martino in the late 16C. Upstairs are lovely landscapes by Domenico Gargiulo in collaboration with, or following, Micco Spadaro (late 17C) both of whom had also been employed at San Martino. On the upper floor is also the richly decorated **Chapel of St Anne** with gilt stuccowork of Sicilian inspiration (18C). The lower loggia and some of the rooms beyond are decorated with frescoes of sacred and profane themes by Francesco de Martino (early 18C)

From the courtyard the **church** is entered through a wooden door dated 1374 and carved with reliefs of the *Annunciation* (on the left) and the *Life of St Lawrence* (on the right). The single nave interior has cross-vaults borne by ogival arches. Its Baroque decorations fortunately do not mask its simple Gothic structure, dating from the 14C. Magnificent intarsia **choir stalls** (c 1507) grace the nave and chancel. The Coro dei Conversi has 24 stalls decorated with the four Evangelists, bishops, martyrs, saints who founded religious orders, as well as landscapes and architecture. The work is signed (above the last three stalls to the left of the entrance) with the name Giovanni Gallo and dated 1507. Beyond is the Coro dei Padri, with 36 stalls reserved for the monastic brothers who led a fully secluded life. It depicts episodes from the New Testament, saints and hermits, stories of martyrs and illusionistic architecture.

The fine majolica floor comes from the same workshop that produced the beautiful cloister of Sta. Chiara in Naples (18C). The high altar, executed around 1680, is made of *scagliola* (plaster inlaid with powdered coloured marbles bound together with glues), here enriched with mother of pearl and fragments of stones, set in swirling floral patterns. Even though the altar was designed by the Neapolitan Giandomenico Vinaccia, the technique, rather than coming from a Campanian milieu, was first used in northern Italy (in Emilia Romagna and Tuscany) in the 16C and was adopted at Padula for all the altarpieces of the monastery. Scagliola is cheaper in terms of material than marble inlay, but technically more difficult; so it is likely that the actual execution was left to the patience of the monks. The stucco work and ceiling frescoes, representing scenes from the Old Testament, were originally executed towards the end of the 17C although the painted surface was heavily retouched in the mid 19C by the Neapolitan Salvatore Brancaccio, a Carthusian monk who is also the author of the three canvases at the sides of the altar with the *Martyrdom of St. Lawrence*, the *Death of St. Bruno* and the *Apotheosis* of both saints. Other paintings had been stolen after Napoleon's suppression of the monasteries, as testified by the seven empty fields framed by stucco decorations.

The door to the sacristy has intarsia panels depicting the entrance to the monastery and church as it was at the beginning of the 16C. Inside the sacristy is a fine bronze **tabernacle** that had been lost in 1813 and only recently identified in the Museum of Capodimonte. It has been attributed to Iacopo del Duca, a pupil of Michelangelo, whose influence is clear in the reliefs showing the Passion of Christ. The vault has an 18C fresco depicting the *Assumption of the Virgin*.

To the right of the church is a series of small chapels, the most interesting of which is the **Chapel of the Relics**. These are treasured in a reliquary conceived like a Spanish retablo and closely influenced by the reliquaries of the church of Gesù Nuovo at Naples.

Restoration has brought to light a 15C fresco of *St John the Baptist* that had been painted over in the Baroque refurbishment of the complex.

To the left of the church is the **treasury** with fine Baroque stucco work. It once housed fabulous riches including gold chalices, silver crosses and busts covered in gems by Neapolitan silversmiths, as well as a famous ivory Crucifix attributed to Michelangelo. All of these have disappeared during and after the suppression.

Passing out of the treasury you come to the small, intermediate 'room of the bells' named after the bell tower which rises above it. It is actually a recreational antechamber where the monks met and exchanged a few words (elsewhere they observed silence) before entering the chapter room. Interesting is the notice board with letters indicating the location of the monks and the office they attended to.

Beyond is the **Sala del Capitolo**, or chapter room, with more stucco work executed by Neapolitan artists at the beginning of the 18C and statues of St Lawrence, Tobias with the Angel, St John and St Joseph. The latter two refer to the coexistence in the monastery of the contemplative life of the hermit monks and the active life of the 'conversi'. All the stucco frames remained empty after the Napoleonic spoliation: as Abbé Saint-Non recounts in his *Voyage Pittoresque* (1781–86) there once was a marvellous painting of the *Virgin and sleeping Child* by Luca Giordano. The only extant canvas of the room is the altarpiece by Ippolito Borghese, an artist of the Counter-Reformation, representing the *Madonna and Child with St Lawrence and St Bruno*. The frescoes decorating the vault, of modest quality, represent the Miracles of Christ and were executed at the end of the 18C. The putti with flowers belong to an earlier phase (early 18C) and follow the style of Francesco de Martino.

Returning to the antechamber, access is gained to the **old cemetery** (1522), rebuilt in the 18C once the cemetery was moved to the great cloister (see below), and featuring architectural elements derived from Antonio Vaccaro. Around the portico are antique architectural fragments found on the site during building work. The Cappella del Fondatore, at the far end, contains a 16C tomb of Tommaso Sanseverino. Next to the chapel is the **refectory** with a splendid 18C portal, a much larger majolica floor, a marble pulpit and a fresco of the *Marriage at Cana* by Alessio d'Elia (1749), following the style of his master F. Solimena. The refectory was used on Sundays and feast days only, for a communal meal that was taken in absolute silence. All other meals were consumed by the hermit monks in their own cells, while the lay brothers used the refectory of the *conversi* which today houses a museum (see below).

The old cemetery also gives access to the interesting and well-preserved kitchen complex, with storage rooms, a mill and a giant oak press (1785). Originally the kitchen served a different function, possibly a chapter house, as testified by the incongruous presence of a 17C fresco of the *Deposition*.

Adjoining the storage rooms is the main corridor of the monastery. From here you enter the 18C **Chiostro dei Procuratori** with a fountain in the centre and symmetrically arranged flower beds holding lemon and orange trees. The architecture is reminiscent of the work of Ferdinando Sanfelice. Here were the apartments and offices of the *procuratore*, the monk who was entrusted with the economic and practical administration of the monastery. Depending on the size of the property, there could be more than one procuratore. This was the case at Padula, whose community owned land and buildings as far afield as Naples.

Looking out onto the cloister, on the right hand side, are the **apartments of the prior**, the head and spiritual leader of the convent. These can be entered from the main corridor and consisted of ten rooms with additional services and a private chapel. This is dedicated to the Archangel Michael, patron of Padula, whose wooden statue is signed and dated 'Giuseppe Feriello 1649'. The four paintings on the walls illustrate the apparitions of the Archangel and were executed by an unknown artist from the circle of Solimena. There is also an interesting wall cupboard decorated with prints of imaginary landscapes. The loggia, opening out to the garden, is beautifully painted with *trompe l'oeil* landscapes showing strong analogies with the frescoes on the upper floor of the Chiostro della Foresteria. A pathway in *opus spicatum*, leads through the recently restored Italian garden.

The library and Great Cloister

Returning to the main corridor, on the left is a narrow and bold **staircase**, closed at the time of writing, winding up like a ribbon without balustrades. At the top is the library, with exquisite Baroque doors of inlaid coloured marbles and a good majolica floor. The ceiling is decorated with allegorical canvases from the 18C. Today only 1940 volumes survive at Padula, much of the rest was sent in cart-loads to Naples shortly after the suppression, ending up in what is today the National Library.

Now descend to the immense Great Cloister, which measures a staggering 104 x 109m and is articulated by 84 pilasters of smoothly rusticated stone. A heavy Doric frieze, decorated with scenes of martyrdom and of the Passion of Christ, runs between the upper and lower storeys. In the centre is a fountain, and on the south side the monks' cemetery, enclosed by an elegant balustrade. Although its architects are unknown they owe much to G. Antonio Dosio and Cosimo Fanzago who had been architects at S. Martino between the late 16C and early 17C. The sense of space, peace and melancholy the cloister imparts is memorable. Its atmosphere and poetic charm were recorded by François Lenormant in 1883:

> 'I went to sit in the Great Cloister. There were many clouds, driven by a violent wind, passing swiftly in front of the full moon, producing continuous sudden changes that ranged from profound darkness to brilliant light ... There is nothing more enchanting than the effect of these drops of nocturnal light which at times reveal the architecture in all its extraordinary purity down to the smallest detail, and at times conceal it completely. These sudden changes in light seemed to conjure up white phantoms in the depths of the porticos, as though the ghosts of the old inhabitants of the monastery had risen, as was their custom, to celebrate night office.'

Off the great cloister are the **monks' quarters** and gardens. The 26 cells consisted of two rooms, a portico, an open loggia and a garden with a fountain. Each monk had his own orchard where he would grow fruit and vegetables for his own consumption as well as herbs and flowers carrying a symbolic meaning (the lily, the violet etc). Since nature was considered an emanation of God, the gardens were conceived as an aid towards contemplation. They opened out onto a communal park. On the north side is an octagonal tower containing the elliptical **grand staircase** by Gaetano Barba (1761–63), a structure of singular elegance leading to an upper gallery (now closed to the public). Also accessible from the cloister is the **Museo Archeologico della Lucania Occidentale** (opening times as for the Certosa), set up in 1957 to display material from local sites. It contains interesting finds from a nearby Villanovan necropolis.

Basilicata and Calabria

> Calabria is not a land to traverse alone. It is too wistful and stricken; too defi-
> cient in those externals that conduce to comfort. Its charms do not appeal to
> the eye of romance, and the man who would perambulate Magna Graecia
> as he does the Alps would soon regret his choice .... The joys of Calabria are
> not to be bought, like those of Switzerland, for gold.

So wrote Norman Douglas, whose 1915 classic, *Old Calabria*, remains one of
the more brilliant, incisive portraits of this rough, wild region—as true to life
today as when it was written. Calabria, indeed, is a severe land, a place of steep,
harsh mountains, cactus and agave. Noisy and lively along the coast, inland it is
silent and sometimes mournfully desolate. Yet it is precisely this disquieting,
haunted character that makes it a land of great fascination. Like the summer
temperatures, emotions run high here, and the thrill of reaching the peaks of
the Pollino massif on foot, or of that first glimpse of Stilo in its desert landscape
as you descend from the wooded shades of Serra San Bruno, is truly memorable.

The same is even more true, if such a thing is possible, of Basilicata. Here the
landscape is so different from anything you've seen before, and so striking at
every turn that it will make your heart race. You won't forget places like Matera,
or overcome your surprise at the richness of its ancient heritage. And the spicy
tang of sun-dried tomatoes and the rich fruitiness of Cirò wine will return to
mind for years to come. But do heed Douglas's advice: when you come here,
bring a friend.

A region corresponding roughly to the ancient *Lucania*, **Basilicata** occupies
a three-cornered area between the Gulf of Taranto, the Tyrrhenian Sea and the
lowlands of Apulia. The country is almost entirely composed of steep parallel
ranges of limestone and dolomitic mountains, preventing easy communication.
It was colonised from Greece in the 7C BC and reached a high degree of prosperity, but was later drawn into the struggles between Rome and the Samnites and
the campaign against Pyrrhus and Hannibal, and in the Middle Ages it suffered
from the continual vicissitudes of the Kingdom of Naples.

Its present name was assumed in honour of Emperor Basil II (976–1025), who
overthrew Saracen power in Sicily and southern Italy. Despite recent progress
the region is one of the poorest in Italy: the soil is poor, and industries remain
undeveloped. **Potenza** and **Matera**, the only towns of any size, are the provincial capitals. In the forests, wild boar and wolves are not uncommon.

Calabria, the mountainous peninsula between the Tyrrhenian and the
Ionian seas, is the toe of the Italian 'boot'. Roughly 223km long, its northern
point culminates in Monte Pollino (2248m), and in the south it terminates in the
Aspromonte group (1955m). Central Calabria expands into the granite plateau
of the Sila (1928m). The rivers are short but copious. The vegetation along the
coast is typically southern, but fine forests and mountain flora prevail inland.

Calabria enjoyed an age of prosperity as part of Magna Graecia, and Croton
(where Pythagoras taught), Sybaris, Locri and Rhegion were flourishing cities.
Many traces of the past have been destroyed by frequent earthquakes. The chief
towns of the region are **Cosenza**, **Catanzaro** and **Reggio**, the provincial capitals.

On the whole Calabria is now a poor country, though emigration to northern
Italy, the United States, and Australia has largely been halted. The work of the post-

war development programme known as the *Cassa per il Mezzogiorno*, in particular in encouraging hydro-electric schemes in the Sila, has brought considerable improvement; an excellent olive oil is produced in several places (the olive groves at Gioia Tauro are amongst the best in Italy); and a blossoming tourist trade along the Tyrrhenian riviera has actually led to over-development, especially around Reggio and between Praia a Mare and Amantea. In spite of its charms, Calabria is still little known to the English-speaking traveller, though improvements in accommodation have brought most of the country within reach.

NORTHERN BASILICATA

There is still something distinctly Norman about this area, with its broad horizons, neatly tilled fields and imposing castles. Not by chance, northern Basilicata draws large numbers of German tourists every year. This and recent industrial development—there are a Fiat factory at Melfi, and Agip petrol-chemical works at Candela—have brought a gradual influx of wealth to the region, which has been skilfully transformed into pleasant (though by no means luxurious) hotels and fine restaurants serving traditional dishes based on lamb, game and mushrooms. It was a land much loved by Frederick II, who left two of his finest architectural achievements at **Melfi** and **Lagopesole**. Walkers, birders and nature-lovers in general will enjoy the wild woodlands of **Monte Vulture**, an extinct volcano. Dozens of **windmills**, on the hilltops between Venosa, Atella and Acerenza, provide clean, renewable electrical power.

Practical information

Information offices
M A T E R A *Ufficio Informazioni e di Accoglienza Turistica*, Via de Viti de Marco 9, ☎ 0835 331983.
P O T E N Z A *Azienda di Promozione Turistica*, Via Cavour 15, ☎ 0971 411839.
Ufficio Informazioni e di Accoglienza Turistica, Via Cavour 15, ☎ 0971 274485.
Ufficio Informazioni e di Accoglienza Turistica, Via Alanelli at Via Plebiscito, ☎ 0971 21812.
Assessorato Regionale al Turismo, Via Anzio 44, ☎ 0971 448647.

Getting there and getting around
By road

Melfi and its region is best reached via

Autostrada A16 and Road 658, an expressway that follows roughly the same route as the older (and slower) state highway, Road 96. Road 658 also provides access from the south via Potenza, which has its own fast road link to Autostrada A3/E45 (Salerno–Reggio Calabria). Two good roads link Potenza with Matera: the older and slower one, the Appian Way, is described below; the other is an expressway along the valley of the Basento, Road 407. It terminates at Metaponto, on the Ionian coast. Country buses provide infrequent but punctual services throughout the region.

By rail

Travelling to northern Basilicata by train is a problem. The main Salerno–Taranto line serves Potenza, with fast Intercity trains making the run from Salerno in c 1hr 45mins, or from Taranto, in 1hr 50mins. But there is no line in the Melfi area, and you have to get a bus at Ferrandina for Matera. Slow local trains cover the 76km from Bari to Matera via Altamura in c 1hr 40mins. There are also slow trains from Altamura to Potenza. Potenza, by the way, has two railway stations: **Inferiore** (Trenitalia) on the main Salerno–Taranto line, with a branch to Foggia, and **Città** for Altamura and Bari.

Where to stay

ACERENZA € *Il Casone*, 6km northwest at Bosco San Giuliano, ☎ 0971 741141, 📠 0971 741039. Modern, quiet and comfortable, in the wooded countryside of the upper Bradano valley.

MATERA €€ *Italia*, Via Ridola 5, ☎ 0835 333561, 📠 0835 330087, 📧 albergo-italia@tin.it. An old, established place near the Sassi and the archaeological museum.

€ *Il Piccolo Albergo*, Via de Sariis 11, ☎ 0835 330201, 📠 0835 333122. Small and atmospheric, in a former patrician townhouse.

€ *I Sassi*, Via San Giovanni Vecchio 89, ☎ 0835 331009, 📠 0835 333733, 📧 hotelsassi@virgilio.it. Central and comfortable, with views of the cathedral and the Sassi.

PIETRAPERTOSA (42km south-east of Potenza) € *Il Frantoio*, Via M. Torraca 15/17, ☎ 0971 983190. A simple place with just twelve rooms, overlooking the village and the mountains of central Basilicata.

POTENZA € *Vittoria*, Via della Tecnica 11, ☎ 0971 56632, 📠 0971 56802. A comfortable place, with hardwood floors and good bathrooms, just outside the city centre.

RIFREDDO (12km south of Potenza) € *Giubileo*, Strada Statale 92, ☎ 0971 479910, 📠 0971 594584, 📧 hgiubileo@tin.it. A quiet place in a shady garden in the hills near Potenza, good restaurant.

RIONERO IN VULTURE € *Masseria delle Sorgenti*, Road 167 km13.50, at Monticchio, ☎ 0972 731300. Beautifully situated farm with simple rooms, good food and excellent home-made Aglianico wine.

TRIVIGNO € *La Foresteria di San Leo*, Contrada San Leo, ☎ 0971 981157. 6 rooms on a lovely farm, with restaurant; open Apr–Dec.

VENOSA € *Orazio*, Corso Vittorio Emanuele II 142, ☎ 0972 31135, 📠 0972 31464. In a 17C palace, with antique majolica and inlaid marble floors.

Eating out

ACCETTURA (82km south-east of Matera on Road 277) € *Pezzolla*, Via Roma 21, ☎ 0835 675008. Restaurant with rooms and good home-made pasta, across from the town hall; closed Fri (except in summer).

ACERENZA € *Palazzo Gala*, Via Consigliere Gala 16, ☎ 0971 741163. Refined restaurant in the historic centre conscientiously managed by two brothers; closed Mon.

AVIGLIANO (26km north-west of Potenza on Road 7) € *Pietra del Sale*, Strada Provinciale 50, at Frusci-Monte Carmine, ☎ 0971 87063. Good trattoria in a former hunting lodge of the Doria family; closed Mon.

€ *Vecchio Lume*, at Sarnelli, ☎ 0971 87080. Trattoria; closed Fri and Sept. *La Radice*, Via Colle San Martino 5, is a **delicatessen** known for its fresh and conserved truffles, meat and vegetable patés and other goodies.

The **pasticcerie** in Via Coluzzi and Via Petruccelli make delicious traditional sweets: try the almond *mustazzuol* and anice-glazed *raffioli con naspro*. Fresh and mature cheeses at nearby (9km) Filiano, *Caseificio Pian della Spina*, via Piano della Spina.

CASTELMEZZANO (42km south-

east of Potenza on SS 407) €€
Dolomiti, Via Volini 7, ☎ 0971
986075. Restaurant with rooms with
good grilled meats and wines; closed
Mon.

€ *Al Becco della Civetta*, Vicolo I
Maglietta 7, ☎ 0971 986249. Osteria
with great home cooking in the heart of
the 'Lucanian Dolomites'; closed Tues.

MATERA €€ *La Buca*, Via San
Pardo 95, ☎ 0835 261984. Restaurant
on the outskirts of town famous for
dishes using the delicious local variety
of veal (called *podolico*); closed Sun
evening, Mon and July.

€€ *Tommaso*, Via degli Aragonesi 13,
☎ 0835 261971. Quiet, refined,
panoramic traditional restaurant; closed
Wed and mid-Aug.

€€ *Venusio*, Via Lussemburgo 2,
☎ 0835 259081. Good family-run
restaurant; closed Sun evening and
Mon, two weeks in Jan and Aug.

€ *La Stalla*, Via Rosario 73, ☎ 0835
240455. Trattoria in a former stable
carved out of the rock and overlooking
the Sasso Barisano; closed Mon and one
week in Aug.

€ *Le Botteghe*, Piazza San Pietro
Barisano 22, ☎ 0835 344072.
Trattoria in the heart of the Sasso
Barisano, with outdoor seating in sum-
mer; closed Wed.

€ *Lucanerie*, Via Santo Stefano 61,
☎ 0835 332133. Materan country
cooking in a restaurant in the historic
centre; closed Sun evening, Mon and Aug.

€ *Trattoria Lucana*, Via Lucania 48,
☎ 0835 336117. Trattoria; closed Sun
(except Aug) and late Aug–mid-Sept.

€ *Il Terrazzino sui Sassi*, Vico San
Giuseppe 7, ☎ 0835 332503.
Restaurant overlooking the Sassi; closed
Tues evening.

Forno a Legna Cifarelli, Via Istria 17.
Wood-oven bakery making excellent
bread and foccacia.

Il Buongustaio, Piazza Vittorio Veneto
1. Delicatessen selling local specialities

and a good selection of wines.

MELFI € *Farese*, Via Foggianello 1 at
Fogianello, ☎ 0972 236478.
Restaurant with rooms at the foot of
Monte Vulture; always open.

€ *Novecento*, Contrada Incoronata,
☎ 0972 237470. Low-key popular trattoria; closed Sun evening, Mon and late
July.

MURO LUCANO € *Delle Colline*,
☎ 0976 2284, 🖷 0976 2192. Trattoria
with rooms; open all year.

PICERNO (21km west of Potenza on
Road 94 or Autostrada A3) € *Re
Alessio*, at the expressway interchange,
☎ 0971 712200. Restaurant/pizzeria;
closed Mon and Oct.

PIGNOLA (10km south of Potenza
on Road 92) €€ *La Fattoria sotto il
Cielo*, Contrada Lago di Piglona,
☎ 0971 420166. Sheep farm and fruit
farm serving and selling home-grown
products; closed Wed.

€ *Amici Miei*, Strada Comunale
Pantano 6, ☎ 0971 420488. Simple
but good, popular with the locals; closed
Mon.

POTENZA €€ *Antica Osteria
Marconi*, Viale Marconi 233–235,
☎ 0971 56900. Osteria offering trati-
tional Lucanian cuisine; closed Sun
evening, Mon and mid-Aug.

€ *Da Mimmo il Ciclista*, Via Vaccaro
47, ☎ 0971 54840. Trattoria lovingly
managed by a passionate cyclist; closed
Sun and mid-Aug.

€ *Fuori le Mura*, Via IV Novembre,
☎ 0971 25409. Restaurant just outside
the old city walls, near the churches of
San Francesco and San Michele.

€ *Triminedd'*, Contrada Bucaletto 127,
☎ 0971 55746. Down-home cooking
in a fine country trattoria; closed Mon
and Aug.

€ *Zi Mingo*, Contrada Botte 2, ☎ 0971
442984. Excellent inexpensive trattoria
often crowded with locals, closed Mon.

Latteria Capece, in Via Vaccaro near Zi
Mingo, sells home-made cheeses.

Panetteria Giovanna Salvatore, Contrada Poggio Cavallo 84b, and *Forno di Lucia Pace*, Contrada Dragonara, are wood-oven bakeries producing bread, focaccia and sweet and savoury pastries.

RIONERO IN VULTURE €€
Pescatore, Località Monticchio Bagni, ☎ 0972 731036. Restaurant offering great traditional food (and fine views); closed Wed and Feb.

 Special events
MATERA *Madonna della Bruna*, on 2 July, an annual religious festival commemorating the recovery of a Byzantine Madonna stolen by the Turks and consisting of a colourful triumphal procession, ending in the destruction of the papier-mâché float on which the image is borne through the streets.

POTENZA *Sacra Rappresentazione del Venerdì Santo*, a re-enactment of Christ's Passion, on Good Friday; *Maggio Potentino* (May), with artistic, cultural, and sports events, culminating in the *Sagra di San Gerardo*, with the *Sfilata dei Turchi*, at the end of the month; also, *Sagra di San Rocco* (16 Aug), with traditional celebrations.

In the footsteps of the Normans

Melfi (population 16,000), set on a hill like a natural fortress, was the first Norman capital. It is now the capital of Fiat's industrial development scheme in the south. In the **castle** the investiture of Robert Guiscard was confirmed by Pope Nicholas II in 1059, at the first of four papal councils held at Melfi between that year and 1101. The first crusade was proclaimed here in 1089, and during his sojourn at Melfi Frederick II set forth his comprehensive body of laws, the *Constitutiones Augustales*. The **Museo Nazionale del Melfese** (open daily 09.00–20.00, Mon 14.00–20.00 ☎ 0972 238726), in the castle, contains Bronze and Iron Age finds, Greek and Roman objects and burial treasures from a Daunian necropolis. Highlights include an extraordinary marble sarcophagus of a woman, of the 2C AD, displayed in one of the towers. The reliefs, ascribed to artists from Asia Minor, represent the deceased asleep (on the lid) and the Roman heroes who represented the mythic 'references' of her aristocratic family (in niches).

A little further up the hill is the church of **Sant'Antonio di Padova**, with its pleasing rose window. It contains two amusing holy-water stoups; the one on the left, dating from the 16C, is the more complete.

Via Garibaldi leads on towards the cathedral, passing on the right the 13C portal of the former church of Santa Maria la Nuova (now a cinema) with its dogtooth carving.

The **duomo** has a campanile of 1153 with fine decorative brickwork, including the representations of two griffins (emblems of the Norman dynasty in Sicily); the pyramidal top is a modern addition. The interior has a wooden ceiling and a Baroque high altar and surround. The latter also encloses an elaborate bishop's throne of gilded and painted wood. At the end of the north aisle is a fresco of the *Madonna and Child Enthroned*, a late imitation of a Byzantine model; and in the second chapel on the south side is the much revered *Madonna dell'Assunta*, protectress of the city. In the adjoining **bishop's palace** can be seen holy objects from the cathedral and other churches in the town.

What to buy in Melfi

There are thousands of Fiats here, but you can't buy one. One does wonder, however, if the Turin-based automobile firm didn't choose Melfi as the site of its new factory because of the town's long-standing tradition of excellence in the wrought-iron trade. Or perhaps the terracotta horns sold for the Feast of the Holy Spirit at Pentecost had something to do with it. The Melfians' reputation as woodcarvers is unlikely to have been a deciding factor.

The district around Melfi contains several painted chapels hollowed in the rock (apply to the municipio for assistance), of which one of the more easily accessible is to be found on the road to Venosa. About 1km outside Melfi a small lane leads left towards the cemetery and, almost at once, a track leads left again to the **Cappella Santa Margherita**, containing 13C frescoes.

From here it is a short drive to **Rapolla** (population 4000), a thermal resort, where the **cathedral** dates from the late 13C. Set into the south wall are two bas-reliefs, one representing Original Sin, and the other an Annunciation. Both date from the early 13C and show a marked Byzantine spirit. The church of **Santa Lucia**, a beautiful little building with two cupolas, is built to a Byzantine plan (the key may be obtained from the sacristan of the cathedral).

Venosa and environs

Venosa (population 12,000), the ancient *Venusia*, is famous as the birthplace of the Roman poet and satirist Horace (Q. Horatius Flaccus, 65–8 BC), whose statue adorns the piazza; and of Manfred (born 1232), son of Frederick II and King of Sicily.

History of Venosa

The surrounding territory was inhabited in prehistoric times and constitutes one of the more prolific archaeological areas in Basilicata. Traces of Chellean and Acheullean settlements have been found at the borders of the Venosa basin, which at one time probably held a large lake. Some of the objects brought to light by recent excavations may be seen in the modest Briscese collection (described below) although the bulk of the material is distributed among the museums of Potenza, Matera, Rome, Florence and Milan. Venusia, originally an Apulian town, became the largest colony in the Roman world in 290 BC; Hannibal ambushed and killed the celebrated Roman general Marcellus (208 BC) here.

In Piazza Umberto I stands the great 15C **castle**, with cylindrical corner towers, a broad moat and a lovely arcaded courtyard. The interior hosts the **Museo Archeologico Nazionale** (open daily 09.00–20.00; ☎ 0972 36095) with a fascinating display of Greek, Italic, Roman and medieval antiquities from exca-'vations in Venosa and its territories. The collection focuses on the Roman colony of Venusia, with epigraphs, coins, architectural fragments, and ceramics documenting the city's political and cultural history (including the presence of a large Jewish population that buried its dead in catacombs adjoining those of the Christians). Also interesting are the bone fragments and other traces of *homo erectus* (who lived c 300,000 years ago), among the oldest such finds in Europe.

Across the square from the castle is a 13C monumental fountain built by order of Charles II of Anjou and guarded by two Roman lions. To the west the undistinguished remains of the supposed tomb of Marcellus can be seen. The **cathedral** dates from the 16C; its walls contain fragments of Roman buildings. The church is entered by a rustic Renaissance portal and contains a painting of the *Martyrdom of St Felix* attributed to Carlo Maratta. Behind the cathedral to the north are the 15C fountain of San Marco (which takes its name from a demolished church) and an interesting early 20C public laundry. In Via Vittorio Emanuele, near the town hall, is the **Museo Briscese** (open daily 09.00–19.00), containing Palaeolithic finds including Acheulean hand axes and some implements of the so-called Clactonian culture, the third phase of which is named after Venosa.

La Trinita Abbey

To the north-east of the town (at Località San Rocco) lie the considerable remains of La Trinita, one of the more impressive monastic complexes in Basilicata. Founded by the Benedictines c 1046, the abbey pre-dates the Norman invasion. It stands on the ruins of an early Christian church, which in turn overlies a Roman temple. The new church (incomplete) dates from 1063. Note the Cluniac form of the building, including a splendid ambulatory; also the beginnings of two campanili and the fine carvings of the capitals. To the south of this part of the group can be seen the remains of an early Christian baptistery. The earlier church dates from the time of the abbey's foundation, but was later enlarged and redecorated. It has a fine façade with, inside the first porch, a beautifully carved second portal with horseshoe arches. Many carved pieces belonging to the buildings are displayed to the right.

The **interior** contains what is said to be the tomb of Robert Guiscard (d. 1085) and of his first wife Alberada, divorced on the grounds of consanguinity. Robert's sarcophagus also contains the remains of his half-brothers, William Bras-de-Fer, first Count of Apulia (d. 1046), Drogo (murdered in 1051), and Humphrey (d. 1057). Numerous frescoes decorate the walls, including one that is possibly a portrait of Joan I of Naples, under which is a 14C *Pietà* attributed to Roberto Oderisius. The extensive remains of Roman baths, including walls in *opus reticulatum* and some fine mosaic pavements, flank the baptistery. Across the road (in an archaeological park open 09.00–19.00 or an hour before sunset) are remains of a Roman amphitheatre and, further on, Jewish catacombs hewn out of the rock c 50m above the road.

Time permitting, a further excursion can be made from Venosa to another ruined abbey. Head for the town of **Banzi**, 25km south-east, where the parish church encloses the remains of the ancient abbey of **Santa Maria**. These can be seen from the sacristy; a room leading from the end of the north aisle; and in the walls of the adjoining habitations, including one of the entrances (an arch leading from the main street). The church also contains, in the chapel to the left of the high altar, a 12C or 13C wooden polychromed statue of the *Madonna and Child* and the remains of a triptych attributed to Andrea da Salerno. Over the high altar is a *Madonna* in the Byzantine manner. High over the west front of the church a relief of the *Madonna and Child* can be seen.

On the slopes of Monte Vulture

Leave Venosa from the south-west, via Road 167 to reach **Rionero in Vulture** (population 13,000). Located 11km south of Melfi and 20km east of Venosa, Rionero is the starting point for excursions to **Monte Vulture**, an extinct volcano whose summit commands nearly all Apulia.

The area to the west, now much frequented by local tourists, is renowned for its natural beauty. Its main attractions are the beautiful little Laghi di Monticchio (652m), of which you may make a circuit. Near the point where these two nearly-circular lakes meet are the ruins of the **abbazia di Sant'Ippolito**, dating from the 11C and 12C. On the heights above the smaller of the two lakes you can see the late 17C abbazia di San Michele, of little interest. The **Bosco di Monticchio**, a splendid wood, contains over 970 varieties of flora, some rare.

A small road from Rionero leads (in about 8km) to the village of Ripacandida, in a commanding position at the top of a hill. Just beyond the village stands the **Santuario di San Donato**, where the small church is almost completely covered with 14C frescoes (repainted) depicting scenes from the Old and New Testaments, figures of saints and representations of miracles.

Barile (population 4000) is an Albanian colony founded in the 15C; the inhabitants retain their ethnic and linguistic traditions. Weddings and funerals are particularly interesting, as are the ceremonies for religious holidays. In the Scescio and Solagna del Fico areas are a number of curious caves carved in the tufa, formerly inhabited, now used as wine cellars. A troglodytic settlement has been found in the area of San Pietro.

The red castle of Lagopesole

At Atella, 6km south of Rionero Vulture, the Apulian aqueduct crosses the valley. The village (population 4000) has a 14C Romanesque-Gothic cathedral. 14km further south stands Lagopesole (829m), huddled at the foot of the last of Frederick II's great castles, begun in 1242. The emperor spent the last summer of his life here. The castle was built as a mountain retreat and as a bulwark against the rebellions that became frequent in Basilicata towards the end of Frederick's reign. It was also frequented by Manfred and by Charles of Anjou, who restored it in 1266 and made it the prison of Elena, Manfred's wife.

The reddish tone of the walls is due to the oxidation of iron salts in the rock. The entrance, on the west side (open daily, 09.30–13.00, 16.00–19.00), leads to a vaulted hall and then to the imposing courtyard, flanked on the north and west by the royal apartments and containing a series of fine mullioned windows. The chapel, in the south-east corner, is linked by a covered gallery to the emperor's apartments. A double staircase on the south side ascends to a smaller court, at the centre of which stands the massive square **keep**. The entrance, 8m above ground, is marked by corbels that at one time supported an external platform. The roof was carried on the two carved heads visible above, one of which is traditionally said to represent Beatrice, second wife of Emperor Barbarossa, and the other, with ass's ears, to be a likeness of the emperor himself.

About 25km due east of Castel Lagopesole (40km north-east of Potenza, with a station on the Potenza–Bari line) stands **Acerenza**, a small town (population 3000) splendidly situated on a calcareous hill. The Romanesque **cathedral**, rebuilt n 1281 (open by appointment; ☎ 0971 741112), has an ambulatory with three radiating chapels and a splendid west portal. The crypt contains early 16C frescoes of rustic charm. Within the church is a small museum with a marble bust, said by some to represent Julian the Apostate and (more doubtfully) by others to be a likeness of Frederick II. The curious cylindrical tower is a later addition.

The road to Avellino

Near the northern outskirts of Potenza, Road 7 diverges north-west. Rising in sinuous curves, the road offers magnificent rugged scenery, passing **Muro Lucano**, with the castle in which Joan I (see p 135)was suffocated (1382), possibly the site of the battle of Numistrum between Hannibal and Marcellus (210 BC) and continuing to Avellino (as Road 400) via Sant'Angelo dei Lombardi. At the Sella di Conza pass (697m) near Caposele, some of the headwaters of the Sele are conducted through a tunnel, 12km long, to the eastern slope of the Apennines, forming the first stage of the Apulian aqueduct. Near the town is the abbey of Materdomini (1748), a pilgrimage centre with a hotel.

Potenza

Potenza (population 68,000), the highest provincial capital of mainland Italy (820m; only Enna, in Sicily, is higher), has suffered much from war and earthquakes, and its architecture is undistinguished. The overall atmosphere of the city is nevertheless quite pleasant.

In Piazza Pagano is the church of **San Francesco** (1274), with a 15C carved door and a good 16C marble tomb. Behind the theatre lies the Romanesque church of San Michele Arcangelo. The duomo, reconstructed in 1799, stands at the highest point of the town. In Via Lazio is the **Museo Archeologico Provinciale Lucano** (entrance in Via Cicotto; open Tues–Sun 09.00–13.00 and Tues, Thur afternoon 16.00–19.00; ☎ 0971 444833). The museum contains a fine collection of objects from Metapontum and other Lucanian excavations, notably local antique ceramic ware, archaic bronze statuettes, terracottas, a bronze helmet from Vaglio, an early 5C kouros and a 5C marble tempietto from Metapontum. A short distance to the south of the museum stands the church of **Santa Maria del Sepulcro**, originally 13C but altered in the 14C and again in the 17C. It has been restored to its original state. The church contains a fine polyptych attributed to Andrea Solario.

Through the hills to Apulia

The area east of Potenza is studded with small sleepy villages in a magnificent landscape. **Vaglio Basilicata** is the first of the little towns of medieval aspect that crown small hills above Road 7, which rises and falls along the wooded north slopes of the wide valley of the Basento River. At the entrance to the village is a piazza containing two fountains; to the right is a pleasing Renaissance portal, near to which stands an ex-Franciscan monastery (now an orphanage) that encloses the church of **Sant'Antonio** (ring at convent for admittance). The latter contains many excellent examples of Baroque gilded and painted wood-

work, including a particularly outstanding 17C carved and painted wooden pulpit. There are also several statues, among the best of which is a terracotta of S¹
Anthony Abbot, in the centre of the screen behind the high altar.

Tolve and Irsina

About 5km beyond Vaglio Basilicata a lonely road diverges left to Altamura and
Bari, passing the little village of **Tolve** (population 4000). The west portal of the
church of San Pietro has a carved architrave containing curious symbolic
images. The road continues across an arid, lonely landscape to **Irsina** (population 7000), overlooking the Bradano Valley. The **cathedral** has a fine campanile
with mullioned openings (some of which are modern replacements) and contains Baroque altars with good marble inlay. The church of **San Francesco**
founded in the 12C, remodelled in the Baroque period and now returned to it
Romanesque-Gothic form, was built on to a castle of Frederick II, parts of which
including a good tower, remain. The church contains fine marble inlaid Baroque
altars, a 17C crucifix behind the high altar and a crypt with 14C frescoes.

Approaching Matera

A magnificent oak forest leads up to the Valico del Cupolicchio pass (1028m); the
road then descends the east side of the mountain.

Just outside **Tricarico** (population 7000) lie the monasteries of the **Carmine**
and of **Sant'Antonio**. The latter is of little interest, but the former contains a
cloister with decorative frescoes (much damaged) and, in the church, 17C frescoes that display a certain liveliness in content and execution, the best being
those in the choir and the two figures of saints on the choir arch. In the town
itself is the fine cylindrical tower of the Norman castle. The church of Santa
Chiara, entered through a chapel containing a 17C crucifix, has a fine gilded
ceiling. The **duomo**, erected by Robert Guiscard but many times restored, contains interesting woodwork, exuberant Baroque stucco in the chapel to the right
of the high altar and the tomb of Diomedo Carafa (1639).

Several traces of Lucanian settlements can be seen in the environs of Tricarico
These include remains of two concentric wall circuits at (3km) Tempa
dell'Altare, traces of habitations and defensive walls at Piano della Civita, and
some 4C BC tombs at Cancello (west of Tricarico on Road 7). Also of interest, but
less readily accessible, is the ruined village of **Calle di Tricarico** (19km north
east), which contains elements dating from Hellenistic times to the early Middle
Ages, including a Roman villa with well-preserved baths.

The road continues east with broad views over the Basento Valley. **Grassano**
(population 6000) is reached by a road on the left. In the municipio (a former
convent of the Minori) you can see two 17C frescoes, one of the *Last Supper*
showing affinities with 16C Venetian painting.

Grottole stands at the north-west end of the Val di Basento industrial district
which developed in the 1960s following the discovery of an extensive methane
gas field. The district extends along the valley floor from the Salandra-Grottole
area to Pisticci and draws upon the population and resources of Grottole
Salandra, Ferrandina, Pomarico, Pisticci and Matera. Methane is piped from here
to Matera, Monopoli and Bari.

The road climbs away from the Basento to **Miglionico**. The impressive castle is
thought to be the place where Sanseverino and his barons hatched their unsuc-

:essful conspiracy against Ferdinand I of Aragon in 1481 (see p 159). The church of **San Francesco** contains a splendid *Madonna and Child with Saints* by Giovanni Battista Cima (1499). The crucifix over the high altar is flanked on one side by the *Madonna* and on the other by *St Francis*. The church of the **Matrice** has a Romanesque campanile, with sculptured figures set into its higher regions (*Madonna and Child*, *Saints*, etc). At its east side can be seen a Renaissance-Baroque portal with a Pietà in the lunette. The west portal is also of interest.

Matera

Beyond the Bradano, which runs through a deep gorge here, and Lago San Giuliano, a lake made by damming the river, you climb through ever-wilder scenery scarred by deep ravines carved out of the chalk. Matera, capital of its province, is beautifully situated (399m) on the edge of a ravine.

History of Matera

The environs of Matera appear to have been inhabited since Palaeolithic times, and for this reason make up one of the more important archaeological zones of southern Italy. However, little is known of the city's ancient history. Although Greek tombs have been discovered in the area of the old town or *civita*, it is generally agreed that the Greek settlement at Matera was of little importance. The town was destroyed by the Saracens in 944 and its inhabitants killed or dispersed. In 1638 it became the capital of Basilicata, a position which it retained until Potenza rose to primacy in 1806. Today Matera is a very pleasant modern city; a few of its 55,000 inhabitants have moved back to the **Sassi**, ancient cave dwellings which have been renovated.

Enter the town by Via Ridola. Here is the former seminary, now called the **Palazzo Lanfranchi**, which houses an interesting collection of paintings, mostly of the Neapolitan school (closed to the public except when the building is open for special events; ☎ 0835 256211). Further on, on the left, stands the church of Santa Chiara, with 18C woodwork of a certain rustic charm. Next to this, in the former convent, is the **Museo Nazionale Domenico Ridola** (open Tues–Sun 09.00– 20.00, Mon 15.00–20.00, Sat 09.00–23.00 June–Sept; ☎ 0835 310058), which contains changing displays of material from the local excavations, including Corinthian helmets in bronze dating from 5C BC, Roman bronze vases, Greek vases, etc.; and an extraordinary prehistoric collection, ranging from Palaeolithic finds from Matera and its environs, to late Bronze Age material from Timmari, 14km west. The ambience of the museum is very pleasant, and the exhibits are well displayed and marked.

Further on, to the left, stands the church of the **Purgatorio**, with its charming Baroque façade decorated, in part, with strange, somewhat gruesome 18C sculptures. Piazza San Francesco has a **church** dedicated to St Francis dating from the 17C, also with a decorative façade. The second south chapel contains an 18C Baroque altar and the 16C tomb of Eustachio Pavlicello. Set into the organ case behind the high altar are panels from a polyptych by the 15C painter Bartolomeo Vivarini. In the fifth chapel on the north side is the entrance to the earlier church of Santi Pietro e Paolo (closed), over which the present church stands. In the first north chapel is a polychromed wood statue of St Francis. The holy-water stoup at the entrance rests on a Romanesque capital.

Crafts in Matera

Matera's craftsmen are famous for their work in terracotta and papier-mâché. The two materials are often combined in the locally crafted Christmas crêches.

If you're in town on the Festa della Madonna di Picciano (first Sunday in May) you can pick up a terracotta *cuccù* (it's just what it sounds like); if you're here for the Madonna della Bruna (2 July) you can rip off a piece of the great float and take it home, as the Materans do. If you don't have the nerve, you can buy a piece on the street after the event.

The street on the south side of San Francesco leads into Piazza Vittorio Emanuele. The decorative entrance to the Conservatorio di Musica can be seen on the right. From here Via del Duomo leads into Piazza del Duomo; along the way, notice the fine palace on the right, opposite which there is a splendid view along the Sasso Barisano Valley.

The duomo

The duomo dates from the 13C and is Apulian Romanesque in style. The west end has a large rose window carried by angels; and the central portal, fine basket-work carving and a sculptural group representing the *Madonna and Child with Saints Peter and Paul*. The south side has a carved central window. The door to the west (Porta della Piazza) has another good surround and a carved central relief of monks with the word 'Abraham' inscribed above it. The east door (Porta dei Leoni) has two lions at its base.

The **interior** is built to a Latin cross plan with a tall nave of typically Lombard conception and aisles divided by columns (some from Metapontum) with extraordinary capitals. In the first north chapel are a 13C *Madonna and Child* of Byzantine taste, and the finest inlaid altar in the church. Further on is the **Cappella dell'Annunciata**, a sumptuously decorated 16C edifice containing good sculpture by Altobello Persio, a local artist, and helpers. At the end of the north aisle, set into an elaborate carved surround, are other figures by Persio and Sannazaro d'Alessandro. To the left of this is a chapel containing an immense *Nativity* with a host of sculpted figures, also by Altobello Persio and Sannazaro d'Alessandro (1534). The choir contains 15C inlaid stalls by Giovanni Tantino da Ariano Irpino, above which hangs a great painting of the *Assumption and Saints* of the early 17C Venetian school. Other paintings of interest are those over the third altar on the south side, *Madonna and Child with St Anne*, attributed to Sebastiano Majieski (1632); and over the first altar on the same side, *Assumption of the Virgin with Saints*, by Giovanni Donato Oppido di Matera, both of which are in fine carved frames. Next to the Cappella dell'Annunciata a door leads into a passageway, at the end of which can be seen the portal of the small church of Santa Maria di Constantinopoli, with worn carving and a 13C relief in the lunette showing the carriage procession of the Madonna della Bruna.

The Piazza del Duomo, from which there is another fine view over the Sasso Barisano, and Via del Duomo split the Sassi into two parts. You can enter both the Sasso Barisano and the Sasso Caveoso from the piazza, or Via Ridola.

Retrace your steps along Via del Duomo, branching off to the right along Via Margherita. This leads into Piazza Vittorio Veneto, which divides the old town om the new. Just off the piazza is **San Domenico**, a 13C church with a rustic çade. The interior contains a repainted statue of the *Madonna and Child*, of determinate date. Above the first altar on the south side hangs a 17C copy of aphael's *Holy Family*, near which is the coeval tomb of Orazio Persio. Beyond e church Via San Biagio leads to the church of San Rocco, which contains a utally realistic crucifix of the early 17C.

Almost opposite stands the early 13C church of **San Giovanni Battista**, with fine carved portal on the south side (through which you enter the church) with elicate foliate decoration of Byzantine inspiration and a Saracenic arch embeded in the door recess. The interior is of a strangely inarticulate nature, with teresting carved capitals and an extremely high central elevation, showing gns of early northern Gothic inspiration.

From the opposite end of Piazza Vittorio Veneto, Via Lavista leads south-west a public garden, from which steps ascend to the unfinished Angevin castle. Its uilder, the tyrannical Count Tramontano, was killed in a popular revolt on his ay out of the cathedral in 1515, in the side street still known as *Via del Riscatto*, reet of vengeance.

In the central Piazza Pascoli are the Pinacoteca d'Errico (to be moved to the earby Palazzo Sangervasio, autumn 2003) and the **Collezione Carlo Levi** pen Mon–Sat 08.00–13.00), which holds a fine collection of works by the celbrated 20C artist.

he Sassi

o visit this part of the town it is essential to find some sort of a guide (see below) mong the inhabitants of the place, likewise to arrange a price; do not expect to e allowed to enter all the churches and chapels. In this strange valley dwellings, hurches and frescoed chapels, some of which are built, but most of which are arved out of the rock itself, are to be found. The Sassi, which are under the proction of UNESCO, are undergoing systematic restoration and rehabilitation; the uunicipality has begun assigning the renovated homes to newly-weds. The area divided into 22 work sites, some of which will be closed to the public on any iven day.

ours of the Sassi

ours may be arranged through the iformation office and the affiliated *ooperativa Turistica*. The young oys who generally offer their services to visitors arriving in Matera are less knowledgeable, but competent (haggling necessary).

ome of the rock chapels worth visiting are **Santa Maria d'Idris** and **Santa ucia**, both of which contain 13C wall paintings, the latter having a particularly ne fresco of *St Michael* and architectural devices carved on the rough stone pilrs. Of the churches constructed in a more conventional way (identifiable by their ampanili) the most interesting are those of **San Pietro Caveoso** (constructed in e 17C and 18C) and **San Pietro Barisano** (dating from the 12C–13C).

Many more chapels are cut into the hillsides elsewhere in the ravine; some of em contain frescoes of a surprisingly high quality but a guide is necessary. Of articular interest are **Santa Maria della Valle**, popularly called La Voglia, arved out of the rock near the Altamura road, with an interesting façade of 280 and 17C frescoes within; the **Cristo alla Gravinella**, a crypt-church of which the façade and frescoes were reworked in the 17C; and **Santa Maria dell Colomba** (or Santo Spirito), popularly La Palomba, in a picturesque position over looking the Gravina di Matera, with a Romanesque façade incorporating a ros window and 15C bas-reliefs.

The well-preserved church of **S. Barbara**, on the other side of the town, i entered through an arched portal flanked by columns and contains 13C frescoe an iconostasis and, in the ceiling, false domes carved out of the rock.

Neolithic trench villages

The area around Matera is also noted for its Neolithic trench villages, curious se tlements centring around circular or elliptical trenches, up to 3m in depth, tha originally held hut-like habitations and burial chambers—excavated with th sole aid of simple stone wedges. The material gathered from these sites, nov chiefly at the Museo Ridola, includes incised and painted ceramic ware, the la ter of a type peculiar to Matera; and numerous broken or discarded tool Excavations in the area have also brought to light a burial ground wit Villanovan cinerary urns and objects decorated in bronze; a Greek necropol with Apulo-Peucetian tombs of the 4C and 3C BC containing ceramic war bronzes, votive vases and statues; and a sanctuary dedicated to Persephon Further information and guides may be obtained at the Museo Ridola.

An excursion to Montescagliosa

A pleasant trip may be made from Matera to Montescagliosa, a large, most whitewashed village (25km south by Road 175). The **Chiesa Maggiore** has a imposing Baroque façade and inlaid altars, of which the high altar is particular fine. **Santo Stefano**, a tiny church, has an attractive main portal. At the top the village stands the imposing abbey of **Sant'Angelo**, a monastic foundatio dating from the 11C, reconstructed by Charles II of Anjou and again part rebuilt in the late 15C. The exterior now has the look of a Renaissance buildin It contains two interesting cloisters. The territory around Montescagliosa ha yielded traces of Lucanian settlements dating from the 6C BC. Beyon Montescagliosa, you may rejoin the main road (175) leading to Metaponto an the coast.

The Sassi ~ ancient cave dwellings, Matera

SOUTHERN BASILICATA AND NORTHERN CALABRIA

One of the chief attractions of this rugged, mountainous region is the variety of beautiful back roads connecting the Tyrrhenian and Ionian coasts, providing endless possibilities of leisurely exploration. Other highlights in the area include the breathtaking landscape of the Monte Pollino National Park, a paradise for walkers, and **Mormanno** and **Morano Calabro**, two charming old towns forgotten by time. **Maratea**, on the west coast, is one of Italy's more beautiful seaside resorts, famous at home but unknown abroad. Calabria's best restaurant is at Castrovillari, and the Gothic church of Santa Maria della Consolazione at **Altomonte** is well worth a side-trip, as is the little Romanesque church of **Santa Maria d'Anglona** near Tursi. Even the medieval centre of **Cosenza** has a certain charm—a rare quality in the cities of Calabria.

Practical information

Information offices

CASTROVILLARI *Ufficio Informazioni e di Accoglienza Turistica*, Autostrada A3, IP Service Area, ☎ 0981 32710.

COSENZA *Ufficio Informazioni e di Accoglienza Turistica*, Corso Mazzini 92, ☎ 098 427271.

Azienda di Promozione Turistica, Corso Mazzini 92, ☎ 098 427485.

MARATEA *Azienda di Promozione Turistica*, Piazza del Gesù 40, Fiumicello di Santa Venere, ☎ 0973 876908.

REGIONE CALABRIA
✉ turismo.regione.calabria.it.

Getting there and getting around
By air

Southern Basilicata and northern Calabria are served by **Lamezia Terme** airport, on the Tyrrhenian coast 61km south of Cosenza; direct flights to/from Naples, Palermo and Rome.

By road

Fast north/south access to the area is provided from Naples and Reggio Calabria by Autostrada A3/E45. Road 106, which is being widened at the time of writing to make a four-lane express-

way, runs along the Ionian coast from Taranto to Reggio Calabria. The many minor roads are safe and well maintained, but not for those who suffer motion sickness.

By rail

Maratea has a station on the main Salerno–Reggio Calabria railway, and there is a branch line connecting Cosenza to the west coast at Paola. The Taranto–Reggio line hugs the Ionian coast. Note that Cosenza has 3 railway stations: Centrale (Ferrovie dello Stato), Piazza IV Novembre, with lines for Paola and Sibari; Cosenza Città (Ferrovie Calabro-Lucane), Via Catanzaro, just east of the central station; Cosenza Casali, Via dei Martiri, lines for Catanzaro and San Giovanni in Fiore.

Where to stay

ALTOMONTE €€
Castello di Altomonte, Piazza Castello 6, ☎ 0981 948933, 🖷 0981 948937, ✉ www. altomonte.it, castello@altomonte.it. Eleven quietly luxurious rooms in a historic setting at the very top of the town.

€ *Barbieri*, Via San Nicola 30, ☎ 0981 948072, 🖷 0981 948073. A homely place owned and managed by the Barbieri family, with comfortable rooms, particularly fine breakfasts and one of the region's better restaurants.

CASTROVILLARI €€ *La Locanda di Alia*, Via Jetticelle 55, ☎ 0981 46370, ▤ 0981 46370, ▨ www.alia.it, alia@alia.it. A charming, romantic hotel with just 14 rooms, set in a beautifully scented garden. The restaurant is the best in Calabria.

FRASCINETO (in the Monte Pollino National Park) **€** *Skanderbeg*, Via Arcuri 24, ☎ 0981 32117, ▤ 0981 32818. A small (16-room) family-run hotel with comfortable rooms, offering hiking, riding and mountain-biking in the park.

MARATEA €€€ *Santavenere*, ☎ 0973 876910, ▤ 0973 877654. Overlooking the sea from a lovely garden, with large luminous rooms, pool and tennis courts; open Apr–Oct.

€€ *Locanda delle Donne Monache*, Via Mazzzei 4, ☎ 0973 877487, ▤ 0973 877687, ▨ locdonnemonache@ tiscalinet.it. In a former convent, with four-poster beds, private garden, magnificent views; open Apr–Oct.

€€ *Villa Cheta Elite*, Via Timpone 46, Acquafredda, ☎ 0973 878134, ▤ 0973 878135, ▨ villacheta@tin.it. Quietly elegant turn-of-the-century villa in a superb garden with magnificent sea views and good restaurant.

€ *La Tana*, Via Nazionale 26, at Castrocucco, ☎ 0973 871770, ▤ 0973 871720, ▨ latana@tiscalinet.it. In a pleasant garden 10km south of Maratea, with good views over the bay of Policastro, shuttle service to the best beaches, and an excellent restaurant; open Feb–Dec.

TERRANOVA DI POLLINO € *Picchio Nero*, Via Mulino 1, ☎ 0973 93170, ▤ 0973 93170, ▨ picchionero.com, picchionero@ picchionero.com. A small place frequented by hikers, in the Monte Pollino National Park.

 Eating out

CASTELLUCCIO INFERIORE € *Beccaccino*, Largo Marconi 12, ☎ 0973 662129. Country restaurant serving excellent regional dishes, especially lamb; closed Tues and Nov.

CASTROVILLARI €€ *La Locanda di Alìa*, Via Jetticelle 69, ☎ 0981 46370 Restaurant, in a renovated farm house adjoining the hotel (see above), closed Sun.

CIVITA (near Castrovillari, in the Monte Pollino National Park) **€** *Agorà*, Piazza Municipio 30, ☎ 0981 73410. Restaurant specialising in Calabro-Albanian dishes; closed Mon and Nov.

€ *La Kamastra*, Piazza Municipio 3–6, ☎ 0981 73387. Another good place for *arbreshe* (Albanian) fare; closed Wed.

FIRMO € *La Capricciosa*, Via Angelo Viscardi, at Piano dello Schiavo, ☎ 0981 940247. A genuine academy of Calabro-Albanian cuisine; closed Mon

FRANCAVILLA IN SINNI € *Fontana del Tasso*, Contrada Scaldaferr 40, ☎ 0973 644566. A farm in the Monte Pollino National Park, traditiona dishes prepared with flair, closed Tues and in autumn.

LAGONEGRO € *Valsirino*, Contrada Aniella at Monte Sirino, ☎ 338 815 8496. Country cooking on a beautiful farm between Lagonegro an Maratea; always open.

NEMOLI € *Da Mimì*, Contrada Lago Sirino, ☎ 0973 40586. Restaurant with rooms by the lovely little Lago Sirino, along the old highway (Road 19 from Naples to Calabria.

MARATEA € *Vincenzo a Mare*, Via Grotte 26 at Maratea Porto, ☎ 0973 876002. Trattoria; closed Mon (except in summer).

€€ *Za Mariuccia*, Via Grotte 2, at the port, ☎ 0973 876163. Restaurant; closed Thur and Jan.

€ *Zu Pascali*, Via Varacia 4, at Massa, ☎ 0973 870242. Simple country

trattoria; closed Oct–Easter.
Pasticceria Panza, Via Angiporto Cavour 9, Maratea Porto; pastry shop and confectioner, with delicious local sweets.

MARSICOVETERE (47km south of Potenza near Road 276) € *Osteria del Gallo*, Largo Nazionale 2, Villa d'Agri, ☎ 0975 352045. Osteria in the Agri valley, at the foot of Monte Vulturino; closed Tues (except in summer).

RENDE € *Il Setaccio*, Contrada Santa Rosa 62, ☎ 0984 837211. Restaurant; closed Sun and mid-Aug.

ROTONDA (on Road 653 near Lauria) € *Da Peppe*, Corso Garibaldi 13, ☎ 0973 661251. Restaurant; closed Mon.
Da Raimondo, Piazza Vittorio Emanuele 14, for traditional breads and pastries.

ROTONDELLA € *La Mangiatoia*, Via Giotto 23, ☎ 0835 504440. Restaurant in a village (near Roads 380 and 106) known as the Balcony of the Ionian; closed Mon.

SAN SEVERINO LUCANO (in the Monte Pollino National Park) € *La Taverna del Brigante*, Contrada Taverna Magnano 15, ☎ 0973 576284. Trattoria with rooms; closed Tues (except in summer).

TERRANOVA DI POLLINO (in the Monte Pollino National Park) € *Luna Rossa*, Via Marconi 18, ☎ 0973 93254. Restaurant; closed Wed (except in summer) and 10 days in Jan.

TRECCHINA € *Aia dei Cappellani*, Contrada Maurino, ☎ 0973 826937. Farm serving home-grown products on a panoramic terrace in summer; closed Tues (except June–Sept) and Nov.
€ *Lanterna Verde*, Piazza del Popolo 22, ☎ 0973 826216. Family-run restaurant in a pleasant little village above Maratea; closed Mon (except in summer) and Nov–Mar.
€ *Mamma*, Via del Popolo 85, ☎ 0973 826129. Another family-run place offering old-time Lucanian fare; closed Wed.

VIGGIANELLO (14km outside the village, in the Monte Pollino National Park) *L'Oasi*, Contrada Falascoso 6, ☎ 0973 57692. Café/trattoria with rooms; closed Tues.

Special events
MARATEA hosts a drama festival in August.

Across the Apennines

The Apennines create a formidable barrier between south-western Italy's Tyrrhenian and Ionian coasts, creating two distinct bioregions. On the Tyrrhenian side the moist west wind brings abundant rainfall. The vegetation is therefore quite lush, and where they have not been felled for firewood or pasture, tall shady forests still grow. In summer they provide welcome relief from the sweltering heat on the coast.

The prevailing westerlies are blocked by the peaks of the Maddalena, Pollino and Serra Calabra ranges, leaving the Ionian shores of Basilicata and Calabria in a state of semi-aridity. Only relatively recently has large-scale irrigation made it possible to convert areas of the Ionian bioregion from sheep-grazing to agriculture.

To cross this natural bulwark has always been an arduous undertaking. But if you're not in a rush, it can actually be one of the highlights of a trip to the south.

Backroads into Basilicata

A few kilometres south of the Certosa di San Lorenzo (see Campania), near Montesano station, a road to the left (Road 103) gives a choice of two mountainous routes to the Ionian Sea, crossing into Basilicata by the Sella Cessuta (1028m) to **Moliterno**, an interesting old town with a much altered Lombard castle. Beyond **Grumento Nova**, above the River Agri (right) is the Roman *Grumentum*, site of two Carthaginian defeats in the Second Punic War. The extensive ruins, not systematically explored, yielded the Siri Bronzes in 1823 now in the British Museum.

Beyond another ridge, at **Corleto Perticara**, our route is joined by Road 92—the other mountainous route to the east coast—from Potenza. The steep and lonely road (no. 103) continues left to **Stigliano**, a superbly sited old town, then descends via Montalbano Ionico to Scanzano, on the Ionian seaboard.

Road 92 (right) re-crosses the River Agri, then joins the Latronico road (described below) in the Sinni Valley, reaching the coast near Nova Siri Alternatively, Road 598, a fast road, bears east after Grumentum, skirting the north shore of the lovely **Lago di Pietra di Pertusillo**, then follows the Agri Valley to Scanzano. All three roads are remarkable for the dramatic quality of the **landscape**, which increases its power and beauty as you near the sea.

Sapri to Policoro

Another beautiful but arduous route from the west coast to Policoro on the east coast (Road 104 and 585) climbs up from Sapri, on the Policastro Bay (see *Campania*) to **Rivello** (479m, population 3254) a small town perched on a hill scenically dominating the valley of the river Noce. Founded by a Basilian community, it was the object of a long dispute among Lombards and Byzantines While the Lombards conquered and fortified the lower town, the Greeks retreated to the top of the hill with the result that the inhabited centre was divided in two parts: one following the Latin rite and concentrating around the church of **Santa Maria Maggiore**, the other, of Greek rite, concentrating around the fortress-like church of **San Nicola** (under restoration at the time of writing). The division, which lasted until the 17C when the Greek rite was abolished, has left its traces in the names of streets, squares and fountains. Byzantine traces are also visible in the architectural structure and the tiled cupolas of some churches like **San Michele dei Greci**, Sant'Antonio (see below) and **Santa Barbara**, which is decorated with frescoes of saints by the local 16C painter Antonio Ajello Unfortunately, a great part of the lower town was heavily damaged by the earthquake of 1998; while it is awaiting a more adequate use of reconstruction funds (many of which have hitherto landed in private hands) it maintains the charm of its narrow streets enlivened with balconies, loggias and architectural decorations.

Below the historic centre lies the interesting monastery of **Sant'Antonio** Begun as a Basilian foundation, it was turned into a Benedictine and later a Franciscan convent. The entrance porch has 16C–17C frescoes and a Catalan door flanked by two lions. The interior, refurbished in the Baroque style, is decorated with stucco work and 17C paintings. Behind the altar are choir stalls (1623–53) charmingly carved with religious and lay themes ranging from saints and episodes from the Old Testament, to amusing genre scenes of everyday life hunting, seasonal arts and crafts, and fantastic animals. They were executed and signed by a Benedictine monk, Fra'Ilario da Montalbano, and provide a provincial counterpart to the much earlier and more refined choir stalls of the monastery at Padula. The adjacent cloister has 17C frescoes and the refectory a colourful *Last Supper* animated by a wealth of anecdotal details.

Road 585 continues to **Lagonegro** (666m, population 6000), a small town somewhat bleakly situated high in the mountains. In the wooded Piazza Grande are three Baroque churches, Sant'Anna (1665), San Nicola (1779–1839), and the **Madonna del Sirino**, flanked by an open chapel containing Romanesque pillars and two lions from another building. Monna Lisa del Gioconda (d. 1505) is said to be buried in the 10C church of San Nicola, in the old town. Monte del Papa (2005m), to the east (ascent in 3–4 hours), commands views of both the Tyrrhenian and Ionian seas.

From Lagonegro Road 19 winds southwards towards Lauria; from a junction 5km north of the village (take the Lauria Sud exit if you come by autostrada), a fine new road (no. 653) runs east via Latronico and the **Parco Nazionale del Monte Pollino**, a nature reserve established in 1990 to protect the wilderness highlands of this great massif (2248m), to the Ionian Sea at Nova Siri. It commands exceptional **views** down the Sinni Valley to the coast, passing through **Chiaromonte**, where the parish church contains a medieval crucifix, two paintings of the Neapolitan school and a good inlaid marble altar; and **Senise**, where the church of San Francesco has a polyptych by Simone da Firenze and good choir stalls. Senise stands on a lake formed by Europe's first earthwork dam, visible from the road just east of the town.

Roughly half-way between the lake and the coast a minor road leads north to **Tursi**, to which the see of Anglona was transferred in 1546. In the lower town is the **cathedral**, which has two interesting representations of the Annunciation, a good painted ceiling, and a majolica floor. A fine monstrance (1741) can be admired in the sacristy.

In the upper town, reached by a stiff climb, the Chiesa della Rabatana, once the cathedral, dates from the 16C but was much altered in the 18C. It has a fine inlaid marble high altar and a 14C triptych representing the Madonna dell'Icona, with scenes from the life of Christ and the Virgin. Steps lead down to an earlier crypt, where a chapel contains 16C frescoes and, in an adjoining room, a *Nativity* composed of carved stone figures. It dates from the 16C and has great, though somewhat naive charm.

On a ridge between the Sinni and Agri valleys, near the coast, is the isolated church of **Santa Maria di Anglona**, a Romanesque construction initiated in the 11C, but today consisting mainly of alterations and additions from later centuries. It has a good west portal, a fine apse and a number of interesting but crude carvings let into different parts of the building. The interior contains 11C, 12C and 13C frescoes and the curious *Madonna Nera*, of uncertain date and provenance.

Maratea to Villapiana

Maratea, pleasantly situated on a hill-slope above the villages of Acquafredda, Fiumicello and Marina di Maratea, is Basilicata's finest seaside resort. The town (population 5000) commands a marvellous view of Policastro Bay. At Maratea Inferiore is the church of **Santa Maria Maggiore** containing very fine 15C Gothic choir stalls, a marble *Virgin in Glory* and paintings of the Neapolitan school. The former church of the Francescani has an interesting cloister. From Maratea Superiore the road continues for c 1km to the sanctuary of **San Biagio**, with good views back to Capo Palinuro and Monte Bulgheria.

Local roads and a short stretch of Road 585 link Maratea with Lauria, from where Road 19 winds along the south slopes of the Pollino Massif to Calabria. The landscape is a harmonious medley of forest, pasture, and fields of grain.

You enter Calabria just short of **Mormanno** (population 4000), a popular refuge from the heat of summer, where the church of **Santa Maria del Colle** contains much good gilded and carved woodwork, fine Baroque altars, a Tuscan relief to the right of the main altar and, in the sacristy, a good painting of the 18C Neapolitan school. The narrow side streets are well worth wandering down. A mountain road descends via Papasidero to Scalea, on the Tyrrhenian coast.

From Mormanno, cross the Passo di Campotenese, a rich pastoral plateau nearly 900m high. The road descends abruptly, into the valley of the Coscile, passing just east of **Morano Calabro** (population 5000), dominated on its conical hill by the church of **San Pietro**, which contains, at the first altars on the north and south sides, marble statues of *St Catherine* and *St Lucy* by Pietro Bernini; and, to the left and right of the high altar, statues of *Saints Peter* and *Paul* by followers of Bernini. Also of fine workmanship are the late 18C and early 19C choir stalls by the local artist Agostino Fusco and a beautiful processional cross, dated 1445, from the Abruzzese workshop of the Guardiagrele. At the bottom of the hill stand the churches of **San Bernardino**, with a superb carved wooden pulpit of 1611, and **La Maddalena**, with its tiled cupola, a beautiful 18C organ, and a polyptych of Bartolomeo Vivarini, signed and dated 1477, temporarily moved here from San Bernardino.

Castrovillari (population 23,000), 7km away, stands on an upland plain at the southern end of the Pollino massif. The old town or *civita* has a massive **castle** built in 1490 by Ferrante I of Aragon to keep the citizens of Castrovillari under his thumb. It was used as a prison by the Spinelli, Dukes of Castrovillari—a function it retained until the late 20C.

A small collection of finds from local excavations, including prehistoric, protohistoric, Roman and medieval material, can be seen at the **Museo Civico** in Corso Garibaldi (open daily 08.00–14.00, Tues and Thur 15.00–18.00; ☎ 0981 25249). The museum's other facility, in the 18C **Palazzo Gallo** in Piazza Vittorio Emanuele II, has paintings by A. Alfano and others.

A long winding road leads on, past the church of San Giuliano, with its pleasing Renaissance façade, to **Santa Maria del Castello**, a church dating from the 11C and reconstructed in the 14C. Here, in the Cappella del Sacramento, a fine Baroque altar encloses a fresco of the *Madonna del Castello*, a much revered image in the Byzantine style. On the right wall of the staircase leading up to the cantoria you can see the remains of frescoes, possibly dating from the 13C. The church also contains two paintings by Pietro Negroni, 17C choir stalls and, on a pillar in the south aisle, a 17C olive-wood figure of the *Crucified Christ*. The Baroque high altar and the bishop's throne likewise warrant attention. The sacristy houses a minute museum, which includes a 15C copper plate made in Nuremburg and a cope given to the church by Pope Pius IV.

From Castrovillari, Road 105 and its continuation, Road 92, wind eastwards along the southern spur of Monte Pollino, reaching the Ionian Sea at the uninteresting village of Villapiana Scalo.

Monte Pollino

There are two explanations for the name Pollino: the first is based on the Latin *pullus* (young animal) whence *Mons Pullinus*, the Mountain of the Young Animals, referring to the ancient custom of driving new-born cattle up to graze on the massif's high pastures in spring; the second derives Monte Pollino from the Latin *Mons Apollineus*, the Mountain of Apollo, god of health and the first physician, because of the great variety of medicinal herbs that grow on its slopes.

Whatever the case may be, Monte Pollino is one of southern Italy's higher, wilder and more beautiful mountain systems. If you arrive from the south by autostrada, it appears as an immense rocky wall running 'across the grain' of the Apennine chain. For centuries it has formed the boundary between Calabria and Basilicata, isolating the latter from the rest of Italy.

Formed largely of limestone, dolomitic limestone, flysch and ophiolite and populated by wolves, eagles and a unique variety of pine, **pino loricato**, it is one of the last remaining wilderness areas in the Mediterranean. Myth and mystery come together here, in a setting of rugged natural beauty punctuated by austere stone hamlets and villages. Together, the variety and beauty of its landscape, the unspoilt character of its natural environment, its broad, open horizons and bright, crystalline skies make Monte Pollino an ideal place for walking. A few, relatively easy itineraries follow.

1 • Pedarreto ~ Piano Ermite ~ Monte Grasta ring walk

This 6.5km circuit (4 hours) entails an altitude gain of just 200m (skiing possible). It starts and ends on the highland known as Piano Pedarreto (1350m), a broad, panoramic terrace overlooking the Valle del Mercure. The plateau is made up of a series of rolling, grassy hills backed by the superb beech forests of the Coppola di Paola (Dome of Paola) and bordered on the north by the spectacular Vallone di Mauro. The presence of numerous cold springs, copious even in late summer, makes it an excellent place to picnic.

Your trailhead is a mountain refuge called Rifugio Fasanelli (☎ 0973 661008, parking), near Rotonda. Leaving the refuge, follow the road that descends to Rotonda for about 200m, then turn left along a dirt forest road. After c 1.5km you reach (right) the Fontana di Ermite, where the spring water flows into a basin carved out of a beech trunk. Though *piano* means plateau, Piano Ermite is actually a series of grassy terraces. Beyond the little clump of trees near the centre of the meadow the road forks; bear uphill left, round a curve, and after a brief steep climb reach the Passo della Tavolara (1455m). From here the trail, which may be barely visible, descends into the woods, coming out in the broad clearing of Piano di Marolo. Skirt the left (uphill) side of the clearing, walk around a small pond, then enter the forest again near an obvious stone marker. At the lower end of the clearing is a little spring known as the Fontana di Marolo.

You now follow an old mule track through the beech forest, which here is characterised by small sinkholes even on the mountainside to the left (the north slope of the Cozzi dell'Anticristo). After a considerable tract between moss-covered boulders, emerge from the woodland onto the grassy Piano Coppone. Cross the meadow, bearing right on a trail that climbs over the small wooded spur between Piano Coppono and Piano Morfino. The latter appears as a series of grassy steps progressing upwards towards the broad meadows of the Sella di Monte Grasta. From the saddle, the summit of the mountain is just a few paces away.

Return to the saddle from the summit and continue along the trail, which enters the forest on the left, rejoining your outbound trail at Piano Ermite.

2 • Colle dell'Impiso ~ Serra del Prete ring walk

Four and a half hours, moderately strenuous. This is a more challenging, 8km circuit with an altitude gain of 670m (skiing possible), overlooking the broad, beautiful Valle del Frido. It starts from Colle dell'Impiso (1570m), the pass between the Timpone di Mezzo and Serra del Prete (Colle dell'Impiso means Hangman's Hill in dialect—a haunting reminder of the times of brigandage). The nearest towns are San Severino Lucano and Viggianello, both in the Parco Nazionale del Pollino.

At Colle d'Impiso you take the clearly-marked trail that begins on the uphill side of the road, at the highest point of the pass. Follow this easy trail until it emerges from the forest in the open pastures that cover the morainic highlands of the Piani di Vacquarro.

Turn downhill and right along a forest road, which, after a few hundred metres, ascends the Valloncello di Viggianello. Continue to climb along the main road, ignoring all turnings. The road ends in the broad, grassy meadow of the Colle Gaudolino (there is a shepherd's hut on the right, at the edge of the forest). About 100m before entering the meadow, a few metres below the road, is a copious spring, called Sorgente Spezzavummola, so-named because the force of its waters are enough to break a *vummola*, or traditional terracotta jug.

A few paces further on, you come out onto the hill of Colle Gaudolino. Turn right, skirting a group of rocks, beyond which begins the broad, clear trail that climbs to the south-east bastion of the Serra del Prete. Beyond the forest you reach the peak (2180m) across broad open meadows, without a fixed path.

From the peak descend along the north crest, which leads directly to the Colle dell'Impiso. Keep right all the way down; the minor crest that diverges left will put you on the paved road to Piano Ruggio, several kilometres from your car.

3 • Colle d'Impiso to Monte Pollino by the north-east crest

Five and a half hours, strenuous. This is a tough but rewarding climb (3.5km up and 2km back) to the top of Monte Pollino (2241m), altitude gain 800m (skiing possible). From Colle dell'Impiso take the forest road that descends to the Piani di Vacquarro; when you reach the first plateau, ignore the trail that turns uphill right and follow the one that skirts a brief wooded stretch of the Torrento Frido before entering the second Vacquarro plateau. Continue along the forest road until, after a long stretch along the hillside, it turns sharply right and enters a broad, flat clearing with large, lone beech trees: the Radura di Rummo.

Beyond the clearing continue straight on, following the straight trail that rises gently towards the east, ignoring the turning on the left. You reach a small, flat clearing where the trail ends. Carry on in the same direction, leaving the clearing and climbing through the woodlands by a steep path.

Several hundred metres later you leave the forest and reach the first sinkholes at the south-east end of the Piano di Toscano, the first of the three Piani di Pollino, or Pollino highlands. Turn immediately right, climbing up the clearly distinguishable crest of the round spur of Monte Pollino, without a fixed path but exploiting the openings in the brush.

Leaving the latter behind, climb to the peak keeping slightly left, towards the top of the gully that marks the mountain's north-east face. For the best views, stick to the more exposed part of the spur all the way to the summit.

The Crati Valley

Road 105 winds south from Castrovillari to Firmo, beyond which a turning on the left leads to **Altomonte** (9km), and the splendid Gothic church of **Santa Maria della Consolazione**. This is one of the more interesting Gothic buildings in Calabria, constructed, possibly by Sienese architects, under the patronage of Filippo Sangineto, Count of Altomonte, during the Angevin period. The simple façade, which dates from 1380, contains a large rose window. Within is the splendid tomb of the founder, by a follower of Tino di Camaino (c 1350).

The former Dominican convent adjoining the church houses a small museum (open daily 08.30–13.00, 16.00–20.00; ☎ 0981 948464) with works of art removed from the church. These include small remains of frescoes, three parts of a triptych by an artist close to Bernardo Daddi, a *Madonna and Child* of the 15C Neapolitan-Catalan school, and two small panels in alabaster of 1380, related to French art of the period.

Beyond Castrovillari the autostrada and Road 19 descend towards the Coscile Valley. **Spezzano Albanese** (320m, population 8000) is pleasantly spread out on a hillside and the local medicinal springs are exploited as a spa. The costume and dialect of the inhabitants proclaim their descent from Albanian refugees who fled before the Turks and settled here in the 15C. The people are noticeably tall and fair among the small, dark Calabrians.

A few kilometres south of Spezzano on Road 19, another road (106b) leads east to **Terranova**, where the convent of Sant'Antonio contains rich Baroque work and the cloister has charming rustic frescoes. The road continues to the Ionian coast via Corigliano Calabro and Rossano.

The autostrada enters the Crati Valley, notable for its wide expanses of gravel. In summer, the temperature here can reach scorching heights. In the hills to the east lie Bisignano and Acri, both towns of growing importance in the Calabrian hydro-electric scheme. At Bisignano remains of a Byzanto-Norman castle can be seen and, in the church of the Riformati, a *Madonna della Grazia* of the school of Antonello Gagini (1537).

Isolated in the mountains 15km north of Acri is **San Demetrio Corone** (population 4000), the most important Albanian colony in Calabria, with an Italo-Albanian college founded in 1791 by Ferdinand I. The 11C or 12C church of **Sant'Adriano** contains a Norman font with a representation of a monkey sitting on two dragons(?) and four pieces of pavement with snakes, birds and leopards, also dating from the Norman construction.

Cosenza

Cosenza (population 104,000), a provincial capital of Calabria, stands at the confluence of two rivers. The old town, overshadowed by its castle, descends to the River Crati, whereas the growing modern city lies to the north, beyond the Busento, on level ground. The historic city centre is crossed by the winding Corso Telesio.

History of Cosenza

Cosenza succeeds *Cosentia*, the capital of the Bruttians, which came early under the influence of the Greek settlements of Magna Graecia. Taken by

Rome in 204 BC, in Imperial times it was an important stop on the Via Popilia, linking Rome with Reggio and Sicily. Alaric the Visigoth died here in AD 412 (probably of malaria) on his way back to Sicily after the sack of Rome. Legend holds that he was buried along with his treasure in the bed of the Busento River, the waters having been diverted for the occasion and then restored to their natural channel. Twice destroyed by the Saracens, the town was conquered by Robert Guiscard, but it rebelled against the rule of his half-brother Roger, who managed to restore his authority only after a siege (1087). In the 13C, 14C, and 15C the city shifted its loyalties several times in the struggle between the Aragonese and the Angevins, and Louis III of Anjou died here in 1434 while campaigning against the Aragonese.

A notable centre of humanistic culture in the 16C, Cosenza was the birthplace of the philosopher Bernardino Telesio (1509–88), whose ideas were instrumental in freeing scientific research from theological restrictions. The city contributed freely to the liberal movement in the 19C and participated in the uprisings of 1848 and 1860. It was damaged by earthquakes in 1783, 1854, 1870 and 1905, and frequently bombed in 1943. Today it is an important commercial and agricultural centre. The University of Calabria, Italy's newest and most modern, lies on the outskirts to the north.

Though there are fewer hairdressers today, old Cosenza retains much of the charm that so struck Gissing. The **cathedral**, in the Gothic style of Provence, was consecrated in 1222 in the presence of Frederick II. The inside was reworked in the Baroque style in 1750 and the façade made over in 1831; both, however, have been restored to their original states. The **façade**, with its three Gothic portals, large central rose window and two smaller rose windows at the sides, is one of the more graceful in Calabria. It is ideally complemented by its surroundings.

The **interior** is simple, with a nave and two aisles divided by piers, and an elevated presbytery. The apse was restored in a neo-Gothic manner and frescoed at the end of the 19C. In the south aisle, at the foot of the stairs to the presbytery, is a Roman sarcophagus; in the north transept is the lovely **tomb of Isabella**, wife of Philippe la Hardi, who died in 1270 after falling from her horse while returning to France from Sicily (some authorities say her body was returned to Saint-Denis).

Behind the cathedral, beyond the Provincial Office Building, extends the newly restored **Villa Comunale**, a lovely public garden with native and exotic plants, arranged and lighted (for evening viewing) with great care. In the nearby Piazza XXV Marzo, with monuments commemorating Telesio and the brothers Bandiera, martyred patriots of the Calabrian rising of 1844, stand the Biblioteca Civica and the Museo Civico Archeologico (open Mon–Fri 08.00–14.00, Mon and Thur 15.30–18.30; ☎ 0984 813324), housing a modest collection of antiquities from excavations in the city and in the environs.

From a point in Via Telesio opposite the cathedral, Via del Seggio climbs to an old quarter with many interesting details. The church of **San Francesco d'Assisi** has a 13C doorway and a plain cloister. Within (open daily 09.00–13.00) is a small collection of paintings by local artists of the 15C to the 18C. The adjoining offices of the Soprintendenza contain an extraordinary **Byzantine reliquary cross** in gold and enamel work with Greek lettering, presented by Frederick II on the occasion of the consecration of the cathedral (visi-

George Gissing's observations

'To call the town picturesque is to use an inadequate word', wrote George Gissing in his 1901 travelogue, *By the Ionian Sea*. 'At every step, from the opening of the main street at the hill-foot up to the stern medieval castle crowning its height, one marvels and admires. So narrow are the ways that a cart drives the pedestrian into shop or alley; two vehicles (but perhaps the thing never happened) would with difficulty pass each other. As in all towns of southern Italy, the number of hairdressers is astonishing, and they hang out the barber's basin—the very basin (of shining brass and with a semicircle cut out of the rim) which the Knight of La Mancha took as substitute for his damaged helmet.'

ble on request). The small enamel panels depict the four Evangelists, the Madonna, and the symbols of Christ. The pedestal dates from the 18C.

The ruined **castle** (383m) was the site of Louis II of Anjou's marriage to Margaret of Savoy (1434). It commands good views. A steep staircase to the right of the church of San Francesco descends to the point at which the two rivers meet. The 16C church of San Francesco di Paola stands beyond the River Crati.

A scenic route to Catanzaro

Beyond Cosenza, Road 19 leaves the autostrada and crosses the peninsula to Catanzaro, 81km south-east. Though highly scenic, this route is notorious for its hills and bends and requires attentive driving. Proceeding south, pass (left) a road offering alternative routes across the Sila highland, via either Lago Arvo or Lago Ampollino to Santa Severina. **Rogliano** has an elegant church of 1544, restored in 1924. The road descends in curves to the Savuto (the *Sabutus flumen* of the ancients), then mounts to **Carpanzano,** where the parish church has a Renaissance façade and inlaid wooden altars. The vista opens over the Savuto Valley, known for its wines.

The road climbs steeply to the Passo di Agrifoglio, 928m, then through dense forests to a second pass 936m high, beyond which it crosses the wooded Borboruso highlands. At Soveria Manelli, a road diverges right to Nicastro and Sant'Eufemia Lamezia. Bear south-east, crossing the watershed between the Ionian and Tyrrhenian seas. The view extends over broad woodlands and, at a certain point, embraces the Gulfs of Sant'Eufemia and Squillace in a single glance. The road continues to wind, offering magnificent **views** over the two seas. Monte di Tiriolo lies ahead. **Tiriolo** (population 4000), where the women wear a charming native costume, is delightfully situated on a ridge. The road descends in zigzags, affording more beautiful views.

Alternatively, the fast way to Catanzaro follows Autostrada A3 from Cosenza to (61km) Sant'Eufemia-Lamezia, from where Road 280 crosses the narrow Isthmus of Catanzaro, reaching the city in 34km.

LA SILA

The plateau of La Sila, inhabited by descendants of the Bruttians, is an irregular expanse of gneiss and granite 1000–1300m above sea level. It occupies the area between the Ionian Sea on the east, the steep Crati Valley on the north and west and the Marcellinara ridge beyond the Corace Valley on the south-west. It is divided into three parts: the **Sila Greca** to the north (which includes the Albanian colonies in Calabria); the **Sila Grande** and the **Sila Piccola** to the south, divided roughly by the Rogliano–Crotone road. The highest peak is Monte Botte Donato (1928m).

The forests of the Sila plateau were renowned by the ancients for the wood they supplied for shipbuilding, but deforestation has left much of the area free for pasture. This condition is being slowly corrected by controlled cutting and careful replanting. The climate is harsh in winter (snow does not disappear from the mountain tops until May) and mild in summer, offering a pleasant escape from the often stifling heat of the Calabrian coast. Olive, oak, poplar and fruit trees grow at the lower altitudes, intermixed with vineyards and the typical, low-growing macchia mediterranea. Above 700m these give way to chestnut, turkey oak and broad expanses of cereal crops. The area above 1200m is characterised by alders, aspens, maples and a native pine (*Pino larico calabrico*) that grows to over 40m in height, often in dense groves. On the higher peaks are beech trees and, in some areas, silver fir, once much more common. Snowdrops bloom in February/March, followed, in late April–June by daffodils, jonquils, violets and small orchids. In June/July the pine forests abound with wild strawberries, and in September/October, with exquisite mushrooms. In autumn, the contrast of red beech trees against dark firs is splendid. Woodland animals, particularly foxes, hares, martens, wild boar, roe deer, squirrels and a rather ferocious variety of wolf, are still present in large numbers. Wildfowl include interesting native species of partridge. Vipers may be found in all the wilder areas, and the lakes and streams abound with trout.

Practical information

Information offices

COSENZA *Ufficio Informazioni e di Accoglienza Turistica*, Corso Mazzini 92, ☎ 098 427271.
Azienda di Promozione Turistica, Corso Mazzini 92, ☎ 098 427485.
REGIONE CALABRIA
✉ turismo.regione.calabria.it.

Getting there and getting around
By road

North/south access to the Sila is provided from the Tyrrhenian coast by Autostrada A3/E45 and from the Ionian coast by Road 106. The best routes across the highlands are from Cosenza to Crotone (126km) by Roads 107/E93

and 106; and from Camigliatello or San Giovanni in Fiore to Catanzaro (c 100km) by Roads 107, 108b, 179d, 109b and local roads.
By rail

The only station serving La Sila is San Giovanni in Fiore from Cosenza Casali station in 2hrs 30mins.

Where to stay
CAMIGLIATELLO SILANO € *Aquila-Edelweiss*, Via Stazione, ☎ 0984 578044, 🖷 0984 578753, ✉ haquila@fidad.it. A modest place with adequate rooms and excellent restaurant; open all year.
CROTONE €€ *Costa Tiziana*, Via per Capocolonna, ☎ 0962 25601,

0962 21427. In a garden near the sea a few kilometres outside the town, with tennis courts and two pools.

Eating out
CAMIGLIATELLO SILANO € *La Tavernetta*, Contrada San Lorenzo 14, ☎ 0984 579026. Tasty dishes prepared with native Sila mushrooms (and more); closed Wed (except in summer) and late Nov–early Dec.

CERVA € *Mundial 82*, Via Daniele 221, ☎ 0961 939481. Trattoria-pizzeria in a quiet village of the Sila Piccola, between Sersale and the sea; closed Tues (except in summer).

TAVERNA €€ *Sila*, Via Villaggio Mancuso 3, at Villaggio Mancuso, ☎ 0961 922032. Good home cooking in a small hotel restaurant; closed Tues.

Sila Grande

The route over the Sila from Cosenza to the Ionian coast crosses some of the finer countryside in Calabria. The first part of the journey passes through rolling green highlands, touching upon the lovely **Lago di Cecita** and running near **Lago Arvo**. Beyond San Giovanni in Fiore the landscape becomes more arid and dramatic as the road descends to the sea and town of Crotone.

From Cosenza the road winds up the west slope of the Sila. The air becomes noticeably cooler on approaching Celico (805m, population 3000), birthplace of the Abbot Gioacchino da Fiore, a hermit and mystic whose writings are still important today in the study of theology and depth psychology (see below). Immediately afterwards, you touch upon **Spezzano della Sila** (850m, population 5000), a locally important centre in a splendid position overlooking Cosenza. The sanctuary of San Francesco has a 15C Gothic door and 17C wooden choir stalls. The neighbouring village of Spezzano Piccolo (750m), with its unusual campanile, is reached by a turning on the right. The landscape takes on a more alpine appearance.

Camigliatello Silano (1275m) is a summer and winter sports resort. From here a minor road leads west to Fago del Soldato, a village of small wooden houses among pine woods, from which the Botte San Donato may be climbed in c 3 hours. Springs along the way offer excellent mineral waters. The combined use of timber and corrugated steel is characteristic of local architecture.

A few kilometres north of Camigliatello, **Lago di Cecita**, also called Lago di Moccone, sits in a wide valley among pastures and fields of grain, at an altitude of 1135m. It was created by damming the Moccone, and like Lakes Arvo and Ampollino, its waters are used to generate electricity. To the south lies Monte Botte Donato, to the east Monte Pettinascura, to the north Monti Altare and Sordello, to the west the Serra la Guardia. The road from Camigliatello winds along the east shore. At Forge di Cecita, a turning on the right leads through dense forests to (4km) **La Fossiata**, a hamlet named after the nearby torrent. Planted with a variety of Silan flora, it is the showcase of the Forest Administration and a starting point for the ascent of the Serra Ripollata (1682m).

The road to San Giovanni in Fiore and Crotone leaves Camigliatello from the south. Woods gradually give way to broad fields of grain and pasture, affording views to the left of Lago di Cecita and the magnificent wood, Bosco di Gallopane, beyond. Further to the right the verdant slopes of Monte Pettinascura can be seen. The landscape is relatively flat here—you are crossing the highland plain at an altitude of roughly 1350m. Croce di Magara is a small hamlet. From here a secondary road follows the Neto Valley to Germano, at the foot of Monte Ruggiero. The route continues through rolling countryside, paralleled by the one-track railway. The road is joined by the road from Lorica, beyond which you follow the valley of the Garga. A few kilometres further on, a turning on the right winds south-west to Lago Arvo, shortly after entering the valley of the Arvo River, and the vista opens up to the Ionian Sea.

San Giovanni in Fiore (population 21,000), the chief town of the Sila, is somewhat mean and shabby in appearance. It grew up in the 12C around the Badia Florense, founded by Abbot Gioacchino, who enjoyed a wide local reputation as a prophet. The attractive costumes of the women are celebrated and the town is famous for its textile trade. The abbey, a 13C Cistercian Gothic edifice of bare aspect, stands in the lower part of the town.

Gioacchino da Fiore

The theologian and mystic Gioacchino da Fiore (b. Celico, c 1130—d. San Giovanni in Fiore, 1202) lived at roughly the same time as St Francis of Assisi and Frederick II of Hohenstaufen. Originally a Cistercian monk, he soon came into conflict with the order, leaving it in 1190 to form the Florensi Order. Considered for centuries the work of a visionary or a prophet, his writings are among the higher achievements of monastic theology. They are still important today, because of their interpretation of the relationship between the godhead and the three persons of the Trinity as demonstrated in *Libellus de unitate et essentia Trinitatis* (now lost), and their critique of the Christocentric notion of history in favour of a markedly Trinitarian conception (explained in *Liber concordiae Novi et Veteris Testamenti*, in which the 'end of history' is not perceived as the Second Coming of Christ, but as an age of freedom and harmony on earth ushered in by the Holy Spirit). Da Fiore accused those who held the traditional views of his time of *quarternitas*—of considering the divine substance as disjoined from the three persons, constituting an independent, fourth element. His position was formally condemned in 1215 by the Fourth Laterna Council.

Continuing to the east, you cross the River Neto (the *Neaethus* of Theocritus) and reach (10km) the turning for Caccuri, birthplace of Cecco Simonetta, secretary to Francesco Sforza, and of his brother Giovanni, who wrote a biography of the prince. After 12km bear right, leaving the new road for Crotone on the left. Across the Neto Valley lies Strongoli Petilia, on a ridgetop; ahead is the Ionian Sea. The deeply eroded landscape is known for its conical formations of clay, called *timpe*.

Santa Severina (population 3000), on an isolated outcrop of sheer rock, was a Byzantine and Norman fortress with a scholastic tradition. John of Salisbury notes that its inhabitants helped him with difficult passages of Aristotle. The sainted 8C pope Zacharias was a native. Here in 1950 began the expropriation of latifondia estates under the Sila reform act. The church of **San Filomeno** is built to a Byzantine plan, with three apses (only one being visible from the exterior).

he high cupola is reminiscent of Armenian constructions. Underneath is the
hurch of the Pozzolio, the exterior of which is adorned with good carved sur-
ounds. The Norman **cathedral** has been largely rebuilt; it has a main portal of
he 13C enclosed in a later surround showing provincial Renaissance-Baroque
aste. A Byzantine **baptistery** (8C–9C), built to a circular plan and incorporat-
ng pillars from a pagan edifice, is attached to the north side of the church; and
here is a small collection of liturgical objects in the former Palazzo Arcivescovile.
he old cathedral, or Addolorata, dates from the 10C. The castle, of the same
eriod (now a school), was rebuilt by Robert Guiscard.

Beyond Santa Severina there are beautiful views of the Neto Valley and the
ast coast. The village of Scandale (population 4000) stands on a site inhabited
ince prehistoric times. Beyond, Crotone and the sea dominate the horizon.

Sila Piccola

rom Camigliatello there are any number of routes you can take to reach **Lake
Arvo** (1280m). The most scenic passes near the summit of Monte Botte Donato
1928m); the easiest involves following Road 107 eastwards for a few kilometres.
Lorica (1350m) is a small summer and winter resort set on the north shore of
he lake, between dense forests and rolling grain fields. Lake Arvo was created by
lamming the River Arvo near Nacelle. Tunnels convey its waters, together with
hose of Lago Ampollino, to the hydro-electric plants at Orichella, Timpa Grande
und Caluria, on the River Neto.

Twenty two kilometres west lies **Aprigliano** (population 3000), the medieval
Aprilianum, birthplace of the poet Domenico Piro. Nearby is the hermitage of San
Martino, where the Abbot Gioacchino is believed to have died (see above). The
hurch, with its single nave, wide transept and three semicircular apses, recalls
rench monastic architecture of the 11C.

The view opens up on all sides as you reach Colle Ascione (1384m). Beyond,
ou descend through forest to the valley of the River Savuto. Here Road 179d
ranches south towards Taverna and the Sila Piccola.

Lago Ampollino

Bearing left soon after the Colle Ascione pass you follow the Savuto Valley east to
ts source, crossing woods, pastures and fields planted with wheat and rye. You
hen descend the wooded Ampollino Valley, which widens below the forested
summit of Montenero (1881m) to form **Lago Ampollino** (1279m). The lake,
created by damming the Ampollino at the foot of Monte Zigomarru, is approximately 13km long and its waters are used to generate electricity. The road winds
around the wooded south bank. The view over the water is splendid. At the east
end of the lake you leave a road to (19km) Cotronei on the left and loop around
he south shore of the lake to the junction with Road 179d. The road descends
hrough dense pine woods, then climbs to Villaggio Racise, a much-frequented
summer resort. Further on lies **Villaggio Mancuso**, another important tourist
centre. Taverna lies 16km south.

At Taverna Road 109 leads east to the little village of **San Pietro**, where the
church of Santa Maria della Luce contains an interesting 17C wooden crucifix.
At **Zagarise**, the church of the Assunta has a fine Gothic façade of local granite,

with an ogival portal and rose window. Beyond, the road winds among the hills with good views at times to the coast. **Sersale** enjoys a position dominating the hills of the Marchesato.

Mesoraca (population 10,000) is built on a ridge between two mountain torrents. The former conventual church of the Ritiro (the monastery was destroyed by earthquake in 1783) contains some unusual paintings of the late Neapolitan school. At the church of the **Annunciata** a good 16C Madonna and Child graces the central portal. The church contains a series of marble inlaid Baroque altars of which the finest is the high altar, upon which stands a silver tabernacle. The sacristy has 18C woodwork. In the environs are the ruins of the Basilian monastery of Sant'Angelo di Frigilo and the **Santuario del Santissimo Ecce Homo**, which contains a *Madonna and Child* by Antonio Gagini (1504) and, in a chapel to the right, a venerated wooden figure of *Christ* attributed to Fra'Umile da Petralia (1600).

The town visible on the horizon beyond Mesoraca is **Petilia Policastro** (population 11,000). It was initially called simply Policastro (from the Byzantine *palaiokastron*, old castle). The second name was added in the mistaken belief that the town stood on the site of the Greek settlement of Petilia, now believed to have been located near Strongoli.

Taverna (population 3000) is set among the foothills of the Sila Piccola. Its name suggests that the village might have been a post-stage on the road from the Ionian coast to the Sila. The old town, which was located to the east of the present centre, was destroyed once by the Saracens and again by the *condottiere* Francesco Sforza.

Mattia Preti (1613–99), the Cavalier Calabrese, one of the more renowned painters of the 17C Neapolitan school, was a native of Taverna, and several of the town's churches contain paintings by him. The former convent of **San Domenico** (open Tues–Sun 09.30–12.30; May–Sept also 16.00–19.00 ☎ 0961 924824) houses the most notable of these, including, on the north side (first altar), *St John the Baptist*, in the lower right corner of which is a self-portrait of the artist dressed as a Knight of Malta (an honour bestowed on him by Pope Urban VIII after he had worked in the cathedral on the island); second altar, *Madonna with Saints*; third altar, *Crucifixion*; fifth altar, *Madonna of the Rosary*; behind the main altar, *Christ in Majesty*, possibly inspired by Michelangelo's Christ of the *Last Judgement*; on the south side (first altar) *Martyrdom of St Peter*; second altar, *St Francis de Paola*, resembling the painting of the same subject in the church of Sant'Agata degli Scalzi in Naples; third altar, *St Sebastian* (patron saint of the town); fourth altar, *Madonna and Saints* an early work; fifth altar, the *Infant Christ*. The furnishings of the church also merit inspection, as does the wooden ceiling. In the sacristy are Neapolitan paintings of later date as well as 17C and 18C furnishings.

Above the high altar in the nearby church of **San Nicola** is the handsome *Madonna della Purità*, commissioned by Giovanni Antonio Peorio and Lucrezia Teutonica, his wife, and probably executed in Emilia between 1636 and 1644. The painting is movable; in a niche behind is a large carved and painted bust of St Nicholas of Bari (1699).

The church of **Santa Barbara**, which formerly belonged to the Order of the Minims, contains several more of Preti's paintings, including a *Baptism of*

Christ, St Barbara being received into Heaven and the large *Patrocinio*, sent by the artist from Malta, in which the dead Christ is supported in the arms of his father. In the lower part of the painting appears a portrait of *Marcello Anania, Bishop of Sutri and Nepi*, once priest at Santa Barbara and Preti's first master. The church also contains finely crafted Baroque altars and figures, especially that of *St Sebastian* to the right of the entrance; and a *Crucifix* of the school of Fra'Umile da Petralia. On the outskirts of the village, in the church of San Martino, is a panel by Preti and his school.

As you descend beyond Taverna the character of the vegetation changes, with olive groves gradually mixing with oak and chestnut woods. **Catanzaro** is described on p 362.

THE TYRRHENIAN COAST OF CALABRIA

The Tyrrhenian coast of Calabria is famous in Italy for its superb beaches and picturesque villages. Beyond the lovely resort of **Maratea**, in Basilicata, the highway and railway run the whole length of Calabria beside the sea. To the east steep mountains separate the seaboard from the rest of the region, rising to heights of well over 1000m: in fact there are just two direct roads—from Lamezia to Catanzaro, and from Gioia Tauro to Gioiosa Ionica—between Calabria's Tyrrhenian and Ionian coasts. From Maratea all the way to Reggio Calabria the scenery is varied, the vegetation luxuriant, and there are spectacular views of the coastline, the Aeolian Islands, Sicily and the Straits of Messina. The white sandy beaches around **Tropea**, on the Monte Poro headland, are among the finest in the south. Motorists should bear in mind that traffic can be quite slow during the summer, when the seaside resorts are crowded.

Practical information

Information offices

PALMI *Ufficio Informazioni e di Accoglienza Turistica*, Piazza 1 Maggio, ☎ 0966 22192.

REGIONE CALABRIA
✉ turismo.regione.calabria.it.

VIBO VALENTIA *Ufficio Informazioni e di Accoglienza Turistica*, Via Forgiani 1, ☎ 0963 42008, ✉ www.costadei.net, aptvv@costadei.net.

Azienda di Promozione Turistica, Via Forgiani 8, ☎ 0963 42008, ✉ www.costadei.net, aptvv@costadei.net.

The tourist information offices at **Reggio Calabria** also provide information on this area, see p 366.

Getting there and getting around

By air

Airport at **Lamezia Terme**, on the Tyrrhenian coast 61km south of Cosenza, with direct flights to/from Bologna, Florence, Milan, Rome and Venice. Also at **Ravagnese**, 4km east of Reggio Calabria, with direct flights to/from Milan, Bergamo and Rome.

By road

The best way to explore the area from the north is to take Road 18, the *Costiera Tyrrenica*; or Autostrada A3/E45, the *Autostrada del Sole*, to Lagonegro, then Roads 585 and 18; from the south, a ferry or hydrofoil from Messina to Reggio di Calabria or Villa San Giovanni, then Autostrada A3/E45.

By rail

FROM NAPLES (Campi Flegrei, Mergellina, Centrale or Porta Garibaldi) to Reggio Calabria (Centrale), 476km in 4hrs 30mins by Eurostar or Intercity, stopping at Paola, Lamezia Terme, Vibo Valentia-Pizzo, Gioia Tauro and Villa San Giovanni. To Villa San Giovanni (where through trains to Sicily cross the Straits of Messina), in c 15mins less.
FROM MARATEA to Reggio, 283km in c 2hrs 45mins. To (139km) Lamezia Terme Centrale, junction for Catanzaro, in c 1hr 15mins. With a few exceptions, fast trains bear inland after Lamezia, returning to the coast at Gioia Tauro. A branch line serves Tropea and the picturesque towns of the Monte Poro headland.

By sea

Ferries and **hydrofoils** run throughout the year from Messina, in Sicily, to Reggio Calabria and Villa San Giovanni (20mins). There are also daily hydrofoils between Reggio Calabria, Messina and the Aeolian Islands (15mins–c 2hrs). For information and tickets, *Trenitalia Reggio Calabria*, ☎ 0965 97957 (ferries to Messina); *Aliscafi SNAV*, Stazione Marittima, ☎ 0965 892 012 (hydrofoils), ✉ www.snav.it. In summer (June–Sept) boats run between the Aeolian Islands and Tropea and Vibo Marina. Contact the information office in Vibo Valentia for details.

Where to stay

AMANTEA €
Mediterraneo, Via Dogana 64, ☎ 0982 426364, 🖷 0982 426247, ✉ mediterraneo1@libero.it. In a former townhouse in the historic centre of Amantea, with private beach.
CETRARO €€ *Grand Hotel San Michele*, SS18 at Bosco, ☎ 0982

91012, 🖷 0982 91430, ✉ www.sanmichele.it, sanmichele@sanmichele.it. In an early 20C villa overlooking the sea, with private beach, windsurfing, golf, tennis, pool, etc.; open Dec–Oct.
CITTADELLA DEL CAPO €€€
Palazzo del Capo, Via Cristoforo Colombo 5, ☎ 0982 95674, 🖷 0982 95676, ✉ www.palazzodelcapo.com, capo@palazzodelcapo.it. In a renovated 18C palace on the sea, with private garden, spacious rooms, pool and private beach; closing time varies.
GIZZERIA LIDO €€ *Marechiaro*, Strada Statale 18, ☎ 0968 51251, 🖷 0968 51854. Small (8 rooms), tasteful and on the sea, with outstanding breakfasts and restaurant; closed mid-Dec–mid-Jan.
PARGHELIA €€€ *Baia Paraelios*, Contrada Fornaci, ☎ 0963 600300, 🖷 0963 600074. Set in a luxuriant garden on the sea, with outdoor dining, private beach, three pools, tennis, windsurfing, sailing, diving and waterskiing; all rooms are suites with private patio; open Easter–Sept.
€€€ *Porto Pirgos*, Contrada Fornaci, ☎ 0963 600351, 🖷 0963 600690, ✉ www.portopirgos.com, info@portopirgos.com. A faux village set in luxuriant surroundings with pool, outdoor dining, private beach, etc.; open Easter–Sept.
SCALEA €€ *Grand Hotel De Rose*, ☎ 0985 20273, 🖷 0985 920194, ✉ hotelderose.it, info@hotelderose.it. A quiet place with comfortable rooms, garden and pool; closed Nov–Mar.
TROPEA € *Punta Faro*, Capo Vaticano, ☎ 0963 663139, 🖷 0963 663968. A small (25-room), family-run place overlooking the rocky headland and white-sandy beaches of Capo Vaticano; open June–Sept.

Eating out

AMANTEA € *Locanda di Mare*, Via Stromboli 20, ☎ 0982 428262. Trattoria run by a family of fishermen; closed Mon.

BAGNARA CALABRA € *Taverna Kerkira*, Via Vittorio Emanuele 217, ☎ 0966 372260. Restaurant serving Greek-Calabrian dishes; closed Mon, Tues and Dec–Jan.

BELVEDERE MARITTIMO € *Sabbia d'Oro*, Piano delle Donne, ☎ 0985 88456. Good seafood, by the water; closed Tues and Nov.

BUONVICINO € *Il Mulino*, Contrada Maucera, ☎ 0985 85188. A farm serving local delicacies in a shady vale by a mill-stream; open July–Aug, daily except Mon.

DIAMANTE €€ *La Guardiola*, Via Lungomare Riviera Bleu, ☎ 0985 876759. Restaurant-pizzeria; closed Tues (except in summer) and Nov–Mar. Nearby (Via Amendola 3) is the *Accademia del Peperoncino*, a shop selling every possible variety of hot red pepper.

NICOTERA € *Da Vittoria*, Via Stazione 16, Nicotera Scalo, ☎ 0963 81358. Trattoria; open daily.

PALMI €€ *Rosa dei Venti*, Strada Provinciale per Marinella, ☎ 0966 21080. Seasonal and fish dishes, with summer seating outdoors; closed Wed (except in summer) Aug and late Dec.

PIZZO € *A Casa Janca*, Via Riviera Prangi at Marinella, ☎ 0963 264364. Farm serving traditional local cuisine; closed Wed (except in summer) and Nov, Jan, Feb.

RIZZICONI € *Osteria Campagnola della Spina*, Contrada Audelleria 2, ☎ 0966 580223. Trattoria; closed Mon and mid-Aug–mid-Sept.

SCALEA € *La Rondinalla*, Via Vittorio Emanuele III 31, ☎ 0985 91360. Family-run trattoria with summer seating outside; closed Sun (except in summer).

SCILLA €€ *Glauco*, at Chianalea di Scilla, ☎ 0965 754026. Family-run trattoria by the sea, with summer seating outside; closed Tues and Oct–Mar.
€€ *Grotta Azzurra*, Lungomare Cristoforo Colombo, ☎ 0965 754889. Good fish restaurant with outdoor seating and sea views; closed Mon and Dec.

SERRA SAN BRUNO € *Roseto*, at Roseto in Agro, ☎ 0963 70670. Lovely farm serving great country meals; open May–Oct.

TROPEA €€ *El Sol*, Largo Mercato, ☎ 0963 61174. Good regional cuisine with outdoor seating in summer; open all year.
€ *Osteria del Pescatore*, Via del Monte 7, ☎ 0963 603018. Good fish (but slow service) in a simple osteria in a picturesque lane near the cathedral; closed Wed (except in summer) and Nov–Mar.
€€ *Pimm's*, Largo Migliarese 2, ☎ 0963 666105. The fanciest place in town, overlooking the sea from a clifftop; closed Mon (except in summer) and Jan.
Delicious ice cream (especially fruit flavours) at *Gelateria Tonino*, Corso Vittorio Emanuele 52; and (chocolate, vanilla, etc.) at *Pasticceria Gelateria Tre Stelle*, Via IV Novembre.

VIBO VALENTIA MARINA €€ *L'Approdo*, Via Roma 22, ☎ 0963 572640. The best fish restaurant on the coast; closed Mon (except in summer).

VILLA SAN GIOVANNI €€ *Antica Osteria Vecchia Villa*, Via Gribaldi 104, ☎ 0965 751125. Old-fashioned trattoria just off the station square; closed Wed and Aug.

Into Calabria

Regardless of whether you arrive from Maratea or from Lagonegro, you enter Calabria just before **Praia a Mare** (population 6000). Above the town you can see the Santuario della Madonna della Grotta (reached by steps), containing a medieval wooden statue of the *Madonna and Child*, and another marble *Madonna* of the school of Gagini. Off the coast lies the **Isola di Dino**, a triangular plateau rising 65m above the sea, with grottoes showing the same light effect as at the Blue Grotto of Capri. The island may be reached by boat from Praia a Mare in c 20 minutes.

The road continues beside the sea to San Nicola Arcella, a charming little town (population 1000) on a hilltop, then it crosses Capo Scalea and descends once again to the sea. A turning on the left ascends to **Scalea** (population 9000), an attractive old town rising in steps above a good beach, now largely spoilt by development, and commanding good views of the cape, the sea and the fertile Lao delta. The latter is believed to be the site of the Sybarite colony of *Laos*, a flourishing commercial centre of the 6C and 5C BC that later fell to the Lucanians. Some Greek and Roman remains can be seen in Largo Cimalonga (open summer 09.00–13.00, 16.00–19.00; winter 09.00–13.00, 16.00–18.00). A Lucanian necropolis has recently come to light south of the river, near the site of the Roman *Lavinium*, remains of which are no longer visible. The church of **San Nicola** contains a tomb of 1343 that recalls the graceful Pisan Gothic style of Tino di Camaino. On the road from Scalea to Mormanno, deep in the hills, lies Papasidero, near which (car park; marked) is the rock shelter of **Il Romito**, with Palaeolithic graffiti depicting bulls and oxen (c 10,000 BC) discovered in 1961.

Back on the coast road, above Cirella, the ruined medieval town of Cirella Vecchia, destroyed by the French in 1806, is prominent on its hill. South of the town, on the beach before the fortified Isola di Cirella, are the remains of a Roman tomb.

Diamante, a fishing centre and resort, is noted for its cedar trees. Beyond, the road hugs the narrow coastal plain to **Belvedere Marittimo** (population 9000), which commands a splendid view of the sea and the coast. The Chiesa Matrice has a 15C Tuscan relief above the main door and the Chiesa del Crocifisso, a great wooden crucifix. The ruined medieval castle also merits a glance.

Cetraro has three statues by Giovanni Battista Mazzola (1533) in the church of the Ritiro. Guardia Piemontese and Montalto Uffugo, in the hills near here, were colonised by Waldensians in the late 14C, but these Protestant colonies were destroyed with great cruelty in 1559–61. Terme Luigiane is a sulphur spa. Fuscaldo (378m, population 9000) has a ruined castle and several Baroque churches.

Paola, once an attractive town (population 18,000), has been entirely transformed by unchecked development as a resort. It was the birthplace of San Francesco da Paola (1416–1507), founder of the Minims, the strictest order of the Franciscans. The **Santuario di San Francesco**, above the town to the north, dates from 1435 and is fronted by a long piazza with a modern statue and an obelisk commemorating the Holy Year of 1950. The basilica, dedicated to Santa Maria degli Angeli, has been restored in recent times; its façade is an unusual mixture of Renaissance and Baroque motifs. The interior contains the 16C Cappella del Santo and 15C and 16C artworks of the Neapolitan school; adjacent is a small cloister. In central Paola are several churches of minor interest. The **Santissima Annunziata**, high in the town, built in the 13C and later redecorated in the Baroque manner, has been restored to its former state. Above the high altar, with its marble inlay, is a 16C painting of the *Annunciation*. A descent may be made by steps (left), passing a pleasing Baroque fountain, through the Porta San Francesco, with another fountain at its centre. Rising at the back you can see the Baroque façade of the church of Santa Maria di Monte Vergine. **Santa Caterina**, with a Gothic portal of 1493, houses a painting of the *Madonna delle Grazie* attributed to Domenico Beccafumi.

A mountain road to Cosenza

Road 107 runs inland from Paola to Cosenza (32km). A bus runs several times daily from Paola station to Cosenza in one and a half to two hours, substituting for the train. The appeal of this route lies in the striking views from the high mountains of the **Catena Costiera**, the range that separates the Tyrrhenian seaboard from the plain formed by the rivers Crati and Busento. After leaving Paola, the road climbs steeply up the west slope of the Catena Costiera among vineyards and orchards, and through dense forests of oak, chestnut, and beech trees. There are splendid **views** through the trees to the sea. The **Passo della Crocetta** (950m) offers a breathtaking panorama that extends from the volcanic cone of Stromboli and the other Aeolian Islands to the west across the broad Crati Valley and east to the Sila. The descent to Cosenza begins here, through the fields and forests that dominate the Crati Valley.

San Fili (population 3000) enjoys a good location on a hilltop, among woods and farms. The Chiesa Parrochiale dell'Assunta has a Baroque portal and interesting choir stalls of inlaid wood (1801). At seven kilometres a road diverges right to **Rende**, where the Palazzo Municipale was built in the 12C or 13C by remodelling a castle initially dating from 1095. The Palazzo Zagarese (Via del Bartolo; open daily 09.00–13.00) contains a small museum of folk art and painting. The descent continues among woodlands and olive groves to the valley floor. At ten kilometres turn right onto Road 19 and enter Cosenza from the north (see p 333).

South of Paola

Beyond Paola, the road runs parallel to the main railway line (and the coast) past the convent of Sant'Antonio to **San Lucido**, a charming little town (population 6000) on a promontory overlooking the sea. Cardinal Fabrizio Ruffo (1744–1827), the Bourbon politician and collaborator of Fra' Diavolo, was born in the castle here. 8km along a minor road leads left to **Fiumefreddo Bruzio** (population 4000), where parts of the medieval town walls and two gates can still be seen. The church of the Matrice possesses an 18C wooden crucifix. **Santa Chiara** has a wooden coffered ceiling, coloured majolica-tile floors and three carved and gilded wooden altars. In San Francesco da Paola is a tomb of the Mendoza family. The church of the **Carmine**, on a hill east of the village, has a 15C Gothic portal and remains of a cloister. A dirt track to the north leads in c 1 hour to the ruined abbey of **San Domenico** or Fonte Laurato, originally dating from 1020–35, interesting for its mixture of Byzantine and Norman architectural elements.

Amantea (population 12,000) extends downwards from its ruined castle to the beach. A modest centre in Roman times, the town has been identified with the

Clampetia of Livy. It was vehemently defended against the French under Verdier in 1806, but has resisted the recent onslaught of builders and holiday-makers less successfully. The ruins of the medieval church and convent of **San Francesco d'Assisi**, in the upper part of the town, and those of the vast **castle** on its hilltop, offer splendid views of the sea and the coastline. In the lower town, the 15C church of **San Bernardino da Siena** is fronted by a portico with five Gothic arches on octagonal piers, with ceramic decorations. The first north chapel contains a *Madonna* by Antonio Gagini (dated 1505) and other sculpture.

Beyond Capo Suvero, where you have a view of the whole curve of the Gulf of Eufemia and, on a clear day, of Stromboli and the Aeolian Islands, you enter the Piana di Sant'Eufemia. This intensely cultivated plain is encircled by beautiful mountains, the lower slopes of which are covered with olive groves. **Sant'Eufemia Lamezia**, a modern town, is the road and railway junction for Catanzaro and the Ionian resort areas. It is the sum of five distinct villages, the most impressive being **Nicastro** (11km north-east), the old *Neocastrum* of Byzantine or Norman origin, almost entirely destroyed by an earthquake in 1638. Charmingly built, on the mountainside, it is dominated by the ruins of one of Frederick II's **castles**, the prison of his rebellious son Henry, who escaped only to die mysteriously at Martirano, 16km north-west. The local costumes worn by women are beautiful. From here you may join the Cosenza–Catanzaro road at Soveria Mannelli or Tiriolo.

> ### Maida Vale
> East of Lamezia rises the plateau of Maida. The Battle of Maida, by which the British, under Sir John Stuart, expelled the French from Calabria in 1806, gave its name to Maida Vale in London. This battle proved the value of the rifle and the 'thin red line' tactics put to successful use in the Peninsular War.

Pizzo, a prosperous little town (population 9000) traditionally engaged in fishing for tuna and swordfish, is now also a resort. In the old **castle** (erected in 1486 by Ferdinand I of Aragon and partially restored) Joachim Murat, ex-king of Naples, was tried by court-martial and shot on 13 October 1815, five days after he had landed in an attempt to recover his throne. The church of **San Giorgio** contains a number of marble statues, among which may be noted a 16C St John the Baptist and a regal figure of St Catherine of Alexandria. From the narrow streets of the medieval town there are extensive views of the coast; below, the rock on which the settlement stands (*Lu Pizzo* in local dialect) plunges straight into the sea.

Vibo Valentia

The Greeks called Vibo Valentia (population 34,000), *Hipponion*, after the horses they bred on the high pastures of the Monte Poro plateau. It was a place of some military importance described by Cicero as an *illustre et nobile municipium*. An important intellectual centre in the late 18C, it was the provincial capital under Murat, a status it has recently regained. It contributed enthusiastically to the cause of unity during the Risorgimento.

The church of **Leoluca** (or Santa Maria Maggiore) is splendidly decorated with fine 18C stucco work and large bas-reliefs of an excellent Baroque exuberance. The last chapel on the north side contains a superb marble group of the *Madonna between St John the Evangelist and Mary Magdalen* (notice the fine bas-reliefs on the bases). These are the last works of Antonio Gagini (1534). In the chapel opposite can be seen statues of the *Madonna and Child and St Luke*, of the Gagini school. On the high altar is a *Madonna and Child* attributed to Girolamo da Santacroce. Two Romanesque lions in the sacristy once formed part of an earlier façade of the church. The **Chiesa del Rosario** (1280, rebuilt in the 18C) contains a strange Baroque wooden pulpit rising from a confessional. Beyond the balustrade to the high altar, on the right, stands the Cappella Crispo, a Gothic construction dating from the 14C. **San Michele** is an exquisite little Renaissance church dating from the early 16C with a fine but somewhat over-shadowing campanile of 1671.

The magnificently restored **Castello Normanno-Svevo**, on a hilltop over-looking the town, houses the **Museo Archeologico Statale Vito Capialbi**. The museum (open daily 09.00–20.00; ☎ 0963 43350) preserves a fascinating col-lection of finds from the necropoleis of *Hipponium*, beautifully displayed and lighted. The visit begins on the first floor, with rooms devoted to the Greek sanc-tuaries at *Scrimbia* (7C–5C BC) and *Cofino* (6C–4C BC), and the city walls of Hipponion (6C–3C BC). Highlights include a splendid group of bronze helmets on the first floor, and a fascinating gold laminate bearing an Orphic inscription, on the ground floor. The other ground-floor rooms host temporary exhibitions.

A cypress-lined road at the north edge of the town leads to the cemetery; half-way along on the left are the imposing remains of the **Greek walls** (best seen at sunset), which include the foundations of several large towers. The huge sand-stone blocks are weathering badly and have been enclosed in a temporary pavil-ion. On the other side of the road, in the Parco della Rimembranza or Belvedere, can be seen the somewhat scanty remains of a late 6C or early 5C Doric temple.

South of Vibo Valentia the autostrada crosses rolling countryside with farms and olive plantations, returning to the coast near Palmi. From here it runs high above the coast towns, offering more stunning **views** of the Tyrrhenian Sea and, finally, of the Strait of Messina and Sicily before entering Reggio Calabria.

The Monte Poro headland

The coast road continues along the sea, past the busy industrial port of Vibo Marina to Briattico, a farming and fishing town located between two lovely beaches, La Rocchetta to the north and Le Galere to the south. From here the road follows the railway to Tropea (population 7000), still perhaps the most pic-turesque of the several small fishing towns that line the rocky coast between Sant'Eufemia Lamezia and Gioia Tauro.

Tropea

Huddled on a cliff above the sea, Tropea commands stunning views of the coast and, on clear days, of the Aeolian Islands. Below, broad white sandy beaches extend to the north and south for more than 4km.

History of Tropea

The origin of the town is uncertain. The most likely hypothesis holds that it was founded by the Greeks, whose initial interest probably focused on its nat-ural harbour (which Pliny the Elder calls *Portus Hercules*, in reference to the popular belief that the hero was the first to realise its importance). Excavations have revealed remains of Greek and Roman settlements, now chiefly in the archaeological museum in Reggio Calabria, as well as an extensive proto-Villanovan necropolis. A Siculan centre has recently been identified at Torre Galli, c 4km south-east of the town. During the Middle Ages Tropea provided a natural fortress for those members of the lesser nobility and the middle class who sought respite from their feudal obligations. The numerous extant palaces, with fine sculpted doorways, attest to this tradition.

From Piazza Ercole, at the centre of the town, Via Roma leads north to Largo Duomo and the **cathedral**, a Norman construction rebuilt several times in the 17C and 18C and restored to its 'original' state in 1926–32. The east flank, with its false arcade and inlaid ornamentation, and the Gothic arcade adjoining the main façade, give the church a rare grace and beauty. The three-aisled interior is impressive in its simplicity. It contains a 14C wooden crucifix, a marble ciborium of Tuscan workmanship and an interesting double tomb with effigies of a brother and sister, to which the tondos representing the Annunciation, now mounted on the interior walls, also belonged. At the end of the south aisle stands an extremely fine statue of the *Madonna and Child* by Giovanni Angelo Montorsoli. Behind the high altar, enclosed in a silver frame, can be seen the *Madonna di Romania*, supposedly painted by St Luke.

Throughout the old town are the once luxurious residences constructed by the lesser nobility and the rising middle class, now largely reduced to flats. The houses, distinguished by their carved **granite doorways** (often crowned by grotesque masks to ward off the evil eye) follow a common plan, with living quarters on the second and third floors and a spacious atrium on the ground floor. Although originally medieval, most were redesigned and rebuilt to Baroque canons; some, like Palazzo Toraldo, Via Glorizio 2, have beautiful courtyards with dramatic open staircases. Others, such as the Palazzo Toraldo di Francia (Via Lauro 12), were done over at the turn of the 19C in the Liberty style, an austere variant of Art Nouveau. More such designs may be seen in the early modern villas at the south-west edge of the old town.

Grocery shopping in Tropea

It's no secret that underdevelopment has its positive side, especially where the production and distribution of food is concerned. Generally speaking, the less you do to a fruit, vegetable, meat or cheese, the better (and more nutritional) it is. Calabria's slow entry into the twenty-first century has meant that many traditional products arrive in the shops with their flavours (and nutrients) intact: Calabrian beef, for instance, is among the best in Italy. What is more, the younger and more sensitive farmers of the region have been quick to capitalise on the fact that chemical fertilisers have never been used on their lands. They're now among the country's leading producers of organic fruits and vegetables and their spin-offs—jams, marmalades, olive spreads, sun-dried tomatoes, etc. Many of these products are whisked away to northern Europe. Others, however, can be found in the places where northern Europeans congregate in Calabria, and especially in Tropea, where there are several shops that sell nothing else.

Corso Vittorio Emanuele, the main street of Tropea, connects Piazza Ercole with the **affaccio**, a scenic overlook on a clifftop at the seaward end of the town.

Opposite, on a steep rock, are the remains of the Benedictine sanctuary of **Santa Maria dell'Isola**. This is reached from the Belvedere del Canone, another scenic overlook just a few blocks south of the affaccio, from where steps descend to the beach. The path that climbs to the church is lined with fishermen's caves; the garden behind offers outstanding views of the town, the coast and the Aeolian Islands. In mid-August the sun sets directly over Stromboli.

A day trip to Serra San Bruno

A good day trip can be made from Tropea to Serra San Bruno, 59km away by Roads 522, 18, and 182. From here you have the further option of descending to the Ionian coast.

Leave Tropea by the road to the station, passing beneath the railway and bearing left into open country, with good views back to the town and the sea. The road winds upwards through switchback turns amid woods and farmland; to the north-east the Serre Calabre range, dominated by the wedge-like mass of Monte Cocuzzo (1030m), is visible in the distance. A small road leads left to Drapia; further on, another leads right to Brattirò, known for its vineyards. At Caria, follow a sharp bend to the left and climb through a second series of curves to the Monte Poro plateau, an isolated formation rising little over 700m above the sea, particularly rich in archaeological finds. At Torre Galli, excavations conducted in 1922–23 revealed an extensive **necropolis** dating initially from the 9C BC and used for some 300 years thereafter. Over 330 trench or pit tombs were unearthed, as well as a few instances of cremation attributed to the infiltration of Greek influences. The artefacts found at the site are now in the National Museum in Reggio Calabria.

The road is crossed by another leading to Zungri and Spilinga. At the former airport of Vibo Valentia (now a military airfield) turn left on road 18 then right onto Road 182 to **Soriano Calabro** (population 3000), an important centre for agriculture and handicrafts, founded by the Normans and acquired in fee by the Dominican Order in the mid-17C. The monastery of San Domenico, founded in 1501, was one of the wealthier and more illustrious Dominican houses in Europe; it produced four popes and was visited by Charles V on his return from Tunisia (1535) and the philosopher Tomaso Campanella. The convent was destroyed by an earthquake in 1659 and again in 1753, rebuilt and destroyed by fire in 1917, and restored on a smaller scale in the 1920s. The earthquake of 1783 also devastated the town, causing extensive landslides and altering the river course.

The main street ascends to the town hall, then turns abruptly left. Steps at the right of the turning descend to the former main façade of the monastery, now a solitary ruin. The new church of **San Domenico**, constructed in the 19C, contains portraits of Benedict XIII and Innocent II (two of the four monks from Soriano who became pope) by a follower of Caravaggio, handsomely carved choir stalls and a painting depicting St Dominic dating from the late 15C or early 16C. The road continues to the village of Sorianello (in the church of San Giovanni, wooden Crucifix by the Flemish artist David Müller), then it ascends, in a series of curves, through dense forests of chestnut and holm oak. Higher up, firs and pines predominate.

Serra San Bruno

Serra San Bruno (population 7000) lies on a broad, wooded plateau. Founded in the late 11C by Bruno of Cologne, founder of the Carthusian Order, the town was originally intended to house the families of the lay dependants of the nearby monastery of Santo Stefano del Bosco and was held in fee by the latter until 1765. It now enjoys relative prosperity as a result of its woodworking industry. Its small wood and stone houses, often entered from external steps; the lace-like decoration around eaves and gables; and the graceful balconies with 17C iron-work make this one of the more charming mountain towns of Calabria.

The Baroque churches are notable for their carved granite façades. Chief among them is the **Chiesa Matrice** (also called San Biago) at the north end of the wide main street, constructed in 1795. Within, marble statues of St Stephen, St Bruno of Cologne, the Madonna and Child and St John the Baptist, originally in the certosa, stand against the first and third piers on either side of the nave. On their bases are bas-reliefs depicting the Stoning of St Stephen, St Bruno making peace between Count Roger and Robert Guiscard, the Nativity, and scenes from the Life of St John the Baptist, signed by David Müller and dated 1611. The figure of the Matrice (above the high altar), a fertility figure identified by the fruit or grain that she holds or that decorates her image, is rich in pagan allusions.

Further along the main street stands the church of the **Addolorata**, built in 1794. The bold curvilinear façade, with its broken lines and unusual proportions, reflects a taste that prevailed earlier in the century in more cosmopolitan centres. The interior contains a ciborium with bronzes and coloured marble reconstructed from the one designed for the certosa by Cosimo Fanzago in 1631 and destroyed by earthquake in 1783 (other fragments are in the cathedral of Vibo Valentia). Continue down the main street to the church of the **Assunta** (also called San Giovanni), which dates from the 13C. The Baroque façade, with its campanile and clock, was added in the 18C. In the suburb of Spineto, the church of the Assunta allo Spineto dominates a long, narrow piazza.

The abbey of **Santi Stefano and Brunone** enjoys a splendid location in a valley 2km south-west. Founded by St Bruno of Cologne at the end of the 11C on land donated by Roger, brother of Robert Guiscard, it houses an independent community of Carthusians. The members are bound by vows of silence, permanence, poverty and solitude, in emulation of the primitive monks of Egypt and Palestine. The present abbey, with its low walls and cylindrical towers, was built in the late 18C and early 19C. It adheres to the canons of Carthusian architecture, with two cloisters adjoining the church, surrounded by the living quarters of the lay brothers and the monks' cells. The visitable areas are entered from the **museum** (entrance marked; open 09.00–13.00, 15.00–18.00/20.00; ☎ 0963 70608). Here are displays regarding St Bruno and monastic life, and the ruins of the magnificent buildings of the earlier monastery destroyed by the earthquake of 1783. On top of the free-standing Doric façade of the former abbey church stand two massive stone pinnacles, turned out somewhat by the tremors. Behind rise the first two arches of the nave arcade (the church was built to a Greek cross plan with three aisles on double Doric piers and a dome at the crossing); in front and to one side stand the remains of the cloister. The new abbey (generally closed to visitors) is built in an austere Gothic-revival style. The church contains interesting woodwork by local craftsmen and a silver bust of St Bruno, containing the founder's skull.

Further along the road that leads from the village to the abbey is the little church of **Santa Maria del Bosco**, set in a charming valley and surrounded by a dense fir forest (paid parking, refreshments). Here Bruno of Cologne lived and died, in the company of a handful of followers from the Chartreuse of Grenoble. At the foot of the broad stairway before the church is the pool into which the saint plunged as penance. The waters of the pool are held to be miraculous. More walks, through lush vegetation and offering splendid views, may be made to Colle di Arena (locally, *La Crista*, 1104m) in c 3 hours and to Monte Crocco (1268m), in c 4 hours; both with broad views of the Serre, Monte Poro and the bays of Gioia Tauro and Sant'Eufemia.

To drive on to Stilo, on the Ionian coast, return towards the village, bearing sharply right at the Parco della Rimembranza onto road 110 for Monasterace. The road ascends through a magnificent forest of firs, pines and beech to a broad, open plateau occupied chiefly by farm and pasture land. At Passo di Pietra Spada (1335m) the descent to the Ionian sea begins, with spectacular views of the rocky, arid landscape that characterises the east side of the Serre. A road on the right diverges to Nardodipace (1086m), a new town built in 1955 to accommodate the inhabitants of a village destroyed by floods. The descent continues; after crossing a beech wood the road winds through some of the wildest and most dramatic landscapes in Italy. On a clear day the **view** stretches as far as the sea, with good prospects of Monte Consolino to the north-east and the steep slopes of Monte Stella, ahead. Mount Pazzano (410m) develops vertically along the slope of the latter. Leave Road 110 on the left for **Stilo** (described on p 363).

Around the cape

Head south from Tropea along the coast, following the road signs for Capo Vaticano. On the outskirts of the town, leave the cemetery on the right, following the road around to the left through verdant farmland, with good views to the sea, to Santa Domenica, where pleasant excursions may be made along the beaches at the base of the cliffs (footpath from the station). Soon after the road turns inland toward Ricadi, a village (population 4000) among fields of olives, wheat and onions. **Capo Vaticano**, a magnificent headland with good bathing beaches, lies to the south-west (overlook). After Coccorino the road hugs the coast, the cliffs falling straight into the sea on the right. The **view** is one of the more striking in all of Calabria. Ioppolo is a charming little village with a splendid prospect over the coastline to the south.

Nicotera (population 8000), an old town on a hill, has magnificent views of the sea and Gioia plain. Built on its present location by Guiscard, its name, recorded in ancient itineraries, remains unaltered. A walk through its winding streets can be rewarding. The **cathedral** (1785) has a *Madonna della Grazia* by Antonio Gagini, some fragments of bas-reliefs, and a wooden Crucifix, often displayed in the Museo Diocesano di Arte Sacra (Piazza Duomo 10; open 09.00–12.00/12.30, 15.30/16.00–18.00/19.00; ☎ 0963 81308). The Museo Civico Archeologico (open summer Tues–Sun 09.00–12.00, 16.00–20.00; winter 08.00–13.00; ☎ 0963 886166), on the main road, houses a collection of objects unearthed nearby, in the area between Marina di Nicotera (6km, bus) and the mouth of the River Mesima. Here archaeologists hypothesise the existence of a Roman emporium that may have served the Greek *Medma* (Rosarno); remains can be seen in the small *area archeologica* at Piano delle Vigne (open daily 08.30–13.30, 14.30–dusk). Iron Age tombs similar to those at Torre Galli have also been found in the area.

The Gioia plain

Beyond Nicotera you leave the coast and descend to the plain of Gioia Tauro, entering the area (extending south to Scilla) devastated by the earthquake of 1783. After 11km the road meets up with Road 18 and enters **Rosarno** (population 14,000), a busy modern town much ruined by unchecked building. The ancient colony of *Medma* is believed to have stood at Pian delle Vigne, nearby. Founded by the Locrians in the 6C BC, it passed back and forth between its parent city and Croton before finally gaining independence in the late 5C. It was the home of Philip of Medma, friend of Plato and possibly the author of the latter's posthumous works.

Across the plain lies **Gioia Tauro**, a sprawling city (population 18,000) with a small harbour and a popular beach, known principally for its olive production. The city is thought to stand on or near the site of the Locrian colony of *Metauron*, and excavations have revealed traces of the Greek necropolis and remains of Roman buildings.

On a hill, 15km south of Gioia Tauro, lies **Seminara**, once the most formidable fortress in Calabria. Here, in 1495, the Sieur d'Aubigny, Charles VIII's general, defeated Gonzalo de Cordoba in the only battle that Gran Capitan ever lost, and in 1503 was himself defeated by the Spaniard, Ugo de Cardona. The battles are commemorated in four contemporary bas-reliefs in the Casa del Comune. Now a centre of ceramic production, Seminara commands good views.

Sinopoli, 12km further on the same road, is a starting point for the ascent, by bridle path and footpath, of Montalto (1955m), the highest peak of the Aspromonte.

At the foot of the Aspromonte

Leave Gioia amid the heavy traffic that will characterise the route from here to Reggio Calabria. Cross the Petrace, beyond which the foothills of the Aspromonte (a wild, mountainous area described on pp 374–376) reach to the sea. The road, offering wide views across the Straits of Messina to Sicily, passes east of **Palmi** (population 19,000), which lies among olive groves half-way up the north slope of Monte Sant'Elia. More early 20C Liberty designs can be seen here. The centrally located **Casa della Cultura** houses several museums. The Museo Calabrese di Etnografia e Folklore Raffaele Corso (open Mon–Fri 08.00–14.00, Mon and Thur 15.00–18.00; ☎ 096 626 2250) has an extensive collection of ceramic materials, hunting and fishing equipment, tools and articles related to shepherdry, and sections devoted to religious life, popular superstitions, weaving and costumes. In the same building is a museum dedicated to Francesco Cilea, composer of *Adriana Lecouvreur*, born in Palmi in 1866. Also of interest are the Museo d'Arte Moderna and Museo Guerrisi (open as above) and the antiquarium, with a collection of materials from *Taurianum*, an ancient city destroyed by the Saracens, of which scant remains are visible between Palmi and Lido di Palmi.

Five kilometres south of Palmi a road (marked) on the right climbs to the summit of Monte Sant'Elia, commanding a splendid **view** across the Straits of

Messina to Sicily. On a clear day, Stromboli is also visible. To the south the high cliffs drop sheer into the sea.

Bagnara Calabra, in a lovely position on steep slopes terraced and planted with vineyards, is known for its sword-fishing in Apr–June. It has been destroyed several times by earthquakes, most recently in 1908. The Museo Angelo Versace (open daily except Thur 09.00–12.30, 15.30–19.30; ☎ 096 637 6007) houses a modest collection of antiquities from the Stone Age to Norman times, and religious art.

Scilla

Scilla (population 6000) is built on a spur behind the famous **Rock of Scylla**. Crowned by a castle (now a youth hostel) it rises 73m sheer from the sea. It faces the Punto del Faro, in Sicily, across the Straits of Messina, which is four nautical miles wide at this point.

History of Scilla

Although the rock of Scylla, personified in the *Odyssey* as a marine monster with seven heads, and the whirlpool of Charybdis were placed by the ancient poets exactly opposite each other, modern geographers have transferred Charybdis to a spot nearer the harbour of Messina. At certain tides there are still strong currents and whirlpools off the Faro point, but these are not very dangerous, even to small craft. The conditions may have been changed since antiquity by earthquakes. More probably, 'Charybdis' may have been the collective name given to the many waterspouts that commonly form off the Sicilian coast. Scilla fell to the Saracens in the 9C and to the Normans in the 11C.

The **castle** was fortified by Pietro Ruffo in 1225; in 1282 the fleet of Charles I of Anjou took shelter here after failing to take Messina. The castle was occupied by the British after the Battle of Maida and defended for 18 months against the French. Huddled around the northernmost of the two small bays is the fishermen's quarter; the main bathing beach is on the south side of the headland. The recently rebuilt church of the Immacolata, at the foot of the road leading to the castle, was once an important Basilian monastery.

Beyond Scilla the scenery, with its luxuriant vegetation characterised by aloes, prickly pears and orange groves, becomes even more beautiful. At Villa San Giovanni (population 13,000) there are train and car ferries to Messina (see *Blue Guide Sicily*). Habitation is continuous from here to Reggio Calabria.

THE IONIAN COAST

The Ionian Coast or 'instep' of Italy is itself uninteresting but the villages in the hills to the north and west, particularly the Calabrian towns of **Stilo** (with the little Byzantine church of the Cattolica) and **Gerace** (with its magnificent cathedral), are well worth visiting. In addition, major archaeological sites, **Metapontum**, **Policoro**, and **Locri**, where excellent museums afford an insight into life in the Greek colonies of Magna Graecia, lie on the plain near the sea.

Practical information

Information offices

BOVA MARINA *Ufficio Informazioni e di Accoglienza Turistica*, Palazzo del Municipio, ☎ 0965 761004.

CATANZARO *Assessorato Regionale al Turismo*, Via San Nicola 8, ☎ 0961 720260, ✉ www.regione. calabria.it, turinet@abramo.it.
Ufficio Informazioni e di Accoglienza Turistica, Via Spasari 3–Galleria Mancuso, ☎ 0961 74961, ✉ apt.catanzaro.@tiscalinet.it.
Azienda di Promozione Turistica, Via Spasari 3–Galleria Mancuso, ☎ 0961 743901, ✉ apt.catanzaro.@tiscalinet. it.

CROTONE *Azienda di Promozione Turistica* and *Ufficio Informazioni e di Accoglienza Turistica*, Via Torino 148, ☎ 0962 23185.

GERACE *Ufficio Informazioni e di Accoglienza Turistica*, Accademia Filarmonica, Piazza Tribuna 10, ☎ 0964 356888.

LOCRI *Ufficio Informazioni e di Accoglienza Turistica*, Via Fiume 1, ☎ 0964 29600; Via Matteotti 90, ☎ 0964 29600.

SOVERATO *Ufficio Informazioni e di Accoglienza Turistica*, Via San Giovanni Bosco 192, ☎ 0967 25432

TARANTO *Azienda di Promozione Turistica*, Corso Umberto 113, ☎ 099 453 2397; ✉ www.apt.ta.it, info@apt.ta.it apt99.@libero.it.
Ufficio Informazioni e di Accoglienza Turistico, Corso Umberto 113, ☎ 099 453 2392.

See also Reggio Calabria listings, p 364.

Getting there and getting around
By air

Airport at **Lamezia Terme**, on the Tyrrhenian coast 61km west of Catanzaro (air terminal in Piazza Matteotti), with direct flights to/from Bologna, Florence, Milan, Palermo, Rome and Venice. Also at **Crotone**, with one daily flight to Rome, and Ravagnese, 4km east of Reggio Calabria with direct flights to/from Milan and Rome.

By road

Road 106 covers the entire 500km from Taranto to Reggio Calabria. Motorists should bear in mind that the road is perennially under construction, and roadwork can cause major delays. Where there is no interruption, the flow of traffic is fast and wild, an oncoming vehicle rarely being viewed as an obstacle to overtaking.

By rail

From Taranto to Reggio Calabria, 471km in c 6hrs. To Metaponto, junction for Potenza and Naples, 44km in c 30mins. To Catanzaro Lido (junction for Lamezia Terme and the Tyrrhenian coast line) in c 3hrs 30mins. Catanzaro has two railway stations: **Catanzaro** (Ferrovie dello Stato), with lines for Catanzaro Lido and Sant'Eufemia Lamezia, and **Catanzaro Città** (Ferrovie Calabro–Lucane), with lines for Cosenza and Catanzaro Lido.

By sea

Ferries and **hydrofoils** run throughout the year from Messina, in Sicily, to Reggio Calabria and Villa San Giovanni (20mins). There are also daily hydrofoils between Reggio Calabria, Messina and the Aeolian Islands (15mins–c 2hrs). For information and tickets, *Trenitalia Reggio Calabria*, ☎ 0965 97957 (ferries to Messina); *Aliscafi SNAV*, Stazione Marittima, ☎ 0965 892 012 (hydrofoils)

Where to stay

CASTELLANETA MARINA €€ *Golf Hotel*, ☎ 099 6439251, 🖷 099 6439255. A

iet, comfortable place with a large,
ne-shaded garden; open May–Oct.

OLICORO ☆ *Callà 2*, Via Lazio;
: 0835 981098, 📠 0835 981090,
📶 hotelcalla.it, info@hotelcalla.it. A
odest, Mediterranean-style establish-
ent with 20 luminous rooms.

TILO € *San Giorgio*, Via Citarelli 1,
: 0964 775047, 📠 0964 731455.
'ell-decorated rooms in the 17C
alazzo Lamberti, with stunning views
cross the Stilaro Valley to the sea.
arden and small pool, fireplaces in
iblic rooms.

■ Eating out

BERNALDA € *Da Fifina*,
Corso Umberto 63, ☎ 0835
43134. Simple family-run trattoria;
osed Sun (except in Aug) and Sept.

IVONGI € *La Vecchia Miniera*,
ontrada Perrocalli at Lavaria, ☎ 0964
31869. Country restaurant not far
om Stilo; closed Mon.

ORGIA €€ *L'Ovile*, Contrada
iordano, at Roccelletta; seasonal
gional cuisine in a historic farmhouse
ith garden and views, on an archaeo-
gical site; closed Nov.

ANOLO € *Da Cosimo*, Via Pertini
☎ 0964 385931. Regional dishes of
e Aspromonte in a village near
erace; closed Wed (except in Aug) and
pt.

ATANZARO € *Da Filippo*, Via
omenico Marincola Pistoia 247,
: 0961 751067. Popular osteria;
osed Sat.

Da Pepè, Vico I–Piazza Roma, 6, no
. Osteria; closed Sun.

Da Salvatore, Salita I del Rosario 28,
: 0961 724318. Osteria-pizzeria
iown for its local delicacies; closed
on and Aug.

Da Santo, Via Scesa Poerio 4, no ☎.
mple trattoria; closed Sun.

Da Teresa, Via degli Angioini 81, no
. Popular osteria; closed Sun and early
pt.

€ *Palazzo Turco*, Via Alessandro Turco
14, ☎ 0961 745179. Trattoria; closed
Sun.

Lanzo, Via Daniele 10–12. Delicatessen
with excellent meats, dairy products,
olives, sun-dried tomatoes, etc.

CATANZARO LIDO €€ *La Brace*,
Via Melito Porto Salvo, ☎ 0961 31340.
Hotel restaurant with garden and views;
closed Mon and early July.

€ *La Fattoria*, Via Magna Grecia 83, at
Chiattine, ☎ 0961 780064; closed
Mon.

CAULONIA € *Da Giglio*, Contrada
Carrubara 20, ☎ 0964 861572. Classic
osteria halfway between Roccella Jonica
and Caulonia; closed Mon (except in
summer) and Nov.

€ *Trattoria del Pesce Fresco*, Strada
Statale 106, Contrada Canne, at Marina
di Caulonia, ☎ 0964 82746. Trattoria
run by a former ship's cook, between
Roccella and Marina di Caulonia; closed
Sun (except in summer).

CIRÒ € *Fattoria San Francesco*, at
Quattromani. Farm making excellent
wines and fruit and vegetable preserves
(mushroom, aubergine, chestnut).

€ *L'Aquila d'Oro*, Via Sant'Elia,
☎ 0962 38550. Trattoria; closed Mon
and late Dec–early Jan.

CIRÒ MARINA € *Max*, Via
Togliatti, ☎ 0962 373009. Simple, genuine trattoria-pizzeria with a good wine
list; closed Mon and late Oct.

CITTANOVA € *La Mora*, Via
Florimo 3, ☎ 0966 661969.
Restaurant-pizzeria; closed Mon and July.

CROTONE €€ *Casa di Rosa*, Via
Cristoforo Colombo 117, ☎ 0962
21946. Traditional restaurant known
for its meat and fish dishes, and its traditional Calabrian sweets; closed Sun and
Dec–Jan.

€€ *Hostaria Le Lanterne*, Strada
Statale 106, at Poggio Pudano,
☎ 09662 948004. Fine country cooking in a former farmhouse; closed Mon
and late Sept.

€€ *Lido degli Scogli*, Via per Capocolonna, ☎ 0962 28625. Hotel restaurant by the sea; closed Mon and Nov.

€€ *Peppone*, Via Santa Maria delle Grazie, ☎ 0962 23855. Friendly and hospitable, with good regional food; closed Sun and Dec–Jan.

€€ *Sosta da Marcello*, Via Corrado Alvaro, Palazzo Merigliano, ☎ 0962 23831. Delicious traditional dishes, refined ambience; closed Sun (except May–Sept).

€€ *Sparviero Due*, Via Interna Marina 39, ☎ 0962 25009. Restaurant near the harbour, run by a family of fisher-men; closed Mon and late Aug–early Sept.

CRUCOLI €€ *Pollo d'Oro*, Corso Garibaldi 87–89, at Torretta, ☎ 0962 34005. Restaurant-enoteca with rooms; closed Sun.

€ *Al Ficodindia*, Viale Kennedy, at Torretta, ☎ 0962 34637. Simple but good restaurant in the Cirò wine dis-trict; closed Mon and late Sept.

GERACE €€ *Lo Sparviero*, Via Luigi Cadorna 3, ☎ 0964 356826. Great trattoria in an old stone building in the historic city centre; closed Mon (except in summer) and Oct.

€ *La Tavernetta*, Strada Provinciale Locri-Antonimina 112, at Azzuria, ☎ 0964 356020. Trattoria on the road from Gerace to Antonimina; closed Tues (except in summer).

GUARDAVALLE MARINA € *Mamma Assunta*, Via Pietro Nenni, ☎ 0967 86121. Trattoria; open daily July–Sept.

ISOLA DI CAPO RIZZUTO €€ *Annibale*, Via Duomo 35, at Le Castella, ☎ 0962 795004. Hotel restaurant with good food and views.

€€ *L'Ancora*, Via Faro, ☎ 0962 799253. Seafood and seasonal dishes by the water; closed Mon (except in sum-mer) and Nov.

€€ *La Scogliera*, Via Fosso, at Le Castella, ☎ 0962 795071. Excellent fish restaurant romantically situated on a rock overlooking the sea; closed Nov–Mar.

MAMMOLA € *Santa Barbara*, at Santa Barbara, ☎ 0964 414401. Trattoria-pizzeria; closed Wed (except in summer) and mid-Nov–mid-Dec.

MELITO DI PORTO SALVO €€ *Casina dei Mille*, Strada Statale Ionica 106, at Annà, ☎ 0965 787434. Restaurant with rooms (Garibaldi slept here!); closed Sun evening (except in summer) and late Dec.

MONTEPAONE LIDO € *Il Cantuccio*, Via Di Vittorio 6, ☎ 0967 22087. Good fish restaurant in an otherwise uninteresting beach resort; closed Wed and late Oct–early Nov.

NOVA SIRI € *Ai Tre Limoni*, Viale Siris 134, ☎ 0835 877178. Restaurant, closed Mon and Nov.

ROCCELLA IONICA € *Giare*, Strada Statale 106, km 111, ☎ 0964 85170. Restaurant with rooms and pool, on a farm by the sea; closed Nov–Mar.

ROTONDELLA € *La Mangiatoia*, Via Giotto 23, ☎ 0835 504440. Restaurant in a village (near Roads 380 and 106) known as the Balcony of the Ionian; closed Mon.

SAN GIORGIO MORGETO € *La Scaletta*, Via Florimo 14, ☎ 0964 946390. Trattoria; closed Tue (except in summer).

SIDERNO € *La Vecchia Hosteria*, Via Matteotti 5, ☎ 0964 388880. Restaurant-pizzeria; closed Wed (except July–Aug).

SIDERNO SUPERIORE € *Zio Salvatore*, Via Annunziata 1–3, ☎ 0964 385330. Simple trattoria in the old town centre; closed Tues.

SIMERI-CRICHI € *La Bottegaccia*, Contrada Apostolello, ☎ 0961 79918. Simple trattoria; closed Mon (except in summer).

Pastificio la Golosa, Via Don Minzoni

2. Pasta factory making excellent *usilli al ferretto* and other shapes.
OVERATO €€ *La Perla*, Via Cristoforo Colombo 6, ☎ 0967 25815. Traditional seafood restaurant; closed Mon (except in summer) and Nov. €€ *Riviera*, Via Regina Elena 4–6,

☎ 0967 25738. Restaurant belonging to the hotel of the same name; closed Mon and late Dec–early Jan.
TREBISACCE € *Trattoria del Sole*, Via Piave 14bis, ☎ 0981 51797. Trattoria crowded with locals; closed Sun (except in summer).

Through ancient Lucania

Before the Byzantine Emperor Basil II (976–1025) evicted the Saracens from southern Italy, Basilicata (the land of Basil) was known by its ancient Latin name, *Lucania*. Today numerous archaeological sites testify to the importance of this region in the Greek and Roman world.

Metapontum

The River Bradano marks the border between Apulia and Basilicata. On the river bank, to the north of the road, is the acropolis of the ancient *Metapontum*, the entrance to which is marked by the disused antiquarium.

History of Metapontum

Founded in the 7C BC possibly from Pylos in the Peloponnesus, Metapontum may have served initially as a buffer state between the Achaean colony at Sybaris and the Spartan *Taras* (Taranto). Archaeological evidence suggests that it was built on the site of an earlier, indigenous settlement. The city prospered due to the suitability of the surrounding land to agriculture and its excellent location for trade with *Poseidonia* (Paestum) and the Tyrrhenian colonies.

Pythagoras transferred his school here after his expulsion from Croton, giving rise to a philosophical tradition that was carried on long after his death in 497. Alexander, King of Epirus, killed in battle against the Bruttians and Lucanians, was buried at Metapontum. During the Second Punic War the city sided with Hannibal, who, on his retirement from Italy in 207 BC, evacuated the inhabitants to save them from Roman vengeance. Later, the city was sacked by Spartacus.

Air surveys of the area have revealed the limits of the city walls (c 6km in circumference); the grid-like street plan, with wide avenues at regular intervals and rectangular insulae measuring c 190 x 38m; the agora; and an artificial harbour at the mouth of the Basento, linked to the town by a canal.

The **Tavole Palatine**, a peripteral hexastyle temple of the Doric order, is the most extensive remnant of the ancient colony and one of the better-preserved monuments of Magna Graecia. Built in the late 6C as a sanctuary, probably dedicated to Hera, it stands 3km from the urban centre. Of its 32 Doric columns, 15 are still upright; some bear traces of their original stucco. Although parts of the lower course of the architrave have been preserved, the entablature has disappeared altogether. Much remains, however, of the stilobate and the foundations of the cella, which seems to have been divided into two unequal parts.

The remainder of the town may be reached by following Road 106 c 2km

south to the junction with Road 175 and turning left (immediately on the le[
remains of a monumental tomb from the Hellenistic period; further on, on th
right, another tomb from the 5C). From the modern village of Metaponto, wher
there is an **antiquarium** (open Tues–Sun 09.00–20.00, Mon 14.00–20.0(
☎ 0835 745327) mounting temporary exhibitions of finds from the excava
tions, a country road follows the railway north to (c 3km, left) the **theatre** an
the **Temple of Apollo Lycius**, a Doric construction of the 6C BC. From the fra[
mentary remains archaeologists have deduced that this temple, like that of th
Tavole Palatine, had 32 columns, 6m high. Numerous sections of these, as we
as several Doric capitals and pieces of the architrave, have been found on the sit
and a reconstruction is underway. Excavations around the perimeter of the tem
ple have revealed traces of smaller religious buildings and numerous archa
votive statuettes.

A brief turn inland

The Agri Valley Road 598, near Metapontum, is one of the more spectacular in southern Italy; the landscape, deeply eroded by wind and rain, affords views of a strange and wild beauty that certainly merit a short detour (20 minutes up and 20 minutes back are sufficient to get a taste of what the countryside can offer, here). Along the road are numerous villages, of little artistic merit but fascinating by virtue of their strong intrinsic character.

Another road worth exploring (653) runs up the Sinni Valley, and a loop of 122km may be made via Tursi, returning to the coast near Nova Siri, 8km south of Scanzano.

Heracleia

Just west of **Policoro**, excavations after magnetic soundings in 1961–67 have located the site of *Heracleia*, a joint colony of Taras and Thurii founded in 433 BC at the end of a ten-year struggle for control of the fertile Siri Valley. The painter Zeuxis was born here in the 5C BC, and Pyrrhus achieved his first victory over the Romans here in 280 BC; terrified by the appearance of a herd of elephants.

The **Museo Nazionale della Siritide** (open daily except Tues morning, 09.00–20.00; ☎ 0835 972154), close by the ruins, contains the result of excavations from the site of Siris-Heracleia and others in the Valle d'Agri (Roccanova, Sant'Andrea, Castranova, Chiaromonte, etc.). The museum is customarily used as a way-station for burial treasures excavated in the environs and awaiting restoration. The entrance hall sometimes holds entire tombs, complete with earth, in open crates. The museum follows an open plan: the rooms to the left of the entrance are mostly concerned with diggings from the Siris-Heracleia and those to the right with the Valle d'Agri excavations. The rooms are excellently laid out and clearly labelled, with an abundance of plans and photographs to show the sources of the excavations.

To the left are terracottas from the 6C–1C BC, including a disc with a votive inscription; an ivory figure (4C BC); fictile bust of Hephaistos (second half of the 4C BC); results of excavations in the Sanctuary of Demeter at Heracleia, including heads of divinities; fragments of painted vases; several bronze plates with dedicatory inscriptions and the representation of the divinity Eleusinie (late 5C BC); a large Laconic krater (archaic) used in Classical times for libations and filled with small votive vases, coins, etc.; terracotta fragments and remains of metalwork from archaic times up to the Roman; prehistoric fragments.

To the right are two fine burial treasures, one from the tomb of a man, the other from that of a woman; Corinthian helmet, remains of armour and other bronze ware of the 7C and 6C BC; Roman glass; skull of a young girl still bearing her jewellery; lekythos (black figure) by the Painter of Edinburgh; coins from the Sanctuary of Demeter and Bendis; metal axe and agricultural implements; terracotta statuettes, etc; Greek vases, including a **hydria** showing a conversation between young people in the presence of Eros, by the Painter of Amykos, group of vases by the Painter of Policoro; and a superb *pelike* (wide-mouthed jar) portraying Poseidon and Athena, attributed by some to the Painter of the Carnee, and by others to the Painter of Policoro.

Near Policoro a road leads inland to the isolated church of **Santa Maria d** **Anglona**, see p 329.

Ionian Calabria

The coast road (106) now traverses the Pantano di Policoro, a thicket of myrtle oleander and lentisk, crosses the Sinni (formerly the Siris) and enters Calabria The hills come close to the sea. Rocca Imperiale, with a castle built by Frederic II, stands on an eminence 4km west of the road. Beyond Trebisacce is the larg alluvial plain of Sibari surrounding the mouth of the River Crati.

History of Sibari

The ancient *Sybaris*, from which Sibari takes its name, probably stood on the le bank of the Crati (*Crathis*). This Achaean colony, whose luxury and corruptio have become a byword, was destroyed by the men of Croton (510 BC), wh flooded it with the waters of the Crathis. The descendants of the survivors, wit the help of a band of Athenian colonists, founded *Thurii* in 443 BC, 6km furthe inland, near Terranova di Sibari. Among the Athenians were the orator Lysia (d. 402) and Herodotus, who died at Thurii between 430 BC and 425.

Romanised after 290 BC under the name of *Copiae*, the town lasted until th decline of the empire. Drainage operations, which have greatly improved th former malarial condition of the plain, have brought some traces of Copiae t light, though the exact site of Greek Sybaris remains a mystery. Some of th material discovered to date may be seen in the Museo della Sibaritide e Parc Archeologico (on SS 106 at Parco Del Cavallo–Casa Bianca, open dail June–Sept 09.00–19.30; closed first and third Mon of every month; ☎ 098 79391).

To the south there is a splendid view of the mountains of the Sila area and, to th north, the steep limestone crags of Monte Pollino, snowcapped except in th height of summer.

At **Corigliano Calabro** (population 40,000) the large church c Sant'Antonio di Padova has a decorative Baroque interior and a good inlaid mar ble high altar. In the hills south-east of the town lies the **Convento del Patir** (Santa Maria del Patirion), founded by St Nilus (see below) on a rugged peak in magnificent surroundings. In the 12C it rivalled Mount Athos, in Greece, as seat of monastic learning; the church preserves traces of a mosaic pavement.

Rossano (population 35,000) lies 6km south of the road. The little town wa the birthplace of St Nilus (910–1001), founder of the convents of Grottaferrata near Rome, and Patire. The cathedral has a Baroque altar, attached to a pillar o the north side of the nave, which encloses a Byzantine *Madonna* of the 8C or 9C and a wooden ceiling. In the archbishop's palace is the Museo Diocesano (ope summer daily 09.00–13.00, 16.30–20.30; Oct–June 09.30–12.30, 16.00 19.00, closed Mon; ☎ 0983 525263) in which you can see the celebrated **Code Purpureus**, an extremely rare Greek work of the 6C (see p 63).

The narrow Via Arcivescovado, to the right of the cathedral, leads down to th small church of the **Panaglia**, a 12C building with an interesting apse contain ing *opus spicatum*. Within is a fresco of San Giovanni Crisostomo. At the top c the town stands the 10C church of **San Marco**, built to a Byzantine plan with five domes and three apses. The Passeggiata di Santo Stefano commands a view across the Gulf of Taranto.

Further along the coast, at **Cariati**, you can make a circuit of the old city walls and bastions, into which houses have been built. The **cathedral**, whose tiled cupola can be seen from the marina, has an impressive interior and contains 18C choir stalls by Girolamo Franceschi. The **cemetery church** (just outside the town) is a bare and pleasing late Gothic building with a well proportioned ribbed dome, completely vested inside with patterned tiles of Moorish inspiration.

Torre Melissa is known for its excellent Cirò wine. **Strongoli**, 9km inland, is the ancient *Petilia* which, faithful to Rome, held out against Hannibal in 206 BC. Here and in neighbouring villages textiles are handwoven to traditional designs.

Crotone

South of the River Neto lies the Marchesato, a former fief of the Ruffo family. Its main city, Crotone (population 62,000), stands on a promontory c 2km east of the road. An industrial centre of some importance, it has the only harbour between Taranto and Reggio. George Gissing wrote much of his *Ionian Sea* here in 1897.

History of Crotone

The Achaean colony of Croton, founded in 710 BC by settlers sent, as legend narrates, by the Oracle of Delphi, became the most important city of the Bruttians. Its dominion, together with that of Sybaris, extended over much of Magna Graecia and included colonies on both the Ionian and the Tyrrhenian coasts. Pythagoras (c 540 BC) made it the chief centre of his school of philosophy, but was expelled some 30 years later when the oligarchy that he supported and justified was overthrown. In the same century, Croton was conquered by the Locrians but, thanks to the prowess of its champion, Milo (one of a series of famous Crotonian athletes) it vanquished the Sybarites in 510. It submitted to Agathocles of Syracuse in 299. Hannibal embarked here after his retreat from Rome.

In the 13C its status was revived, and it became the capital of the Marchesato. Most of its ancient buildings were used by Don Pedro of Toledo in the construction of his castle. From the 11C to 1929 the town was known as Cotrone.

On the road to the town are storehouses for olives, oranges and liquorice. The castle dates from the 16C. The church of San Giuseppe has a decorative façade with two domed chapels. Nearby is the excellent **Museo Archeologico Nazionale** (open daily 09.00–20.00; closed first and third Mon of every month; ☎ 0962 23082). The museum was established in 1910 and its collection largely constructed by the famous early 20C archaeologist, Paolo Orsi. What you see today is essentially a teaching collection, enriched by maps, plans and photographs of archaeological sites in and around Crotone. The **ground floor** displays document the development of Crotone from prehistoric times to the Middle Ages, with particular emphasis on the founding of the city and the School of Pythagoras. The **first floor** is devoted to the surrounding territory; the finds include tomb treasures, red- and black-figure Attic pottery, terracotta votive statuettes and architectural details. On the **top floor** are some extraordinary jewellery (*Gioielli delle* *dea del Lacinio*) and an assortment of votive offerings from the newest dig, at Capo Colonna. The visit culminates in the room devoted to the **Tesoro di Hera**, a group of bronze, silver and gold objects including a splendid gold diadem.

A hilly peninsula lies south of Crotone. Calypso's island of Ogygia was supposed to lie off the coast here. Isola di Capo Rizzato was one of the centres of the 1948 agrarian reform, when large feudal estates were broken up and redistributed. This was one of the first social reforms of the Italian Republic. **Capo Colonna** (11km) takes its name from the scant remains of a Greek temple (notably a single standing column) and **Le Castella** (25km), from the Aragonese fortress built on an island just offshore.

Catanzaro

An expressway (Road 19b) diverges inland to Catanzaro (12km), an animated city of 104,000 inhabitants, capital of its province. Situated high up between the gorges of two mountain torrents, it boasts a glorious record of opposition to tyranny.

From Catanzaro station a unique funicular tramway ascends through a tunnel to Piazza Roma and crosses Corso Mazzini. To the west of the corso, near the rebuilt cathedral, is the church of the **Rosario** (or San Domenico), a Baroque edifice with paintings of the *Madonna del Rosario* and the *Madonna della Vittoria*, celebrating the victory of Lepanto; as well as some marble altars, all 17C. On the south side of the church is the Oratorio della Congrega del Rosario, with elaborate stucco work. The **Museo Provinciale**, in the public gardens of the Villa Margherita (open Tues–Fri 10.30–13.30, 15.30–17.30, Sat–Sun 09.00–12.30; ☎ 0961 720019), contains antiquities from Catanzaro and its province: some 8000 coins, the remains of an equestrian monument of the 2C AD; prehistoric material; a marble head from Strongoli and a Greek helmet from Tiriolo, of fine workmanship. Adjacent to the museum is the Villa Margherita, a public park commanding exceptional sea views. More good views may be had from all sides of the town from the ring road (*circonvallazione*).

George Gissing's impression of Catanzaro

The sun was setting when I alighted at the Marina, and as I waited for the branch train my eyes feasted upon a glory of colour which made me forget aching weariness. All around lay orchards of orange trees, the finest I had ever seen, and over their solid masses of dark foliage, thick hung with ripening fruit, poured the splendour of the western sky. It was a picture unsurpassable in richness of tone; the dense leafage of deepest, warmest green glowed and flashed, its magnificence heightened by the blaze of the countless golden spheres adorning it. Beyond, the magic sea, purple and crimson as the sun descended upon the vanishing horizon. Eastward, above the slopes of Sila, stood a moon almost at its full, the yellow of an autumn leaf, on a sky soft-flushed with rose.

In my geography it is written that between Catanzaro and the sea lie the gardens of the Hesperides. (*By the Ionian Sea*, 1901.)

Between Catanzaro and Locri

Just 2km south of Catanzaro Marina, an important industrial town and a crowded, built-up resort, is one of the region's more majestic monuments, the ruined church of **Santa Maria della Roccella** (open 09.00–dusk). Although its date of construction is disputed, the church is generally believed to be an 11C building modelled on the large Cluniac churches of the north and conditioned by local building traditions. It is built to a Latin cross plan, with a simple nave, three semicircular apses, and a broad transept. The crypt follows the plan of the presbytery and apses. The façade, nave walls and transept have largely fallen down, and access to the crypt is difficult; nevertheless the contrast between the warm red brick of the remaining walls and the cool silver-green of the olives that grow around the ruin is striking. Excavations nearby have begun to bring to light the ruins (forum and theatre) of a Roman settlement, *Scolacium*.

Squillace (7km, population 3000), the Greek city of *Schilletion*, which became the Roman *Scolacium*, was the birthplace of Cassiodorus (480–575), secretary to the Byzantine emperor Theodoric, and of General Guglielmo Pepe (1782–1855), commander of the Neapolitan army in Lombardy. The cathedral contains 16C sculptures and the castle commands a view.

Soverato stands below **Soverato Superiore**, where the Chiesa Arcipretale contains a fine *Pietà* by Antonio Gagini (1521) and, to the right of the main entrance, a 16C bas-relief also depicting a *Pietà*.

Monasterace Marina stands about a kilometre south of the ruins of *Caulonia*, an Achaean colony destroyed by Dionysus I in 389 BC, consisting of a rampart and a fragmentary Doric temple (*area archeologica* open daily 08.00–dusk).

Stilo and the Cattolica

From Monasterace Marina, Road 110 winds up the valley of the Fiumara Stilaro to (15km) **Stilo** (population 3000), beautifully situated on the side of Monte Consolino.

Tommaso Campanella (1568–1639), the philosopher, was a native of Stilo, and its environs were a favourite resort of Basilian anchorites. Emperor Otho II was defeated by the Sicilian Saracens here in 982.

The town is overlooked by the **Cattolica** church, a gem of Byzantine architecture resembling church of San Marco at Rossano (see above), perhaps the best-preserved monument of its kind in Europe.

The Cattolica was the church of all those who lived as monastic hermits in the surrounding hills. Built in the 10C, it survived the earthquake of 1783, which destroyed much of the town, and was restored in the first quarter of the 20C. Built to a square plan, it has five conical domes on circular drums. The interior measures 6 x 6m and is divided into nine quadrants by four rough columns. The latter, taken from antique buildings, have been placed on top of their capitals to symbolise the defeat of paganism. The first column on the right bears the Greek inscription, 'God is the Lord who appeared to us,' surmounted by a carved cross. On the walls and ceiling can be seen traces of Byzantine frescoes in three

Byzantine Cattolica, Stilo

strata, corresponding to three different epochs, discovered and restored in 1927.

From the vantage point of the Cattolica, other interesting remains of domed churches can be seen. These include the ruined convent of San Domenico, where Campanella lived and worked.

South of Stilo, in the valley of the Allaro, the former Sagras, 10,000 Locrians defeated 130,000 Crotonians c 540 BC. **Caulonia**, 8km inland, was founded by the refugees from ancient Caulonia. The church has a Carafa tomb of 1488.

At Roccella Ionica, the ruined castle stands on a striking cliff overlooking the sea, and near the station Gioiosa Ionica are remains of a small Roman theatre. Plantations of bergamot trees line the coast between here and Siderno, a sprawling modern town with a popular beach.

Locri and Gerace

Locri (population 14,000) lies 5km north of the ruins of its ancient namesake, the famous *Locri Epizephyrii*. The latter was founded by colonists, probably from the *Opuntian Locris* in Greece, in either 710 BC or 683 BC, on a site that had already been inhabited by native Siculian peoples for several centuries.

History of Locri

The Greek colony flourished, perhaps by virtue of its location on a major road (the *dromos*, which bisects the site) and its contacts with Sicily and Tyrrhenian colonies. Locri was the first Greek city to possess a written code of laws, attributed to Zaleucus (664 BC), and it was praised by Pindar as a model of good government. Religious life centred on the goddess Persephone, and the city contained a celebrated sanctuary dedicated to her (see below). The Locrians conquered the Crotonians (see above), allied themselves with Dionysius I and finally surrendered to Rome (205 BC). The town dwindled and was eventually destroyed by the Saracens.

Although the finest remains from the site are housed in the Museo Archeologico Nazionale in Reggio Calabria, the little **Antiquarium Statale di Locri** (open daily 09.00–19.00; Sat 09.00–19.00 and 21.00–24.00, June–Sept; closed first and third Mon of the month; ☎ 0964 390023) contains clear plans and photographs illustrating the history and artistic development of the city, a well-displayed collection of pottery and bronzes from Greek and indigenous tombs, architectural fragments, a vast assortment of small votive statues (the craftsmen of Locri specialised in producing these), Roman inscriptions and Locrian and Greek coins.

Visits to the **ruins** (open daily 09.00–19.00; closed first and third Mon of the month) begin at the museum, from where a dirt path leads inland to (500m) the remains of an Ionic temple believed to have been dedicated to Zeus. Originally constructed in the 7C BC, it was enlarged in the 6C and completely rebuilt in the following century.

Further on, a footpath leads from a modern hamlet situated on the dromos to a Doric temple (called Marafioti) and the neighbouring Hellenistic theatre, much altered in Roman times. In 1959 thirty bronze tablets dating from 3C BC recording civic expenditures were found here. The visible stretches of the town walls (behind the antiquarium and c 1km further south, along a track perpendicular to the coast road) probably date from the 6C. Traces of the earlier walls may be seen at the Centocamere, an area only partially excavated, entered from a dirt

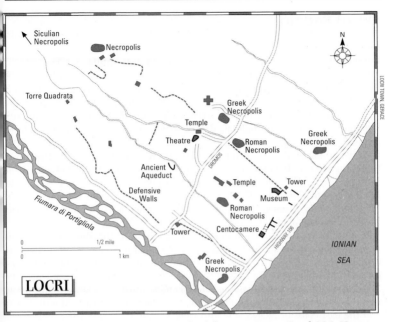

Siculian
Necropolis

Necropolis

Torre Quadrata

Greek
Necropolis

Temple

Greek
Necropolis

Theatre

Roman
Necropolis

Ancient
Aqueduct

Temple

Tower

Defensive
Walls

Museum

Fiumara di Portigliola

Roman
Necropolis

Tower

Centocamere

HIGHWAY 106

IONIAN

Greek
Necropolis

SEA

0   1/2 mile
0   1 km

LOCRI TOWN GERACE

LOCRI

track (marked *Locri scavi*) c 500m south of the museum on Road 106. Here too
are the foundations of houses and parts of a water system, as well as the beaten-
earth streets dividing the insulae. The shrine of Persephone stands in a ravine
outside the city wall, just above which are the foundations of a small temple of
Athena. Little, however, remains to be seen of these monuments, and access is
difficult. Greek and Roman tombs lie close to the dromos, and a Siculian necropolis, further inland.

From the centre of modern Locri, Road 111 climbs inland through olive groves
to (9km) **Gerace** (population 3000), situated on an impregnable crag overlooking the road. Founded by refugees from Locri in the 9C, it possesses a remarkable
cathedral, the largest church in Calabria. Consecrated in 1045, this was rebuilt
under Swabian rule and restored after an earthquake in the 18C. The spacious
interior is built to a Latin cross plan. The nave and aisles are divided by 20 granite and coloured marble columns, possibly from Locri, above which rounded
arches of differing heights spring from high stilt-blocks. At the end of the south
aisle is the Gothic Cappella del Sacramento (1431); in the adjacent south
transept the 14C tomb of Giovanni and Battista Caracciolo and of Niccoló Palazzi
can be seen. Antique columns also support the vault of the much-restored crypt.

The church of the Sacro Cuore has a distinctive dome and contains pretty
Baroque decoration. San Francesco d'Assisi (1252) has two fine portals, of
which the larger bears Arabic and Norman decorative elements. Within are a
tomb of Niccoló Ruggo (d. 1372), of Pisan influence, and a marvellous inlaid
marble high altar. The small church of San Giovanello is also of Byzanto-
Norman construction.

On to Reggio

Continue south along the coast. Just north of Ardore Marina, a road turns inland to (5km) Bombile, near which lies the **Santuario di Bombile**, constructed in a most astonishing way inside a large cave. The sanctuary, reached by a track through olive groves, has a charming façade into which an attractive Baroque portal, dated 1758, is set. Inside, the edifice is completely built and vaulted as would be any free-standing church and exhibits somewhat later decoration. Over the high altar stands the *Madonna della Grotta*, a fine marble statue, possibly by a close follower of Antonello Gagini.

At Bovalino Marina a turning on the right mounts to (5km) **Bovalino Superiore**, where the church of the Matrice contains a marble *Madonna della Neve* by the Gagini school. Set into the south wall is a fragment of a marble *Madonna and Child*, mutilated by Turkish pirates. Also to be noted is the *Madonna of the Rosary*, clothed in fine 18C garments. The Chiesa del Rosario has a richly decorated 14C portal.

Beyond Brancaleone you round Capo Spartivento, the Roman *Heracleum Promontorium*, at the south-east extremity of Calabria. Some of the villagers in this area retain a dialect of Greek origin, though scholars dispute whether it originates from antiquity or the Middle Ages. Garibaldi landed in 1860 and again in 1862 at Melito di Porto Salvo, the southernmost town (population 10,000) on the mainland. A beautiful mountain road ascends to Gambarie. Mount Aetna and the east coast of Sicily come into view. On the right rises the five-pronged crag of **Pentedattilo**, whose name translates from the Greek as 'five fingers', with a picturesque ruined village at its foot. Further on, the road winds around the Punta di Pellaro and Messina is visible across the strait.

REGGIO CALABRIA AND THE ASPROMONTE

Reggio Calabria is the regional capital and the last major city on the Italian peninsula before crossing to Sicily. It is known above all for its **Museo Nazionale della Magna Grecia**, which houses an extraordinary collection of prehistoric, Graeco-Roman and medieval antiquities. The city stands at the foot of the **Aspromonte**, a wild, mountainous region, for centuries isolated from the rest of the world. In some villages, the dialect spoken is still based on ancient Greek.

Interesting day trips may be made from Reggio and its environs, the usual starting points being Melito di Porto Salvo, on the south coast, and Bagnara Calabra, to the north.

Practical information

Information offices
REGGIO CALABRIA *Ufficio Informazioni e di Accoglienza Turistica*, Corso Garibaldi 329, ☎ 0965 892012. Branch offices at Ravagnese Airport, ☎ 0965 643291;

Stazione Centrale, ☎ 0965 27120. *Azienda di Promozione Turistica*, Via Roma 3, ☎ 0965 21171, ✉ www.netonline.it/apt/, apt.reggiocalabria infinito.it.
REGIONE CALABRIA ✉ www.

turismo.regione.calabria.it.

SANTO STEFANO IN ASPROMONTE–GAMBARIE

Ufficio Informazioni e di Accoglienza Turistica, Piazzale Mangeruca, ☎ 0965 743295.

Getting there and getting around
By air

Airport at **Ravagnese**, 4km south, with direct flights to/from Milan and Rome.

By road

Reggio Calabria is the southern terminus of Autostrada A3/E45, the *Autostrada del Sole*. It is also reached by Road 18, the Tyrrhenian coast road, from Praia a Mare, and Road 106, the Ionian coast road, from Taranto.

Three main routes provide access to the Aspromonte region. From Reggio Calabria to Gambarie take Roads 18 and 184; from Bagnara Calabra to Gambarie take roads 18 and 112; and from Melito di Porto Salvo to Gambarie use local roads.

By rail

From Naples (Campi Flegrei, Mergellina, Centrale or Porta Garibaldi) to Reggio Calabria (Centrale), 476km in 4hrs 30mins by Eurostar or Intercity, stopping at Paola, Lamezia Terme, Vibo Valentia-Pizzo, Gioia Tauro and Villa San Giovanni. To Villa San Giovanni (where through trains to Sicily cross the Straits of Messina), in c 15mins less. From Maratea (on the Tyrrhenian coast) to Reggio, 283km in c 2hrs 45mins. To (139km) Lamezia Terme Centrale, junction for Catanzaro, in c 1hr 15mins. From Taranto to Reggio Calabria, 471km in c 6hrs.

Reggio has three train stations: Centrale, Piazza Garibaldi, at the south end of the town, for all trains; Lido, more centrally placed near the hotels and the museum is served by most; Marittima is the terminus of trains from the east, but is not served from the north.

By sea

Ferries and **hydrofoils** run throughout the year from Messina, in Sicily, to Reggio Calabria and Villa San Giovanni (20mins). There are also daily hydrofoils between Reggio Calabria, Messina and the Aeolian Islands (15mins–c 2hrs). For information and tickets, *Trenitalia Reggio Calabria*, ☎ 0965 97957 (ferries to Messina); *Aliscafi SNAV*, Stazione Marittima, ☎ 0965 892 012 (hydrofoils). Timetables at www.calabriaweb.it/rcportal/it/trasporti/traghetti.html.

Where to stay

REGGIO CALABRIA €€
Excelsior, Via Vittorio Veneto 66, ☎ 0965 812211, ▯ 0965 893084, ✉ excelsior@reggiocalabriahotels.it. A classic place across the street from the national museum.
€€ *Miramare*, Via Fata Morgana 1, ☎ 0965 812444, ▯ 0965 812450, ✉ miramare@reggiocalabriahotels.it. Sober but comfortable, on the Lungomare.
€€ *Palace Masoanri's*, Via Vittorio Veneto 95, ☎ 0965 26433, ▯ 0965 26436. Pleasant, centrally located near the national museum.
€ *Fata Morgana*, Via Lungomare, at Gallico Marina (8km north of the city centre), ☎ 0965 370008, ▯ 0965 370000. Simple but comfortable.
€ *Lido*, Via Tre Settembre 1943 6, ☎ 0965 25001, ▯ 0965 899393. Near the sea between the Lido station and the national museum.

Eating out

BAGNARA CALABRA €
Taverna Kerkira, Via Vittorio Emanuele 217, ☎ 0966 372260. Restaurant serving Greek-Calabrian dishes; closed Mon, Tues and Dec–Jan.
MELITO DI PORTO SALVO €€
Casina dei Mille, Strada Statale Ionica 106, at Annà, ☎ 0965 787434.

Restaurant with rooms (Garibaldi slept here!); closed Sun evening (except in summer) and late Dec.

REGGIO CALABRIA €€
Cantuccio Club, Via Nuova Friuli 9, ☎ 0965 891614. Warm, genuine restaurant with a strong local following; closed Sun, Mon and June–Sept.

€€ *Fuori Porta Club*, Via Vecchia Provinciale 37, at Archi, ☎ 0965 45199. Creative cuisine in a pleasant garden restaurant; closed mid-day, Sun (in summer), Wed (in winter) and Sept.

€€ *Gabbiano*, Contrada San Gregorio, ☎ 0965 758174. Seaside restaurant with good views and food; closed Sept–May.

€€ *Galà*, Via Vittorio Veneto 66, ☎ 0965 812211. Restaurant at the *Grand Hotel Excelsior*, with good panorma; open all year.

€€ *Garden*, Via Fata Morgana 1, ☎ 0965 812444. Restaurant at the *Hotel Miramare*, with good traditional cuisine; open all year.

€€ *London Bistro*, Via Osanna 2F, ☎ 0965 892908. Creative cuisine;
closed Mon, mid-day Sat and Aug.

€ *Taverna degli Ulivi*, Via Eremo Botte 32, ☎ 0965 891461. Trattoria-pizzeria; closed Sun.

Torrone Giuseppe Malavenda, Via Santa Catarina 85–91. Confectioner producing almond paste and *torroncini* flavoured with mandarin oranges, orange blossom honey, etc.

SANTO STEFANO IN ASPROMONTE € *Villa Rosa*, road 184, at Schiccio, ☎ 0965 740500. Trattoria; open all year.

SCILLA €€ *Glauco*, at Chianalea di Scilla, ☎ 0965 754026. Family-run trattoria by the sea, with summer seating outside; closed Tues and Oct–Mar.

€€ *Grotta Azzurra*, Lungomare Cristoforo Colombo, ☎ 0965 754889. Good fish restaurant with outdoor seating and sea views; closed Mon and Dec.

VILLA SAN GIOVANNI €€
Antica Osteria Vecchia Villa, Via Gribaldi 104, ☎ 0965 751125. Old-fashioned trattoria just off the station square; closed Wed and Aug.

Reggio Calabria

Reggio is a flourishing city (population 178,000), with wide streets and low buildings, many constructed in the early 20C Liberty style.

History of Reggio Calabria

Reggio Calabria still carries a reference to *Rhegion* or *Rhegium*, founded c 723 BC by the Chalcidians, who were afterwards joined by the Messenese. The colony grew in size and wealth under Anaxilas, but it was sacked by Dionysius the Elder of Syracuse in 387 BC and was later subject to the Mamertines and repopulated by the Romans. Its propitious situation secured it continuous prosperity and enabled it to survive the repeated ravages of both pirates and earthquakes.

Reggio was rebuilt with wide and regular streets after the earthquake of 1783, only to be practically demolished again on 28 December 1908, when 5000 of its 35,000 inhabitants perished and every house that was not completely ruined was seriously damaged. Heavily bombed in 1943, it was occupied on 3 September by the Allies, who crossed the Straits of Messina practically unopposed.

Corso Garibaldi, roughly parallel to the sea, forms the main thoroughfare of the city, with Piazza Italia at its centre. To the north-east of the piazza the severe

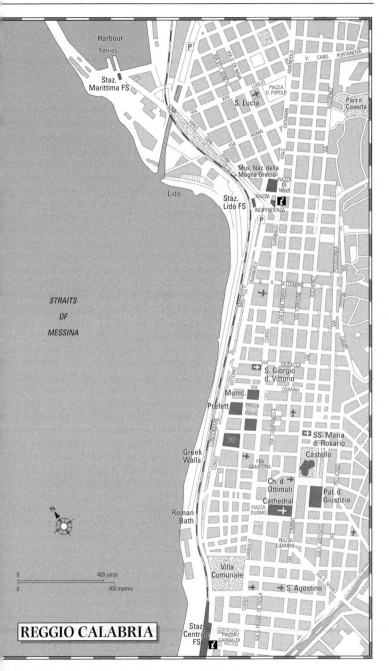

Harbour
Ferries

Staz.
Marittima FS

P

VIA XXV LUGLIO

VIALE GEN.

VIA DE NAVA

VIA ROMA

VIA GIOVANNI

V. CARD. PORTANOVA

AMENDOLA

SCENZ.

Parco
Caserta

PIAZZA
D. POPOLO

S. Lucia

Mus. Naz. della
Magna Grecia

PIAZZA
DE
NAVA

Lido

Staz.
Lido FS

PIAZZA
INDIPENDENZA

i

P

GARIBALDI

EMANUELE

VIA MATTEOTTI

II SETTEMBRE

VIA D. ROMEO

VIA TURBIONE

ASCHENZ.

VIA

CORSO

CORSO GARIBALDI

PASSAGINEA

STRAITS

OF

MESSINA

VIA VITTORIO

VIA GIUDECCA

S. Giorgio
d. Vittorio

VIA OSANNA

VIA

Munic.

Prefett.

PIAZZA
ITALIA

VIA CAMPAGNA

VIA PANETTA

SS. Maria
d. Rosario

PO

Castello

Greek
Walls

LUNGOMARE

CORSO

PZA
CAMAGNA

Ch. d.
Ottimati

Cathedral

Pal. d.
Giustizia

FELICIANO

Roman
Bath

PIAZZA
DUOMO

VIA CAMINI

VIA G. AGOSTINO

VIA

GARIBALDI

PIAZZA
CARMINE

Villa
Comunale

S. Agostino

VIA A. SPANO

CORSO GARIBALDI

VIA FRANZ. DE BIOLA

Staz.
Centrale
FS

i

PIAZZA
GARIBALDI

REGGIO CALABRIA

N

0 _____ 400 yards
0 _____ 400 metres

Tempio della Vittoria (1939) serves as a war memorial. Two massive towers of the castle survive, further south, and afford a fine view over the city and the straits. There is a mosaic pavement of the Norman period, taken from two ancient Calabrian churches destroyed, like so many others, by earthquakes, in the nearby Chiesa degli Ottimati.

The Museo Nazionale della Magna Grecia

To the north-east, in Piazza de Nava, is the Museo Nazionale della Magna Grecia (open daily May–Oct 09.00–20.00, mid-summer weekends until 23.00; Nov–Apr Mon 09.00–13.30, Tues–Sat 09.00–13.30, 15.30–19.00; Sun 09.00–12.30; closed first and third Mon of every month; ☎ 0965 812255), by far Reggio's chief attraction for the visitor. It contains an extensive collection of antiquities, including beautiful terracottas, marbles, and small bronzes of fine workmanship, from Sibari, Locri, Medma and other sites throughout Calabria. The museum is open on a rotating-gallery basis; displays on the mezzanine and first floors may be closed; the hall of the Riace Bronzes is always open.

Ground floor The Neolithic, Iron and Bronze Age collections (flint implements, iron and bronze swords, spear heads, pottery, bones) are well displayed and clearly labelled in the ground floor rooms. At the beginning of the section are large cases containing instructive scale models of prehistoric villages and a cast of a graffito representing an ox from Papasidero, the only such Italian find dating from the Upper Palaeolithic period. The rooms that follow display material from localities throughout the region: ceramics and tools from Favella della Corte, Cosenza, Girifalco, Catanzaro, Cassano Ionio, Praia a Mare, Opido Momentina, Tropea, Drapia, Cirò, Calanna, Torre Galli, Grotterie and Serra Aiello.

The Greek collection starts with a small sampling of the treasures unearthed at **Locri Epizephyrii**: terracottas, ointment jars, mirrors, fibulae, jewellery and bronze statuettes, dating from the 7C to the 4C BC. The next room (4) displays an extraordinary collection of **pinakes** (clay tablets intended as ex-voto offerings, once brightly painted) from the Sanctuary of Persephone (see p 365), the most famous shrine of the goddess in Magna Graecia. These small clay bas-reliefs (*pinax* in the singular) were manufactured in Locri and distributed throughout the Greek world. Archaeologists have counted 176 different types representing ten basic subjects. The reliefs shown here have been assembled from fragments: they were found in a 'bank' where offerings were deposited after being ritually broken. Although they have lost most of their colouring and are marred by chips and cracks, the refinement of their forms and liveliness of their compositions still testify to the extraordinary skill of the Locrian craftsmen, who worked between 490 and 450 BC.

The next room (5) focuses on the terracotta **equestrian group** from the Marafioti Temple (see p 364). Believed to be a pediment sculpture, it shows a nude horseman riding above a winged sphinx. The latter supports the horseman's feet with her hands and his steed with her head, suggesting to scholars that the group may represent one of the Dioscuri, the twin sons of Zeus, who were thought to have led the Locrians to victory against superior forces from Croton, around 550 BC. Set against a beautiful green ground in a room of their own (Plan 6) are the most celebrated ancient representations of this subject, the Parian marble **Dioscuri** from the Ionic Sanctuary of Contrada Marasà. Here Castor and Pollux are shown leaping off their mounts to rush to the aid of the Locrians. The horses this time are carried by Tritons, who raise their front hoofs to make horse and rider fit the ideal triangle of the pediment. The centre of the omposition is believed to have held a winged victory, a considerable part of which survives. The sculptures, it seems, were made in Greece around 400 BC and imported to Locri; discovered in the late 19C, the original fragments were integrated' with plaster reconstructions, as was the custom of the time.

Basement The Marine Archaeology collection, installed downstairs, displays the museum's most famous treasures. Beyond an atrium with Greek, Punic and Roman amphorae, anchors and other objects recovered from wrecks along he Calabrian coast and in the treacherous Straits of Messina, glass doors admit o the climate-controlled main hall. Here you are immediately greeted by two plendid bronze heads recovered near Porticello, at the north entrance to the straits of Messina. That nearest to the door, labelled *Bearded Mask*, shows the idealised features characteristic of the Severe Style (the face is symmetrical, arranged horizonatally around the double arch of the eyebrows and vertically around the straight, strong axis of the nose; hair and beard are stereotyped). It is thought to represent a god or an aristocrat and has been dated to the early 5C BC. The adjacent *Head of a Philosopher* is much more naturalistic (the face's inherent asymmetries have been preserved, as have distinctive traits such as the long beard and thinning hair). It is ascribed to the Classic period of Greek sculpture 450–400 BC) and is considered the only Greek portrait head in existence. Both heads show signs of damage inflicted by violent impact: they are thought to have belonged to a cargo of deliberately smashed sculptures on their way to the oundry to be recycled.

The hall is dominated by the celebrated heroic nude statues discovered off Riace, on Calabria's Ionian shore, in 1972. Standing high above the floor on special anti-seismic plinths, the **Riace Bronzes** are among the very few surviving examples of Classic Greek bronze statuary. They spent eight years in Italy's most sophisticated restoration laboratories before being revealed to the public in Florence in 1980. Produced by the lost-wax method (in which molten bronze chases' a wax simulacre of the sculpture out of a clay mould), both figures stand over 2m tall and weigh around 160kg. They are finished in ivory and glass (eyes), ilver (teeth) and copper (lips and nipples), and signs suggest they each held a hield and lance. The statues have been attributed to Phidias (460 BC) and Polyclites (430 BC) respectively, and they have been associated with the Temple at Delphi, built by the Athenians to commemorate the victory of Marathon. In the absence of documentary evidence, however, any hypothesis regarding the provenance to the statues remains just an educated guess. Mystery also shrouds the ssue of how the statues got to be where they were. X-ray analysis has shown hat Statue B was altered after the initial casting to resemble its companion (the ight arm and left forearm are not original). On this basis some experts suggest hat the sculptures were en-route to a new (perhaps Roman) location when they were thrown overboard from a ship in distress.

Mezzanine On the landing is more material from Locri: architectural fragments from the Temple of Zeus (5C BC) and 38 bronze tablets (account books) inscribed in Locrian dialect (350 BC–250 BC) from the temple archive. There is also a fine collection of **coins**, nearly all Greek and Roman, well displayed, and representative of all sites. It includes the silver stater, typical of Magna Graecia, of standard weight (8g), stamped with the symbol of the mint and the name of he city where it was made (tripod = Croton; bull = Sybaris; hipogriff = Locri; eagle and serpent = Hipponion; wheat = Metapontum).

The Story of Persephone

In Ovid's *Metamorphoses* (V, 345-571), Calliope tells the touching tale of the rape of Proserpina (the Greek *Persephone*, often simply called *Kore*, the girl) by the king of the lower world, Dis or Tartarus, and of the desperate effort of her mother, Ceres (*Demeter* in Greek), to win her back. Ceres finds her daughter, but Jupiter rules that the young girl must spend half the year with her captor, and half with her mother. The girl's absence from her earthly homeland, and her mother's sorrow (Ceres is goddess of the harvest) account for the changing of the seasons. Here is Calliope's story, in an abridged version of the beautiful translation of Frank Justus Miller (1915):

The king of the lower world had left his gloomy realm and, in his chariot was traversing the land of Sicily, carefully inspecting its foundations. After he had examined all to his satisfaction and found that no points were giving way, he put aside his fears. But Venus Erycina from her mountaintop saw him wandering to and fro and ordered Cupid to pierce his heart with an arrow of love. For he was the last of the three sons of Saturn to remain unmarried. Already Pallas and Diana had revolted against her, choosing to remain virgin, and Ceres' daughter, too, would follow suit if she, Venus, should suffer it; for she aspired to be like them. 'Go', she entreated, 'and join the goddess to her uncle in the bonds of love'. The god of love loosed his quiver at his mother's bidding and selected from his thousand shafts the sharpest and the surest and the most obedient to the bow. With this barbed arrow he smote Dis through the heart.

Not far from Henna's walls is a deep pool of water called Pergus. A wood crowns the heights around its shores, and the cool, shady ground bears bright-coloured flowers. There spring is everlasting. Within this grove Proserpina was playing and gathering violets or white lilies. While with girl-ish eagerness she was filling her basket and her bosom and striving to sur-pass her friends in gathering, almost in one act Dis saw and loved and car-ried her away: so strong was his passion, fired by Cupid's arrows. The terri-fied girl called plaintively on her mother and her companions; but her cap-tor urged on his horses, shaking the dark reins on their necks and manes. Through deep lakes and over high mountains they sped until, near Arethusa, they reached the pool of Cyane.

Here, the most famous of the Sicilian water-nymphs, recognizing the god-dess, stood forth from her waters and blocked the way, crying to Dis: 'No fur-ther shall you go! Thou canst not be the son-in-law of Ceres against her will. The maiden should have been wooed, not ravished'. Dis, urging on his terri-ble steeds, whirled his royal sceptre and smote the pool to its bottom. The stricken earth opened up a road to Tartarus and received the down-plunging chariot in its cavernous depths. Cyane, grieving for the rape of the goddess and for her fountain's rights thus offended, nursed an incurable wound in her heart and dissolved all away in tears. Into those very waters whose divinity she had been but now, she was melted, her body vanishing into thin streams, her living blood into clear water.

Meanwhile the frightened mother sought her daughter in every land and on every deep. Not Aurora, rising with dewy tresses, not Hesperus saw her pause in the search. Over what lands and what seas the goddess roamed it would take long to tell. When there was no more a place to search in, she came back to Sicily, and in the course of her wanderings here she came to Cyane. Having no means of speech, the nymph showed on the surface of her pool Proserpina's girdle, which had chanced to fall upon the waters. As soon as she saw the garment, as if she had for the first time learned that her daughter had been stolen, Ceres tore her hair and beat her breast. As she did not know as yet where her child was, she reproached all lands, but especially Sicily, where she had found traces of her loss. There with angry hand she broke the plows that turn the soil, and in her rage she gave to destruction farmers and cattle alike and bade the plowed fields to betray their trust and blighted the seed. The fertility of this land, famous throughout the world, lay false to its good name: the crops died in early blade, now too much heat, now too much rain destroying them. Stars and winds were baleful, greedy birds ate up the seed as soon as it was sown, and stubborn grasses choked the wheat.

At this juncture Arethusa lifted her head from her pool and prayed the goddess of fruits to cease her boundless search and stop punishing the land, which had been true to her. Imploring the goddess's mercy, she explained that she herself had seen Proserpina in the earth's lowest depths. The maiden had seemed sad and her face had been perturbed with fear; but yet she was a queen, 'the great queen of that world of darkness, the mighty consort of the tyrant of the underworld'. The mother, upon hearing these words, stood as if turned to stone and was for a long time like one bereft of reason. But when her overwhelming frenzy had given way to overwhelming pain, she set forth in her chariot to heaven. There, with clouded countenance, she appeared before Jove, her brother, father of her daughter and brother of the girl's abductor. 'My daughter, sought so long, has at last been found', she said, 'if you call it fiding more certainly to lose her, or if you call it finding merely to know where she is. That she has been stolen, I will bear, if only he will bring her back; for your daughter does not deserve to have a robber for a husband—if now she is not mine'. And Jove replied: 'She is, indeed, our daughter, yours and mine, our common pledge and care. But if only we are willing to give right names to things, this is no harm that has been done, but only love'. If Ceres wished to separate them, Jove remarked, Proserpina would be allowed to return to heaven on one condition only: if in the lower-world no food had yet touched her lips—for so had the fates decreed.

Ceres was resolved to have her daughter back. Not so the fates; for the girl had already broken her fast. Simple child that she was, while she wandered in the trim gardens, she had plucked a pomegranate hanging from a bending bough and eaten seven of the seeds. But Jove, seeking to balance the claims of his brother and his grieving sister, divided the revolving year into two equal parts and ruled that the goddess, the common divinity of two realms, should spend half the months with her mother and with her husband, half. Proserpina's expression and bearing changed straightaway: she who but lately had seemed sad even to Dis, donned a joyful countenance—like the sun which, long concealed behind dark and misty clouds, disperses the clouds and reveals its face.

First floor The first-floor rooms display material from the Greek colonies a Rhegium, Metauros, Medma, Laos and Kaulonia. The finds from Rhegiu (rooms 1–3) include architectural terracottas, some bearing traces of the orig nal painting; a large Hellenistic sarcophagus in the form of a foot (the decease was buried in a sitting position); and a goblet of Alexandrian glass with huntin scenes in gold leaf. The better displays from Metauros (room 4) include importe ceramics from Attica and Chalcis. From Medma (room come an interesting group of fictile votive offerings and th moulds for making them (notice the small statue of seated deity holding a dove); bronze objects, including mirror handle with Silenus approaching a seated nuc youth. The finest material from Laos (room 6) is the trea sure from a 4C chamber tomb used for the burial of Lucanian warrior and his wife, including a fine cereme nial suit of armour and diadem. From Kaulonia (room 7 notice the clay lion-head decoration of a temple, head of statue, and coloured mosaic with a sea monster from a patricia house. Room 8 houses finds from the Temple of Apollo Alaic that stood alone on the headland today known as Punta Alic near Cirò Marina, notably a 5C head of Apollo attributed Pythagoras of Rhegium, and fragments of feet and hands.

Second floor The works which the National Museu inherited from the Provincial Gallery, which it superceded, ar displayed here. Byzantine artefacts: reliquary crosses ar medals of the 6C–11C. Arabo-Norman gesso-work: columr and panels with peacocks, etc. Two small panel paintings b **Antonello da Messina**, *St Jerome* and *Three Angels*. Two late 15C panels b Pietro Cararo. A fine but small, late 14C *St Lucy*. Mattia Preti, **Return of th Prodigal Son**. Fede Galizia, **Judith and Holofernes**. Various 17C canvases, dar and anonymous. Paintings of the 18C and 19C by Vincenzo Cannizzaro, Adria Mangland and others.

Bronze mirror found at Locri

Near the post office are remains of the Greek walls and a Roman bath. Th **Lungomare**, described by D'Annunzio as the most beautiful kilometre in Ital though now busy with traffic commands a magnificent panorama.

Aspromonte ~ the great southern spur

The Aspromonte, the last great spur of the Apennines, is an old massif with so contours descending in several terraces to the sea. The name denotes the distri bounded by the Tyrrhenian Sea, the Straits of Messina and the Ionian Sea and b the Petrace, Plati and Careri Rivers on the north. At the centre of th Aspromonte rises Montalto (1956m), the highest peak of southern Calabri from here, numerous ridges radiate in all directions, most of these droppin abruptly into the sea. The longest ridge, which extends to the north-east, form the main watershed.

The four terraces or *Piani dell'Aspromonte*, as they are known locally, wer made by bradyseisms and reflect successive alterations in the relative levels c land and sea. Earthquakes have afflicted the area with uncommon frequency, the most disastrous being that of 1783, which destroyed much of the inhabited area between Reggio and Palmi, 46km up the west coast.

Almonds, peaches, figs, and citrus fruit flourish in the coastal areas, and the lowlands between Scilla and Capo Spartivento are famous for their plantations of bergamot orange, used for scent and eau de cologne. Jasmine is also grown in the area around Brancaleone. In the hill zones are groves of giant olives. Above 650m chestnuts and oaks prevail, then beech and conifers. The highland areas were once covered by dense forest, unfortunately destroyed over the centuries, so that much of the region is now given over to pastures and to the cultivation of grain and potatoes. The forests of the Aspromonte are constantly expanding, however, due to an active reafforestation programme. The spectacular views—which at some points span the north and west coasts of Sicily—winter sports at Gambarie (see below), and woodlands are the region's main attraction and a considerable part of the area was set aside as a National Park in 1991.

Garibaldi's untimely advance on Rome (he had been ordered to attack Austria in the Balkans, but decided instead to attack the Papal States, without the approval of king and cabinet) was checked by Cialdini at the Battle of Aspromonte in September 1862 and in later years its fastnesses were the haunt of Musolino, a 19C Robin Hood. Even today, the mountains are a favourite hiding-place of fugitives from the law.

Reggio Calabria to Gambarie

This road climbs through the foothills of the Aspromonte, offering good views across the Straits of Messina and along the densely populated coast north of Reggio.

Sambatello (286m) is known for its dry rosé wine. Beyond, the road follows the Gallico Valley, dominated by the ruined castle of Calanna, a structure of strategic importance in Byzantine, Norman and Swabian times. Below, the river-bed is strewn with small orchards protected against the violent winter currents by dykes. The road crosses the river and is joined by the road from **Calanna**, perched on the ridge above. The village (population 2000) enjoys a splendid view. In the parish church fragments of medieval sculpture from a ruined Byzantine church, a 15C bell and sculptural fragments dating from the 16C and 17C can be seen. In 1953 excavations nearby revealed a necropolis dating from the 9C–6C BC. The material recovered is now in the Museo Nazionale in Reggio.

As the valley narrows, the ascent becomes more tortuous. Laganadi is set among olive groves. The road crosses a deep ravine, then resumes its climb, with views of the villages of Cerasi and Ortì in the distance. Beyond Sant'Alessio in Aspromonte, continue through wooded glens and past a river-bed graced by flowering junipers in summer to **Santo Stefano in Aspromonte** (population 2000), a small town with a distinctive mountain character (the upper floors of many houses are wood), the birthplace of Musolino (see above). Beyond, the road loops back to the west. The **view** spans the Straits of Messina and the Sicilian coast from Punto Faro to Mount Etna. The road terminates at **Gambarie** (1300m), a popular summer and winter resort in a magnificent position among beech and fir forests.

Bagnara Calabra to Gambarie

The first part of this route winds up to a broad plain covered with olives and dwarf oaks. Through further loops and turns, the road mounts to Sant'Eufemia d'Aspromonte (440m), where you leave the main road on the left and cross the Piani dell'Aspromonte. The **view** to the west is magnificent. You emerge onto Road 183, which you follow to the south. A dirt track on the left leads to the site of Garibaldi's capture at the Battle of Aspromonte (see above). Beyond it, the road ascends steeply to Gambarie.

Melito di Porto Salvo to Gambarie

The road (marked) from Melito to Gambarie initially follows the west bank of the Fiumara Melito. Beyond the turning for Prunella (right) the ascent of the Aspromonte begins. At (9km) Chorio the valley narrows. You pass a small hamlet, and a road on the right diverges to San Lorenzo and Roghudi. **Bagaladi** (475m) derives its name from the Arabic *Baha' Allah*, the beauty that comes from God. The road continues to climb, with views over the Pristeo and Melito valleys. At the head of the latter, the Punta d'Atò rises vertically to a height of 1379m. Continue the ascent through forests of oak and chestnut, with broad views over the sea and the Strait of Messina to Aetna and the Monti Peloritani in Sicily. Cross a rolling plain planted with forage and grain, followed by a forested glen between two high mountains. Further on, the view to the left embraces the Campi di Sant'Agata and the Calopinace Valley. The Strait and Mount Aetna are once again visible. A little later the road to Reggio via the Passo di Petrulli (1056m) branches left. Continue across a broad pasture, then descend rapidly between beach trees to a large clearing and Gambarie.

Among the many pretty excursions from Gambarie, the following are particularly pleasant; all have good views. **Puntone di Scirocco**, 1660m, is c 2km by chairlift from Bivio di Gambarie, where the roads from Gallico and Dellanuova meet. **Montalto** summit, 1985m, can be reached on foot in 4 hours by a steep mule-track (also on mule-back, May–Oct, conditions permitting). On the summit stands a large bronze Christ turned towards Reggio in benediction. From the top of the mountain the Strait of Messina is out of sight, and Sicily and Calabria appear to form a single, continuous land mass. Just below the summit, a track to the north leads to (3 hours) Dellanuova. A steep path to the north-east winds through forests of beech, fir, oak and chestnut to the Santuario di Santa Maria dei Polsi, of Byzanto-Norman origin. The **Cippo di Garibaldi** commemorates the Battle of Aspromonte. From Bivio di Gambarie, road 183 crosses a plateau. A signpost indicates a way through the woods to the *cippo* (1204m), a modern monument built on the site where the general was captured.

Abruzzo and Molise

Abruzzo and Molise represent a hidden treasure, a land of mountains at once rugged and soft, clothed here in a mantle of dark forest, there in a golden cloak of grain. Whatever you think of the towns, which in the more remote areas can be rather grim, you'll be favourably impressed by the particular character of the landscape, 'these impressive Abruzzi ridges that combined in so special a way hard temper with soft color—as if there were steel underneath blue silver, yet a blue so etherealized that one peak, with its pencilled veins of snow, seemed to merge into the slate-blue heavens' (Edmund Wilson, *Europe without Baedeker*, 1947).

These two relatively small regions occupy the east centre of the Italian peninsula, with their seaboard on the Adriatic. They are bordered on the north by the Marches, on the west by Lazio and on the south by Campania and Apulia. With a total area of 15,232sq km, they comprise the hilly provinces of L'Aquila, Teramo, Pescara, Chieti, Campobasso and Isernia. Formerly a single region, they became administratively independent in 1963.

The highest peaks of the Apennines are to be found in Abruzzo. They diverge slightly from the main north-west to south-east axis here to form the Meta Massif, in the Abruzzo National Park. The Lago-Gran Sasso-Maiella range—which culminates in the Corno Grande (2912m), the 'roof' of the peninsula—divides the region into two fundamentally different landscapes and climates: one maritime, the other alpine. Between this and the central range lies the so-called Abruzzo highland, with the basins of L'Aquila and Sulmona.

The first human presence in Abruzzo seems to date from the Lower Palaeolithic period. Evidence from the Upper Palaeolithic and Neolithic periods has been found throughout the region, particularly in the Fucino basin, rich in cave finds, and at Corropoli, where the so-called Ripoli culture, distinguished by a particular type of painted ceramics, appears to have lasted over a millennium. The Neolithic Apennine culture was introduced at a fairly advanced stage, in the Middle Bronze Age, probably by small groups of shepherds from Apulia or the Marches; and Neolithic traditions persisted even in the later, sub-Apennine phase. Especially in the mountain areas, the sub-Apennine cultures maintained their autonomy, contributing later to the formation of numerous allied tribes, of mixed origin, who were subdued by the Romans only after a long, bitter struggle culminating in the Social War (91–82 BC).

After the fall of the Roman Empire, the region was partitioned between the Dukes of Spoleto and Benevento and was later united by the Normans to the Duchy of Apulia. Frederick II Hohenstaufen transformed Abruzzo into an independent province with Sulmona as capital, but after the arrival of the Angevins the region followed the fortunes of the Kingdom of Naples. The Bourbons in 1684 divided it into Abruzzo Citeriore, Ulteriore Primo and Ulteriore Secondo (corresponding to the three northern provinces of today), and Molise.

The name, Abruzzo, originally *Aprutium*, seems to be derived from the Praetuttii, one of the aboriginal tribes. The Tronto river, which today separates Abruzzo from the Marches, is the historical border between the Kingdom of Naples and the Papal States. On the west, the boundary with Lazio still follows the dividing line between the ancient IV Regio Samnium and I Regio Latium. The title of Duke of Abruzzi was borne by Luigi Amedeo, grandson of Victor Emmanuel II, the distinguished explorer and mountaineer (1873–1933).

Medieval Abruzzan art is characterised by severe simplicity and Abruzzan churches are distinguished by their flat, gableless façades. The region is noted for its pottery and goldsmiths' work and for its attractive local costumes; and the people are famous for their pride, their industry and their hospitality. The origin of the name Molise, which is first mentioned as a region in the 13C, is uncertain.

THE ADRIATIC COAST

The Adriatic coast of Abruzzo and Molise is flat and unremarkable, but just a few kilometres inland are areas known for their natural beauty, their magnificent castles and their austere medieval churches. Particularly fine examples of the latter may be seen at **Atri** and **Lanciano**.

The little resorts by the sea are good starting points for exploring these areas—as well as Abruzzo's mountainous interior. Day trips can easily be made to **L'Aquila** and to the **Gran Sasso**, or to the churches, castles and archaeological sites of the western highlands. Whatever you do, don't miss the archaeological museum in **Chieti**, which won a European Union award for its excellent layout. Chieti itself is a lively, pleasant town. **Pescara** is a busy provincial capital.

Practical information

Information offices

ALBA ADRIATICA *Ufficio Informazioni e di Accoglienza Turistica*, Lungomare Marconi 1, ☎ 0861 712426.

CHIETI *Amministrazione Provinciale, Settore Turismo*, Corso Marruccino, ☎ 0871 408282.
Ufficio Informazioni e di Accoglienza Turistica, Via Spaventa 29-31, ☎ 0871 63640.

FRANCAVILLA AL MARE *Ufficio Informazioni e di Accoglienza Turistica*, Piazza Sirena, ☎ 085 817169.

GIULIANOVA LIDO Via Mamiani 2, ☎ 085 800 3013.

LANCIANO Piazza Plebiscito, ☎ 0872 714959.

ORTONA *Ufficio Informazioni e di Accoglienza Turistica*, Piazza della Repubblica 9, ☎ 085 906 3841.

PESCARA *Amministrazione Provinciale Settore Turismo*, Piazza Italia, ☎ 085 372 4232.
Assessorato Regionale al Turismo, Viale Bovio 425, ☎ 085 7671, ✉ www.

regione.abruzzo.it/turismo, quirino.morelli@regione.abruzzo.it;
Azienda Regionale per la Promozione Turistica, Via Nicola Fabrizi 171, ☎ 085 7671.
Ufficio Informazioni e di Accoglienza Turistica, Corso Vittorio Emanuele 301, 429001; free phone 800 502520.
Ufficio Informazioni e di Accoglienza Turistica, Via Mazzini 146, ☎ 085 421 5933.

PINETO *Ufficio Informazioni e di Accoglienza Turistica*, Via Mazzini–Centro Polifunzionale, ☎ 085 949 1745.

ROSETO DEGLI ABRUZZI *Ufficio Informazioni e di Accoglienza Turistica*, Piazza della Libertà 37–38, ☎ 085 899 1157.

SILVI MARINA *Ufficio Informazioni e di Accoglienza Turistica*, Lungomare Garibaldi 208, ☎ 085 930343.

TERMOLI *Azienda Autonoma di Soggiorno e Turismo*, Piazza Bega, ☎ 0875 703913.

VASTO *Ufficio Informazioni e di Accoglienza Turistica*, Piazza del Popolo 18, ☎ 0873 367312; *Rotonda Lungomare Dalmazia*, Marina di Vasto (June–Sept), ☎ 0873 801751.

Getting there and getting around
By air

There is a regional airport (Pasquale Liberi) 6km north of **Pescara**, with flights to/from Frankfurt, London, Olbia Rome, Milan and Turin.

By road

Autostrada A14 follows the coast closely from the Marches, on the north, to Apulia on the south, and is the best road to use when visiting the area. Road 16, which parallels the autostrada, is satisfactory for short hops but may prove tiresome over long distances. Autostrade A25 and A24 link Pescara to Rome.

By rail

The main line connecting Milan with Bari, Brindisi and Lecce keeps close to the road all the way. Fast Intercity trains stop at San Benedetto del Tronto, Giulianova, Pescara and Termoli; slow local trains stop at most other towns on the line. There is also an Intercity service from Rome to Pescara (240km in c 3hrs 25mins). Pescara has two railway stations: Centrale, the main station and the terminus of the line from Rome, and Porta Nuova, for the southern part of the town.

By sea

Termoli, Vasto (Punta Penna) and Ortona are connected by boats and hydrofoils to the Tremiti islands. To/from Termoli: daily ferries 1hr to 1hr 40mins, hydrofoils 50mins. Vasto: daily hydrofoils June–Sept in 1hr. Ortona: daily hydrofoils June–Sept, 2hrs. For further details contact offices in Ortona: *Adriatica di Navigazione*, c/o *Agenzia Fratino*, Via Porto 34, ☎ 085 906

3855, www.adriatica.it; *Termoli: Navigazione Libera del Golfo*, at the harbour, ☎ 0875 704859 (ferries) and *Adriatica di Navigazione*, c/o *Agenzia Adriashipping*, at the harbour, ☎ 0875 705343 (hydrofoils); *Vasto*, *Adriatica di Navigazione*, c/o *Agenzia Massacesi*, Piazza Diomede 3, ☎ 0873 362680.

Where to stay

CHIETI €€ *Abruzzo*, Via A. Herio 20, ☎ 0871 41940, 🖷 0871 41960, ✉ gaa@alicom.com. The traditional place to stay in Chieti, with comfortable rooms and cordial staff.

CITTÀ SANT'ANGELO (near Silvi) €€€ *Villa Nacalua*, Contrada Fonte Umano, ☎ 085 959225, 🖷 085 959263, ✉ www.nacalua.com, info@nacalua.com. In the country near the autostrada at Pescara Nord; elegant rooms, marble baths, pool.

€ *Giardino dei Principi*, Viale Petruzzi 30, at Moscarola, ☎ 085 950235, 🖷 950254. Simple butcomfortable, with an excellent restaurant.

FRANCAVILLA AL MARE €€ *Sporting Hotel Villa Maria*, Contrada Pretaro, ☎ 085 451 1001, 🖷 085 693042. Distinguished establishment with lovely rooms, pool and shady gardens.

LANCIANO € *Anxanum*, Via San Francesco d'Assisi 8, ☎ 0872 715142, 🖷 0872 715142, ✉ hotelanxanum@tin.it. A modern place with spacious rooms, pool and sauna.

LORETO APRUTINO €€ *Castello Chiola*, Via degli Aquino 12, ☎ 085 829 0690, 🖷 085 829 0677. Refined and comfortable, in a historic building.

€ *La Bilancia*, Contrada Palazzo 11, ☎ 085 828 9321, 🖷 085 828 9610. In the hills 5km from the town, with an excellent restaurant; closed mid-Dec–mid-Jan.

ORTONA € *Ideale*, Via Garibaldi 65, ☎ 085 906 3735, 🖷 085 906 6153. Simple and quiet, with good views.

PESCARA € *Ambra*, Via Quarto dei Mille 28–30, ☎ 085 378247, 🗐 085 378183. Central and comfortable; closed mid-Dec–mid-Jan.

€€ *Esplanade*, Piazza Primo Maggio 46, ☎ 085 292141, 🗐 085 421 7540, 🖾 www.esplanade.net, themanager@ esplanade.net. Refined and comfortable, with an excellent restaurant, in the very centre of town.

SPOLTORE (8km north west of Pescara) €€ *Montinope*, Via Montinope, ☎ 085 496 2836, 🗐 085 496 2143. Just 18 rooms and 2 suites, with good views and an excellent restaurant.

Youth Hostel

VASTO € *Ostello Antoniano*, Via Spalato 19, ☎ 0873 801640.

 Eating out
ALBA ADRIATICA (near Giulianova)

€€ *Mediterraneo*, Via Mazzini 148, ☎ 0861 752000. Traditional fish dishes with a creative twist; closed Tues evening.

CAMPOMARINO (near Termoli) € *Nonna Rosa*, Via Biferno 41, ☎ 0875 539948. Tiny trattoria in the historic town centre; closed Tues (except in July–Aug) and first two weeks of Oct.

CARPINETO DELLA NORA (near Chieti) € *La Roccia*, Contrada Versante al Bosco, ☎ 085 849142. Good country trattoria; closed Tues (except in July–Aug) and two weeks in Oct.

CHIETI €€ *Caminetto d'Oro*, Via Aterno 36, ☎ 0871 561349. Restaurant offering good regional fish and meat dishes; closed Mon and late Aug.

D'Orazio, Vicolo Storto Teatro San Ferdinando 1. Pastry shop for biscuits, pastries, cakes and pies.

CITTÀ SANT'ANGELO (near Silvi) € *La Locanda dell'Arte*, Vico II Santa Chiara 7, ☎ 085 96669. The art of cooking *farro* (spelt), in a simple oste-

ria; closed Sun (except in summer).

CIVITELLA CASANOVA (west of Chieti) € *La Bandiera*, Contrada Pastini 32, ☎ 085 845219. Authentic regional cuisine at its best, in the countryside miles from anywhere; closed Wed, Jan and July.

COLONNELLA (near Giulianova) € *Zenobi*, Contrada Rio Moro, ☎ 0861 70581. Farm serving excellent country meals; closed Tues (except in summer) and Nov.

CONTROGUERRA (near Giulianova) € *La Credenza*, Via Pianura del Tronto 80, ☎ 0861 89757. Wine estate (Controguerra d.o.c.) and farm serving country meals, open for dinner (lunch by reservation); closed Mon and Jan.

CORROPOLI (near Giulianova) € *Locanda della Tradizione Abruzzese*, Via Piane, at Piane, ☎ 0861 810129. Restaurant-pizzeria in a former farmhouse; closed Wed (except in summer) and a few days in Oct and Dec.

FARA FILIORUM PETRI €€ *Belvedere*, Via San Giacomo 50, ☎ 0871 70282. Traditional restaurant with great regional food and wines; closed Mon and Nov.

GIULIANOVA €€ *Osteria dal Moro*, Lungomare Spalato 74, at Giulianova Lido, ☎ 085 800 4973. Trattoria with good fish; closed Mon and Tues, Thur and Sat evening, late Sept–early Oct and late Feb–early Mar.

€€ *Osteria della Stracciavocc*, Via Trieste 159, at Giulianova Lido; ☎ 085 8005326. Osteria serving delicious regional seafood; closed Mon and 10 days in Oct.

€ *Beccaceci*, Via Zola 28, ☎ 085 800 7073. Traditional fish restaurant; closed Mon evening, Tues and Dec–Jan.

Salumeria Antonio, Via Nazario Sauro 120. Delicatessen with a wide assortment of cold meats, cheeses, olive oil, wine, etc.

GUARDIAGRELE € *Santa Chiara*,
Via Roma 10, ☎ 0871 801139.
Delicious regional cuisine in the heart of
the historic town centre; closed Tues
and late July.

€ *Villa Maiella*, Via Sette Dolori 30,
☎ 0871 809319. Locally famous
restaurant offering outstanding regional
cuisine and good ambiance; closed Mon
and late July.

GUGLIONESI (near Termoli)
€ *Il Pagatore*, Corso Conte di Torino
71, ☎ 0875 680550. Good local
recipes in a pleasant hill town; closed
Sun (except in Aug) and two weeks in
Nov.

€€ *Ribo*, Contrada Malecoste, ☎ 0875
680655. Restaurant known for its
creative interpretations of traditional
fish and game dishes; closed Mon.

LANCIANO €€ *Ruota*, Via per
Fossacesia 40, ☎ 0872 44590.
Restaurant known for its good regional
cuisine, especially fish; closed Sun.

LORETO APRUTINO
€€ *La Bilancia*, Contrada Palazzo 10,
☎ 085 828 9321. Small hotel restaurant with great local cooking, often
crowded; closed Mon and Dec–Jan.

MARTINSICURO (near Giulianova)
€€ *Il Sestante*, Lungomare Italia, at
Villa Rosa, ☎ 0861 713268. Excellent
fresh fish in a locally famous restaurant;
closed Sun evening and Mon, and late
July–early Aug.

€€ *Mare*, Lungomare Europa 40,
☎ 0861 762100. Another good restaurant for fresh fish; closed Sun evening
and Mon, and late Oct–early Nov.

NOTARESCO €€ *Tre Archi*, Via
Pianura Vomano 36, at Guardia
Vomano, ☎ 085 898140. Great old-
fashioned country cooking in the hills
above the coast; closed Wed and Nov.

ORTONA €€ *Cantina Aragonese*,
Corso Matteotti 88, ☎ 085 906 3217.
Good traditional restaurant; closed Sun
evening and Mon.

€€ *Il Sestante*, Via Marina 72, ☎ 085

9061878. Pleasant restaurant and
pizzeria near the harbour; closed Mon
(except in summer) and Nov.

PESCARA €€€ *Michele al Sea
River Club*, Via Roveto 37, ☎ 085
28056. Outstanding fish restaurant
overlooking the River Pescara; closed
Sun evening, Mon and Jan.

€€ *Da Attilio*, Viale La Figlio di Iorio
20, ☎ 085 451 4920. Good seafood
reasonably priced; closed Sun evening
and Mon and late Aug–early Sept.

€€ *Franco*, Via Andrea Doria 28,
☎ 085 66390. Delicious traditional fish
dishes; closed Mon.

€€ *Guerino*, Viale della Riviera 4,
☎ 085 421 2065. Good fish restaurant
with outdoor seating by the sea; closed
Thur and Dec–Jan.

€€ *La Locanda Manthoné*, Corso
Manthoné 58, ☎ 085 454 9034.
Refined, friendly osteria in the heart of
Pescara's restaurant district; open
evenings only, closed Sun.

€ *Enoteca-Osteria Visaggio*, Via De
Cesaris 44, ☎ 085 421 6692. Wine bar
with a wide selection of wines and cold
snacks.

€ *La Figlia di Attilio*, Via Pepe 117,
☎ 085 451 1500; reasonably priced
family-run fish restaurant; closed Sun
evening, Mon and Aug.

€ *La Lumaca*, Via delle Caserme 51,
☎ 085 451 0880. Osteria with an
excellent wine list and good local
cheeses, open evenings only; closed Tues.

€ *Osteria dei Miracoli*, Corso
Manthoné 57, ☎ 085 66986. Osteria
with a strong local following, known for
its seasonal cooking, open evenings
only; closed Tues and late July–early Aug.

€ *Taverna 58*, Corso Manthoné 58,
☎ 085 690724. Authentic trattoria
offering good seasonal cuisine; closed
mid-day Sat, Sun, holidays and Aug.

D'Alessandro Enoteca & Dolcezze, Via
Trento 126, for local delicacies and wines.
Berardo, Corso Umberto I 120, for
delicious ice cream.

Pandora Dolci Artigianali, Via Pisano 33–35. Pastry shop making traditional and imaginative pastries, cakes and pies.
Pasticceria Camplone, Corso Umberto 36; confectioner selling traditional candies, cakes and *semifreddi*.
PIANELLA €€ *Il Club dei Buongustai*, Via Francesco Verrotti 10, ☎ 085 973393. Family-run restaurant with good regional food, especially fish; closed Sun evening, Mon and Nov.
€ *Poggio del Sole*, Contrada Nardangelo 12, ☎ 085 972233. Creative interpretations of local dishes, with fair-weather seating outdoors; closed Mon and Sept.
PINETO € *Al Bacucco d'Oro*, Via del Pozzo 6, at Mutignano, ☎ 085 936227. Restaurant-pizzeria in the hills above Pineto; closed Wed (except in summer) and Nov.
€€ *Italia*, Via al Mare 8, ☎ 085 946 2117. Good fish restaurant by the sea; closed Mon and Nov.
RIPA TEATINA (between Chieti and Francavilla) € *Casa di Filippo*, Contrada Santo Stefano 152. Good regional cooking in a historic setting, with garden; closed Mon and mid-Aug.
ROSETO DEGLI ABRUZZI
€€ *Tonino da Rosanna*, Via Volturno 9, ☎ 085 899274. Garden restaurant serving innovative fish dishes; closed Mon and Nov–Mar.
SAN MARTINO IN PENSILIS (near Termoli) € *Castello*, Piazza Vittoria 23, ☎ 0875 604902. Fine local dishes from the hills and mountains, in a historic setting; closed Wed and Sept.
SAN SALVO (near Vasto) € *Osteria delle Spezie*, Corso Garibaldi 44, ☎ 0873 341602. Fine osteria in an otherwise uninteresting village; closed Wed and late Sept.
Caffé Roma, Corso Garibaldi 7. Café with excellent pastries and ice cream.
SAN VALENTINO IN ABRUZZO CITERIORE (near Chieti)
€ *Antichi Sapori*, Contrada Cerrone 4,

☎ 085 854 1234; closed Wed (except in summer).
SAN VITO CHIETINO (between Francavilla and Termoli) €€ *L'Angolino di Filippo*, Via Nazionale Adriatica, ☎ 0872 61632. Good, elegant fish restaurant by the sea, in the same family for over a hundred years; closed Mon and late Dec–early Jan.
SILVI €€ *Gabbiani del Faro*, Via Garibaldi 196, at Silvi Marina, ☎ 085 930 0589. Good fish restaurant by the sea; closed Mon and Oct–Nov.
€ *Don Ambrosio*, Contrada Piomba 49, ☎ 085 935 1060. Restaurant (with rooms) offering regional food and good wines, at Piomba Alta, in the hills above Silvi; closed Tues and Nov.
€ *Vecchia Silvi*, Via Circonvallazione Boreale 22, at Silvi Alta, ☎ 085 930141. Traditional recipes from mountain and shore; closed Tues.
Taberna Imperiale, Via Roma 130–136. Delicatessen offering a broad selection of regional specialities.
TERMOLI €€ *Cian*, Lungomare Cristoforo Colombo 48, ☎ 0875 704436. Another good seafood restaurant, on the water; closed Mon and Nov.
€€ *San Carlo*, Via Giudicato Vecchio 24, ☎ 0875 705295. Excellent regional cuisine in a historic building in central Termoli; closed Tues (except in summer).
€€ *Torre Saracena*, Strada Statale 16, ☎ 0875 703318. Good fish restaurant with sea views, in a historic setting; closed Mon and Nov.
€€ *Z'Bass*, Via Oberdan 8, ☎ 0875 706703. Warm, sometimes crowded trattoria known for its outstanding seafood; closed Mon (except in summer).
TORANO NUOVO (near Giulianova) € *La Sosta*, Via Regina Margherita 34, ☎ 0861 82085. Good trattoria-pizzeria in the Montepulciano and Trebbiano d'Abruzzo wine country; closed Tues and late Aug–early Sept.
VASTO €€ *All'Hosteria del Pavone*,

Via Barbarotta 15–17, ☎ 0873 60227. Warm, friendly trattoria in the historic town centre; closed Tues (except in summer) and Jan–Feb.

€ *Villa Vignola*, Strada Statale 16 at Marina di Vasto, ☎ 0873 310050, 🖷 0873 310060. Restaurant with 5 rooms, on the sea just outside town; open all year (except a few days in late Dec).

Special events

CHIETI *Stagione di Prosa e di Musica*, music and theatre, *Teatro Marruccino* (Nov–May); Good Friday procession; Sagra di San Giustino (May); *Vivi l'Estate*, various cultural and folk events (July–Aug).

FARA FILIORUM PETRI *Sagra di Sant'Antonio Abate* (16 Jan), celebrated by burning a forest of farchie, bamboo columns up to 12m high.

PESCARA *San Cetteo* (10 Oct); *Stagione Teatrale e Musicale* (theatre and music, Nov–May); *Stagione Estiva di Prosa* (open-air theatre, July–Aug); *Festival Internazionale del Jazz* (July); *Concorso Ippico* (horse show, July); *Premio Internazionale Ennio Flaiano* (international theatre, cinema, literature, and television awards, July).

White sands and pines

Most of the towns along the coast have become summer resorts, usually with sandy beaches backed by cool pine woods. The towns can be curiously quiet in low season, which here extends from mid-September to mid-June.

Giulianova, a seaside resort (population 23,000) was founded in 1470 by the people of San Flaviano (the ancient *Castrum Novum*) and named in honour of Giulio Antonio Acquaviva, Duke of Atri. It consists of a medieval town set on a hill 1km from the coast and a new quarter, Giulianova Lido, which stands between the road and the sea. The Renaissance **duomo**, built to an octagonal plan, contains a 14C reliquary. The fine Romanesque church of Santa Maria a Mare was ruined in 1944, but has been restored. The **Pinacoteca Comunale Vincenzo Bindi** (Via Garibaldi 14; open Mon–Fri 09.00–12.00 and 15.00–18.30; ☎ 085 802 1215) has a modest collection of Neapolitan School paintings and Capodimonte ceramics; and there is a small collection of modern art in the former convent of the **Madonna dello Splendore** (open Tues–Sat 10.00–13.00 and 16.00–18.30, Sun and holidays 10.00–12.30 and 16.00–18.30; ☎ 085 800 7157).

Pineto lies near **Atri** (population 11,000), on a hill to the west. This is the legendary *Hatria*, which became a Roman colony in 282 BC. Its coins are among the heaviest known, exceeding the oldest Roman coins in weight. The **cathedral** (1285), with a graceful campanile and a beautiful, though simple façade, contains 15C frescoes of Old and New Testament scenes, and of evangelists, doctors, and saints, by Andrea Delitio, and a fine tabernacle (1503) by Paolo de Garvi. The crypt, entered from the handsome cloister behind the church, is a Roman *piscina;* in the sacristy are two carved polyptychs. The Museo Capitolare (open Tues–Sun 09.00–20.00; ☎ 085 879 8140), also in the cloister, houses a small collection of medieval art.

The churches of Sant'Agostino and Sant'Andrea have good portals. The severe façade of the **Palazzo Acquaviva dei Duchi** (town hall and post office) masks an attractive 14C courtyard.

Inland to Penne

From Montesilvano country roads run west to Città Sant'Angelo, with a 14C church, and south-west to Penne. **Moscufo**, on the Penne road, is situated on a hilltop with views over the sea and mountains, from the Gran Sasso to the Maiella. The church of Santa Maria del Lago, 5km south of the road, has a fine pulpit of 1158. To the south of **Loreto Aprutino** the church of Santa Maria in Piano contains notable frescoes (*Last Judgement*, stories from the life of St Thomas Aquinas, New Testament scenes and saints) by 13C and 14C artists **Penne** (population 12,000) is an ancient city of the Vestini. The church of San Giovanni contains a processional cross attributed to Nicola da Guardiagrele (in the treasury). The 14C cathedral, almost completely destroyed in 1944, has been restored. Santa Maria in Colleromano, 1km south-east, has fragmentary 15C and 16C frescoes; and at Pianella, 18km south-east near the road to Chieti, is an interesting little Romanesque church.

Pescara

Pescara (population 129,000), capital of the province of Pescara, is the most active commercial town in Abruzzo as well as an important fishing port and a popular bathing resort. The completely modern town, charmingly situated among pinewoods, is divided into two parts by the River Pescara. The northern section, known as Pescara Riviera, was formerly the separate commune of Castellammare Adriatico. Pescara proper, on the south, is on the site of the Classical *Aternum*, the common port of the Vestini, Marrucini, and Peligni, and at the seaward end of the Via Valeria (today Highway 5).

Pescara was the birthplace of Gabriele D'Annunzio (1863–1938), the controversial early 20C writer and politician whose life and work may be admired in the **Museo Gabriele D'Annunzio** (Corso Manthoné 101; open Mon–Sat 09.00–14.00, Sun and holidays 09.00–13.00, last admission 30 mins before closing; ☎ 085 60391). The Museo Civico e Pinacoteca Basilio Cascella (Via Guglielmo Marconi 45; open daily 09.00–13.00, 16.00–19.00) contains paintings, sculpture, and prints by three generations of the Cascella family, also natives. The **Museo delle Genti d'Abruzzo** (Via delle Caserme 22; open June–Sept, Mon–Fri 09.00–13.00, Tues–Sun 21.00–00.30; Oct–May, Mon–Sat 09.00–13.00, Tues and Thur 15.30–18.00, Sun 10.00–13.00; ☎ 085 451 0026.) has sections devoted to ethnography, prehistory and protohistory, religion, popular festivities, and agriculture. South-east of the city centre is the attractive Pineta di Pescara.

Chieti

Chieti, capital of the province of the same name, is a lively little town with a population of 58,000. It is famous for its wide **views** of Abruzzo, from the Gran Sasso and the Maiella to the sea. Chieti railway station is at Chieti Scalo, 5km west (bus connection).

Chieti stands on the site of the ancient *Theate Marrucinorum*. Gian Pietro Carafa, Bishop of Chieti (afterwards Paul IV), gave the name of his see to the Theatines, the religious order that he founded in 1524, with St Cajetan (Gaetano da Thiene). The **cathedral**, many times rebuilt, has a graceful campanile silver (1335–1498); within are a Baroque pulpit and stalls, and (in the treasury) a statue of *St Justin*, by Nicola da Guardiagrele. Behind the post office are interest

A figure of controversy

Gabriele D'Annunzio is known as much for his political activism as for his dark, turbulent literary works. D'Annunzio was born in Pescara on 12 March 1863. He studied literature in Rome, where he also wrote for several magazines and soon distinguished himself as a socialite. Elected to parliament in 1897 (his home district was Ortona), on a whim he suddenly swung from the extreme right to the extreme left. In the same year he took a villa at Settignano near Florence, but at the insistence of his creditors he fled to France in 1910.

He returned to Italy in 1915 as an ardent champion of Italian intervention against Austria in the First World War. Convinced (rightly) that the example of an internationally famous poet would be influential, he flew over Austrian-held Trent and Trieste in 1915, lost an eye in a forced landing near Grado, took part in the Italian bombings of Pula and Kotor in 1917 and rode Italy's infamous manned torpedos (MAS) against Austrian warships. In 1919, he led a band of irregulars to occupy Rijeka (Croatia), which had been denied to Italy at the peace conference, holding the city until the arrival of the Italian army in 1920. A firm supporter of Fascism in its early stages, in 1921 he retired from public life to his villa, the Vittoriale, at Gardone Riviera, where he remained until his death on 1 March 1938. His most famous literary achievements are the four volumes of verses known as the *Laudi del cielo, del mare, della terra e degli eroi*, composed between 1899 and 1912. He was also a prolific novelist and playwright.

ng remains of three small Roman temples. The Palazzo Municipale, in the cathedral square, was erected in 1517, as the palace of the Valignani, and rebuilt in Neo-classical style in the 19C.

The **Museo d'Arte Costantino Barbella** (open Tues–Sat 09.00–13.00, Tues and Thur 16.00–18.45, first Sun of every month 09.00–12.00; ☎ 087 133 0873) occupies the Palazzo Martinetti-Bianchi, a former Jesuit college, in the central Via Cesare de Lollis. It has a few paintings by Francesco Paolo Michetti and other works dating from the 16C to the present. The Museo di Arte Sacra, adjoining the Baroque church of San Domenico (1642), is mainly notable for its examples of local woodcarving (open daily 08.00–12.00 and 16.30–19.00). Santa Maria Mater Domini (to the south-east) contains a *Madonna* carved in wood, by Gagliardelli.

National Archaeological Museum of Abruzzo

In the Villa Comunale is the Museo Nazionale Archeologico degli Abruzzi (open daily 09.00–19.30; ☎ 087 133 1668), which won the European Community's European Museum of the Year award in 1984 for its extraordinarily rich and well-displayed collections of Italic and Graeco-Roman antiquities. The museum was undergoing renovation at the time of writing but should follow this arrangement when work is completed.

Rooms 1, 3, and 4 are devoted to **burial cults in pre-Roman Abruzzo**, ranging from the 9C–4C BC. The objects displayed were found at grave sites throughout the region; their provenance is labelled and they are numbered progressively. Although most are made of inorganic materials (which do not decay), rare fragments of fabric, leather, and wood (see below, room 4) also survive. The finds include vessels for food and drink, arms and armour, jewellery, and personal

adornments, which indicate the social status of the deceased, and the commer
cial and cultural ties that the Italic communities in Abruzzo enjoyed with othe
Mediterranean and continental European peoples.

Room 1. Especially interesting are two of the 272 tombs excavated a
Campovalano (Province of Teramo). The first, belonging to a man, yielded
Corinthian-type bronze helmet and a bronze shin-guard; the second, of
woman, contained embossed bronze sandals imported from Etruria and a glas
sceptre. Both are 'patrician' tombs of the 7C or 8C BC. In the same room are bu
ial treasures from the excavations conducted at Penna Sant'Andrea (Teramo) i
1973, including masks and pearls of Phoenician–Punic origin; similar objec
have been found only at Carthage, in Spain, and in Sardinia. Particular impoi
tance is given to the stone stelae from the same site, which bear the first writte
evidence (7C or 6C BC) of the ethnic term Safin (Sabines).

Room 2, devoted to **Italic sculpture**, holds the famous **Warrior o
Capestrano**, the burial stele of an Italic monarch of the 6C BC, flanked by
series of presumably contemporary archaic sculptures: the so-called Devil's Leg
from Collelongo (L'Aquila), the Atessa torso (Chieti), the Leopardi head froi
Loreto Aprutino (Pesaro), and a fragment from Rapino (Chieti). **Room 3** contain
a variety of material from Iron Age necropoleis, notably the treasures of sever
tombs unearthed at Capestrano (one is probably that of the warrior); a stele froi
Guardiagrele (Chieti); material from Paglieta and Torricella Peligna (excavated i
the 19C but never before displayed); finds from the necropoleis of Alfeden
(L'Aquila); an iron sword and bronze belt with traces of fabric from the necroj
oleis of Pennapiedimente (Chieti), dating from the 4C BC and treasures from tw
of the 300 tombs identified in 1983 at Le Castagne, dating from the 7C or 6C B
and representing one of the larger necropoleis of Abruzzo.

In addition to the 'cultural' material of the archaeological collections, th
museum houses a number of important human remains, mainly from Iron Ag
necropoleis, housed in the **anthropological section** (**room 5**). Explanator
panels outline how knowledge about a person (sex, age at death, degree of isola
tion, state of health, blood group, nutritional habits, etc.) is obtained centuries o
even millennia after the individual's death by examining his or her bones
Fundamental in evolutionary terms is the Ortucchio jaw (8000–9000 years BC
which demonstrates a marked decrease in the size of teeth compared to othe
specimens of the late Iron Age.

Rooms 6–9 are devoted to finds from a Roman sanctuary on Monte Moron
near Sulmona; the highlight is the small bronze **Curino Hercules**, a votiv
statue attributed to the Greek sculptor Lysippus (4C BC).

The **Pansa collection** (**rooms 10–11**). This private collection, recently left t
the museum, reflects the tastes and interests of an *amateur* of the late 19C an
early 20C, an eminent local solicitor with a predilection for small bronzes, object
from daily life, jewels, glass, and ivory. Next comes the **numismatic collectio**
(**rooms 12–13**), where the exhibits have been selected from among c 15,00
coins from various areas of Abruzzo, ranging in date from the 4C BC–18C AD. Th
coins have been arranged to reflect the economic history of the region from pre
Roman times onward; the thematic display cases and panels show the prove
nance, technical characteristics, and site of each find. The coins are also colou
coded for clarity (yellow = Greece and Magna Graecia, red = republican Rome
and so on). Especially interesting are the Roman Aureo of Gauda (case 7), one o

ree known examples of this type (the other two are in the British Museum);
d the medieval pieces, many of which were minted in northern Italy and illus-
ate the prosperity brought to the region by the trade in wool, silk and spices.
agnifying glasses are provided on request.

Rooms 14–16 are devoted to **Roman portraiture**, public, private, and funer-
y; whereas **rooms 17–18** constitute the **lapidarium**, with Roman funerary and
norary epigraphy, including two extraordinary **burial beds** in bone and ivory.

t the eastern edge of the town, in the shadow of a high-rise development, lie the
mains of **Roman thermae**, consisting of a large (60 x 14m) cistern and
merous rooms, one of which retains its mosaic pavement. The complex prob-
ly dates from the early Imperial Period.

round Chieti

he Roman Via Valeria (now Road 5) ascends the valley of the River Pescara,
king the Adriatic coast with Rome. A bit further west of Chieti, on the north
de of the valley, is the Cistercian church of **Santa Maria d'Arabona** (1208),
ntaining a noteworthy aumbry and paschal candlestick (the way is marked;
ng for admittance).

A road with fine views runs further south towards the Maiella Massif from
afa–San Valentino station to (27km) Sant'Eufemia a Maiella. The village of
n Valentino is near the ancient *Interpromium*. San Tommaso has a fine 12C
urch. **Caramanico** is a summer resort, with sulphur baths on the west slopes
the Maiella range. Its church of Santa Maria Maggiore has a fine portal of
476 and a reliquary by Nicola da Guardiagrele; San Domenico has two good
orways. Beyond Sant'Eufemia a Maiella a fair road, rising to 1282m, leads
uth over the mountains to Campo di Giove, a mountain village (1064m), with
station on the railway from Roccaraso to Sulmona.

orre dei Passeri is a picturesque village, bypassed by the Via Valeria, between
afa and Popoli. About 2km south (marked) is another fine church, **San
lemente in Casauria**, rebuilt by the Cistercians in the 12C, but retaining its
riginal crypt of 871, the date of its foundation by Emperor Louis II. The façade
fronted by a magnificent portico, with three broad arches (that at the centre is
unded, whereas the others are slightly pointed) on compound piers. The capi-
ls and archivolts are richly carved. Above, two orders of attached shafts termi-
ate in a delicate band of arched corbels, above which rises the fenestrated upper
orey, an addition of 1448.

The main portal, with its complex sculptural programme, is a splendid work of
e 12C. The bronze doors, with 72 relief panels (some of which are missing), are
ughly contemporary. The interior, built to a Latin cross plan with shallow
ansepts, ends in a semicircular apse, unusual in Cistercian architecture, but in
eping with the Romanesque tradition. The first four bays of the nave arcade are
ller than the others and are lighted by clerestory windows. Above the door is a
othic loggia. The magnificent ambo (right), candlestick (left) and altar canopy
re of the same date as the sculptures of the portal. Steps lead down to the crypt.

Castiglione a Casauria, 4km west, has a fine 14C church and palazzo.

Heading southwards

Francavilla al Mare, just south of Pescara, was the home of the paint Francesco Paolo Michetti (d. 1929), whose work is the focus of the Museo Mur (open summer, Tues–Sun 18.00–24.00) in the former town hall. In the treasu of the modern church of Santa Maria Maggiore is a monstrance by Nicola Guardiagrele.

Ortona (population 23,000), a town several times devastated by earthquak and badly damaged in the Second World War, is the most important port Abruzzo. The cathedral (San Tommaso) is a restoration, having been half demo ished in the Second World War. The **Palazzo Farnese**, begun in 1584 Giacomo della Porta for Margaret of Parma, was left unfinished on her dea here in 1586. It lies between the municipio and a piazzetta named after the com poser F.P. Tosti (1846–1916), a native of Ortona. The palazzo is home to th pinacoteca and museo, with works by regional artists and material from loc archaeological sites, which are opened on request (☎ 085 906723). More inte esting, perhaps, is the **Museo Musicale d'Abruzzo** in the Palazzo Corvi (ope summer Mon–Fri 10.00–13.00, Tues and Thur 15.00–18.00; winter Mon–S 10.00–13.00; ☎ 085 906 6310), dedicated to the composer of the classic 'Neapolitan' songs *A vucchella* and *A Marechiare.*

About 3km south of the town, beyond the Moro River, is Ortona (Moro Rive British Military Cemetery, with 1614 graves.

From the Ortona Autostrada exit a road (538) runs inland along the ridge the north-west side of the Moro Valley, crossing most of its Second World Wa battlefield. The castle at **Crecchio** (reached by a turning on the right) gav refuge to Victor Emmanuel III and the Italian Command when they escaped fro Rome following the armistice of 8 September 1943. Today the castle hosts th **Museo dell'Abruzzo Bizantino ed Altomedievale** (open daily July–Se 10.00–12.00 and 15.00–19.00; Oct–June Sat 15.00–19.00, Sun 10.00–12.0 and 15.00–19.00; ☎ 087 194 1392), which displays an extraordinary colle tion of early medieval artefacts, mainly of Byzantine and Lombard origin.

At Guardiagrele station the railway turns left for Lanciano, to regain the coa at San Vito (see below). Bear right on the Chieti road for (3km; lef **Guardiagrele**, a little town noted in the 15C for its goldsmiths, of whom Nico di Andrea was the most famous. The 14C Romanesque church of **Santa Mari Maggiore** was damaged in 1943, but the external fresco of St Christopher, Andrea Delitio (1473) survived. The noted silver crucifix by Nicola di Andr (1431), stolen from the treasury and dismembered, has been almost entire recovered and is now the focus of a Museo di Arte Sacra (open by appointmen ☎ 0871 82117). The 14C church of **San Francesco** has a carved Romanesqu Gothic portal and a 15C cloister. The Biblioteca Comunale has a small collectic of architectural fragments and sculptures from churches in the area.

A scenic road (81) leads to Chieti via the Bocca di Valle, where a huge inscri tion on a cliff and a cave chapel serve as the Abruzzo Memorial to the First Wor War. At Fara Filiorum Petri, the Feast of St Anthony Abbot (16 January) is cel brated by burning a forest of *farchie*, bamboo columns up to 12m high. To th south rises the Maielletta.

Road 363, also with good views, leads from Guardiagrele to Lanciano.

anciano

om the Lanciano interchange it is a short drive inland to Lanciano (population 5,000), the Roman *Anxanum*, originally a city inhabited by the Frentani. The andsome cathedral, with its 17C campanile, is built on a bridge dating from the me of Diocletian and restored in 1088. It dates from 1788 and is one of the few eo-classical churches in Abruzzo. **Santa Maria Maggiore**, a Cistercian edifice 1227, has a Gothic portal of 1317 and, in the handsome Burgundian Gothic terior, a crucifix by Nicola da Guardiagrele (1422) and a triptych by Polidoro di nzo (1549). Sant'Agostino contains other interesting examples of goldsmiths' ork. The 13C church of San Francesco is traditionally held to contain evidence the first eucharistic miracle recorded by the Church, which took place around e year 700 during a mass celebrated by a Basilian monk who doubted the icharistic presence. The reliquary is kept in a marble tabernacle over the cibo- im and is composed of a silver monstrance (1713) and a chalice below it in crys- l, the former containing the flesh, the latter the blood into which the bread and ine were transubstantiated. The 11C **Porta San Biagio** is the only remaining wn gate; near it is the 14C campanile of the disused church of San Biagio.

a road fork beyond the Aventino bridge, the turning on the left (Road 652) fol- ws the Sangro Valley to Castel di Sangro (74km). On the way is **Bomba**, with a onument to Silvio Spaventa (1822–93), a native hero of the Risorgimento, a useo Etnographico documenting rural culture in Abruzzo (open summer, t–Sun 18.00–20.00, winter Sat–Sun 15.30–17.30; ☎ 087 286 0128) and mains of cyclopean walls. From here a winding country road ascends to illascoso, near which lie the ruins of the Roman *Iuranum*. The extensive mains include a forum, a theatre, foundations of several temples and numerous uses and streets. A parallel road on the east (road 364) passes **Atessa**, where e church of San Leucio contains a monstrance by Nicola da Guardiagrele.

asto and Termoli

ie village of **Fossacesia** lies 4km inland from Fossacesia Marina. Here the agnificent conventual church of **San Giovanni in Venere** overlooks the driatic above the railway station. Documented from the 8C, it was rebuilt in)15 by Trasmondo II, Count of Chieti, and after 1165 it was enlarged in the stercian style by Abbot Oderisio II. The lower part of the façade is in stone, the pper part in brick. The remarkable marble **Portale della Luna** (1225–30) has tall quatrefoil archivolt, and in its lunette, Christ enthroned between the Virgin ad St John; below are the remains of small statues of St Benedict and Abbot iinaldo. At the sides of the door stand broad, flat engaged pilasters with bas- liefs depicting Old and New Testament scenes, of Apulian Romanesque inspi- tion. Above rises the tympanum, divided into three parts like a tripytych and obably conceived in relation to a group of frescoes that was never executed.

The basilican **interior** (1165) has a nave and aisles separated by cruciform ers. Above these, in the nave, are attached shafts designed to support a vaulted iling that was never carried out. The raised presbytery is covered by cross ults; in the apses are 12C, 13C, and 14C frescoes. Steps in the aisles descend to e crypt, which contains some late 12C frescoes and columns from a temple of nus that occupied this site in antiquity. At the rear of the church the three ele- nt apses are visible. The **cloister** (ring for entrance) was rebuilt in 1932–35.

Across the River Sangro on road 16 is Torino di Sangro Marina, south
which lies the Sangro River British Military Cemetery, with 2619 graves. Beyo
Casalbordino station a road diverges for the much visited Santuario de
Madonna dei Miracoli (festival, 11 June).

Vasto (population 34,000) is a pleasant town 3km from its railway station. Vas
is the mythical *Histonium* and for centuries was subject to the powerful D'Ava
family. The painter, Dante Gabriel Rossetti, was the son of a blacksmith from Vas
He is honoured by a statue in Piazza Diomede. The church of San Pietro contains
picture painted at the age of 80 by Filippo Palizzi (1818–99), a native of the tow
The **castle** dates from the 13C. The plain **duomo** (1293) has a Gothic port
Across the square, the Museo e Pinacoteca Civici, in the 18C Palazzo D'Aval
(open summer Tues–Sun 10.30–12.30, 18.00–24.00; winter Thur–St
09.30–12.30 and 16.30–20.30, Tues and Weds 16.30–20.30; ☎ 087 336 777
contains antiquities, including Oscan inscriptions, and works by Palizzi.

The River Trigno forms the boundary between Abruzzo and Molise. **Termo**
probably the ancient *Buca* of the Frentani, has suffered repeatedly from eart
quakes and was largely destroyed by the Turks in 1566, though it was little da
aged in the Second World War. The town, with 27,000 inhabitants, has mediev
walls, a **castle** built in 1247 by Frederick II, and a 13C **duomo**. The striki
stone façade, in the Apulian Romanesque manner, dates from the 12C–15C; t
arcading continues along the right flank of the church to the apse. The vie
from the promontory on which the old town stands are exceptional: to the we
is the Maiella Range; to the east the mountainous Gargano Promontory; se
ward, 25 nautical miles distant, the Tremiti Islands, for which Termoli is t
main departure point.

THE WESTERN HIGHLANDS

Welcome to the most spectacular natural environment in south-central Italy.
this area you'll find wooded mountains and fertile valleys—wild countrysi
punctuated with medieval castles and villages that economic development h
not yet had time to spoil. Even the most sedentary will feel the temptation
explore the region on foot, and with good reason: the cool, pine-scented air a
magnificent views more than compensate the effort of walking. And the mo
adventurous have excellent chances of encountering the small wolves a
brown bear native to the region (there are dedicated wildlife study centres in t
fabulous **Parco Nazionale d'Abruzzo**), as well as deer and chamois. The dri
from L'Aquila to Teramo also offers unequalled views over the **Gran Sas
d'Italia** and the **Vomano Valley**. **Roccaraso**, **Sulmona**, **Popoli**, and **Camp**
are fine old cities that are well worth strolling round and **L'Aquila** (see p 41
and **Teramo** remain pleasant places despite being bustling provincial capitals

Practical information

Information offices
CAMPOBASSO
Assessorato Regionale al

Turismo, Via Mazzini 94, ☎ 0874
429514.
Ente Provinciale per il Turismo, Piazz

ella Vittoria 14, ☎ 0874 415662.
SERNIA *Ente Provinciale per il
urismo*, Via Farinacci 9, ☎ 0865 3992.
ESCASSEROLI *Ufficio
nformazioni e di Accoglienza Turistica*,
'ia Piave 2, ☎ 0863 910461.
ESCOCOSTANZO *Ufficio
nformazioni e di Accoglienza Turistica*,
'ico delle Carceri 4, ☎ 0864 641440.
IVISONDOLI *Ufficio Informazioni
di Accoglienza Turistica*, Piazza
Municipio 6, ☎ 0864 69351.
OCCARASO *Ufficio Informazioni e
i Accoglienza Turistica*, Palazzo del
omune, Via Mori 1, ☎ 0864 62210.
CANNO *Ufficio Informazioni e di
ccoglienza Turistica*, Piazza Santa
Maria della Valle 12, ☎ 0864 74317.
ULMONA *Ufficio Informazioni e di
ccoglienza Turistica*, Corso Ovidio
08, ☎ 0864 53276.
AGLIACOZZO *Ufficio
nformazioni e di Accoglienza Turistica*,
'ia Veneto 6, ☎ 0863 610318.
ERAMO *Amministrazione
rovinciale Settore Turismo*, Via G:
lilli 2, ☎ 0861 3311.
*Ufficio Informazioni e di Accoglienza
uristica*, Via del Castello 10, ☎ 0861
44222.

Getting there and getting around
By air

'here is a regional airport (**Pasquale
iberi**) 6km north of Pescara, with
ights to/from Frankfurt, London, Olbia
ome, Milan and Turin.

y road

he most convenient approaches to the
vestern highlands are, from the south,
oads 87 and 17 from Termoli and
ampobasso; and Roads 88 and 87 from
enevento; from the north, Road 81
om Ascoli Piceno; and from the east
nd west, Autostrada A25 from Rome
nd Pescara. Throughout the region,
ie driving may be difficult in winter
ecause of snow. Bus connections are

too infrequent to be useful.

By rail

Most of the places in this chapter are
served by slow local trains. One possible
itinerary, touching upon the major
sights, is: **Campobasso** to **Isernia**,
59km in c 1hr. To visit **Sulmona**,
change at (48km) **Carpinone**, saving
11km and 15mins each way. Isernia to
Sulmona, 129km in 2–3hrs. Sulmona
to **L'Aquila**, 60km in 1hr–1hr 15mins.

Where to stay

PESCASSEROLI
€€ *Duca degli Abruzzi*,
Piazza Duca degli Abruzzi, ☎ 0863
911082, 📠 0863 911839, ✉
ducadegliabruzzi@ pescasseroli.net.
Delightful small hotel with excellent
restaurant, in the centre of the village.
€€ *Daniel*, Viale Colli dell'Oro,
☎/📠 0863 912896, ✉ www.
hoteldaniel.it. Modern and tidy, with
pool and private balconies.
€€ *Edelweis*, Viale Colli dell'Oro,
☎ 0863 912577, 📠 0863 912798.
Comfortable family-run establishment
in a garden, known also for its delicious
food.
€€ *Paradiso*, Via Fonte Fracassi,
☎ 0863 910422, 📠 0863 910498,
✉ www.albergo-paradiso.it. Friendly,
quiet and restful, with a large garden a
short walk from the village.
€ *Pagnani*, Viale Colli dell'Oro 5,
☎ 0863 912866, 📠 0863 912870,
✉ h.pagnani@ermes.it. In a wooded
garden just outside the village. Warm,
quiet, luminous rooms, indoor pool and
gym.
ROCCARASO € *Grande Albergo*,
Via Roma 21, ☎ 0864 6023523,
📠 0864 602372, free phone 167
820080. A comfortable, family-run
establishment in the town centre;
closing times vary.
€ *Iris*, Viale Iris 5, ☎ 0864 602366,
📠 0864 602366, ✉ iris@roccaraso.
net. Another owner-managed place,

clean and cordial.

TERAMO €€ *Sporting*, Via De Gasperi 41, ☎ 0861 210285, ☐ 0861 210285. Modern and comfortable, with an excellent restaurant.

VASTOGIRARDI € *Vecchio Granaio*, Via Trigno, ☎ 0865 836255. Farm offering simple rooms and meals, and delicious home-made cheeses; season varies.

See also L'Aquila and the Gran Sasso (p 411).

Youth Hostels

CANSANO € *Ostello del Parco*, ☎ 0864 408464. Hostel serving the Parco Nazionale d'Abruzzo.

CEPPO € *Ostello del Ceppo*. Hostel serving the Parco Nazionale del Gran Sasso, managed by *Cooperative Iride*, Via Vidacillo 16, Ascoli Piceno, ☎ 0736 256417, ☐ 0736 258377.

CIVITELLA ALFEDENA € *Ostello La Torre*, ☎ 0864 890121. Another hostel for the park.

LEOFARA € *Ostello di Leofara*. Hostel serving the Parco Nazionale del Gran Sasso, managed by Cooperative Iride, Via Vidacillo 16, Ascoli Piceno, ☎ 0736 256417, ☐ 0736 258377.

Eating out

ANVERSA DEGLI ABRUZZI € *La Fiaccola*, Via Duca degli Abruzzi 12, ☎ 0864 49474. Warm, rustic trattoria on the road from Sulmona to Scanno; closed Mon.

AVEZZANO €€ *Jardin*, Via Sabotino 36, ☎ 0863 414710. Garden restaurant offering delicious traditional dishes; closed Tues and Aug.

€ *Il Gioco dell'Uva*, Corso Garibaldi 133, ☎ 0863 25441. Wine bar with cold meals; closed Mon.

BELLANTE € *Casale*, Via De Luca 1, ☎ 0861 611925. The best ingredients intelligently cooked and presented. On the road from Teramo to Giulianova; closed Tues.

BOIANO € *Filomena*, Via Garibaldi 16, ☎ 0874 773078. Good, old-fashioned osteria, open mid-day (and Fri and Sat evenings); closed Mon and July.

Pastificio Bernardo, Corso Amatuzio 100, pasta maker producing over 60 shapes.

CAMPLI €€ *Locanda del Pompa*, Bivio Campli 5, ☎ 0861 569011. Trattoria with rooms just outside the town, on the road to Ascoli; closed Wed and one week in Jan.

Mancini road 81. Wood-oven bakery with excellent breads and pastries.

CAMPOBASSO € *Da Concetta*, Via Larino 9, ☎ 0874 311378. Good home cooking and attentive service; closed Sat, Sun and Aug.

€ *Da Nonno Cecchino*, Via Larino 32, ☎ 0874 311778. Trattoria serving largely local fare in the old town centre; closed Sun evening (except in summer).

€ *Miseria e Nobiltà*, Viale del Castello 16/18, ☎ 0874 94268. Rustic country restaurant, with garden; closed Sun and July–Aug.

€ *Sagittario*, Via Ziccardi 74, ☎ 0874 698413. Creative interpretations of local recipes, in the historic town centre; closed Tues and July.

€ *Vecchia Trattoria da Tonino*, Corso Vittorio Emanuele 8, ☎ 0874 415200. Good selection of local delicacies; closed Sun and late Aug.

Palazzo Via Ziccardi 5. Wood-oven bakery for bread and pizza.

CAMPOTOSTO € *Barilotto*, Via Roma 18, ☎ 0862 900141. Simple trattoria with rooms; closed Tues and Feb.

€ *Trattoria del Pescatore*, Via Rio Fucino, ☎ 0862 900227. Trattoria; closed Mon (except in summer).

CANTALUPO DEL SANNIO € *Trattoria del Riccio*, Via Sannio 7, ☎ 0865 814246. Trattoria; open for lunch only, closed Mon, 10 days in June and 10 days in Sept.

CANZANO € *La Tacchinella*, Via

Roma 18, ☎ 0861 555107. Best place
around for *tacchino alla canzanese*, the
famous (turkey) delicacy of this town
between Teramo and Giulianova; closed
Mon (except in summer).

CAROVILLI € *Adriano*, Via Napoli
14, ☎ 0865 838688. Trattoria offering
the finest local ingredients, prepared
with care; closed Mon evening and Tues
(except in summer), and Sept.

CARSOLI € *Al Caminetto*, Via degli
Alpini 95, ☎ 0863 995105. Restaurant
and wine bar with plenty of mushroom
and truffle dishes, plus wood-fired pizza
oven; closed Mon (except in Aug) and
early July.

€€ *L'Angolo d'Abruzzo*, Piazza Aldo
Moro 8, ☎ 0863 997429. Outstanding
regional cuisine and good wine list;
closed Mon and early July.

CASACALENDA €€ *Villa
Continelli*, SS 87, Contrada Monte. Fine
country restaurant with views; closed
Mon.

CIVITELLA DEL TRONTO
€ *Zunica*, ☎ 0861 91319. Restaurant
with rooms, closed Wed and late Nov.

FERRAZZANO € *Da Emilio*, Via
Spensieri 21, ☎ 0874 416576.
Restaurant serving local dishes with a
creative twist, in the main square of this
panoramic village near Campobasso;
closed Tues and July.

FROSOLONE *La Tana dell'Orso*, at
Colle dell'Orso, ☎ 0874 890785. Café-
restaurant; closed Tues, Jan and Feb.

ISERNIA € *Dai Due Vagabondi*, Via
Berta 131, ☎ 0865 410233. Lamb in
every possible manner, and more; closed
Mon.

DOLCIARIA VALENTINO
Contrada Pettoranello. Pastry shop selling traditional Molise sweets.

€ *Taverna Maresca*, Corso Marcelli
186, ☎ 0865 3976. Delicious traditional food, in the heart of the old town;
closed Sun, Aug and late Dec–early Jan.

LUCOLI € *Macondo*, at Collimento di
Lucoli, ☎ 0862 73636. Warm, friendly

trattoria near the Campo Felice ski area;
closed Tues and one week in Sept.

MAGLIANO DE' MARSI
€ *Laghetto di Magliano*, Piazza Uno del
Serpentone, ☎ 0863 517346. Friendly
family-run restaurant; closed Mon and
early Sept.

MASSA D'ALBE € *La Conca*,
Corso Umberto I 30, ☎ 0863 510249.
Trattoria; closed Wed.

MONTEREALE €€ *Palazzetto*,
Largo San Lorenzo 1, ☎ 0862 901340.
Refined restaurant in a small hotel,
serving original interpretations of
traditional dishes; closed Mon.

MONTORIO AL VOMANO
€ *Totò*, Via Gramsci 3, ☎ 0861
598508. Restaurant and pizzeria with
good local recipes; closed Mon.

OVINDOLI € *Il Pozzo*, Via
Monumento all'Alpino, ☎ 0863
710191. Warm, friendly restaurant in a
former stable carved out of the rock;
closed Wed and late Sept–early Oct.

PACENTRO (near Sulmona)
€€ *Taverna de li Caldora*, Piazza
Umberto I, ☎ 0864 41139. Fine traditional trattoria in the town centre, with
outdoor seating in summer; closed Sun
evening, Tues and mid-Jan–mid-Feb.

PESCASSEROLI €€ *Alle Vecchie
Arcate*, Via della Chiesa 41, ☎ 0863
910781. Warm, cosy, family-run
restaurant in the centre of the village.

€€ *Plistia*, Via Principe di Napoli 28,
☎ 0863 910732. Small, family-run
hotel restaurant; closed Mon.

€ *A Cavu't*, Piazza Vittorio Veneto 17,
☎ 338 267 2842. Simple, rustic trattoria known for its fresh pasta and grilled
meats; closed Mon except in July-Aug.

RIVISONDOLI €€ *Giocondo*, Via
del Suffragio 2, ☎ 0864 69123.
Traditional dishes of Abruzzo in a small,
amiable restaurant; closed Tues.

€ *La Portella*, Via Sulmontina 44,
☎ 0864 69372. Restaurant and pizzeria just outside the village; always open.

Eno Giò, Via Roma 30. Wine shop also

selling local delicacies such as saffron and truffles.

SAN PIETRO AVELLANA
€ *Il Perticone*, Masserie di Cristo 35, ☎ 0865 940139. Café-trattoria; open daily.

SCANNO €€ *La Fonte*, Via Fontana Saracco 3, ☎ 0864 747390. Delicious local cooking in the heart of old Scanno; closed Wed and Oct–Nov.
La Volpe e l'Uva, Piazza San Rocco 6, ☎ 0360 526529. Wine bar with cold meals, open for lunch; closed Wed (except in summer) and Feb.

SCHIAVI DI ABRUZZO € *Templi Italici*, Contrada Taverna 1, ☎ 0873 976173. Café-restaurant by the archaeological site; open evenings only, closed Wed.

SEPINO € *L'Imperatrice*, Contrada Rio Verdaro 18, ☎ 0874 790005. Trattoria near the archaeological site offering great local cooking; closed Wed.

SULMONA €€ *Rigoletto*, Via Stazione Introdacqua 46, ☎ 0864 55529. Warm, traditional restaurant with outdoor seating in summer; closed Mon.
€ *Clemente, Osteria della Quercia*, Vico Quercia 5, ☎ 0864 52284. Traditional restaurant in the 14C Palazzo Sardi de Letto; closed Thur and a few days in June and Dec.
€ *Frangiò*, Via Ercole Ciofano 51, ☎ 0864 212773. Delicious regional cuisine in a historical setting, with garden seating in summer; closed Mon and Nov.
€ *Gino*, Piazza Plebiscito 12, ☎ 0864 52289. Old-fashioned osteria in the centre of town; open mid-day only, closed Sun.
Confetti Pelino Via Introdacqua 55. Confectioner, with a wide assortment of Sulmona's famous candies.
Reginella d'Abruzzo Via Aroto 1. For fresh and matured cheeses made with milk from local pastures.

TERAMO € *Angolo Divino*, Via Crucioli 10, ☎ 0861 247354. Creative interpretations of traditional recipes; closed Sun evening, Tues and Aug–Sept.
€ *Antico Cantinone*, Via Ciotti 5, ☎ 0861 248863. Quiet, traditional restaurant; closed Sun and Aug.
€ *Duomo*, Via Stazio 9, ☎ 0861 241774. Excellent family-run restaurant in a historic building; closed Mon.
€ *Enoteca Centrale*, Corso Cerulli 24–26, ☎ 0861 243633. Wine bar offering light meals; closed Sun and two weeks in Aug.
€ *Gran Sasso*, Via Vinciguerra 12, ☎ 0861 24530. Good regional dishes from hills and shore; closed Sun evening.
€ *Moderno*, Costa Sant'Agostino, ☎ 0861 414559. Fine regional cuisine; closed Mon and Aug.

VALLE CASTELLANA € *Remigio II*, Valle Castellana–Monte Pisello, ☎ 0861 930123. Hotel restaurant with great mountain food and views; closed Mon.

VASTOGIRARDI € *La Taverna*, Via Mazzini 13, ☎ 0865 836156. Trattoria with delicious mountain cooking; closed Mon.
See also L'Aquila and the Gran Sasso (p 411).

VINCHIATURO € *Hotel Residence Le Cupolette*, SS 87 at Santa Maria delle Macchie, ☎ 0874 340030. Hotel restaurant known for its delicate cuisine and attentive service; open all year.

Special events
LARINO *Sagra di San Pardo*, celebrated on 25–27 May, featuring a torchlight procession of elaborately decorated *plaustri* or pseudo-Roman ox carts.
SCANNO Peasant New Year, 11 November, celebrated by igniting immense bonfires (the *Glorie di San Martino*) in the hills around the town.
TERAMO San Berardo (19 Dec); *Giugno Teramano* (theatre, opera, folklore and cuisine; June); *Stagione*

Lirica e del Balletto (opera and ballet, Nov–Dec); *Mostra-Mercato*

dell'Agricoltura (agricultural fair, May).

Approaching Campobasso

Our exploration begins in the verdant farmland east of Campobasso. **Larino** (population 8000; bus from the station in 5 minutes), in charming surroundings, is the ancient *Larinum*, a town of the Frentani, Samnites who lived on the Adriatic coast between the *Sagrus* (Sangro) on the north and the *Frento* (Fortore) on the south. The medieval town, damaged by earthquake in 1300, was destroyed by the Saracens shortly thereafter. It was rebuilt in 1316, but in 1656 plague claimed the lives of 9625 of its 10,000 inhabitants.

The **duomo** (1319), with an attractive façade, has a 16C campanile and a fine Gothic portal by Francesco Petrini, the sculptor of the portal of Santa Maria Maggiore in Lanciano. In the lunette, Crucifixion with the Virgin and St John. The large rose window is similar to those that characterise Apulian churches; the mullioned windows on either side open above the level of the aisle roofs. The interior has three tall, narrow aisles separated by pointed arches (six on the south side, five on the north) on cruciform piers with carved capitals. In the south aisle is an *Immaculate Conception* attributed to Francesco Solimena. The chapter house contains a marble altar, built to a design by Andrea Vaccaro, and other interesting objects.

The **Palazzo Comunale**, in the cathedral square, contains a monumental staircase of 1818, adorned with Roman architectural fragments and, in the biblioteca, mosaic floors from Roman villas discovered in the environs of the amphitheatre (see below). Also of interest are a 14C wooden Madonna and numerous ceramic and bronze objects, some dating from the second millennium BC.

The wooded avenue that ascends to the station passes (left) the so-called *Ara Frentana*, a cylindrical altar of pre-Roman origin; and other archaeological material (chiefly inscriptions and architectural and sculptural fragments) brought here from nearby excavations. The ruins of *Larinum*, including the conspicuous remains of an amphitheatre of the late 1C or early 2C BC, lie north-east of the station, in and around Piazza San Lorenzo, and in the vicinity of the Torre Sant'Anna and Torre De Gennaro.

From Larino there is an almost continuous ascent to Casacalenda. Beyond Taverna Cerrosecco, the town of Morrone del Sannio comes into view, on its hilltop (839m); a road further on leads up to the town. Beyond Taverna Clemente the road descends in broad curves. On a hill to the right stands the splendid Romanesque church of **Santa Maria della Strada**, reached by a turning.

Campobasso

Campobasso, with 51,000 inhabitants, is the chief town of the province of the same name, formerly the county of Molise. The local cutlery industry has dwindled to a handful of artisans who make and engrave scissors and knives, hawked by pedlars. The *Sagra dei Misteri* (Corpus Domini) is celebrated with 18C iron contrivances in which children assume impossible poses (flying angels, etc.) depict-

> ### Molisan metals
>
> In many Molisan villages Christmas Eve culminates with torchlit processions or with bonfires of wood and grass, and at Agnone Carnival fires 'burn away' the end of winter. In a strictly spiritual context, fire is an element of purification and transformation but a popular saying recites, 'fire is the father of metals,' and in these parts the culture of fire is accompanied by that of metals. Metalworking in Molise, in fact, dates as far back as the ancient Samnites.
>
> The working of iron, copper and bronze is common throughout the region. Campobasso's goldsmiths are famous for creations that still echo Spanish designs—and more often than not, are made for the statues that adorn religious feasts rather than for flesh-and-blood clients.
>
> Other famous centres are Agnone, where Molisans have been producing bronze church-bells for over a thousand years, and Frosolone, from which knives and scissors are exported throughout Europe. The beautiful horn-handled jack-knives are particularly popular in rural Italy. Not least of Molisan metal crafts is copper-working, practised throughout the region thanks to the cheese industry, which still uses immense copper cauldrons in which to boil milk.

ing Christian mysteries or miracles of the saints. These human sculptural configurations are borne through the streets on wooden platforms.

In the old upper town are two churches preserving Romanesque portions: San Bartolomeo, with a fine 14C portal, and San Giorgio, with delicate 12C bas-reliefs. The **Nuovo Museo Provinciale Sannitico** occupies the 19C Palazzo Mazzarotta, at Via Chiarizia 12 (open daily 08.30–19.30, ☎ 087 441 2265). Here you'll find material ranging in date from the dawn of history to the Samnite age, all found in Molise. The museum is divided into four sections: clothing and accessories (bronze belts, helmets, spear points, bracelets and jewellery); housewares (vases, lamps, keys, etc.), tools and equipment (knives, weights, bricks and tiles), religious and burial cults (bronze and clay votive statues, burial treasures). There are also a reconstructed tomb from the Lombard necropolis at Campochiaro, and some epigraphs. Above rises the 15C **Castello Monforte**, square in plan with six rampart towers. The square before the entrance offers good views over the town and the surrounding countryside.

On the south of the castle hill is the church of Sant'Antonio, with a painting of *St Benedict* by Fabrizio Santafede. An inscription beneath the portico of the Municipio, in the lower town, records the death, near Campobasso, of Amadeus VI, the Green Count of Savoy (1383). Nearby, in Piazza Vittoria, is a Museo Internazionale del Presepio in Miniatura, containing a fine private collection of Italian and foreign nativity scenes (open by appointment, ☎ 0874 63370).

Saepinum

More rolling hills separate the regional capital from Vinchiaturo, an attractive little town (population 51,000) rebuilt after the earthquake of 1805. A road to the east leads through more splendid landscape to **Cercemaggiore**. Above this town, near the summit of Monte Saraceno (1086m) are the walls of a Samnite village intermingled with the ruins of medieval fortifications. The view from the summit spans vast areas of Molise, Campania and Apulia.

Beyond Vinchiaturo take road 17 (the Benevento–Isernia road) south-east. **Sepino**, on a hill 4km south, is the successor of the Roman *Saepinum*, the ruins of which lie along the road on the right. Later named *Atilia*, Saepinum was founded by survivors from the Samnite *Saipins*, destroyed in 293 BC. Its history was not particularly eventful; it was destroyed by the Saracens in the 9C.

The defensive walls, 1250m in circumference, still surround the ancient town. Fortified by 27 bastions, they are pierced by four gates, today known as the Porta di Baiano (north-west), Porta del Tammaro (north-east), Porta di Benevento (south-east) and Porta di Terravecchia (south-west).

Enter by the Porta del Tammaro and cross the site to the Porta di Terravecchia, outside which is an improvised car park surrounded by low walls in *opus reticulatum*. Within (open daily, 09.00–1hr before sunset; ☎ 0874 790207), the *cardus maximus* leads past modern farmhouses built with the stones of the ancient city. Further on, the road preserves its ancient pavement. The **basilica**, on the left, has a peristyle made up of 20 slender Ionic columns. Turning right, follow the decumanus past the **forum** and a series of public buildings that includes the **curia**, or town hall, and a temple believed to have been dedicated to the Capitoline triad (Jupiter, Juno and Minerva).

Further on, on the left, are the Casa del Frantoio, an olive press (note the brick-lined wells for storing the oil); the Mulino Idraulico or water mill; and the so-called **Casa dell'Impluvio Sannitico**, a house with a graceful fountain, built to the typical Samnite plan around an atrium with impluvium, preceded by shops. Beyond the Porta di Benevento stands a monumental tomb with an inscription describing the civic and military career of the defunct. To the left is a small museum (open Tues–Sun 09.00–13.00) with photographs and texts describing the town and its discovery, and a collection of Roman inscriptions.

Returning to the centre of the town, pass behind the basilica to the octagonal market and what appears to be a small temple. Beyond are the remains of private dwellings and, at the end of the street, the imposing **Porta di Baiano**, in *opus tesselatum*, flanked by cylindrical bastions, another of which can be seen along the wall to the north. At the sides of the arch are statues of prisoners on plinths; that on the right is headless. The keystone is carved with a bearded head, possibly of Hercules; the inscription above the arch tells us that the fortification of the town was financed by the future emperor Tiberius and his brother Drusus.

Steps ascend to the top of the gate, from where there is a fine view over the excavations; the rectangular **tomb of the Numisi**, in a field to the north, and the **thermae**, the remains of which extend along the town wall between the decumanus and the **theatre**. The latter is reached by a minor gate, an unusual feature suggesting that theatrical performances were combined with fairs held outside the walls. Surrounded by farmhouses, it preserves large portions of the cavea and orchestra.

On the stage, another farm building houses a beautiful collection (open 09.00–13.30, 15.00–1 hour before sunset) of objects found on the site and in the vicinity, chiefly funerary sculpture from a necropolis brought to light along the extramural portion of the decumanus. Photographs and texts explain the finds. On the first floor are numerous maps and plans describing the territory, the town and its monuments.

Through western Molise

Molise's south-western boundary is formed by the **Monti del Matese**, a large, high massif extending crescent-like between the rivers Volturno (north), Calore (south), Tammaro (east) and Biferno (north-east). The lofty, forested massif is one of the more beautiful and unspoilt areas of southern Italy. On the south or Campanian side, it rises like a steep wall, whereas the north slopes ascend more gradually. The central region, which contains highland plains at altitudes of 1400–1900m, culminates in the triple peaks of *Colle Tamburo* (1982m), **Monte Gallinola** (1923m) and **Monte Miletto** (2050m). The latter is the *Tifernus Mons* of Livy and the site of the last Samnite struggle against the Romans.

The valleys and gorges of the interior are largely calcareous, and the porosity of the rock permits the absorption of large quantities of water, giving rise to numerous springs at various altitudes and, on the south side, to the large Lago del Matese. The smaller lakes of Gallo and Latino are man-made. The Matese is covered by vast beech woods, with lesser numbers of oaks, maples, ashes, spruces, chestnuts, walnuts, hazel-trees, hornbeams, etc, and by pastures. The native fauna include wild pigs, roe-deer (rare), wolves, foxes, badgers, wildcats, hares, weasels, martens and squirrels. Eagles nest on the Miletto and Gallinola as well as in the Tre Finestre district. Moorhens, ducks, lapwings, woodcocks and snipe inhabit the areas along the lakes and streams, and trout abound. The more isolated villages preserve traditional customs and dress.

Campitello, Boiano and San Massimo in Molise, and Piedimonte Matese, San Gregorio and Letino in Campania, are the best starting points for excursions and climbs. San Gregorio and Campitello are year-round resorts.

Campochiaro, in the foothills of the Matese, is a walled medieval village with an Angevin keep. Excavations have brought to light nearby an Italic sanctuary of the 2C BC, incorporating the largest known Samnite temple after that of Pietrabbondante (described below). Evidence of earlier buildings, dating from the 4C–3C BC, has also been found.

Boiano (population 8000), a chilly place, is the ancient *Bovianum*, one of the main centres of the Samnites and the meeting place of the Italic chiefs during the last phase of the Social War, before the capital was moved to Isernia. The upper town preserves some megalithic walls and remains of a castle.

An afternoon's ramble

From Boiano you can climb **Monte La Gallinola** (1923m) in c 2 hours. A road mounts to the Rifugio Sant'Egidio, from where a steep trail, later a footpath, climbs through the forest to the Costa Alta, a pass 1680m high (view). The way crosses ski slopes at Sogli di Boiano, to the base of Monte La Gallinola. A narrow path climbs to the summit. The **view** is extraordinary, embracing the entire peninsula from the Gulf of Naples to the Adriatic, with the Lago del Matese directly below. You may also climb **Monte Miletto** in c 3 hours, from Sogli di Boiano; or in c 1 hour from Campitello Matese. The latter, a winter sports centre (1417m), has a refuge maintained year-round by the *APT* in Campobasso.

North-west of Boiano, reached by road 17, are Cantalupo del Sannio, whose name means wolfsong; Pesche, presenting medieval walls with cylindrical bastions; and Carpinone, with a handsome castle belonging to the Caldora family.

Some ancient hill towns

Isernia (population 22,000) is the Samnite *Aesernium*, headquarters of the Italics after the fall of *Corfinium* (89 BC). Though a provincial capital, it is a modest town with one main street. It is well known for its onions and lace.

The Romanesque Fontana Fraterna was damaged in the Second World War. Bomb damage to the church of **Santa Maria delle Monache** exposed a 14C fresco of the *Last Judgement* that was covered with 18C plaster. The church complex now houses a museum documenting prehistoric settlements in the area, the **Museo Archeologico Sannitico Romano** (open daily except Mon 08.30–19.30; ☎ 086 541 5179). The cathedral tower, rebuilt after the earthquake of 1805, stands on a medieval archway. One of the Roman bridges is partially intact. Recent excavations nearby have revealed some monumental tombs.

From Isernia road 85 turns south-west past Macchia d'Isernia and Monteroduni, both with fine castles, to Ponte a Venticinque Archi (25 arches), by which you cross the Volturno.

Venafro, with its cyclopean walls and the remains of an amphitheatre, is the ancient *Venafrum*, praised by Horace for its olive oil. The 18C **Chiesa del Purgatorio** contains a *Madonna and Child with Saints* by Fedele Fischetti. In the adjacent Piazza Cimorelli is the 15C Palazzo Caracciolo, a fortified residence built by Maria di Durazzo, who also enlarged the castle. Beneath the Baroque veneer of the church of the **Annunziata** is a Romanesque building of 1387. Within, the second south altar incorporates seven English alabasters dating from the 15C and representing scenes from the Passion. The former convent of Santa Chiara houses the **Museo Archeologico di Venafro** (open Tues–Sun 09.00–12.00, 15.00–18.00; ☎ 0865 900742), containing inscriptions, statues, architectural fragments and miscellaneous objects relating to the Roman colony of *Venafrum*. On the south-west edge of the town is the 15C **cathedral**; in a transitional Romanesque-Gothic style, it is a conglomerate of several churches, the oldest of which dates from the 5C. Recent excavations have revealed remains of a Roman theatre on Monte Croce, near the ancient walls. Road 85 continues from Venafro to Capua and Naples.

Stunningly situated in the hills 28km north of Isernia are the ruins of **Pietrabbondante** (open 09.00–1hr before sunset). Excavations here have revealed a religious sanctuary of Samnite construction, the largest yet discovered, consisting of two temples and a theatre, and dating from the 2C BC. At nearby **Agnone** the cathedral has a good Romanesque portal. At **Schiavi di Abruzzo,** where St Anselm retired in 1098 after his attendances at the conclave of Bari, you can see two Italic temples of the 3C and 2C BC.

The Parco Nazionale d'Abruzzo

Road 17 climbs through splendid countryside to Rionero Sannitico, where dairy cattle are raised. A turning leads south to **Cerro al Volturno**, with a ruined castle in an imposing position above the town; the nearby **Badia di San Vincenzo**, a Benedictine abbey dating from the 8C, possesses a small **crypt** containing frescoes of the life of Christ and martyrdom of Saints Lawrence and Stephen, the only surviving examples of the 9C Benedictine school. In the hills to the west lie the beautiful lake of Castel San Vincenzo.

From Rionero Sannitico there is a descent to Ponte Zittola. From here, road 8 runs west to **Alfedena**, on the Sangro, with a 15C church. On the opposite side of the river are the cyclopean walls of the Samnite town of *Aufidena* and, beyond the station, the Madonna del Campo, with frescoes by Cola dell'Amatrice. Beyond the Vallico de Barrea, a pass 1164m high, lies the **Parco Nazionale d'Abruzzo**

Italy's second-oldest national park was established in 1923 and enlarged in 1925 and 1976. It now occupies an area of 400sq km in one of the wilder and more spectacularly beautiful zones of the Apennines. Its grassy valleys, vast beech woods and alpine meadows compare favourably with those of the Alps or the Pyrenees. Its rare wildlife, which includes the Abruzzo brown bear (*Ursus arcto marsicanus Altobelli*), the highest concentration of wolves in Italy and a sub-specie of the chamois (about 500 of which inhabit the so-called Camosciara between Monte Amaro and the Meta Massif) is known to naturalists throughout the world. Within the park lie the sources and upper valleys of the Sangro, Giovenco and Melfa. The eastern boundary is formed by the Montagna Grande range, the south and south-west boundary by the watershed between the Sangro and the Liri, which also includes the highest peak of the park, Monte Petroso (2247m).

A threat to the natural environment was posed in the early 1960s by private speculation; but this trend has been brought to a halt, largely due to the awakening of public opinion, in which a leading role was played in Italy and throughout the world by the World Wide Fund for Nature (WWF). Hunting, fishing, and the gathering of native flora are forbidden and special hunting regulations are enforced in a wide area around the park. The park is a refuge for golden eagles, wrynecks, firecrests, Sardinian warblers, blue rock thrushes, middle spotted great spotted and white-backed woodpeckers, alpine choughs, snow finches and the most southerly breeding population of dotterel in Europe. Small predator include wild cats, foxes, otters, badgers and pine martens. There are numerou red squirrels and a significant number of wild pigs. The park is also rich in wild flowers and butterflies.

At **Pescasseroli**, birthplace of the philosopher Benedetto Croce, is a park visitors' centre with an excellent small museum and wildlife area (Museo Naturalistico e Area Faunistica, open daily 10.00–13.00, 15.00–19.00 ☎ 0863 91131). Maps and camping permits may be acquired at the *Ufficio di Zona*, Via Santa Lucia. Other park-related museums and wildlife areas, open as above, may be seen at Civitella Alfedena (Museo del Lupo Appenninico e Area Faunistica: wolves); Opi (Museo del Camoscio e Area Faunistica: chamois); San Sebastiano (Museo degli Insetti: insects) and Villavallelonga (Museo del Cervo Area Faunistica: deer).

Castel di Sangro

Castel di Sangro is a picturesque town with a population of 5000 situated partly on a hill and partly on level ground, at the confluence of the Sangro and the Zittola rivers. A resort, it is also known for its traditional ironworking, wood working and woollen industries. The town was reduced to ruins during the Second World War and has been largely rebuilt. The 16C Convento dell Maddalena houses the Museo Civico Aufidenate (open 10.30–12.30, 17.00 20.00 in Aug; other summer months as above except Mon and Tues; winter Wed–Sun 10.00–13.00, 17.00–19.00; t 0864 840826), with the municipal

Benedetto Croce

Benedetto Croce (1866–1952) is arguably the most important Italian philosopher, historian and literary critic of the 20C. He established his idealist philosophical system in the first decade of the century, with seminal works dedicated to aesthetics, logic, economics and ethics. In the journal, *La Critica*, he carried out a sharp critique of positivism and other dominant schools of thought of his time. The journal evolved from his friendship with another early 20C luminary, Giovanni Gentile; but their friendship was broken after political choices led the two philosophers in opposite directions— Gentile becoming an idealogue of the Fascist movement, Croce of liberal anti-Fascism. Today Croce is studied chiefly for his critique of Hegelian dialectics, his aesthetics, and his works on the relationship between philosophy and history, notably *La Storia come Pensiero e come Azione* (History as Thought and Action), which gives a philosophical basis to the struggle against Fascism.

archaeological collection (two headless Roman statues, architectural fragments and a collection of antique bronzes unearthed along the river Zittola in 1957). In the central Piazza del Plebiscito stands the church of the Annunziata (or San Domenico), originally 15C and rebuilt after the Second World War. Steps opposite ascend to the upper town.

Here the two-towered church of **Santa Maria Assunta**, rebuilt in 1695–1727 over an earlier edifice, escaped the war with minor injuries. The Baroque façade incorporates modern statues. At the far end of the portico on the right is a 14C *Pietà* in a Gothic aedicule. The interior, entered from the sides, is built to a Greek cross plan with four small domes in the arms and a large dome at the crossing. In the south arm are a *Madonna and Child with Saints* by Paolo De Matteis, and *Adoration of the Shepherds* and *Disputa* by Domenico Antonio Vaccaro. Behind the marble high altar (1738), *Last Supper* by De Matteis, *Ecce Homo* and *Christ on Calvary* by Francesco de Mura. In the north arm are a painted wooden altar frontal of the 16C and minor paintings.

Several medieval and Renaissance houses can be seen in the upper town. A mule track leads through pine woods up to the ruined castle, near which are traces of cyclopean walls.

Roccaraso and the road to Lanciano

Roccaraso, with its ruined castle, is a pleasant summer resort and winter sports centre, connected by rail with Sulmona. About 2km north-west of the town road 17 bears west and road 84, north. The magnificent **views** afforded by the latter road on its descent have won for it the name of Ringhiera dell'Abruzzo (Balcony of Abruzzo).

Just north of the fork lie Rivisondoli (1320m), a summer and winter resort, and **Pescocostanzo** (1395m), once famous for its lace and other local arts. The little town, with its characteristic deep eaves and porches, is now also a popular summer and winter holiday centre. The church of **Santa Maria del Colle**, a remarkable work of the 16C, 17C and 18C, has elaborately carved wood detailing. Particularly noteworthy are the ceiling of the nave and the high altar, the latter incorporating, in a central niche, an 11C Madonna and Child, the so-called *Madonna del Colle*. A station on the Sulmona railway serves both resorts.

Sulmona

Sulmona (405m) is a pleasant town with a population of 25,000, delightfully situated in a ring of mountains, on a ridge between two small streams. Its many attractive old houses, medieval or later, give it a charming air of antiquity.

History of Sulmona

Sulmona, the *Sulmo* of the Paeligni, was the birthplace of the poet Ovid (P. Ovidius Naso, 43 BC–AD 17) and of Innocent VII (Cosimo de'Migliorati, 1339–1406), collector of Peter's Pence (the pope's tribute) in England in 1376–86. Emperor Frederick II made Sulmona the capital of an independent province. It was bestowed by Charles V as a principality upon Charles de Lannoy (1487–1527), Viceroy of Naples, to whom the French king Francis I surrendered at Pavia (1525). In the 14C and 15C, the goldsmiths of Sulmona were famous. Today it is renowned for its sweets and liqueurs.

The **duomo** (San Panfilo), at the north end of the town, is built on the ruins of a Roman temple and has a Gothic portal and an 11C crypt. Beyond the Villa Comunale the Corso Ovidio, the main street of the town, leads to (right) Via Ciofano, where the 15C **Palazzo Tabassi** (no. 44) has a fine Gothic window.

In the corso are the church and Palazzo of the **Annunziata**, founded in 1320 and showing a happy combination of Gothic and Renaissance elements. The left portal is surmounted by a richly carved Gothic arch embracing statues of *St Michael* and, in the lunette, the *Madonna and Child*, originally gilded, painted and set against a fresco background. Inscribed in the architrave is the date 1415. The monumental central portal recalls the Tuscan Renaissance style. It dates from 1483, as does the central portion of the façade. The smaller right portal is somewhat later.

Along the base of the façade, on tall plinths, are statues of the doctors of the Church (Saints Gregory the Great, Jerome, Ambrose and Augustine); St Pamphilus, titular of the cathedral; and the Apostles Peter and Paul. Above, a delicately carved frieze runs the length of the façade, forming the base of the ornamental windows, which offer the same interesting contrast of styles as the portals below. On the first floor is a museum of local antiquities and paintings (open Tues–Sun 10.00–13.00; ☎ 0864 210216), including the church treasury, with interesting examples of goldsmith's work. The church, rebuilt after an earthquake in 1706, preserves a campanile of 1565–90. More archaeological finds, from Italic, Roman and medival sites in and around Sulmona, can be seen in the little Museo Civico (open as above).

A 20C statue of Ovid stands in the nearby Piazza XX Settembre. Further on, opposite a fountain of 1474, is a rich Romanesque portal leading to the presbytery of the church of San Francesco della Scarpa. The aqueduct that powered local industries during the Middle Ages terminates here. Behind this lies the broad Piazza Garibaldi, containing the church of San Filippo Neri, at the far end. Still further is Santa Maria della Tomba, mainly of the 15C and 16C.

About 6km north of here is the abbey of **Santo Spirito**, or Badia Morronese, founded in the 13C by Pietro Angeleri, afterwards St Celestine V, who dwelt in a hermitage high upon the Montagna del Morrone. The convent (dating from the 17C and 18C, with a fine chapel of the original foundation) and hermitage can be visited by appointment with *Ufficio Informazioni e di Accoglienza Turistica* (Corso Ovidio 208, ☎ 0864 53276). On the way to the hermitage are the remains of a Temple of Hercules, called Ovid's Villa.

The undulating upland plain of Sulmona was referred to by Ovid in his lament for his homeland as the 'fresh land of copious springs'. Poplars are a feature of the landscape here, their growth encouraged by the many streams.

North-west of Sulmona lies Pratola Peligna. To the east is Roccacasale, crowned by a castle finely positioned against a barren peak of the Montagna del Morrone (2061m), known as the *Cunza*. From the road junction near Corfinio station and towards Popoli (described below), roads 5 and 17 coincide.

A trip to Scanno

A brief excursion (31km) can be made from Sulmona to Scanno, a village forgotten by time in a beautiful, rugged setting due south of the city. Leave Sulmona by the imposing 14C Porta Napoli and cross the Gizio River. Near Anversa–Scanno station the road passes beneath a lofty railway viaduct. At **Anversa degli Abruzzi** the church of the Madonna delle Grazie in the piazza has a doorway dated 1540 and a painting of *Saints Michael and Francis*, of the 15C Sulmona school, in the sacristy. San Marcello has a Gothic portal. The road beyond Anversa threads through the deep, narrow gorge known as the **Gola del Sagittario**. A bit further on, the Lago di Scanno (c 2km long) is stocked with trout.

Scanno (1015m), an ancient little town in a striking situation, is popular for summer holidays. The local women still wear their handsome traditional costume. The country New Year, 11 November, is celebrated by igniting immense bonfires (the *Glorie di San Martino*) in the hills around the town. The road goes on over the watershed to (17km south) Villetta Barrea, 6km west of Alfredena.

The Piana del Fucino

Between Pratola and Popoli the Via Valeria turns westward, passing the village of **Corfinio**, known until 1928 as Pentima and given the name of the ancient Italic capital (*Corfinium*) by Mussolini. Beyond the village is the 13C Romanesque **Basilica of San Pelina**, with a characteristic apse and a finely carved ambo. The adjoining church of **Sant'Alessandro** incorporates antique architectural fragments. The former seminary, on the north side of the church, contains the small Museo delle Antichità Corfiniensi (open by appointment; ☎ 0864 728350), with antiquities from the widely scattered ruins of *Corfinium*, the chief town of the Paeligni. In 91 BC, at the beginning of the Social War, it became the capital of the insurgent Italic tribes, who renamed it *Italica* and intended that it should supplant Rome. In 49 BC, after Julius Caesar had crossed the River Rubicon, Lucius Domitius Ahenobarbus, leader of the conservative senatorial aristocracy that opposed his claim to power, held out against him for a short time at *Corfinium*.

Raiano has a station on the railway from Sulmona to L'Aquila. Road 5, the Via Valeria, follows this line up the Gola di San Venanzio, the steep gorge of the Aterno, as far as Molina Aterno (448m).

Another road (road 261), parallel with the railway, leads north from Molina to (47km) L'Aquila, passing Beffi on its castle-crowned height, and the oil well of Vallecupa, joining road 17 at San Gregorio.

At Molina Aterno, the Via Valeria turns south-west past Castelvecchio Subequo, with an interesting church, after which, rising in sharp curves, it reaches the summit at Forca Caruso (1107m). At Collarmele you cross the Pescara–Rome railway and motorway and descend to the north side of the Piana del Fucino, the dried-up basin of **Lake Fucino**.

A lake without water

The ancient *Lacus Fucinus* was the largest lake in central Italy (155sq km); it had no visible outlet and was subject to sudden variations, often flooding the countryside. Emperor Claudius first attempted to drain it by digging a tunnel to connect it with the basin of the Liri, 6km south. The tunnel was opened with great rejoicing in AD 52, but without much result; a second attempt met with equal failure, and the tunnel, the most important work of underground engineering until the construction of the Mont Cenis Tunnel, became blocked.

Frederick II attempted to reopen it in 1240, but it was not until 1852 that the work was seriously undertaken. A company was then formed which entrusted the plans of a new scheme to Hutton Gregory, an English engineer, and later the operations passed under the control of Alessandro Torlonia, a wealthy Roman, who was aided by Swiss and French engineers. The old route was more or less followed, but the new tunnel is nearly 500m longer than the old one. The work was successfully finished in 1875. The outflow is used by electrical installations at Capistrello, to the southwest. In the spring of 1951 the reclaimed lake area, which formed part of the Torlonia estate, was expropriated. About 14,000 hectares were handed over to 8000 families.

Celano

Celano, which stands on a hill (800m) crowned by a castle of the Piccolomini, was the birthplace of Thomas of Celano (d. 1253), the first biographer of St Francis of Assisi and author of the hymn *Dies Irae*. Its churches have been well restored after an earthquake in 1915, as has the imposing **castle**. This was begun in 1392 and completed after 1463, and consists of a rectangular core with four square towers and projecting battlements, surrounded by an irregular enceinte with cylindrical towers at the corners and square bastions along the ramparts. The attached loggie and mullioned windows were added in the 15C, possibly by Antonio Piccolomini. Within, a ramp ascends to the keep, at the centre of which is a courtyard encircled by a Gothic portico, and above, a fine loggiato with rounded arches carried by columns bearing the Piccolomini seal in the capitals. The ramparts command good views over the surrounding countryside.

The Museo Marsicana di Arte Sacra

The Museo Marsicana di Arte Sacra (open summer, daily 09.00–20.00, winter Mon–Fri 09.00–13.30, Sat & Sun 09.00–19.00; ☎ 0863 792922), with examples of religious art from western Abruzzo, is situated on the castle's Gallery Floor.

The visit begins in **room 2**: panels illustrating the history, economy, and art of he region; in the same room, model representing the Marsica area before the draining of Lake Fucino. A computer gives general information about the works displayed, their media, and the techniques used in their restoration. **Room 3**: early medieval sculptural fragments, most from the church of San Pietro at Alba Fucens, where they were found after the earthquake of 1915. Of particular interest is the little pillar, once part of an **iconostasis** now lost, inscribed with the names of its patron and makers. Other fragments from the iconostasis include a lion and a capital with acanthus leaves and human and animal figures.

Room 4: two sets of wooden **doors**, one from the church of Santa Maria in Cellis, Carsoli (1132), the other from the church of San Pietro at Albe (late 12C), both formerly displayed in the Museo Nazionale d'Abruzzo. **Room 5**: panel painting from the church of Santa Maria delle Grazie at Collelongo (13C); two sculptures representing the *Madonna and Child*, from Carsoli and Colli di Monte Bove (13C); panel painting of the *Madonna del Latte* from Carsoli; some detached frescoes from the church of San Pietro at Albe (14C–15C); two panels representing the *Virgin and St John*, ascribed to Giovanni da Sulmona (15C); and an interesting fragment representing the *Virgin*, from Cese di Avezzano, recently attributed to Andrea Delitio (1439–42).

Room 6: tabernacle with scenes from the life of Christ, from Scurcola Marsicana; small wooden Saint from Magliano dei Marsi; paintings, by an unknown artist, of *Christ carrying the Cross*, the *Assumption of the Virgin*, and the *Resurrection of Christ* from the church of St Angelo, Celano; 15C frescoed *Crucifixion* from the Palazzo Ducale, Tagliacozzo.

Room 7: four wooden sculptures representing St Peter, St Paul, St Benedict, and St Andrew, from the church of Santa Maria at Luco dei Marsi; two 17C paintings, of the *Holy Trinity* and the *Crucifixion*. **Rooms 8–9**: goldsmiths' **art**, including precious objects formerly kept at the Museo di Palazzo Venezia in Rome, notably a cross-shaped Byzantine reliquary (13C), a gilded chalice from Celano (14C), the silver Croce degli Orsini with enamels (dated 1334), a small ivory box of the Embriachi school, two silver crucifixes from the church of San Nicola in Albe (15C), and a silver crucifix from Magliano dei Marsi (17C); around the walls are more 15C frescoes from the Palazzo Ducale, Tagliacozzo. **Rooms 10 and 11** contain vestments dating from the 15C to the 19C, notably two silk hempen **chasubles** from the church of San Cesidio in Trasacco (15C–16C).

A scenic mountain road winds northwards from Celano to **Ovindoli** (1379m), situated at the foot of a rock-girt, grassy valley. The village is a starting point for the ascent of **Monte Velino** (2487m) reached in c 4 hours via the *CAI* Sebastiani Refuge (1996m; key at Ovindoli), and the **Colle di Pezza** (2070m). The road (5b) continues northwards to L'Aquila, winding at a high level between Monte Velino and Monte Sirente (2349m).

Road 5 skirts the north side of the Piana del Fucino, closely followed by Autostrada A25. **Avezzano** (695m), a town of 37,000 inhabitants, was completely destroyed by an earthquake on 13 January 1915, but, in common with the surrounding villages, it has been rebuilt and has the atmosphere of a garden city. It suffered further damage in the Second World War, when the Palazzo Torlonia, used by the Germans as a headquarters, was bombed. The Castello degli Orsini dates from 1490. The present building has been largely reconstructed. The

Museo Lapidario Marsicano (closed at the time of writing; ☎ 0863 5011) contains tomb inscriptions, and sculptural and architectural fragments from sites in the ancient Marsica (Alba Fucens, Marruvium, Ortona dei Marsi).

The Roman town of Alba Fucens

Alba Fucens, also called *Alba Fucentia*, lies near the village of Albe, 8km north of Avezzano. It is reached by a minor road (marked). Alba received from Rome in 304 BC a colony of 6000 citizens and became the chief Roman stronghold in the uplands of central Italy. Its three hilltops, the north-east one of which is occupied by the old village (ruined by the earthquake of 1915), were united by a strong wall of polygonal masonry, constructed in the 3C and 2C BC, part of which was incorporated in the medieval town wall on the west. Another well-preserved stretch, reinforced by an external rampart and a rectangular platform probably built during the Social War, is visible to the north-west of the modern village.

Excavations conducted jointly by a Belgian mission and the Soprintendenza Archeologica di Chieti have brought to light a considerable stretch of the ancient Via Valeria, the main street of the town, as well as part of the parallel Via dei Pilastri—so-called after the tall shafts (rebuilt) that line the north side of the road. Also excavated were a **forum**, and remains of numerous buildings, including the **basilica**, the **market**, shops and the partially excavated thermae. The much-ruined **theatre** is opposite the latter. The excavated amphitheatre lies on the east slope of the Collina di San Pietro.

At the top of the hill stands the church of San Pietro, with Corinthian columns and Cosmatesque ornament, which has been expertly restored; on the hill of Pettorino (south-east) are further remains of walls and the houses of the rebuilt

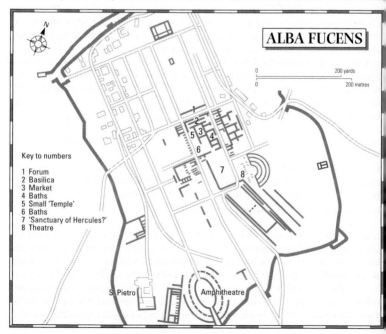

ALBA FUCENS

0   200 yards
0   200 metres

Key to numbers
1 Forum
2 Basilica
3 Market
4 Baths
5 Small 'Temple'
6 Baths
7 'Sanctuary of Hercules?'
8 Theatre

S. Pietro   Amphitheatre

village. It is interesting to note that the walls of Alba Fucens had no towers or bastions other than those at the four gates.

Through the hills to Rome

West of Avezzano **Scurcola Marsicana**, dominated by a castle of the Orsini (1269), preserves in its parish church a fine polychrome wooden Madonna, a relic of the ruined church of Santa Maria della Vittoria built by Charles of Anjou to mark the site of his victory over Conradin, last of the Swabians, at the battle of Tagliacozzo (12 August 1268). To the south and further on, is the large convent of Santa Maria d'Oriente.

Tagliacozzo (823m) is an attractive town (population 7000) built on a slope above the Salto river. The **Palazzo Ducale**, in the imposing piazza, is a fine building of the 14C and 15C. The first floor loggia has 15C frescoes (partially ruined). More frescoes are in the adjoining chapel. **San Francesco**, a 14C convent of Franciscan simplicity, has a Gothic portal and rose window of the mid-15C and a fine frescoed cloister. Within are a 16C wooden crucifix and a 15C Madonna and Child. There are two other churches with 13C doorways and many interesting old houses in the town.

Road 5 continues westwards to Rome, passing several interesting little villages. **Carsoli** (population 5000) stands beneath an ivyed keep. The charming medieval houses in the principal square were completely destroyed in the Second World War, but the 12C church of Santa Maria in Cellis, south-west of the station, escaped injury. Oricola–Pereto station is near the site of *Carseoli*, a stopping place on the ancient Via Valeria from which the town of Carsoli derives its name.

Up the Fioio Valley to the south is **Rocca di Botte**, whose two churches contain 15C and 16C frescoes. In San Pietro are a 13C Cosmatesque pulpit and high altar. The road crosses the regional boundary of Abruzzo into Lazio.

Arsoli (546m), on the Riofreddo, was built, like Carsoli, from the ruins of *Carseoli*. Above the town rises the **Castello Massimo**, dating from the 11C, but rebuilt in the 16C, with two rooms frescoed by the Zuccari and a chapel with Cosmatesque decoration. Pleasant excursions may be made in the surrounding hills. The river provides water for the Aqua Claudia and Aqua Marcia aqueducts. The road descends a long steep slope into the Anio Valley and joins the road from Subiaco.

Abruzzo's green heart

Popoli (population 6000), with its mantle of emerald fields and dark forests, marks the heart of Abruzzo, the point where the roads from Pescara to Rome and Campobasso to L'Aquila cross. The little town is dominated by the ruined castle of the Cantelmi, dukes of Popoli. The war-damaged church of **San Francesco** preserves its important façade and a good medieval Crucifixion group above the high altar. The 14C Gothic Taverna Ducale was built as a storehouse for the ducal tithes; adjoining is the so-called Taverna dell'Universita, added in 1574.

Near Popoli station road 17 begins an immediate, steep and winding ascent, called the **Strada delle Svolte**, reaching a height of 746m. From Navelli (760m) a byroad descends on the right to **Capestrano**, the birthplace of St John Capistran

(1386–1456), an early reformer of the Catholic church. The fine castle, built by the Piccolomini, dates from the 15C, as does the nearby Convento di San Giovanni.

From here a country road descends to Bussi, passing near (right) the ruined abbey of Santa Maria di Cartignano and (left) the lonely Romanesque church of **San Pietro ad Oratorium**, with 12C frescoes and 13C sculptures. Another road crosses the hills to Penne via the Forca di Penne (918m), a pass marking the south-east limit of the Gran Sasso range.

Frescoes in the forest

Just north of Navelli, a turning ascends westwards to **Bominaco** (3km), where two remarkable **churches**, relics of a fortified monastery, have been preserved (if closed, call the custodian, ☎ 0862 93765; a small donation to the church fund will be appreciated). The lower church (San Pellegrino) was built in 1263 over an earlier foundation and has a small porch with three rounded arches. The rectangular interior is covered by a pointed barrel-vault divided into four bays by transverse arches and reflects on a humble scale the Burgundian Gothic style introduced to southern Italy with the abbey of Fossanova. The walls and ceiling are completely decorated with **murals** of the period, of which the most extraordinary are those above the cornice, a cycle representing the Calendar of the Diocese of Valva, with the months, the signs of the Zodiac and feast days. Two stone *plutei*, carved with a dragon (left) and a griffin (right), and originally painted, separate the nave from the sanctuary. Hidden on the north side of the altar is a small hole through which, according to tradition, you can hear the heartbeat of the saint, buried below. The upper church (Santa Maria Assunta) is a splendid example of 12C architecture (note in particular the sculptural decoration of doors, apse, capitals, etc.). It contains a contemporary pulpit, signed and dated 1180, a bishop's chair of 1184, and a fine paschal candlestick. The columns may have been salvaged from a temple of Venus that rose here.

Onwards to Teramo

On the outskirts of L'Aquila (described in Chapter 27) road 17 feeds into Autostrada A24. This continues to Assergi, then passes immediately below the main peaks of the Gran Sasso (tunnel), descending towards (60km) Teramo through the Mavone Valley.

An alternative route from L'Aquila to Teramo, 10km longer but incomparably more beautiful, climbs over the Gran Sasso d'Italia by the Passo delle Capanelle (1299m). Road 80 branches to the right of road 17 just west of L'Aquila and at first ascends the valley of the Aterno. **San Vittorino**, a 12C village on a hill, is reached by a turning on the right. Beneath the Romanesque church of San Michele (1170, rebuilt 1528), you can see the **Catacomba di San Vittorino**, with walls in *opus reticulatum* and *opus incertum*, 14C and 15C frescoes and the presumed tomb of the saint. The church, which is broken into two parts by a dividing wall, contains 13C frescoes and reliefs.

Near Ponte Cermone are the ruins of *Amiternum*, comprising a theatre, an amphitheatre, and the remains of a building with frescoes and mosaics, excavated in 1978. This ancient Sabine town was the birthplace of Sallust. At **Arischia**, you begin to ascend the north-west flank of the Gran Sasso. **Taverna**

della Croce (1270m) marks the beginning of a saddle preceding the road's summit-level at the Passo delle Capannelle, the west-north-west limit of the Gran Sasso range. 4km beyond, a secondary road leads left to the lovely **Lago di Campotosto**, an artificial lake 64km round, taking its name from the village of Campotosto, on the north shore. The fishing in the lake is excellent.

Beyond La Provvidenza (1100m), a starting point for the ascent of the Gran Sasso, the descent of the narrow, picturesque Vomano Valley begins. A by-road climbs south to Pietracamela (1005m), passing the village of **Fano Adriano**, where the 12C church of San Pietro has a simple, characteristic façade of 1550. Monte Corvo and other peaks of the Gran Sasso appear on the right. **Montorio al Vomano** is dominated by its ruined castle. In the main square stands the church of San Rocco, with a curious composite façade, added piecemeal over the centuries. About 16km south, on a by-road, is Isola del Gran Sasso, one of the approaches to the Gran Sasso. To the south-east is Castelli, another approach to the mountains. From Montorio the road climbs out again, then descends, in view of the Monti della Laga, to Teramo.

Teramo

Teramo (population 52,000), the modern-looking capital of the province of the same name, is situated between the Tordino and the Vezzola rivers. It was the ancient *Interamnia Praetuttiorum*, which became a Roman city in 268 BC. Under the Angevin dukes of Apulia it flourished in the 14C; but later, distracted by feuds between the Melatini and the Antonelli, it became part of the Kingdom of Naples.

The **cathedral**, at the centre of the town, has a handsome campanile and a singular Romanesque-Gothic **portal** incorporating mosaic decoration, a rose window, and statues of *Saints Bernard* and *John the Baptist*, and *Christ Blessing*. In the architrave is the date 1332. On either side of the door are statues of the *Archangel Gabriel* and the *Virgin Annunciate*, by Nicola da Guardiagrele, on columns borne by lions; several other lions scattered about the façade probably belonged to the porches of the lateral doorways, now destroyed.

The austere **interior** was begun in the 13C and extended in the following century. The two parts meet at a slight angle, with steps separating the earlier church from the Gothic addition. The high altar is faced with a fine silver frontal by Nicola da Guardiagrele (1433–48), with 34 relief panels depicting New Testament scenes, apostles and saints. On the south wall of the presbytery is a notable polyptych by Jacobello del Fiore, formerly in the church of Sant'Agostino; and in the south transept, a fine, 13C wooden Madonna set in a marble tabernacle. The church incorporates numerous antique architectural fragments and part of the wooden ceiling of the original building. Above the arches of the nave are the arms of the churchmen who helped in its reconstruction. The holy-water stoups at the west end of the nave arcade have been reassembled from medieval sculptural fragments.

The **Museo Archeologico** was opened in 2001 at Via Delfico 30, a few blocks from the cathedral. The collections (open daily, except Mon, Sept–June 09.30–13.00, 16.00–20.00; July–Aug 17.00–22.00; ☎ 0861 247772) document human settlement in the Teramo area, with particular emphasis on the Roman city of *Interamnia*. Highlights include statuary and architectural fragments from the forum, the theatre and three villas, plus burial treasures from the necropolis at Ponte Messato.

Near the east end of the town are the **Madonna delle Grazie**, with a 15C wooden *Virgin* attributed to Silvestro dall'Aquila; Sant'Antonio, with a portal of 1309; and the 14C Casa dei Melatini. Remains of the walls of a Roman amphitheatre may be seen in Via San Bernardo, on the left side of the cathedral, and in Via Vincenzo Irelli, which branches south to the recently excavated Roman theatre. In the Villa Comunale is the **Pinacoteca Civica** (closed for renovation at the time of writing; reopening winter 2003, with the same hours as the Museo Archeologico; ☎ 0861 247772), containing 15C works by local artists and 17C and 18C works by Roman and Neapolitan artists.

North of Teramo

In the hills to the north of Teramo lies the little town of **Campli** (393m), where the lovely, central Piazza Vittorio Emanuele is paved with brick and marble. The cathedral of Santa Maria in Platea from the 14C. Within are a painted wooden ceiling and a good reproduction of Raphael's *Visitation* (now in the Prado in Madrid). The crypt has 15C frescoes.

Opposite the church stands the **Palazzo Farnese**, the former Palazzo Parlamentare, erected in the 14C, rebuilt in 1520 and restored in 1888. It has a portico on heavy piers and mullioned windows. Along the main street are the Casa della Farmacia with a 16C loggia, and the coeval Casa del Medico.

A museum in the former convent of **San Francesco** (Museo Nazionale Archeologico; open daily, 08.30–13.30, 15.30–19.30; ☎ 0861 569158) houses material from an Italic necropolis discovered at Campovalano, nearby. Excavation of the site, which began in 1967, has revealed more than 200 pit tombs dating from the 7C–5C BC. The church, an early 14C Romanesque building, has a fine portal and simple but elegant decorative details. Within are a 14C crucifix, 15C frescoes, and a panel depicting *St Anthony of Padua* by Cola dell'Amatrice (1510).

The little church of **San Giovanni** also dates from the 14C and contains a 14C wooden crucifix and 15C frescoes, as well as two 16C wooden altars. Just beyond is the Porta Orientale, part of the medieval walls.

From the centre of the town a country road leads to (c 1km) the church of **San Pietro**, founded—together with the adjacent ruined Benedictine convent—in the 8C and rebuilt at the beginning of the 13C. The three-aisled interior, restored 1960–68, has votive frescoes on the piers and, on the north wall, a panel, from an early Christian sarcophagus, with bas-reliefs of biblical scenes.

Further north, **Civitella del Tronto** rises in a magnificent position on a hillside below its ruined castle, which was almost the last stronghold of the Bourbons to yield to the Italian troops (1861). It also resisted Guise's attack in 1557 after he had taken Campli in his campaign against Alva's Spaniards. Civitella is interesting for its Renaissance mansions.

The road to Ascoli Piceno descends, with good views back towards Civitella, crossing the Salinello River by a tall bridge. A road branches left to Ripe, near which caves inhabited from the Upper Palaeolothic to the Bronze Age have been found. Beyond Lempa you enter the Marches and begin a long, winding descent. The road passes beneath the expressway linking Ascoli Piceno and San Benedetto del Tronto, then turns west, followed by the railway, to Ascoli Piceno, a handsome town with an extraordinary main square and a provincial capital of the Marches.

L'AQUILA AND THE GRAN SASSO D'ITALIA

L'Aquila is a regional capital in a setting of great natural beauty. Its air of detached serenity is still largely unspoilt, notwithstanding Baroque and Neo-classical attempts to redesign the city and the modern building that has invaded the surrounding countryside. In the city and its environs you can see some of the finest churches in Abruzzo, notably **Santa Maria di Collemaggio**, the highest achievement of Abruzzan religious architecture. The 16C castle houses a truly outstanding collection of polychrome wooden statues removed for safekeeping from these churches, many of which are in a state of partial or total abandon and the former convent of Santa Maria dei Raccomandati is being renovated to hold a new archaeological museum. The **Gran Sasso d'Italia** rises above the city, and is largely responsible for L'Aquila's chilly climate. The peaks of this chain are the highest in the Apennines, rising to 2912m at the Corno Grande. The area is now a national park and certainly repays a visit. Wild horses roam the grasslands of the Campo Imperatore plateau. The Gran Sasso is icy in spring or autumn, and can be cool even in midsummer.

Practical information

Information offices
L'AQUILA
Amministrazione Provinciale Settore Turismo, Piazza Santa Maria di Collemaggio 4, ☎ 0862 2991.
Ufficio Informazioni e di Accoglienza Turistica, Via XX Settembre 8, ☎ 0862 22306.
Ufficio Informazioni e di Accoglienza Turistica, Piazza Santa Maria di Paganica 5, ☎ 0862 410808.

Getting there and getting around
By air
There is a regional airport (**Pasquale Liber**i) 6km north of Pescara, with flights to/from Frankfurt, London, Olbia Rome, Milan and Turin.
By road
The approach to L'Aquila may be made from Rome by Autostrada A24. This goes on to Assergi, then it passes immediately below the main peaks of the Gran Sasso in a tunnel, descending towards Teramo by the Mavone Valley. An alternative approach may be made by the Via Salaria to Antrodoco (see

Blue Guide Umbria), from where Road 17 (here called the Via Sabina) runs across the Apennines to L'Aquila.
By rail
The Rome–Antrodoco route is followed by a secondary railway linking L'Aquila to the Rome–Ancona main line (Rome to L'Aquila in c 3hrs, with a change of trains at Terni).

Where to stay
ASSERGI €€ *Campo Imperatore*, ☎ 0862 400 000, 🖨 0862 400 004. In a splendid position (2130m; 10mins by chairlift) at the foot of the Gran Sasso, with an excellent restaurant.
L'AQUILA € *Duca degli Abruzzi*, Viale Giovanni XXIII 10, ☎ 0862 28341, 🖨 0862 61588, ✉ htlduca@mbox.vol.it. Large, quiet rooms and restaurant with views over the city centre.
€ *Duomo*, Via Dragonetti 6/10, ☎ 0862 410893, 🖨 0862 413058. Centrally located, in a renovated 18C palazzo with terracotta floors and wrought-iron beds.
€ *Rifugio Campo Imperatore*, Via

Campo Imperatore 1, ☎ 0862 400011. Simple lodge.

PAGANICA €€ *Villa Dragonetti*, Via Oberdan 4, ☎ 0862 680222, 🖷 0862 681902, ✉ www.villadragonetti.it. Beautiful 18C villa in a park, with delightful frescoed interiors, antique furniture, impeccable service and one of the better restaurants in L'Aquila and environs.

 Eating out

CAMPOTOSTO

€ *Barilotto*, Via Roma 18, ☎ 0862 900141. Simple trattoria with rooms; closed Tues and Feb.

CASTEL DEL MONTE (at the foot of the Gran Sasso, 41km east of L'Aquila) € *Il Gattone*, Via Campo della Fiera 9, ☎ 0862 938446. Traditional trattoria; closed Wed.

CASTELNUOVO (at the foot of the Gran Sasso, 23km south-east of L'Aquila) €€ *La Cabina*, Via Aufinate 1, ☎ 0862 93567. Small hotel restaurant; closed Mon (except in Aug), Jan–Feb.

FONTE CERETO € *Geranio*, ☎ 0862 606678. Good food and wines, and unique ambience, in the old station of the Gran Sasso cableway; closing times vary.

ISOLA DEL GRAN SASSO (at the foot of the Gran Sasso, 37km south of Teramo) € *Il Mandrone*, at San Pietro, ☎ 0861 976152. Trattoria; closed Tues and Wed (except in Aug), late Nov–early Dec and late Jan–early Feb.

L'AQUILA €€€ *Tre Marie*, Via Tre Marie 3, ☎ 0862 413191. The only place in town where the menu, as well as the décor, is landmarked; closed Sun evening, Mon and late Dec–early Jan.

€€ *Elodia*, SS 17 at Camarda, ☎ 0862 606219. Fabulous country cooking, just outside the city on the Gran Sasso road; closed Sun evening, Mon and Oct.

€ *Antiche Mura*, Via XXV Aprile 2, ☎ 0862 62422. Warm, friendly osteria;

closed Sun.

€ *Il Caminetto*, Via Antica Arischia, at Cansatessa, ☎ 0862 311410. Exquisite renditions of traditional recipes from the city and its environs; closed Mon and Jan.

€ *Mangiatoie*, Via Dragonetti 22, ☎ 0862 24639. Warm atmosphere, good food and great wines in the historic city centre; closed Tues and Nov.

€ *Matriciana*, Via Arcivescovado 5A, ☎ 0862 26065. Fine old-fashioned trattoria with fin-de-siècle interiors; closed Wed and late June–early July.

€ *Taverna del Duomo*, Via Roi 45, ☎ 0862 25392. Good, simple home cooking; closed Wed.

La Fenice, Piazza della Prefettura. Wine bar with an impressive assortment of regional, national and internaltional wines and spirits.

Norcineria Paolo Giuliani, Via Patini 21. Butcher making traditional cold meats and salame.

Panificio Eredi Celso Cioni, Via San Sisto 35. Bakery with delicious breads.

POGGIO PICENZE (20km east of L'Aquila on SS 17) € *Osteria della Posta*, Via Palombaia 1, ☎ 0862 80474. Lovely warm country trattoria, with good food and atmosphere; open evenings (and mid-day Sat and Sun); closed Tues, July and Nov.

PRATA D'ANSIDONIA €€ *Casa Baroni Cappa*, Via della Fonte 33, at San Nicandro, ☎ 0862 93419. Restaurant in a historic building, offering innovative interpretations of traditional dishes; closed Mon and Nov.

 Special events

L'AQUILA *Teatro Internazionale dei Burattini* (international puppet theatre, June–July), *Rassegna musica e architettura* (music and architecture review, July–Aug); historical-religious pageant of the *Perdonanza papale* (28–29 Aug).

L'Aquila

L'Aquila is the capital (population 68,000) of Abruzzo, as well as of the province that bears its name. Prosperous despite frequent earthquakes, the town is notable for its broad streets and imposing public buildings. There are two seasons for visitors: from June to September and a fortnight at Christmas. The summer climate is delightfully cool. L'Aquila is the main centre from which to ascend the peaks of the Gran Sasso d'Italia (see below).

History of L'Aquila

Founded in 1240 by Frederick II as a barrier to the encroachments of the popes, L'Aquila was peopled with the inhabitants of the numerous castles and fortified villages that had grown up in the valley and on the surrounding hills following the destruction of the ancient centres of *Amiternum*, *Forcona*, *Foruli* and *Peltuinum*. In 1423, the combined armies of Joan II, Pope Martin V and the Duke of Milan successfully assaulted the town, and Braccio Fortebraccio, the famous *condottiere*, who held the place for Alfonso of Aragon, was killed. Attendolo, first of the Sforza (later lords of Milan), was drowned in the Pescara, nearby, in the same battle while fighting for the allies.

In later years L'Aquila became, on the strength of its wool trade, one of the chief cities of the Kingdom of Naples, extending its commercial ties to the major centres of north Italy and Europe. It was at this time that the Franciscan Saints Bernard of Siena, John of Capistran and Giacomo della Marca came to the town, increasing its importance as a centre of religious activity. L'Aquila suffered especially severely from the earthquakes of 1461 and 1703.

The city centre

The main approaches to the town unite at Piazza delle Acacie; Via XX Settembre comes in from Rome (and the railway station) and Viale Francesco Crispi enters from the southwest. The piazza is linked by Corso Federico II to Piazza del Duomo, the town centre and market-place.

Pedestrians coming from the station may turn to the right and go through the town wall by Porta Rivera, inside which is the **Fontana delle Novantanove Cannelle**, a singular fountain with 99 spouts (an allusion to the 99 castles from which the town was formed) in the shape of a courtyard of red and white stone. The water issues from 93 grotesque masks (six of the spouts are unadorned) of human, animal and fantastic figures, each of which differs from the others. Set into the end wall is a tablet inscribed *Magis. Tangredus de Pontoma de Valva fecit hoc opus* and dated 1272. Tancred's fountain is believed to have included two sides only; the third, that on the left of the entrance, is generally thought to have been added in 1582. The complex was restored and the right wall rebuilt in the 18C (as the Baroque character of the masks attests), probably following damage in the earthquake of 1703. Further restorations were carried out in 1871 and 1934.

On the west side of Piazza del Duomo is the **duomo** (San Massimo), dating from 1257 and rebuilt after 1703. The Neo-classical façade is a 19C work; the upper storey, with its twin bell-towers, was added in 1928. The original wooden doors are covered by an awkward bronze composition of 1976. Traces of the 13C church can be seen along the right flank. Within is a monument to Cardinal Amico Agnifili by Silvestro dall'Aquila (1480), reconstructed after the earthquake of 1703. Other fragments of this work may be seen at the left of the door to the sacristy and above the portal in the south flank of the church of San Marciano (see below).

On the south side of the square stands the 18C church of the Suffragio. The church of San Giuseppe, in the nearby Via Sassa, contains the Camponeschi tomb (1432) by Gualtiero Alemanno.

On the immediate right of the cathedral Via di Roio leads past Palazzo Dragonetti De Torres and Palazzo Rivera (left) to Palazzo Persichetti, three 18C mansions. Other fine houses from this and earlier centuries may be seen in the neighbourhood. The churches of Santa Maria di Roio, across the street from Palazzo Persichetti, and San Marciano, behind Palazzo Rivera, have plain Romanesque façades.

Aquilaean architecture

No account of L'Aquila's extraordinary architectural heritage could be as curious and colourful as this passage from Edmund Wilson's 1947 travelogue, *Europe without Baedeker*:

'The town looked as if it were constructed of hard panes of light and shade that made the most violent contrasts. Above white blinding sidewalkless streets stood façades built of local stone that had a richness despite their austerity, with their juxtaposed orange and sepia, burnt siena and café au lait, neutral liver and greenish grey, that made a double scale of colors, one darkened and cold, one glowing. The tall doorways were impressively hooded with heavy ornamental architraves, and the windows, well-proportioned and brown-shuttered, were capped with a variety of pediments that resembled now triangular crests, now crowns with twin peaks, now coronets, and contributed to a standard of dignity that ... attained something akin to grandeur ... Aquila had a unity and harmony which made it seem all to have been built in one piece like those wasps'-nests in the hills that had given her the creeps, but which here imposed themselves upon her and compelled her to respect and admire. This, she saw, was what architecture could do—not merely lay out a plan as at Washington, but dominate a whole city and actually provide the medium in which human beings lived.'

From Piazza del Duomo return along Corso Federico II and take a side street to the right to Piazza San Marco, in which are the churches of **San Marco**, preserving two portals dating respectively from the 14C and 15C, and Sant'Agostino. In the other direction is the church of **Santa Giusta** (1257), the simple façade of which incorporates a Romanesque portal and a splendid rose window adorned with grotesque figures. The uninteresting interior contains, in the first south chapel, a *Martyrdom of St Stephen* by Cavalier d'Arpino. In the choir are Gothic stalls. Opposite the church is the 18C Palazzo Conti, a sumptuous building with an unusual balcony.

Santa Maria di Collemaggio

Returning to Corso Federico II, you reach again Piazza delle Acacie (see above), and cross it into Viale Francesco Crispi, which runs alongside the Villa Comunale. Turn left into Viale di Collemaggio, an avenue that leads east to Santa Maria di Collemaggio, a majestic Romanesque church (1287) founded by Pietro dal Morrone (1221–96), who was crowned here as Pope Celestine V in 1294 and canonised as St Peter Celestine in 1313. The façade is a graceful composition of red and white stone, with three doors and three rose windows; the central one is particularly splendid. The large central portal, embellished with spiral moulding and delicate carvings, is flanked by Gothic niches, some of which retain fragments of statues. The wooden door dates from 1688. Carved surrounds also adorn the lateral portals. The façade is divided horizontally by a prominent frieze, the linear value of which lends emphasis to the flat roof line, a recurrent characteristic of the churches of Abruzzo. The low octagonal tower at the south corner was possibly intended for open-air benedictions. On the north side of the church is a Holy Door, unusual outside Rome.

The impressive **interior** was restored in 1973. The floor is paved with red and white stones in square and diamond patterns. The graceful nave arcade consists of broad pointed arches on massive piers, supporting a wooden ceiling. In the aisles are 15C frescoes revealed during the restoration, a 15C terracotta statue of the Madonna and paintings by the 17C artist Charles Ruther. The church also contains the Renaissance tomb (1517) of Celestine V, in a chapel at the right of the apse.

San Bernardino and vicinity

Leaving the church, go back along Viale di Collemaggio for a short distance and then take Strada di Porta Bazzano to the right. This road leads to the Porta Bazzano, from where Via Fortebraccio leads to a flight of steps at the head of which rises San Bernardino. This is an imposing church of 1454–72 with an elaborate Renaissance façade by Cola dell' Amatrice (1524). The Baroque interior, with a splendid, 18C carved ceiling by Ferdinando Mosca, contains (south aisle, second chapel) a *Coronation of the Virgin*, *Resurrection*, and *Saints*, by Andrea della Robbia; further on are the **tomb of San Bernardino** (1505) and (in the apse) the **monument of Maria Pereira** (1496), two fine works in stone by Silvestro dall'Aquila, the latter showing the influence of Antonio Rossellino. Behind the altar (right) is a huge *Crucifixion* by Rinaldo Fiammingo. A fascinating photographic display in the north aisle tells the story of the Holy Shroud.

The Renaissance façade of San Bernardino

From the piazza in front of the church, Via San Bernardino leads left to a busy crossroads called Quattro Cantoni. Keep straight on here, across the corso, to Piazza del Palazzo. Here is a statue of the historian, Sallust (Sallustius Crispus, 86–34 BC), a native of Amiternum, by Cesare Zocchi (1903). Palazzo di Giustizia and its bell tower dominate the piazza; the bell sounds 99 strokes every day at Vespers. The palace was rebuilt in 1573 for Margaret of Austria, illegitimate daughter of Charles V, wife of both Alessandro de'Medici and Ottavio Farnese, and Governess of the Abruzzi.

On the opposite side of the square is the **Biblioteca Provinciale Salvatore Tommasi**, the most important library in Abruzzo, with over 100,000 volumes, including 150 incunabulae, among them two books printed at L'Aquila in 1482. Adjacent is the Convitto Nazionale, in which St Bernard of Siena (1380–1444) died. The **Casa Museo Signorini Corsi** (Via Patini 27, near Piazza del Palazzo; open Tues–Sun 16.00–19.00, Sat, Sun 10.00–13.00, ☎ 0862 241 0900) was given to the city by the descendants of the Signorini Corsi family. It preserves the appearance of a patrician house of the early 18C, with interesting period furniture, as well as a coin collection, icons from Russia, Crete and Dalmatia, and paintings from the 14C to the 20C.

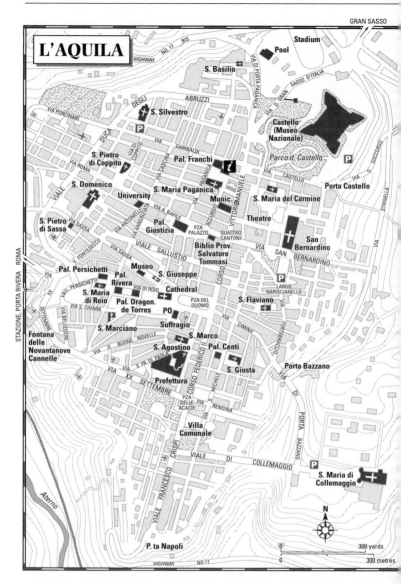

Return to the corso, here dedicated to Vittorio Emanuele, and proceed north (left) passing, in the side streets, the churches of **Santa Maria di Paganica** (1308) on the left and Santa Maria del Carmine on the right. Both have 14C façades, the former with a handsomely carved portal. From the end of the corso cross the busy Piazza Battaglione Alpini, with its rhetorical fountain, to the Parco del Castello.

The Museo Nazionale d'Abruzzo

The **castle**, built by Pier Luigi Scriva in 1530, now houses the Museo Nazionale d'Abruzzo (open summer Tues–Sun 09.00–21.00; winter Mon–Sat 09.00–14.00, Sun 09.00–13.00, ☎ 0862 6331) and the Auditorium, one of the halls used by the Societa Aquilana dei Concerti. The museum, the finest in east central Italy, incorporates the collections formerly held by the Museo Civico and the Museo Diocesano d'Arte Sacra, as well as works from ruined churches throughout the region.

You enter through a monumental doorway surmounted by the arms of Charles V and huge horns of plenty carved by Salvato Salvati and Pietro di Stefano and dated 1543. Beyond the entrance hall lies the large, rectangular court; turn right and proceed beneath a vaulted portico to the large, domed room in the south-east bastion, at the centre of which stands a **prehistoric elephant** (*Archidiskodon Meridionalis Vestinus*), partly reconstructed with plaster casts, found at Scoppito, 14km west of L'Aquila. Plant fossils are exhibited on the wall. In an adjoining room is a group of works donated to the museum in 1993 by the contemporary artist Emilio Greco.

The nearby **Sala del Gonfalone** displays the **banner** of the city of L'Aquila, a curious work painted in 1579 by the local artist Giovanni Paolo Cardone. The banner shows Aquila as it looked before the 1703 earthquake, presented to Christ the Redeemer by the four patrons of the city (Saints Maximus, Equizio, Nernardino and Celestine). At the sides of the Saviour are the Virgin, interceding for the city, and an angel holding an amphora. The influence of Roman mannerism is particularly evident in the figure of Christ holding the Cross, which seems to be derived from the Christ sculpted by Michelangelo for the church of Santa Maria sopra Minerva in Rome.

The archaeological collection

Return to the courtyard and, passing the entrance, turn right to the archaeological section. Outside the entrance are various architectural fragments of Roman manufacture and a large Roman Hercules from 1C AD. Highlights of the collection include inscriptions; tomb relief from Coppito (*Pitinum*); stele of Q. Pomponius Proculus, from Scoppito (*Foruli*); calendar from *Amiternum*; milestone of the Via Claudia Nova (*Foruli*); tympanum with head of Medusa from Preturo; headless lion holding the head of a ram; bas-relief with a funeral procession; **tympanum** with butcher's tools; tympanum with relief of carpenter's tools; vases in terracotta and impasto, bronze jewellery, painted vases, Etruscan ware in bucchero and clay (6C BC); terracotta votive statues (3C–2C BC); and a fine collection of small cups, plates and bowls (1C BC–1C AD).

Religious art collection

Steps ascend to the **first floor**, where the religious art collection occupies the corridor and adjoining rooms. In the corridor are (left) fresco of **Christ with the Virgin and St John** by Armanino da Modena, for an apse (the work is dated 1237 and signed by the artist, which was unusual at the time); below, stone altar frontal with plant and animal reliefs; nearby, a large *Baptism of St Augustine* by Mattia Preti; a polychrome wooden sculpture of the **Virgin and Child** by an anonymous local artist of the 16C; and (right) detached frescoes from ruined churches of Abruzzo: *Madonna del Latte* (14C–15C); a Byzantine fresco with the **Madonna and Child**, **St Sebastian**, and a mandorla with the **Virgin in Glory**

(15C), Byzantine fresco with the *Madonna and Child, Saints and an Archangel* a fresco with a *Crucifixion* by Francesco da Montereale (16C).

Room 1: polychrome wooden crucifix (13C); *Madonna and Child enthroned* (13C); 12C–13C fresco fragments. **Room 2**: polychrome wooden figure group of the *Madonna and Child* (dated 1262); polychrome *Madonna and Child* (13C); Byzantine panel painting of the *Madonna del Latte* (1270–80); panel of the *Madonna and Child* (signed Gentile da Rocca and dated 1283); a wooden figure of *Christ deposed* (early 15C). **Room 3**: *St Balbina*; polychrome *Madonna and Child* (early 14C); wooden statue of *St Catherine of Alexandria* between panels representing episodes from her life; *Madonna enthroned*; polychrome wooden statue of *St Leonard* (15C); wooden figure of *St Bartholomew* showing French influence. **Room 4**: more polychrome wooden statues, including a poorly preserved but evocative *Santa Coronata*; in the glass case, gilded silver processional cross (dated 1434 and signed by Nicola da Guardiagrele). **Room 5**: *Tree of the Cross* (early 15C); triptych (15C); *Madonna and Child with Saints*, altarpiece by Jacobello del Fiore (15C); *St Bernardino of Siena*, by Sano di Pietro; triptych with the *Madonna and Child enthroned, Nativity, Annunciation to the Shepherds* and *Transito della Vergine*, showing Sienese influence (15C). **Room 6**: polychrome wood sculpture of the *Madonna and Child*, by Silvestro dall'Aquila (late 15C); minor sculptural works; *St Sebastian* (1478) by Silvestro dall'Aquila, showing the influence of the Florentine Renaissance sculptor Verrocchio; panel paintings of the 15C and 16C; fragmentary panel of the *Virgin* by Andrea Delitio, showing the strong influence of Piero della Francesca and Benozzo Gozzoli. Note the painted ceilings in this and the following room. The ceiling of **room 6** represents mythological scenes, including the *Rape of Ganymede* and the story of *Amor and Psyche*, from Ovid's *Metamorphoses*; the ceiling of **room 7** is adorned with heads of Roman emperors.

Room 7: 15C panel paintings: *St John Capistran* with episodes from the life of the saint, by the Master of St John Capistran (15C); *Stigmatisation of St Francis* by the Master of St John Capistran (15C); a poorly preserved terracotta *Madonna and Child* (16C); at the centre, terracotta *Nativity* (late 15C). **Room 8**: 15C and 16C stained glass; church furnishings and 16C panel paintings; three polychrome wooden figures of *St Joseph*, the *Virgin Mary* and a *Bagpipe Player*, by an anonymous 15C artist following Silvestro dall'Aquila. **Room 9**: assorted paintings by local artists of the 15C, including two paintings by Pietro Alemanno, one of Carlo Crivelli's disciples. **Room 10**: other assorted paintings by local artists of the 15C–16C, including two paintings attributed to Saturnino Gatti.

The **coin collection**, also reached from the first-floor loggia, displays over a hundred pieces offering a good sample of Abruzzan numismatics from the 4C BC to the Unification of Italy. The **gold room**, on the landing between the first and second floors, contains an arrangement of objects (notably processional crosses and shrines) from Sulmona, Teramo, and L'Aquila.

The religious art section continues on the **second floor**, with works from the 16C up to the 18C. The first two rooms, off the corridor on the right, are dedicated to artists native to L'Aquila, notably Francesco da Montereale, Giovanni Paolo Cardone and his master, Pompeo Cesura, all active in the 16C. In the third room are Flemish painters, followed by the 17C artist Giulio Cesare Bedeschini in the fourth room. Next are works by 17C Neapolitan and Roman artists, and paintings by Carl Ruther, a Benedictine monk of Flemish origin and member of he community of Santa Maria di Collemaggio. Rooms 7 and 8 are being earranged. They will display locally made ceramics and lace, respectively. nother section on this floor will show Abruzzan gold and silver liturgical items.

he Cappelli collection

eturn to the corridor from the far end to view the Cappelli collection, with vorks by Neapolitan artists, including a *Madonna and Child* by Fabrizio antafede; *St Agatha* by Andrea Vaccaro; *Mary Magdalen* by Giuseppe Ribera; *ribute Money, Christ and the Adulteress, Martyrdom of St Bartholomew and ob in the Dung Pile* by Mattia Preti; and *Triumph of Charles of Bourbon* by rancesco Solimena.

The **modern art collection** contains works by contemporary painters such s Mino Maccari, Giuseppe Capogrossi, Mario Mafai, Domenico Cantatore, and iiovanni De Santis, as well as numerous minor artists.

round the castle

he road to the right of the castle leads to (15 minutes) the Madonna del occorso, with a good Renaissance façade (1496) and two early 16C tombs in the tyle of Silvestro dall'Aquila.

From the end of Corso Vittorio Emanuele, Via Garibaldi leads north-west to the 4C church of **San Silvestro**, with an elegant rose window in its simple façade nd 15C frescoes in the apse. From here, Via Coppito and Via San Domenico lead o San Domenico, a church dating in part from the 14C, now used as an audito-ium. Of the many 18C mansions, perhaps the most interesting is the **Palazzo 3enedetti**, in Via Accursio (near Santa Maria Paganica), with its finely propor-ioned courtyard. The Convento di San Giuliano, just outside the town, houses a mall natural history museum (Museo di Scienze Naturali; open Tues–Sun, 0.00–13.00, 15.00–18.00, ☎ 0862 314201).

The Gran Sasso d'Italia

'he Gran Sasso d'Italia, a predominently limestone formation, containing the ighest mountains in southern Italy (apart from Etna), is part of the east wall of he Abruzzo mountain group. With an average depth of c 15km, it extends in a vest north-west–east south-east direction for c 35km from the Passo delle 'apannelle, on road 80 from L'Aquila to Teramo, to Forca di Penne, on a sec-ndary road from Popoli to Penne.

The Gran Sasso comprises two almost parallel chains separated by a central lepression interrupted by peaks of its own. The south chain is a uniform rampart xtending from Monte San Franco (2132m) in the west to Monte Bolza (1904m) n the east, with the Pizzo Cefalone (2533m) in the centre. The north chain ncludes the formidable peaks of Monte Corvo (2623m); the Pizzo Intermesoli 2635m), the Corno Piccolo (2655m), the Corno Grande with its three summits, ne of them the highest of all (2912m), Monte Brancastello (2385m), Monte 'rena (2561m) and Monte Camicia (2570m). Deep valleys extend from this hain to the north: the Venacquaro, between Monte Corvo and the Pizzo ntermesoli; the Valmaone, between the Pizzo Intermesoli and the Corno Grande; he Valle dell'Inferno, between the Corno Grande and Monte Brancastello. To the outh are the Passo di Portella (2260m) and the Vado di Corno (1924m).

The ski runs of the Gran Sasso compare favourably with the most famou Alpine runs. Of the shelters, which provide rudimentary accommodation fo hikers and skiers, the Duca degli Abruzzi refuge (2388m) is habitable (key at th Albergo Campo Imperatore); that of Carlo Franchetti (2433m) was built in 195 (key with Lino d'Angelo at Pietracamela); the old Garibaldi refuge is derelict.

Much of the central depression consists of the **Campo Imperatore**, a vas tableland (2130m) inhabited by herds of wild horses. It is connected with th road from L'Aquila by cableway (see below). Other approaches include thos from La Provvidenza, on road 80 from L'Aquila to Teramo; Pietracamela, at th foot of the Corno Piccolo; Isola del Gran Sasso, below the Corno Grande; an Castelli, below Monte Prena. All these localities are mentioned below.

Ascent of the Gran Sasso

The Funivia del Gran Sasso d'Italia (Gran Sasso cableway; operative 08.00 17.00 except in high winds) enables travellers to reach the Campo Imperator and return to L'Aquila in a day. An alternative approach to the Camp Imperatore may be made in fair weather by an extension of road 17b, whic links the upper and lower stations of the cableway.

To reach the funivia's lower station, at **Fonte Cerreto**, above Assergi, take th Viale del Gran Sasso d'Italia out of L'Aquila, past the castle, heading east alon road 17b to (9km) **Paganica** (660m). Alternatively, leave L'Aquila by the Port Napoli and take road 17 to Bazzano and from there by a secondary road t Paganica. From Paganica the road ascends north-east to (7km) **Assergi** (867m a tiny village of importance to mountaineers; its church has a Gothic façade an a 12C crypt. Beyond Assergi the road climbs sharply to (4km) Fonte Cerret (1120m) and the lower station of the cableway (*Stazione Inferiore Funivia* Autostrada A24 follows roughly the same course to Assergi. Buses from L'Aquil (50–60 minutes) connect with the cableway services.

The cableway climbs several times daily to (3km) Campo Imperatore in 3 minutes. Above the terminus is the Albergo di Campo Imperatore. The hotel is a the top of a ski-lift (*sciovia*), 600m long, which ascends from Le Fontari (1980m during the winter season (Dec–Apr). It was the scene of the daring Nazi 'rescue of Mussolini on 12 September 1943. Now it is the usual starting point for walk and ascents.

Tunnels link the hotel to the little church of the Madonna della Neve, the astro nomical observatory and the adjacent Giardino Botanico, created for the study o high altitude pastures.

Hiking the Gran Sasso

From the Albergo di Campo Imperatore there are several recognised hiking trai across the Gran Sasso and up to its various summits. The hotel sells trail maps Those who would like a guide should apply to the **Ufficio Informazioni e a Accoglienza Turistica**, in L'Aquila. Detailed information about the area is give in the *Guida dei Monti d'Italia*, volume *Gran Sasso*, published by the *CAI (Clu Alpino Italiano)* and *TCI (Touring Club Italiano)*. A selection of the recognise itineraries, all starting from the Albergo di Campo Imperatore, is given below. Th times shown for each trip are for *one way* only.

Why Mussolini was imprisoned and how he got away

The story is a bit confusing, but it goes something like this. Following the talks between Mussolini and Hitler at Feltre (19 July 1943), the Gran Consiglio del Fascismo voted to remove the *duce*. King Victor Emmanuel III accordingly dismissed Mussolini and had him arrested (25 July). The next day a new cabinet, formed under General Pietro Badoglio, disbanded the Fascist Party (28 July) and, while publicly expressing the wish to remain at the side of Italy's Nazi ally, secretly began talks with the Allies (3 August, in Lisbon). After the announcement of the armistice, signed in Sicily on 3 September between the Allied Command and the Italian government, on 8 September the Germans occupied the principal strategic points of northern and central Italy, and Rome. The disoriented Italian troops were largely disarmed or taken prisoner. The Badoglio government, without making any provision for armed resistance against the Nazis, fled with the royal family to Brindisi, where they found Allied protection.

On 12 September an SS assault team freed Mussolini from his prison on the Gran Sasso and flew him away to Salò, on Lake Garda. Here, with Hitler's support, Mussolini formed the *Repubblica Sociale di Salò*, a puppet state of Nazi Germany. On 13 October the Badoglio government declared war on Germany. You know the rest.

• To La Provvidenza via the Sella dei Grilli

hours, moderately strenuous. Skiing is possible all the way. From the lbergo di Campo Imperatore turn round the left of the observatory and follow ie mule track to the Passo di Portella (2260m). From the pass, a track descends the Capanne di Val Maone. From here continue to the left to the Sella dei Grilli ?110m). Skirting the south slopes of the Pizzo Intermesoli, the trail passes irough the Fonte dei Grilli to reach the Casa Venacquaro, from where there is n easy climb to the Sella Venacquaro (2300m). A track leads to the Masseria accareccia (1503m). Cross the Piano del Castrato and, keeping left, descend the alle del Chiarino to the Masseria Cappelli (1262m). A road follows the aqueduct ist the source of the Vomano to the village of La Provvidenza.

• To La Provvidenza via the Sella dei Cefalone

hours 30 minutes, moderately strenuous. From the Passo di Portella (see 'alk 1) climb the crest that ascends towards the Pizzo Cefalone for c 500m, pass- ig over the summit (2163m), which looks out over the wide valley on the east ink of Pizzo Cefalone. Descend into the valley and keep left to reach a second est which, with the first, forms a small valley and which leads easily to the val- y's head. A steep slope leads to the Sella del Cefalone. Descending beneath the ella dei Grilli, turn left to reach the Casa Venacquaro (2001m). From here to La rovvidenza, follow Walk 1.

• To Pietracamela via the Valmaone

hours 45 minutes, moderately strenuous. Skiing possible. From the Passo Portella (Walk 1), descend to the Capanne di Val Maone, continuing with the ist wall of the Pizzo d'Intermesoli on your left and the north-east slope of the east eaks of the Corno Grande and the east summit of the Corno Piccolo on your ght. Pass under the Grotta d'Oro, leave the Valle dei Ginepri on the right and

reach the Sorgenti di Rio d'Arno. From here you descend through the woode
Valle di Rio d'Arno, avoiding a turning to the left, to Pietracamela, see below.

4 • To Pietracamela via the Sella dei Due Corni

6 hours 15 minutes, strenuous. Skiing possible for experts; route for th
ascents of the Corno Grande. From the hotel climb to the Duca degli Abruz
refuge (2388m), then north to the Sella di Monte Aquila. Cross the Camp
Pericoli and climb steeply to (2 hours) the Sella di Brecciaio. You now cross a wid
plateau to the northeast of the Conca degli Invalidi. After another steep clim
you reach (1hr 15mins) a fork. The right branch leads up in 3 hours 15 minute
by the north-west slope to the west peak of the Corno Grande, the highest of th
three summits (2912m).

Climb up to the Passo del Cannone (2697m) and descend (care needed) to th
Sella dei Due Corni. From the saddle descend on a steep path into the Valle del
Cornacchie, and, keeping left, reach the Franchetti refuge (2613m), facing the ea
side of the Corno Piccolo. From here the route is to the Passo delle Scalette and int
the Regione Arapietra. Enter the Prati di Tibo and descend to Pietracamela.

5 • To Isola del Gran Sasso via the Sella dei Due Corni

7 hours 45 minutes, strenuous. To the Regione Arapietra, see above. Turnin
right, descend by a steep mule track past the little church of San Nicola (1096m
An easy descent follows to Casale San Nicola, where the road begins. For Isola d
Gran Sasso, see Walk 6.

6 • To Isola del Gran Sasso via the Vado di Corno

5 hours, moderately strenuous. Practicable on skis. Descend a little valley t
the east of the hotel as far as Le Fontari. Bear left here and take the path skirtin
the slopes of Monte Aquila to Vado di Corno (1294m) with a **view** of the Val
dell'Inferno. From here there is a climb of 3 hours to Monte Brancastell
(2385m), to the east. From Vado di Corno the route leads to Vaduccio; you the
descend through woods to Fosso Vittore. Cross the river, reach a roofless shed an
descend by a track to the bridge at Casale San Nicola. Isola del Gran Sasso is 8k
by road from here.

7 • To the Garibaldi refuge via the Passo di Portella

2 hours, easy. Follow Walk 1 to the Passo di Portella. From the pass descend an
follow a track to the right, which at first descends and then gently ascends to
hump (on which there is a rain-gauge). From here, you go through a valley to th
Garibaldi refuge (2231m).

APULIA

Apulia (Puglia) occupies the extreme south-east of the Italian peninsula, from the 'spur' (Monte Gargano) to the 'heel' (Salentine or Iapygian Peninsula) of the 'boot'. For the most part it is flat, rising gently inland to a long plateau (Le Murge), with no considerable elevations except the Gargano promontory. It is the ancient Apulia, originally inhabited by the Pelasgians and the Oscans, the Daunians and the Peucetians. Among its towns were several Greek colonies, including Taras. It flourished under the Roman rule which followed the defeat of Pyrrhus, and with the rest of southern Italy it has passed through the hands of innumerable overlords, its most prosperous period being under the Swabians.

The great period of church-building in Apulia was under the Normans, who combined diverse influences from France, Pisa, the Lombards and the Orient into the style known loosely as Apulian Romanesque. This style is generally characterised by the massive solidity, rounded arches and flat ceilings found in the contemporary architecture of northern Europe, though here embellished with delicately detailed ornamental features of Byzantine or Saracen origin. The details of these churches and of Frederick II's fine castles amply repay study.

As in Abruzzo and Lazio, there are still nomad shepherds in parts of Apulia. In these three provinces together there are about 3000km of grassy drove-roads, known as *tratturi* (with side-tracks known as *tratturelli* or *bracci*), under the administration of the State, by which the sheep are driven up to the lofty pastures of Abruzzo in spring, returning to the Apulian lowlands in autumn.

Apulia largely consists of flat expanses of limestone, almost destitute of rivers, as the surface water disappears into the limestone fissures. The rainfall is very light, and the region deserves its epithet of *seticulosa* or thirsty. However, the soil is well cultivated. Wheat is the chief crop in the almost treeless plain of the *Tavoliere della Puglia*, known also as the *Capitanata*, around Foggia. Further south, vineyards predominate, with groves of olives, almonds, and figs.

The great Apulian aqueduct, the largest in the world, with 2700km of channels, supplies drinking water to 268 communes in the region. From the sources of the Sele, on the west side of the Apennine watershed, it carries c 15,000,000 litres of water per hour into Apulia.

FOGGIA AND THE GARGANO

Most people enter Apulia from the north, by the motorway or railway that runs along the Adriatic shore. Coming this way, you gradually leave the rolling hills of Molise for much flatter country. Ahead stretches the great plain of Foggia, an area rich in prehistoric sites, few of which have been systematically excavated. In Roman times the plain was centuriated—that is, partitioned into farms of uniform area with a regular network of roads between them. This pattern, which can still be traced, gives the district its popular nickname, *tavoliere* (chessboard). Its modern prosperity was greatly increased by an improvement scheme of 1934–38. Photographic reconnaissance in 1945 revealed upwards of 2000 settlements, many confirmed as Neolithic on excavation. Passo di Corvo, which is the largest known Neolithic site in Europe, has yielded tools, implements and masses of pottery.

Standing watch over Apulia's northern gateway are the fabulous **Gargano Peninsula** and its offshoot, the quiet little archipelago known as the **Tremiti Islands**. Here you'll find respite from the hustle and bustle of the Apulian coast as well as immense natural beauty. The region has more in common geologically with the eastern Adriatic than with the rest of Italy: the Gargano and the Tremiti Islands in fact form a single geological unit, composed largely of white limestone identical to that of southern Croatia. Unlike the neighbouring plain, they are densely forested, and the combination of glistening stone, dark forest and azure sea is unforgettable. The forested highlands of the Gargano were declared a national park in 1991, and the unique pine woods of the Tremiti Islands are a specially protected nature reserve.

Practical information

Information offices

FOGGIA *Azienda di Promozione Turistica*, Via Senatore Emilio Perrone 17, ☎ 0881 723650.

MANFREDONIA *Ufficio Informazioni e di Accoglienza Turistica*, Piazza del Popolo 11, ☎ 0884 581998.

SAN GIOVANNI ROTONDO *Ufficio Informazioni e di Accoglienza Turistica*, Piazza Europa 104, ☎ 0882 456240.

VIESTE *Ufficio Informazioni e di Accoglienza Turistica*, Corso Fazzini 8, ☎ 0884 707495. *Ufficio Informazioni e di Accoglienza Turistica*, Piazza Kennedy, ☎ 0884 708806.

Getting there and getting around

By air

Helicopters fly twice daily in summer and around Christmas and Easter, from Foggia's **Gino Lisa** airport to the Tremiti Islands. Details from *Ali Daunia*, ☎ 0881 617944.

By road

To reach the Gargano from the north, take Autostrada A14 from Termoli to Poggio Imperiale, then continue along local roads; from the south, take Road 9 from Foggia or Roads 545 and 159 from Cerignola to Manfredonia. You can make a 223km circuit of the peninsula from Foggia via 40km Manfredonia—52km Vieste—26km Peschici (short cut: Foggia to Peschici via Monte Sant Angelo, 59km)—14km Rodi Garganico—53km Foggia. Travel time is 3hrs 30mins, plus stops.

By rail

Foggia is the junction between the main lines from Milan and Rome to Bari, Brindisi and Lecce, and the terminus of a secondary line to Manfredonia. Fast Intercity trains run to Foggia from Pescara in c 2hrs and from Bari in c 1hr. Eurostar trains run from Rome via Caserta in c 3hrs 15mins; and Expresses, from Naples, in c 3hrs. Through trains to/from Switzerland and Germany. There are slow local trains from Foggia to Manfredonia Città, 36km in c 25mins, with bus connections to Vieste.

By sea

The Tremiti Islands are best reached by hydrofoil from Ortona (daily June–Sept, 2hrs), Vasto (daily June–Sept, 1hr), Termoli (daily all year, 50mins), and Rodi Garganico (daily June–Sept, 50mins). Ferries daily from Termoli (1hr 40mins). Details in Rodi Garganico from

driatica di Navigazione, c/o VI.PI.,
iazza Garibaldi 10, ☎ 0884 966357;
n the Isle of San Domino, from
driatica di Navigazione, c/o Cafiero,
ia degli Abbati 10, ☎ 0882 463008.

Where to stay

FOGGIA €€ *Cicolella*,
Viale XXIV Maggio 60,
☎ 0881 566111, ▤ 0881 778984,
hotelcicolella@isnet.it. Traditional,
entral, quiet and comfortable, with a
ood restaurant; open all year.

MANFREDONIA €€ *Gargano*,
iale Beccarini, 2, ☎ 0884 587621,
▤ 0884 586021. Overlooking the sea,
with antiques, plants and flowers, pool,
astefully furnished rooms, and an
xcellent restaurant; open all year.

MARGHERITA DI SAVOIA
€ *Delle Terme*, Via Garibaldi 1, ☎
883 656888, ▤ 0883 654019. On
he sea with great views, luminous well-
urnished rooms, spa and private beach;
pen Apr–Oct.

MATTINATA €€ *Baia delle Zagare*,
t Baia dei Mergoli, 17km north-east,
☎ 0884 4115, ▤ 0884 4884,
◪ www.hotelbaiadellezagare.it,
nfo@hotelbaiadellezagre.it. In an olive
rove overlooking the sea, with private
each; open June–Sept.

€ *Dei Faraglioni*, at Baia dei Mergoli,
7km north-east, ☎ 0884 49584,
▤ 0884 4965. As above, with views of
he Faraglioni rocks; open June–Sept.

Apeneste, Piazza Turati 3, ☎ 0884
50743, ▤ 0884 550341, ◪ info@
otelapeneste.it. On the outskirts of the
own, surrounded by oleander, olive and
mon trees; good views, great cuisine;
pen all year.

PESCHICI € *Solemar*, at Baia San
icola, 3km north-east, ☎ 0884
64186, ▤ 0884 964188, ◪ hotel.
olemar@tiscalinet.it. In a pine grove
km ouside the town, towards Vieste;
rivate beach, pool, cinema; closing
me varies.

RODI GARGANICO €€ *Baia
Santa Barbara*, at Santa Barbara,
☎ 0884 965253, ▤ 0884 965414. In
a pine grove 1km west of the village,
with pool; open Apr–Oct.

€€ *Parco degli Aranci*, at Mulino di
Mare, ☎ 0884 965033, ▤ 0884
98481. In an orange grove 2km east of
the village, also with pool; open Apr–Oct
and Dec–Jan.

TREMITI ISLANDS €€ *Kyrie*,
San Domino, ☎ 0882 663241, ▤ 0882
663415. Quiet and comfortable, in a
pine grove; open Apr–Sept.

€€ *Gabbiano*, San Domino, ☎ 0882
463410, ▤ 0882 463428, ◪ hotel-
gabbiano.com, gabbiano@hotel-
gabbiano.com. Panoramic location,
courteous staff, wholesome local
cuisine, shuttle to harbour and beach;
open all year.

€ *San Domino*, San Domino, ☎ 0882
663404, ▤ 0882 663221,
◪ hdomino@tiscalinet.it. Small,
friendly and tranquil; open all year.

VIESTE €€€ *Pizzomunno Vieste
Palace*, Spiaggia di Pizzomunno,
☎ 0884 708741, ▤ 0884 707325,
◪ www.pizzomunno.it. A luxury hotel
complex in a beautiful park on a great
sandy beach; pool, gym, archery, sail-
and motor-boats, windsurfing, tennis
courts, etc.; open Apr–Oct.

€ *Seggio*, Via Vieste 7, ☎ 0884
708123, ▤ 0884 708727. In the old
(17C) town hall, on a cliff above the sea,
at the heart of the pedestrian district;
pool and private beach; open Apr–Oct.

Eating out

FOGGIA €€ *Chacaito*, Via
Arpi 62, ☎ 0881 708104.
Osteria near a wonderful fruit and
vegetable market; closed Sun and Aug.

€€ *Conca d'Oro*, Via Bari, at Borgo
Incoronata, ☎ 0881 638160.
Restaurant with garden on the outskirts
of town; closed Mon and one week in
Aug.

€€ *Da Pompeo*, Vico al Piano 14,
☎ 0881 724640. Traditional trattoria
in the historic city centre; closed Sun
and Aug.

€€ *Il Ventaglio*, Via Postiglione 6,
☎ 0881 661500. Restaurant; closed
Sat–Sun in July–Aug and Sun
evening–Mon in other months, closed
late Dec and late Aug.

€€ *La Locanda di Malì*, Via Arpi 86,
☎ 0881 723937. Romantic restaurant
offering fine creative cooking; closed
Mon, Tues and Aug.

€ *Zia Marinella*, Via Saverio Altamura
23–31, ☎ 330 654510. Warm, friendly
osteria, centrally located; closed Sun
and mid-Aug.

Pasticceria Pietro Moffa, Viale
Michelangelo 50, for delicious pastries,
cakes and candies.

€€ *Il Baraccio*, Corso Roma 38,
☎ 0884 583874. Trattoria famous for
its skillfully prepared local delicacies;
closed Thur and 10 days in July.

MATTINATA € *Montesacro*,
Contrada Stinco, ☎ 0884 558941.
Farm serving country meals, in a grove
of olives and almonds near the sea;
open daily, Jan and Feb by reservation
only.

MINERVINO MURGE
€ *La Tradizione*, Via Imbriani 11,
☎ 0883 691690. Trattoria with good
traditional fare; closed Thur and a few
days in Sept and Feb.

MONTE SANT'ANGELO
€ *Da Costanza*, Via Garibaldi 67,
☎ 0884 561313. Simple trattoria;
closed Fri (except in summer) and in
winter.

€ **MEDIOEVO**, Via Castello 21,
☎ 0884 565356. Traditional restaurant; closed Mon (except in summer)
and Nov.

SAN GIOVANNI ROTONDO
€€ *Abete*, Via Sant'Adele 9, ☎ 0882
456886. Curiously alpine cuisine, with
a focus on game; closing times vary.

€ *Antica Piazzetta*, Via al Mercato 13,
☎ 0882 451920. Restaurant known
for its wholesome regional food; closed
Wed, July and Jan.

SAN SEVERO €€ *Fossa del Grano*
Via Minuziano 63, ☎ 0882 241122.
Osteria, with good wine list, in an old
granary; closed Tues, Sat–Sun in
July–Aug.

Foggia and its environs

Foggia (population 160,000), Apulia's northern gateway, is a city of moder
aspect with important paper and textile mills. As the marketing centre of a va
agricultural region, it is also the focus of communication for northern Apulia.

History of Foggia

Founded by the people of the abandoned Italic town of *Arpi* (the site of whic
may be traced 3km north), Foggia probably takes its name from the *foveae* o
trenches made to store grain. Frederick II often resided here; on Palm Sunda
in 1240 he summoned the Third Estate to a *colloquia*, an event almost ce
tainly noted by Simon de Montfort, who passed through Apulia shortly afte
wards, embarking from Brindisi to join the crusade led by Richard o
Cornwall, second son of King John of England. Frederick's third wife, Isabell
daughter of King John of England, died here in 1241, as did Charles I o
Anjou in 1285.

In 1528 Lautrec took the town and massacred the inhabitants. It wa
almost totally destroyed by an earthquake in 1731, when the casket contai
ing Frederick's heart was lost (he died suddenly, perhaps of dysentery, i

nearby Castel Fiorentino, in 1250). Foggia became an important airbase in the Second World War and was much damaged by bombing, the remaining portions of Frederick's palace being destroyed. Umberto Giordano (1867–1949), composer of *Andrea Chenier*, was a native.

From Piazza Cavour, the older part of the city lies to the north-west. Follow Via Lanza and Corso Vittorio Emanuele to Via Garibaldi. Here turn left, then immediately right in Via Duomo. The **cathedral**, built in 1172, retains part of its Romanesque façade and crypt; the remainder, shattered in 1731, was rebuilt in the Baroque style. An interesting portal with primitive bas-reliefs, brought to light in 1943 when bombs levelled the building which adjoined the cathedral, can be seen along the north flank.

The **interior**, built to a Latin cross plan with a single nave, has modern (1932) stained-glass windows and, above the door, a painting of the *Miracle of the Loaves*, by Francesco De Mura. The Cappella dell'Icona Vetere, to the right of the presbytery, contains a Byzantine icon that was found in a pond in 1073, according to tradition. The restored crypt has vaulted ceilings and stout columns with delicate Romanesque capitals, possibly by Nicola di Bartolomeo da Foggia.

Via Arpi, to the north, leads (right) to Piazza Nigri, where the small **Museo Civico** (open daily 09.00–13.00; Mon, Tues, Thur, Fri 09.00–13.00 and 17.00–19.00; closed for renovation at the time of writing; ☎ 0881 711134) has several rooms devoted to archaeology, displaying finds from the Belgian excavations at Ordono, from Arpi and from Ascoli Satriano. There is also material from Siponto, a section devoted to folk traditions and a modern picture gallery.

On the plain

Several of the towns in the environs of Foggia warrant a visit. **San Severo**, the ancient centre (population 55,000) of the area known as the Capitanata, is noted for its vines (Sansevero white is particularly dry and delicate). It is a starting point for exploring the Gargano. The church of **San Severino** has an elegant rose window in its Romanesque façade. The small Museo Civico (Piazza San Francesco 48; open daily except Sat and hols 08.00–14.00, 16.00–19.00; ☎ 0882 334409), with Stone, Bronze and Iron Age finds, Daunian material of the 4C and 3C BC, Roman inscriptions (from *Teanum Apulum*), and medieval ceramics.

Serracapriola, with a castle, stands on a hill near the border with Molise. Between the Ponte di Civitate over the River Fortore and San Paolo di Civitate the road passes the scanty ruins of the Roman *Teanum Apulum*, and, higher up (left) those of the medieval *Civita*, where the Normans defeated and captured Pope Leo IX in 1053, immediately afterwards imploring his pardon, which was accorded and accompanied with a grant of the suzerainty of Apulia, Calabria and Sicily to Humphrey and Robert Guiscard.

Troia

Troia, a small town (population 8000) founded in 1017 as a Byzantine fortress on the site of the ancient *Aecae*, commands a wide view. The **cathedral** (1093–1125) is perhaps the most remarkable example of the successful Apulian marriage of Byzantine sculptural ornament of Saracen inspiration to the Pisan Romanesque style. The well-proportioned façade, plain below (with blind arcades and lozenge motifs that continue around the sides and rear of the church) and of

Troia cathedral

singular richness above (note the projecting lion and bull consoles and the beautifully carved moulding of the arch beneath the gable), is pierced by a rose window. The west and south **doors** (1119 and 1127), by Oderisius of Benevento, are in bronze; some panels are executed in high relief, others are incised. They show both eastern and Classical influences, as do the reliefs of the lintel and the capitals above the main door. The apse has double tiers of free-standing columns. The sombre **interior** has three aisles separated by semicircular arches on columns with singularly rich capitals. In the penultimate bay is an ambo of 1169 with curious sculptures, formerly in the nearby domed 11C church of San Basilio (shown by the cathedral sacristan). The rich treasury contains various silver statues and liturgical objects, including a chalice by followers of the famous Florentine goldsmith, Benvenuto Cellini (1521).

Lucera

Lucera, a town (population 35,000) with a magnificent castle, was a provincial capital until 1806 and preserves many relics of its former greatness.

History of Lucera

Luceria Augusta, already Roman in 314 BC, became a *colonia* under Augustus. Destroyed by Constans II, Emperor of Byzantium, in 663, it was rebuilt by Frederick II, who repopulated it in 1233 with 20,000 Saracens from Sicily, to whom he granted liberty of worship. It then took on the appearance of an Arab town. It became the stronghold of the Ghibellines in southern Italy and in 1254 was the refuge of Manfred and, later, of his widow. The city was taken in 1269 by Charles I of Anjou. After the revolt of 1300 Charles II massacred all the Saracens that he could not forcibly convert and repopulated the town with Provençal families.

The **cathedral** (Santa Maria Assunta), a curious blend of Romanesque and Gothic, was founded by Charles II of Anjou and built in 1300–17. It is one of the less altered monuments of its age. The simple façade has three Gothic portals, that at the centre incorporating Roman columns and sculptural representations of *St Michael* and the *Madonna and Child*. The low campanile is crowned by an octagonal lantern of the 16C. The streets at the sides of the church lead round the protruding transepts to the magnificent **apse**, attributed to Pierre d'Agincourt, where massive buttresses and tall lancet windows betray an unmistakably French design.

The **interior** is built to a Latin cross plan, with a tall nave and aisles separated by pointed arches on rectangular piers with attached columnar shafts. The nave and aisle ceilings are in wood, whereas those of the three polygonal apses are vaulted and ribbed. In the south aisle are a *Last Supper* attributed to Palma Giovane and an elegant pulpit of 1560, obtained by reworking a tomb of the

Scassa family. The south apse contains two cenotaphs, one of 14C Neapolitan workmanship; and a 14C wooden crucifix. Above the altar is a 15C fresco of the *Pietà;* on the walls, Martyrs, Apostles and Saints frescoed by Belisario Corenzio.

The stone high altar came in part from Castel Fiorentino, the castle (14km north-west; now a ruin) where Frederick II died on 13 December 1250; the choir stalls date from the 17C, the frescoes of the apse from the 18C. In the north apse are a 17C tomb and a heavily repainted,14C wooden statue of the *Madonna della Vittoria*, commemorating the Angevin rise to power. In the north aisle can be seen a *Madonna with Saints Nicholas and John the Baptist*, by Fabrizio Santafede, a fine baptismal font with Renaissance baldachin and a 15C taberna-cle. Below the organ, the *Madonna delle Stelle*, a late 14C sculpture. To the right of the entrance, a relief of *God the Father*, of the 16C Neapolitan school.

Opposite the cathedral stand the bishop's palace and Palazzo Lombardi, both 18C. Via de'Nicastri, at the rear of the church, leads to the **Museo Civico Giuseppe Fiorelli** (open Wed, Thur, Sat, Sun 09.00–13.00, Tues and Fri 09.00–13.00, 15.00–18.00; closed for renovation at the time of writing; ☎ 800 767606), which contains a Roman Venus, a fine mosaic pavement (1C), terra-cottas (3C BC) and ceramics of the Saracen and Angevin period, as well as 17C paintings and ethnographical exhibits.

About 500m west of the town on an eminence (250m) stands the **castle**, the most magnificent in Apulia, built by Frederick II in 1233 and enlarged by Charles I (1269–83). The enceinte of nearly 1km, with 24 towers, is still complete, and encloses the ruins of the Swabian palace. To the north-east of the town (10mins; open daily 09.00–14.00) are the ruins of a **Roman amphitheatre** of the Augustan period with two imposing entrance arches (reconstructed).

Canosa and Cannae

Canosa di Puglia (population 31,000) a flourishing agricultural and trade cen-tre on a hilltop overlooking the Tavoliere, is the ancient *Canusium* which, accord-ing to legend, was founded by Diomedes. It may well have been of Greek origin, as archaeological evidence (chiefly silver and bronze coins inscribed in Greek) and later records (its inhabitants were bilingual at the time of Augustus) suggest. In antiquity the town was well known for its polychrome and red-figure pottery and large *askoi* decorated with relief figures, examples of which may be seen in the museums of Ruvo, Bari and Taranto. An early and steadfast ally of Rome, it supported her in the Hannibalian wars, taking in survivors from the battle of Cannae (216 BC). This was its most prosperous period, with commercial activities at their peak. The town retained its importance after the opening of the Via Traiana and in the 4C AD it became the capital of the region. Its diocese, docu-mented from AD 343 but moved to Bari following the destruction of the town by the Saracens, is the oldest in Apulia.

The **cathedral**, dating from the 11C, is uninteresting externally. Within, the *chiesa antica* or old church is readily identifiable despite 17C alterations and modern additions (the latter corresponding to the first three bays of the nave). It is built to a Latin cross plan, with five domes in the Byzantine manner and cross vaults, in the aisles, carried on arches that spring from 18 antique columns. The columns, taken from the ancient monuments of Canusium, have beautiful white marble capitals with carved volutes and acanthus leaves. On the north side of the nave stands a masterfully carved pulpit of the 11C. Behind the altar, with its modern tabernacle and 13C silver-gilt icon of the *Madonna della Fonte*, is a splendid **bishop's throne** borne by elephants and decorated with plant and animal motifs, carved by the sculptor Romualdo for Ursone, Bishop of Bari and Canosa (1079–89). Steps in the aisles descend to the crypt, rebuilt in the 16C. A door in the south transept leads to a small court where the remarkable **tomb of Bohemond** (d. 1111), son of Robert Guiscard, has a fine door fashioned from solid bronze by Roger of Melfi. The walls of the tomb are faced with marble. Within are two columns with good capitals and the simple tomb slab, inscribed *Boamundus*. Around the walls of the court architectural fragments, inscriptions and a Greek torso of the 4C BC can be seen.

Adjacent to the church are the public gardens of the Villa Comunale, containing more architectural fragments. Across the town, Via Cadorna leads to the three **Ipogei Lagrasta**, underground burial chambers, excavated in 1843 which yielded a number of gold, ivory and glass objects; and a variety of vases including the famous Anfora dei Persiani, now in the Museo Archeologico Nazionale in Naples. The largest of the tombs has nine chambers and an interesting atrium with painted and stuccoed Ionic columns.

The **Museo Civico Archeologico** (open Tues–Sat 09.00–13.00, 16.00/17.00–18.00/19.00, Sun 08.00–14.00; ☎ 0883 663685) has a small collection of Canosan ceramic ware, Hellenistic and Roman material from the district and finds from the nearby Tomba Diurso, which also yielded objects (now in the Museo Nazionale in Taranto). The ruined medieval **castle** incorporates large (1.5x1m) blocks of tufa from the ancient acropolis; the **view** ranges across the Tavoliere from the mountains of the Basilicata to those of the Gargano.

On the banks of the Ofanto, the ancient Aufidus, some 10km nearer the sea, lies the site of **Cannae** (open daily 08.30–1 hr before sunset; ☎ 0883 510993 where, in 216 BC, Paullus Aemilius and Terentius Varro, the Roman consuls, were defeated by Hannibal. Many Romans perished in the battle. The **Antiquarium di Canne della Battaglia** (open daily as the archaeological site) houses finds from the immense necropolis and the scanty remains of the ancient city, including native Apulian painted vases (among the oldest painted ceramic ware in Italy), ivories, bronzes and coins and numerous other objects demonstrating the continuous importance of the site from prehistoric times to the Middle Ages. The Cittadella di Canne, situated on a hill above the museum, has been excavated in the more superficial strata only and shows mainly medieval remains.

About 7km east of Canosa, a road diverges (right) to **Minervino Murge** (population 11,000), known as the Balcony of Apulia on account of its panorama. The road continues to Gravina in Puglia.

Cerignola (population 55,000) is an important market town with an agricultural school and a modern cathedral. Near here Gonzalo de Cordoba defeated the French in 1503. To the east are San Ferdinando di Puglia, an important wine-producing centre founded by Ferdinand II in 1843; and Margherita di Savoia, a town on the edge of a very important salt field (the bromo-iodide salts are used for medicinal cures). There is also a good beach.

The Gargano

A mountainous peninsula rising in Monte Calvo to 1065m, the Gargano is still thickly wooded, especially with oak. The Boschi Umbra, Quarto and Spigno are the three main forests in this area. The whole of the promontory is streaked with limestone, and the streams have no outlet except in the fissures, where they are swallowed up. There are many unexplored pot-holes and stalactite grottos. The Gargano has the same geological composition as Dalmatia and in the tertiary period was separated from Italy by a narrow stretch of water.

The most common approach to the Gargano is from Foggia by road 89. Near the coast, on the south side of the road, are the ruins of an abbey whose 11C church (San Leonardo) has a simple façade with blind arcades, a plain portal and a small rose window. Along the left flank of the church is a richly sculptured doorway, probably 13C, in a shallow porch with griffins in the impost blocks and (modern) columns supported by lions.

Santa Maria di Siponto

Sipontum was an ancient coastal town abandoned in 1256 probably on account of malaria. Conrad landed here in 1252 to claim the crown of Sicily. An important Daunian centre, it was conquered by Hannibal and, soon after, by the Romans. By the early Middle Ages it had become the chief port of northern Apulia and, as such, it attracted the attention of the Lombard princes of Benevento, under whose dominion it remained from the 7C–11C. Sipontum was occupied in 1039 by the Normans, under whom its influence extended over most of the Gargano promontory. In the 13C the slow-quake phenomenon known as bradyseism caused much of its territory to degenerate into swampland, and the earthquake of 1223 virtually levelled the town. The inhabitants and the diocese were transferred to the new town of Manfredonia.

Little remains of the town proper, other than the scanty ruins visible from the road. But a few metres before the archaeological zone, in a small pine grove, stands **Santa Maria di Siponto**, the beautiful 12C cathedral, built above an underground church dating probably from the 5C and modified in the 13C and later centuries. The simple but elegant façade, restored in 1975, has a fine **doorway** of local workmanship framed by a shallow porch and flanked by columns borne by lions. At the sides are blind arcades enclosing rhomboid decorative motifs, which are carried around to the south and east walls.

The interior, built to a square plan with a central vault (reconstructed) carried by four rectangular piers and two small apses, has a distinctly Oriental flavour. On three of the four walls are blind arcades with attached shafts, like those of the exterior. On the north wall you can see mosaic fragments from an early Christian basilica found nearby. The high altar is made from an early Christian sarcophagus; above is a copy of the *Madonna and Child* in the cathedral of Manfredonia. The circular chapel to the right of the altar is, in all probability, a later addition.

Steps on the north side of the church descend to the **crypt**, with vaulted ceiling, four squat columns corresponding to the piers above, and 16 small columns, some ancient, with sculptured capitals of Classical and Byzantine design. Remains of a still earlier (4C–7C) church—chiefly bases, capitals and fragments of columns, as well as some Roman and medieval tombs—have been discovered nearby.

Manfredonia and the Foresta Umbra

Manfredonia, a town with a population of 59,000, on the bay of the same name stands at the foot of the Gargano promontory. It was founded in 1256 by Manfred (1231–66), King of Sicily and Naples, and peopled by the inhabitants of *Sipontum*. Much of the town was destroyed by the Turks in 1620. The first act of Austrian aggression against Italy was carried out here in 1915, with the bombing of the railway station and the sinking of the *Turbine* in the bay. Now a developing industrial centre, Manfredonia is not a particularly pleasant place; however, it is an excellent starting point for excursions in the Gargano.

The **Castello Svevo-Angioino**, begun by Manfred in 1256, originally stood outside the town walls. The primitive core, which is still visible today, is a square plan with massive bastions—three cylindrical and one rectangular—at the corners and a tall enceinte surrounding a central court entered by archways in the east and west walls. Charles of Anjou enclosed this earlier fortification within a new set of walls, also built to a rectangular plan with cylindrical towers at the corners. The great spear-head bastion was added in the 16C.

The castle houses the **Museo Archeologico Nazionale del Gargano Meridionale** (open daily 08.30–19.00, closed first and last Mon of each month; ☎ 0884 587838), which has an interesting collection of material from local excavations, notably 6C bronze and ceramic objects of Daunian workmanship and an unusual series of 6C and 5C Daunian grave slabs, carved to represent people and animals. The church of San Domenico (1299, rebuilt in later centuries) has a Gothic doorway and 14C frescoes. The late 17C cathedral, of little architectural interest, contains a 12C wooden crucifix.

Leaving Manfredonia by Road 89, the road climbs in steep zigzag turns to **Monte Sant'Angelo**, a town with a population of 16,000 situated on a south spur (884m) of Monte Gargano. It owes its origin to the foundation of the **Santuario di San Michele Arcangelo** in a grotto, now in the centre of the town (open daily 07.30–18.30). From the portico with two Gothic doorways (that on the right dates from 1395; the other is a modern imitation), flanked by a fine octagonal belfry of 1281, 89 steps descend to the inner vestibule built by Charles I of Anjou, where a bronze door made in Constantinople in 1076 fills the Romanesque portal. From here you enter the church, built of stone (1273), and finally the grotto, consecrated, according to tradition, by the archangel Michael himself when he revealed it to St Laurence, Bishop of Sipontum, on 8 May 490. The grotto contains a 16C statue of St Michael and an 11C stone bishop's throne.

In front of the campanile steps lead down (left) to the ruined church of San Pietro, through which you enter the so-called **Tomba di Rotari**, probably a baptistery, with a cupola and 12C decorations. To the right is the church of **Santa Maria Maggiore** (1198). Above the town the massive ruined castle started by the Normans, affords a wide view. In the lower town, the church of San Francesco contains the supposed tomb of Joan I. Here also is the **Museo delle Arti e Tradizioni Popolari del Gargano Giovanni Tancredi** (open summer Mon–Sat 08.30–13.30, 15.00–19.00, Sun 10.00–12.30, 15.30–19.00, closed Mon morning; winter Mon–Fri 08.00–14.00, Tues and Thur 16.00–19.00, closed Sat and Sun; ☎ 0884 562098), with an interesting collection of folk art.

From Monte Sant'Angelo follow the Valle Carbonara (leaving to the left a road that runs along the spine of the promontory via San Giovanni Rotondo and San Marco in Lamis to San Severo) then climb over the arid Piano della Castagna towards the Foresta Umbra (marked). The Rifugio Foresta Umbra (29km) is charmingly situated shelter in the heart of the forest. It has a small but interesting display of the forest's ecology and wildlife. Descend by Vico del Gargano, through olive and orange groves, and through the splendid Marzini pine forest to the coast road, turning right to reach Peschici (described below).

If you take the left turn (west) after Monte Sant'Angelo you soon come to **San Giovanni Rotondo** (567m), a small village on a plateau below Monte Calvo (1065m), highest peak of the Gargano. In 1177 it belonged to Joan Plantagenet, wife of William II of Sicily. The 14C church of **Sant'Onofrio** and the contemporary towers are interesting, but the **Rotonda di San Giovanni**, a baptistery of uncertain date, is more mysterious. It was reputedly built on the ruins of a Temple of Jupiter. At the west end of the village, the tree-lined Viale dei Cappuccini leads to the 16C convent of **Santa Maria delle Grazie**. The conventual church, consecrated in 1629, contains a much-venerated Madonna delle Grazie. In the crypt of the modern church nearby is buried **Padre Pio** da Pietralcina (1887–1969), the Franciscan monk (beatified in Rome on 2 May 1999 by Pope John Paul II), whose reputation for working miracles has made the village a centre of pilgrimage, especially for the sick. The Fiorello La Guardia Hospital, named after a mayor of New York City, is supported largely by American funds. The road continues back to Foggia.

The coast road

Beyond Manfredonia the coast road begins to climb. At Mattinata (population 6000), Road 89 climbs over the east end of the promontory through rocky and wooded country. Bear right and follow the coastline to **Vieste**, a small town (population 14,000) with a castle in a fine position on the north-east tip of the Gargano. Celestin V was arrested here in 1295 by order of Boniface VIII.

Peschici (90m, population 4000) is a picturesque village perched above a rocky cliff. Beyond, the headland of Monte Pucci commands an admirable view along the coast. West of Peschici the coast road is joined by road 528 from Vico del Gargano and Monte Sant'Angelo (see above). Beyond, San Menaio has a sandy beach that extends to Rodi Garganico, a fishing village (population 4000) below hills ringed with orange groves and pine woods.

The Lago di Varano is a shallow lagoon separated from the sea by a strip of sand dominated by Cagnano Varano. From here a new, fast road flanks the shallow lake, Lago di Lesina, to Termoli. Road 89 bears inland via Sannicandro Garganico and the last foothills of the Gargano to Foggia.

The Tremiti Islands

The **Isole Tremiti**, a group of small limestone islands 22km north of the Gargano peninsula, are known throughout Italy for their natural beauty, clear waters and mild climate. These are the *Insulae Diomediae* of Classical mythology, where the companions of Diomedes allegedly changed into herons.

Of the three main islands, the largest, **San Domino**, was the scene of the death of Julia, granddaughter of Augustus. In recent years the island has experienced a sudden rush of 'green' tourists drawn by its pine forests, marine caves, and other natural assets.

San Nicola, though smaller than San Domino, is the administrative centre of the group and is of greater interest from a historical point of view. From the marina at the south-west tip of the island, a narrow, walled road passes through two medieval gates to the town proper and the abbey church of **Santa Maria a Mare**, founded in 1045 and rebuilt in the 15C, 17C and 18C. From the abbey's foundation, in the 8C, to the mid-12C, it was governed by the Benedictines of Monte Cassino. In the 12C it passed to the Cistercian Order and was fortified by Charles II of Anjou. In the 14C corsairs, who managed to enter the convent by trickery, laid waste to it and massacred the monks; it was not until 1412 that the Laterans of San Frediano di Lucca, by concession of Gregory XII, took over the complex, embellishing the church and building a new defensive system. Their monastic fortress successfully held off an assault by Süleyman II in 1567.

In 1783, after a period of gradual decline, Ferdinand IV of Naples suppressed the abbey, the possessions of which had once included vast areas of the Gargano, the Terra di Bari, Molise and Abruzzo, establishing in its place a prison, which remained active until 1926. From that year until 1945 it was used for the detention of political prisoners.

The 15C façade of the church incorporates a Renaissance doorway (1473) flanked by double Corinthian columns and surmounted by weather-worn sculptures. The interior has retained its original 11C plan, with a rectangular nave preceded by a double narthex. The painted wooden ceiling dates from the 18C and replaces an earlier dome. The colourful mosaic pavement, of which substantial areas remain, was executed c 1100. The church contains a 12C painted Greco-Byzantine Crucifixion and a fine, early 15C Venetian polyptych.

The island of **Capraia** (also called Caprara or Capperara), to the north of San Nicola, is interesting for its many small rock arches or *archetielli*. **Pianosa**, 20km north-east, is not served by commercial passenger craft.

THE TERRA DI BARI CATHEDRAL TOWNS

The area between Barletta and Bari possesses the richest architectural heritage on the Adriatic south of Venice. Here are the splendid **Terra di Bari cathedrals**, great churches which combine northern and eastern influences in a unique way, giving rise to a characteristic local style broadly referred to as the Apulian Romanesque. The first and, in a sense, the most typical expression of this local tradition is the magnificent 12C **Basilica of San Nicola in Bari**, for it is to this model that the builders of later churches turned for inspiration, at least initially.

In its last phase, the Apulian Romanesque style aspired to an elegance and grace of form which in northern Europe was to become a guiding aesthetic principle. This architectural taste, coupled with rich and eclectic decorative schemes that unabashedly combine Byzantine, Norman, Pisan, Lombard and Provençal motifs, makes these some of the more interesting and curious churches in southern Italy. Conical rural constructions called *caselle* are also characteristic of the area.

Practical information

Information offices

BARI *Assessorato Regionale al Turismo*, Via Bozzi 45C, ☎ 080 540111, ✉ www.pugliaturismo.com.
Ufficio Informazioni e di Accoglienza Turistica, Piazza Moro 33a, ☎ 080 524 2244; Corso Vittorio Emanuele 68, ☎ 080 521 9951.
BARLETTA *Ufficio Informazioni e di Accoglienza Turistica*, Corso Garibaldi 208, ☎ 0883 531555.
TRANI *Ufficio Informazioni e di Accoglienza Turistica*, Piazza Trieste 10, ☎ 0883 588830.

Getting there and getting around
By air

Palese airport, 8km west of Bari, has regular flights to/from Athens, Bologna, Brescia, Bucharest, Catania, Corfu, Genoa, Milan, Munich, Paris, Pisa, Rome, Timisoara, Tirana, Turin, Trapani and Verona.
By road

If you come from the north, Bari and the Terra di Bari cathedral towns lie just beyond the junction of Autostrada A14 from Ancona and Autostrada A16 from Naples. The A16, in particular, crosses extraordinarily beautiful countryside, offering broad, open horizons and dramatic skies in addition to gently rolling hills and vast forests.

From Cerignola the coastal towns are conveniently reached by a new road (16b) which parallels the old coast road to Bari and is slowly being extended southwards. It has replaced Road 16 beyond Bari and some parts are open as

far as Maglie, in the Salentine Peninsula.

The A14 is also the quickest way to reach the area from Taranto and the Ionian region.
By rail

The towns in this section lie on the main rail lines from Rome, Naples and Milan to Bari, Brindisi and Lecce. Eurostars make the run from Rome to Bari in 4hrs 30mins, stopping at Barletta; Expresses from Naples Centrale, Piazza Garibaldi, Mergellina and Campi Flegrei to Bari in 4–5hrs, stopping Barletta, Trani, Bisceglie and Molfetta. Intercity trains from Pescara reach Bari in 3hrs 10mins, stopping at Barletta, Trani, Bisceglie and Molfetta. Through trains to/from Switzerland and Germany.

Where to stay

BARI €€€ *Palace*, Via Lombardi 13, ☎ 080 521 6551, 🖷 080 521 1499, ✉ palaceh@tin.it. An elegant and well-managed hotel conveniently located on the edge of the old town; open all year.
€€ *Mercure Villa Romanazzi Carducci*, Via Capruzzi 326, ☎ 080 542 7400, 🖷 080 556 0297, ✉ mercure@villaromazzi.com. A registered landmark encompassing a Neo-classical villa and a 2000 sq m park; comfortable, refined rooms, competent staff, pool, sauna, gym; open all year.
€€ *Vittoria Parc*, Via Nazionale 10F, Palese, ☎ 080 530 6300, 🖷 080 530 1300, ✉ avasi@tin.it. In a garden in a northern suburb of Bari; modern and comfortable, with a shuttle bus to the city centre; open all year.

BISCEGLIE €€ *Salsello*, Via V. Siciliani 32, ☎ 080 395 5953, 📠 080 395 5951, ✉ barsasso@tin.it. A modern, well-managed place in a large park on the beach just outside the town; open all year.

TRANI € *Royal*, Via De Robertiis 29, ☎ 0883 588777, 📠 0883 582224. Centrally located in a Liberty-style townhouse; quiet, comfortable rooms; open all year.

 Eating out

ANDRIA €€ *Antica Cucina*, Via Milano 73, ☎ 0883 521718. Very good regional cuisine and wines; closed Mon and July.
€€ *Arco Marchese*, Via Arco Marchese 1, ☎ 0883 557826. Osteria serving great seasonal dishes; closed Tues and two weeks in Aug.
€€ *Madama Camilla*, SS 170, ☎ 0883 546545. Lovely old farm serving local delicacies, outside in summer, on the road to Castel del Monte; closed Mon and Jan.
€€ *Masseria Barbera*, SS 97, ☎ 0883 692095. Another fine old farm with great local fare, on the road to Minervino; closed Mon and late Aug.
€€ *Taverna Sforza*, SS 170, ☎ 0883 569994. Trattoria-pizzeria with rooms and good views; closed Tues and late Jan.
€€ *Tenuta Cocevola*, SS 170, at Cocevola; good county restaurant with garden and views; closed Mon.
€ *Antichi Sapori*, Piazza Sant'Isidoro 9, at Montegrosso, ☎ 0883 569529. Wholsesome family-run trattoria; closed Mon and a few days in July and Aug.
€ *Au Coq d'Or*, Via Santa Maria dei Miracoli 259, ☎ 0883 291361. Osteria in the hills just outside of town; closed Mon and mid-Aug.
€ *Locanda de la Poste*, Via Bovio 49, ☎ 0883 558655. Creative interpretations of seasonal dishes of the region; closed Wed and two weeks in Aug.
Fratelli Mucci, Via Gammarotta 12;

confectioner selling traditional candies.
BARI €€€ *Santa Lucia*, Lungomare Starita 9, ☎ 080 534 4860. Apulian *haute cuisine*, famous especially for its creative renderings of traditional fish dishes; closed Mon and late Dec–early Jan.
€ *Al Focolare da Emilio*, Via Principe Amedeo 173, ☎ 080 523 5887. Simple but delicious restaurant-pizzeria; closed Sun evening, Mon and Aug.
€ *Osteria delle Travi*, Largo Chiurlia 12, ☎ 330 840438. Simple, traditional trattoria in the old town; closed Sun evening, Mon and two weeks in Aug.
€ *Verde*, Largo Adua 19, ☎ 080 554 0870. Simple restaurant-pizzeria; closed Sun and mid-Aug.
De Carne, Via Calefati 128. Venerable old delicatessen with fine regional specialities and ready-made take-out dishes.
Enoteca De Pasquale, Via Marchese di Montrone 87. Wine shop with an extraordinarily wide variety of Apulian wines.
Il Germoglio, Via Puntignani 204. Organic foods, from jams to cheeses to pasta.
Marazia, Via Manzoni 217 and *Veneto*, Corso Cavour 125. Bakeries selling traditional breads, pizze and foccace.
Stoppani, Via Roberto da Bari 79. Famous pastry shop.
BARLETTA €€ *Baccosteria*, Via San Giorgio 5, ☎ 0883 534000. Warm atmosphere, delicious food, excellent wines; closed Sun evening, Mon and Aug.
€€ *Il Brigantino Uno*, Viale Regina Elena 19, ☎ 0883 533345. Good fish restaurant by the sea, with panoramic terrace, garden and pool; open all year.
€€ *Cascina del Borgo*, Via Canosa 315, at Palombaro, ☎ 0883 510941. Lovely garden restaurant known for its fresh seasonal cooking; closed Mon.
CORATO €€ *Corte Bracco dei Germani*, Via Ruvo, ☎ 080 872 2698. Country estate offering great seasonal dishes; closed Tues.
€€ *Il Mulino*, Via Castel del Monte

135, ☎ 080 872 3925. Characteristic restaurant; closed Mon and Jan.
MOLFETTA €€ *Borgo Antico*, Piazza Municipio 20, ☎ 080 696 4236. Fine seafood restaurant by the water; closed Mon and Nov.
€ *Bistrot*, Corso Dante 33, ☎ 080 397 5812. Simple, straightforward cooking in the old town, near the harbour; closed Wed, Sun evening and Aug.
Pasticceria Barese, Via Cavallotti 15. For *bocconotti*, *spume di mandorla*, *cassatine*, *postaccioli* and other local pastries.
Gelateria San Marco, Piazza Giovene. For ice cream, especially fruit flavours.
PALO DEL COLLE € *La Stalla del Nonno*, Via XXIV Maggio 26–28, ☎ 080 629598. Wine-bar serving hot and cold meals; open evenings only, closed Sun and Aug
RUVO DI PUGLIA €€ *Ristor*, Via Alberto Mario 38, ☎ 080 361 3736. Restaurant offering country cooking from the Murge; closed Mon and July.
€ *L'Angolo Divino*, Corso Giovanni Jatta 11, ☎ 080 362 8544. Wine-bar serving hot and cold meals, including good vegetarian dishes; open evenings only, closed Mon and two weeks in Aug.
Berardi, Via Jatta 37. Has the best pastries in Ruvo.

TRANI €€ *La Nicchia*, corso Imbriani 22, ☎ 0883 482020. Excellent seafood restaurant with a strong local following; closed Thur, Sun evening and July.
€€ *Melograno*, Via G. Bovio 189, ☎ 0883 486966. Good regional cooking in a warm atmosphere; closed Wed and Jan.
€€ *Torrente Antico*, Via Fusco 3, ☎ 0883 487911. Good creative cooking and great wines; closed Sun evening, Mon, July and early Jan.
€ *Ai Platini*, Via Commeno 16, ☎ 0883 482421. Fresh seafood in an osteria in the old city centre; closed Mon and Oct.

Special events

BARI *San Nicola* (8 May and 6 Dec), celebrated with a colourful historical parade of St Nicholas and *Processione dei Pelligrini* (procession on the sea) on 7–8 May; *Processione dei Misteri* (Easter Week). The *Fiera del Levante*, inaugurated in 1930 to increase Bari's trade with the Levant, is held annually in September near the Punta San Cataldo.
BARLETTA *Disfida di Barletta* (last Sun in July) historic pageant (see below).

Barletta

Barletta, an agricultural centre (population 89,000) and port, with a considerable trade in vegetables and wine, has recently regained some of the prosperity it enjoyed in the Middle Ages, when it was Manfred's favourite residence.

History of Barletta

Archaeological evidence has demonstrated the existence of an indigenous centre on the site dating from the 4C or 3C BC. However, the first mention of the town—which was variously known as *Barduli*, *Baruli*, *Bardulo*, *Baretum* and finally, in common speech, *Barletta*—dates from Roman times. Under the Normans it became an important trade centre and fortress. Its population increased in 1083 with refugees from Cannae, who fled when the city was destroyed by Robert Guiscard.

Frederick II proclaimed his son Henry heir to the throne here in 1228, before embarking on a crusade. The inhabitants rebelled after the king's death, but the uprising was put down by Manfred, who established his court here. The city was the seat of the Archbishop of Nazareth from 1291 until 1818. It reached greatest prosperity under the Angevins, from whom it received special privileges and concessions, soon becoming one of the more important fortresses of the kingdom. During this period it traded actively with the Orient, and its merchant fleet was one of the finest in the region. Here in 1459 Ferdinand I of Aragon was crowned King of Naples, and later suffered an Angevin siege.

On 13 February 1503, while the French were besieging the town, the famous Challenge or *Disfida di Barletta* was staged as a means of ending the conflict. Thirteen Italians and 13 Frenchmen met in mortal combat. Prospero Colonna and Bayard umpired the struggle, which ended in victory for the Italians. The champions were greeted by the clergy in procession, bearing aloft Serafini's *Madonna*, now in the cathedral. On the last Sunday in July the citizens of Barletta re-enact the (locally) famous Challenge for control of the besieged town. The Italians win today as they did then, amid a flurry of medieval pageantry.

Barletta was damaged by earthquakes in 1689 and 1731, and stricken by plague in 1656–57, after which it suffered a long period of decay. Since 1860 it has grown rapidly in wealth and size and it now hosts important electrical, chemical, automobile manufacture, leather-working and food-processing industries.

From the west side of town, follow Corso Vittorio Emanuele, passing (right) **San Giacomo**, with its eccentric plan, pyramidal tower, and pointed arches. At the far end of the avenue stands (right) the **Colosso**, a 5C bronze statue, over 5m high, possibly representing the Emperor Marcian. The head and torso are original; the hands and legs were recast, somewhat clumsily, in the 15C. The statue was restored in 1980.

Behind is the 13C **Chiesa del San Sepolcro**, built over an earlier church documented from the 11C. The north flank has blind arcades with pointed arches enclosing monoforum windows and a good Gothic portal. The Baroque façade conserves, on the right, a small Gothic doorway; at the left corner stand the remains of the campanile brought down by the earthquake of 1456. The church was completely restored in 1972.

The **interior** is built in the Burgundian Gothic style with three aisles, three apses and a shallow transept preceded by a vestibule or narthex incorporating a gallery in the upper part. The aisle ceilings have simple cross vaults, whereas those of the nave and transept are ribbed. Over the presbytery is an octagonal dome, possibly of Byzantine inspiration. In the gallery are 14C frescoes representing the *Life of St Anthony Abbot*, the *Annunciation*, and *Saints*. The south apse contains a 16C Byzantine-style panel portraying the *Madonna di Costantinopoli*. The baptismal font, near the entrance door, dates from the 13C.

From the rear of the church, Corso Garibaldi leads towards the harbour, passing (right) the pleasant Baroque façade of San Domenico. The **duomo**, nestled among the narrow streets at the end of Corso Garibaldi, was built in the 12C, enlarged in 1307 and again in the 15C; it underwent a thorough restoration in 1996. The tripartite façade has blind arcades, a rose window and a profusely carved monoforum window in the central section flanked by elegant bifora windows on either side. The main entrance dates from the 16C. The lateral entrances, which belong to the original building, have historiated arches. An inscription above the left portal records the participation of Richard Coeur-de-Lion in the building's construction. The Romanesque campanile has monoforum, bifora and trifora windows on successive levels. The campanile, with its octagonal spire, was added in 1743.

The first four bays of the basilican **interior**, carried on antique columns, are built in the Apulian Romanesque style, with decorative bifora above the nave arcade. They date from the 12C and reflect the plan and character of the original church. The remaining bays, which date from the 14C, have pointed or rounded arches on compound piers and ribbed cross vaults. The polygonal apse, with its ambulatory and shallow radiating chapels, was erected during the following century and shows French Gothic influence. It contains carved tomb slabs of various ages. The 13C tabernacle above the high altar was dismantled in the 17C and reassembled, with modern additions, in 1844.

The *Madonna della Disfida* by Paolo de'Serafini da Modena (1387), the only signed work of that artist, hangs in the ambulatory. The fine pulpit on the south side of the nave was executed in 1267. Steps at the end of the north aisle descend to the crypt, where the semicircular apses of the 12C cathedral have been revealed by recent excavations. In a room adjoining the church (usually closed) is a small collection of paintings and ecclesiastical objects, including some 13C illuminated codices.

To the north-west of the cathedral is the little church of **Sant'Andrea**, with a fine 13C portal signed by Simeone da Ragusa and a *Madonna* by Alvise Vivarini (1483). The massive **castle**, to the east, was built in the 13C on top of the earlier construction that hosted both the court of Manfred and Frederick II's assembly of barons and prelates at the time of the Third Crusade (1191–92). It was enlarged by Charles of Anjou to a design by Pierre d'Agincourt later in the 13C; and fortified again some 200 years later by the Aragonese, in the face of the impending Saracen invasion. The four corner bastions were erected in 1532–37 by Charles V to a plan by Evangelista Menga, architect of the castle of Copertina.

Within, the impressive court is lined by vaulted rooms, no doubt used as workshops, stables and barracks. On the east side a ramp mounts to the bastions. A fine staircase gives access to the first floor rooms, opposite. Along the walls are three 13C windows, two of which bear reliefs of eagles in the tympana. The halls of the castle interior house the municipal **Museo e Pinacoteca** (open Tues–Sun 09.00–13.00, 15.00/16.00–19.00/20.00; ☎ 0883 578613). The ground-floor **archaeological section**, displaying mainly finds from the battlefield at Cannae, will reopen to the public after renovation in 2004. The first-floor **pinacoteca** has a modest collection of southern Italian painting and sculpture, ranging from 14C–19C; some early modern paintings from northern Italy, and a fine collection of paintings, drawings and prints by the Giuseppe De Nittis (1846–84), a native.

South of Barletta

Four kilometres south of the motorway is **Andria** (population 90,000), the largest city in the province after Bari. Founded by the Normans in c 1046, it was sacked by the French in 1527 and again in 1799. Its earlier fidelity to Frederick II is recalled by the inscription on the Porta Sant'Andrea. The Gothic **cathedral**, several times restored (the façade is a modern reconstruction), has a large crypt with remains of sculptures and frescoes; here lie Yolande of Jerusalem and Isabella of England, two of Frederick's consorts. The **Museo Diocesano** (open by appointment, ☎ 0883 593032) houses paintings, sculptures and decorative objects from several of the town's churches. Sant'Agostino (1230) has a highly individual 14C portal with rich decoration. In San Domenico is a bust of Francesco II del Balzo (1442), perhaps by Francesco Laurana.

By far the most important monument in this area, however, is **Castel del Monte**, 18km further south, a massive octagonal castle with Gothic corner towers, crowning an isolated peak (540m) of the Murge and known as the Spia delle Puglie. On UNESCO's World Heritage list since 1996, it was built by Frederick II c 1240 and for 30 years was the prison of Manfred's sons. It is notable for its harmony of proportion, its fine windows in the Italian style and the principal entrance in the form of a Roman triumphal arch, most unusual for the 13C. The **interior** (open Mon–Fri 09.00–18.30, Sun 09.00–20.00, May–Oct 09.00–18.30 and 21.00–24.00 June–Sept) is built round an octagonal courtyard and has two storeys with spacious rooms, virtually identical in plan and decoration. The capitals of the pillars are remarkable for their beauty and variety. Official

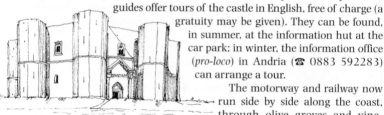

guides offer tours of the castle in English, free of charge (a gratuity may be given). They can be found, in summer, at the information hut at the car park; in winter, the information office (*pro-loco*) in Andria (☎ 0883 592283) can arrange a tour.

The motorway and railway now run side by side along the coast, through olive groves and vineyards.

Castel del Monte

Trani

Trani, a pleasant white-painted town (population 51,000) with whitewashed buildings and a small harbour, is an important centre of the wine trade, its strong, dark red wines being mostly exported for blending.

History of Trani

It succeeds the ancient city of *Tirenum* or *Turenum*, which probably dates from the 3C or 4C AD, although popular legend attributes its foundation to Tirenus, son of Diomedes. Before the year 1000 it was, together with Bari, one of the easternmost outposts of the Roman church.

Under the Normans it was an important embarkation point for the Orient. Its commercial activity attracted considerable colonies of merchants from Genoa, Pisa, Ravello and Amalfi, as well as a large Jewish community. Its *Ordinamenta Maris* (1063) is the earliest maritime code of the Middle Ages.

The town enjoyed its greatest prosperity at the time of Frederick II, when it rivalled Bari in importance. It suffered greatly from the struggle that shook Apulia under the Angevins, and in 1308–16 it engaged in a political and economic conflict with Venice. It repeatedly shifted its loyalty between the

Angevins and the Aragonese, finally siding with the latter in 1435. Here in 1259 Manfred married his second wife, Helena of Epirus; here also (a few days after Conradin's execution) Charles of Anjou married Margaret of Burgundy. Trani was the birthplace of the sculptor, Barisano (late 12C) and of Giovanni Bovio (1841–1903).

The cathedral

The cathedral (San Nicola Pellegrino), next to the sea, was begun at the end of the 11C, over the earlier church of Santa Maria della Scala. Its imposing form and refined decoration, together with the dramatic beauty of its location (best appreciated at dawn) make it one of the more striking churches of Apulia.

The façade, reached by a flight of steps preceded by a porch with a finely carved frieze, has a richly sculptured portal with bronze **doors** by Barisano da Trani (1175–79), who also cast the doors of the cathedrals of Ravello and Monreale. The iconographic and decorative schemes of both the bronze and the stone reliefs reflect Byzantine, Saracenic and Romanesque models. The door jambs are decorated with bas-reliefs of biblical scenes, plant and animal motifs, and geometric patterns that are carried over into the arch above. To either side, blind arcades with cylindrical shafts and finely carved capitals traverse the façade to enclose the lateral portals.

The upper storey consists of a broad, smooth surface of warm stone pierced by a fine rose window and several smaller windows, all with carved surrounds. The beautiful, tall, 13C campanile stands upon a graceful archway open to the sea. The octagonal belfry and spire date from 1353–65.

The flanks of the church are traversed by prominent blind arcading surmounted by a double clerestory. High up on the south transept are a second rose window and two large bifora, above a curious sculpture of two men and a bull. The triple apsidal ending, like the transepts, has finely carved eaves with projecting animal corbels and, at the centre, a great window with a rich surround. More windows and carving can be seen on the north transept.

The **interior** is entered by a small door on the north flank. It has been restored to its original Romanesque form, with a nave arcade of six semicircular arches supported by double columns. Above runs a triforium, the left and right halves of which are joined by a characteristic gallery spanning the west façade; and a clerestory with simple monoforum windows. The ceilings of the nave and transept are in wood, whereas those of the aisles have stone cross vaults.

At the sides of the presbytery you can see fragments of a 12C mosaic pavement; in the chapel on the north side is a 13C relief of the *Crucifixion*. The crypt has an interesting vaulted ceiling carried on 28 marble columns with intricately carved capitals.

A door in the west wall admits to the lower church of **Santa Maria della Scala**, which may also be entered from the archway beneath the porch of the façade. The area of this church corresponds to that of the nave above, and is divided into three narrow aisles by Roman columns, probably

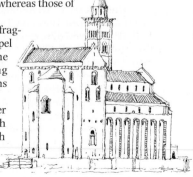

Trani cathedral

brought here from Canosa, supporting low cross vaults. Here a Gothic tomb, Lombard sarcophagi (under the porch), some 14C and 15C frescoes and fragments of an early mosaic pavement are to be seen. Beneath is the interesting **Ipogeo di San Leucio**, a burial area preserving fresco fragments. At Piazza del Duomo 4 is the Museo Diocesano (open Tues–Fri 10.00–12.30, Sat 17.00–19.00; if closed ☎ 0883 584632), with architectural and sculptural fragments and paintings, chiefly from the Middle Ages.

Use as a prison has spoilt much of the **castle** (open daily 08.00–20.00; guided visits, in English, at 09.30, 10.30 and 11.30), which was built for Frederick II in 1233–49 by Phillip Chinard, Stefano di Trani and Romualdo di Bari, as an inscription on the sea-wall records.

Near the harbour are the 15C Palazzo Caccetta, the Baroque chapel of Santa Teresa (adjacent); and by an arch over the street, the church of **Ognissanti**, erected by the Knights Templar in the 12C. The latter is preceded by a sort of pronaos with a double file of piers and columns, beyond which three sculpted 13C doorways admit to the simple interior.

Of the four surviving Romanesque churches, Sant'Andrea, in the form of a Greek cross, is the oldest. San Francesco has a quaint, pleasant façade with a modest portal and an oculus; the interior has been redecorated in a Baroque style and contains three little Byzantine domes. Both churches flank Via Mario Pagano. Rising from the shore at the south edge of the town is the 11C Benedictine abbey of Santa Maria della Colonna, now a museum for temporary exhibitions.

Bisceglie and Molfetta

Bisceglie, a town (population 49,000) that exports excellent cherries, has a Romanesque **cathedral**, begun in 1073 and completed in 1295. The façade, altered by Baroque additions, has an ornate central portal with a shallow porch borne by griffins on columns. Along the south flank is a Renaissance doorway with crude sculptures; more interesting is the apsidal end, with its richly decorated window and blind arcades. The interior, completely restored in 1965–72, is basilican in plan with compound piers and a graceful triforium above the nave arcade. Over the main entrance is a 13C relief of *Christ with Saints Peter and Paul*. The Renaissance choir stalls, brought here from the destroyed abbey of Santa Maria dei Miracoli, are carved with the likeness of 70 eminent figures of the Benedictine Order.

The **Museo Civico Archeologico** in the former monastery of Santa Croce (Via Frisari 5, open Tues and Thur 09.00–13.00, 16.00–18.00, Sat 09.00–12.30; ☎ 080 395 7576, contains Palaeolithic and Neolithic material as well as palaeontological finds. The little church of **Santa Margherita**, set in a courtyard in Via Santa Margherita, is one of the simpler achievements of the Apulian Romanesque style (1197). Along the south side are three tombs of the Falcone family, the largest of which dates from the 13C.

Molfetta is an active commercial centre (population 64,000) with light industries and one of the larger fishing fleets on the Adriatic. On the sea at the edge of the old town stands the **Duomo Vecchio** (San Corrado), an unusual building begun in 1150 but not completed until the end of the 13C. The highly original design, probably of Byzantine inspiration, has a short nave covered by three domes, on polygonal drums, with pyramidal roofs. Compound piers with rounded arches separate nave and aisles; on top of the engaged columns are intricately carved capitals. More carvings (dating from the 13C) may be seen in the second chapel on the south side. The west front of the church is without a façade, whereas the apsidal end, which presents, as elsewhere in Apulia, a flat wall masking the semicircular apse, has delicate interlacing blind arches, a fine window with a sculptured archivolt flanked by

View of the medieval town and duomo from the harbour, Molfetta

columns supported by lions, and two tall campanili of Romanesque design. You enter the church from the court of the bishop's palace, adjacent.

The Baroque Duomo Nuovo dates from 1785. The interior, asymmetrical in plan, is of harmonious design. The Museo Diocesano (in the bishop's palace), and the Museo Archeologico (Seminario Regionale Pugliese) house local archaeological finds including Peucetian and Hellenistic ceramics (open by appointment; ☎ 080 911559).

Ruvo di Puglia

Ruvo di Puglia (population 25,000) succeeded the ancient *Rubi*, famous for its terracotta vases (5C–3C BC). An excellent collection of these (together with other finds from local excavations) may be seen in the **Museo Archeologico Nazionale Jatta** (Piazza Giovanni Bovio 35; open daily 08.30–13.30, Fri–Sat 08.30–13.30 and 14.30–19.30; ☎ 080 361 2848).

The 13C **cathedral** is a fine example of the late Apulian Romanesque style, richly ornamented. The vertical thrust of the façade, evident in the tall central gable and steep roof line, has been somewhat lessened by the widening of its base to accommodate the chapels added to the interior in later centuries. Along the edges of the roof, blind arcades spring from delicate human- or animal-head corbels, a motif that continues along the right flank of the building. High up at the centre of the façade is a superb 16C rose window, surmounted by a seated figure that some identify with Frederick II, others with an Apocalyptic person. Below are a mullioned window (in the lunette, St Michael in bas-relief) and an oculus surrounded by angels' heads. On the ground level, the three portals stand beneath supporting arches that redistribute part of the weight of the massive wall above. The jambs and archivolts of the doorways are carved with figurative and decorative reliefs by local artists, in a style that fuses Lombard, French and Oriental elements. On either side of the main entrance are unusually slender columns borne by crouching telamones and surmounted by griffins. The sculptural decoration of the apse, transept and south flank of the church also merits close inspection. The campanile, set apart at the rear of the church, was originally a defensive tower.

The **interior**, like the façade, foreshadows the Gothic sensibility for soaring height and delicate ornamentation. It is built to a basilican plan with semicircular apses and high wooden ceilings in the nave and transept. Above the nave arcade runs a balcony on sculptured corbels; higher up is a graceful triforium articulated, as is the nave arcade, by pilaster strips. Recent restoration has closed off all but two of the lateral chapels. The tabernacle above the main altar is a modern construction.

Bitonto

Bitonto (population 54,000) produces olive oil. Free tours of Bitonto are given, in English, by the police (!), who have been cross-trained as official guides; ☎ 080 375 1014.

The town is renowned for its Romanesque **cathedral** (1175–1200), the most complete and harmonious in Apulia. The church follows a T-plan, the apse being concealed behind a single uniform wall surface that unites the arms of the transept and that is a recurrent characteristic of the Apulian Romanesque style. The façade, the design of which faithfully follows that of San Nicola in Bari (see below), is divided into three parts by bold pilaster strips. Blind arcades surmounted by a chessboard cornice run along the pointed gable and the eaves above the aisles.

The upper portion of the façade is dominated by the magnificent rose window, protected by a foliated archivolt on hanging columns. Below are bifora windows. The central portal has strongly projecting foliated arches resting on griffins atop columns borne by lions and surmounted by the pelican pecking her breast, a symbol of the Passion. Above the door are reliefs of the *Annunciation*, *Visitation*, *Epiphany* and *Presentation at the Temple*, in the lintel; and of the *Descent into Limbo*, in the lunette. The lateral portals have door-joints and architraves carved with plant motifs. A loggia on the left connects the façade with the 16C Palazzo De Lerma, now a tenement. Along the right flank, deep arches enclose lancet windows and, in the last bay, the Gothic Porta della Scomunica, with sawtooth mouldings of Siculo-Norman workmanship. Above runs a graceful hexaform gallery, with splendidly carved arches, columns and capitals; and a clerestory with intricate tracery in the windows.

The south transept is adorned with tall blind arcades surmounted by bifora and a rose window, with a handsomely carved architrave. On the east wall is a finely carved window, similar in form and workmanship to the main portal, and, higher up, a broad Moorish arch. The 13C campanile was remodelled in 1488 and in 1630.

The **interior**, simple and dignified, is built to a Latin cross plan with three semicircular apses and a shallow transept. The nave arcade is borne by columns alternating with compound piers in a rhythmic order of two to one. The capitals are profusely carved. Along the aisle walls are half columns from which spring simple cross vaults. The nave arcade is surmounted by a triforium, the two parts of which are joined by a 19C balcony on the west wall. Along the south side of the nave are a pulpit made with fragments of the high altar of 1240 and a magnificent **ambo** by Maestro Nicola (1229) with a bas-relief representing Frederick II and his family. Stairs in the aisles descend to the crypt with 30 fine columns.

In the little alleys behind the cathedral, the church of **San Francesco** has a façade of 1286; that of the **Purgatorio**, bizarre reliefs of human skeletons above the portal (cf. Gravina in Puglia, p 456). Several good Renaissance palazzi survive in the town.

The Museo Civico E. Rogadeo (Via Rogadeo 52, inside the library; open

Bitonto cathedral

Mon–Fri 09.30–13.30, Tues and Thur also 15.30–18.30; ☎ 080 375 1877) houses a small collection of antiquities from local excavations as well as a gallery of paintings by 19C regional artists.

Bari

Bari, the capital of Apulia, is the second largest town in southern Italy (population 353,000) and a frequent port of call for ships bound for the eastern Mediterranean. It has important oil refineries.

History of Bari

The ancient *Barium* was founded by the Illyrians, civilised by the Greeks and developed as a commercial centre under the Roman Empire. Seized from the Romans by the Ostrogoths who in turn lost it to the Byzantines, it eventually came under the rule of the Lombard dukes of Benevento. In 847 it became a Saracen emirate, only to be liberated, some 34 years later, by Emperor Louis II. After the fall of Sicily to the Saracens it became the capital of the Byzantine province of Lombardy and, in 975, the seat of the 'catapan' or Byzantine governor.

In the 11C the city became one of the more important Adriatic ports in Italy, rivalling Venice, with whose help it was freed from a Saracen siege in 1003. The anti-Byzantine revolts that shook the town and much of north-central Apulia in the first half of the century paved the way for the Norman conquest of the region, which was made final in 1071 with the fall of Bari to Robert Guiscard. In 1087 the remains of St Nicholas of Myra, patron saint of Russia, stolen from Asia Minor by sailors from Bari, were brought here to be deposited in the basilica of San Nicola (begun in 1089). In the following years the city became a major religious centre: at the Council of Bari in 1098, St Anselm of Canterbury defended the doctrine of the procession of the Holy Ghost against the Greek Church. In 1156 the town rose against the Normans. As a reprisal William the Bad levelled it to the ground, except for the shrine of St Nicholas.

Bari flourished under Frederick II (who granted it considerable powers and privileges, despite the dubious loyalty of the townspeople), but it declined under the Angevins. At the end of the 15C it passed into the hands of the Sforza, and Isabella of Aragon, widow of Galeazzo Sforza, held her court here. At her daughter Bona's death in 1558 it became part of the Kingdom of Naples and, like many southern Italian towns, suffered the grievous effects of absentee government. Torn by famine (in 1570 and 1607), class strife and internal political struggles, it fell into a century-long period of decay. The plague of 1656–57 claimed the lives of four out of five inhabitants, reducing the population to a mere 3000. In the 18C Bari was subject to the Austrians, then to the Bourbons; the latter, under Ferdinand IV, drew up an ambitious plan for enlarging the city. This, however, was not to be carried out until 1813, when Joachim Murat issued a decree authorising construction of a Borgo Nuovo outside the old town walls.

Bari has grown steadily in wealth and population over the last century and a half, expanding to over ten times its previous size. The present city consists of three parts; the old town, new town and industrial area. The **Città Vecchia** or

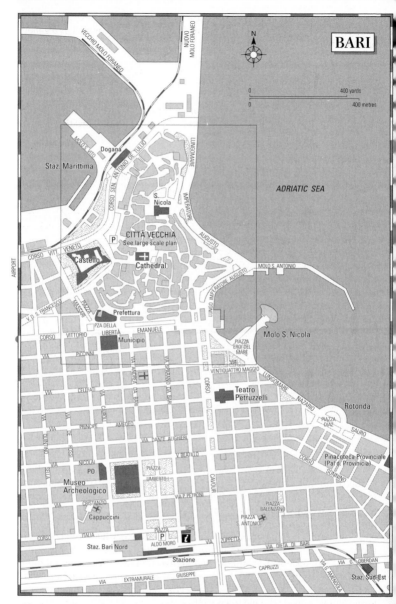

old town, where the major medieval monuments are located, stands compactly on a peninsula. It is characterised by a maze of narrow, winding streets where life is still closely tied to the maritime activities of the adjacent port. Its peculiar, baffling town plan (it is almost impossible to wind your way from one end of the quarter to the other without getting lost) protected the inhabitants from the vind as well as from their enemies (Saracen invaders were lured into the narrow streets and blind alleys and attacked from the windows and rooftops above).

The **Città Nuova** or modern quarter, broadly laid out to a chessboard plan with wide, straight avenues, is the financial and administrative centre of the city. The museums, theatres, concert halls and university (one of two in Apulia, the other being at Lecce) are also located here. The industrial area spreads inland, sandwiched between the city proper and the semicircular ring of satellite towns.

Via Sparano da Bari—the high street—bisects the new town, connecting the Città Vecchia at one end with Piazza Umberto I and the railway station at the other. Corso Vittorio Emanuele II, running east and west, divides the modern city from the old town. In Piazza della Libertà, an expansion of the corso, are the Municipio, the Teatro Puccini, the prefettura and a monument to Puccini.

The castle

To the north, beyond Piazza Massari, is the **Castello Normanno-Svevo**. The castle was built by Frederick II over an earlier fortress, in 1233–39 and extended with massive bastions by Isabella of Aragon in the 16C. It is frequently used for special exhibitions (open daily except Wed, 09.00–19.00; ☎ 080 528 6263). Its predecessor saw the traditional meeting of Frederick and St Francis in 1221. The earlier structure, which stands at the centre of the complex, is readily distinguishable from the 16C additions. It is trapezoidal in plan, with a tall enceinte made of warm brown tufa laid in rusticated rows, and block-like corner towers. You reach it by crossing the moat (now a public garden) to a vaulted entrance hall, from where an archway on the right leads to the outer courtyard. Here the walkway leads around the massive south tower to a second archway with 13C bas-reliefs, the entrance to the elegant atrium. Beyond lies the inner courtyard. The more monumental rooms are used to house the **Gipsoteca del Castello** (open as the castle). The vaulted hall on the west side contains a collection of plaster-cast reproductions of sculptural and architectural fragments from Romanesque monuments in Apulia. On the floor above are the offices of the Soprintendenza ai Monumenti e Gallerie di Puglia and laboratories for the restoration of paintings.

The nearby Molo Pizzolo hosts a modest aquarium (open daily 10.00–13.00, Tues also 15.00–18.00; ☎ 080 521 1200; closed for renovation at the time of writing) with examples of local marine life.

The cathedral

To the east lie the narrow streets of the old town. One block west is the cathedral, an apsidal church of the 12C, built over the remains of an earlier church destroyed by William the Bad in 1156. Basilican in plan, with shallow transepts surmounted by an octagonal drum, it is one of the more noteworthy medieval cathedrals of Apulia. The façade is Romanesque in spirit, with a modern rose window and three Baroque portals incorporating the simpler 12C doorways. Deep arcades run along both flanks, surmounted by a gallery that corresponds to the triforium level of the interior. Two towers, of which that on the south side was damaged by earthquake in 1613, rise just east of the transepts and are joined at the rear of the church by a wall that masks the apse. The east window, a masterpiece of Apulian sculpture, is set beneath a hanging baldachin and ornamented with plant and animal motifs of Oriental inspiration. The cylindrical structure on the north side, now the sacristy, was built in the 11C as a baptistery and converted to its present function in 1618.

The **interior** has been restored to its original simplicity, with a nave and two aisles supported by tall, slender columns probably taken from the earlier church. Above the rounded arches of the nave arcade runs a false matroneum, which opens directly onto the side aisles. The nave contains remains of a 14C marble pavement with a rose design matching that of the façade. Steps in the crossing mount to the raised presbytery; the dome above rises to a height of 35m.

In the semicircular main apse marble choir stalls and a bishop's throne recomposed from fragments of the original can be seen. The ciborium on the high altar and the marble pulpit in the nave are likewise modern reconstructions. The north apse contains remains of 13C and 14C frescoes and the tomb of Bishop Romualdo Grisone (d. 1309). A door in the north aisle opens onto the sacristy and steps at the ends of both aisles descend to the Baroque crypt.

Excavations below the church floor have brought to light an early Christian basilica dating from the 8C–10C, with extensive remains of a mosaic pavement now visible in the south apse. In the archives is a precious early 11C exultet, an illuminated scroll with medallions of Greek saints and liturgical scenes on the verso. Also of interest are the late 11C *Benedizionario* of Apulian workmanship and two smaller exultets. More works from the cathedral and the diocese are preserved in the bishop's palace (shown by appointment, ☎ 080 521 2725).

The basilica of San Nicola

From the north flank of the cathedral follow Strada del Carmine and Strada della Crociate to (right) the **Arco di San Nicola**, a large Gothic arch adorned with a relief of the saint. (This is an area of town dear to pickpockets: watch out!) Pass beneath and emerge in a small piazza dominated by the Romanesque basilica of San Nicola, the first great church built by the Normans in Apulia.

The basilica was founded in 1087 to receive the relics of St Nicholas, stolen from Myra in Lycia by 47 sailors from Bari. It stands in the centre of four piazze known as the Corti del Catapano, after the Byzantine governor's palace, which once stood here.

Owing something to the churches of Caen, but deriving more from Lombard models, San Nicola became the model for the cathedral and the inspiration of later Apulian churches. The majestic façade, flanked by unfinished towers, is clearly divided into three parts reflecting the tripartite division of the interior. The tall central section terminates in a steep gable, whereas the lateral sections end in gently sloping semi-gables. The entire roof line is edged with blind arcading that culminates in the large, slightly pointed arch at the apex. The vast surface of the façade is enlivened by an oculus and eight arched windows, of which the uppermost are mullioned. Lower down its flatness is relieved by blind arches and attached columns. The central portal is set beneath a shallow porch with a pointed gable surmounted by a sphinx and carried by two bulls. The surface surrounding the door and the arch and gable above are richly carved with ornamental and symbolic motifs combining Arabian, Byzantine and Classical influences.

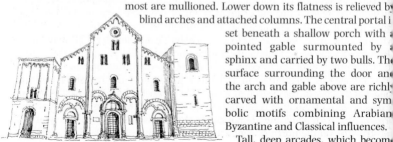

Basilica of San Nicola

Tall, deep arcades, which become noticeably shallower in the arms of the transept, run along both flanks of the church, surmounted by a graceful gallery below the eaves of the roof. In the third arch on the north side is the magnificent **Porta dei Leoni**, so-called after the lions that support the columns at the sides of the doorway. The sculptural decoration, including two figures of months on the impost blocks and scenes of chivalry below the arch, are signed by the sculptor Basilio. Another fine doorway is to be seen on the south side. The east wall, like that of the cathedral, masks the apsidal endings of the nave and aisles. The bas-relief of the *Miracles of St Nicholas* below the central window dates from the 15C.

The nave and aisles are separated by tall, stilted arches on marble columns with elaborately carved capitals. The three great transverse arches were added in 1451; the church seems to have been completed c 1105, although it was not consecrated until 1197. An arched choir screen on tall columns with fine

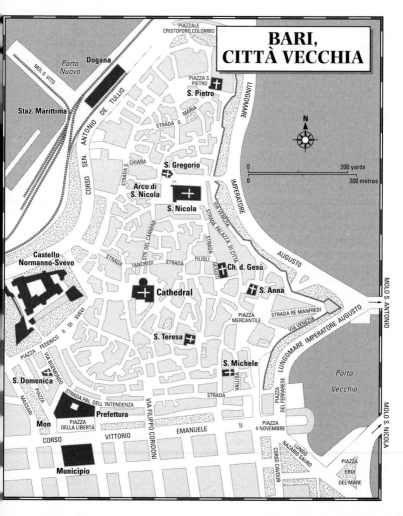

Romanesque capitals (note particularly that on the left) separates the nave from the transept. Beyond it is the high altar. The **bishop's throne**, probably made for the council of 1098, stands in the apse below the monument (1593) of Bona Sforza, Queen of Poland and Duchess of Bari.

The crypt, reached by steps in the aisles, has 28 columns with diverse capitals; the vaulted ceiling was freed of its stuccoes in 1957. The altar contains the relics of St Nicholas, said to exude a 'manna' to which miraculous powers are attributed; the silver and gold reliefs were executed in 1684 by Domenico Marinelli and Antonio Avitabili over a Byzantine icon donated in 1319 by the King of Serbia. Notice the mosaic detail of the floor and the low bench in the apse. In the galleries above the aisles are housed the remains of the treasure of St Nicholas, together with fragments of paintings and sculpture brought to light during restoration.

On the north side of San Nicola is **San Gregorio**, an 11C church with fine windows and façade, and three semicircular apses. The Romanesque interior has particularly good capitals. The Museo di San Nicola (Largo Abate Elia 13, open by appointment; ☎ 080 573 7254) preserves a small collection of religious and historical objects.

The Pinacoteca provinciale

Lungomare Imperatore Augusto meets Corso Vittorio Emanuele II at the vast Piazza Eroi del Mare. From here, Lungomare Nazario Sauro diverges south-east past the Rotonda, a semicircular terrace overlooking the sea, to the Palazzo della Provincia.

On the top floor of the palazzo is the **Pinacoteca provinciale** (open Tues 09.30–13.00, 16.00–19.00, Sun 09.30–13.00; ☎ 080 541 2421) containing works of the 11C–19C, mainly by southern Italian artists. **Room 1. Medieval sculptural fragments and paintings** of local provenance, including low reliefs, fragments of capitals, and two fine icons of the 13C, representing *St Margaret* and *St Nicholas*, from Santa Margherita, Bisceglie.

Room 2. In the first part of the room, more 11C, 12C and 13C sculpture and paintings, notably architectural details that fell from the rose window of San Nicola in 1943, when an American ammunition ship blew up in the harbour. The second part of the room hosts 15C panels for altarpieces produced by the Venetian painters Antonio and Bartolomeo Vivarini for the churches of Surbo, Altamura, Andria, and Modugno; especially noteworthy is Bartolomeo Vivarini's altarpiece for the convent of Santa Maria Vetere in Andria; at the end of the room is a *presepio* composed of fragmentary figures that were once painted in naturalistic colours, by the Apulian sculptor Paolo da Cassano.

Room 3 is dominated by Giovanni Bellini's *St Peter Martyr*, painted for the Indelli Chapel in the church of San Domenico in Naples; the painting is set away from the wall, to give a glimpse of the fine drawings by the artist on the back. Also in the room are a small *St Peter*, a *Pietà with Saints*, a *Head of a Saint* and minor paintings by anonymous artists.

Room 4 is devoted to **Apulian Renaissance painting** showing affinities with Neapolitan trends of the period; there is also a polytych by the Maestro di Cassano. **Room 5** highlights a particularly fascinating neo-Byzantine trend fostered by artists who worked in the Terra di Bari during the 16C, many of whom came to the area from the eastern Mediterranean after the fall of Constantinople. The works include a *Madonna and Saints* and a *Nativity* by Donato Bizamano, a

Madonna and Child with St John by Angelo Bizamano showing a mixture of Oriental and Venetian elements, and a fine panel with miniatures of the *Lives of Christ and the Virgin* by Giovanni Maria Scupula. The other great 16C trend, Mannerism, is represented by Marco Pino (*Holy Trinity*).

The **Venetian school** returns in **room 6** with three outstanding paintings executed for Bari cathedral: *Sacra Conversazione* by Paris Bordone, *Virgin in Glory with Saints* by Paolo Veronese and a *St Roch* by Jacopo Tintoretto, completed after the artist's death probably by Domenico Tintoretto.

Rooms 7–9 are devoted to **17C painting** by Neapolitan artists (Paolo Finoglio, Pacecco De Rosa) and local painters trained in Naples, which eventually replaced Venice as the leading point of reference for the cultural élite of Apulia. Conventional painters working in the tradition of Domenichino, for whom local patrons expressed a preference, and the more radical *caravaggeschi* (Andrea Vaccaro, Matteo Stomer), are both represented.

Access to the Baroque collections is through **room 10**, a corridor lined with glass cases displaying examples of Neapolitan *presepi* and popular ceramics. **Room 12** is occupied by two large genre scenes by the early 18C Neapolitan painter Giuseppe Bonito and, in a small showcase, a composition of statuettes (of shepherds) possibly inspired by the paintings.

Room 13. Dramatically placed so that it is framed by the marble doorway is Luca Giordano's painting of *St Peter of Alcantara*. The original study for the painting is also displayed here. The room contains other works by Giordano (*Deposition of Christ*, *Departure of Rebecca*) by his follower Andrea Miglionico, and altarpieces by the local painter Nicola Gliri.

Rooms 14–15 are devoted to **Rococo painting**, represented in particular by the Apulian artists Corrado Giaquinto (who worked in Rome, Naples, Madrid, Turin, and Vienna) and Oronzo Tiso.

Room 16. The tone changes abruptly as you enter this room, which hosts 19C works of more secular subjects on a smaller scale, for middle-class patrons. There are several paintings by the local artists Francesco Netti and Giuseppe de Nittis, as well as works by Telemaco Signorini, the Macchiaiolo, Anton Sminck Pitloo, Teofilo Patini and Domenico Morelli.

A separate section of the gallery, dedicated to the **Anna** and **Luigi Grieco Collection**, provides an outstanding panorama of 19C, and early 20C Italian painting by artists ranging from Giovanni Fattori to Giovanni Boldini, Tranquillo Cremona, Giuseppe de Nittis, Silvestro Lega, Filippo Palizzi, Pellizza da Volpedo, Raffaello Sernesi, Telemaco Signorini, Massimo Campigli, Carlo Carrà, Felice Casorati, Giorgio de Chirico, Filippo de Pisis, Mario Mafai, Giorgio Morandi, Ottone Rosai, Mario Sironi and Lorenzo Viani.

Museo Archeologico

Returning to the Rotonda, follow Via Imbriani, then Via Dante Alighieri west, turning left in Via Andrea da Bari to reach the Palazzo dell'Università (or dell'Ateneo), which houses the Museo Archeologico (open daily 09.00–18.00. Closed for renovation at the time of writing; partial reopening scheduled for 2004; ☎ 080 541 2422).

The **vestibule** contains Roman inscriptions; Tarentine and indigenous antefixes (6C–4C BC); large vases recovered from a sunken Roman ship; in cases (left of centre), coins from the Greek colonies at *Sybaris*, *Metapontum*, *Croton*, *Laos*, *Caulonia* (6C–4C BC); right of centre, coins from *Nuceria*, *Bruttiorum*, *Petelia*,

Hipponium, Vibo, Bretii, Paestum and *Lucania* (3C–1C BC); Apulian coins from *Arpi* *Barium, Ausculum, Butuntum, Azetium, Brundisium, Rubi, Caelia, Canusium, Uria* *Graxa, Salapia, Mateola* and *Venusia*, showing the transition from the Tarentine to the Roman type; against the pillar, on the right, Campanian coins from *Cumae* *Neapolis, Poseidonia, Velia, Thurii* and other centres (6C–1C BC); at the right of the central window, Tarentine coins from the 6C–2C BC; on either side, cases with Byzantine coins; in the case opposite the window, various objects in bone and amber, mainly from Taranto and Canosa.

Turn left to enter the **Corridoio delle Terracotte Figurate**; against the corner pier, terracotta statue of a woman in prayer, from Canosa (3C BC) in glass cases, bronze objects of the 7C–5C; Apulian vases of various types and provenance; Classical and Hellenistic statuettes in terracotta.

The following hall, the **Corridoio degli Scavi Recenti**, displays a sampling of material brought to light in excavations conducted since 1950, mainly sculptural fragments and small vases from Egnatia, proto-Italic ceramic vases from Bitonto, Peucetian vases and bronzes from Monte Sannace (Gioia del Colle) and Apulian material from necropoleis at Bari and Conversano.

Now turn right to the **Corridoio della Ceramica Apula**. This collection is arranged topographically and embraces Attic black figure (5C BC) and red figure (4C BC) vases; indigenous geometric ceramics, including Peucetian ware bichrome and monochrome vases from Gioia del Colle, and proto-Italic vases from Ceglie del Campo; a bronze Apollo of Greek workmanship, also from Ceglie a krater decorated by the Amykos painter, from Ruvo, and geometric and red figure vases from Canosa. Particularly noteworthy for their beauty and rarity are 2736, Gnathian pelike (4C BC); 1627, Messapian *trozzella* with deer-hunting scene; and (no number) a large Apulian krater with battle and theatrical scenes.

Retrace your steps to the beginning of the corridor and enter **room 1**, the **Sala dei Bronzi**. Beginning on the entrance wall: bronze objects of various date and provenance; armour, spear heads, Corinthian helmets; bronze humeral, preserving original gilt (6C BC); **complete suit of armour** of an Apulian warrior, from Canosa. The glass cases at the centre of the room contain glass and alabaster ware; jewellery in bronze, gold, coral and precious stones; bronze mirrors. **Room 2**, **Salone**: material from private collections, arranged by type; note in particular case 12, Gnathian ware, and (at the centre of the room) bronze armour of Corinthian workmanship, including a fine embossed belt bearing a representative of a chariot race. **Room 3**, **Sala di Canosa**: material from the tombs at Canosa, including vases with characteristic sculptural decoration (more of these are in room 2).

Return to the **Corridoio della Ceramica Apula** and follow it to its end, then turn right to the **Corridoio della Preistoria**, containing Protoapennine (early 2nd millennium BC) and Apennine ceramics (18C–17C BC), bronze and ceramics from Bari, Monte Sannace, Andria and Bisceglie and Neolithic material from Molfetta. From here return to the vestibule.

The Facoltà di Agraria (Via Amendola) has a modest botanical garden, shown on request (open by appointment; ☎ 080 242152); and the Museo Etnografico Africa Mozambico (Convento Cappuccini, Via Gen. Beltomo 9, at Poggiofranco open by appointment, ☎ 080 551 0037), houses a small but interesting collection of ethnographical material from East Africa.

SOUTH OF BARI

This region embraces the rocky highlands between Bari and Taranto, the inhabitants of which took refuge in the Middle Ages in caves in the deep, narrow ravines (*gravine* in Italian) to escape the Saracen massacres. Later, as more conventional settlements grew up on the cliff tops nearby, the caves were frequently made into chapels and decorated with rough frescoes or carved designs. The finest examples of this unusual architectural genre are to be found at Matera, in neighbouring Basilicata; but there are many others strewn about the region, such as those at **Massafra**. Between the two towns, in the country around Castellaneta (which, with its pristine whitewashed houses is well worth a stop) is another fascinating form of local architecture, the *masseria fortificata*, or fortified farm. Many of these walled agricultural complexes, which usually include a noble residence for the landowner, simple but harmonious peasant homes, and barns and other out-buildings, are now being turned into country inns.

Practical information

Information offices
BARI See p 433.
TARANTO See p 461.

Getting there
By air
Palese airport, 8km west of Bari, has a daily service to Milan, Rome, Turin, and Venice; and frequent flights to Verona and Tirana.

By road
Autostrada A14 is the quickest and most convenient way to drive from Bari to Taranto. Roughly paralleled by Road 100, it passes close to Acquaviva delle Fonti, Gioia del Colle, Mottola, Castellaneta and Massafra. From Gioia del Colle good roads run east to Alberobello, Locorotondo, Ostuni, Martina Franca and Putignano (described in the next section); and west to Altamura and Gravina in Puglia. Altamura and Gravina are also served by an excellent road (no. 96) from Bari. Another good road (99) connects Altamura with Matera, in Basilicata. Due to a recent increase in highway robbery, the Carabinieri discourage visitors from travelling the more isolated country roads.

By rail
The main line from Bari to Taranto touches upon Modugno, Bitetto, Acquaviva delle Fonti, Gioia del Colle, Mottola, Massafra. Intercity trains cover the 115km in c 65mins, stopping at Gioia del Colle. Slow local trains, stopping at all stations, take just 30mins more. Secondary lines run from Gioia to Altamura and Gravina in Puglia, and from Bari to Altamura and Matera.

Where to stay
GIOIA DEL COLLE
€ *Svevo*, Via Santerano 319, ☎ 080 348 2739, 🖷 080 348 2797, ✉ www.hotelsvevo.it,hotelsvevo@hotelsvevo.it. Modest but comfortable hotel; regional recipes with a creative twist in the well-known restaurant.

Eating out
GRAVINA IN PUGLIA
€ *Osteria di Salvatore Cucco*, Piazza Pellicciari 4, ☎ 080 326 1872. Simple osteria on the edge of the old town; closed Sun evening, Mon and mid-Aug.

LATERZA €€ *Tenuta dell'Aquila*, Via San Falco 1, ☎ 099 829 6842. Delightful small country restaurant with rooms; closed Mon and Nov. *Atelier della Carne*, Via Roma 51, ☎ 099 821 8788 and *Tamborrino*, Via Roma 58, ☎ 099 821 6192. Two outstanding examples of a traditional local eatery: the *fornello*, or wood oven at the back of butchers' shops where steaks and chops chosen by the client are cooked up and served with utter simplicity; open evenings only; closed, like the shops, Thur and Sun.

PALO DEL COLLE € *La Stalla del Nonno*, Via XXIV Maggio 26–28, ☎ 080 629598. Wine-bar serving hot and cold meals, open evenings only; closed Sun and Aug.

SAMMICHELE DI BARI € *Cavaliere*, Via De Gasperi 28, ☎ 080 891 0220. Cordial country restaurant with good service; closed Sun evening, Tues and Aug.

On the beach and in the hills

Several places of interest along the coast and in the hills lie just outside the city limits of Bari. **Modugno** is a large town (population 38,000) with a 17C campanile. The ancient church of San Pietro (or San Felice), 3km south-east on the Bitetto road, is the sole survival of the medieval town of Balsignano.

Palo del Colle has a 12C cathedral. Its railway station also serves **Bitetto** where the **cathedral** (San Michele), originally 11C, was remodelled in 133 using Romanesque forms. The handsome façade has a richly decorated central doorway, with reliefs of the *Madonna and Child* in the lunette, *Christ and the Apostles* on the architrave, and New Testament scenes on the doorposts. At the north-east corner of the church stands a Romanesque campanile, probably belonging to the original building. The Baroque bell-tower to the left of the façade probably dates from 1764. The interior has been extensively altered, especially in the 16C, but recent restoration has returned it more or less to its 14C form. It is basilican in plan, with long, narrow aisles, wooden ceilings, slightly pointed arches and a triforium. Behind the main altar is an *Assunta* by Carlo Rosa (1656)

Altamura

In the midst of a lonely landscape lies Altamura (population 58,000), a flourishing agricultural and industrial centre built along the top of a ridge.

History of Altamura

Altamura was a Peucetian centre of considerable importance, the name of which is still unknown. The ancient city was destroyed by the Saracens and the area remained uninhabited until 1230, when Frederick II founded a new town on the site of the former acropolis, with a population of Italians, Greeks and Jews drawn from neighbouring villages by the concession of special privileges.

In the centuries that followed, the town was granted in fee to the Del Balzo and Farnese families, among others. In 1799 it was ruthlessly sacked and burned by the Sanfredisti under Cardinal Ruffo for its adherence to the Parthenopean Republic. It became a major intellectual centre in the 18C and possessed its own university from 1748 until the end of the century. Altamura was the seat of the first provisional government of Apulia during the Risorgimento.

Piazza Unità d'Italia marks the entrance to the town. From here Viale Regina Margherita descends to the station, passing the Strada Panoramica, from which considerable remains of the 5C BC **Peucetian city walls** may be seen. Approximately 3700m in circumference, the walls stand over 4m high in some areas, with an average thickness of c 5m.

The **Porta di Bari**, originally a medieval gateway, was later absorbed by the massive Palazzo Del Balzo. Corso Federico II di Svevia, beyond, leads to the heart of the old town. To the left of the gateway are remains of the 13C walls that give the town its name (Altamura, high walls). Pass, on the left, the little church of **San Niccolo dei Greci**, erected in the 13C by Greek colonists, where the Orthodox rite was celebrated until 1601. The simple but attractive façade has a rose window and an interesting portal decorated with Old and New Testament scenes in bas-relief. Beyond, the corso ends in Piazza Duomo, with its monument to the citizens of Altamura who were slain in the sack of 1799.

The cathedral

The cathedral (Santa Maria Assunta) is one of the four Palatine basilicas of Apulia (Palatine churches were those frequented by the Holy Roman Emperor; the others are San Nicola di Bari and the cathedrals of Barletta and Acquaviva delle Fonti). Begun by Frederick II in 1232 and rebuilt after the earthquake of 1316, it was further altered in 1534, when its orientation was inverted and the main portal and rose window were dismantled and reassembled in their present position, on what was formerly the apse.

The façade stands between two 16C campanili to which Baroque pinnacles were added in 1729. In a loggia beneath the pediment can be seen a figure of the Assunta, flanked by Saints Peter and Paul above the arch. Below is the beautiful recessed **rose window**, with delicate fretted stonework and multiple bands of ornate carving. The Gothic window of 1232, which originally stood in the apse wall and which was removed to make way for the rose window, is now located in the left portion of the façade, next to three heraldic stems, the largest of which bears the arms of Charles V.

The 14C–15C **main portal** is one of the more richly decorated doorways of Apulia. It is set beneath a shallow porch with four slender columns and a pointed gable, within which bands of moulding carved with foliate motifs and scenes from the *Life of Christ* establish a formal and visual link between the doorposts and the delicately pointed arches above. In the lintel is a relief of the *Last Supper*. The lunette contains an exquisitely carved *Madonna and Child with Angels*.

Along the unaltered north flank of the church, broad semicircular blind arches enclose slender lancet windows and the elegant Porta Angioina, named for Robert of Anjou whose arms, together with a Gothic inscription commemorating its construction, appear above. Between the tops of the arches and the roof run 12 trefoil windows with intertwining arches. The transept, a 16C addition to the church, incorporates a tall Gothic window from the earlier façade.

The vast, sombre three-aisled basilica retains its original flavour despite the 19C additions. The nave is divided into three broad bays by semicircular arches on piers alternating with columns with good capitals. Above the nave arcade is a triforium with

Detail of the cathedral portal

semicircular arches on slender columns, also bearing interesting capitals. The aisles contain a number of paintings, chiefly by local artists. The inlaid choir stalls, the bishop's throne and the carved marble pulpit all date from the mid-16C.

The **Museo Archeologico Statale** (Via Santeramo; open summer 08.30–19.15, winter Tues–Sat 08.30–13.30, 14.30–19.30; Sun and holidays 08.30–13.30; ☎ 080 314 6409) contains material from local excavations. The collection includes Bronze Age pottery, bronze and ceramic ware from nearby tombs (8C–5C BC), locally painted pottery (6C–5C), a bronze helmet and Gnathian and Peucetian ware.

Around Altamura

In the environs of Altamura you can visit numerous *specchie*, free-standing sepulchral monuments of a type quite common in prehistoric Apulia. Interesting excursions may be made to the **Pulo**, 7km north-east of Altamura, a circular sinkhole 500m in diameter and c 75m deep; and to **Casal Sabini**, a village 9km east on the Santeramo road, where there are several Bronze Age **rock-cut tombs** as well as Peucetian trench-graves dating from the 6C–3C BC. The site lies to the right of the road just beyond the village. Matera (see p 321) lies 17km south on Road 99.

Gravina in Puglia

Gravina in Puglia (population 40,000), 12km west of Altamura, is set in a breathtaking position on the edge of a deep ravine. It succeeds the Peucetian centre of *Sidion*, which in Roman times became known as *Silvium*, probably located on the nearby hill of Petramagna, today known as Botromagno. During the Barbarian invasions its inhabitants took refuge in the *gravina* or ravine, and many continued to live in its limestone caves even after the present town began to take shape around the 5C. This town was destroyed in the 10C by Saracen mercenaries and was occupied in the following century by the Normans. In 1420 it passed to the Roman Orsini family, who held it in fee until 1807. The old town is interesting for its winding streets and ancient houses with balconies supported by corbels.

In the centre of town is Piazza della Republica, flanked by the much-altered Palazzo Orsini. From here Corso Matteotti leads to Piazza Notar Domenico, where the church of the **Purgatorio** (or Santa Maria dei Morti) has a bizarre portal with a *memento mori* of reclining skeletons in the tympanum. The columns, carried by bears, allude to the Orsini family who commissioned the building in 1649. Within are a painting of the *Madonna and Saints* by Francesco Solimena and the tomb of Ferdinando III Orsini (d. 1660).

To the left of the church is the Biblioteca Finya, founded by Cardinal Angelo Antonio Finya (1669–1743). From here a narrow street on the left descends to the Rione Fondovico, the oldest quarter of the town, where the church of **San Michele di Grotti** is hewn entirely out of the rock. The interior has five aisles and a flat ceiling borne by monolithic piers; scant remains of frescoes; and in one corner, human bones that tradition attributes to the victims of the Saracen attack of 983. More of these are heaped together in the Grotta di San Marco, above.

In Piazza Benedetto XIII is the **duomo**, originally of 1092, enlarged in 1420, destroyed by fire in 1447 and rebuilt in 1482. The basilican interior has three aisles separated by semicircular arches on columns with finely carved capitals.

The gilded wooden ceiling incorporates rather indifferent paintings. Above the fourth altar on the south side is a 16C relief of the *Presentation of the Virgin*. The wooden choir stalls date from 1561.

Returning to Piazza Notar Domenico, take Via Ambrazzo D'Ales and Via Lelio Orsi to **Palazzo Somarici Santomasi**. Here are collections (open Tues–Sat 09.00–12.30, 16.00–18.00/19.00, Sun 09.30–12.30; ☎ 080 325 1021) of archaeological material from Botromagno; coins and medallions; a section devoted to rural life; a reconstruction of the Byzantine crypt of San Vito Vecchio, with 13C frescoes of local workmanship; architectural fragments and ethnographical collections.

Nearby is the small church of **Santa Sofia**, in the presbytery of which you can glimpse the tomb of Angela Castriata Scanderbeg, wife of Ferdinand I Orsini (d. 1518). The Renaissance church of **San Francesco** has a fine rose window and sculptured portals; the Baroque campanile dates from 1766. Also worthy of attention is the church of the **Madonna delle Grazie**, near the station, the unique façade (1602) of which incorporates three crenellated towers in rusticated stone and an enormous eagle with outspread wings in low relief.

The lonely interior

South-west of Altamura, beyond Matera (to which it is joined by the Roman Via Appia (now road 7) rises **Laterza** (population 14,000), an agricultural town huddled on the brink of a ravine that is lined with cave dwellings and churches carved from the rock. The ancient **castle**, situated at the north end of the old town, has been extensively rebuilt. The main entrance, on the north side, consists of two double pointed archways preceded by a stone bridge; on the south side a similar doorway gives access to the maze of narrow, winding streets that make up the old town. The Romanesque church of the **Assunta** is the last remaining vestige of the Cistercian monastery of Santa Maria la Grande. Within is an interesting baptismal font with 12C sculptural decoration. The **Chiesa Matrice** (also called San Lorenzo) has a curious Veneto-Dalmatian façade dating from the 15C.

Ginosa, 7km south, is the ancient *Genusia* mentioned by Pliny and the site of important archaeological finds. It is surrounded on three sides by a deep ravine containing cave-churches with frescoes dating from the 12C–14C.

Castellaneta (population 16,000), dramatically perched on a spur above its ravine, is the birthplace of the silent-movie star Rudolph Valentino (Rodolfo Guiglielmi, 1895–1926). The old town is divided into two quarters, known locally as *Sacco* and *Muricello*, on either side of the **cathedral**. Begun in the 13C and rebuilt in the 17C, the cathedral has a façade of 1771. The campanile retains blind arcades and mullioned windows belonging to the original Romanesque structure. Via Seminario, on the right of the church, leads to the bishop's palace, where there is a fine polyptych depicting the *Madonna with Saints, Angels and Apostles*, signed by Girolamo da Santacroce and dated 1531. Reached by a dirt track on the south edge of the town is the little church of the **Assunta**, now restored to its original 14C appearance. The Romanesque façade contains a finely crafted portal and rose window. Within are 14C and 15C frescoes. More fresco fragments can be seen in the ruins adjoining the church.

Road 7 descends steeply along the west wall of the deep Gravina di

Castellaneta, dominated to the north by the lofty railway bridge, then crosses the torrent and climbs up onto a small plateau.

Turn left for **Palagianello** (population 7000). The castle, rectangular in plan with sharp corner bastions, dates from the 18C. It stands in a dominant position on the outskirts of the village. To the left of the castle can be seen the *gravina*, which holds several cave-churches. San Nicola, to the south of the village, contains remains of 14C frescoes. San Girolamo, the largest in the area, has a badly damaged fresco of the Madonna dating from the 15C.

Beyond the turning, Roman ruins mark the course of the ancient Via Appia. Road 7 descends gently through olive groves. **Mottola** is visible on its hill, to the left. There are numerous cave-churches in the environs of Mottola, some with 12C–15C frescoes.

Massafra

Massafra (population 30,000), situated at the top of a deep ravine, is divided into two distinct parts: the *Terra* or old town on the west, and the more modern Borgo Santa Caterina on the east. Two lofty bridges—the Viadotto Superiore or Ponte Nuovo, and the Viadotto Inferiore or Ponte Vecchio—span the abyss between the two quarters. To see Massafra to full advantage, arrange for a free **guided tour** (in English). Many of the monuments are open sporadically, but tour guides (Via Vittorio Veneto 15, ☎ 099 880 4695) have the keys.

From Piazza Vittorio Emanuele, at the centre of the modern Borgo, Corso Italia bears across the Ponte Vecchio (spectacular view of the ravine with its caves and terraces) to the ancient Terra. Here Via La Terra leads to the imposing **castle**, built in the mid-15C on the site of a Norman fortification and rebuilt in the late 17C or early 18C for Michele Imperiali, whose eagle emblem can be seen on the entrance wall. Rectangular in plan with cylindrical towers and a massive octagonal bastion at the south-east corner, it incorporates in one rampart the church of San Lorenzo (or Chiesa Matrice), built in the 15C and remodelled in 1533. The terrace below commands a view of the entire coastal plain west of Taranto.

Returning to Piazza Garibaldi at the foot of the bridge, follow Via Vittorio Veneto then Via del Santuario to a terrace on the outskirts of the town, from which a monumental staircase descends to the sanctuary of the **Madonna della Scala**. Built in 1731, the church contains an unusual 12C or 13C fresco of the *Madonna and Child* with two kneeling deer from the Basilian crypt over which it stands. The latter, believed to date from the 8C or 9C, is reached by steps in the atrium. Several incised crosses can be seen on the walls and piers. The adjacent Cripta della Buona Nuova, partially ruined by the building of the sanctuary, contains a 13C representation of the *Madonna della Buona Nuova* and a large frescoed *Christ Pantocrator*.

At the bottom of the valley, c 200m distant, lies the so-called **Farmacia del Mago Greguro**, a complex of adjoining caves, the walls of which contain hundreds of small hollows where, according to tradition, the monks stored their medicinal herbs.

Returning to the town, take Viale Marconi to Via Frappietri (also called Via del Cimitero). Here turn left to (300m, left) the 13C crypt of **San Lorenzo**. The primitive church, only partially intact, contains frescoes of saints, on the arches of the presbytery, and of *Christ enthroned*, in the apse. Viale Marconi leads on to the Ponte Nuovo, near which three arches cut in the rock mark the entrance to the recently restored **Cappella-cripta della Candelora**. Located in a private garden, the chapel may be reached from Via dei Canali. 8.5m long and 6m wide, it has three aisles, a low dome, and arched niches in the walls. On the capitals, incised Greek crosses. The walls also bear extensive remains of 13C and 14C frescoes with Greek and Latin inscriptions, including a well-preserved *Presentation in the Temple*.

In the east wall of the ravine is the unusually well-preserved **Chiesa-cripta di San Marco**, of uncertain date. Access is afforded through a gate at the end of Via Fratelli Bandiera (reached by crossing the bridge to Via Scarano and turning right, then right again; ring for key at the house next door). A stairway carved out of the rock descends to the church. Entry is through a vestibule; on the left is a well, presumably a primitive baptismal font; on the right, a large fresco depicting *St Mark*. Piers with rough carvings, inscribed in Greek and Latin and surmounted by rounded arches, divide the church into nave and aisles. Steps lead to the raised presbytery and the main apse; another apse, on the right, is closed off by a parapet, possibly used as a pulpit. In the walls are carved niches that may have served as arcosolia. Of the frescoes they once contained, only a 13C representation of *Saints Cosmas and Damian* remains, the others having been destroyed by humidity.

Just outside Massafra, to the south, stands the 10C Byzantine chapel of **Santa Lucia**. Parts of the original building can still be seen; of particular interest are the distinctive cupolas, pyramidic on the outside but rounded within. The road is straight from here to Taranto. The railway parallels its course across the Aranceta Valley to a broad plain dominated, on the right, by orchards and fields planted with vegetable crops.

Gioia and Acquaviva

From Massafra you can return to Bari by road 100, touching upon at least two more towns of strong medieval character. **Gioia del Colle** (population 28,000) is a busy market town with a massive, austere **castle** that was begun at the end of the 11C and enlarged by Frederick II, who used it mainly as a hunting lodge. The fortress is built to a rectangular plan with the four walls of the enceinte facing the cardinal points. The walls and towers are heavily rusticated and originally displayed a single, impregnable surface to the outside, the windows being later additions. The interior has been extensively altered; nevertheless, the grace and refinement of the original structure and of the Angevin and Aragonese additions are still visible. According to tradition, the castle was the birthplace of Manfred, son of Frederick and Bianca Lancia, who the emperor, out of jealousy, imprisoned in the smaller of the two towers.

The rooms now house the Biblioteca Comunale and the small Museo Archeologico Nazionale (open daily 09.00–13.00, 16.00–19.00; ☎ 080 348 1305), displaying material from the nearby excavations at Monte Sannace, where explorations in 1957 and 1961 revealed an unidentified Apulian settlement, believed to be a major Peucetian town. The extensive site includes remains of houses, public buildings, city walls and an acropolis and in some places the street plan can be discerned. The **defensive walls** (including the remains of a gate) average 4m in width and reach 6m in height. The necropolis, in part composed of small tombs beneath the floors of houses, also extends beyond the city walls. It has yielded much material now in the museums of Gioia, Bari and Taranto.

The name of the other big town on this road, **Acquaviva delle Fonti** (population 21,000), reflects the abundant and accessible water supply that distinguishes this, now prosperous agricultural district, from neighbouring areas. The elegant **cathedral**, a Norman edifice begun under Roger II, was transformed in the 16C in a late Renaissance style. The bipartite façade has a delicate rose window, bold pilasters and a triangular pediment surmounted by statues of the *Madonna and Child* at the apex, and of *Saints* at the ends. Free-standing columns borne by lions, a vestige of the earlier Romanesque building, support the broken pediment above the tall central doorway. In the lunette is *St Eustace with the stag*, in bas-relief. The **Municipio**, formerly the Palazzo dei Principi, erected in the 17C by the De Mari family, has an open loggia crowned by a decorative course of niches and masks running the length of the façade. The two towers belong to the Norman castle that originally stood on the site.

At **Sammichele di Bari** (population 7000), a former Serbian colony, the 17C castle houses a modern museum (Museo della Civittà Contadina D. Bianco, open Tues–Fri 08.30–12.30) documenting rural life and peasant culture. Nearby **Capurso** (population 14,000) has a Renaissance baronial palace and a venerated icon of the Madonna (reputedly found in a well) in the 18C church of the Madonna del Pozzo.

Just outside Bari a road leads west to Bari British Military Cemetery, the burial place of 2000 officers and men killed in local fighting.

BRINDISI, TARANTO AND THE MURGE

The area covered in this chapter includes the Adriatic coast of Apulia between Bari and Lecce, and the interior between the seaboard and Taranto. Though the coast between Bari and Lecce is flat and monotonous, the beaches are generally quite good. **Monopoli** and **Ostuni** are pleasant places to stay if you are looking for a central base from which to explore Apulia; Monopoli is closer to Bari and the main roads leading north and west, whereas Ostuni, an attractive town with a distinct Oriental air, is nearer **Alberobello** and the **Valle dell'Itri**. All around Alberobello the rolling countryside is planted with vines, olives and almond trees and dotted everwhere by clusters of *trulli* (see below). **Taranto** warrants a visit for its magnificent Museo Archeologico Nazionale. **Brindisi**, like Bari, is crowded and busy, and though its museums and monuments repay a visit, you are better off staying elsewhere. South of Brindisi the only place worth a stop is the Romanesque abbey of **Santa Maria di Cerrate**, near Squinzano (which also houses a small ethnographic museum).

The **Murge** is a great limestone plateau (473m above sea level) that extends south-east of Bari. Here are two jewels of Apulian architecture, medieval **Conversano** and Baroque **Martina Franca**.

Beyond Taranto, **Grottaglie** is the best place in Apulia to buy ceramics. **Francavilla Fontana** and **Oria** both offer insight into the evolution of Apulian baronial architecture, and the county is dotted with pre-Roman archaeological finds. Throughout the region the scenery is among the most impressive in southern Europe.

Practical information

Information offices

BARI see p 435.

BRINDISI *Azienda di Promozione Turistica*, Via Cristoforo Colombo 88, ☎ 0831 562126.
Ufficio Informazioni e di Accoglienza Turistica, Lungomare Regina Margherita, ☎ 0831 523072.

FASANO *Ufficio Informazioni e di Accoglienza Turistica*, Piazza Ciaia 10, ☎ 080 441 3086.

FRANCAVILLA FONTANA *Ufficio Informazioni e di Accoglienza Turistica*, Via Municipio 16, ☎ 0831 811262.

MARTINA FRANCA *Ufficio Informazioni e di Accoglienza Turistica*, Piazza Roma 3, ☎ 080 4805702.

NOCI *Ufficio Informazioni e di Accoglienza Turistica*, Piazza Plebiscito, ☎ 080 497 8889.

OSTUNI *Ufficio Informazioni e di Accoglienza Turistica*, Corso Mazzini 6, ☎ 0831 301268.

TARANTO *Azienda di Promozione Turistica*, Corso Umberto 121, ☎ 099 453 2397, ✉ www.apt.ta.it, info@apt.ta.it.
Ufficio Informazioni e di Accoglienza Turistica, Corso Umberto 113, ☎ 099 453 2392.

Getting there and getting around

By air

There are two airports in the region. **Palese**, 8km west of Bari, has regular flights throughout Italy and Europe. **Casale**, 16km north of Brindisi, has a daily service to Milan, Rome and Venice.

By road

The towns of the Adriatic seaboard—Mola di Bari, Polignano a Mare, Monopoli, Ostuni and Brindisi—are most conveniently reached by the coastal road, E55/S16, and its variants (E55/S379, S613 and local roads). The interior towns lie along the main roads from Bari to Taranto (Roads 634, 172/172r and 7ter), and from Taranto to Lecce (Roads 7ter, 174, and 613).

By rail

The coastal towns lie on the main Bari–Lecce railway. Fast Eurostar trains make the 150km journey in c 1hr 40mins, stopping at Monopoli, Ostuni and Brindisi; slow local trains stop at Mola di Bari, Polignano a Mare, Monopoli, Egnazia, Fasano, Cisternino, Ostuni, San Vito dei Normanni, Brindisi and Squinzano. Through trains to/from Switzerland and Germany.

The *Ferrovie del Sud-Est*, a private railway, links Bari to Taranto via Rutigliano, Conversano, Castellana Grotte, Putignano, Alberobello, Locorotondo and Martina Franca. The same company operates trains from Martina Franca to Lecce via Cisternino, Ceglie Messapico, Francavilla Fontana and Manduria. Another private line, the *Ferrotramviaria SpA*, runs from Bari to Palese airport, Bitonto, Ruvo, Corato, Andria and Barletta.

A secondary line of the State Railways (*FS*) connects Brindisi and Taranto; trains stop at Mesagne, Oria, Francavilla Fontana and Grottaglie. The main rail line from Bari to Taranto runs to the west of the area discussed in this chapter (see South of Bari chapter). Intercity trains cover the 115km in c 65mins, stopping at Gioia del Colle.

By sea

Car ferries daily to/from Corfu, Igoumenitsa and/or Patras, moor at Brindisi, Stazione Marittima. Timetables and ticketing information from the information office.

Where to stay

ALBEROBELLO
€€ *Dei Trulli*, Via Cadore 29, ☎ 080 432 3555, 🖷 080 432 3560. A complex of *trulli*, naturally with all modern comforts, in the historic centre of the village; open all year.

CASTELLANA GROTTE
€€ *Relais & Le Jardin*, Contrada Scamardella 59, ☎ 080 496 6330, 🖷 080 496 5520. A small (10 rooms), cosy place in the country, with lots of flowers and plants, private balconies, good cuisine.

CEGLIE MESSAPICO
€ *La Fontanina*, Strada Provinciale Ostuni-Francavilla, Contrada Palagogna, ☎ 0831 380932, 🖷 0831 380933, 🖾 www.fontanina.it, lafontanina@fontanina.it. Set amid olive and almond groves 9km outside the town, on the Ostuni–Francavilla road; pool, playground, free bikes and a great restaurant; open all year.

CISTERNINO € *Villa Cenci*, Strada provinciale per Ceglie Massapico, ☎ 080 444 8208, 🖷 080 444 3329. A renovated country manor, with simple rooms (suites in *trulli*) and pool; open Apr–Oct.

FASANO €€€ *Masseria San Domenico*, Strada Litoranea Provinciale 379 at Savelletri di Fasano, ☎ 080 482 7990, 🖷 080 482 7978; 🖾 www.imasseria.com, info@masseriasandomenico.com. Fine old manor house, on an estate with basilian cave churches and an olive press in a natural cave; spacious rooms with wrought-iron beds; pool, tennis courts, etc.; open Apr–Dec.
€€ *Masseria Marzalossa*, Contrada Pezze Vicine 65, ☎ 080 441 3780, 🖷 080 441 3780, 🖾 www.marzalossa.it, masseriamarzalossa@marzalossa.it. Lovely 18C manor with just 8 rooms; open Mar–Oct and 25–31 Dec.

MARTINA FRANCA € *Dell'Erba*, Viale dei Cedri 1, ☎ 080 430 1055, 🖷 080 430 1639, 🖾 dellerbahotel@

tin.it. In a large garden in the historic town centre; comfortable rooms, pool, sauna, gym, riding; open all year.

MONOPOLI €€€ *Il Melograno*, Contrada Torricella 345, ☎ 080 690 9030, 🖷 080 747908, 🖾 www.melograno.com, melograno@melograno.com. A 16C fortified manor surrounded by groves of olive, pomegranate, lemon, orange and prickly pear; beautiful rooms, excellent cuisine, pool, sauna, tennis, etc.; closed Feb.

OSTUNI €€ *Masseria Santa Lucia*, SS 379, km 23 (Costa Merlata exit), ☎ 0831 35560, 🖷 0831 304090, 🖾 masseriasantalucia.it, infomasseriasantalucia.it. A renovated country manor; spacious rooms with garden patios, Olympic pool, tennis, riding, private beach; open all year.
€€ *Tutosa*, Contrada Tutosa, ☎ 0831 359046, 🖷 0831 330630, 🖾 www.tutosa.it, info@tutosa.it. Fine old fortified manor with garden and pool; open all year.

POLIGNANO A MARE
€€ *Castellinaria*, road 832, at Cala San Giovanni, ☎ 080 424 0233, 🖷 080 424 0489, 🖾 hotelcastellinaria.it, info@hotelcastellinaria.it. Immersed in Mediterranean vegetation in a rocky little cove, with sea views from most rooms; open Dec–Oct.
€€ *Grotta Palazzese*, Via Narciso 59, ☎ 080 424 0677, 🖷 080 424 0677. Also on the coast, with cosy rooms and a locally famous restaurant in a cave; open all year.

Eating out

ALBEROBELLO
€€€ *Il Poeta Contadino*, Via Independenza 21, ☎ 080 432 1917. Restaurant famous for its outstanding Apulian cuisine, in the heart of Alberobello; closed Mon (except July-Sept), Jan and late June–early July.
€ *La Cantina*, Vico Lippolis 9, ☎ 080 432 3473. Simple but delicious local

fare in the heart of the old town; closed Tues (except in summer) and late June–early July.

Caseificio Notarnicola, Viale Notarnicola 2. Dairy selling good local cheeses.

Pastificio Pmc, Via Girolamo 34. Pasta factory selling antique bronze-tooled pasta, including *orecchiette* and other traditional shapes.

BRINDISI €€€ *La Lanterna*, Via Giovanni Tarantini 14, ☎ 0831 564026. Elegant, refined seafood restaurant in the 15C Palazzo Seripando; closed Sun and Aug.

€€ *Penny*, Via San Francesco 1, ☎ 0831 563013. Excellent fish restaurant (with pizza) near the harbour; closed Mon and early Sept.

€€ *Trattoria Pantagruele*, Via Salita di Ripalta 1–3, ☎ 0831 560 605. Restaurant offering good regional dishes from land and sea; closed Sun evening and Mon in winter, Sat and Sun in July–Aug (completely closed two weeks in Aug).

€ *Il Cantinone*, Via De Leo 4, ☎ 0831 562122. Characteristic trattoria; closed Tues and mid-Aug.

Pasticceria Esmeralda, Via De Leo 42. Pastry shop specialising in almond-based recipes.

CAROVIGNO €€ *Fornello da Ricci*, Contrada Montevicoli, ☎ 0831 377104. Delightful traditional restaurant with garden; closed Mon evening, Tues and Jan–early Feb.

€€ *Già sotto l'Arco*, Corso Vittorio Emanuele 71, ☎ 0831 996286. Restaurant; closed Mon and a few days in June and Jan.

Bar Centrale, Corso Garibaldi 27. Café with outstanding ice cream, pastries and biscuits.

CEGLIE MESSAPICA € *Cibus*, Via Chianche di Scarano 7, ☎ 0831 388980. Warm, family-run trattoria with commendable local dishes; closed Tues and early July.

CISTERNINO €€ *Osteria Cantone*, Contrada Fantese, ☎ 080 444 6902. Traditional restaurant in an old manor house on the Martina Franca Road; closed Nov.

€ *Il Capriccio*, Via Libertà 71, Contrada Caranna, ☎ 080 444 2553. Agreeable restaurant-pizzeria; closed mid-day Mon, Wed and Oct–Nov.

€ *La Botte*, Via Santa Lucia 38, ☎ 080 444 7850. Characteristic trattoria in the old town centre, with summer seating in the piazza; closed Thur (except in summer) and late Sept–early Oct.

FASANO €€€ *Il Fagiano*, Viale Toledo 13, at Selva di Fasano, ☎ 080 433 1157. Elegant, refined garden restaurant with delicious seasonal dishes; closed Sun evening and Mon (except in summer), and Jan.

LOCOROTONDO € *Centro Storico*, Via Eroi di Dogali 6, ☎ 080 431 5473. Trattoria offering great seasonal dishes; closed Wed.

MARTINA FRANCA €€ *Al Ritrovo degli Amici*, Corso Messapia 8, ☎ 080 483 9249. Restaurant indeed full of 'friends' attracted by good food and wines; closed Sun evening and Mon (except in summer).

€€ *Trattoria delle Ruote*, Via Monticello 1, ☎ 080 483 7473. Trattoria in a *trullo*, with simple *menù du jour*; closed Mon and one week in Sept.

€€ *Villa Bacco*, Via Madonna del Pozzo 46, ☎ 080 483 8615. Warm, romantic restaurant (with rooms), with good traditional fare; closed Mon and Jan.

€ *La Murgetta*, Strada Statale 172, Contrada Lanzo, ☎ 080 449 0016. Characteristic restaurant with good local fare, closed Wed.

MOLA DI BARI €€ *Van Westerhout*, Via De Amicis 3–5, ☎ 080 474 6989. Innovative interpretations of traditional dishes, *fin-de-siècle* ambience; closed Sun evening and Tues.

MONOPOLI € *Osteria Perricci*, Via Orazio Comes 1, ☎ 080 937 2208. Old-fashioned osteria in the same family for four generations; closed Wed, Sept and late Jan–early Feb.

€ *Il Sagittario*, Contrada San Nicola 42A, ☎ 080 690 0059. Restaurant-pizzeria; closed Tues (except in Aug).

NOCI €€ *L'Antica Locanda*, Via Spirito Santo 49, ☎ 080 497 2460. Fine, friendly osteria in the old town centre; closed Sun evening, Tues and in July–Aug.

Gourmandise, Via Petrone 32. For cakes, pastries, candies and ice cream.

OSTUNI €€ *La Taverna*, Contrada Rosa Marina, ☎ 0831 350433. Good fish restaurant in a rennovated farmhouse by the sea just outside town; closed Wed and Jan.

€€ *Masseria Il Frantoio*, SS 16 km 874, ☎ 0831 330276. Fine regional fare in a lovely manor house (with rooms); closed Sun evening and Nov–Feb.

€€ *Osteria del Tempo Perso*, Via Vitale 47, ☎ 0831 304819. Characteristic osteria in the historic town centre; closed Mon and late Dec–early Jan.

€€ *Porta Nuova*, Via G. Petrarolo 38, ☎ 0831 338983. Creative cuisine and great views, in the old town centre; closed Wed.

PUTIGNANO €€ *Il Cantinone*, Via San Lorenzo 1, ☎ 080 491 3378. Characteristic trattoria with tables among wine vats; closed Wed and two weeks in July.

Pastificio Sbiroli, Via Conversano 10. For traditional hand-made pasta.

TARANTO €€ *La Fattoria*, Via Abruzzo 7–9, ☎ 099 737 1161. Characteristic seafood restaurant with good wines and service; closed Sun and late Aug.

€€ *Vecchie Cantine*, Via Girasoli 90, at Lama, ☎ 099 777 2589. Creative fish dishes in a restaurant (with rooms) by the sea; closed Wed and Sept.

€ *Da Mimmo*, Via Giovinazzi 18, ☎ 099 459 3733. Simple osteria near the Villa Comunale; closed Wed and late Aug.

Special events
TARANTO Holy Week celebration, with representations of the Passion and Death of Christ and procession through the city streets. Taranto is also the site of the annual conference of scholars of Magna Graecia.

Along the coast

South of Bari the road and railway hug the coast, providing broad sea views and the occasional glimpse inland, over fields and orchards, to the Murge.

Mola di Bari (population 27,000) was a crusader port. Today it consists of an old town on a headland and a new quarter that extends inland to the railway. The **cathedral**, erected in the mid-16C on the site of an earlier church, combines Romanesque and Dalmatian architectural motifs. The rose window is probably a remnant of the earlier structure. Within is a curious nave arcade, taller at the east end and shorter, with a gallery in the walls above the arches (again a vestige of the old church), at the west. In the south aisle a baptismal font with dancing putti can be seen. Near the head of the promontory rises the **castle**, built by Pierre d'Agincourt for Charles of Anjou in 1278. Irregular in plan, it has a tall enceinte and polygonal corner bastions with steep scarps.

Near Polignano a Mare is the former abbey of **San Vito**, which dates from the 9C but has been repeatedly altered, particularly in the 16C. The abbey church, preceded by a porch, has an unusual nave surmounted by three domes. A medieval watch-tower stands nearby.

Polignano a Mare (population 16,000) rises abruptly from the rocks. The Chiesa Matrice, in Piazza Vittorio Emanuele, was consecrated in 1295. The 16C interior contains a contemporary stone *presepio* by Stefano da Putignano, 17C choir stalls and, in the sacristy, several panels of a polyptych by Bartolomeo Vivarini (1472). Steps descend from the village to two large (25–30m diameter) caves collectively called the Grotta Palazzese; these and the Raccolta Archeologica, in Viale Rimembranza, may be seen on request (open by appointment, ☎ 080 740144).

Monopoli and its environs

Monopoli (population 47,000), a large, busy town, derives its livelihood from fishing, farming and industry.

The polygonal **castle** was built in 1552 and remodelled in 1660. Beyond is the harbour, frequented by merchant and fishing vessels. The **cathedral**, founded in 1107 and rebuilt in 1742–70, is one of the more prominent Baroque buildings in the district. It has a tall façade of grey stone connected, on the right, to a blank wall with statues in niches, a scenographic addition to the piazza. The **interior** is a Latin cross with nave and aisles faced in coloured marble. It contains paintings by several prominent artists, including (first south altar) *Fall of the Rebel Angels* by Palma Giovane; (south transept) *Last Supper* and (in tondi on the walls) *Sacrifice of Abraham* and *Supper at Emmaus*, by Francesco de Mura; (further on) *Madonna in Glory with Saints Roche and Sebastian*, attributed to Palma Giovane, and *Circumcision*, by Marco da Siena. Steps mount to the presbytery; above the altar is a 13C Byzantine *Madonna*, possibly by a Campanian painter.

In the sacristy and the adjoining room you can see architectural fragments from the 12C church, including an architrave with bas-reliefs and a capital bearing a representation of Daniel in the lion's den. The treasury contains an extraordinary 10C or 11C reliquary, possibly from Constantinople, with panels that open to form a triptych representing the *Crucifixion and Saints Peter and Paul*; a 17C processional cross of Neapolitan workmanship and other precious objects. In the Vescovado are a *Crowning of the Virgin* by Palma Giovane, and a *Madonna and Saints* by Paolo Veronese and pupils.

The church of **San Domenico** is distinguished by an elegant Renaissance façade. Within is Palma Giovane's canvas of the *Miracle of Soriano*, one of the more noteworthy of the artist's Apulian paintings. The graceful chapel of **Santa Maria Amalfitana**, erected in the 12C by merchants from Amalfi, stands over a Basilian cave-church. The apse and the south flank belong to the original Romanesque structure; later additions were made in the Gothic and Baroque styles. The interior has a nave and two aisles divided by compound piers with good Romanesque capitals. Above, semicircular arches support the nave walls and simple wooden ceiling. From the south aisle, steps descend to the Basilian *laura*, now the crypt. A doorway at the end of the aisle opens onto a small court, from which the east end of the church (restored) may be seen. The largest of the three apses is adorned with slender half-columns, grotesque consoles and a fine window framed between two small columns—motifs which link the chapel to the Lombard Romanesque churches of northern Italy.

In the suburb of Cozzana, on the Conversano road, the private **Villa Meo-Evoli** has another collection of antiquities (open by appointment; ☎ 080 803805) from sites in Apulia and Campania.

If you're driving, leave Monopoli from the south following the railway as far as the turning for Santo Stefano, then bear slightly east for the coast and Torre Cintola. At Torre Egnazia (Egnazia station if you're travelling by train) the road crosses the ruins of **Egnathia** (*Egnazia* in Italian; open summer daily 08.30–dusk; winter daily 08.30–13.30, 14.30–dusk; ☎ 080 482 9056), a Graeco-Messapian town set on the frontier between Messapia and Peucetia where Horace and his companions were amused at a pretended miracle (*credat Judaeus Apella, non ego*; Judaeus Apella believed it, I didn't). The **Museo Archeologico di Egnathia**, at the edge of the archaeological zone (open as the excavations), contains vases, terracottas and Messapian inscriptions discovered in the course of excavations, late antique and early Christian mosaics and a large Messapian chamber tomb of the 4C or 3C BC. The site is especially important to archaeologists for the so-called **Gnathian ware** (characterised by small coloured designs on a black background, and sometimes ribbed) that was made here in the 4C and 3C BC.

The walled acropolis and the town proper lie respectively on the east and west sides of the road. The town contains a Roman **forum** paved with large blocks of stone and flanked by remains of a colonnaded portico; at the centre of the square are a well, a tribune and other remains. To the north lies the foundation of a **basilica**, of uncertain date. Further east are remains of what is believed to be the amphitheatre. The south side of the forum is bordered by shops and houses. Beyond lies a well-preserved stretch of the **Via Traiana**, which crossed the town at this point. Remains of walls and an arch stand to the east; further south across the Via Traiana, is a ruined early Christian basilica built with materials from pagan edifices. Also visible are numerous rock-cut tombs and an imposing (7m high) section of the town walls.

Savelletri is a fishing village and a developing resort to the south of Egnathia. Extensive views over the sea and the Murge plateau are revealed as you continue south. Near Villanova, a modest village with a low castle, a road on the right diverges to Ostuni (see below). The coast beyond is full of modern bathing establishments and tourist villages. Another turning leads inland to Carovigno (see below). From here the road crosses a somewhat monotonous landscape dominated by vineyards to link up with SS 16 from Fasano and San Vito just before entering Brindisi.

Ostuni and its environs

An alternative to the coast road passes slightly inland, bearing south-east from Monopoli in a straight line through groves of olives and almond trees.

On this road is **Fasano** (population 39,000), a thriving agricultural town with a Palazzo Comunale dating from 1509. It is developing rapidly as a holiday centre, thanks to its location between the wooded hills of Selva di Fasano (6km west) and the attractive shoreline (7km east). It is known principally for its **Zoo-Safari** (open daily 09.30–dusk), a large drive-through zoological park with amusements. A *strada panoramica*, which runs along the north rim of the Murge dei Trulli, connects the town with Castellana Grotte.

From Fasano the road skirts the lower edge of the Murge, past dense olive groves. Beyond Pezze di Greco, roads lead north to (6km) Torre Canne and south to (9km) Cisternino. Just before Montalbano, a dirt track leads left to the Masseria Ottava, a farm, near which lies the so-called Dolmen of Cisternino or Tavole Paladine, a prehistoric stone monument thought to be a tomb. The straight course of the road ends as you round the northernmost spur of the Murge. The road begins to climb, with views ahead to Ostuni, its white houses silhouetted against the sky.

Ostuni (population 32,000) is a town of pre-Roman origin built on three hills. Its centre, composed of steep medieval alleys, is still circled by ramparts. The focus of town life is the triangular Piazza della Libertà, at one end of which stands the exuberant Guglia di Sant'Oronzo (1771). Slightly set back from the square is the little church of the **Spirito Santo** (1637), with its handsome Renaissance portal bearing reliefs of the *Annunciation* and of the *Crowning and Death of the Virgin*. From here Via Vicentini climbs to the old town, passing an 18C Carmelite convent and, next door, the Baroque church of Santa Maria Maddalena, with its cupola of coloured majolica.

The **cathedral** stands at the heart of the old quarter. Begun in 1435 and completed some 60 years later, it has an unusual façade of Spanish inspiration, with three rose windows and late Gothic decorative details. The Latin-cross interior was remodelled in the 18C; in the last chapel on the south can be seen a *Madonna and Child with Saints* by Palma Giovane.

The **Museo di Civiltà Preclassiche della Murgia Meridionale e Parco Archeologico di Santa Maria di Agnano**, in the Convento delle Monacelle at Via Cattedrale 15 (open Tues–Sat 08.30–13.00, Tues–Thur 15.30–19.00, Sun 15.30–19.00; ☎ 0831 336383), displays the 25,000-year-old skeleton of **Delia**, the Palaeolithic woman carrying a foetus, found in the cave of Santa Maria di Agnano. Here also are Neolithic, Bronze-Age and Iron-Age finds as well as an exhibition on ancient Mediterranean agriculture. The 13-hectare archaeological park where the Palaeolithic burial ground was found can be visited by appointment.

Behind the cathedral stands the bishop's palace, with its elegant 18C loggia. Further on lie the remains of a castle erected in 1198 by Geoffrey, Count of Lecce, and destroyed in 1559. The church of the Annunziata, in the modern town, contains a *Deposition* by Paolo Veronese (stolen in 1975 and recovered in 1977).

Carovigno (population 14,000) is a large town built on the site of the Messapian *Carbina*. Remains of megalithic walls may be seen to the north and west. The **castle**, erected in the 14C and 15C as a defence against pirates, was restored in 1906. The almond-shaped bastion at the north-east corner is unusual in Italian military architecture, whereas the triangular ground plan and tall enceinte are typical of late medieval fortifications. Within are rooms with 19C period furniture.

San Vito dei Normanni (population 21,000) has a 12C castle, transformed into a fortified residence in the 15C. Beyond the town, near its station, lie the **Grotto di San Biagio**, with paintings by Mastro Danieli (1197), and the Grotto di San Giovanni, also with frescoes.

Up on the Murge plateau

The Italic tribes of Apulia considered the long, low massif of the Murge an ideal place to live—close to the Adriatic, but high enough above it to be out of the sight of travellers passing by land or sea. **Rutigliano** (population 17,000) stands on the site of an ancient Apulian settlement 22km south-east of Bari. The church of **Santa Maria della Colonna**, founded by the Normans, was consecrated in 1108. The main portal retains the original carved architrave depicting *Christ* *and the Apostles*, and the *Annunciation;* the Gothic porch dates from the 13C or 14C. Within is a polyptych of 1450 by Alvise Vivarini.

Some 8km south-east of the town is the conventual church of **Santa Maria dell'Isola**, built to an unusual plan with two aisles, Gothic arches and vaults and three domes in a row. The church contains the tomb of Giulio Antonio Acquaviva, Duke of Atri, executed in 1482 by Nuzzo Barba di Galatina.

Conversano

Conversano (population 23,000) stands on a hill overlooking the Adriatic. It appears to have been a Peucetian town, possibly the *Norba* described in the *Tabula Peutingeriana*, an Italic document in the Oscan language, as lying on the inland route from Bitonto to Egnathia. It was bitterly contested by the Normans and Byzantines during the late Middle Ages. It changed hands several times in the following centuries, ending up among the possessions of the Acquaviva, Counts of Conversano, who retained it until 1806.

From the public gardens of the Villa Garibaldi, at the edge of the town, the view embraces the coastal plain to Bari. Nearby, at the centre of a sloping piazza, stands the **castle**, originally Norman, transformed over the centuries into a lordly manor with numerous wings and towers. Above the tiled roofs rises the rectangular Norman keep; the low polygonal bastion and the taller cylindrical one, respectively located at the north-east and north-west corners, date from the 15C; the remaining structures are chiefly 17C. The main entrance, which faces Piazza della Conciliazione, and the elegant gallery in the atrium, were built in 1710 by order of Countess Dorotea Acquaviva. The interior contains private dwellings and the Biblioteca Civica.

The **duomo** was restored after a fire in 1911. The 14C façade combines Romanesque and Gothic forms, with interesting sculptural decoration above the main portal. At the ends of the transept are two low campanili. The interior, with nave and aisles divided by piers, a trefoil matroneum and triple apse, contains a 13C icon of the Virgin (left aisle), a 14C wooden crucifix, traces of frescoes and a modern pulpit.

From the rear of the cathedral, Via San Benedetto, to the left, leads to the ancient Benedictine monastery. Founded, according to tradition, by St Mauro or St Placid and documented from the 10C onwards. The conventual church, erected in the late 11C and extensively altered in the 16C and 17C, stands beneath a Baroque campanile of 1655. Part of its original decoration can be seen in the rough mosaic frieze that runs along the top of the entrance wall. The richly decorated interior has a nave surmounted by three consecutive domes with 17C frescoes. Along the left flank of the church is a pleasing 11C **cloister** with trefoil arches and delicately carved capitals. From here you may enter the crypt, originally a 6C–9C Byzantine cenobium. In the apse are some repainted frescoes. The small Museo Archeologico Nazionale (open Mon–Sat 09.00–12.00, 15.30–19.30), houses finds from local excavations.

About 1km north-east of the town stands the unusual little church of **Santa Caterina**, with four semicircular arms arranged in a clover-leaf pattern around a central dome. The building is believed to date from the 12C.

From Conversano the road bears south-east through farmland and rugged terrain. The Torre del Castiglione, on a hilltop (right), marks the site of an ancient indigenous settlement, later a medieval fortified town but abandoned in the 15C

Caverns near Castellana Grotte

Castellana Grotte (population 18,000) takes its name from the spectacular caverns 2km south-west of the town, the Grotte di Castellana. Possibly the most exciting series of caverns in the whole of Italy, they are 1.5km long with an average depth of c 65m. A series of corridors connects various chambers, rich in stalagmites and stalactites, in alabaster and other coloured stones. The short guided tour (open Apr–Sept 11.00, 13.00, 16.00, 19.00; in English at 11.00 and 16.00), which terminates at the Grave al Precipizio, takes about an hour; the full tour to the **Grotta Bianca** (considered by some the most beautiful cavern in the world because of its brilliant crystalline formations; hourly Apr–Sept 09.00–19.30; Oct–Mar 09.00–13.00) takes two hours. The temperature inside the caverns remains constant at around 15°C. The nearby observation tower offers good views over the surrounding countryside.

Putignano (population 27,000), a busy market and manufacturing town, is a former fief of the Knights of Malta. The Museo Civico, in Piazza Plebiscito, is closed indefinitely for restoration. More interesting caverns (**Grotta di Putignano**, chiefly in pink alabaster; open 09.00–12.00 and 15.00–18.00) can be seen 1km north-west of the town.

Alberobello is a small town (population 11,000) with a quarter wholly composed of story-book-like *trulli*, flanking narrow streets. The name, Alberobello, derives from the *Sylva Arboris Belli*, the vast oak forest that once covered the area. The town was probably founded by the Acquaviva, Counts of Conversano, in the 15C. In the following century it grew up around a mill and a tavern built by Count Gian Girolamo II. The area comprising the Rioni Monti and the Aia Piccola, composed of over 1000 *trulli*, has been declared a national monument. Although it is now crowded with tourists from May to October, with shops selling trinkets that only vaguely recall the region's rural craft tradition, it neve theless remains a fascinating place to visit.

About trulli

Trulli are curious dwellings, built without mortar from local limestone and usually whitewashed. Their conical roofs, formed from the flat-pitched, spiral courses of the same stone are capped with diverse finials. They are found all over the region, isolated or in groups, and their origin is very remote. It is no doubt related to the rocky nature of the soil, and in many cases the same limestone used for the *trulli* is also adopted in the drywork walls used as boundary markers, which give the agrarian landscape of this area its distinctive appearance.

Religious or folk symbols are traced in white on many of the grey conical roofs. Inside, the rooms are small and usually windowless; the interior walls, like those of the exterior, in most cases receive one or two coats of whitewash each year, which accounts for their immaculate appearance. The Trullo Sovrano, in Piazza Sacramento, has two storeys; and the pretty church of Sant'Antonio derives its inspiration from the trullo style.

Locorotondo (population 13,000) is a strikingly beautiful town designed in a circular plan (hence the name, round place) set on a hilltop at the heart of the Murge. From the Villa Comunale at the top of the hill there are splendid views over the Itria Valley, with its constellations of *trulli*, to Martina Franca (see below). The church of **San Marco della Greca**, a late Gothic building erected by Piero del Balzo, Prince of Taranto, has pilasters and half-columns with interesting capitals and bases. A road to the east connects Locorotondo to Ostuni via **Cisternino**, a town of almost Greek appearance, made up of white terraced houses with external staircases.

South of Locorotondo stretches the Valle d'Itria, one of the more beautiful and exotic areas of southern Italy, where the neat *trulli*, low stone walls, and small meticulously planted farms all combine to create the atmosphere of a story-book.

Martina Franca (population 46,000) is a graceful 18C town known for its strong white wine (used in preparing vermouth and spumanti) and for its many Baroque and Rococo buildings. The town was established in the 10C by refugees from Taranto, forced inland by the Saracen invasions. It was enlarged in the early 14C by Philip of Anjou, who granted it the fiscal immunities from which it derives its appellative, *franca*. In the years that followed it was given defensive walls and no fewer than 24 bastions, to which Raimondello Orsini added a castle in 1388. The town was held in fee by a branch of the Caracciolo family of Naples from 1506 to the extinction of the line in 1827.

The central Piazza XX Settembre is flanked by the Villa Comunale, beyond which stands the 15C Gothic church of **Sant'Antonio**. Across the square rises the Porta Sant'Antonio, an 18C structure surmounted by an equestrian statue of *St Martin*, patron of the city. In the triangular Piazza Roma, beyond, stands the former **Palazzo Ducale**, now the town hall, attributed to Bernini (1668), with a fine ironwork balcony running the length of its façade. The building stands on the site of the Orsini castle. The Palazzo Martucci, across the square, has an elegant, restrained Baroque façade.

The narrow Corso Vittorio Emanuele winds past charming Baroque and Rococo townhouses to the collegiate church of **San Martino** (1747–75), its tall graceful façade dominated by the sculptural group of St Martin and the beggar above the main door. The Romanesque-Gothic campanile is from a 15C church over which the present edifice was built. The richly adorned interior consists of a single nave with transept. The main altar, in coloured marble, has 18C statues of Charity and Maternity. The paintings above the minor altars are by local artists. The Palazzo della Corte (1763) and the Torre dell'Orologio (1734) stand at the left of the church.

From nearby Piazza Plebiscito, Via Cavour leads past some more 17C and 18C townhouses to Piazza Maria Immacolata. From here, Via Principe Umberto runs past the church of San Domenico and the Conservatorio di Santa Maria della Misericordia (both 18C). Further on, in Via Pergolesi outside the town gates, is a terrace offering marvellous views over the Valle d'Itria.

From Martina Franca road and railway descend the southern edge of the Murge, crossing the plateau abundant with grain, vines and olive groves. Near **Crispiano** are Basilian cave-churches with 13C frescoes, and a small but well-displayed collection of traditional agricultural tools (at the 16C Masserie Lupoli). The Ionian Sea and Taranto, preceded by the Mare Piccolo, stretch out before you as you cross the last low foothills to the coast. A turning (left) bypasses the city centre.

Taranto

Taranto, at the northern extremity of the gulf that bears its name, is an important commercial port and industrial centre (population 244,000) and the second naval dockyard in Italy after La Spezia.

History of Taranto

The Spartan colony of *Taras*, founded in 708 BC after successful struggles against the Messapians and Lucanians, became the greatest city in Magna Graecia, famous especially for the purple dye it produced from the murex, a marine mollusc, for the wool of its flocks, which grazed on the banks of the Galaesus, and for its wine, figs and salt. It was also a centre of Pythagorean philosophy. The mathematician, Archytas, president of the town (430–365), was visited by Plato here, and Aristoxenes (4C BC), author of the earliest known treatise on music, was also a Tarantine.

Threatened by Rome in the 3C BC, the city summoned Pyrrhus, King of Epirus to its aid, but after ten years of war it lost its independence (272 BC). In 209 BC the city surrendered to Hannibal, for which, after being taken by Fabius Maximus, it was severely punished. It was subsequently Latinised as *Tarentum*.

Of little importance under the Roman Empire, it was destroyed by the Saracens (927), but rebuilt by Nicephorus Phocas, the Byzantine emperor, in 967. It retained its importance under the Normans, Swabians and Angevins, and by the 14C its territory had come to include much of Apulia and Basilicata. Although it was made an independent Signoria under Raimondello del Balzo Orsini (1393–1406), it was captured by Consalvo di Cordova in 1502. In 1647–48 it was torn by a popular uprising inspired by that of Masaniello in Naples.

The town came under Bourbon rule in 1734 and adhered to the Parthenopean Republic in 1799. Occupied by the French in 1801, it proved to be one of Napoleon's strongest bases against the English and the Russians. With the opening of the Suez Canal, it grew to be one of the newly united Kingdom of Italy's more strategic harbours. During the First World War the port became familiar to British troops proceeding to and from the Eastern Fronts; in 1940–43 it was attacked repeatedly by Allied aircraft. On 9 September 1943, the Royal Navy entered the harbour and landed troops unopposed.

Taranto was the native town of the composer, Giovanni Paisiello (1740–1816). It gives its name to the tarantula, a species of spider, whose bite was the reputed cause of a peculiar contagious melancholy madness (tarantism), curable only by music and violent dancing. This hysterical mania reached its height in southern Italy in the 17C and has left its memory in the *tarantella*, the graceful folk dance of that region.

The town occupies an unusual site. The industrial **Borgo**, with the railway station, is on the mainland to the north-west. The **Città Vecchia** stands on the site of the Roman citadel on an island between the Mare Grande and the Mare Piccolo. The Mare Grande is a bay in the Gulf of Taranto, separated from the open sea by the fortified Isole Cheradi. The Mare Piccolo is a large lagoon extending some 8km north-east of the town and divided by a peninsula into two bays: the first is used as a naval harbour, the second for oyster culture. The **Città**

Nuova, separated by a navigable canal dating from the Middle Ages, stands on a peninsula to the south-east.

The Città Vecchia

The Città Vecchia, connected with the Borgo by the long Ponte di Porta Napoli, is oblong in plan and crossed by four parallel avenues and many narrow alleys. In the animated Via Duomo is the **duomo**, dedicated to San Cataldo (St Cathal of Munster), who remained at Taranto after a pilgrimage to the Holy Land in the 7C. Constructed in the 11C over an earlier building, it has been rebuilt several times, most notably in 1596 and 1657. The Baroque façade was added in 1713. Much of the building has recently been restored to its original form. The outside walls of the nave and transept are decorated with charming geometric motifs and blind arcading, as is the cylindrical drum of the Byzantine cupola at the crossing. The campanile, originally of 1413, was completely rebuilt during the recent restoration.

You enter the church through a 15C vestibule, at the left of which is the baptistery, containing a covered font (1571) incorporating antique columns, and the 17C tomb of Tommaso Caracciolo, Archbishop of Taranto. The **interior** of the church, a three-aisled basilica, has rounded arches rising from 16 columns of ancient marble (the first on the left is fluted) and marvellous **capitals** of Byzantine and Romanesque craftsmanship (note particularly the figures of bird with foliage, second on the left). On the right of the entrance is a holy-water basin carried by female herms, one of which is missing. The 17C coffered ceiling of the nave bears reliefs of *St Cathal and the Virgin*. In the floor are scanty remains of the original mosaic pavement. From the aisles, steps mount to the raised transept, which has vaulted ceilings and blind arcading high up on the walls. The cupola, rebuilt in 1657, rises above the crossing.

To the right of the apse, the Baroque **Cappella di San Cataldo**, with inlaid marble walls, 18C statues and richly frescoed ceiling, is enclosed by ornate bronze- and iron-work gates. The statue of the saint on the altar dates from 1984, replacing an earlier piece that was stolen. Steps in front of the high altar descend to the Gothic **crypt**, built on low columns belonging to the first phase of the building. On the walls are fragments of Byzantine frescoes dating from the 12C–14C. Also in the crypt is an early Christian sarcophagus.

All the fault of a spider?

In Taranto it is always afternoon. 'The Tarentines', says Strabo, 'have more holidays than workdays in the year' (Norman Douglas, *Old Calabria*, 1915).

Behind the duomo is the church of **San Domenico Maggiore** (also called San Pietro Imperiale), built in the late 11C and remodelled in the Gothic style in 1302. It is preceded by a high Baroque double staircase. The façade has a fine main portal with a baldachin, a graceful rose window and blind arcading. The interior is built to a Latin cross plan with a single nave and a rectangular apse. Along the north wall are 16C chapels with coloured marble decoration; the third of these contains a painting of the *Circumcision* by Marco Pino.

At the east end of the island, preceded by two antique columns thought to have belonged to a 6C Greek temple dedicated to Neptune, stands the **castle**, built by Ferdinand of Aragon in 1480, enlarged by the Spaniards in the 16C, and further modified in the 19C. It is now home to the Taranto naval command.

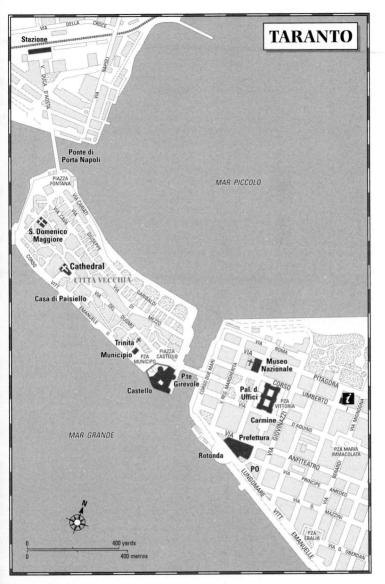

The Città Nuova

A swing bridge crosses the channel to the Città Nuova. Here, in Piazza Archita, its principal square, are the imposing Palazzo degli Uffizi and the **Museo Archeologico Nazionale** (open Mon–Sat 08.30–13.30, 14.30–19.30, Sun and holidays 08.30–13.30, 14.30–22.00; closed for renovation at the time of writing; ☎ 099 453 2112), containing the largest collection of antiquities in southern Italy after that of the Museo Archeologico Nazionale in Naples. While the museum is gradually being renovated and rearranged, parts of the collection may be seen at **Palazzo Pantaleo** (Corso Vittorio Emanuele II, open daily 08.30–13.30, ☎ 099 471 8492). Installed on a rotating basis, the display range from prehistory to the 1C BC. Finds are articulated in sections regarding **prehistory**, **small mass sculptures** and, most significantly, **Greece and Magna Graecia** with a beautiful selection of pottery, gold and jewellery. Highlights include proto-Corinthian and Corinthian ceramics (dating from the 8C–6C BC), Laconic ceramics (7C–6C BC), and superb examples of Attic black and red figure pottery (5C–3C BC). Most of the gold objects are of Tarentine workmanship.

The original display in the **Palazzo degli Uffizi** may be reinstated withiin the lifetime of this edition. From the entrance, on the ground floor, steps ascend to the **first floor**. **Tarentine collection**. Room 1. Greek sculpture. 2092 Archaic kore; 3885 *Head of a Female Divinity* (Hera or Aphrodite, 5C BC) attributed to a Greek sculptor working at Taras; 6138 Small kore (c 500 BC); 3881 *Apollo* (5C BC) by a Greek sculptor working at Taras; 2348, 6142, 52926, 6141, 52925, fragments of small sculptures (4C BC); 3899 *Athena* (5C); 388 *Athena* (5C); no number *Eros*, attributed to the school of Praxiteles (after 350 BC); 3897 *Head of Aphrodite* or *Artemedes*, attributed to the school of Praxiteles (325 BC); 3905 Female head from a tomb sculpture (4C BC), 3893 *Aphrodite or Kore* (400 BC), both by Tarentine artists; 6137 Female head (400 BC); 3930 funerary stele of a Nude warrior offering a pomegranate to a serpent; no number, *Heracles at Rest*, male torso, copy after an original by Skopas the Younger (4C BC).

Room 2. 3895 *Heracles* (4C BC) or *Boxer Resting* (1C BC); 3887 *Dionysus* attributed to the school of Praxiteles (after 350 BC); 3918 *Dionysus*, copy after the school of Praxiteles (4C BC); no number, Female head of Tarentine workmanship (3C BC); 10774, 4998, 6139, 2092, 5000, 10137 small heads and fragments (4C BC); 4999 herm (bearded Dionysus? 4C BC); 6143 *Athena*; no number, Roman mosaic pavement; 3916 Headless female figure in the Hellenistic manner (3C–2C BC); 3914 late Hellenistic decorative statue (nymph?); 3709–12 **Hellenistic kline tomb** decorated with caryatids at the corners and reliefs of battle scenes (reconstruction); no number, two Tarantine decorative reliefs one of which represents a chariot race; 119142 Female head from a funerary statue.

Room 3. **Roman sculpture**. No number (right of entrance) portrait head of *Augustus with Veil* and (left) of other figures of the Julio-Claudian period; no number (in case on wall) series of folk art portraits from a Roman urn field (1C BC–1C AD); Roman mosaics, including (left and right of entrance) decorative mosaics (2C AD); fragment of mosaic with a deer (4C or 5C); **mosaic pavement** with representation of a hunting scene, and two tondi from the same pavement (4C or 5C BC); **mosaic** of a lion and a wild pig fighting (3C AD).

Room 4. **Architectural and sculptural fragments**. Here are assembled numerous reliefs and sculptures of local workmanship from the 4C–2C BC, which decorated the small temples (*naiskoi*) that stood above the burial chambers of monumental tombs; as well as terracotta architectural ornaments and antefixes also from the naiskoi, and the painted doors and fronts of burial beds of the chambers below. At the centre of the room is a large architectural sarcophagus with extensive traces of the original painted decoration, containing the remains of an athlete (c 500 BC). Around the sarcophagus were found three Panathenaean amphora with paintings of games or contests; these are displayed in glass cases. Note also (right of entrance, no number), capital of a funerary column surmounted by a kalathios and decorated with female heads and bucrania; 50777–50783 *Nikai in Flight* and architectural elements (late 6C BC).

Rooms 5–8 contain a beautiful and extensive collection of objects recovered from the necropolis of Taranto, illustrating the development of Greek ceramics from the 8C BC onwards. The more interesting items are marked by the museum with one to four red stars. A summary description of the collection is given below.

Room 5. Proto-Corinthian and Corinthian Ceramics. Cases 1–2, Proto-Corinthian vases (8C–7C BC), including numerous small *unguentaria* painted with geometrics and (later) human or animal motifs. Cases 3–4, Palaeo-Corinthian vases (late 7C–early 6C BC), notably a fine *alabastron* with winged panther, *aryballos* with griffins and more *unguentaria*. Cases 5–11, Meso-Corinthian (6C BC) and Ionian vases, including a good *pyxis* with warriors, Meso-Corinthian *skyphos* with griffins and wild animals, Meso-Corinthian *alabastron* with sirens, Corinthian and Ionian *unguentaria* (many in animal forms), late Corinthian *skyphos* with lion and wild pig, Egyptian statuette, anthropomorphic *unguentaria* (one of which is from Rhodes), *skyphos* with sirens, Meso-Corinthian *amphora* by the Dodwell Painter and a *thymiaterion* with Artemis running.

Room 6. Laconic ceramics (7C–6C BC). This room contains objects from those tombs in which vases of Corinthian production were mixed with those of other centres (chiefly the Greek islands), as well as some of the earliest Attic pottery. Particularly important are the so-called Laconic vases, after which the room is named, an extremely rare category whose presence at Taras is explained by the continuing trade relations that were maintained between the Spartan colony and its mother city throughout the 7C and 6C BC. Made of highly refined clay, with extremely thin walls and sober decorations, they are among the more elegant products of the archaic period.

Among the finer objects displayed are: case 13, two Laconic cups with fish and dolphins, by the Painter of the Fish (c 600 BC). Case 15, Laconic ceramics (600–550 BC), late Corinthian *hydria*, *aryballos* with lion and wild pig, Meso-Corinthian *kylix* (600–575 BC). Case 16, Attic *kylix* with dance scene (579 BC). Case 17, Meso-Corinthian *skyphos* with dancers and lions, Attic *kylix* decorated by the Falmouth Painter (c 560 BC). Case 18, Laconic *kylix* with scenes of votive offering and dance, in the manner of the Arkesilas Painter (540 BC), Laconic *kylix* with *Zeus and the Eagle* by the Naukratis Painter (c 575 BC). Case 20, Corinthian, Attic and Ionic vases, including Attic *kylix* with scenes of battle and Palaeo-Attic *oinochoe* (580–570 BC).

Rooms 7–8 are dedicated to Attic black and red figure pottery, of which the more outstanding examples are a large *kylix* by the Heidelberg Painter (case 28) and the Lydos Cup, with superimposed colours and fine drawing representing battle scenes on one side and Hercules and Athena on the other. **Rooms 9–10** contain material of local provenance, including Proto-Italiot (430–380 BC) and Apulian vases, Hellenistic and Roman pottery and a very fine collection of Gnathian ware.

Room 11: Sala degli Ori. Here are gathered gold and silver ornaments and jewellery from Taranto and other locations throughout Apulia, most of which can be considered of Tarentine workmanship. Among the more striking pieces are several diadems with oak, olive, laurel and rose-patterned laminae; many elegant earrings, some with filigrained pendants; a large ring with female head, woven gold necklace and ram's-head bracelet, from Mottola; a shell-shaped jewellery case in gilded silver, flower-patterned diadem, laminated tubular sceptre and mirror case, from Canosa. Also in the room are Greek and Roman ivories and bronzes, gilded terracottas (ornaments of burial beds), Byzantine jewellery of the 6C and 7C AD, and (oddly out of place among these minute treasures) an archaic bronze **Poseidon** from Ugento. There follow four corridors (**Rooms 12–15**) dedicated to terracotta statuary (mainly small votive statues, with some grotesque masks), generally of the Hellenistic age.

The **second floor** houses the **Regional Prehistoric Collection**, with Palaeolithic and Upper Palaeolithic finds from Terranera di Venosa, the Gargano Peninsula and the Grotta Romanelli (Otranto); Neolithic and late Neolithic ceramics from the Grotta della Scaloria and Grotta dell'Erba (Avetrana) and the Grotta Sant'Angelo (Ostuni); a substantial collection of (mainly) Bronze Age pottery, and bronze and bone objects from Scoglio del Tonno (Taranto); material from Porto Saturo (Leporano) and Torre Castelluccia (Taranto), including Mycenaean pottery; a cinerary urn of the 10C or 9C BC, from Timmari (Matera) and a collection of protogeometric vases from Taranto, among the oldest examples of indigenous Apulian ceramics.

In the **ground floor** rooms adjoining the entrance to the museum is the **topographical collection**, with material (mainly pottery) from various localities in Apulia, Basilicata, and Calabria arranged to reflect the ancient territorial divisions of Messapia (the present provinces of Taranto, Brindisi and Lecce), Peucetia (province of Bari), Daunia (province of Foggia) and Lucania (Basilicata-Calabria).

In nearby Via Roma is the Museo Oceanografico dell'Istituto Talassografico (no. 3; open Mon–Fri 09.00–12.30), with specimens of marine life from the Gulf of Taranto and elsewhere.

Towards Brindisi

North-east of Taranto, on the road (and railway) to Brindisi, lies **Grottaglie**, a town (population 31,000) taking its name from the grottoes in its limestone rocks. The **Chiesa Matrice**, at the centre of the town, was erected in the late 11C or early 12C. The façade, which dates from 1379, includes a fine Apulian Romanesque portal with octagonal piers on zoomorphic supports. To the right of the façade can be seen the polychrome tile cupola of the Cappella del Rosario. The church of the **Carmine**, further up the hill, has a beautifully carved *Nativity* of 1530. Behind the massive castle lies the quarter of the celebrated Grottaglie ceramic workers, many of whom still use traditional methods. The countless vases that line the streets and the flat roofs of the houses are a strange sight.

Six kilometres north-west of Grottaglie on the Martina Franca road lies the 17C sanctuary of **Santa Maria Mutata**, erected on the site of a small basilica built by Basilian hermits and containing a heavily repainted medieval fresco of the *Madonna and Child*. The image of the Madonna is said to have turned to face Grottaglie during a dispute between that city and Martina Franca over the land on which the church stood. The sanctuary also contains a 15C wooden crucifix. In the environs are the scanty remains of a Messapian settlement, consisting of low walls and tombs, as well as Roman tombs with Latin inscriptions.

At **Francavilla Fontana** are several interesting palazzi. The most impressive of these is the **Palazzo Imperiali**, a castle erected in 1450 by Giovanni Antonio del Balzo Orsini, enlarged in the mid-16C and rebuilt in 1730 by Michele Imperiali to plans by Ferdinando Sanfelice. Rectangular in plan with crenellated battlements and imposing corner bastions, the building is adorned with a graceful loggia and balcony surmounted by large windows in richly carved surrounds, all of Baroque workmanship. A wide doorway leads to the courtyard, where there are a portico, another loggia, and a 15C or 16C baptismal font. In the Sala del Consiglio, where the town council now meets, 16C and 17C paintings and a fireplace bearing the Imperiali arms can be seen. Nearby is the **duomo**, a sober Baroque edifice with colossal statues of Saints Peter and Paul in the façade and a coloured-tile dome.

An interesting excursion can be made to the **Specchia Maiano**, north-east of Francavilla. Leave the town by the road signposted Ceglie Messapica. After c 8km a country lane diverges left to the Masseria Bottari, a farm; proceed on foot through the field on the right to (c 500m) the Specchia Maiano, a mysterious dry-work stone edifice of Messapian origin, 20m in diameter and 11m high, made up of six concentric steps of varying heights. Its purpose is unknown.

About 6km south-east of Francavilla Fontana is **Oria** (population 15,000), on a low ridge in view of the sea on either side. It was the ancient *Hyria*, capital of the Messapians. During the Middle Ages an important Jewish colony lived here, and the Giudecca quarter is still distinguishable. The massive **castle**, built by Frederick II in 1227–33 and enlarged in the 14C, possibly to plans by Pierre d'Agincourt, stands in an indomitable position on top of the ancient acropolis. It is triangular in plan, the tall enceinte surrounding a spacious garden. The south wall, which faces the town, had three towers: one of these, the four-sided bastion at the south-west corner, was originally the keep of the primitive fortification (see below); the others, built in the Angevin period, are cylindrical in form with rings of corbels that once supported wooden battlements.

Within (open 08.00–12.30, 15.30–18.30; closed at the time of writing; ☎ 0831 840009) are a vaulted hall containing a modest collection of antiquities and the rebuilt Norman keep, a tall room with pointed vaults on heavy piers which was once divided, with two floors, as the remains of a fireplace high up on one wall attest, and now contains a collection of arms and armour. A small stairway mounts to the battlements and the Angevin towers, from the tops of which there is a marvellous view of the town and the Tavoliere di Lecce. The much-restored Palazzo del Castellano extends along the north-west wall. Across the garden (open by special permission only; apply to custodian), among the cypresses at the foot of the south-east tower, steps descend to the **Cripta di Santi Crisante e Daria**, an underground chapel dating from the 9C or earlier. The interior is basilican in form, with three aisles, cruciform piers and four shallow domes (a fifth dome, in the left arm of the transept, was destroyed to make the present entrance). The **Centro di Documentazione Messapica** in Via Russo (open Mon–Sat 08.30–13.30; ☎ 0831 845703) has interesting Messapian artefacts and a dig on the premises.

The Museo Civico (in the Palazzo Comunale, open by appointment; ☎ 0831 845703) houses a small collection of Messapian and Graeco-Roman material. The Baroque cathedral, rebuilt after an earthquake of 1743, has a tall, coloured-tile dome of a kind common in this area.

The road follows the final courses of the ancient Via Appia, through olive groves and vineyards. **Latiano** (population 16,000) has a Palazzo Comunale, originally 12C, rebuilt in 1526 and 1724. At Muro Tenente (also called Paretone), to the south-east of the town, are the remains of Messapian walls and tombs identified by some with the *Scamnum* mentioned in the *Tabula Peuntingeriana* as lying along the Via Appia between Taranto and Brindisi.

Latiano can be reached directly from Oria by a country road that follows more or less the same course as the railway, passing (3km left) the ruined church of the Madonna di Gallana, which contains, in the apse, a large Byzantine fresco of the **Blessing Christ between Two Angels**, in poor repair. From here you may proceed directly to Mesagne (see below) without returning to the main road.

Mesagne, a prosperous market town (population 31,000), is the ancient *Messania*. In the old town is the **castle**, built by Robert Guiscard in 1062, destroyed (together with the town) by Manfred's Saracens in 1254, rebuilt by Manfred himself in 1256 and enlarged and embellished in the 15C and 17C. Originally a heavily bastioned stronghold against pirates, it was transformed into a lordly residence, as the Renaissance loggia that runs along the north and east façades clearly demonstrates. The Palazzo del Municipio, formerly a Celestine convent, houses the Museo Archeologico U. Granafei (open Tues–Sat 09.00–12.00, 18.00–21.00, Sun and hols 18.00–22.00), which contains Messapian ware of the 7C–2C BC, Roman inscriptions, and other material of interest. The Baroque Chiesa Madre has a Gothic crypt with a 16C crucifix and numerous paintings by local artists. On the outskirts of the town lies the little 7C church of San Lorenzo, partially rebuilt in the 17C. Recent restoration has brought some frescoes to light, probably dating from the 15C.

Brindisi

Brindisi, a provincial capital (population 93,000) of modern appearance, has the safest natural harbour on the Adriatic and consequent importance as a trading port with the East.

History of Brindisi

Of Messapian origin, the *Bentesion* of the Greeks and the *Brundisium* of the Latins became a Roman city in the 3C BC and was used as a naval base in the Second Punic War. In 49 BC Caesar tried unsuccessfully to contain Pompey's ships here on his return from Greece. It was the birthplace of Pacuvius (219–129 BC), painter and dramatic poet, and the goal of the journey described by Horace (*Satire i*, 5). Virgil died here in 19 BC.

The city flourished under Roman rule, was taken by the Saracens in 836, and rose to prosperity again during the Crusades. It was sacked by Louis of Hungary in 1352 and by Louis of Anjou in 1383. Pestilence and the earthquake of 1456 contributed to its decline, and its modern importance dates only from the opening of the Suez Canal in 1869. An important base in both world wars, Brindisi was occupied by Allied troops on 10 September 1943, and on the same day Badoglio's interim government with King Victor Emmanuel arrived here, having fled before the German advance on Rome.

Today Brindisi derives its wealth largely from agriculture, the processing and packaging of agricultural products, and its chemical industries.

The city centre

The city is built on a peninsula between two land-locked bays, the Seno di Ponente on the north-west and the Seno di Levante on the east. The bays form an inner harbour and are connected with the outer harbour by the Canale Pigonati. The outer harbour is protected by the Pedagne islets and the large island of Sant'Andrea, on which stands the fortress built in 1481 by Ferdinand I of Aragon after the fall of Otranto to the Turks.

Piazza Vittorio Emanuele opens out onto the inner harbour. To the right is the Stazione Marittima; to the left the Lungomare Regina Margherita leads to a marble column, with a remarkable capital, and the base of a second column (ruined in 1528 and later removed to Lecce), which are said to mark the end of the Appian Way. On the opposite bank, to the west of the Canale Pigonati, rises the **Monument to the Italian sailor** (1933), by A. Bartoli and L. Brunati, in the form of a rudder, 52m high. This may be reached by ferry and the terrace (lift) commands a fine view of the whole city.

Via Colonne leads away from the harbour and passes beneath the campanile of the cathedral to Piazza del Duomo, the religious centre of the city, comprising the 18C duomo (begun in the 11C, rebuilt in 1749) and Seminario, the 14C Loggia Balsamo, and the so-called Portico dei Cavalieri Templari. Frederick II married his second wife Yolande in the **duomo** in 1225. Around the main altar are

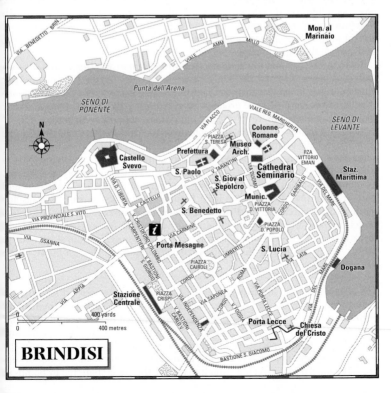

remains of the original mosaic pavement of 1178, with representations of animals, discovered in 1957 and 1968. The inland choir stalls date from the late 16C; the silver altar frontal, from the 18C.

The Museo Archeologico Provinciale

To the left of the church is the Portico dei Cavalieri Templari, a 15C construction with Gothic-style arches that gives access to the Museo Archeologico Provinciale (open Mon–Sat 09.00–13.00, Tues 15.00–19.00; ☎ 0831 565501). The museum is arranged to form four itineraries devoted to antiquities and collections from Brindisi and its province, statues and inscriptions, prehistoric civilisations and marine archaeology, though this arrangement will change significantly in 2004, when the museum's greatest treasure, the Punta del Serrone bronzes (described below) will be installed in new, climate-controlled quarters on the first floor.

Portico Medieval sculptural fragments, notably four capitals from the 11C abbey of Sant'Andrea all'Isola (no longer extant).

Rooms 1 and **3** Antiquarium. Archaeological material from excavations in the city and the surrounding territory, notably architectural fragments and capitals; a plaster cast from **Trajan's Column** in Rome showing the emperor's departure from the harbour at Brindisi during the Dacian campaign; Apulian, Proto-Corinthian, Messapian, and Attic ceramics—including Gnathian ware from the excavations at Valesio, an Attic red-figure *krater* showing a Dionysiac procession and robed figures (5C BC), an Attic bell crater showing Athena with Hercules and Hermes, and an Apulian wine jug with a wedding scene—and several groups of minor sculpture, principally votive statuettes, portrait busts, antefixes, and Gorgon masks.

Room 2 Statues and inscriptions. *Armoured Roman warrior* with a Medusa and a Winged Victory on his cuirass; effigy of *Diana* (or by another interpretation, *Roma Virtus*); lower part of a seated woman, of Greek workmanship; headless female figure probably representing a Victory or a Muse, in the Hellenistic manner. Several of the inscriptions are in Greek or Hebrew.

Room 4 Prehistoric section, with finds from the Palaeolithic to the Bronze Age (stone tools, clay vases and so on).

Rooms 5 and **6** are devoted to temporary exhibitions.

Room 7 Marine archaeology section. Here you can see a variety of material, including a colossal bronze foot from the Secca di Sant'Andrea (4C AD) and numerous amphorae recovered from Roman shipwrecks, as well as a display tracing the discovery of the **Punta del Serrone bronzes**, a find of over 300 sculptures and fragments of sculptures (including two complete statues and seven bronze heads) recovered from the waters just outside Brindisi harbour in 1992. The material is of Hellenistic Greek workmanship, though many of the subjects are Roman.

The Loggia Balsamo, at the beginning of Via Tarantini, was part of an Angevin palace. Via Tarantini and Via San Giovanni (left) lead to **San Giovanni al Sepolcro**, an 11C baptistery of circular plan, erected by the Knights Templar over an early Christian building. The main entrance is decorated with reliefs and fronted by a shallow porch resting on columns (interesting capitals) carried by lions. The interior follows a horseshoe plan. Eight columns (some antique) support the modern roof, which was built to replace the dome shattered by bombs in the Second World War. An ambulatory runs round the perimeter of the room; on the walls are 13C and 14C frescoes of *Christ*, the *Madonna and Child*, and *Saints*. A little south-west is **San Benedetto**, a Romanesque church of 1080, with an elegant cloister.

Overlooking the shore, to the north-west, stands the **castle**, built by Frederick II (1227) and enlarged under Ferdinand I of Aragon and Charles V. West of the castle, in the Strada Provinciale San Vito, is the **Fontana Tancredi** (1192), erected by Tancred to celebrate the marriage of his son Roger to Urania of Constantinople. The crusaders are said to have watered their horses at this fountain. To the south-east, along the busy Via Cristoforo Colombo, is the **Porta Mesagne**, a 13C Gothic arch in the city rampart, reinforced in the 16C by Charles V, near which you can see the remains of five tubs, which collected mud brought by the Roman aqueduct.

From Piazza Vittorio Emanuele, Corso Garibaldi runs south-west to Piazza del Popolo, the modern centre. From here, Corso Umberto leads to the Stazione Centrale. Just south of Piazza del Popolo is the little church of **Santa Lucia**, preserving traces of its original Romanesque decoration on the south side. Within are fragmentary frescoes from the original building and a fine crypt of 1225. At the southern end of the town, near Porta Lecce, the **Chiesa del Cristo** (1230) has a polychrome façade. Inside is a 13C wooden crucifix and statue of the Madonna.

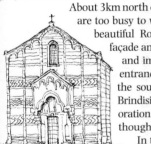

About 3km north of the city centre (the way is marked, but the roads are too busy to walk comfortably) is **Santa Maria del Casale**, a beautiful Romanesque church (1322) with a polychrome façade and Byzantine frescoes, of which the most complete and impressive is the immense *Last Judgement*, on the entrance wall. Note also the *Madonna with Knights* on the south nave wall, an image clearly connected with Brindisi's importance as a crusader port. The profuse decoration of the apse and transepts is equally fascinating, though less well preserved.

In the Cimitero Comunale are 86 graves of officers and men of the British navy who served with the Adriatic Drifter Fleet (1915–18).

Santa Maria del Casale

LECCE AND THE SALENTINE PENINSULA

The old town of **Lecce**, with its small squares and winding streets, owes its distinctive charm to the richly decorated Baroque architecture of its churches and houses, which skilfully exploits the properties of local building stone. This *pietra leccese*, a sandstone of warm golden hue, is easy to work when first quarried, but hardens with the passage of time to form a surface which stands up remarkably well to erosion. The style to which it gave rise, generally known as *Barocco Leccese*, flourished from the 16C–18C and was applied both to monumental and to private architecture, so that even the most unassuming buildings sometimes have carved window frames, sculptured balconies, and elaborate portals. Of the style's leading exponents, Gabriele Riccardi and Francesco Antomio Zimbalo were most firmly rooted in Renaissance classicism. Giuseppe Zimbalo (Lo

Zingarello) was perhaps the most extravagant, whereas Achille Carducci and Giuseppe Cino developed an elegant and (relatively) restrained architectural idiom. Cesare Penna produced much refined sculpture. However, it is perhaps misleading to concentrate on a few 'masters', since in a profound sense this became a popular style, an essential part of the repertory of local artisans. The *Barocco Leccese* remained more a decorative phenomenon than an architectural one, for it never really broke away from the spatial models of 16C Rome. Instead, it affirmed itself in the embellishment of traditional architectural forms with imaginative and ingenious sculptural designs.

The **Salentine peninsula**, devoted largely to the cultivation of vines and olives, also has important tobacco-growing districts. Megalithic remains (dolmen, menhir, etc.) are widespread, though unfortunately somewhat difficult to find; and traces of the Messapian period are visible in cyclopean walls.

Practical information

 ### Information offices
LECCE *Azienda di Promozione Turistica*, Via Monte San Michele, ☎ 0832 314117. *Ufficio Informazioni e di Accoglienza Turistica*, Via Vittorio Emanuele II 24, ☎ 0832 248092.
OTRANTO *Ufficio Informazioni e di Accoglienza Turistica*, Via P. Presbitero, ☎ 0836 801436.
SANTA CESAREA TERME *Ufficio Informazioni e di Accoglienza Turistica*, Via Roma 209, ☎ 0836 944043.

 ### Getting there
By air
Lecce is served by **Casale** airport, 16km north of Brindisi, with daily flights to/from Milan, Rome and Venice. Air terminal in Piazza Mazzini, with coach service connecting with flights.
By road
The quickest route to Lecce from Brindisi is by Roads 16 and 613, and local roads; from Taranto, Roads 7, 7ter and 613. A good way to tour the Salentine peninsula is to make a 184km loop beginning and ending at Lecce. Take Roads 543 and 611 to (46km) Otranto, then road 173 to (51km) Leuca. From Leuca, a secondary road follows the coast to (50km) Gallipoli, from where road 101 returns to (37km) Lecce.

By rail
Lecce is the south-eastern terminus of the State Railway (*FS*) network. There are Eurostar and Intercity trains from Brindisi and points north, non-stop in 20–25mins, and through trains to/from Switzerland and Germany, Turin, Milan and Rome. Many towns of the Salentine peninsula (notably Otranto, Maglie, Gallipoli, Casarano, Nardò and Copertino) are served by local trains of the *Ferrovie del sud-est*. The same company operates trains from Martina Franca to Lecce via Cisternino, Ceglie Messapico, Francavilla Fontana and Manduria.

By sea
Car ferries from Corfu to Otranto and vice-versa. Details from the Information office.

 ### Where to stay
GALATINA €€ *Palazzo Baldi*, Corte Baldi 2, ☎ 0836 568345, 🖨 0836 564835, ✉ hbaldi@ tin.it. Refined elegance in a 16C palace.
€ *Hermitage*, road 476 18km, ☎ 0836

65422, ▯ 0836 528114. Outside the village in a 22,000sq m park, with pleasant rooms, pool, gym, *bocce*; open all year.

LECCE €€€ *Patria Palace*, Piazzetta Gabriele Riccardi 13, ☎ 0832 245111, ▯ 0832 245002, ✉ patria.palace. hotel@mail.clio.it. A beautiful renovated townhouse, with good restaurant, across the square from Santa Croce; open all year.

OTRANTO € *Rosa Antico*, SS 16, ☎ 0836 801563, ▯ 0836 801563, ✉ hotelrosantico@tiscalinet.it. On the outskirts of town, in a 16C villa with park and orange grove; 10 comfortable rooms, courteous staff; open all year.

Eating out

CAVALLINO € *Osteria del Pozzo Vecchio*, Via Silvestro 16, ☎ 0832 611649. Osteria with a strong local following, open evenings (lunch also on Sun and holidays); closed Mon and 10 days in Feb.

CORIGLIANO D'OTRANTO € *Anichirio*, Via Capiterra 5, ☎ 0836 320839. Simple trattori; open evenings, closed Mon and in July–Aug.

GALLIPOLI €€ *Bastione*, Via Riviera Nazario Sauro 28, ☎ 0833 263836. Romantic restaurant by the sea, with good fish and wonderful views; closed Tues and Nov.

€€ *Capriccio*, Via Bovio 14, ☎ 0833 261545. Lively trattoria known for its fresh seafood; closed Mon (except in summer).

€€ *La Puritate*, Via Sant'Elia 18, ☎ 0833 264205. Restaurant by the water, in a little square with outside seating in summer; closed Wed (except in summer) and Oct.

€ *Al Pescatore*, Riviera Cristoforo Colombo 39, ☎ 0833 263656. Hotel restaurant famous for fresh fish; closed Mon.

LECCE €€ *Borgo Antico*, Via Brancaccio 16, ☎ 0832 241569.

Traditional Salentine seafood and broad selection of regional wines; closed Mon and late July–early Aug.

€€ *Picton*, Via Idomeneo 14, ☎ 0832 332383. Characteristic restaurant in a historic building; closed Mon and late Sept, June and Nov.

€ *Cucina Casereccia*, Via Costadura 9, ☎ 0832 245178. Popular trattoria near the Villa Comunale; closed Sun evening, Mon and early Sept.

€ *Da Guido & Figli*, Via XXV Luglio 14, ☎ 0832 305868. Restaurant in a cool crypt, popular with locals at lunch time.

Lecce is famous for its apple jam, best at *La Cotognata Leccese*, Viale Marconi 51.

LIZZANELLO €€ *Fucazzeria da Francesco*, 10km south-east of Lecce, Strada Provinciale per Cavallino, Contrada Caprarica, ☎ 0832 654481. Farm serving traditional local dishes; open for dinner (lunch by reservation), closed Tues (except in summer).

MINERVINO DI LECCE
€ *Da Cazzatino*, Via Manzoni 40, Cocumola, ☎ 0836 954455. Good country restaurant; closed Tues (except in summer) and Oct.

NARDÓ € *La Barchetta*, Via Mastro Gioffreda 5, at Santa Caterina, ☎ 0833 574124. Restaurant-pizzeria near the Porto Selvaggio park; closed Mon (except in summer) and Dec.

€ *Paglialunga*, Via Lamarmora 117 at Santa Maria al Bagno, ☎ 0833 573018. Fresh fish in a pleasant restaurant by the sea; closed Mon (except in summer) and Dec.

OTRANTO €€ *Da Sergio*, Corso Garibaldi 9, ☎ 0836 801408. Exquisitely prepared fresh fish, in the historic town centre; closed Wed (except in summer) and Jan–Feb.

PORTO CESAREO €€ *L'Angolo da Beppe*, Via Zanella 22, ☎ 0833 565305. Creative interpretations of traditional fish recipes; closed Mon.

SAN DONATO DI LECCE
€ *Da Bruna*, 11km south of Lecce, Via Risorgimento 8, ☎ 0832 658207. Popular restaurant-pizzeria, open evenings only; closed Mon and Sept.
SANNICOLA € *La Casina del Doganiere*, 8km north-east of Gallipoli, Via Sferracavalli, ☎ 0833 232072. Popular pizzeria; closed Mon.
TAVIANO € *A Casa Tu Martinu*, Via Corsica 95, ☎ 0833 913652. Traditional osteria in an 18C town-house, with garden seating in summer, open evenings only; closed Mon and Sept–Oct.

Special events
LECCE National Wine Fair in May–June; Saints Orontius and Cataldo (patron saints of the city), 24–26 Aug, Salentine celebrations, including exhibitions, literary contests/sporting events, etc., in October.

Lecce

The chief town (population 102,000) of the Salentine peninsula, Lecce is clear and spacious. Because of its 17C and 18C architecture, it has been called the Florence of the Baroque. It was the birthplace of the painter, Antonio Verri (c 1639–1707).

History of Lecce

A Messapian settlement, afterwards a Greek town and the Roman *Lupiae*, Lecce is the 10C *Licea* and the *Litium* of the Swabian epoch. The ancient city reached its greatest prosperity in the Imperial Roman period, at which time its harbour (today San Cataldo), built by Hadrian, was the most important on the Adriatic after Brindisi. Sacked by Totila in 549, Lecce remained under the Eastern Empire for the next 500 years. During this period it was overshadowed by Otranto, which became Byzantine Italy's busiest port; but it regained its primacy following the Norman conquest and from 1053 to 1463 (the date of its inclusion in the Kingdom of Naples) it was ruled as an independent county.

Later it was known as the Apulian Athens because of its tradition of scholarship, maintained despite the continuous peril of Turkish invasions, from the 15C–18C. Today the city hosts one of Apulia's two universities, the other being in Bari.

In 1647–48 Lecce was the scene of a broadly based anti-Spanish and anti-feudal revolt which, although brutally repressed, continued to smoulder until modern times. In 1734 a second uprising won concessions from the Bourbons that the aristocracy failed to implement; violent social struggle again erupted against the wealthy middle class that had emerged during the period of French domination, without success. Only with the establishment of the Italian Republic has oppression slowly begun to ease. The city suffered no damage in the Second World War.

The central Piazza Sant'Oronzo, which is mainly modern in appearance, lies roughly midway between the castle and the cathedral. It is dominated by a Roman column (from Brindisi) bearing a statue of St Orontius, tutelary of the city, appointed Bishop of Lecce by St Paul in AD 57 and martyred during Nero's perse ution of AD 66 or 68. The square is partly occupied by the **Roman amphithe-atre**, built in the 1C BC and excavated in 1938. Only half of the monument is visible. The piers around the outside probably rose in superimposed orders to a height considerably greater than that of the extant fragments; several of their arches are still standing. Only the lower of the two orders of seats remains.

The amphitheatre may be entered from the south-west corner of the square. Within, the elliptical passage that provided access to the lower order of seats, partially hewn out of the rock and partially built in *opus reticulatum*, can be followed to the left or right. Many fragments of the bas-reliefs that decorated the high wall separating the cavea from the arena (depicting wild animals, gladiators, etc.), and a few Roman inscriptions, are still visible. More reliefs, in infinitely better condition, can be seen at the Museo Provinciale (see below). Several tombs dating from the 5C BC to Roman times were found in the environs.

Adjoining the amphitheatre on the west are the **Sedile** (1592), formerly the own hall, and the ex-chapel of San Marco. The lion over the doorway recalls the chapel's restoration by Venetian merchants (1543). Opposite is the Baroque church of Santa Maria delle Grazie, behind which lies the 16C **castle**. The latter, currently a military installation, consists of two concentric trapezoidal structures separated by a courtyard. The outer fortification, nearly 1km in circumference, was built by Charles V; the inner structure dates from the 12C.

Santa Croce

A narrow street leads north from Piazza Sant'Oronzo to the impressive church of Santa Croce, the most celebrated of the town's Baroque monuments. Begun in 1549 by Gabriele Riccardi, the church was completed in 1679 and bears testimony to the styles of the city's most prominent architects. The façade is built to a general plan by Riccardi, who is only directly responsible for the lower portion, with its columns (note the unusual capitals), blind arcading, and elegant frieze. The elaborate main portal and the two lateral doorways were added in 1606 by Francesco Antonio Zimbalo. The upper portion, which rests on a balcony supported by richly carved mensoles, centres around an ornate rose window flanked by saints in niches and sculpted columns. It was executed in 1646 by Cesare Penna to a design by Giuseppe Zimbalo (Lo Zingarello). The pediment is also designed by Zimbalo.

The **interior**, begun in 1548 by Riccardi and completed after the artist's death by his followers, embodies a conception of spatial elegance reminiscent of Brunelleschi. Built to a Latin cross plan, it has a nave and aisles separated by columns (note the ornate composite capitals with heads of apostles, and at the crossing, symbols of the evangelists), and 14 lateral chapels. The smaller rectangle of the sanctuary has an elegant apse and sculptured portal. Above the crossing, the luminous cupola (1590) and slightly pointed arches bear a rich sculptural decoration that is carried over into the vaults of the transept. In the coffered ceiling of the nave is a 19C representation of the Trinity. In the south transept stands the Altare della Croce, by Cesare Penna (1637–39), with a small loggetta for the exhibition of relics. The high altar, of coloured marble, was brought from the

Chiesa di Santa Croce

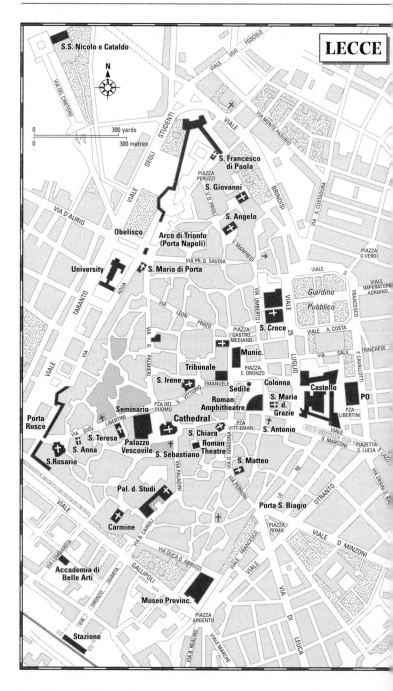

LECCE

S.S. Nicolo e Cataldo

N

0 — 300 yards
0 — 300 metres

VIALE UGO FOSCOLO

VIALE STUDENTI

VIALE DEGLI STUDENTI

VIA DEL CIMITERO

VIA D'AURIO

VIALE

VIALE MONTE PASUBIO

BRINDISI

VIA A. COSTADURA

S. Francesco di Paola

PIAZZA PERUZZI

S. Giovanni
VIA V. D. PRIOLI

S. Angelo

VIA MANFREDI

Obelisco

Arco di Trionfo
(Porta Napoli)

University

VIA D'AURIO

VIA PR. D. SAVOIA

S. Maria di Porta

VIA ADUA

VIA LEON PRATO

VIA G. PALMIERI

VIA UMBERTO I

PIAZZA CASTRO MEDIANO

S. Croce

Giardino Pubblico

VIALE IMPERATORE ADRIANO

PIAZZA G. VERDI

VIALE A. COSTA

VIALE 25 LUGLIO

VIA SALV.

Munic.

Tribunale

S. Irene

VIA VITTORIO EMANUELE

PIAZZA S. ORONZO

Colonna

S. Maria d. Grazie

Castello

PO

PZA LIBERTINI

F. CAVALLOTTI
TRINCHESE

Sedile

Roman Amphitheatre

Seminario

PZA DEL DUOMO

Cathedral

VIA GIOV. LIBERTINI

S. Chiara

PZA VITT-EMAN

Roman Theatre

S. Antonio

VIALE

G. MARCONI

PIAZZETTA S. LUCIA S

VIA LAZ

Porta Rusce

S. Teresa

S. Anna

Palazzo Vescovile

S. Sebastiano

VIA D. ARAGONA

VIA PADULINI

S. Matteo

RE

VIA ORSINI D. BA

S.Rosario

Pal. d. Studi

VIA FERRONI

Porta S. Biagio

OTRANTO

VIA DI LEUCA

Carmine

VIA B. CAIROLI

PIAZZA ROMA

VIALE FRANCESCO

VIALE D. MINZONI

VIALE

Accademia di Belle Arti

VIA LOMBARDIA

VIA DUCA D. ABRUZZI

GALLIPOLI

VIA L. ORONZO — QUARTA

Museo Provinc.

PIAZZA ARGENTO

VIA B. REALINO

VIALE MARCHE

Stazione

church of Santi Nicola e Cataldo (described below). In the chapel on the north side of the sanctuary is the **Altare di San Francesco di Paola** with bas-reliefs of the saint's life by Francesco Antonio Zimbalo (1614–15).

Across the public gardens from Santa Croce is the Museo Missionario Cinese (Via Imperatore Adriano 79; open Tues, Thur and Sat 09.00–12.00, 17.00–19.00 or by appointment, ☎ 0832 392580), with a modest collection of Chinese art and crafts.

Adjoining the church is the **Palazzo del Governo** (1659–95), initially built as a Celestine convent to a plan attributed to Zingarello. From here turn southwest, past the church of the Gesù or Buon Consiglio (1575–79) and the former Jesuit college adjacent, and cross Via Rubighi. Via Vittorio Emanuele leads west, passing the Theatine church of Sant'Irene (completed 1739). Further down on the left) is Piazza del Duomo, with its fine Baroque buildings.

Piazza del Duomo and vicinity

The duomo, founded in 1114 but rebuilt by Giuseppe Zimbalo in 1569–70, has an unusually high campanile (68m), terminating in an octagonal aedicule and two main façades. One of the façades, at the west end of the nave, incorporates statues also by Zimbalo, in a sober Classical design. It fronts onto the smaller square of the elegant Palazzo Vescovile (described below). The other, facing the piazza, is a sumptuous composition containing a statue of St Orontius in a monumental triumphal arch.

The **interior** is a rather ponderous Latin cross with nave and aisles divided by compound piers. The coffered ceiling displays scenes from the *Life of St Orontius* and, in the transept, a *Last Supper*. The first and second south altars were designed by Cesare Penna. Above the altar in the south transept is a painting depicting St Orontius, by Giovanni Andrea Coppola, perhaps the most prominent painter of the Baroque period in Lecce. The crypt, which dates from 1517, was restored in 1956. The custodian will let you in if it is closed.

The **Palazzo Vescovile**, with a fine loggia, is set back a little from the main square. Constructed in 1420–38, it was rebuilt in 1632 and restored in the 18C. To the right stands the magnificent **seminario**, built between 1694 and 1709 to a design by Giuseppe Cino. In the spacious courtyard you can see a richly decorated well, also by Cino.

From Piazza del Duomo Via Libertini continues west past (left) the unfinished church of Santa Teresa, built, together with the adjacent convent, between 1620 and 1630. Across the street is the little church of the Assunzione (or Santa Elisabetta), constructed in 1519 but rebuilt in the 19C. The street continues past the church of Sant'Anna (left) to the church of the **Rosario** (also known as San Giovanni Battista), Giuseppe Zimbalo's last work, begun in 1691 and completed in 1728. The unusual interior follows the plan of a Greek cross developed around a central, octagonal space. A profusion of sculpture decorates the altars. Across the street stands the former Ospedale Civile (1548), now occupied by the Tobacco Administration. Further on is the 18C Porta Rusce (see below).

The southern neighbourhoods

Returning to Piazza Sant'Oronzo, follow Via Augusto Imperatore south to the church of Santa Chiara. A street on the right leads to the small (40m diameter), but well preserved, **Roman theatre**, the only known example of its kind in Apulia. The extensively restored *cavea* has 12 rows of seats, although in all likelihood there were initially several more. These are divided into *cunei* by steps that converged upon the orchestra, which was separated from the cavea by a parapet, now replaced by a modern wall. On the performers' side are three rows of broad seats reserved, as was the custom, for the town dignitaries; access to the orchestra was provided by lateral passages (*paradoi*), one of which is still partially intact. The orchestra floor is particularly well preserved. The *skene* is pierced by numerous holes: some of these may have served for anchoring scenery, but others are more recent. The sculptural decoration of the *proskenion* and the skene itself are missing, but excavations of the site have unearthed numerous fragments (mainly Roman copies of well-known Greek originals). At the entrance of the street leading to the theatre is a small antiquarium with finds from the site and reconstruced rooms with mosaics and frescoes. The lower floor gives an orchestra-level view of the theatre and displays models of the theatre and the amphitheatre.

Via Augusto Imperatore continues south to the church of **San Matteo** (1667–1700), the curvilinear façade of which recalls Borromini's San Carlo alle Quattro Fontane in Rome. The church was designed by the little-known architect, A. Carducci. The elliptical interior has shallow chapels and 12 statues of apostles on tall plinths. The high altar, an exemplary expression of local workmanship, dates from 1694. To the left Via Perrone leads past former mansions and through the 18C Porta S. Biagio to Piazza Roma and the Monumento ai Caduti (1928).

The Museo Provinciale

Follow Viale Francesco Lo Re south to the Palazzo Argento and the superbly appointed Museo Provinciale Sigismondo Castromediano (open daily 09.00–19.30–19.30, Sun 09.00–13.00; ☎ 0832 307415).

The **archaeological collection**, which begins on the **first floor**, is reached by a spiral ramp along which projecting platforms hold texts and illustrations relating to the Palaeolithic period in Italy; the Neolithic, late Neolithic and Bronze Ages in southern Italy; Greek and indigenous pottery; and Greek and Roman coins. **Case 1**, Greek and Roman coins. **Cases 2–9**, Attic black figure vases. **Case 10–71**, Apulian ceramics, including a comprehensive collection of Gnathian ware and a fine, extensive collection of Messapian *trozzelle*; small bronzes and terracotta statuary from Egnathia and Ruvo; large vases with reliefs, from Canosa; and a singular large basin painted in red, yellow, black and white. **Cases 78–79**, large bronzes, including hemispherical and conical helmets; bronze belts and belt buckles; cups, bowls, etc., chiefly from Rudiae. **Case 80**, small bronzes, including numerous *fibulae*, mirrors, statuettes, etc.; **Cases 81–82**, terracotta statuettes and architectural ornaments. **Case 83**, terracotta children's toys (*tintinnabula*) from Rudiae. **Cases 84–87**, fragments of large jugs, oil lamps, fossils, small terracottas, keys, spear heads, etc. in iron. Around the ironwork dividing walls: Roman and Messapian inscriptions dating from the 3C BC–2C AD. A new installation, to be completed by 2004, will illustrate themes related to the life of the Messapians —the home, religious beliefs, etc.

Return to the **ground floor** and follow the corridor around to the left, turning right at the second bank of windows to the **topographical collection**, which contains material dating from the Palaeolithic to the late Roman Imperial period, an eloquent testimony to the cultures that continuously inhabited Apulia over the last 20,000 years. Here also is a room devoted to 19C and 20C Salentine painters who rose to more than local fame: Toma, the Futurist Delle Pite, Ciardo, Calò, Barbieri.

The **picture gallery**, on the **third floor**, may be reached by lift. **Room 1**: on the right, 13C gold and enamel psalter cover; 12C architectural fragments of local workmanship; Jacobello di Bonamo, polyptych (c 1380); Jacobello del Fiore, *Madonna dell'Umiltà*; 15C Venetian school polyptych from the church of Santa Caterina at Galatina; Gerolamo da Santacroce, *Bishop Saint*; 15C and 16C architectural fragments and bas-relief of local workmanship; 18C Byzantine icons and a small reliquary, also of Byzantine craftsmanship; compasses, goods case made from a horn, jewellery box (16C).

Cross the atrium. In cases, on the left, is a collection of coins and medallions ranging from 1220 (Frederick II) to the late 19C. **Room 2**: on the walls, paintings by southern Italian artists of the 17C and 18C. Cases 1–2, ivories, cameos. **Cases 3–4** fans, and local paper and silk compositions (18C); against the pillar, wooden jewellery cabinet with ivory inlay. **Case 5** (centre right), Castelli d'Abruzzo ceramics, from the 17C and 18C. **Case 6**, Venetian glass (also 17C and 18C). **Case 7**, Salentine ceramics. Against the right wall is a large, gaily painted wardrobe of Neapolitan manufacture (17C).

Porta Rusce, the south-west city gate, recalls the city of *Rudiae* (3km south-west) where Ennius (239–168 BC), the father of Latin poetry, was born. The ruins, which may be reached from Via San Pietro in Lama, are of little interest. They include some Roman streets, the scanty remains of public buildings and ramparts and numerous tombs.

To the north-west, beyond Porta Napoli (a triumphal arch erected in honour of Charles V in 1548) is **Santi Nicola e Cataldo**, the most important Romanesque church of the Salentine and one of the finer Norman monuments in Italy. Founded in 1180 by Tancred, Count of Lecce, its unique character results from a confluence of Byzantine, Arabian and proto-Gothic styles. The Baroque façade, attributed to Giuseppe Cino, incorporates a richly decorated portal (note the heads of women on the architrave and the three orders of freely carved arabesques; the badly damaged fresco in the tympanum dates from the 16C), and the rose window from the original 12C building, together with pilaster strips and statues of saints.

The austere **interior** consists of a tall nave, narrow aisles, and a shallow transept, with Saracen arches on compound piers that recall the cathedral of Monreale in Sicily. A marked Burgundian feeling is evident in the nave, particularly in its proportions and in the sense of soaring height they produce. Above the crossing the elliptical dome rises from an unusually high drum. The vaulted roof is also typically northern. Traces of frescoes can be seen along the walls. In the north aisle is an undistinguished statue of *St Nicholas* by Gabrieli Riccardi; in the south aisle, the 17C tomb of Ascanio Grandi, a native poet. The paintings above the lateral altars are by Giovanni Bernardo Lama.

A door to the right of the façade leads to the monumental 16C **cloister**, at the centre of which stands an elegant Baroque aedicule with spiral columns. To the right is a second, smaller cloister. In the south flank of the church can be seen a fine portal with a fresco of *St Nicholas* and an inscription regarding the building of the church in the lunette. From the cemetery, on the north side of the building, you can see the blind arcading that runs along the top of the wall, and the singular octagonal cupola, clearly Oriental in derivation.

West of Lecce

Far and away the most interesting place west of Lecce is **Manduria** (population 33,000). One of the chief centres of Messapian civilisation, it was known even in ancient times for its heroic opposition to the Tarentines, whose mercenary general, Archidamus of Sparta, was killed beneath its walls in a fruitless siege in 338 BC. Now known primarily for its vineyards, it conserves several interesting monuments including Messapian necropoli and a fine stretch of the ancient walls.

At the centre of the town is the triangular Piazza Garibaldi, dominated on the left by the **Palazzo Imperiali**, built in 1719 over a bastion of the ancient walls, part of which can still be seen. A balcony with an ironwork balustrade runs the length of the façade; inside are an elegant courtyard and two covered staircases. Across the piazza, the municipio occupies the 18C Convent of the Carmine. On the upper floor is the **Biblioteca Comunale** (open Tues, Wed and Fri 08.30–13.30; Mon and Thur 08.30–13.30, 16.00–19.00), containing incunabula, manuscripts and an extraordinary collection of first-edition 16C medical texts, as well as a small collection of Messapian antiquities.

The **duomo** (San Gregorio Magno), originally a Romanesque building, was remodelled in Gothic and Renaissance forms. The tripartite façade has a large rose window and three Renaissance portals; the finest, at the centre, incorporates reliefs of the Trinity with Angels and the Annunciation. On the right side stands the Gothic-Renaissance campanile. The apse, with its two orders of columns, dates from the 16C. The **interior**, restored in 1938, has three aisles with rounded arches in the nave and pointed arches and ribbed cross-vaults in the choir. At the beginning of the south aisle is a 16C baptismal font with figures of Christ and the apostles; the 12 statues of saints in the apse date from the 17C. The two large Baroque chapels, with paintings by local artists, were added in the 18C. The **medieval ghetto**, beside the cathedral, survives intact in its original form.

The **ancient ruins** are crossed by both the road and the railway, and take about one hour to visit. At the heart of the archaeological area, north of the town, is **Pliny's Well**, identified with the lacus recorded in the *Natural Histories* (III, 6), in which the water maintains a constant level however much is drawn from it. To reach the site, leave Manduria by Via Sant'Antonio; just before the modern church of the Cappuccini, a road on the right leads to the cave (visit accompanied by a caretaker) where you can see the famous spring.

Just beyond the Cappuccini lies a well-preserved stretch of the ancient **walls**, the remains of which consist of three more or less concentric circuits surrounded by broad, deep ditches. They suggest that Manduria was for several centuries a strategic bastion against Hellenistic penetration of Messapian territory. The three sets of walls belong to different phases of the city's history. The innermost circuit, which probably dates from the 5C BC, is c 2km in circumference and 2m thick. It is made of large, irregular blocks laid lengthwise. The second circuit, attributed to the 4C BC, is made with carefully cut ashlars placed at right-angles to one another in a typically Greek way, suggesting that its builders adopted Greek architectural methods—presumably from the enemy at Taras—while they struggled vehemently to maintain their political independence. The third and most impressive circuit is over 5km in circumference and 5.5m thick. The remains stand in some points at a height of 6–7m. The wall has two distinct faces: one, on the inside, composed of irregular blocks and small stones; the other, on the outside, made of regular blocks laid longitudinally; the middle zone having been filled in with rubble and covered over. It appears to have been erected in the 3C BC, perhaps as a defence against Hannibal.

Just north of Pliny's Well is a curious triple gate where converging roads penetrated the outer walls in points a few metres apart, merging in the space between the walls and entering the innermost wall through a single gate. Other gates have been located in the east wall and near the present Via del Fosso. In addition, three of the underground passages that connected the city with the surrounding countryside and were used during sieges (to smuggle in supplies, to send out troops or to evacuate the population) have been found near the Cappuccini and in the wall to the south and east of the church.

The Viale Panoramico, which follows the perimeter of the walls, passes numerous rock-cut tombs arranged in groups beside the ancient roads leading out of the town. These tombs, of which over 2000 have been identified, have yielded large quantities of Gnathian and other wares of the 3C BC, now at the Museo Nazionale in Taranto. Those situated along the north wall also have painted decorations.

At **Avetrana**, south-east of Manduria, the **castle** was probably built around the end of the 14C over an earlier fortification. It incorporates a tall rectangular keep surrounded by walls, and on the north a cylindrical bastion with a projecting battlement on Renaissance corbels. Adjoining this structure is a feudal residence of somewhat later date; the large rectangular courtyard, with loggia and portico, is characteristic of 17C feudal architecture.

North of Manduria, Erchie and Torre Santa Susanna both have Basilian cave-churches and 17C and 18C feudal residences.

At **Campi Salentina** (population 12,000), a large agricultural centre, the Palazzo Marchesale was built in 1627 over an earlier castle, of which traces are still visible along the east front. The 15C church of the **Madonna delle Grazie** has a dramatic façade (1579) and a richly sculpted portal (1658) by Ambrogio Martinelli.

Four kilometres north-east of **Squinzano** is the charming abbey of **Santa Maria di Cerrate**, a Romanesque complex of the early 12C. The simple façade of the abbey church is graced by a richly carved portal and characteristic portico. Within (open Mon–Fri 09.00–13.00, 14.30–19.30; Sun 09.00–13.00), pointed arches spring from columns with interesting sculptured capitals. A ciborium of 1269 and 13C–16C frescoes may also be seen. Housed in a former olive press next to the church is the Museo delle Arti e delle Tradizioni Popolari del Salento (open daily except Mon 09.00–13.00, 14.30–19.30), which has an entertaining collection of farm tools and folk objects.

The white peninsula

From Lecce, road 543 runs through verdant farmland to San Cataldo, where there is a popular bathing beach. Just west of this, road 611 branches south for Otranto. Near the crossroads are the scanty remains of **Porto Adriano**, the harbour constructed by Hadrian in AD 130. Many of the large stones from this site were removed in the 19C to build the breakwater of the modern harbour.

The road (611) bears south through woods and farmland, parallel to the coast. A road to the right climbs to **Acaia**, a small village still largely enclosed by walls, with an interesting, though somewhat run-down **castle**. This is a typical

Renaissance fortification furnished with imposing enceinte and large bastions with steep scarps and projecting battlements (only partially visible). Begun in 1506 by Baron Alfonso dell'Acaja and completed in 1535 by his son Gian Giacomo (known for his contributions to the castle of Lecce, the walls of Crotone and Castel Sant'Elmo in Naples), it is perhaps the purest example of Aragonese military architecture in Apulia. A road to the south returns to the coast via Vanze.

At San Foca a road leads inland to Melendugno, with another fine 15C and 16C castle. At **Rocca Vecchia** a grass-covered mound of rubble and a few metres of low walls are all that remain of the Rocca built by Gualtiero VI de Brienne, Count of Lecce, in the early 14C and destroyed by Charles V in 1544. The ruin stands on a rocky ledge overlooking the sea, amid the remains of a Messapian village, which in turn overlays a prehistoric settlement. Here excavations have revealed c 1200m of **megalithic walls** with a gate and two square towers, remains of several buildings and cave dwellings cut into the rocky walls of the bay, and numerous graves that have yielded material from the 4C and 3C BC, now at the Museo Provinciale in Lecce.

Otranto

Continuing south, you pass the popular bathing beach at Torre dell'Orso, flanked by pine woods. The road goes through the Alimini lakes district, a growing tourist resort area. A few kilometres further on, the road enters Otranto, a fishing centre and resort (population 5000) situated on a pleasant bay.

History of Otranto

This was *Hydruntum*, a Greek city and a Roman municipium, possibly founded by the Tarentines. It took its name from the stream (the Idro) that runs into the sea here; the townspeople still refer to themselves as *Idruntini*. Located at the mouth of the Adriatic, and separated from the coast of Albania by less than 60 miles of water (now known as the Strait of Otranto), it was one of Republican Rome's leading ports for trade with Greece and Asia Minor, and it is generally thought that the Via Traiana was extended to Otranto to handle this traffic.

Although eclipsed by its rival, Brindisi, in the Imperial Age, *Hydruntum* enjoyed renewed activity under the Byzantines, becoming one of the more important centres of the Eastern Empire in Italy and capital of the region still known as the Terra d'Otranto. Together with Taranto and Bari, it was one of the last Byzantine cities to fall to the Normans, finally surrendering in 1070 to Robert Guiscard. At the time of the Crusades it became an embarkation point for the Orient and a leading centre of trade between Venice, Dalmatia and the Levant. In 1480 a Turkish fleet, allied to the Venetians in the latter's struggle against the Kingdom of Naples, ruthlessly attacked the city and slaughtered its inhabitants. The 800 survivors were promised their lives if they renounced their Christian faith, but none did so; they too were killed on the nearby hill of Minerva, together with their executioner, who confessed himself a Christian after witnessing the unwavering faith of his victims.

Alfonso of Aragon recaptured the city in 1481 and provided it with new and more formidable fortifications, including the castle, featured in Horace Walpole's *Castle of Otranto*. But the town shrank in size and population, its port deserted. The surrounding countryside was abandoned and the marshes, only recently improved, once again bred malaria. Today, Otranto has a modest fishing fleet and is a departure point for the car-ferry to Corfu.

The **castle**, at the centre of the town, was built under Alfonso of Aragon between 1485 and 1498 and reinforced by the Spanish in the late 16C. It is irregular in plan with cylindrical towers at the corners and a massive spearhead bastion facing the sea. Most of the visible structure (open Tues–Sun 09.00–13.00 and 16.00–19.00; ☎ 0832 930722) dates from the 16C; nevertheless, the enceinte shows traces of Roman and medieval masonry, as well as 19C restorations. You enter through the archway on the north side. Within, a narrow entrance hall opens onto the central courtyard; an external staircase climbs to the rooms of the upper floor. Above the main arch are the monumental arms of Charles V.

The road opposite the entrance to the castle descends to the **cathedral** (Santa Maria Annunziata), founded by the Normans in 1080 and reworked in 1481. In the façade are a fine 15C rose window and a Baroque portal of 1764. The basilican interior is divided into a nave and two aisles by 14 marble columns, some antique, from which spring stilted arches. A beautiful **mosaic floor** (1163–65) representing the *Tree of Life*, the *Months* (with the relevant sign of the Zodiac and agricultural or domestic activity), biblical scenes (*Expulsion from the Garden, Cain and Abel, Noah's Ark* and the *Tower of Babel*), scenes of chivalry (Alexander the Great and King Arthur) and mythological episodes, occupies the nave and aisles; probes have revealed a Roman mosaic underneath. The roughly made but fascinating Norman work is the largest of its kind. In the south arm of the transept is a rather gruesome chapel with the bones of the inhabitants slain by the Turks.

Steps in the aisles descend to the **crypt**, with five aisles, semicircular apses, and a vaulted ceiling carried by 42 antique, Byzantine and Romanesque columns with sculptured capitals. On the walls are fresco fragments of various ages and relief panels from a dismantled pluteus.

Descend along the north flank of the cathedral to Corso Garibaldi, one block before the sea. To the left lie the two main gates to the old town—the Torre Alfonsina (1481), with cylindrical bastions; and the Napoleonic Porta di Terra. To the right is a house where the door-jambs incorporate inscriptions dedicated to Marcus Aurelius and Lucius Verus. Further on, Via San Pietro mounts to the little Byzantine church of the same name, built in the form of a Greek cross inscribed in a square. It is said to have been the first cathedral of the city. The interior is covered with frescoes of various epochs, some with Greek inscriptions. It has barrel-vaulted ceilings and a cylindrical cupola supported by four squat columns at the crossing. In the walls are indented arches corresponding to the blind arcades of the exterior.

A diversion inland

Though the road around the coast is more scenic, the interior of the Salentine Peninsula possesses several commendable sights. From Otranto road 16 runs inland to Maglie, at the centre of the peninsula. Just before reaching the town of **Palmariggi** turn left. After a few metres turn left again to the Masseria Quattro Macini, a farm, near which you can see a group of seven dolmens and standing stones. 5km further south of these lies Minervino di Lecce, with a fine Renaissance chiesa parrocchiale. Just outside the town, on the road to Uggiano la Chiesa, is the **Dolmen di Scusi**, the largest and best preserved of these primitive structures.

Maglie is a manufacturing town containing several Baroque buildings, including the church of the Madonna della Grazia; the Chiesa Parrocchiale, the campanile of which recalls that of the duomo at Lecce; and the monumental Palazzo Capece. The latter houses the Museo Comunale di Paleontologia e Paletnologia (open 09.00–12.00, 18.00–22.00, closed Sun morning; ☎ 0836 485820), which has a collection of fossilised fauna from the Pleistocene period and archaeological material from nearby caves.

The coast south of Otranto

Leave Otranto by the castle. A road on the left climbs to the hill of Minerva, the name of which may allude to an ancient temple to the goddess. A staircase ascends past the spot where the survivors of the attack of 1480 were executed; at the top of the steps is the 16C church of San Francesco di Paola, incorporating the chapel (Santa Maria dei Martiri) erected by Alfonso of Aragon to commemorate the massacre. Two kilometres further south, along the rocky promontory that terminates in the Cape of Otranto, the easternmost point of Italy, lie the ruins (right) of the Basilian abbey of **San Nicola di Casole**, founded in the late Middle Ages, rebuilt in the 12C and destroyed by the Turks in 1480. In clear weather the **view** stretches across the Strait of Otranto to Albania and further south, to Corfu.

Beyond the cape the road bears inland and descends, returning to the coast at Porto Badisco, a small hamlet on a rocky cove. Nearby is the **Grotta dei Cervi**, a complex of caves, several kilometres long, containing Neolithic paintings of hunting scenes and magic symbols and rich formations of stalactites. The caves are not open to the public; however, numerous objects (ceramic, bone and flint) found on the site as well as colour photographs of the paintings will be housed in an antiquarium. The road climbs and falls along the coast to **Santa Cesarea Terme**, a bathing resort and spa commanding views to the mountains of Albania. Beyond, the coastal road winds past Porto Miggiano, along sheer cliffs covered with prickly pear.

After 4km a road on the left descends to a small car park. Ramps and steps lead down the rock wall to the **Grotta Zinzulusa** (open by appointment, ☎ 0836 943812). A long (140m) marine cavern, rich in stalagmites and stalactites (*zinzuli* in local dialect), this was occupied in the Upper Palaeolithic period (c 10,000 BC) and in the Copper Age. It is beloved by zoologists for its peculiar species of small crustacea, which seem to have originated in the eastern Adriatic and suggest that this part of Italy was at one time united to the Balkan peninsula. Nearby, but somewhat difficult to access, is the **Grotta Romanelli**, discovered in 1879 and also inhabited in the Upper Palaeolithic period. The flint implements found here have given their name to a variant of the so-called Gravettian industry. Figures of animals, stylistically similar to groups in France and Spain, have been found engraved on the walls and on loose blocks of stone. Among the other items brought to light here is a stone with schematic drawings in red ochre, considered the oldest painting in Italy. Fossil animal remains discovered in the sediment include warm-climate animals (elephant, hippopotamus and rhinoceros) in the lower levels and cold-climate creatures (goat, northern and steppe birds) in the upper levels. They provide evidence of a variance in the sea level in the Quarternary period, as a result of climate change.

Continuing south, you round a headland to Castro Marina, a fishing village and resort with a small, cliff-bound harbour. From here a winding road climbs up to **Castro** (population 2000), a fortified town with a Romanesque cathedral, perhaps the ancient *Castrum Minervae*, where Aeneas first approached the Italian shore (*Aeneid* III, 521). The **castle**, erected in 1572 and fortified in the following century, stands on the site of a Roman fortification later used by the Byzantines and the Normans. The former **cathedral** retains parts of its 12C façade, transept and lateral portals. The north aisle incorporates the remains of a 10C Byzantine church. The town offers magnificent views of the sea and the coastline.

At nearby **Andrano** the 13C castle was made over into an imposing palazzo by the Caracciolo in the 17C. Further on is Marina d'Andrano, with its medieval tower. Tricase Porto is a fishing village and resort. **Tricase**, 4km inland, is a large (population 17,000) agricultural town with a 14C castle rebuilt and extended in the 16C, and a Chiesa Matrice (1770) containing a Deposition and an Immacolata by Palma Giovane.

From Tricase Porto the road climbs to Marina Serra and Marina di Novaglie, then crosses a relatively uninhabited stretch of coastline before reaching **Capo Santa Maria di Leuca** (deriving its name from the Greek *leucos*, white), a conspicuous limestone cliff (60m), the *Iapygium* or *Salentinum Promontorium* of the Romans, with a lighthouse. The actual southernmost point of Apulia is the Punta Ristola, to the west. Marina di Leuca, below the cape, is popular for bathing. The church of Santa Maria Finibus Terrae stands on the site of a Temple of Minerva, close to the point where the Apulian aqueduct ends in an artificial cascade (usually dry).

Boat trips can be made to the several caves on the north-west shore of the cape, beyond Punta Ristola. Among these are the **Grotta del Diavolo**, which has yielded fossil remains of warm-climate animals and Neolithic flint, bone and ceramic objects; the **Grotta della Stalla** and **Grotta Treporte** with their beautiful effects of light and colour, and the **Grotta del Bambino**, also inhabited in prehistoric times. To the east lie the **Grotta Cassafra** and the **Grotta Grande di Ciolo**, both of which present interesting structural and atmospheric effects.

Along the Ionian Sea

The road rounds Punta Ristola and bears north-west, offering good views in all directions. At Torre San Gregorio, a turning on the left leads inland to **Patu** where, opposite the Romanesque church of San Giovanni, you can see the Centopietre, a small (7 x 5.5m) rectangular structure of large ashlars with a pitched roof. Some believe the building to be Messapian in origin, while others hold that it was built during the Middle Ages, using stones belonging to earlier buildings.

Continue along the coast, which is distinguished by rocky bays, many dominated by medieval watch-towers. Beyond Sant'Antonio, the road is straight and somewhat monotonous, the countryside virtually uninhabited. Near Marina San Giovanni lie the scanty remains of the Roman harbour of *Usentum*. Just beyond the 16C Torre Suda (left) a road on the right leads inland to Taviano and **Casarano**, birthplace of Pope Boniface IX (reigned 1389–1404). The church of **Casaranello** (or Santa Maria della Croce) contains the only known early Christian mosaics in Apulia. The ancient building, initially comprising a single nave, was enlarged during the late Middle Ages and remodelled in the 11C, 13C and 17C. The mosaics occupy the vault of the chancel and the cupola; in the former are geometric designs with animals; in the latter, the Cross set against the night sky. Along the nave walls are 13C frescoes representing the life of St Catherine and New Testament scenes.

Gallipoli

The road turns inland, returning to the sea along the shore of a broad bay. 15km further on, enter Gallipoli (population 21,000), the *Kallipolis* of the Greeks and the *Anxa* of Pliny, by its modern borgo on the mainland, pass a fountain decorated with antique reliefs, and cross an old bridge (1603). The old city, its narrow streets tightly packed onto a small island, was the last of the Salentine Terre to capitulate to the Normans (1071). Sacked by the Venetians in 1484, it was strong enough to drive off a British naval squadron in 1809. Beyond the bridge is the **castle**, where 34 rebel barons held out for seven months against Charles of Anjou in the 13C. Rectangular in plan with an imposing enceinte and massive corner bastions, it is fronted by the keyhole-shaped annexe built in 1522 to plans by Francesco di Giorgio Martini, who visited the fortification in 1491–92. The original Byzantine fortress has been incorporated into the polygonal bastion at the south-east corner.

Further west, the Baroque **cathedral** (1630), with an elaborate façade of 1696, is adorned with many paintings by local artists, including a *Madonna and St Orontius* by Giovanni Antonio Coppola, the artist's last work. In the nearby bishop's palace are an Assunta by Francesco De Mura and other paintings.

The **Museo Civico** (Via De Pace 108; open Mon–Sat, 09.00–13.00, 16.00–19.00; closed for renovation at the time of writing; ☎ 0833 264224) houses a collection divided into ten sections, encompassing antiquities (largely Messapian sarcophagi and vases), natural history, weapons and clothing, historical and ethnographic relics and curiosities, and prints and paintings of the city.

The Baroque church of **San Francesco** contains wooden carvings of the *Two Thieves* by Vespasiano Genuino, an outstanding achievement of the realistic school of local sculpture. The church of the **Purità** has a richly stuccoed interior and many paintings; the floor is paved with 18C majolica tiles depicting baskets of flowers and fruit.

Beyond Gallipoli, the road bears inland through farmland. **Galatone** is a large town (population 16,000) with several Baroque monuments, and the birthplace of the humanist, physician and cosmographer Antonio de Ferrariis (Galateo, 1444–1517). Road 101 leads straight to Lecce (24km). There are two alternative and more interesting routes to Lecce via Galatina and Soleto (respectively 9km and 15km north-east), or Nardo and Copertino (respectively 5km and 11km north-west).

Galatina and Soleto

Galatina (population 29,000) is one of the more populous cities on the Salentine peninsula and an important wine-producing centre. It hosted an important Greek colony during the Middle Ages, and the Greek dialect and customs were maintained until the dawn of the modern era. Later, it was incorporated into the county of Soleto (see below). The Franciscan church of **Santa Caterina d'Alessandria** reflects the wealth and influence of the town's feudal lords, the barons Orsini. Begun by Balzo Orsini in 1384 and completed by his son Giovanni in 1460, it has a façade in the late Apulian Romanesque manner, with three gables lined with arched corbel tables. The central portal (1397) is flanked by slender columns on much-worn lions. It has three bands of intricately carved moulding; those nearest the door show a marked Oriental influence. In the lintel are relief figures of Christ and the apostles and, above the rounded arches, a Classical pediment, surmounted by a fine rose window. The lateral doorways are placed asymmetrically to the gables above, creating a disturbing sensation of imbalance.

The **interior** (apply for admission at the monastery) is remarkable for its construction and its decorative scheme. Massive walls pierced by wide drop arches separate the nave from the double side aisles. The nave, like the aisleless nave of San Francesco in Assisi, is articulated into bays by clusters of columns and pilasters from which ribbed cross vaults spring. On the walls and in the vault, numerous frescoes (badly damaged) illustrate the Old and New Testaments and provide insight into the nature of feudal life in Apulia. Superficially resembling the frescoes of Giotto's school at Assisi, they are attributed to central Italian artists working in the early 15C. Also of interest are the apocryphal account of the *Life of the Virgin* depicted in the south aisle and the episodes from the *Life of St Catherine of Alexandria* in the presbytery. Here, against the north wall, is the tomb of Raimondello del Balzo Orsini, with the deceased depicted supine in a Franciscan habit and again, kneeling, on the sarcophagus. Beyond the sanctuary is the octagonal apsidal chapel constructed by Giovanni Andrea Orsini. The latter's tomb, surmounted by a baldachin with four columns carried by lions, stands against the rear wall.

The **treasury** contains a silver reliquary shrine and other precious objects, possibly of Apulian workmanship, a portable Byzantine mosaic of the *Redeemer* set on wood and an icon of the *Madonna* in a silver-gilt frame.

Four kilometres east of Galatina is **Soleto** (population 5000), also interesting for its medieval monuments. A Messapian town, it has been identified with the *Soletum* of Pliny. Like Galatina, it adhered closely to eastern cultural and religious traditions throughout the Middle Ages; the Latin rite was not instituted in its churches until 1598. The parish church of **Santa Maria Assunta**, rebuilt in 1770–83, is flanked by a campanile begun in 1397 by Raimondello Orsini and completed in the early 15C by Giovanni Antonio Orsini. The structure, which is commonly referred to as the Guglia di Raimondello, represents a graceful compromise between Romanesque and Gothic building canons. A similar confluence of styles distinguishes the façade (1347) of the small chapel.

Nardò and Copertino

Nardò (population 30,000) is the third-largest city in the province of Lecce. Founded by the Messapians, it became a Roman municipium under the name of *Neritum*. It retained a decidely Oriental stamp throughout the Middle Ages, despite repeated efforts to westernise it, and the Greek and Latin rites were practised side-by-side in its churches until the 15C. It was taken by the Turks in 1480. Attacked by the Venetians in 1484, it suddenly surrendered after five days of strenuous resistance, an event which has perplexed historians. It participated in the anti-Spanish revolt that shook Lecce and sent repercussions throughout the peninsula, and it adhered enthusiastically to the cause of the Risorgimento.

The triangular Piazza Antonio Salandra, at the centre of the city, is a theatrical piece of town planning that revolves around the exuberant Guglia dell'Immacolata (1769). The **Palazzo della Prefettura**, rebuilt in 1772, has an open arcade on the ground floor and a vaulted loggia on the floor above, both with trefoil arches. Above the shop fronts along the other sides of the piazza are ironwork balconies and elegant loggie, some of which have been wholly or partially walled up. The adjacent piazza takes its name from the church of **San Domenico**, built in the late 16C but restored, in Baroque form, after 1743. The façade hosts a strange colony of grotesque herms and caryatids.

The former **castle** of the dukes of Conversano, now the town hall, was begun by Giovanni Antonio Acquaviva d'Aragona, who built the central block (distinguished by its crenellated battlements on unadorned arched corbels) and the mandorla-like corner bastions in the early 16C. The other parts are clearly later additions. Adjoining the medieval town walls is a largo containing the curious octagonal aedicule (1603) called the **Osanna**, composed of eight small columns joined by polyfoil arches, surmounted by a segmented stone cupola with eight pinnacles and a sculptured finial.

The **cathedral**, founded on the site of a Basilian church by Benedictines in 1090, was partially rebuilt after an earthquake of 1230, enlarged in the following century, and modified several times after that, particularly in 1721 by Ferdinando Sanfelice, when additions were made to the façade and interior. The latter was restored in 1900 to an earlier, though not original form. Within, the nave and aisles are separated by compound piers with engaged columns. The rounded arches on the south side are those of the original building; the pointed arches on the north are part of the 13C reconstruction. Above the altars are paintings by local artists and a 13C Catalan crucifix which, according to legend, began to bleed when the Saracens attempted to carry it off. On the walls and piers are frescoes dating from the 13C to the 15C.

In the bishop's palace you can see a *Madonna with Saints Peter and Paul* by Francesco Solimena.

Copertino (population 24,000) is known for its imposing **castle**, which stands at the north-west corner of the old town. The overall design of the castle was drawn up by Evangelista Menga, who was also the architect of the castles at Mola and Barletta. The fortress is made up of two distinct parts: a Renaissance exterior, rectangular in plan with pointed bastions and a broad moat; and an inner structure of earlier date, which includes the high Angevin keep and the rooms in the north wing, referred to as the *Castello Vecchio*. The east wall, nearly 120m long, contains an elaborate Renaissance portal surmounted by rosettes and medallions with effigies of illustrious figures. Beyond is a vaulted entrance-hall with arrow-loops and offset doorways. The inner court (open daily 08.30–13.30; ☎ 0832 931612) is surrounded by buildings of different epochs: the Renaissance **Cappella di San Marco**, on the right, has a fine portal and a small rose window. Inside you can see frescoes by a local artist and the sarcophagi of Umberto and Stefano Squardiafico (d. 1562 and 1568 respectively).

Adjacent to the chapel is a room with a large fireplace. From this room you enter the vaulted corridor that runs round the north, west and south walls. Steps in the south-west corner of the courtyard mount to a terrace from which you enter the monumental apartments of the Castello Vecchio, entering the Angevin keep through an archway in the south-east corner of the courtyard.

The shortest route from Copertino to Lecce is by local roads, passing through the village of San Pietro in Lama. The fast way back is by road 101, which passes 6km east of Copertino.

Glossary of art terms

Note: explanation of further terms used in classical architecture will be found in the description of the Pompeian house, page 226.

Aedicule, a small edifice or room

Agora, public square or marketplace

Ala (pl. *alae*), literally, 'wing', the lateral part of a buidling

Ambo (pl. *ambones*), pulpit in a 'hristian basilica' two pulpits on opposite sides of a church from which the gospel and epistle were read

Amphora, antique vase, usually of large dimensions, for oil and other liquids

Antefix, ornament placed at the lower corner of the tiled roof of a temple to conceal the space between the tiles and the cornice

Antis, *lit antis* describes the portico of a temple when the side-walls are prolonged to end in a pilaster flush with the columns of the portico

Architrave, lowest part of the entablature

Archivolt, moulded architrave carried round an arch

Athenaion, sanctuary dedicated to Athena

Atlantes (or *Telamones*), male figures used as supporting columns

Atrium, forecourt, usually of a Byzantine church or a classical Roman house

Badia, *abbazia*, abbey

Basilica, originally a Roman building used for public administration; in Christian architecture, an aisled church with a clerestory and apse, and no transepts

Benedizario, a prayer book

Biclinium, a Roman dining bed for two; also, the room where it is located

Bifora, a window divided externally into two equal lights by a column

Borgo, a suburb; street leading a way from the centre of a town

Bottega, the studio of an artist; the pupils who worked under his direction

Bucchero, Etruscan black terracotta ware

Bucrania, a common form of melope decoration—heads of oxen garlanded with flowers

Caldarium, or Calidarium, room for hot or vapour baths in a Roman bath

Campanile, bell-tower, often detached from the buidling to which it belongs

Camposanto, cemetery

Capital, the top of a column

Capitolium, a temple of Jupiter, Juno and Minerva

Cardo, the main street of a Roman town, at right-angles to the decumanus

Caryatid, female figure used as a supporting column

Cavea, the part of a theatre or amphitheatre occupied by the row of seats

Cella, sanctuary of a temple, usually in the centre of the building

Chiaroscuro, distribution of light and shade, apart from colour in a painting; rarely used as a synonym for grisaille

Ciborium, casket or tabernacle containing the Host

Cipollino, onion-marble; a greyish marble with streaks of white or green

Cippus, sepulchral monument in the form of an altar; a stone marking a grave or boundary

Coemeterium, a cemetery

Cosmatesque, inlay work, usually dating from the 12C–16C of the famous marbleworkers of Lazio conventionally called 'Cosmall' from the name 'Casma' frequent in their families

Cryptoporticus, a semi-underground covered portico used in Roman architecture for the construction of terraces or as a covered market

Cuneus, wedge-shaped block of seats in an antique theatre

Cyclopean, the term applied to walls of

unmortared masonry, older than the Etruscan civilisation, and attributed by the ancients to the giant Cyclopes

Daunii, ancient inhabitants of Apulia, a fraction of the Iapigi (the others being the Mesapii and Peucilli), who came from the Illrian (east) shore of the Adriatic

Decumanus, the main street of a Roman town running parallel to its longer axis

Dipteral, temple surrounded by a double peristyle

Diptych, painting or ivory tablet in two sections

Dolium (pl. *dolia*), a very large ceramic jar, like the Greek pithos, used for storage of wine, water, grain, etc. The Villanovans and Etruscans often used dolla for cremation burials. The width of the mouth of the jar ranges from 40cm to 80cm; the overall height anywhere from 1m to 1.5m

Dolmen, a prehistoric monument (possibly a tomb) made up of two or more upright stones supporing a horizontal stone slab

Duomo, cathedral

Entablature, the continuous horizontal element above the capital (consisting of architrave, frieze and cornice) of a classical building

Enneastyle, temple with a portico of nine columns at the end

Ephebos, Greek youth under training (military or university)

Etruscan, of, relating to, or characteristic of Etruria, an ancient country in central Italy, its inhabitants, or their language

Exedra, semicircular recess in a Byzantine church

Exultet, an illustrated scroll

Ex-voto, tablet or small painting expressing gratitude to a saint; a votive offering

Fauces, the entrance passage of a Roman house (well seen at Herculaneum)

Fictile, moulded of earth, clay, or other soft material

Forum, open space in a town serving a a market or meeting-place

Frigidarium, room for cold baths in a Roman bath

Fumarola, volcanic spurt of vapour (usually sulphurous) emerging from the ground

Graffiti, design on a wall made with iron tool on a prepared surface, the design showing in white. Also used loosely to describe scratched designs or words on walls

Heptastyle, temple with a portico of seven columns at the end

Herm (pl. *hermae*), quadrangular pillar decreasing in girth towards the ground, surmounted by a bust

Hexastyle, temple with a portico of six columns at the end

Historiated, adorned with figurative painting or sculpture, usually comprising a narrative

Hypogeum, subterranean excavation for the internment of the dead (usually Etruscan)

Iconostasis, a screen or partition that divides the public part of a church from that reserved for the clergy

Intarsia, inlay of wood, marble, or meta

Kore, maiden

Kouros, boy; archaic male figure

Krater, antique mixing-bowl, conical i shape with rounded base

Kylix, wide shallow vase with twin handles and short stem

Largo, an urban space resulting from the intersection of two or more streets or from the widening of a single street

Laura, monastery of the Eastern church

Loggia, covered gallery or balcony, usually preceding a large building

Lunette, semiciruclar space in a vault or ceiling, often decorated with a painting or relief

Matroneum, gallery reserved for women in early Christian churches

Menhir, a single upright monolith, usually of prehistoric origin

Mesapii, ancient inhabitants of Apulia, a fraction of the Iapigi (the others being the Daunii and Peucitii), who came from the Illyrian (east) shore of the Adriatic

Metope, panel between two triglyphs in the frieze of a Doric temple

Mithraeum, a shrine of Mithras, a Persian sun-god worshiped in imperial Rome

Monoforum, a single-light window, without subdivisions

Narthex, vestibule of a Christian basilica

Naumachia, a mock naval combat for which the arena of an amphitheatre was flooded

Nymphaeum, a sort of summer house in the gardens of baths, palaces, etc., originally a temple of the Nymphs, decorated with statues of those goddesses, and often containing a fountain

Octastyle, a portico with eight columns

Odeion, a concert hall, usually in the shape of a Greek theatre, but roofed

Oecus (pl. *oeci*), generic term used to describe a room in a Roman building

Oinochoe, wine-jug usually of elongated shape for dipping wine out of a krater

Opisthodomos, the enclosed rear part of a temple

Opus Alexandrinum, mosaic design of black and red geometric figures on a white ground

Opus Incertum masonry of small irregular stones in mortar

Opus Musivum, mosaic decoration with cubes of glass (usually on walls or vaults)

Opus Quadratum, masonry of large rectangular blocks without mortar; in *opus Etruscum* the blocks are placed alternatively lengthwise and endwise

Opus Reticulatum, masonry arranged in squares or diamonds so that the mortar joints make a network pattern

Opus Sectile, mosaic or paving of thin slabs of coloured marble cut in geometrical shapes

Opus Spicatum, masonry or paving of small bricks arranged in a herringbone pattern

Opus Tessallatum, mosaic formed entirely of square tesserae

Opus Vermiculatum, mosaic with tesserae arranged in lines following the contours of the design

Oschi, a nationality born of the fusion of the Samnites with the Opici following the elimination of Etruscan power in the second half of the 5C BC

Palazzo, any dignified and important building

Paliotto, a vestment, hanging, or covering of any material that covers the front part of a Christian altar

Pantokrator, the Almighty

Pediment, gable above the portico of a classical building

Pelike, a jug with the round belly, narrow neck, and two handles

Peribolos, a precinct, but often archaeologically the circuit round it

Peripteros, a porch. A peripteral building (temple) is one that is surrounded by a single row of columns on all four sides

Peristyle, court or garden surrounded by a columned portico

Peucitii, ancient inhabitants of Apulia, a fraction of the Iapigi (the others being the Daunii and Mesapii), who came from the Illyrian (east) shore of the Adriatic

Pietà, group of the Virgin mourning the dead Christ

Pinacoteca, an art gallery specialised in the exhibition of painting

Piscina, Roman tank; a basin for an officiating priest to wash his hands before Mass

Pithos, large pottery vessel

Pleistocene, the earlier part of the Quarternary period (c 1.8 million years ago) or the corresponding system of rocks

Pluteus, a low wall that encloses the space between column bases in a row of columns

Podium, a continuous base or plinth supporting columns, and the lowest row of seats in the cavea of a theatre or amphitheatre

Polyptych, painting or tablet in more than three sections

Predella, small painting attached below a large altarpiece

Presepio, literally, crib or manger. A group of statuary of which the central subject is the infant Jesus in the manger

Pronaos, porch in front of the cella of a temple

Propylon, Propylaea. Entrance gate to a lemenos; in plural form when there is more than one door

Proskenion, the area before the stage of a Greek theatre

Prostyle, edifice with free-standing colums,as in a portico

Prothesis, the Byzantine rite of setting forth of the oblation, or the chamber north of the sanctuary where this is done

Prothyrum, Greek: a vestbule or space begfore a door or gate. Latin: a gate or railing before the door itself

Pseudodipteral, a temple with a double peristyle at the front and back

Pseudoperistyle, a false peristyle

Pulvin, cushion stone between the capital and the impost block

Putto, figure of a child sculpted or painted, usually nude

Quadriga, four-horsed chariot

Rhyton, drinking-horn usually ending in an animal's head

Samnite, of, relating to, or characteristic of an ancient people, an offshoot of the Sabines, in south-central Italy

Situla, water-bucket

Skene, the stage of a Greek theatre

Skyphos, a squat stemless cup with two opposing, rim oriented handles. A form particular to Athenian potters

Stamnos, big-bellied vase with two small handles at the sides, closed by a lid

Stele, upright stone bearing a monumental inscription

Stereobate, basement of a temple or other building

Strigil, bronze scraper used by the Romans to remove the oil with which they had annointed themselves

Stylobate, basement of a columned temple or other building

Sudatorium, room for very hot vapour baths (to induce sweat) in a Roman bath

Telamones, see *Atlantes*

Temenos, a sacred enclose

Tempietto a small temple

Tepidarium, room for warm baths in a Roman bath

Tessera, a small cube of marble, glass, brick, used in mosaic work

Tetrastyle, having four columns at the end

Thermae, originally simply baths, late elaborate buildings fitted with libraries, assembly rooms, gymnasia, circuses, etc.

Tholos, a ciruclar building

Tondo, round painting or bas-relief

Transenna, open grille or screen, usually of marble, in an early Christian church separating nave and chancel

Triclinium, dining-room and reception-room of a Roman house

Trifora, a window divided into three lights joined by a common architectura motif

Triglyph, blocks with vertical grooves on either side of a metope on the frieze of a Doric temple

Triptych, painting in three sections

Trullo, rural dwelling of Apulia, built without mortar of local limestone and usually whitewashed, with conical roo formed of flat-pitched spiral courses of the same stone capped with diverse finia

Tympanum, the face of a pediment within the frame made by the upper an lower cornices; also, the space within a arch and above a lintel or a subordinat arch

Villa, country-house with its garden; also, a Roman Farm or estate and, in some southern towns, an urban park

Index

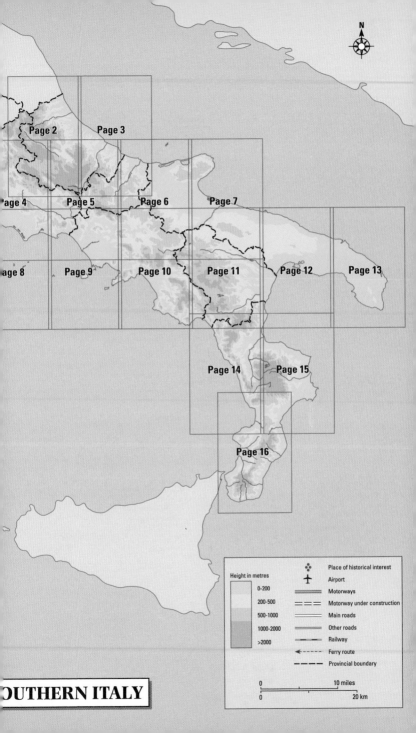

N

Height in metres

0-200
200-500
500-1000
1000-2000
>2000

♣ Place of historical interest
✈ Airport
━━━ Motorways
═══ Motorway under construction
━━━ Main roads
━━━ Other roads
━━━ Railway
◄---- Ferry route
━ ━ ━ Provincial boundary

0   10 miles
0   20 km

SOUTHERN ITALY